CORNERSTONE
BIBLICAL
COMMENTARY

CORNERSTONE
BIBLICAL
COMMENTARY

The Gospel of John
Grant Osborne

1-3 John
Philip W. Comfort & Wendell C. Hawley

GENERAL EDITOR
Philip W. Comfort

with the entire text of the
NEW LIVING TRANSLATION

TYNDALE HOUSE PUBLISHERS, INC. CAROL STREAM, ILLINOIS

Cornerstone Biblical Commentary, Volume 13

Visit Tyndale's exciting Web site at www.tyndale.com

John copyright © 2007 by Grant Osborne. All rights reserved.

1—3 John copyright © 2007 by Philip W. Comfort & Wendell C. Hawley. All rights reserved.

Designed by Luke Daab and Timothy R. Botts.

Library of Congress Cataloging-in-Publication Data

Cornerstone biblical commentary.
    p. cm.
  Includes bibliographical references and index.
  ISBN-13: 978-0-8423-8341-7 (hc : alk. paper)
  ISBN-10: 0-8423-8341-7 (hc : alk. paper)
    1. Biblical—Commentaries. I. Osborne, Grant.   II. Comfort, Philip W.
III. Hawley, Wendell C.
BS491.3.C67 2006
220.7′7—dc22   2005026928

Printed in the United States of America

12   11   10   09   08   07
7   6   5   4   3   2   1

CONTENTS

CONTRIBUTORS TO VOLUME 13

John: Grant Osborne
BA, Fort Wayne Bible College;
MA, Trinity Evangelical Divinity School;
PhD, University of Aberdeen;
Professor of New Testament, Trinity Evangelical Divinity School.

1—3 John: Philip W. Comfort & Wendell Hawley
Philip W. Comfort
BA, Cleveland State University;
MA, Ohio State University;
D. Litt. et Phil., University of South Africa;
Tyndale House Publishers;
Coastal Carolina University.

Wendell C. Hawley
BA, University of Oregon;
MA, Western Baptist Seminary;
LLD, California Graduate School of Theology;
DD, Western Baptist Seminary;
Director of Pastoral Care, Windsor Park Manor.

GENERAL EDITOR'S PREFACE

The *Cornerstone Biblical Commentary* is based on the second edition of the New Living Translation (2004). Nearly 100 scholars from various church backgrounds and from several countries (United States, Canada, England, and Australia) participated in the creation of the NLT. Many of these same scholars are contributors to this commentary series. All the commentators, whether participants in the NLT or not, believe that the Bible is God's inspired word and have a desire to make God's word clear and accessible to his people.

This Bible commentary is the natural extension of our vision for the New Living Translation, which we believe is both exegetically accurate and idiomatically powerful. The NLT attempts to communicate God's inspired word in a lucid English translation of the original languages so that English readers can understand and appreciate the thought of the original writers. In the same way, the *Cornerstone Biblical Commentary* aims at helping teachers, pastors, students, and laypeople understand every thought contained in the Bible. As such, the commentary focuses first on the words of Scripture, then on the theological truths of Scripture—inasmuch as the words express the truths.

The commentary itself has been structured in such a way as to help readers get at the meaning of Scripture, passage by passage, through the entire Bible. Each Bible book is prefaced by a substantial book introduction that gives general historical background important for understanding. Then the reader is taken through the Bible text, passage by passage, starting with the New Living Translation text printed in full. This is followed by a section called "Notes," wherein the commentator helps the reader understand the Hebrew or Greek behind the English of the NLT, interacts with other scholars on important interpretive issues, and points the reader to significant textual and contextual matters. The "Notes" are followed by the "Commentary," wherein each scholar presents a lucid interpretation of the passage, giving special attention to context and major theological themes.

The commentators represent a wide spectrum of theological positions within the evangelical community. We believe this is good because it reflects the rich variety in Christ's church. All the commentators uphold the authority of God's word and believe it is essential to heed the old adage: "Wholly apply yourself to the Scriptures and apply them wholly to you." May this commentary help you know the truths of Scripture, and may this knowledge help you "grow in your knowledge of God and Jesus our Lord" (2 Pet 1:2, NLT).

PHILIP W. COMFORT
GENERAL EDITOR

ABBREVIATIONS

GENERAL ABBREVIATIONS

b.	Babylonian Gemara	Heb.	Hebrew	NT	New Testament
bar.	baraita	ibid.	*ibidem,* in the same place	OL	Old Latin
c.	*circa,* around, approximately	i.e.	*id est,* the same	OS	Old Syriac
cf.	*confer,* compare	in loc.	*in loco,* in the place cited	OT	Old Testament
ch, chs	chapter, chapters	lit.	literally	p., pp.	page, pages
contra	in contrast to	LXX	Septuagint	pl.	plural
DSS	Dead Sea Scrolls	𝔐	Majority Text	Q	Quelle ("Sayings" as Gospel source)
ed.	edition, editor	*m.*	Mishnah	rev.	revision
e.g.	*exempli gratia,* for example	masc.	masculine	sg.	singular
et al.	*et alli,* and others	mg	margin	*t.*	Tosefta
fem.	feminine	ms	manuscript	TR	Textus Receptus
ff	following (verses, pages)	mss	manuscripts	v., vv.	verse, verses
fl.	flourished	MT	Masoretic Text	vid.	*videur,* it seems
Gr.	Greek	n.d.	no date	viz.	*videlicet,* namely
		neut.	neuter	vol.	volume
		no.	number	*y.*	Jerusalem Gemara

ABBREVIATIONS FOR BIBLE TRANSLATIONS

ASV	American Standard Version	NCV	New Century Version	NKJV	New King James Version
CEV	Contemporary English Version	NEB	New English Bible	NRSV	New Revised Standard Version
ESV	English Standard Version	NIV	New International Version	NLT	New Living Translation
GW	God's Word	NIrV	New International Reader's Version	REB	Revised English Bible
HCSB	Holman Christian Standard Bible	NJB	New Jerusalem Bible	RSV	Revised Standard Version
JB	Jerusalem Bible	NJPS	The New Jewish Publication Society Translation (*Tanakh*)	TEV	Today's English Version
KJV	King James Version			TLB	The Living Bible
NAB	New American Bible				
NASB	New American Standard Bible				

ABBREVIATIONS FOR DICTIONARIES, LEXICONS, COLLECTIONS OF TEXTS, ORIGINAL LANGUAGE EDITIONS

ABD *Anchor Bible Dictionary* (6 vols., Freedman) [1992]

ANEP *The Ancient Near East in Pictures* (Pritchard) [1965]

ANET *Ancient Near Eastern Texts Relating to the Old Testament* (Pritchard) [1969]

BAGD *Greek-English Lexicon of the New Testament and Other Early Christian Literature,* 2nd ed. (Bauer, Arndt, Gingrich, Danker) [1979]

BDAG *Greek-English Lexicon of the New Testament and Other Early Christian Literature,* 3rd ed. (Bauer, Danker, Arndt, Gingrich) [2000]

BDB *A Hebrew and English Lexicon of the Old Testament* (Brown, Driver, Briggs) [1907]

BDF *A Greek Grammar of the New Testament and Other Early Christian Literature* (Blass, Debrunner, Funk) [1961]

BHS *Biblia Hebraica Stuttgartensia* (Elliger and Rudolph) [1983]

CAD *Assyrian Dictionary of the Oriental Institute of the University of Chicago* [1956]

COS *The Context of Scripture* (3 vols., Hallo and Younger) [1997–2002]

DBI *Dictionary of Biblical Imagery* (Ryken, Wilhoit, Longman) [1998]

DBT *Dictionary of Biblical Theology* (2nd ed., Leon-Dufour) [1972]

DCH *Dictionary of Classical Hebrew* (5 vols., D. Clines) [2000]

DJD *Discoveries in the Judean Desert* [1955–]

DJG *Dictionary of Jesus and the Gospels* (Green, McKnight, Marshall) [1992]

DOTP *Dictionary of the Old Testament: Pentateuch.* (T. Alexander, D.W. Baker) [2003]

DPL *Dictionary of Paul and His Letters* (Hawthorne, Martin, Reid) [1993]

EDNT *Exegetical Dictionary of the New Testament* (3 vols., H. Balz, G. Schneider. ET) [1990–1993]

HALOT *The Hebrew and Aramaic Lexicon of the Old Testament* (L. Koehler, W. Baumgartner, J. Stamm; trans. M. Richardson) [1994–1999]

IBD *Illustrated Bible Dictionary* (3 vols., Douglas, Wiseman) [1980]

IDB *The Interpreter's Dictionary of the Bible* (4 vols., Buttrick) [1962]

ISBE *International Standard Bible Encyclopedia* (4 vols., Bromiley) [1979–1988]

KBL *Lexicon in Veteris Testamenti libros* (Koehler, Baumgartner) [1958]

LCL Loeb Classical Library

L&N *Greek-English Lexicon of the New Testament: Based on Semantic Domains* (Louw and Nida) [1989]

LSJ *A Greek-English Lexicon* (9th ed., Liddell, Scott, Jones) [1996]

MM *The Vocabulary of the Greek New Testament* (Moulton and Milligan) [1930; 1997]

NA^{26} *Novum Testamentum Graece* (26th ed., Nestle-Aland) [1979]

NA^{27} *Novum Testamentum Graece* (27th ed., Nestle-Aland) [1993]

NBD *New Bible Dictionary* (2nd ed., Douglas, Hillyer) [1982]

NIDB *New International Dictionary of the Bible* (Douglas, Tenney) [1987]

NIDBA *New International Dictionary of Biblical Archaeology* (Blaiklock and Harrison) [1983]

NIDNTT *New International Dictionary of New Testament Theology* (4 vols., C. Brown) [1975–1985]

NIDOTTE *New International Dictionary of Old Testament Theology and Exegesis* (5 vols., W. A. VanGemeren) [1997]

PGM *Papyri graecae magicae: Die griechischen Zauberpapyri.* (Preisendanz) [1928]

PG *Patrologia Graecae* (J. P. Migne) [1857–1886]

TBD *Tyndale Bible Dictionary* (Elwell, Comfort) [2001]

TDNT *Theological Dictionary of the New Testament* (10 vols., Kittel, Friedrich; trans. Bromiley) [1964–1976]

TDOT *Theological Dictionary of the Old Testament* (8 vols., Botterweck, Ringgren; trans. Willis, Bromiley, Green) [1974–]

TLNT *Theological Lexicon of the New Testament* (3 vols., C. Spicq) [1994]

TLOT *Theological Lexicon of the Old Testament* (3 vols., E. Jenni) [1997]

TWOT *Theological Wordbook of the Old Testament* (2 vols., Harris, Archer) [1980]

UBS^3 *United Bible Societies' Greek New Testament* (3rd ed., Metzger et al.) [1975]

UBS^4 *United Bible Societies' Greek New Testament* (4th corrected ed., Metzger et al.) [1993]

WH *The New Testament in the Original Greek* (Westcott and Hort) [1882]

ABBREVIATIONS FOR BOOKS OF THE BIBLE

Old Testament

Gen	Genesis	1 Sam	1 Samuel	Esth	Esther
Exod	Exodus	2 Sam	2 Samuel	Ps, Pss	Psalm, Psalms
Lev	Leviticus	1 Kgs	1 Kings	Prov	Proverbs
Num	Numbers	2 Kgs	2 Kings	Eccl	Ecclesiastes
Deut	Deuteronomy	1 Chr	1 Chronicles	Song	Song of Songs
Josh	Joshua	2 Chr	2 Chronicles	Isa	Isaiah
Judg	Judges	Ezra	Ezra	Jer	Jeremiah
Ruth	Ruth	Neh	Nehemiah	Lam	Lamentations

Ezek	Ezekiel	Obad	Obadiah	Zeph	Zephaniah
Dan	Daniel	Jonah	Jonah	Hag	Haggai
Hos	Hosea	Mic	Micah	Zech	Zechariah
Joel	Joel	Nah	Nahum	Mal	Malachi
Amos	Amos	Hab	Habakkuk		

New Testament

Matt	Matthew	Eph	Ephesians	Heb	Hebrews
Mark	Mark	Phil	Philippians	Jas	James
Luke	Luke	Col	Colossians	1 Pet	1 Peter
John	John	1 Thess	1 Thessalonians	2 Pet	2 Peter
Acts	Acts	2 Thess	2 Thessalonians	1 John	1 John
Rom	Romans	1 Tim	1 Timothy	2 John	2 John
1 Cor	1 Corinthians	2 Tim	2 Timothy	3 John	3 John
2 Cor	2 Corinthians	Titus	Titus	Jude	Jude
Gal	Galatians	Phlm	Philemon	Rev	Revelation

Deuterocanonical

Bar	Baruch	1–2 Esdr	1–2 Esdras	Pr Man	Prayer of Manasseh
Add Dan	Additions to Daniel	Add Esth	Additions to Esther	Ps 151	Psalm 151
Pr Azar	Prayer of Azariah	Ep Jer	Epistle of Jeremiah	Sir	Sirach
Bel	Bel and the Dragon	Jdt	Judith	Tob	Tobit
Sg Three	Song of the Three	1–2 Macc	1–2 Maccabees	Wis	Wisdom of Solomon
	Children	3–4 Macc	3–4 Maccabees		
Sus	Susanna				

MANUSCRIPTS AND LITERATURE FROM QUMRAN

Initial numerals followed by "Q" indicate particular caves at Qumran. For example, the notation 4Q267 indicates text 267 from cave 4 at Qumran. Further, 1QS 4:9-10 indicates column 4, lines 9-10 of the *Rule of the Community*; and 4Q166 1 ii 2 indicates fragment 1, column ii, line 2 of text 166 from cave 4. More examples of common abbreviations are listed below.

CD	Cairo Geniza copy of the *Damascus Document*	1QIsa[b]	Isaiah copy [b]	4QLam[a]	Lamentations
		1QM	*War Scroll*	11QPs[a]	Psalms
1QH	*Thanksgiving Hymns*	1QpHab	*Pesher Habakkuk*	11QTemple[a,b]	*Temple Scroll*
1QIsa[a]	Isaiah copy [a]	1QS	*Rule of the Community*	11QtgJob	*Targum of Job*

IMPORTANT NEW TESTAMENT MANUSCRIPTS

(all dates given are AD; ordinal numbers refer to centuries)

Significant Papyri ($\mathfrak{P}$ = Papyrus)

$\mathfrak{P}$1 Matt 1; early 3rd
$\mathfrak{P}$4+$\mathfrak{P}$64+$\mathfrak{P}$67 Matt 3, 5, 26; Luke 1-6; late 2nd
$\mathfrak{P}$5 John 1, 16, 20; early 3rd
$\mathfrak{P}$13 Heb 2-5, 10-12; early 3rd
$\mathfrak{P}$15+$\mathfrak{P}$16 (probably part of same codex) 1 Cor 7-8, Phil 3-4; late 3rd

$\mathfrak{P}$20 James 2-3; 3rd
$\mathfrak{P}$22 John 15-16; mid 3rd
$\mathfrak{P}$23 James 1; c. 200
$\mathfrak{P}$27 Rom 8-9; 3rd
$\mathfrak{P}$30 1 Thess 4-5; 2 Thess 1; early 3rd
$\mathfrak{P}$32 Titus 1-2; late 2nd
$\mathfrak{P}$37 Matt 26; late 3rd

$\mathfrak{P}$39 John 8; first half of 3rd
$\mathfrak{P}$40 Rom 1-4, 6, 9; 3rd
$\mathfrak{P}$45 Gospels and Acts; early 3rd
$\mathfrak{P}$46 Paul's Major Epistles (less Pastorals); late 2nd
$\mathfrak{P}$47 Rev 9-17; 3rd

𝔓49+𝔓65 Eph 4-5; 1 Thess
   1-2; 3rd
𝔓52 John 18; c. 125
𝔓53 Matt 26, Acts 9-10;
   middle 3rd
𝔓66 John; late 2nd
𝔓70 Matt 2-3, 11-12, 24; 3rd
𝔓72 1-2 Peter, Jude; c. 300

𝔓74 Acts, General Epistles; 7th
𝔓75 Luke and John; c. 200
𝔓77+𝔓103 (probably part of
   same codex) Matt 13-14, 23;
   late 2nd
𝔓87 Phlm; late 2nd
𝔓90 John 18-19; late 2nd
𝔓91 Acts 2-3; 3rd

𝔓92 Eph 1, 2 Thess 1; c. 300
𝔓98 Rev 1:13-20; late 2nd
𝔓100 James 3-5; c. 300
𝔓101 Matt 3-4; 3rd
𝔓104 Matt 21; 2nd
𝔓106 John 1; 3rd
𝔓115 Rev 2-3, 5-6, 8-15; 3rd

Significant Uncials

ℵ (Sinaiticus) most of NT; 4th
A (Alexandrinus) most of NT;
   5th
B (Vaticanus) most of NT; 4th
C (Ephraemi Rescriptus) most
   of NT with many lacunae;
   5th
D (Bezae) Gospels, Acts; 5th
D (Claromontanus), Paul's
   Epistles; 6th (different MS
   than Bezae)
E (Laudianus 35) Acts; 6th
F (Augensis) Paul's Epistles; 9th
G (Boernerianus) Paul's
   Epistles; 9th

H (Coislinianus) Paul's
   Epistles; 6th
I (Freerianus or Washington)
   Paul's Epistles; 5th
L (Regius) Gospels; 8th
Q (Guelferbytanus B) Luke,
   John; 5th
P (Porphyrianus) Acts—
   Revelation; 9th
T (Borgianus) Luke, John; 5th
W (Washingtonianus or the
   Freer Gospels) Gospels; 5th
Z (Dublinensis) Matthew; 6th
037 (Δ; Sangallensis) Gospels;
   9th

038 (Θ; Koridethi) Gospels;
   9th
040 (Ξ; Zacynthius) Luke; 6th
043 (Φ; Beratinus) Matt,
   Mark; 6th
044 (Ψ; Athous Laurae)
   Gospels, Acts, Paul's
   Epistles; 9th
048 Acts, Paul's Epistles,
   General Epistles; 5th
0171 Matt 10, Luke 22;
   c. 300
0189 Acts 5; c. 200

Significant Minuscules

1 Gospels, Acts, Paul's Epistles;
   12th
33 All NT except Rev; 9th
81 Acts, Paul's Epistles,
   General Epistles; 1044
565 Gospels; 9th
700 Gospels; 11th

1424 (or Family 1424—a
   group of 29 manuscripts
   sharing nearly the same
   text) most of NT; 9th-10th
1739 Acts, Paul's Epistles; 10th
2053 Rev; 13th
2344 Rev; 11th

f^1 (a family of manuscripts
   including 1, 118, 131, 209)
   Gospels; 12th-14th
f^{13} (a family of manuscripts
   including 13, 69, 124, 174,
   230, 346, 543, 788, 826,
   828, 983, 1689, 1709—
   known as the Ferrar group)
   Gospels; 11th-15th

Significant Ancient Versions

SYRIAC (SYR)
syr^c (Syriac Curetonian)
   Gospels; 5th
syr^s (Syriac Sinaiticus)
   Gospels; 4th
syr^h (Syriac Harklensis) Entire
   NT; 616

OLD LATIN (IT)
it^a (Vercellenis) Gospels; 4th
it^b (Veronensis) Gospels; 5th
it^d (Cantabrigiensis—the Latin
   text of Bezae) Gospels, Acts,
   3 John; 5th
it^e (Palantinus) Gospels; 5th
it^k (Bobiensis) Matthew, Mark;
   c. 400

COPTIC (COP)
cop^{bo} (Boharic—north Egypt)
cop^{fay} (Fayyumic—central Egypt)
cop^{sa} (Sahidic—southern Egypt)

OTHER VERSIONS
arm (Armenian)
eth (Ethiopic)
geo (Georgian)

TRANSLITERATION AND NUMBERING SYSTEM

Note: For words and roots from non-biblical languages (e.g., Arabic, Ugaritic), only approximate transliterations are given.

HEBREW/ARAMAIC

Consonants

א	*aleph*	= '	מ, ם	*mem*	= *m*
ב, בּ	*beth*	= *b*	נ, ן	*nun*	= *n*
ג, גּ	*gimel*	= *g*	ס	*samekh*	= *s*
ד, דּ	*daleth*	= *d*	ע	*ayin*	= '
ה	*he*	= *h*	פ, פּ, ף	*pe*	= *p*
ו	*waw*	= *w*	צ, ץ	*tsadhe*	= *ts*
ז	*zayin*	= *z*	ק	*qoph*	= *q*
ח	*heth*	= *kh*	ר	*resh*	= *r*
ט	*teth*	= *t*	שׁ	*shin*	= *sh*
י	*yodh*	= *y*	שׂ	*sin*	= *s*
כ, ךּ, ך	*kaph*	= *k*	ת, תּ	*taw*	= *t, th*
ל	*lamedh*	= *l*			(spirant)

Vowels

ַ	*patakh*	= *a*		*qamets khatuf*	= *o*
ַה	*furtive patakh*	= *a*		*holem*	= *o*
ָ	*qamets*	= *a*	וֹ	*full holem*	= *o*
ָה	*final qamets he*	= *ah*		*short qibbuts*	= *u*
ֶ	*segol*	= *e*		*long qibbuts*	= *u*
ֵ	*tsere*	= *e*	וּ	*shureq*	= *u*
ֵי	*tsere yod*	= *e*		*khatef patakh*	= *a*
ִ	*short hireq*	= *i*		*khatef qamets*	= *o*
ִ	*long hireq*	= *i*		*vocalic shewa*	= *e*
ִי	*hireq yod*	= *i*		*patakh yodh*	= *a*

Greek

α	*alpha*	= *a*	ε	*epsilon*	= *e*
β	*beta*	= *b*	ζ	*zeta*	= *z*
γ	*gamma*	= *g, n (before*	η	*eta*	= *ē*
		γ, κ, ξ, χ)	θ	*theta*	= *th*
δ	*delta*	= *d*	ι	*iota*	= *i*

κ	kappa	= k		τ	tau	= t
λ	lamda	= l		υ	upsilon	= u
μ	mu	= m		φ	phi	= ph
ν	nu	= n		χ	chi	= ch
ξ	ksi	= x		ψ	psi	= ps
ο	omicron	= o		ω	omega	= ō
π	pi	= p		ʽ	rough	= h (with
ρ	rho	= r (ῥ = rh)			breathing	vowel or
σ, ς	sigma	= s			mark	diphthong)

THE TYNDALE-STRONG'S NUMBERING SYSTEM

The Cornerstone Biblical Commentary series uses a word-study numbering system to give both newer and more advanced Bible students alike quicker, more convenient access to helpful original-language tools (e.g., concordances, lexicons, and theological dictionaries). Those who are unfamiliar with the ancient Hebrew, Aramaic, and Greek alphabets can quickly find information on a given word by looking up the appropriate index number. Advanced students will find the system helpful because it allows them to quickly find the lexical form of obscure conjugations and inflections.

There are two main numbering systems used for biblical words today. The one familiar to most people is the Strong's numbering system (made popular by the *Strong's Exhaustive Concordance to the Bible*). Although the original Strong's system is still quite useful, the most up-to-date research has shed new light on the biblical languages and allows for more precision than is found in the original Strong's system. The Cornerstone Biblical Commentary series, therefore, features a newly revised version of the Strong's system, the Tyndale-Strong's numbering system. The Tyndale-Strong's system brings together the familiarity of the Strong's system and the best of modern scholarship. In most cases, the original Strong's numbers are preserved. In places where new research dictates, new or related numbers have been added.[1]

The second major numbering system today is the Goodrick-Kohlenberger system used in a number of study tools published by Zondervan. In order to give students broad access to a number of helpful tools, the Commentary provides index numbers for the Zondervan system as well.

The different index systems are designated as follows:

TG Tyndale-Strong's Greek number   ZH Zondervan Hebrew number
ZG Zondervan Greek number   TA Tyndale-Strong's Aramaic number
TH Tyndale-Strong's Hebrew number   ZA Zondervan Aramaic number

So in the example, "love" *agapē* [TG26, ZG27], the first number is the one to use with Greek tools keyed to the Tyndale-Strong's system, and the second applies to tools that use the Zondervan system.

1. Generally, one may simply use the original four-digit Strong's number to identify words in tools using Strong's system. If a Tyndale-Strong's number is followed by a capital letter (e.g., TG1692A), it generally indicates an added subdivision of meaning for the given term. Whenever a Tyndale-Strong's number has a number following a decimal point (e.g., TG2013.1), it reflects an instance where new research has yielded a separate, new classification of use for a biblical word. Forthcoming tools from Tyndale House Publishers will include these entries, which were not part of the original Strong's system.

The Gospel of
John
GRANT OSBORNE

John

THE GOSPEL OF JOHN is so simple that it is often the first biblical book given to seekers and recent converts to help them understand Christian truth, and yet it is so difficult that only experienced scholars attempt to study it. It is paradoxically the most accessible and yet the most complex of the four Gospels. There are many reasons why this is so. John presents the basic gospel, as well as the necessity of having faith, more directly than any of the Gospels. It also brilliantly dramatizes the process of one's decision to have faith. If I were teaching a course in creative writing, I would use John's Gospel along with Shakespeare's plays as examples of brilliant characterization and plot. The longest stories in the synoptic Gospels consist of about 20 or so verses, but John's dramas (chs 1; 3; 4; 6; 9; 11) are closer to 40 verses long, and they are powerfully written, centering on the encounter of various characters with Jesus as the Christ and Son of God.

AUTHOR

It is important to know the author of a document in order to interpret the message and determine the historical veracity of what the document reports. All four canonical Gospels, however, are anonymous—that is, they do not name their authors. In order to determine the author of John, there are two sources of information that must be examined—the external evidence from the early church fathers and the internal evidence from the Gospel itself.

External Evidence for Authorship. The earliest church fathers (such as Ignatius and Polycarp) do not mention John by name. Polycarp, however, quotes 1 John 4:2 (*To the Philippians* 7.1), and Justin Martyr alludes to John 3:3-5 (*First Apology* 61.4-5) and speaks of the "memoirs of the apostles" (*First Apology* 67.4), undoubtedly referring to Matthew and John, the two apostles among the four Evangelists. In addition, John was an apparent favorite of the Gnostics (it was often cited in the *Gospel of Truth*), and this misuse of his Gospel by the Gnostics may have contributed to a reluctance of the orthodox to quote him. Tatian used John as the historical basis of his harmonization of the four Gospels (the *Diatesseron*), and Athenagorus also alluded to it. The first to quote from John's Gospel is Theophilus of Antioch (AD 181). Irenaeus (c. AD 180) attributes the Gospel to John (*Against Heresies* 3.1.1), as does the Muratorian Canon and the anti-Marcionite prologue (both late-second century). Irenaeus, in that same statement, says he heard Polycarp talk about being tutored by John, the apostle who had seen the Lord. By the end of the second century (and from that point on) there was near unanimous acceptance of John's

Gospel. The one exception was the *Alogoi* (those who rejected John's Gospel or *logos* [TH3056, ZH3364]; cf. Irenaeus *Against Heresies* 3.2.9; Epiphanius *Refutation of All Heresies* 51), who opposed it primarily because of its use by the Montanists, a charismatic group who claimed its founder (Montanus) was the Paraclete of 14:16.

One item remains: Eusebius (c. AD 300) believed there had been two leaders of the church named John and quotes Papias (beginning of the second century) as speaking of "the discourses of the elders, what Andrew or what Peter said . . . or what John or Matthew or any other of the Lord's disciples, and things which Aristion and John the elder, disciples of the Lord, say" (*Ecclesiastical History* 3.39.4-5). This is often taken as evidence that the "elder John" rather than the apostle was author of the fourth Gospel, but Carson (1991:69-70) sums up the view of many who believe Eusebius misunderstood Papias, who more likely equated the "elder John" with the John who wrote one of "the discourses of the elders." While Eusebius separated elders from apostles, Papias did not. More likely, Papias was distinguishing eyewitnesses who had died from eyewitnesses who were still alive. Thus, the elder John was identical with the apostle John and wrote this Gospel. (See discussion on this issue in the Introduction to 1 John.) In short, the external testimony strongly favors John's authorship of the fourth Gospel—that is, John the son of Zebedee, one of the twelve apostles.

Internal Evidence of Authorship. As for internal evidence of John's authorship, Morris (1969:218-256, building on Westcott) mounts his evidence in five steps. The writer was (1) Jewish, as seen in his knowledge of Jewish customs and culture, as well as his knowledge of groups like the Pharisees and Sadducees in the time of Jesus and his acquaintance with Aramaic; (2) Palestinian, as seen in his accurate knowledge of the geography of the area—for example, the pools of Bethesda (5:2) and Siloam (9:11), Jacob's well (4:5), and the "Stone Pavement" (19:13); (3) an eyewitness (emphasized in 19:35, 21:24; cf. 1 John 1:1), as demonstrated in the accuracy of the minute details in the Gospel that can be corroborated historically or have parallels with the Synoptics (Stauffer 1960b); (4) one of the twelve disciples, as seen in 21:20-24, which calls the author the "disciple Jesus loved"; and (5) John the son of Zebedee, also linked to the identity of the beloved disciple.

Who was the "disciple Jesus loved"? He is mentioned in five passages (13:23; 19:26; 20:2; 21:7, 20) and is called "the one who testifies to these events and has recorded them here" (21:24). He has been variously identified as Lazarus ("loved" by Jesus in 11:3, 36; cf. "dear friend," NLT); John Mark (Acts 12:12), associated with Peter and traditionally ascribed as the author of the second Gospel; Thomas, a leader among the disciples according to the fourth Gospel (11:16; 20:24); an unknown convert from the Essenes who was living in Jerusalem (Capper 1998: 47-55); the elder John (cf. above); John the son of Zebedee; or a fictional creation intended to portray the ideal disciple (or the ideal author—so Bauckham 1993). When one considers the evidence in the fourth Gospel, certain things seem fairly evident. Few any longer think of this beloved disciple as entirely fictional. First, O'Grady (1998:24-26) argues that he is both a historical person and the archetypal disciple. Second, in 13:23 the beloved disciple is at the Last Supper, and Matthew

26:20 tells us that only the Twelve were present with Jesus. Also, in 21:2 he is with or among a group of seven disciples, all of whom were probably members of the Twelve. This makes Lazarus, John Mark, and a separate "elder John" (cf. above) unlikely. Third, in every story the beloved disciple is paired with Peter, and this would favor John the apostle, one of the inner circle of three that was made up of Peter, James, and John. James could not have been the author because he died at the hands of Herod (Acts 12:2) long before John was written.

Critics (e.g., Brown, Schnackenburg, Barrett) have dismissed John's authorship of the fourth Gospel on the grounds that a nearly illiterate fisherman from Galilee could hardly have written so deep a work and that the detailed knowledge of Judean geography and topography means the person was from Judea not Galilee. They also doubt whether a Galilean fisherman could have had access to Herod's courtyard (cf. note on 18:15). (For a more complete list of criticisms, see Blomberg 2001:31-35.) These arguments are not entirely valid, however. Most Jews were quite literate, and John spent a great deal of time, perhaps years, in Judea (on his access to the court-yard, see commentary on 18:15-16). Charlesworth (1995:225-437) is the major proponent of the view that the beloved disciple was Thomas, but this argument falters when we read in 20:8 that the beloved disciple came to faith at the empty tomb, whereas Thomas did not believe in the risen Christ until Jesus' second post-Resurrection appearance (20:27-29). Therefore, the beloved disciple who penned this Gospel is most likely John the son of Zebedee.

The Johannine Circle as "Author." It has been common for critical scholars in recent decades (e.g., Bultmann, Brown, Schnackenburg, Culpepper [1975], Zumstein) to posit that this Gospel was written by a circle or community of disciples of John rather than by John himself. The reason they do so are the many "aporias," the clumsy transitions that make them think a later editor has inserted material. They point out, for example, the different style of 1:1-18; Jesus going from Judea to Galilee, back to Judea, and then back to Galilee again in chapters 2-4; a similar movement from Samaria to Galilee to Jerusalem to Galilee and back to Jerusalem in chapters 5-6; the mention of Mary anointing Jesus in 11:2 before the event; and so on. The best known reconstruction came from Brown (1966:xxxiv-xxxix), who has five stages: (1) tradition stemming from the apostle himself; (2) elaboration on that tradition with preaching from the Johannine community; (3) the first collection in a Gospel form; (4) further editing from an anonymous disciple; and (5) a final reworking from a later editor. The speculative nature of such reconstructions is startling, and Carson (1991:42-43) speaks of it as "the uncontrolled pursuit of sources and traditions" in a manner that cannot be tested. Is the fourth Gospel really that clumsy? Culpepper wrote a later volume, *The Anatomy of the Fourth Gospel* (1983), which demonstrated the remarkable unity and precision of the plot development. He did not realize that his second book made his first (*The Johannine School,* 1975) unnecessary; if John fits together perfectly, there is no need to posit successive redactions. There are no truly clumsy transitions in John. In short, John is a whole Gospel written by a single person (cf. Hengel 1989:80-83), John the apostle and disciple of Jesus.

DATE

The latest possible date for the writing of John's Gospel is AD 110–120 because there is an early papyrus fragment of John ($\mathfrak{P}$52; John Rylands Papyrus 457) dated to this period. Another papyrus fragment of an unknown Gospel (known as Egerton Papyrus 2) that was based on John's Gospel is dated c. 130–150. These copies evidence the existence of John's Gospel at least to the beginning of the second century, if not earlier. The earliest possible date for John's Gospel is probably the late 60s (if John knew of Mark and perhaps Matthew; Morris [1969] and Burge [2000] place it here). Most assign it to the 80s or early 90s due to 21:23, which probably was penned while John was either near the end of his life or already dead (if he wrote Revelation, he lived past AD 95, when it was most likely composed [cf. Osborne 2002]). Beyond this rough time frame we cannot go with certainty. We simply do not know the order of his writings—the Gospel, the three epistles, Revelation. Many think the phrase "expelled from the synagogue" in 9:22, 12:42, and 16:2 refers to the time after Christians were kicked out of synagogues in the early 80s, but that is an unprovable assumption. The Jewish ban expelling Jews from synagogues probably existed in Jesus' day as well (for examples see Brown 1970:374).

Though there is no absolute proof, the traditional place of writing, Ephesus, remains the most likely. John ministered there for a great deal of time (attested by Irenaeus in *Against Heresies* 3.1.2 and by Eusebius in *Ecclesiastical History* 3.1.1), and the book of Revelation was written for the churches in that area.

AUDIENCE AND PURPOSE OF WRITING

The key to the purpose of the fourth Gospel is found in 20:31— "These are written so that you may continue to believe that Jesus is the Messiah, the Son of God." Scholars, however, debate as to whether this means saving faith on the part of non-Christians or growing faith on the part of Christians. Some (Morris and especially Carson) believe John wrote primarily to evangelize Jews; others (Brown, Kysar, Michaels, Ridderbos) think he wrote mainly for believers. This is certainly a false dichotomy. I am not convinced by either extreme. Rather, John wrote both to awaken faith in the lost and to quicken faith in the followers of Jesus (so Bruce, Beasley-Murray, Whitacre, Burge). This issue is similar to that found in all four Gospels.

It is common today to believe that all four Gospels, including John, were originally intended almost entirely for Christians. Some have thought they were written for specific Christian communities. Bauckham (1998) provides a valuable service in showing that the Gospels were not written to separate communities (the Markan community, the Johannine community), as has been presupposed by critical scholars (who always searched for the *Sitz im Leben* or "situation in the life" of each differing community behind a Gospel). Rather, each Gospel was intended for the whole church. However, Bauckham dismisses in one footnote (1998:9) the possibility of an evangelistic or apologetic purpose and concludes, "On this question the present chapter takes for granted, without arguing the point, the answer given by the scholarly consensus, that all Gospels were intended to reach, in the first place, a Christian audience" (1998:9-10). However, such an assumption should not be made. While this is likely true for Matthew and Mark, it is not true for Luke and John, as seen in the fact that the central theme in both is soteriology (for Luke see Marshall 1970 and Evans 1990:104-111). Though Carson does not prove his point that John centers entirely on evangelistic concerns (1991:87-95), he certainly does prove that evangelism is a major purpose of his Gospel (so also Keener, Köstenberger).

John wanted to win the lost as well as strengthen the believers. In fact, in chapters 1–12, encounters with Jesus and faith-decisions are certainly in the foreground. It is true that the diatribe against the Jewish people (e.g., chs 5–10) is a telling point against a purely evangelistic interest. In fact, Whitacre (1999:28-33) sees conflict both with the synagogue/rabbinic Judaism and with a similar proto-Gnosticism as that which John fought against in his first epistle. The latter is questionable (there is not enough evidence for such a theme), but the former is a definite emphasis. John wanted to encourage the church in light of Jewish persecution.

CANONICITY AND TEXTUAL HISTORY
The fourth Gospel has long been recognized as one of the four canonical Gospels. Irenaeus was among the first to recognize the four Gospels (Matthew, Mark, Luke, and John) as being the exclusively canonized Gospels (*Against Heresies* 3.11.11). The Muratorian Canon (c. AD 200) also affirms John's Gospel as part of the canon, as did Eusebius (*Ecclesiastical History* 6.14.7) in about 325, and Athanasius in 367 (presenting the Canon of the Western church in his *Festal Letter*).

There are more extant early manuscripts for the Gospel of John than for any other book of the New Testament. Manuscripts of the second and third century include: 𝔓5, 𝔓22, 𝔓28, 𝔓39, 𝔓45, 𝔓52, 𝔓66, 𝔓75, 𝔓80, 𝔓90, 𝔓95, 𝔓107, 𝔓108, and 𝔓109. Among these, 𝔓52 belongs to the early second century (c. 110, the earliest extant ms of the NT), 𝔓66 belongs to middle of the second century, and 𝔓75 to the end of the second century (Comfort and Barrett 2001:365-366, 376-379, 501). Of all these manuscripts, 𝔓75 is the most accurate copy of John. The manuscript, produced by a very careful scribe, has the kind of text that was used by another careful scribe—the one who produced the fourth-century manuscript known as codex Vaticanus (cf. Porter 1962:363-376). All textual critics agree that 𝔓75 and B provide the best textual witness to the original wording of John's Gospel. The corrected text of 𝔓66 (notated as 𝔓66ᶜ) is also a good witness, as are 𝔓39 and 𝔓90. Other manuscripts of the fourth and fifth century that provide good witness to the original text of John are codex Sinaiticus (ℵ, from John 9–21), T, and W (Comfort 2007: Introduction).

LITERARY STYLE
John's style is very memorable. His discourses were written in high prose, at times close to poetry, and have a definite "ring" to them. At the same time, his Greek seems clumsy, using a great deal of parataxis (coordinate clauses instead of subordination) and asyndeton (clauses connected without conjunctions), neither of which was

considered good style. He loved variation and double meaning. He favored synonyms for stylistic variety (e.g., four word-pairs in the well-known "do you love me" section in 21:15-17). The synonymous use of "believe," "know," and "see" for salvific encounter is also well known (cf. below). His preference for key terms that he used again and again makes this book a treasure house for word studies on terms like the three above as well as the words "witness," "command," "life," "truth," "world," "abide," "light," "darkness," and "reveal." He also uses a great deal of chiasmus and *inclusio,* in which the last part of a discourse returns to the beginning ideas for emphasis (cf. 6:36-40; and see the trial before Pilate in 18:28–19:16). Finally, his Gospel is filled with misunderstandings (Jesus speaks on the heavenly plane as his hearers misinterpret on the earthly plane) and irony (throughout the Passion narrative, the forces of evil are used by God to accomplish his purposes).

Probably the best known aspect of John is his differences with the synoptic Gospels. Over 85 percent of John's Gospel is unique material. While many believe John is independent from the Synoptics, a lot can be said regarding possible connections. Blomberg (2001:46-48) notes three periods in the debate: (1) Until the 1930s it was assumed John knew of the other Gospels but simply wished to supplement them and go his own way. (2) Due to the fact that there is very little verbal similarity at any point with the Synoptics (even accounts of the same event), later scholars (such as Dodd and Brown in the 1960s) turned to asserting the complete independence of John. (3) Then, in the 1980s, the pendulum began to swing back as several parenthetical remarks in John (e.g., 3:24; 5:33-35; 7:1; 11:2, 56-57; 18:24, 28) have made viable some connection with Mark at least (here Blomberg follows Bauckham 1998). Brodie (1993) even goes so far as to say that John systematically uses all of Mark, most of Matthew, and some of Luke–Acts. Today most believe John's omissions were deliberate, and he was indeed supplementing the synoptic witness. Vogler (1999a) goes too far when he says John was a critic of the synoptic tradition and intended not just to supplement but to correct it. Carson (1991:51-54) is closer when he speaks of "an interlocking tradition, i.e., where they mutually reinforce or explain each other, without betraying overt literary dependence." One of John's purposes was to preserve many stories and sayings not found in the other Gospels. This provided an invaluable service to the church.

To make room for his new material, John omitted many key events in Jesus' life, like the Baptism (the Baptist only briefly and indirectly speaks of it; 1:29-34), the temptation by Satan, the Transfiguration, the words of institution at the Last Supper, and Gethsemane. There is no commission or mission of the Twelve, no Olivet discourse, no exorcisms, and none of the lengthy parables. At the same time, he adds a great deal of material, such as the first calling of the disciples in chapter 1, the two miracles in Cana, Jesus' encounters with Nicodemus and the Samaritan woman, the conflict narratives of chapters 5–8, the healing of the man born blind, the raising of Lazarus, and the *mashal* (see note on 10:6) of the Good Shepherd and of the Vine and branches. John seems to have followed a different chronology, centering on the three Passover festivals (2:13; 6:4; 11:55) and involving several trips by

Jesus to Jerusalem. (In the Synoptics, Jesus does not visit Jerusalem until the end of his ministry.)

Furthermore, the style of Jesus' discourses differs markedly from the Synoptics. There Jesus told people not to tell anyone of his messianic works (the so-called "messianic secret"), but in John he tells everyone who he is, often employing "I am" terminology. The Jesus of John confronts his listeners with the reality of who he is in language that is unique among the four Gospels. This has led many critical scholars to wonder if we have the same Jesus in John as in the other three. But John's presentation of Jesus as Christ is not so different that it warrants such a conclusion. Mark is the primary Gospel centering on the messianic secret; Matthew and Luke contain many of the secrecy passages but also contain passages with high Christology, in which Jesus reveals who he is. The Christology of the latter two is similar to John's. There Jesus is called not only *Messiah* but *Son of Man* and *Son of God*. There Jesus forgives sins (an action attributable only to God; cf. Luke 5:21 and parallels) and declares he is "the Son of Man seated in the place of power at God's right hand and coming on the clouds of heaven" (Matt 26:64). The divinity of Jesus, though not as explicitly stated, is still clear in the Synoptics, and there is no contradiction. For instance, the "Johannine thunderbolt" in Matthew 11:27 says, "My Father has entrusted everything to me. No one truly knows the Son except the Father, and no one truly knows the Father except the Son and those to whom the Son chooses to reveal him." It is difficult to imagine anything closer to John than this. Moreover, Feinberg (1979) has shown that John's language is within the bounds of *ipsissima vox*, "the very voice of Jesus," and that is within the boundaries of a high view of Scripture. Carson (1991:47) speaks "of the liberty he felt to use his own language, of the principles of selection that governed his choice of material"—all within the larger context of historical interest.

HISTORICAL RELIABILITY OF THE GOSPEL OF JOHN

First, it must be said that when the history of John is discussed, it is usually the history of the Johannine community (at the time the Gospel was written, c. 40–70 years after Jesus) rather than of the actual period of Jesus' life. In her discussion of literature (text) and history (context), C. H. Conway (2002:493) says, "Since the dawn of historical criticism of the Bible, history has been privileged over the text in order to discover the meaning of the text." Thus, for example, Conway thinks the meaning of the Gospel of John can be discovered vis-à-vis the context of a historical "Johannine" community. As such, she and many others have redefined the meaning of "historical" until it is no longer the events behind the text but a scholarly re-creation of a community assumed to exist at the time of writing! She and others should take note of Bauckham (1998), who argues that all four Gospels were not written for any specific community but are *The Gospels for All Christians*.

Next, it needs to be said that over the last couple of centuries no Gospel has been more doubted with respect to its historical reliability than John's, largely because of its differences with the Synoptics. Blomberg (1987:153-155) has noted five reasons for doubting its trustworthiness: (1) John's selection of material (as noted earlier, 85 percent of his material is unique); (2) his theological distinctives, like the deity of Christ, the promise of eternal life, and his presentation of when the Spirit was given; (3) his chronology, which contradicts the Synoptics (Jesus' numerous trips to Jerusalem, the three Passover festivals); (4) the book's apparent historical discrepancies (birth in Nazareth, perhaps alluded to in 7:52; the raising of Lazarus as the catalyst for Jesus' arrest); and (5) the different style of his writing (cf. "Literary Style" above).

Recent critical studies have found John's Gospel to have more historically reliable material than heretofore noticed (as in the commentaries of Brown, Lindars, Barrett, Schnackenburg), and numerous commentators have considered it to be almost entirely accurate historically (cf. the commentaries of Morris, Bruce, Beasely-Murray, Michaels, Carson, Witherington, Borchert, Ridderbos, Whitacre, Köstenberger, Burge, Blomberg). While some (e.g., Culpepper 1983) treat John as fiction, Tovey (1997:265-266), after a detailed study of John on the basis of narrative criticism and speech-act theory, concludes that John is "a form of historical discourse" in which historical interests intersect theological interests, yielding "interpretations which are true with regard to the assertions made about events in the real historical world." Jackson (1999:26-28, 32-34) points out that while John utilized Hellenistic conventions in constructing his story, he intended the reader to understand it as a historically accurate eyewitness report, with the author participating in the events via the third-person literary style (i.e., avoiding first-person and calling himself the "beloved disciple"), similar to that of the Roman historian Thucydides. With more and more information becoming available about the times and customs when Jesus was alive, John seems to be increasingly corroborated as a reliable witness. Blomberg (2001:56-57) names four areas of historical evidence demonstrating trustworthiness: (1) the issues Jesus discusses reflect key issues in the pre-70 AD period (ritual purification, the Samaritans, Sabbath rules, the value of testimony about oneself); (2) parallels with the Pauline Epistles show the value of the Johannine traditions (hostility of Jews against Jesus, 1 Thess 2:13-16; revelation and knowledge, 1 Cor 1–4; high Christology, Phil 2:5-11); (3) John differentiates what was known before the Cross from what was realized afterward (2:22; 7:39; 12:16; 16:12-13); (4) John's frequent emphasis on "witness" and "truth" mitigates against an intention to write a fictional account; in fact, he seems to have developed a "prophetic lawsuit" against those who would do such. Moloney (2000:57-58) shows that in the events of Jesus' early ministry, John was even more accurate than Mark, who omits many of the events. Ridderbos (1997:14) says that while "the referential character of the miracles" as signs is stressed, "the historical reality of the miracles themselves does not thereby become a secondary or indifferent matter." In fact, for John they serve as witnesses precisely because they actually occurred in history (10:37-38).

MAJOR THEMES AND THEOLOGICAL CONCERNS

The core of John's thought is the wondrous event that the Son of God came down to earth in human form to reveal God and offer salvation. It is impossible to separate soteriology (the doctrine of salvation) from Christology (the doctrine of Christ) in John, though both emphases come to the fore at different points. Since the fourth Gospel is primarily an encounter Gospel in which Christ challenges each individual character (and reader) about the truths of God and forces them to make a decision based on faith (i.e., no one can remain neutral about Jesus; each must decide to accept or reject Christ), soteriology will be first.

Salvation. John's dramas inevitably stress what I call a "faith-decision." This is seen in the conversion of the five disciples in 1:35-51, Jesus' challenge to Nicodemus in 3:1-15, and the conversions of the Samaritan woman in 4:1-42 and of the man born blind in 9:1-41. The emphasis is on the universal effects of this encounter. Jesus sheds his light on every person (1:4, 7, 9) and is "Savior of the world" (4:42; cf. 1 John 4:14) and of "everyone" (1:7; 5:23; 11:48; 12:32). Here we may observe how John centers on certain key terms. The mission of Jesus and the church (cf. further below) is to "the world," a term found in John's writings in 105 of its 186 occurences in the New Testament. The main thrust is that the world is dominated by sin and rebellion, with Satan being the "ruler of this world" (12:31; 14:30; 16:20). The Jewish people are part of this world (1:10-11); indeed, a tone of hostility coming from the Jewish people dominates the latter half of the Gospel. At the same time, however, God's salvific love extends to the world (3:16), and Jesus was sent to save it (1:29; 3:17; 4:42; 6:33). The world is under God's judgment and is subject to death (8:24) due to unbelief (3:36; 16:9), but Christ has defeated Satan (12:31; 16:11) and brought salvation. So John is not anti-Semitic; he emphasizes Jewish guilt but does so in order to draw the Jews to their Messiah (see Keener 2003:1.227-228).

The challenge to faith is seen in several clusters of terms (many of which are thoroughly discussed by Brown 1966:497-518). I will point out five examples here: (1) The verb "believe" (*pisteuō* [TG4100, ZG4409]; John never uses the noun) is found 98 times versus 34 total in the Synoptics, and the use of the verb shows that for him, faith is a dynamic commitment to Christ. (2) The two verbs for "know" (*ginōskō* [TG1097, ZG1182] and *oida* [TG1097, ZG3857]) are virtually synonymous in John, used a total of 141 times, centering on the intimate knowledge between Father and Son, which is then extended to Jesus' followers (10:14-15). Knowledge is equated with obedience and a life of active trust in God. (3) Five verbs are used for "see" a total of 114 times, and while many are used of physical sight, a number signify spiritual insight (cf. the movement of the man born blind from physical to spiritual sight in ch 9). This idea is often coupled with "know" (14:7) or "believe" (1:50; 2:23-24; 4:48). To "see" means to recognize the true significance of Jesus and his glory (1:14) and to enter a life of discipleship (cf. Keller 2000). (4) The result of grasping, by faith, the significance of Jesus is marked by the centrality of the term "life"/"eternal life" (*zōē* [TG2222, ZG2437]), found in John in 66 of its 135 occurrences in the New Testament (it is found 16 times in the Synoptics). In 20:31, life is the goal of the whole Gospel. Jesus is the source of "living water," the "food" that gives eternal life (4:14; 6:27, 35). In John, eternal life is not just a future possibility but a realized or present reality; those who come to faith "have" eternal life and will be "raised" (6:40, 47). (5) Another characterization of faith in Jesus is "truth" (*alētheia* [TG225, ZG237]), which appears in John 85 of the 163 times it occurs in the New Testament (it is found 10 times in the Synoptics). The term indicates both intellectual and moral truth—not just knowledge but patterns of living (e.g., "walk in truth," 3:21; 1 John 1:6; 2 John 1:4; 3 John 1:3). In Jesus, as "the truth" (14:6), God's redemptive purpose was truly realized, and the way to God was truly revealed. In a sense, it means authentic living in light of the final truth that has been revealed in Jesus.

Jesus Christ, Both God and Man. John shows a remarkable balance between Jesus' divinity and his humanity. The divinity of Jesus is expressed most powerfully in 1:1, 18; 10:30, as well as in the "I AM" sayings, especially those in the absolute form in 8:24, 28, 58; 13:19 ("I AM"); and those with an implied predicate, "I AM (he)." Most agree that these are direct allusions to God's revelation of himself as Yahweh in Exodus 3:14-15 ("I AM WHO I AM") and the use of *'anoki hu'* [TH595/1931, ZH644/2085] ("I [am] he") in Isaiah 51:12 (cf. Isa 43:10; 47:8, 10) to signify "God and God alone." At the same time, as the Son of the Father, Jesus is not only one with him, he is also subordinate to him. The theme is implicit in the prologue with Jesus as the revealing Word and becomes explicit in Jesus as the agent or "sent one" in 3:17 (over 30 instances of Jesus being "sent" in the Gospel as a whole). Köstenberger (1998a:108-111) notes several themes showing a relationship of dependence: the one sent brings glory and honor to the Father, does not do his own will and works but those of the sender, speaks the words of the sender, is accountable to him, bears witness to him, has delegated authority and represents the sender accurately, and knows the sender intimately. In short, Jesus' work is oriented completely to his Father, and he relies completely on the Father. This is developed further in 5:19-30, where he does nothing on his own but only "what he sees the Father doing" (cf. 3:17; 4:34; 5:36; 6:38; 7:16, 33; 8:29; 12:27, 49; 14:28). At every point, he states he has descended from heaven and is returning soon, showing the source of his authority. Jesus is fully God and at the same time submissive to God (cf. Barrett 1982:19-36; Carson 1991:250-251).

In terms of the relationship between Jesus' human flesh and his divine glory, Bultmann said John radicalized the paradox by presenting his glory as "hidden" in his flesh, while Käsemann radicalized his mentor (Bultmann) by saying John had a "naive docetism" in which Jesus carried the divine *doxa* [TG1391, ZG1518] in his incarnation. Both are wrong. John shows that Jesus is the incarnate God-man, and his flesh and glory are in perfect balance (1:1, 14). Jesus is the exemplar of "perfect humanity" (4:7, 31; 11:35; 17:24) and as such is the pattern his followers are to copy (cf. Cadman 1969). In the "glory" theme, there is a major motif that represents the glory of God from the Old Testament attributed to Jesus as the "embodiment of divine glory" and as the "visible divine presence exercising itself in mighty acts" (Brown 1966:503). John is unique in emphasizing how this glory was visible in Jesus, leading to belief (2:11; 11:40; 17:4). The fourth Gospel presents Jesus' death as his glorification, as can be seen from the "lifted up" passages (3:14; 8:28; 12:32) and in others (7:39; 12:16, 23; 13:31). Smith (1995:119) calls this "paradoxical," for the linkage of crucifixion and glory does not normally work. Yet that is Jesus' exaltation, and since glory is also connected to the revelation of God, Jesus' death is to be seen as the complete revelation of God's unceasing love and salvific purpose.

The Living Revealer. Another important theological theme in John is that Jesus is the "living revealer," which is the meaning of *logos* [TG3056, ZG3364] ("Word") in John 1:1-18 (cf. commentary on 1:1-18). It is commonly agreed that the concept of revelation is central in John. Jesus is the One who came from heaven to reveal God to the people of this world. To meet Jesus is to meet God and to encounter the demands of God.

The Son of Man. The name "Son of Man" speaks to Jesus' role as Messiah in John in two special ways. First, he is the Son of Man, "lifted up" on the cross into glory (cf. 3:14; 8:28; 12:32; 13:31). Second, he is the Son of Man as salvific revealer, the descending and ascending redeemer (1:51), with the shekinah glory revealed to mankind through him, the gate to heaven (6:62).

The debate on the intended meaning of "Son of Man" in the Gospels is quite extensive, and centers on whether it follows Ezekiel (93 times to indicate he is a mortal human being) or the one "like a son of man" in Daniel 7:13 (an eschatological figure who has dominion over the whole earth). In other words, was Jesus using it simply as a circumlocution for "I," or did he use it as an exalted title pointing to his glory? Most today accept both uses as stemming from Jesus' own historical uses of the title (cf. DJG 779-780) in three primary motifs—his earthly work ("no place even to lay his head," Matt 8:20), his suffering (the passion predictions; e.g., Matt 20:18), and his apocalayptic glory (highlighted in John). Hengel (2002:343) sums it up well: "The earthly and suffering Son of Man are a cipher with which Jesus, in certain situations, expresses both his authority (indeed, we may say as *Messias designatus*), and his humility and tribulation, which ultimately lead him to suffering and death . . . [including] the coming Son of Man, who appears as a mysterious heavenly figure."

The Messiah, Son of God. In John 20:31, the revelation of Jesus as "the Messiah, the Son of God," is stated as a major purpose of the Gospel, and this theme comes out especially in terms of the Father-Son relationship that dominates the book. Jesus is the "one and only Son" (1:14, 18; 3:16, 18) who shares the Father's divine glory and the authority over life and judgment (5:21-23, 25-28). He is Messiah, especially the royal Messiah and "King of Israel" or "King of the Jews" (1:49; 12:13; 18:33; 19:3, 19), whose throne is the cross—the sign of his glory and the means of atonement for the world (cf. 1:29; 6:51; 10:11, 15; 11:50-52; 15:13; 17:19; for atonement in John, see Morris 1998).

God. Smith (1995:75) says, "The fundamental question of the fourth Gospel is the question of God, not whether a god exists but who is God and how God reveals himself." In her important book, Thompson (2001) successively discusses God as the living Father, the one who reveals himself to the world, the one who gives the Spirit, and the one who is worshiped. Summing up the Old Testament and Jewish teaching, she defines God as first "the Maker and Creator of all that is. God is the life-giving God. Because God is the Creator of all, God is also supreme over all other beings, whether heavenly or human. . . . As Creator and Sovereign, God therefore merits worship and honor" (2001:54). In John, God is called "Father" 120 times, as compared to the 108 times he is called "God." In the majority of cases he is the Father of Jesus Christ, the one who "sent" Jesus as his "agent" and who reveals himself through Jesus. All that the Father is, Jesus is (5:18-30). Thompson (2001:58) sees three major emphases: he is the origin or source of life; he is an authoritative figure, deserving obedience and honor; and he is a being who loves and cares for his children.

The Holy Spirit. As Burge points out (2000:32-33), there are two emphases: (1) The Spirit is integral to Jesus' experience of God, with the Spirit remaining on Jesus (1:32-33) and Jesus receiving the Spirit from God "without limit" (3:34). The Spirit is the source of the living water (4:10) that flows from the innermost depths of Jesus (7:37-39). (2) The Spirit is then given by Jesus to believers (14:16, 26; 15:26; 16:12-15) and to the world (14:16; 16:8-11) as the Advocate, the representative sent from the Father and the Son to guide and empower the faithful and to convict the world. Finally, the Spirit is given to the believers in the Johannine "Pentecost" (20:22) to empower them for mission to the world (see below). I would add a third element: the Spirit becomes the representative of Jesus and continues his work in the lives of believers and in the world. Boice (1970) conceives of the Johannine Spirit in terms of witness and revelation; he provides the internal witness to Jesus and, as revealer, brings to light that which has been hidden in Jesus (14:26; 15:26). As Brown says (1970:1016), there is an intimate connection between Jesus' ascension and the sending of the Spirit (6:62; 16:7; 20:17, 22), as the Spirit becomes the dispenser of life and "will beget the believing disciples as God's children." In so doing, the Spirit indwells the hearts of the believers as the "Spirit of truth" (14:17; 15:26; 16:13), the spiritual guide to all truth revealed in Jesus.

Mission. R. A. Smith calls this "the revelation of the glory to the world" (1995:80). That is good as far as it goes, but the purpose should be added: "In order to bring the world to belief in the Son." The pattern of this revelation is fourfold: (1) The Father reveals himself to the world. (2) He sends his Son as his envoy or "living revealer" to the world. (3) The Father and Son send the Holy Spirit as their envoy to the world to convict it (16:8-11). (4) The Godhead sends the believers as their envoys into the world (20:21-23; cf. 17:18). Köstenberger (1998a:167-169) brings out the use of the disciples in John to depict the future mission of the church, calling the disciples "the messianic community called out by Jesus . . . in terms of fulfillment of Old Testament metaphors for God's people." Moreover, all believers, not just the original Twelve, are sent to participate in God's mission (cf. Köstenberger 1998a:149-152 on the "widening" of the term "disciples" to refer to future believers as well), and their task is to continue Jesus' mission to the world (1998a:198). This is a major emphasis in the second half of John (chs 13–21) and culminates in the mission theme of 20:21-23 and chapter 21.

The Church. Though the term "church" never occurs in the fourth Gospel, the idea is certainly implicit in such phrases as "sheep . . . that are not in this sheepfold" (10:16), Jesus' plan to "bring together and unite all the children of God scattered around the world" (11:52), and his prayer for "all who will ever believe in me" (17:20). The church is seen in such parables as the sheep of the shepherd (10:1-18) and the vine and the branches (15:1-8). The church is the new people of God chosen out of the world (6:37, 39) to become the focus of God's activity in the world through the power of the Spirit (15:26-27). As such, they will perform not only the "works" of Jesus but also "greater works," meaning that they will bring the unsaved to Jesus to find life (see commentary on 14:1-14, esp. 14:12). John stresses the universal church more than the Jewish mission, as Jesus is "Savior of the world" and "Savior of all men" (cf. "Mission" above). The church's mission is directed to the whole world. There is also a great deal of emphasis on the purity and unity of the church. It is likely the thieves and robbers of 10:1 referred to the Pharisees in Jesus' day and to false teachers in John's day. The church must keep itself pure from such false teachers. At the same time, it must be united, as in 10:16 ("one flock with one shepherd"), 11:52 ("unite all the children of God"), and 17:11 ("that they will be united just as we are"). The union of the church on earth is in fact both a reflection of and a witness to the union of the Godhead in heaven, and the very mission of the church is at stake (17:20-23). Our unity as a church is built upon our unity with Christ (6:56; 15:4-5) and is intended to reflect that unity. To do this the church must maintain intolerance regarding deviation from its cardinal doctrines (purity) and tolerance on non-cardinal issues (unity).

The Sacraments. There is considerable debate on the nature and extent of sacramental interest in John's Gospel. Some scholars see a great deal of emphasis on the sacraments (Cullmann, Brown); some are moderate (Schnackenburg, Kysar); and some see no interest whatsoever (Bultmann, Morris, Carson). Eucharistic allusions are often seen in the changing of the water into wine (2:1-11); the feeding miracle (6:1-13); the statements by Jesus about eating his flesh and drinking his blood (6:51-58); the blood and water that flowed from Jesus' side (19:34); and the meal of bread and fish that Jesus gave the disciples (21:11-14). Baptismal allusions are seen in "born of water and the Spirit" (3:5); the water flowing out of Jesus (7:37-39); and the foot-washing scene (13:1-17). In each case, however, my conclusion has been that there does not seem to be sacramental theology in the text. This does not mean John is rejecting the sacraments. As Carson says (1991:99), "The fourth Gospel is neither sacramentarian nor anti-sacramentarian . . . by its consummately careful use of language, it drives people to the reality, to Christ himself, refusing to stop at that which points to the reality." Matsunaga (1981) adds that due to the high Christology of this Gospel, the emphasis is upon the spiritual rather than the sacramental, though the latter is not rejected.

Witness and Signs. John uses two terms to describe miracles: "signs" (*sēmeia* [TG4592, ZG4956]) and "works" (*erga* [TG2041, ZG2240]). Interestingly, he never utilizes the primary Synoptic term *dunamis* [TG1411, ZG1539], translated "miracle" or "act of power." They are "works" from the standpoint that by these acts Jesus was performing the works of God and "signs" because they are symbols that point to the heavenly reality observable in the historical act itself. John selected seven "sign-miracles" from the many Jesus did (20:30) to signify this heavenly reality. In each case, the sign points to a theological truth built into the context. The background may be seen in the Exodus story (Brown 1966:529), in which God multiplied signs through Moses (Exod 10:1; Deut 7:19) but the people refused to believe (Num 14:11). Miracles as signs have salvific value, pointing to the true significance of Jesus, especially his sonship and mission from the Father. Several passages have led some to say that signs do not lead to faith in the Gospel of John (2:23-25; 3:11; 4:48; 6:25-31; 20:24-29), but after examining them, Johns and Miller (1994:525-531) have concluded that they are part of the judicial framework of the book and provide viable evidence that calls for faith. "Ultimately, all signs point to Jesus as the true messenger of God, the giver of life, a reality that finds its fullest expression in Jesus' resurrection from the dead, but a reality that is already given preliminary expression in the signs performed during Jesus' ministry" (Köstenberger 1998a:70). The purpose is to confront the audience and divide it via the necessity of a "faith-decision." Two camps result: those seeking understanding and those enamored only with the outward aspects. The latter fall away (2:23-25; 6:60-66). The miracles as works are part of John's "witness" theme, for they are official witnesses to Jesus (5:36; 14:11). Jesus' witness is self-authenticating (8:14), and his witness to the Father direct and absolute (cf. Boice 1970). Jesus appealed to several witnesses to support the validity of his words and works (5:31-47; 8:14-18).

The signs, along with Jesus' works and the witness of the Father and the Scriptures, serve as evidentiary witnesses, anchoring his claims and demanding faith in him. As Thompson says (1991:96-98), the signs produce faith as people see God in the miracles and respond to Jesus as the divinely sent life-giver.

Eschatology. As in all New Testament books, eschatology is not just the doctrine of last things—that is, the end of human history; it is also the belief that the last days have already begun and that every aspect of the life of the believer is part of that reality. For John, it is the medium of thought through which every doctrine discussed here is presented. It is common among critical scholars to say that John has replaced the final eschatology of the synoptic Gospels with a realized eschatology centering on the present blessings of the believers. In his thematic arrangement, the Olivet discourse has seemingly been replaced by John's farewell discourse (13:31–17:26), and the return of Christ with the coming of the Paraclete (the Holy Spirit; cf. 14:16-17). Yet this is not really true. John clearly has an interest in the event of the Parousia (Jesus' second coming) and the coming of eternity (5:25, 28-30; 6:39-40; 14:2-4; 21:22). Thus, it is best to see in John's emphasis on present blessings an inaugurated eschatology that also views the present blessings as anticipating the final realization of God's promises at the return of Christ.

OUTLINE

While some have detailed outlines involving an intricate pattern of chiasmus (Barnhart 1993, Ellis 1999), such a complex pattern is unlikely. John was primarily interested in theological history, and the book has a structure similar to the other Gospels, including a prologue (1:1-18) and epilogue (21:1-25), a preparatory period (1:19-51), a series of events comprising Jesus' public ministry (2:1–12:50), a lengthy farewell address to the disciples (13:35–17:26), a Passion narrative (18:1–19:42), and a two-pronged Resurrection narrative (20:1–21:25; ch 21 is both an epilogue and part of the Resurrection narrative).

I. Prologue (1:1-18)

II. Jesus Prepares for His Ministry (1:19-51)

    A. John Answers the Pharisees (1:19-28)

    B. John's Witness to Jesus (1:29-34)

    C. The First Disciples Come to Jesus (1:35-42)

    D. Philip and Nathanael Come to Jesus (1:43-50)

    E. Jesus Unites Heaven and Earth (1:51)

III. The Public Ministry of Jesus: Signs and Teaching (2:1–12:50)

    A. Glory Revealed: the Beginning Stages (2:1–4:54)

        1. The first sign: water into wine (2:1-12)

        2. Confrontation in the Temple (2:13-22)

        3. Inadequate faith based on signs (2:23-25)

        4. Jesus speaks to Nicodemus about regeneration (3:1-15)

        5. Life and light confront the world (3:16-21)

        6. John the Baptist exalts Jesus (3:22-30)

        7. The glory of the Son (3:31-36)

        8. Jesus converts the Samaritan woman (4:1-42)

        9. Healing and conversion in Cana (4:43-54)

    B. Jesus and the Feasts of the Jews—Conflict and Fulfillment (5:1–10:42)

        1. Jesus heals a lame man on the Sabbath (5:1-15)

        2. Conflict over Jesus' claim to be the Son of God (5:16-30)

        3. Witness and unbelief (5:31-47)

        4. Jesus feeds five thousand (6:1-15)

        5. Jesus walks on water (6:16-21)

        6. Jesus, the Bread of Life (6:22-58)

        7. Division among Jesus' disciples (6:59-71)

        8. Jesus at the Feast of Tabernacles (7:1-13)

        9. Conflict at the Feast (7:14-52)

        10. Excursus: the woman caught in adultery (7:53–8:11)

        11. Jesus, the Light of the World (8:12-20)

        12. Jesus warns the unbelievers (8:21-30)

        13. The children of Abraham and the children of the devil (8:31-59)

        14. Jesus heals a man born blind (9:1-41)

COMMENTARY ON
John

◆ **I. Prologue (1:1-18)**

In the beginning the Word already
    existed.
  The Word was with God,
  and the Word was God.
² He existed in the beginning with God.
³ God created everything through him,
  and nothing was created except
    through him.
⁴ The Word gave life to everything that
  was created,*
  and his life brought light to
    everyone.
⁵ The light shines in the darkness,
  and the darkness can never
    extinguish it.*

⁶God sent a man, John the Baptist,* ⁷to
tell about the light so that everyone might
believe because of his testimony. ⁸John
himself was not the light; he was simply
a witness to tell about the light. ⁹The one
who is the true light, who gives light to
everyone, was coming into the world.

¹⁰He came into the very world he created, but the world didn't recognize him.

¹¹He came to his own people, and even
they rejected him. ¹²But to all who believed him and accepted him, he gave the
right to become children of God. ¹³They
are reborn—not with a physical birth resulting from human passion or plan, but
a birth that comes from God.

¹⁴So the Word became human* and
made his home among us. He was full of
unfailing love and faithfulness.* And we
have seen his glory, the glory of the Father's one and only Son.

¹⁵John testified about him when he
shouted to the crowds, "This is the one I
was talking about when I said, 'Someone
is coming after me who is far greater than
I am, for he existed long before me.'"

¹⁶From his abundance we have all received one gracious blessing after another.* ¹⁷For the law was given through
Moses, but God's unfailing love and faithfulness came through Jesus Christ. ¹⁸No
one has ever seen God. But the unique
One, who is himself God,* is near to the
Father's heart. He has revealed God to us.

1:3-4 Or *and nothing that was created was created except through him. The Word gave life to everything.*
1:5 Or *and the darkness has not understood it.*   1:6 Greek *a man named John.*   1:14a Greek *became flesh.*
1:14b Or *grace and truth;* also in 1:17.   1:16 Or *received the grace of Christ rather than the grace of the law;*
Greek reads *received grace upon grace.*   1:18 Some manuscripts read *But the one and only Son.*

NOTES

1:1-18 It has often been suggested that the prologue was an addendum written by
another author and added after the Gospel was finished (cf. Brown). However, the
language and style are quite close to the rest of the Gospel, and such a theory is unnecessary. It is also often argued that this was originally a hymn with a couple of prose inser-
tions (1:6-8, 15). Witherington (1995:47-48) calls it John's "hymn to the Emperor" in

four strophes (1-2,   3-5, 10-12a, 14). Others (Harrington) see the hymn in 1:1-5, 10-14, 16 or in 1:1-3; 4-5, 9; 10-12c; 14, 16 (so Hofius 1987:10-15). While it does have poetic elegance, the actual rhythm and organization of the lines of John's prologue do not quite fit either Greek or Hebrew poetry. It is therefore better to understand it as heightened prose (so Barrett, Carson, Michaels). It is indeed possible that John was utilizing the form of prologue found in Greco-Roman drama here (E. Harris 1994:12-16). Others (Boismard, Culpepper, Pryor, Köstenberger) see the prologue as a chiasm (A = 1:1-5; B = 1:6-8; C = 1:9-14; B' = 1:15; A' = 1:16-18).

1:1 *the Word was God.* The Gr. for "the Word was God" (*theos ēn ho logos* [TG2316/3056, ZG2536/3364]) has been misused by Jehovah's Witnesses, who interpret the absence of the article before "God" as equaling the English indefinite article "a," thereby yielding the translation "a god." There are several serious errors here. First, there is no one-to-one correspondence between the Greek article and the English article, as if it has to be "a god." Actually, the absence of the article normally emphasizes the abstract aspect, namely that Jesus partook of "divinity" or "God-ness." Second, it was common in Greek to highlight the subject with the article (the Word) and to designate the predicate nominative (God) when it came before the verb "to be" by leaving out the article (cf. Harris 1992:51-73). Finally, *theos* [TG2316, ZG2536] is also missing the article in 1:18, where it definitely speaks of God the Father ("no one has ever seen God") as well as in 1:6, 12, 13 (cf. Keener 2003:372-374), and the connection between 1:1 and 1:18 has long been recognized (cf. the extensive discussion in M. Harris 1992:51-103). In short, to translate this as "the Word was a god" is an obvious error and a very bad translation.

1:3b-4 *everything that was created.* It is debated whether the words at the end of 1:3 (lit., "that was made/created") belong with 1:3 (so KJV, NASB, NIV, Schnackenburg, Carson, Ridderbos, Köstenberger) or 1:4 (NRSV, NJB, REB, NLT, Brown, Beasley-Murray, Whitacre). If it is the former, 1:4 would simply read "in him was life," but the parallelism of the lines favors the latter option, seen in the NLT. In this sense, 1:3 ends with the statement "nothing was created except through him," and 1:4 begins, "The Word gave life to everything that was created." This fits the developing thought better than the redundant "apart from him nothing was created that was created," and this was the older interpretation. However, when the Arians (fourth-century heretics) began to use this to argue that the Holy Spirit was a created being, the reading that placed the phrase with 1:3 became the accepted one.

1:5 *can never extinguish it.* Translators face a difficult decision as to whether to translate the verb here (*katelaben* [TG2638, ZG2898]) as "understand/comprehend" (so KJV, NASB, NIV, NLT mg) or "overcome" (so NRSV, NJB, NLT, TNIV). The former could be favored by 1:10, 11, where the world does not "recognize" or "know" him, and in fact some (Barrett, Carson, Comfort, Burge, Keener) believe there might be a double meaning in the verb, in which the world cannot understand the light and therefore opposes it. This may well be correct, but the main thrust is on the conflict between darkness and light, making "overcome" the better choice (cf. the only other use of the verb, in 12:35, "so the darkness will not overtake you"; so Brown, Köstenberger).

1:6 *sent.* In this book the verb "sent" occurs 59 times, mainly of four cases in which God is the sender: Jesus (over 30 times), the Holy Spirit, the disciples, and John the Baptist. The verb in these instances partakes of the Jewish idea of the *shaliach* (cf. TDNT 1.414-420), the official envoy or representative sent on behalf of the sender—in this case, God. It is a major term used for the mission theme in John's Gospel. Here, the Baptist is sent on a mission by God. Cf. 3:17.

1:9 *coming into the world.* This expression could modify "everyone," thus meaning the light came to all who were in the world (so KJV), and by the Gr. word order, that is a distinct possibility. But the context is clearly that of the Incarnation, and the style of this expression is quite common in John (*ēn . . . erchomenon* would be a periphrastic, "was coming," similar to 1:28; 2:6; 3:23; 10:40 and others; cf. Schnackenburg). Thus, it is best to see the expression as modifying "the true light," as in the NLT.

1:13 *not with a physical birth resulting from human passion or plan.* Lit., "not of bloods, nor of the will of the flesh, nor of the will of man." Whitacre (1999:56) thinks there is an ABA pattern here, with the emphasis on the middle concept (lit., "the will of the flesh"), borrowing Brown's definition of "flesh" as "the sphere of the natural, the powerless, the superficial, opposed to 'spirit,' which is the sphere of the heavenly and the real."

1:14 *his glory.* With the term "glory," we have another of John's major themes. In the Synoptics it describes primarily the glory of the risen Lord (Luke 24:26) and his second coming (Mark 8:38; 13:26 and parallels). The only use of it for the earthly Jesus is at the Transfiguration, when the disciples "saw Jesus' glory" (Luke 9:32). In John, however, the glory of Jesus is visible to the disciples (2:11), and indeed it is always used of the earthly Jesus (18 times in chs 1-17). The divine glory was evident in the earthly Jesus for those with the faith to see it.

1:15 *John testified.* John's disciples continued to follow him even after his death (Acts 18:25; 19:1-7), and there are indications that the movement lasted well into the second century. In fact, a sect called the Mandaeans in Iran and Iraq still claim a connection with him today. It is widely believed by scholars that many passages in the Gospels about the Baptist (e.g., 1:6-9, 15; 3:22-36) were partly meant to show his followers that he never intended to found a movement apart from Christ.

shouted. There is an interesting change of tense here: the testifying is stated in the present tense, indicating an ongoing witness, while the shouting is in the perfect tense ("has shouted"), which may well add a stative thrust, stressing the comprehensiveness of the witness (so Carson).

1:17 *unfailing love.* The term *charis* ("grace," translated "unfailing love" here) only occurs four times in the fourth Gospel, all of them in 1:14, 16, 17. Yet in one sense, John's whole Gospel is an account of the grace of God in Christ. It is a fitting introduction.

1:18 *unique One, who is himself God.* Lit., "an only one, God" (*monogenēs theos* [TG3439/ 2316, ZG3666/2536]). This is supported by the best mss (𝔓66 ℵ* B C* L), and the reading with *theos* is also supported by 𝔓75 ℵc, though both include the definite article before *theos*. Inferior mss (A C³ Wˢ 𝔐) substitute *huios* [TG5207, ZG5626] (Son) for *theos* (God). The NLT translation follows the evidence of the earlier, better mss. It is likely that later scribes added "Son" under the influence of other passages that have "one and only Son" (3:16, 18; 1 John 4:9). This is one of the clearest statements of Jesus' deity in the fourth Gospel and forms a parallel to the assertion of 1:1 ("the Word was God") to close the prologue. (For a further discussion on this, see Comfort 2007:[John 1:18]).

COMMENTARY

If you were to write a biography of a famous person, you would try to sum up the impact of that person's life and give an overarching theme to your presentation before you provided all the details. This is what John did in his prologue. The purpose of a prologue or introduction in any New Testament book (e.g., Mark 1:1-15) is to introduce the major themes and to help the reader understand who Jesus really is. This is nowhere better exemplified than in John's Gospel. Here, the primary truth of the book is clear—Jesus is God himself!

In his Gospel, John has given us a theological masterpiece centering upon key terms, the most significant of which are introduced in the prologue—life, light, darkness, sent, truth, world, believe, know, receive, witness, new birth, love, glory. Most of all, he has given us a theology of the Incarnation unmatched in the New Testament (with the exception of Phil 2:6-8). Here we see a powerful presentation of what it meant for God to become flesh in order to bring light and life to sinful mankind.

The prologue has an ABAB pattern, from the Word (1:1-5) to John the Baptist (1:6-9), to salvation by believing in the Word (1:10-14), to John and the law (1:15-18). We will explore each of these sections.

The Essence of the Word (1:1–5). It is difficult to imagine a more magnificent introduction. "In the beginning" reiterates Genesis 1:1, "In the beginning God created the heavens and the earth." With Jesus as the Word, there is a new beginning, in a sense a new creation—a spiritual re-creation of the world. This is evident in 1:3-4, where Christ is creator of both physical and spiritual life. Yet at the same time, this says Jesus was in existence "in the beginning." The idea of the Son of God as the preexistent Word is the basis of the incredible claims of this section. Verses 1-2 tell who he was (before creation), and 1:3-4 tell what he did (in creation). This One who was in the beginning is called the "Word" (*logos* [TG3056, ZG3364]), a term that, in Greek thought, connoted the principle of reason that governs the world and makes thinking possible. Closer to the thrust here, however, is the Jewish connotation for "word"— the divine Wisdom, which was at God's side at Creation (Prov 8:30-31) and was viewed as God's living voice (Whitacre 1999:50-51; Keener 2003:339-363). Most of all, Jesus as the "Word" means that he is the living revealer of God, the very voice of God in this world. Carson (1991:127) translates this as God's "self-expression." Psalm 33:6 says, "The LORD merely *spoke*, and the heavens were created." Jesus is God's living "voice" to this world.

John 1:1 tells us three things about the Word: he is/was preexistent (he "already existed"), he enjoys a special relationship "with God," and he is the Deity. Note the progression. Each is more intense. The Word exists prior to Creation, then is in intimate communion "with" God (the idea is not just casual contact but special relationship), and finally is in his very nature God himself. This is a major theme in the fourth Gospel (cf. "Major Themes" in the Introduction), and everything flows from it. Only very God of very God could create the world and bring light and life to it. In fact, this is the most astounding claim John could pen. This Jesus who walked the earth was actually the eternal Word, partaking of the very essence of God! This is a truth so startlingly wondrous that John repeated key elements in 1:2 to make certain the reader caught these essential truths. Only one who had that special relationship "with God" and was there "in the beginning" could create the universe.

To affirm the divinity of the Word, John tells us that he was God's agent in the very act of creation (1:3). To emphasize this truth, John states it positively ("God created everything through him") and negatively ("nothing was created except through him"). The stress is on every single aspect of the created order. This is perhaps more astounding today than it was in John's time: today we know there are more stars in our own galaxy than any human being could count in a lifetime, and there are more galaxies in this universe than there are stars in our own galaxy. And there are more complex cells in our bodies than we could begin to imagine. At both the micro- and macrocosmic levels, our universe is made perfectly. The created universe is beyond scientific understanding, and the Son of God made it all! The work of God's Son in Creation is also stressed in 1 Corinthians 8:6 ("through whom God made everything"), Colossians 1:16-17 ("everything was created through him and for him"), Hebrews 1:2 ("through the Son he created the universe"), and Revelation 3:14 ("the ruler of God's new creation," NLT mg). He is both creator and sustainer of all there is.

Life and light were the two essential aspects of the Genesis 1 creation, but Christ has brought more. There is a double meaning in "the Word gave life to everything that was created" (1:4). In the original creation, he gave physical life and light to all beings, but now he has also made spiritual life available to all. The Word breathed the breath of "life" into Adam; now as the last Adam (Rom 5:12-21), he brings eternal life to mankind—another major theological emphasis of the book. Moreover, the Word does so by bringing "light to everyone," a theme emphasized in 1:7, 9. This has often been labeled "universal salvific will," namely God's desire that no one should perish but rather that all should come to repentance (2 Pet 3:9). Through the Word as "the light of the world" (8:12), God illumines every person with the light of the gospel. This looks to the revelation of God in Jesus, through whom every person is confronted with their sin and with the light that God has brought in the sacrificial death of Jesus. This is the heart of John's message.

The darkness/light dualism (1:5) is a key feature of John's Gospel. The light of the Word "shines in the darkness" of this world. In the original creation, "the earth was formless and empty, and darkness covered the deep waters" until God said, "Let there be light" (Gen 1:2-3). In this new era, a more important darkness—the darkness of sin—has felt God's salvific light. Darkness is a common metaphor for sin in John (3:19; 8:12; 12:35), and here the idea is the war between darkness and light. When the Word shines in this world, "the darkness can never extinguish it." Darkness hates light and fights against it (3:19-20), but the light must triumph. In our normal day-to-day experience, we may think of it this way: when we shine a flashlight into a dark closet, the closet can never say, "I don't want the light; go away," and cause the light to bend into another room. Darkness cannot "overcome" light and bend it to its will! Similarly, every person is brought under the light of Christ and must respond. Since this Gospel is an encounter Gospel (cf. "Literary Style" in the Introduction), this may also refer to the convicting power of the Spirit (16:8-11) as the light of Christ. As we will see throughout this book, the light of Christ will continually confront the darkness of sin and force the sinner to a "faith-decision." That decision will determine their eternal destiny.

The Ministry of John the Baptist (1:6-9). The first five verses speak of the exalted origin and status of the Word. Now we realize that the Word has appeared on the stage of this world, and he was heralded by John the Baptist, "sent" by God as his official envoy to prepare for Christ's coming. John's ministry was one of "witness," another frequent theme that speaks of official testimony to the reality of Jesus (cf. 5:31-40; 8:14-18). John was sent to testify "about the light"—namely, Jesus— "so that everyone might believe." This continues the message of 1:4-5; John was one of the divinely sent heralds who were to enable the light to shine on every person and prompt them to make a decision based on faith. God's purpose in sending John was the salvation of mankind. The mission theme of this Gospel officially begins here, and this prepares the reader for 1:35-49, where John the Baptist's witness about Jesus encourages some of John's disciples to follow Jesus.

To make certain that readers do not misunderstand, the author clarifies that John "was not the light" but was "simply a witness" regarding the light (1:8-9). His entire focus was upon introducing the world to Jesus, "who is the true light," namely the only one who can light the way to God. The word "true" means he is the "genuine" or "ultimate" revelation of God, the final and only answer to the dilemma of sin (so Carson). For the third time (with 1:4, 7), the emphasis is that he "gives light to everyone," meaning that every human being has experienced the light of God in their lives through Christ. This, however, does not support universalism, the belief that everyone eventually will be saved. The "light" does not guarantee that everyone will accept the light, just that everyone will see the truth. They cannot "extinguish" the light (1:5), but those who "love the darkness more than the light" will "hate the light" and reject it (3:18-20). Most wonderful of all is the fact that this true light "was coming into the world," a reference to the Incarnation. He was no Olympian deity, dwelling in a society above humanity with little attachment to humans or their affairs. No, he became one of us so that he could bring us to God. He is the God-man! The fact that the Word came into the "world" (*kosmos* [TG2889, ZG3180]) is significant. Throughout John, the world is characterized as rebelling against God. Yet it is also the focus of God's salvific love (3:16)—so much so that Christ gave his life for the world (6:51) in order to save it (3:17; 12:47). He came to take away the sins of the world (1:29), bring life to the world (6:33), and be the Savior of the world (4:42).

The Incarnate Word (1:10-14). There are three themes here: the rejection of the Word by the world (1:10-11), the new birth given to those who accept Jesus (1:12-13), and the true meaning of the Incarnation (1:14). The incredible fact is that the Word came into the world to experience rejection. John begins by reiterating the truth that the one who came into the world is the very one who created the world (1:3). One would expect that the people would cheer and worship their creator, who had loved them enough to become one of them. Instead, they "didn't recognize him," an idiom that does not mean they simply failed to know who he was but rather that they rejected who he was. As Brown says (1966:10), "Knowledge of Jesus would also imply repentance and a new life in his service." This is similar to Romans 1:18-32; they had experienced divine revelation (cf. 1:4, 9 above) but had rejected it.

Moreover, he did not just come into the world—"he came to his own people," the Jews (1:11). In the fourth Gospel, the Jewish people are regarded as part of the world. The reason is that they too "rejected him." The parallelism between 1:10 and 1:11 is clear. Whitacre says it well (1999:54): the world had experienced "the general revelation of creation" and refused, but God's own people had experienced "the special revelation of covenant" and rejected it. Then the most unbelievable affair of all occurred—God's own Son arrived and they repudiated him. They had long speculated about and anticipated the Messiah, yet when he arrived they rejected him!

John divides mankind into two groups—those who reject and those who accept. In 1:12, the promise is given: all those who "believe" and "accept" the Word have an entirely new status and authority. God gives them "the right to become [his] children." Believing and receiving are virtual synonyms, and they are further described as believing "in his name"—that is, accepting the reality of who he is. In the ancient world, a person's name connoted the essence of who they were; thus, the belief here is focused on Jesus' real self, not just his name. The result is that believers have the "right" or "authority" (*exousia* [TG1849, ZG2026]) to join a new family. While Paul utilizes the metaphor of adoption (Rom 8:15), John uses the image of the new birth (1:13; 3:3, 5). In both cases, the new believers become "children of God," a wondrous truth describing in a powerful way the new status and authority they have.

In 1:13, John emphasizes that this is not controlled by human effort but only by God. This new birth cannot come via "a physical birth resulting from human passion or plan." In other words, we have no power over the process. It is a spiritual reality and so only "comes from God." We cannot produce spiritual rebirth via human passion or family planning. Only God can accomplish it.

It is clear that this salvation will come in an entirely new way, and John spells this out in 1:14, one of the deepest theological statements ever written. The only basis for mankind entering the realm and family of God is for God to enter the realm of humanity himself and provide redemption. John states it unequivocally: "The Word became human." This is the high point of the prologue—indeed, the high point of history. God has entered this world; his Word has become "flesh"; the Creator has become a creature. More than that, he has "made his home among us." John chose a very particular term here (*skēnoō* [TG4637, ZG5012]), which means he has "pitched his tent" or "tabernacled" among us. The image of the tabernacle (*skēnē* [TG4633, ZG5008]) is very prominent, especially with the correspondence between the glory of the Word (1:14) and the "shekinah glory" of God that filled the Tabernacle (and later, the Temple). The shekinah (cf. Heb. verb *shakan* [TH7931, ZH8905], referring to God "dwelling" among his people) or presence of God was seen in the pillar of fire by night and the cloud by day in the Exodus (cf. Exod 13:21). This glory then filled the Tabernacle. This was what made the Tabernacle the most sacred object in the universe; the physical manifestation of God's holy presence was there. The dwelling of God among his people was everything (cf. Exod 25:8-9; Ezek 43:7; Joel 3:17; Zech 2:13; 8:3) and will be the chief characteristic of the new heaven and new earth (Rev 21:3). With this in mind, John was saying that in Jesus as the Word, God's "shekinah" glory had become incarnate.

Since God's indwelling presence was in the Word, John adds that in Jesus "we have seen his glory." No wonder there was no more need for a Temple; God's shekinah glory now walked the earth, visible to all with the eye of faith! As Burge says, "Christ is the locus of God's dwelling with Israel *as he had dwelt with them in the tabernacle in the desert* (Exod 25:8-9; Zech 2:10). Hence, the glory of God, once restricted to the tabernacle (Exod 40:34), is now visible in Christ" (2000:59, italics his). In actuality, the praise and worship of the church are simply the natural result of the recognition and affirmation of the glory of God in Jesus—when we feel God's presence in a tangible way, we shout, "Glory!" as did the Israelites (Ps 29:1, 9). As Comfort indicates (1994:37-38), the image of Jesus being God's Tabernacle "also speaks of God's presence accompanying the believers in their spiritual journey." God dwelt with the Israelites and walked with them (cf. Lev 26:12) via his presence in the Tabernacle. Throughout the Gospel of John, we see Jesus bringing God's presence to people, especially the believers who saw the glory of God in Jesus.

This is even more true when we realize it is "the glory of the Father's *one and only* Son." This used to be translated "only begotten" (KJV), and indeed the term was used of an only child (Judg 11:34; Luke 7:12; Heb 11:17), but that is not the connotation here (contra Dahms 1983). The components of the word (*monogenēs* [TG3439, ZG3666]) mean "only one of a kind" and stress the uniqueness of the Word (cf. Pendrick 1995:597, 600, who argues that the idea of "only begotten" was introduced in the fourth and fifth centuries). He is the unique Son, the God-man, the one who alone shared the divine glory. Finally, this glorious Word is "full of unfailing love and faithfulness" (lit., "full of grace and truth"). It is commonly agreed that the background to this is Exodus 33–34, where Moses asks to see God's glory (Exod 33:18), and God passes in front of him, declaring himself to be "the God of compassion and mercy . . . [full of] *unfailing love and faithfulness*" (Exod 34:6). It is here that God gives Moses the two stone tablets that summed up the loving relationship between God and his people. These last two terms (in italics) are key Old Testament characteristics of God, his *khesed* [TH2617, ZH2876] ("gracious lovingkindness") and *'emeth* [TH571, ZH622] ("covenant faithfulness"), and are reflected here in John's (literal) "full of grace and truth." The Word is the embodiment of God's gracious love and the proof of his absolute faithfulness. John's choice of "grace" and "truth" to express this is critical. In Christ, the "grace" of God is especially seen, and he is the only "truth" or reality (14:6).

The Greatness and Grace of the Word (1:15-18). John now expands on the "testimony" of John the Baptist mentioned in 1:7. That testimony was that Jesus was "coming after me" but was "far greater than I am" (1:15). There is a play on words in the Greek, as Jesus is described as coming "after" (temporally) but is actually "before" John (both temporally and in degree or status). John was the forerunner, but Jesus was the important figure, the one whose "coming" had been anticipated for generations. The fact that "he existed long before me" refers back to the preexistence spoken of in 1:1. The Word had absolute primacy and precedence over John.

Picking up on the phrase "full of unfailing love and faithfulness" (1:14), John now turns to Christ's "abundance" or "fullness," reminding the reader that "we have all received" the benefits of what the Word has given us (1:16). Christ has filled us with blessings. The blessings are then spelled out in what is literally "grace instead of (*anti* [TG473, ZG505]) grace." There are three major options for the term *anti*: (1) accumulation—as NLT, we could take it as "grace upon grace," thus "one gracious blessing after another," as Christ gives an inexhaustible supply of gracious gifts (so Barrett, Bruce, Morris, Schnackenburg, Comfort, Whitacre, Keener); (2) correspondence—it could mean "grace for grace," thus saying that the grace shown the believer corresponds to the grace of the Word (so Bernard, Robinson); (3) replacement—in the more common use of *anti*, and it would be translated "grace instead of grace"—in other words, the grace of Christ replacing the grace of the law (so Brown, Edwards [1988], Michaels, Carson, Blomberg, Köstenberger). While the first makes good sense, the third is favored by 1:17, which spells out the implications of the new covenant blessings replacing the old covenant blessings. The Word has given us the full blessings of the Kingdom he has inaugurated. The previous time of grace was that of Moses, who gave God's people "the law." This was also a gift from the preexistent Word, as hinted at in 1:16-17, but it was a temporary blessing, meant to be replaced by a greater gift (cf. Gal 3:21–4:7). This greater gift is the full expression of "God's unfailing love and faithfulness," and it "came through Jesus Christ." This will become a major emphasis of John's Gospel, as it explores the implications of the final "grace" that Christ brought for the Jewish people.

In 1:18, John frames his prologue with the same truth with which he began—the deity of Christ (cf. 1:1). As Comfort states: "The prologue begins and ends on the same theme; verses 1 and 18, in effect, mirror each other. In both verses, the Son is called 'God' and is depicted as the expression ('the Word') and explainer of God; the Son is shown in intimate fellowship with the Father—'face to face to with God' and 'in the bosom of the Father' " (1994:40).

In this verse, John begins again with the experience of Moses in Exodus 33:18-23 (cf. 1:14, 17, and comments). When Moses asked to see God's glory, he was told to stand in the cleft of a rock as God passed by so that God could cover his face lest he look upon God's face and die. John's statement, "no one has ever seen God," does not mean people have never seen visions of God (as does occur in Exod 24:9-11; Isa 6:1-13; Ezek 1–3). Those visions were partial, however, and no one has ever seen God as he truly is. In the case of the Word, this is no longer correct because Jesus is "the one and only God" (1:18, NLT mg). Note how clear a statement of his deity this is. The Word is uniquely God, and as such he was "near to the Father's heart" (lit., "in the bosom of the Father"). Harris (1992:101) speaks of "the unparalleled intimacy that existed (and still exists) between the Son and the Father." Here, we are at the heart of the doctrine of the Trinity. Jesus is fully God and yet a different person than the Father. This is an expansion of 1:1b, "The Word was with God." They had the deepest relationship imaginable. As a result, the Word "has revealed God to us," the heart of the message. If the Word is indeed God's "self-expression," the living revealer, then he alone is able to make God truly known to us. The rest of this Gospel flows out of this essential truth.

♦ II. Jesus Prepares for His Ministry (1:19-51)
A. John Answers the Pharisees (1:19-28)

¹⁹This was John's testimony when the Jewish leaders sent priests and Temple assistants* from Jerusalem to ask John, "Who are you?" ²⁰He came right out and said, "I am not the Messiah."

²¹"Well then, who are you?" they asked. "Are you Elijah?"

"No," he replied.

"Are you the Prophet we are expecting?"*

"No."

²²"Then who are you? We need an answer for those who sent us. What do you have to say about yourself?"

²³John replied in the words of the prophet Isaiah:

"I am a voice shouting in the wilderness, 'Clear the way for the LORD's coming!'"*

²⁴Then the Pharisees who had been sent ²⁵asked him, "If you aren't the Messiah or Elijah or the Prophet, what right do you have to baptize?"

²⁶John told them, "I baptize with* water, but right here in the crowd is someone you do not recognize. ²⁷Though his ministry follows mine, I'm not even worthy to be his slave and untie the straps of his sandal."

²⁸This encounter took place in Bethany, an area east of the Jordan River, where John was baptizing.

1:19 Greek *and Levites.* 1:21 Greek *Are you the Prophet?* See Deut 18:15, 18; Mal 4:5-6. 1:23 Isa 40:3. 1:26 Or *in;* also in 1:31, 33.

NOTES

1:19 *Jewish leaders.* Lit., "the Jews," occurring 71 times in John versus 17 total in the Synoptics. Most of the time it is used in contexts referring to the Jewish leaders, but John also intends to portray the Jewish people in their hostility and rejection of Jesus. Over half the occurrences are in conflict settings, and the leaders are portrayed as completely opposed to Jesus. Still, there are "Jews" who are believers (8:31; 11:45; 12:11), and the Samaritan woman calls Jesus a "Jew" (4:9). In spite of the conflict John portrays, Israel was still the focus of God's salvific work (EDNT 2.195-196).

1:21 *"Are you Elijah?" "No."* While John denied that he was the Messiah, Elijah, or the Prophet, Jesus identified him as Elijah in Matt 11:14: "If you are willing to accept what I say, he is Elijah" (cf. Matt 17:12; Mark 9:13). While some have held this to be a contradiction or seen Matt 11:14 as a later church reflection read back onto Jesus' lips (so Brown), it is better to see the issue historically, namely that the Baptist "did not detect as much significance in his own ministry as Jesus did" (Carson 1991:143).

1:24 *the Pharisees who had been sent.* There are several ways to understand this. The KJV, due to a definite article in the TR, has "they which were sent were of the Pharisees." The article is missing in the best mss (𝔓66 𝔓75 ℵ* A* B C* L). Even with this reading, there are three ways to translate it: (1) "those sent by the Pharisees"; (2) "some Pharisees who had been sent" (NLT, REB, NIV); or (3) "some Pharisees had been sent" (Phillips). The problem with the first is that the Pharisees were not in charge of the Sanhedrin, and the problem with the third is that there is no hint of a separate delegation from that mentioned in 1:19. Thus, the second is the best translation, meaning that there were some Pharisees in the delegation that was sent from the Sanhedrin, a natural surmise due to Pharisaic membership in that council.

1:28 *Bethany.* This is not the same "Bethany" near Jerusalem where Mary, Martha, and Lazarus lived; this is the Bethany on the other side of the Jordan. There is no record of the location of the place, and some simply consider it another biblical site that has disapeared through the centuries (Brown, Morris, Witherington). Origen believed it was

Bethabara (*Commentary on John* 6.24, 40), which is the reading in some mss and in the TR. This is Tel el-Kharrar in modern Jordan, a Bethany site that is now open to tourists. This place would allow a Joshua–Jesus parallel, since it means "crossing over," but it remains unlikely. A viable possibility is Batanea, an area in the northeast of Judea ruled by Philip, a more benign ruler than Herod Antipas, and therefore a viable site for the Baptist's ministry (Riesner 1987, so also Keener, Köstenberger). However, the timing of the events surrounding the raising of Lazarus (10:40; 11:6, 17) may make Perea (a district south of Batanea, containing Bethabara) a viable option as well (so Burge, see notes on those passages). I will tentatively side with Batanea as the better option because of 10:40.

COMMENTARY

There are two sections in this interrogation, one asking who John is (1:19-23) and the other asking what he does (1:24-28). We know from the synoptic Gospels that John quickly became extremely popular. In Matthew 3:5 we are told he attracted crowds "from Jerusalem and from all of Judea and all over the Jordan Valley." He was perceived as the first prophet to appear in centuries. It was natural that an official delegation came from Jerusalem to test him to see if he were a false prophet. The "Jewish leaders" were probably members of the Sanhedrin, the high council of Judaism, a group of 71 men led by the high priest and composed mainly of the chief priests (Sadducees), the elders or lay aristocracy, and Pharisees. The Sadducees were the major ecclesiastical authority (consisting largely of the leading priests), and the Pharisees were the major lay religious leaders, the religious experts of the land. The Sanhedrin oversaw the civic responsibilities of the nation and would naturally have sent priests and Levites (who assisted in various ways in the Temple) to ask John key religious questions. Since John was the son of a priest (Zechariah; cf. Luke 1:5), this was understandable.

There are three primary questions (1:20-21), all centering on Jewish messianic hopes. The Sadducees were the only ones without a messianic hope; they believed the messianic age had already come with the Maccabean revolt. The nation as a whole longed for a Messiah, but there was still a great deal of confusion regarding the actual figure. The Essenes at Qumran expected a royal Messiah but also a priestly Messiah and a prophet. Still, much of Judaism awaited the Anointed One (the meaning of "Messiah" and of "Christ"). Interestingly, the delegation never asked the primary question. Instead, John provided his own forceful testimony and confession: "I am not the Messiah." He had already pointed to Jesus in 1:15 as the "greater" one. Now he made it clear that he was not the expected one.

Hearing this, the delegation went down the checklist of other expected figures for the last days. It had been prophesied in Malachi 4:5 that Elijah would come "before the great and dreadful day of the Lord." Since John dressed and acted like Elijah did (Mark 1:6, "His clothes were woven from coarse camel hair, and he wore a leather belt around his waist"; cf. 2 Kgs 1:8), this was a natural question. John's answer was unequivocal: "No." They tried a third time and asked if he was "the Prophet," namely, the "prophet like Moses" of Deuteronomy 18:15 and 18, thought to be a legal Torah Messiah (both by those at Qumran and the Samaritans, cf. discussions in Carson, Köstenberger). Again, John answered, "No."

Finally, the delegation allowed John to tell them his own perception regarding his identity (1:22-23). They had to return with some kind of "answer" for their superiors. John responded obliquely, not saying who he was, but quoting Isaiah 40:3. In actuality, this was a proper response. There is no sense in which his inquisitors were actually searching for truth, so there was no reason for John to be direct. Yet it is clear that John knew he transcended a mere rabbinic role. Isaiah 40:3 was used in all four Gospels to identify the ministry of the Baptist (Matt 3:3; Mark 1:3; Luke 3:4), but this is the only one in which John utters it himself. Isaiah speaks of the removal of obstacles (the leveling of roads, the removal of mountains) for the return of Israel from exile, but the Essenes at Qumran also used the verse in an eschatological sense for their study of Torah as preparation for the coming of the Kingdom (1QS 8:13-16). Moreover, this became a theme verse for the primitive church, which at the earliest date called itself "the Way" (Acts 9:2; 19:9, 23; 22:4; 24:14, 22), a name probably taken from this passage. Like Qumran and later the early church, John saw his purpose in life to be the fulfillment of the Isaianic promise as "a voice shouting in the wilderness"—in one sense less than a rabbi but in another sense far more, for he came to "clear the way for the Lord's coming." The Essenes at Qumran sought to bring about the Kingdom passively through reading Torah; John cleared the way actively by being the voice calling the nation to repentance.

There were some members of the delegation, mainly Pharisees, who were not satisfied with John's response. The Pharisees were mainly a lay movement made up of pious groups from the Maccabean period that focused on contemporizing the Torah by introducing an oral tradition that would enable people in their day to understand how to keep the law in their culture, which was entirely different from that of Moses's day. Because they were very concerned about faithfulness to the Jewish laws, they had serious problems with John's practice of baptism. Since he denied that he was "the Messiah or Elijah or the Prophet, what right [did he] have to baptize?" (1:25). This was a viable concern in light of the difference between John's practice and that of the rest of Judaism. Normative Judaism had regular washings for ritual purity (cf. Mark 7:1-4), and the people at Qumran practiced daily washings in a pool to signify their cleanliness before God. John's was quite different from those in that it was a one-time initiation rite and was conducted by John rather than being self-administered. If the Jews practiced proselyte baptism at that time (there is no absolute evidence for it before AD 70; cf. Keener 2003:440-448), there would be an even more powerful message, for John would be saying the Jewish people had become like the Gentiles in needing to repent of their sins and get right with God (DJG 386). The question posed by the Pharisees is perfectly reasonable. Since John had begun an entirely new religious rite without true precedent, where did he get the authority to do such a thing? If he was not a messianic figure, how could he do it?

John answered the question indirectly (1:27; cf. 1:15) by deflecting the attention from himself to the actual source of his authority—Jesus. John was also hinting that his water baptism was a preparation for the coming of the greater one. Everything he did was that of the "voice shouting in the wilderness" (1:23), preparing the highway to Zion. He declared that there in their midst was someone they did not recognize (1:26). There is double meaning here: on one level they had not seen Jesus before; on another level this restates 1:10-11 (the world does not know/rejects) Jesus. He repeated the message of 1:15 that Jesus was the one "coming after" him and also added a metaphor centering on Jesus' transcendent superiority. Since rabbis received no pay for their ministries, it was common for their disciples to perform small services for them. There was a saying that a disciple would do everything for his rabbi that a slave would do except "untie the straps of his sandal" (*b. Ketubbot* 96a). That was considered too menial a task (cf. Morris). John was saying in effect that he was unworthy even to be Jesus' slave. In keeping with 1:7, John provided a powerful witness regarding the true light. Yet there did not seem to be any effect; their unbelief obviously continued. The story closes simply by telling us that "this encounter took place in Bethany, an area east of the Jordan River." John's purpose may simply be to establish a literary connection between this Bethany and the one at the end of Jesus' ministry (11:1), thereby framing his ministry with Bethany appearances.

◆　　## B. John's Witness to Jesus (1:29–34)

29The next day John saw Jesus coming toward him and said, "Look! The Lamb of God who takes away the sin of the world! 30He is the one I was talking about when I said, 'A man is coming after me who is far greater than I am, for he existed long before me.' 31I did not recognize him as the Messiah, but I have been baptizing with water so that he might be revealed to Israel."

32Then John testified, "I saw the Holy Spirit descending like a dove from heaven and resting upon him. 33I didn't know he was the one, but when God sent me to baptize with water, he told me, 'The one on whom you see the Spirit descend and rest is the one who will baptize with the Holy Spirit.' 34I saw this happen to Jesus, so I testify that he is the Chosen One of God.*"

1:34 Some manuscripts read *the Son of God.*

NOTES
1:29 The next day. The phrase "the next day" is used repeatedly, connecting the events of 1:29–2:1 and accounting for over a week's time. The first day was when John was challenged by the questioners (1:19-28); "the next day" (1:29), John bore witness to Jesus as the Lamb of God; then "the following day" (1:35) several of John's disciples followed Jesus. Finally, on "the third day" (2:1, NLT mg) Jesus' ministry began. At first the events may not appear to span a week, but it is possible (cf. Brown, Morris, Carson) to understand it as a week by recognizing that Andrew brought Peter (1:42) the day after he met Jesus and spent the evening with him (1:39), and that Philip brought Nathanael the day after Andrew brought Simon Peter. Finally, the "third day" (2:1) would refer to two days after the events of 1:43-51, which makes sense because it involves a trip from Judea (the scene of 1:19-51) up to Cana of Galilee.

Look. This is a favorite expression in John (15 of the 29 NT uses); it points to an important saying.

The Lamb of God who takes away the sin of the world. While most agree with the idea of a sacrificial understanding in John's Gospel, there are three options for interpreting how the Baptist historically understood "the Lamb of God who takes away the sin of the world": (1) the apocalyptic Lamb who will triumph and crush evil (thus take away sin by force; so Dodd, Barrett, Brown, Beasley-Murray, Carson, Witherington)—this is found in several intertestamental works (*Testament of Joseph* 19:8; *Testament of Benjamin* 3:8; *1 Enoch* 90:9-12), and Revelation 5:5-6 also pictures Jesus as the Lamb who triumphs. (2) The Suffering Servant of the Lord (Boismard; cf. Blomberg)—since the suffering servant theme in Isa 53 is used of Jesus, and since the same Aramaic word for "servant" can also be "lamb," it is possible that John made this connection. (3) The sacrificial Lamb (Hoskyns, Bruce, Morris, Grigsby [1982], Michaels, Whitacre, Burge, Köstenberger)— some link this particularly with the Passover lamb, others with the scapegoat, still others with the lamb of the daily sacrifices, but all center on the sacrificial overtones. The Suffering Servant is linked with the lamb image in Isa 53:7, but this implicitly shows that it should be taken as secondary to sacrificial or paschal lamb imagery. The major argument against the sacrificial Lamb is the statement in Matt 11:2-19, which may show that the Baptist "was *not* prepared for a suffering Messiah" (Carson 1991:149, italics his). This, however, is not clearly indicated in Matt 11, which seems to be centered on Jesus as the expected Messiah in general and represents the Baptist's personal doubts at a later period. On the whole, the sacrificial interpretation is perfectly viable for the Baptist and is in keeping with his general preaching on sin and repentance. It does not mean he understood the implications clearly but that he had a dawning understanding of the purpose of Jesus. In short, the apocalyptic interpretation is historically possible but unnecessary and not indicated by the text here.

1:34 *Chosen One of God.* There is a text-critical debate as to whether this should be "Son of God" (NLT mg) or "Chosen One of God." The word *huios* [TG5207, ZG5626] (son) is found in 𝔓66 𝔓75 A B C W 083 (cf. KJV, NASB, NIV, NRSV), while *eklektos* [TG1588A, ZG1723], (chosen one) is found in 𝔓5vid 𝔓106vid ℵ* ite syrc,s (cf. NJB, REB, NLT). While the ms evidence is slightly stronger for "Son of God," most scholars (Comfort, Barrett, Brown, Schnackenburg, Morris, Carson) tend to prefer the latter because it is unlikely that later scribes would have replaced "Son of God"—a major title in John (cf. 1:49; 3:18; 5:25; 10:36; 11:4, 27; 19:7; 20:31)—with one that does not appear elsewhere in the book. Thus, it is more likely that "Chosen One of God" is original.

COMMENTARY

When John the Baptist called Jesus "the Lamb of God," he used a sacrificial image that had powerful implications. It is hard to know how much he understood about the sacrificial destiny of Jesus. He may have meant it to refer in a very general way to Jesus effecting forgiveness of sins for the people, but the Spirit was using him to introduce the key purpose of Jesus' coming. The lamb was one of the primary animals used in the sacrificial system. In the phrase "takes away the sin of the world," there is certainly an idea of atonement, Jesus bearing the sins of the nation. Did John understand Jesus as the Suffering Servant of Isaiah 53? This is difficult to know because mainstream Jewish interpretation did not understand the Servant of the Lord messianically but rather as symbolic of the nation or perhaps of Isaiah himself. Still, there is no reason why the Spirit could not have led John to that conclusion, especially since the Essenes at Qumran also linked the Servant with messianic expectations (so Morris). Note also that atonement for sin is made for the "world," not just for the Jewish people, in keeping with the world as the focus of the divine mission (3:16; 4:42; 8:12).

John then reminded his listeners of what he had said in 1:15—that this Jesus, the Lamb, was to follow him but would supplant his ministry because of his "greater" status than John as the preexistent one. This has great emphasis, for it tells the reader of the importance of this Jesus and highlights once more the fact that the great significance of the Baptist's ministry was his witness to the identity of Jesus (1:7, 15, 19-20). John then proceeded to relate the moment when he came to his conclusion about Jesus' identity—namely, at Jesus' baptism, which had apparently taken place a few days earlier. First, he said that until that time, he "did not recognize him as the Messiah." It is difficult to know how much time John had spent with Jesus prior to the Baptism; they were relatives (Luke 1:36), but that does not mean they had known each other growing up. Until the Baptism itself, however, he had longed for the Messiah but did not know who he would be. The only thing he was sure about was that his ministry of baptism was messianic in nature—that is, it was preparing for the moment when the Messiah might be revealed to Israel. While in one sense John baptized people "to show that they had turned to God to receive forgiveness for their sins" (Mark 1:4), even the preaching of repentance was preparing for the Messiah who alone could "[take] away the sin of the world."

But then the moment of realization had come when John baptized Jesus. As he testifies in 1:32-33, "I saw the Holy Spirit descending like a dove from heaven and resting upon him." In a sense, this event was Jesus' messianic "anointing" (the meaning of "Messiah" and "Christ") for public ministry, but it was also a sign to John. In the Old Testament, kings were anointed by the high priest or a prophet, but here Jesus was anointed by the Holy Spirit. Throughout the fourth Gospel, the Spirit is seen in his revelatory function as the Spirit of God who infuses Jesus' ministry and carries it on (cf. comments on 14:16). Thus, the Spirit inaugurated Jesus' ministry here. God had previously told John that "the one on whom you see the Spirit descend and rest is the one who will baptize with the Holy Spirit" (1:33). When John saw this occur, he knew Jesus was the designated Messiah. The baptism John administered by water was preparatory for the Spirit-baptism that Jesus would bring about. This is made explicit in 7:38-39, where out of Jesus' heart flow "rivers of living water," namely the Holy Spirit. Through him, the Spirit flows out to all mankind (cf. also 16:8-15).

Then John gave his fourth official "witness" to Jesus' identity (1:34; cf. 1:15, 19, 32, all building on 1:7-8)—"he is the Chosen One of God," that is, the one God had chosen to be Messiah and Redeemer. This is probably an allusion to Isaiah 42:1 ("Look at my servant, whom I strengthen. He is my chosen one, who pleases me"), which was also part of God's testimony at the Baptism (Mark 1:11). This continues the Servant of the Lord imagery from 1:29, pointing forward to Christ as the Suffering Servant who was destined to die as a sacrifice for sin.

◆   ## C. The First Disciples Come to Jesus (1:35-42)

³⁵The following day John was again standing with two of his disciples. ³⁶As Jesus walked by, John looked at him and declared, "Look! There is the Lamb of God!" ³⁷When John's two disciples heard this, they followed Jesus.

³⁸Jesus looked around and saw them following. "What do you want?" he asked them.

They replied, "Rabbi" (which means "Teacher"), "where are you staying?"

³⁹"Come and see," he said. It was about four o'clock in the afternoon when they went with him to the place where he was staying, and they remained with him the rest of the day.

⁴⁰Andrew, Simon Peter's brother, was one of these men who heard what John said and then followed Jesus. ⁴¹Andrew went to find his brother, Simon, and told him, "We have found the Messiah" (which means "Christ"*).

⁴²Then Andrew brought Simon to meet Jesus. Looking intently at Simon, Jesus said, "Your name is Simon, son of John— but you will be called Cephas" (which means "Peter"*).

1:41 *Messiah* (a Hebrew term) and *Christ* (a Greek term) both mean "the anointed one."   1:42 The names *Cephas* (from Aramaic) and *Peter* (from Greek) both mean "rock."

NOTES

1:38 *Rabbi.* This was not a title of office (like "priest") in Jesus' time, and it did not become one until late in the first century. Rather, it referred to a person recognized as a teacher of Torah. These were lay leaders, often scribes or Pharisees. Köstenberger (1998b:108-111) says that half the Gospel occurrences of "rabbi" are in John (8 times); these express the earthly ministry of Jesus, with chs 13–17 moving beyond that designation into an emphasis on Jesus' exalted status.

1:39 *four o'clock in the afternoon.* The Romans counted the hours of the day from midnight on, while the Jewish people counted the hours from dawn. It is most likely that John was using the Jewish system here (Schnackenburg, Carson, contra Westcott), so "the tenth hour" mentioned in the Gr. here would be four in the afternoon.

COMMENTARY

This section continues the theme of 1:10-12. Many of "his own" people rejected him (1:11; 1:29-34), but others "accepted him" (1:12; 1:35-50). This, the first of John's salvation dramas, adds an important bit of historical information regarding the process by which Jesus chose his twelve disciples. It did not begin with the lake scene, when Jesus called the inner circle to be "fishers of men" (Mark 1:16-20); rather, at that time Jesus already knew them. It began when, after his baptism, Jesus spent some time with his relative, John the Baptist. The day after John identified Jesus as "the Lamb of God" and God's "Chosen One," he was with two of his disciples and saw Jesus again. Upon seeing Jesus, he repeated his declaration, "Look! There is the Lamb of God" (1:36). It seems clear that John the Baptist had carefully thought through what he said in 1:15, 30 ("a man is coming after me who is far greater than I am"), and in a sense he was passing on his ministry to his successor. Van der Merwe (1999:288-290) thinks that the entire purpose of the Baptist in John 1 is to witness to Jesus and to bring followers to him; this is how he was "sent" to "witness" (1:6-7). The greater one had come, and John the Baptist wanted his followers to know it. The time of witness had finished; the time of messianic action had arrived. Jesus' first two followers were drawn from the circle of John the Baptist's disciples.

The interaction between Jesus and the two disciples is enigmatic. There is no call as such, and the whole narrative seems fairly innocuous; yet it is filled with double meaning. The two disciples heard the Baptist's witness and followed Jesus. The initiative was theirs; they heard and decided to follow. We know one of them is Andrew, but the other is not named. It may well be Philip (1:43) or perhaps "the beloved disciple," John (the traditional view), who never names himself in his own Gospel. While we cannot know for sure, John's presence would fit in light of the eyewitness touches in this scene. The double meaning begins with "follow"—on one level merely the act of going with Jesus, yet on another level, the first step to discipleship (cf. its use in 1:43; 8:12; 10:27; 12:26; 21:19-20).

This continued when Jesus saw them following and said, "What do you want?" (1:38; lit., "What are you seeking?"). The question is far more than a simple inquiry: "What would you like to talk about?" As Carson says (1991:155), "the Logos-Messiah confronts those who make any show of beginning to follow him and demands that they articulate what they really want in life." This is more confrontation than question. R. A. Smith (1988:52-54) says this introduces a critical theme in this Gospel, as Jesus was in effect asking, "What do you want out of life?" This motif of seeking Jesus is at the heart of the evangelistic purpose in John (cf. "Salvation" in the Introduction).

The conversion of these disciples is never described but, as elsewhere, is rather implied by the dramatic flow in 1:38b-39 (cf. the Samaritan woman in ch 4 and the blind man in ch 9). They called Jesus "rabbi," meaning "teacher." Without even spending time with him, they were ready to accept him as their rabbi. Their question, "Where are you staying?" (1:38), again contains more than appears on the surface. As Brown notes (1966:75, 79), it means on the normal level, "Where are you lodging?" Yet the verb is a major concept in John and implies a desire to "abide" or "dwell" with God at a deeper level. Jesus responded with an invitation to salvation. His response, "come and see," has two terms that imply coming to a faith-decision throughout John ("coming"—e.g., 3:21; 5:40; 6:35; 7:37; "see"—e.g., 6:40; 9:39; 16:16; 17:24). These words are used in a similar invitation by Philip to Nathanael in 1:46.

The clear implication is that the two were searching for a deeper allegiance, and Jesus was offering them the greatest opportunity of all. Witherington (1995:70) says, "Jesus is being depicted not merely as a sage but as Wisdom, who elsewhere in Jewish literature appeals to her audience, 'Draw near to me, you who are uneducated, and lodge in the house of instruction' (Sir 51:23, 25-27, cf. also *Wisdom of Solomon 6*, 'Wisdom . . . is easily discerned by those who love her and is found by those who seek her')." The process of coming to salvation is implied in the rest of 1:39. They went with Jesus at "four o'clock in the afternoon . . . and they remained with him the rest of the day." They did more than change their physical residence at this time; they found a new home with God in Christ. Brown (1966:75) thinks this may have been a Sabbath eve, which means they stayed with Jesus until dusk the next day, observing the Sabbath.

Andrew's conversion is seen in his immediate response (1:40-41). He went to his brother Simon and did what any good evangelism program intends—each one reaches one! He could not wait to share his newfound faith. The first thing he said to his brother was, "We have found the Messiah." This is rather startling after the rather abbreviated story thus far. Yet it is natural in light of the Baptist's testimony, and it is obvious that their night with Jesus had confirmed the reality of the Baptist's confession. Jesus indeed was the "Christ" (*Christos* [TG5547, ZG5986], the Greek equivalent for the Jewish term "Messiah"). For the Jewish people, the Messiah was the expected deliverer who would be anointed by God to destroy their enemies and vindicate them as his people. The redemptive overtones, and especially the idea of a suffering Messiah, were not understood. While the Baptist glimpsed some of this (cf. notes on 1:29), it is doubtful if the disciples ever understood it until after Jesus' death and resurrection (cf. Peter's response to Jesus' passion prediction in Mark 8:27-33). Still, Andrew had become a true follower and wanted to introduce his brother, possibly another disciple of the Baptist, to Jesus.

It is interesting that John used Simon's full name, "Simon Peter," here. "Peter" was not part of his actual name (cf. below) but is the name Jesus gives him in 1:42, where Jesus actually prophesies what Simon would later become. The whole scene shows Jesus' divine foreknowledge (cf. also 1:47). When Andrew brought Simon to Jesus, we are told that Jesus looked intently at him, hinting that he saw into the very heart of Simon. The name of a person in the ancient world spoke of their very essence. When parents named a child, the meaning of that name described their hopes for the destiny of that baby. Jesus began with his actual name ("Simon son of John"—people took the name of their father as their surname, like the Scandinavian names Johan-son, Eric-son, Soren-son, etc.). Then he gave Simon his new name: "You will be called Cephas" (1:42). "Cephas" was an Aramaic name; "Peter" was the Greek equivalent, meaning "rock." This is similar to the time when God gave Jacob the new name "Israel" (Gen 32:28). This spoke not only of Peter's future significance but also of the authority of Jesus in giving him the new name. We see the human Peter in the Gospels—rash and impulsive, unsteady as "shifting sand." God was at work in his life, however, and the post-Pentecost Peter did indeed become the "rock of the church" (as prophesied in Matt 16:18). Jesus was not only a prophet but the all-seeing mind of God.

◆   D. Philip and Nathanael Come to Jesus (1:43-50)

43The next day Jesus decided to go to Galilee. He found Philip and said to him, "Come, follow me." 44Philip was from Bethsaida, Andrew and Peter's hometown.

45Philip went to look for Nathanael and told him, "We have found the very person Moses* and the prophets wrote about! His name is Jesus, the son of Joseph from Nazareth."

⁴⁶"Nazareth!" exclaimed Nathanael. "Can anything good come from Nazareth?"

"Come and see for yourself," Philip replied.

⁴⁷As they approached, Jesus said, "Now here is a genuine son of Israel—a man of complete integrity."

⁴⁸"How do you know about me?" Nathanael asked.

Jesus replied, "I could see you under the fig tree before Philip found you."

⁴⁹Then Nathanael exclaimed, "Rabbi, you are the Son of God—the King of Israel!"

⁵⁰Jesus asked him, "Do you believe this just because I told you I had seen you under the fig tree? You will see greater things than this."

1:45 Greek Moses in the law.

NOTES

1:43 *Jesus decided.* The actual subject of 1:43 is not named. While Peter is the nearest person named, few believe he is the one deciding to go to Galilee here. While it is possible that Andrew (also mentioned in 1:42) brought Philip to Jesus (so Carson), it is most likely that Jesus is the intended subject because he was the main focus of the context (so most commentators).

COMMENTARY

In 1:35-42, the initiative lay with Andrew and the unnamed disciple. Now Jesus took the initiative and encountered Philip and then Nathanael. This is unusual because in the Jewish world disciples chose which rabbi they wished to follow (cf. Köstenberger 1998b:120). Thus, Jesus was acting more like God in choosing his followers. "Come, follow me," is another pairing of two major Johannine terms for coming to salvation (cf. 1:39; 1:46). As was the case with Andrew, the hint is that Philip was converted at that time (note his confession in 1:45). Jesus decided on "the next day" to leave for Galilee. Bassler (1981:246-251) makes a study of "Galilee" in John and concludes that it is used both topographically and typologically—Galilee signifies receiving the Word, and Judea signifies rejecting the Word. John is remarkably different from the Synoptics in another way as well. In Matthew, Mark, and Luke, there are no journeys between Judea and Galilee. Jesus is depicted as beginning his ministry in Galilee and never going to Judea until Passion Week. John tells us that Jesus followed his parents' practice (Luke 2:41, "every year Jesus' parents went to Jerusalem for the Passover festival"), traveling often from Galilee to Judea and back. In just the first few chapters, Jesus is in Judea (1:29-42), returns to Cana of Galilee (1:43; 2:1), travels to Jerusalem for Passover (2:13), and returns again to Galilee by way of Samaria (ch 4). Thus, John's account provides an important historical addendum.

Before leaving for Galilee, Jesus chose another member for his discipleship band—Philip (cf. the list of the Twelve in Mark 3:16-18 and parallels), who may have also been a follower of the Baptist. We do not know much about Philip; John is the only Gospel to give us much (cf. 6:5-7; 12:21-22; 14:7-9). Later tradition tells us that he was martyred at Hierapolis near Laodicea in Asia Minor (cf. the *Acts of Philip*). Philip was "from Bethsaida, Andrew and Peter's hometown," a fishing village northwest of Capernaum just on the other side of the Jordan River going north from the Sea of Galilee (not the same as the Philip of Acts 6:5; 8:4-7, 26-40). Since Mark 1:29 tells us that Peter made his home in Capernaum during Jesus' ministry, Bethsaida is probably where he, Andrew, and Philip grew up.

Following the evangelistic pattern set by Andrew, Philip decided to introduce his friend Nathanael to Jesus (1:45). Nathanael is never mentioned in the lists of the Twelve, but it is commonly held that he is Bartholomew in the lists (Mark 3:18). This is viable for three reasons: (1) Bartholomew is coupled with Philip in the lists; (2) the name "Bartholomew" actually means "son of Tolmai," and he almost certainly had a first name, which is not mentioned in the Synoptics (cf. "Simon son of John" in 1:42); (3) in 1:50, Jesus hints that Nathanael will see "greater things," probably the miracle of Cana in 2:1-11, meaning Nathanael is one of the "disciples" in 2:2. This identification of Nathanael with Bartholomew is an interesting possibility but not ultimately certain (Beasley-Murray 1987:27 calls it "gratuitous"). Still, since the three others in this passage became members of the Twelve, it may be that Nathanael ("son of Tolmai") did as well. Philip's message is similar to that of Andrew in 1:41—"We have found the very person Moses and the prophets wrote about." The emphasis on scriptural fulfillment was a major theme in early Christian preaching (cf. the sermons in Acts 2, 3, 13, and the first part of ch 17), as it is in apologetics today. Philip's point is that the law and the prophets (that is, the entire OT) point to Jesus as the Messiah.

In identifying for Nathanael the person he has in mind, Philip used the formal method, mentioning the father and the hometown: "Jesus, the son of Joseph from Nazareth." This was normal practice at that time. "Jesus" was a common name, so Philip needed to distinguish him from others. Nathanael's reaction—"Can anything good come from Nazareth?" (1:46)—was curt, and there are three possible reasons for this: (1) rivalry between Nathanael's hometown of Cana (cf. 21:2) and Nazareth, so that Nathanael was quoting a "local proverb" (so Brown, Blomberg, Burge); (2) the Messiah was to come from Bethlehem (Micah 5:2), and Nazareth was inconsequential prophetically (so Comfort, Witherington). (3) Nazareth was a small, insignificant town of not more than 2,000 people, about 3.5 miles southeast of the capital of the region, Sepphoris (Köstenberger). From the reaction of people throughout the Gospels to the fact that Jesus was a "Nazarene" (cf. Matt 2:23; Acts 4:10; 24:5), the first or third seems likely. At the same time, the prophetic problem of Nazareth versus Bethlehem is stressed in 7:41-42. Thus, all three are probably part of the reason. The only possible response for Philip is, "Come and see for yourself." Note that Philip repeats the challenge of Jesus in 1:39. It implies an invitation to salvation, not only for Nathanael but also for the reader (so Carson).

Jesus encountered Nathanael via affirmation (1:47). Jesus' approach was quite similar to his prophecy about Simon in 1:42, and it is a sign of Jesus' divine omniscience that he could look so deeply into Nathanael and know his character. To understand what Jesus meant about "a genuine son of Israel—a man of complete integrity" (lit., "in whom there is no deceit"), one must turn to the story of Jacob in Genesis 27. The name "Jacob" connoted deceit, and that certainly characterized the man. His brother Esau, after being tricked out of his birthright, even said, "No wonder his name is Jacob, for now he has cheated me twice. First he took my rights as the firstborn, and now he has stolen my blessing" (Gen 27:36). God renamed him "Isarel," denoting his new character (Gen 32:28). Jesus was saying that Nathanael is not like the old Jacob (filled with deceit) but like the new Israel. L. F. Trudinger (1982:117) translates this well, "Look, Israel without a trace of Jacob left in him." Jesus may have also been alluding to Psalm 32:2, "What joy for those . . . whose lives are lived in complete honesty" (lit., "no deceit"). Whitacre (1999:74) calls Nathanael a "model disciple," saying he has "a clear heart in which there is no deceit and a humble docility that is open to God."

Nathanael was shocked at the insight Jesus had shown and asked, "How do you know about me?" Can we imagine a complete stranger coming up and demonstrating awareness of who we are at the core of our being? Jesus' response seems enigmatic on the surface: "I could see you under the fig tree." Scholars have had all kinds of speculations regarding the meaning of the fig tree, like the place where rabbis studied Torah or an Old Testament symbol for home (Isa 36:16; Zech 3:10). None of these are that helpful, and this is probably simply a historical reference— Jesus actually saw him under a fig tree and knew what kind of person he was. The emphasis is not on the fig tree but on Jesus' supernatural ability.

Nathanael justified Jesus' insight by making an astounding leap of faith. He called Jesus "rabbi" (as did John's disciples in 1:38) but then went far beyond what anyone had ever called a rabbi and declared Jesus the "Son of God—the King of Israel." When he called Jesus "Son of God," it is doubtful that he meant everything the title connotes to modern Christians. He probably meant it in terms of the royal Messiah, for David is called a "son" of God in 2 Samuel 7:14 and Psalm 2:7; 89:27. Moreover, Israel is called God's "child" in Deuteronomy 1:31; Jeremiah 31:9. The later overtones of the special sonship of Jesus were not understood at this early stage by Nathanael but are still present in John's retelling of the story. "King of Israel" was a definite messianic title, used later in John at 12:13 (with "King of the Jews" in 18:33, 39; 19:3, 19, 21). It is remarkable that Nathanael understood this so early, and in John's Gospel it is part of the theme of messianic understanding. The glory of Jesus was indeed observable from the beginning (cf. 1:14; 2:11), and 1:35-49 traces the stages by which the disciples' understanding grew.

As such, this section (1:35-49) contains an extraordinary set of titles attributed to Jesus by his followers: Lamb of God (1:29, 36), Chosen One of God (1:34), Messiah (1:41), a "prophet like Moses" (1:45), Son of God, and King of Israel (1:49). The Synoptics contain nothing like this, and thus many have said that John's Gospel is unhistorical at this point. Still, as several writers have pointed out (Morris, Carson, Blomberg, Keener), there is nothing actually contradictory here. There had to be some reason for these disciples to leave John the Baptist's group and follow Jesus, and they were uttering titles that had to do with messianic expectation—the very thing the delegation had been asking John about (1:19-25). This does not necessarily mean that they understood at a deep level what they were saying. This exemplifies the flowering of faith and understanding. The scene makes sense. Everyone was asking about the coming Messiah, and while the Pharisees rejected Jesus, these men believed he was the Messiah.

Their faith was still inadequate, as is indicated by Jesus' rather surprising response to Nathanael's exclamation (1:50). This must be understood in light of the Johannine view of true faith—actual belief happens when one has both heard Jesus' teaching and observed his works. Nathanael believed when Jesus told him who he was after seeing him "under the fig tree." Soon he would "see greater things than this," and his faith would deepen. The "greater things" comment points forward to the first sign-miracle at Cana in 2:1-11, and this hints that Nathanael was one of the disciples mentioned in 2:2 who saw Jesus' first miracle.

◆   ## E. Jesus Unites Heaven and Earth (1:51)

⁵¹Then he said, "I tell you the truth, you will all see heaven open and the angels of God going up and down on the Son of Man, the one who is the stairway between heaven and earth.*"

1:51 Greek *going up and down on the Son of Man;* see Gen 28:10-17. "Son of Man" is a title Jesus used for himself.

NOTES

1:51 *I tell you the truth.* The Greek is *amēn amēn* [TG281, ZG297] ("amen, amen"). It was used in the ancient world as an official response of affirmation or confirmation for a truth and was also often used to end prayers as an indication that the person or congregation was assenting to its contents. Jesus used it to highlight especially important statements, giving them his divine imprimatur and emphasizing their truthfulness. In the Synoptics we find the use of a single *amēn* and in John, the double *amēn* (doubling a saying [e.g., holy, holy] gives it greater emphasis [so Morris]).

you will all see. Jesus here was not just addressing Nathanael, for the plural "you" in 1:51 includes all the disciples.

Son of Man. The "Son of Man" sayings are particular to Jesus, occurring 83 times in the Gospels, but only found three times outside them—once when Stephen saw Jesus himself in heaven (Acts 7:56) and twice when "someone like the Son of Man" is used of Christ in Rev 1:13; 14:14 (some also see Heb 2:6 as a title). This title is sometimes used as a circumlocution for "I," (this stems from the "son of man" in Ezekiel, used of him as a mortal human), and it is sometimes a reference to the glorified heavenly being of Dan 7:13-14. Both aspects were utilized by Jesus because both apply to him. On the historicity of the title, see DJG 778-781.

COMMENTARY

This is the first "Son of Man" saying in the Gospel of John. Jesus drew the title from the phrase "someone like a son of man" in Daniel 7:13-14, a reference to the heavenly figure who is "given authority, honor, and sovereignty over all the nations of the world." (In other places, Jesus drew from Ezekiel's use of "son of man" [e.g., Ezek 2:1, 3, 6, 8] to designate his earthly aspect.) In John, this title occurs 13 times and is associated with Jesus' heavenly origin and access (3:13; 6:62), his glory (12:23; 13:31), his exaltation on the cross (the "lifted up" sayings, 3:14; 8:28; 12:34), and his authority to judge (5:27) and to give life (6:27, 53). John built on the synoptic "Son of Man" sayings with the emphasis on Jesus' heavenly glory (for the historical authenticity of this material, see Carson 1991:165-166; Blomberg 2001:84-85).

The expression "the stairway between heaven and earth" must be understood by again looking at the story of Jacob—in particular Jacob's ladder or "stairway" in Genesis 28:12. In Jacob's vision, he saw a stairway that reached from the earth up to heaven with the angels of God going up and down it—a strong picture of Jacob's new authority and access to heaven. Jesus is the final Jacob, the new Israel, the one on whom the angels ascend and descend, the "stairway between heaven and earth" (1:51). This being who is one with God has brought heaven down to earth and united the two spheres in himself. In a sense, the "new heaven and a new earth" of Revelation 21:1 is now found in Jesus as the God-man. In fact, even the word order is important: since Jesus is God on earth, the angels first "ascend" from earth rather than descend from heaven (so Schnackenburg). The idea of the "open heaven" is first seen at Jesus' baptism, when "the heavens [split] apart" (Mark 1:10) and indicated that in some sense the last days had begun. The "open heaven" also implies a new period of divine revelation, as heaven is opened to God's people in Jesus (so Rowland 1984:501-505). As Whitacre says (1999:76), "The one Isaiah saw (Isa 6:1-5; John 12:38-41) has come into our midst. Jesus, not heaven, is the focal point of revelation."

◆ III. The Public Ministry of Jesus: Signs and Teaching (2:1–12:50)
    A. Glory Revealed: the Beginning Stages (2:1–4:54)
        1. The first sign: water into wine (2:1-12)

The next day* there was a wedding celebration in the village of Cana in Galilee. Jesus' mother was there, ²and Jesus and his disciples were also invited to the celebration. ³The wine supply ran out during the festivities, so Jesus' mother told him, "They have no more wine."

⁴"Dear woman, that's not our problem," Jesus replied. "My time has not yet come."

⁵But his mother told the servants, "Do whatever he tells you."

⁶Standing nearby were six stone water jars, used for Jewish ceremonial washing. Each could hold twenty to thirty gallons.* ⁷Jesus told the servants, "Fill the jars with water." When the jars had been filled, ⁸he said, "Now dip some out, and take it to the master of ceremonies." So the servants followed his instructions.

⁹When the master of ceremonies tasted the water that was now wine, not knowing where it had come from (though, of course, the servants knew), he called the bridegroom over. ¹⁰"A host always serves the best wine first," he said. "Then, when everyone has had a lot to drink, he brings out the less expensive wine. But you have kept the best until now!"

¹¹This miraculous sign at Cana in Galilee was the first time Jesus revealed his glory. And his disciples believed in him.

¹²After the wedding he went to Capernaum for a few days with his mother, his brothers, and his disciples.

2:1 Greek *On the third day*; see 1:35, 43.   2:6 Greek *2 or 3 measures* [75 to 113 liters].

NOTES

2:3 *Jesus' mother.* Some (e.g., Whitacre) point to Mary as a model disciple here and see similarities with the reaction of the first disciples in ch 1, for instance, in taking the initiative in coming to Jesus (cf. 1:37) and allowing Jesus to set the agenda (cf. 1:38). Her faith in Jesus' ability to solve the situation is another parallel.

2:4 *that's not our problem.* Some (Lagrange, Schnackenburg, Derrett, Beasley-Murray) have tried to give this a softer tone, such as, "What do you want me to do?" or "Why tell me this? I understand it." Such renderings are doubtful. There is some aspect of rebuke or distancing in the question.

2:5 *his mother told the servants.* The symbolism of Mary as developed through the ages is out of keeping with her actual portrait here and in the rest of the NT. Brown calls her "the New Eve, the symbol of the church" (1966:109), not in the sense of the later developed Mariology but as an incipient emphasis in terms of "corporate personality." Schnackenburg is closer (1980:331) when he sees the emphasis on the scene rather than on "theological presuppositions concerning her."

2:9 *the water that was now wine.* Several (Brown, Beasley-Murray, Carson) also see a further theme: the replacement of the old Jewish institutions and rituals with the new life of the Kingdom in Christ. The new wine makes the old unnecessary. While this seems overly allegorical, it is certainly a possible thrust here in light of the messianic themes of John.

2:12 *his brothers.* Jesus' brothers were certainly his half-brothers born to Joseph and Mary. The idea that Mary was a "perpetual virgin" and that these were actually Jesus' cousins arose in the second century (cf. Morris 1995:187).

COMMENTARY

This begins a major section (2:1–12:50), which centers on seven signs that are carefully structured to accord with Jesus' discourses. Thus, this section of John is frequently labeled "the book of signs" because in these signs God reveals the glory of Christ. In these chapters, the Jewish people also encounter the miraculous power of Jesus and the invitation of these sign-miracles to investigate his true identity. The discourses then demand that the people recognize Jesus' God-sent authority and come to a faith-decision. The conflict intensifies as the Jewish people continually reject Jesus and his message. Yet his glory also becomes more and more evident for those with the eyes of faith.

The first portion of this major section (2:1–4:54) is framed by two miracles in Cana of Galilee (2:1-11; 4:46-54); these are the first two "signs." In these and the intervening material, Jesus progressively reveals his new plan of salvation, which requires people to encounter God in him. Beasley-Murray (1987:31) thinks the primary theme is that "'The old things have passed away; see, the new have come' (2 Cor 5:17). The three chapters together present the replacement of the old purifications by the wine of the kingdom of God, the old Temple by the new in the risen Lord, an exposition of new birth for new creation, a contrast between the water of Jacob's well with the living water from Christ, and the worship of Jerusalem and Gerizim with worship 'in Spirit and in truth.'"

This reenactment motif, in which the history of Israel's journey foreshadows Jesus and the disciples' journey, appears throughout John's Gospel. For example, in the first few chapters, Jesus offers himself as the new spiritual habitation for God's people, as he is the new Tabernacle (ch 1) and the true Temple (ch 2). Furthermore, he is the source of a new corporate regeneration (ch 3) and God's gift of life (ch 4). The same pattern continues in the rest of John (for details, see Comfort 1994:15-20).

The First Sign: Changing Water into Wine (2:1-12). As already stated (cf. note on 1:29), "the third day" (2:1, NLT mg) culminates a weeklong ministry of Jesus, involving preparatory events for his public ministry. In these events, the primary theme is awakening awareness to the fact that this Jesus is the Messiah, Lamb of God, and Son of God. This scene culminates with a messianic miracle par excellence. At this time, a wedding was taking place at Cana in Galilee, a village a few miles north of Nazareth that was also the home of Nathanael (21:2). A typical wedding would consist of a procession bringing the bride to the groom's home, a wedding supper, and a week of festivities. Jesus, his family, and his disciples were invited, so Jesus made the lengthy trip from Judea to attend. The presence of his family and the disciples as his guests makes it plausible to suppose that a relative of Jesus was involved in the wedding. An apocryphal tradition even names John himself as the groom (so Brown; on the historicity of the scene, see Blomberg 2001:85).

At some time during the festivities the wine supply ran out, which was a major problem (2:3). Some think that part of the reason was the arrival of Jesus and his disciples (so Whitacre), but if that were true, it is difficult to see why Jesus reacted the way he did in 2:4. In that culture, the groom was responsible for the wedding expenses, and he would at the least face disgrace for a long time to come for allowing the wine to run out. (Hospitality was essential in the ancient world, with weddings presenting the greatest of obligations.) There might even have been legal complications, for the bride's family could have sued them (cf. Derrett 1963:82-89; Collins 1995:103-104 for the honor/shame aspect). This was a desperate situation. Jesus' mother, who may have had some responsibility for planning the wedding (if she and the groom were indeed relatives), brought the problem to Jesus. It is hard to know what she expected Jesus to do. If this was indeed the first of his miracles (which is likely), she could hardly have expected him to do such a thing. There is no evidence (in spite of apocryphal stories) that he had performed miracles while he was growing up, and the reaction of his townspeople when rejecting him (Mark 6:1-6) shows that he was known merely as the village carpenter. His father Joseph had likely died at some time in those years (cf. Carson 1991:292), so Jesus, as the oldest son, took over his father's practice. There is no mention of Joseph in Matthew and Luke after the birth narratives, and Christian tradition favors the idea that Joseph was old when he married Mary (cf. *Protoevangelium of James* 9:2). Thus, Mary had probably learned to depend on Jesus' resourcefulness, and she was doing that here as well.

Jesus' reaction (2:4) to Mary is startling. On first glance, it seems rude and uncaring—yet behind it, there is unbelievable depth. The address, literally just "woman," is not really insulting, as seen in the fact that when he gives her over to John's care in 19:26, he also calls her "woman." The NLT's phrasing, "dear woman," is somewhat valid, but in the context, Jesus was distancing himself from

Mary. He was no longer just her son—the time had come to follow the path his Father had prepared for him (so Michaels, Burge). His reply is quite interesting. It is literally, "What is it to me and to you?" In the Synoptics, demons often use this expression when Jesus is about to cast them out—"Why are you interfering with us?" (Mark 1:24; 5:7 and parallels). In the LXX, it is often used of discord ("What has caused this?"—Judg 11:12; 2 Chr 35:21) or disengagement ("What business is this of mine?"—2 Kgs 3:13; Hos 14:8). Jesus' reply is of the latter kind. In it there may be a slight rebuke: "That's not our problem." That is, Jesus was distancing himself from the situation and showing reluctance to get involved. Most likely the point is that he had to follow the agenda set for him by the Father rather than allow human situations to dictate what he did.

The reason for disengaging himself from the situation is in keeping with this concern for the Father's agenda: "My time has not yet come" (2:4). Throughout John, the theme of his "time" (lit., his "hour") always refers to the time of destiny, the passion events (7:30; 8:20; 12:23; 13:1; 17:1). Jesus was saying here that he was reluctant to begin the series of events that would culminate in his passion. Carson (1991:172-173) gives three points to explain the symbolism: (1) Jesus saw the wine as symbolizing the messianic age and was saying that the hour of his glorification had not yet come; (2) Jesus was very oriented to his Father's will rather than human schedules, and he wanted to be sure the time was right; and (3) as the messianic bridegroom, he would meet the need, but the true hour of the messianic banquet had not yet arrived. All three are likely part of the meaning.

Obviously, there is no way Mary could have understood this. She showed a mother's trust in her son and simply told the servants, "Do whatever he tells you" (2:5). Again, she was the model disciple, humbly leaving it all to Jesus and trusting in his wisdom, even when she did not understand. Jesus' subsequent actions show that her trust was well placed. He saw the "six stone water jars" that were "used for Jewish ceremonial washing," each holding 20 to 30 gallons of water (2–3 measures). Jews would use these jars for washing hands (Mark 7:1-5) or utensils. It is important to realize that their purpose was to render the unclean ritually pure— they represented ceremonial uncleanness. When Jesus had them filled with water and then changed that water into wine, a double miracle occurred. First, the unclean jars were made clean. In fact, the reason they were made of stone was because the Jews would have had to break earthen jars that had been rendered unclean (Lev 11:33-35). Second, the water was turned into wine. Moreover, when the wine was distributed, the "master of ceremonies" (in charge of distributing the food and wine) called it the "best wine" of the entire wedding. His explanation (2:10) provides some interesting background. At celebrations like weddings, it was the custom to buy some expensive wine and some cheaper wine. They would serve the good wine first; then after their palates were satisfied (note that this cannot be grape juice; there is a hint of inebriation in "a lot to drink"), they would serve the cheaper wine.

Jesus gave up his reluctance and performed a powerful miracle. No wonder it "revealed his glory" (2:11); in fact, M. S. Collins (1995:106) thinks the thrust of the story as a whole is to present the true "glory" of Jesus. According to the Old Testament, at the coming of the final Kingdom there will be an abundance of wine (Isa 25:6; Jer 31:12; Hos 14:7), and this banquet is often depicted as a messianic wedding feast (Hos 2:16-23; cf. Rev 19:9-11). The message of the wine, then, is that the messianic age has started, and it is a proleptic anticipation of the final messianic age to come. The "glory of the Father's one and only Son" (1:14) is now unveiled for those with eyes to see. This is the first "sign" miracle demonstrating Jesus' glory. While the synoptic Gospels use "power" or "miracle" (*dunamis* [TG1411, ZG1539]) to describe such events, John uses "sign" (*sēmeion* [TG4592, ZG4956]) because the miracles point beyond themselves to a deeper reality—namely, the "unveiling" of God's work in Jesus (cf. Schnackenburg 1980:515-528). The sign reveals the glory, and the disciples who saw it "believed in him." This is the key moment, linked with all the other encounters to come (cf. 20:30-31, where it is the major purpose of this book). They had experienced God revealing himself in Jesus through this first sign, and they responded with faith.

Finally, in a brief side note (2:12), John tells us that Jesus went down from Cana in the hill country of Galilee to Capernaum (about 16 miles away) with his disciples, his brothers (mentioned again in 7:1-5; Mark 6:3 names them as "James, Joseph, Judas, and Simon") and his mother. This may have been a transition to his move to Capernaum around this time, for we know from the Synoptics that near the start of his ministry Jesus made Capernaum the headquarters (Matt 9:1, "his own town") for his Galilean ministry. That was a natural move, for Capernaum was a central fishing village on the lake with a major north–south thoroughfare passing through it.

◆   ## 2. Confrontation in the Temple (2:13-22)

13It was nearly time for the Jewish Passover celebration, so Jesus went to Jerusalem. 14In the Temple area he saw merchants selling cattle, sheep, and doves for sacrifices; he also saw dealers at tables exchanging foreign money. 15Jesus made a whip from some ropes and chased them all out of the Temple. He drove out the sheep and cattle, scattered the money changers' coins over the floor, and turned over their tables. 16Then, going over to the people who sold doves, he told them, "Get these things out of here. Stop turning my Father's house into a marketplace!"

17Then his disciples remembered this prophecy from the Scriptures: "Passion for God's house will consume me."*

18But the Jewish leaders demanded, "What are you doing? If God gave you authority to do this, show us a miraculous sign to prove it."

19"All right," Jesus replied. "Destroy this temple, and in three days I will raise it up."

20"What!" they exclaimed. "It has taken forty-six years to build this Temple, and you can rebuild it in three days?" 21But when Jesus said "this temple," he meant his own body. 22After he was raised from the dead, his disciples remembered he had said this, and they believed both the Scriptures and what Jesus had said.

2:17 Or "Concern for God's house will be my undoing." Ps 69:9.

NOTES

2:19 *Destroy this temple.* Jesus' challenge to destroy the Temple was turned into a legal accusation at his trial when witnesses recounted it and claimed that he had threatened to destroy the Temple, a capital crime (cf. Mark 14:58 and parallels). Interestingly, the Synoptics do not record the original saying; only John does. As Comfort points out, "Jesus said, '*You* destroy this temple.' (The verb is a second person, plural, aorist active imperative.) He did not say that he would destroy the Temple. But at the time of Jesus' trial, some of his accusers twisted his statement to assert that Jesus said he would destroy the Temple (Matt 26:61; Mark 14:58). This was the only accusation against Jesus that was clearly verbalized— and the accusation was false" (1994:189-190). Though Jesus never said he was going to destroy the Temple, there are still a great number of debates regarding the meaning of this cryptic saying. Many think that Jesus was actually predicting the abolition of the Temple and of Temple worship. Several (Morris, Hoskyns, Bruce) see a double meaning here, primarily Jesus' resurrection but secondarily the destruction of the Temple and its replacement by a "spiritual temple" (= the church), effected by Jesus' death and resurrection. Beasley-Murray (1987:40-41) goes further and believes this is "an ironic challenge" for them to continue their behavior, which would lead to the destruction of the Temple. Others (Dodd, Lindars) take this to be the original meaning, while a prophecy of Jesus' death and resurrection was a Johannine interpretation. Yet these views are very difficult to see in the wording here, for the "third day" motif points exclusively to the Resurrection and does not fit any spiritualizing interpretation. If one could isolate "destroy this temple," Beasley-Murray's view would be possible. However, it is a whole saying, and such prophetic irony is unlikely here. In fact, John himself denies this in 2:21, saying that "temple" referred specifically to "his own body."

2:20 *It has taken forty-six years to build this Temple.* This is an important note for dating the life of Christ. Josephus tells us that Herod began constructing the Temple in the eighteenth year of his reign (*Antiquities* 15.380), and that would be 20/19 BC. Therefore, Jesus began his ministry about AD 27/28.

2:21 *his own body.* Some have interpreted Jesus' "body" to be the church (cf. Eph 1:23; 4:16; Col 1:18) and taken the rebuilding of it (2:20) as a reference to his inauguration of the church. That is Paul's metaphor, however, not John's. The context makes it absolutely clear that this is Jesus' physical body.

COMMENTARY

The first major issue is how to reconcile John's placement of the clearing of the Temple at the beginning of Jesus' ministry with the Synoptics' placement of it at the end (Mark 11:15-17). The majority of scholars (e.g., Barrett, Schnackenburg, Beasley-Murray, Ridderbos, Borchert, Keener) believe that there was only one clearing of the Temple, at the close of Jesus' ministry, which then became a major factor in his arrest. Thus, they think John took it out of order and placed it at the start of Jesus' ministry for thematic reasons. This is possible because of the absence of chronology in the Gospel accounts. As Blomberg says (1987:127), from the "time of Augustine it has been recognized that the gospels did not set out to supply a detailed itinerary of Jesus' ministry with every event in its proper chronological sequence, but frequently arrange passages in topical or thematic order instead." Is this true here as well? There are some differences in the accounts, and this story occurs in a large block of material not found in the Synoptics. Moreover, unlike the Synoptic stories, this does not end in an attempt to arrest or kill Jesus. For these reasons and others, I (along with Hendriksen, Morris, Carson, Köstenberger) believe this is a separate account. In the Synoptics, the emphasis is upon the cleansing as an act of judgment for the apostasy of the nation. In John, it is messianic zeal that is uppermost. It is possible that John intended it as another of Jesus' signs (which would explain the plural "signs" in 2:23; see Köstenberger 1995:95-101 and 1998a:70-74 for the cleansing of the Temple as a sign).

There are two parts to this section: the cleansing of the Temple (2:13-17) and the ensuing debate with the Jewish leaders (2:18-22). This is the first of three Passover festivals that frame Jesus' ministry in John (with 6:4; 11:55), thereby breaking Jesus' ministry into a roughly two-year period. Though found only in John, these stories make perfect sense, for Jesus went to Jerusalem regularly with his parents for Passover (Luke 2:41), and he most likely continued the pilgrimages as an adult. It also shows Jesus' Jewish piety. He did not reject Judaism; the Jewish people rejected him. Passover was one of the most sacred of the Jewish feasts, celebrating the Exodus story of the angel of death "passing over" the homes of the Jewish people who put blood on their doorposts (Exod 12). It was celebrated in early spring (late March to early April).

When Jesus arrived, he found the usual chaos caused by the sale of the sacrificial animals and the exchange of foreign coins. The "cattle, sheep, and doves" were needed for the various sacrifices, and it was much more convenient to buy them in the Temple precincts than to go to the trouble of transporting them to the site. The Jewish authorities greatly profited from this. The number of animals needed was staggering. For a festival like Passover, when the normal population of 50,000 to 70,000 for Jerusalem swelled to 250,000 or so, an incredible number was needed. At this time, as well, the pilgrims would pay the annual half-shekel Temple tax (= two denarii or two days' wages for a day laborer; Passover was one of three times it could be paid during the year) with coins that came from all over the Empire. The pilgrims had to pay in Tyrian silver due to the purity of the silver, and the exchangers set up a month ahead to keep up with the need (so Carson). Also, coins with images of the emperor on them or other pagan symbols were considered idolatrous and could not be used. Once again, high interest would sometimes be charged by the money changers (it was supposed to be 2–4 percent but could be as high as 12 percent; see Barrett, Bruce). The sales and the exchange took place in the court of the Gentiles, where a market was set up.

Jesus was so outraged that they had desecrated the Temple with this buying and selling that he made a whip out of some ropes, possibly by tying together the rushes used as bedding for the animals. With this whip, he then chased them all out of the Temple—the sellers as well as the animals. John emphasizes three actions: driving out all the animals, scattering the coins over the floor, and turning over the tables. The reader should note the stress on Jesus' authority as Son of God in ridding his "Father's house" of impurity. The descriptions in all the Gospels focus not so much on Jesus' use of force as on his moral and spiritual outrage. If ever there were a case of "righteous indignation," this was it! Jesus' messianic zeal for his Father's house probably convicted the majority of bystanders, and this may have kept the authorities from seeking legal repercussions. After the second cleansing of the Temple, Mark 11:18 says the leaders "began planning how to kill him" but were "afraid" because of the people.

To the sellers of doves (the sacrifice for the poor), Jesus gave his rationale: "Stop turning my Father's house into a marketplace" (2:16). Note here that the emphasis is on the act of buying and selling ("marketplace") rather than on the exorbitant interest rates ("den of thieves" in Mark 11:17). Certainly the selling of sacrificial animals and the exchange of coins was necessary but not within the Temple proper. They had replaced worship with commerce. The noise and the chaos were more than Jesus could take. Several Old Testament passages call for such a cleansing of the Temple in light of spiritual impurity (Ezek 43:7; Zech 14:21; Mal 3:3). One wonders if Jesus would do this in some of our contemporary churches where commerce and profit and entertainment have replaced true worship.

The disciples discovered the basic message of the event when they "remembered" Psalm 69:9: "Passion for your house has consumed me" (cf. 2:17). This is one of the most frequent psalms cited regarding Jesus' passion (e.g., 15:25; 19:28). According to Psalm 69, one of the reasons David experienced opposition was that he had zeal for God and his Temple. Carson (1991:180) says that the use of the future "will consume me" points first to Jesus as "David's greater Son" and even more to the ultimate time when Jesus will be "consumed"—namely, at his death. Both in the emphasis on the "Passover" at the beginning of the episode (Jesus fulfilling the Passover feast, see ch 6) and in Jesus' future here, John was preparing the reader for the ultimate destiny of Jesus in his true "passion," his death on the cross. John's language here also indicates that the Temple is no longer the place of God's dwelling, for Jesus has become "the new and true dwelling place of God"; the shekinah has "taken up a new residence," and the new age has begun (Comfort 1994:52).

The result of Jesus' action in the Temple, needless to say, created controversy. There are three levels of understanding. First, at the level of the authorities, they (possibly the Temple leaders) were indignant and demanded a "miraculous sign" to prove that "God gave you authority to do this" (2:18). Their very reaction is telling. They do not seem to question the legality of Jesus' action. There is no attempt to arrest him. Implicitly, they almost seem to accept the rightness of the action and only question his authority. The question itself is valid. The Messiah would give "signs" of his presence. What was invalid was their refusal to consider what Jesus had already said and done—proof that he indeed was Son of God and Messiah. They at least recognized his basic claim, for they were not treating him as a petty criminal. They understood the authority he had shown and wanted proof through a messianic miracle—but as will be seen throughout John, they rejected his heavenly status.

Jesus responded with a confusing retort: "Destroy this temple, and in three days I will raise it up" (2:19). The statement functions at several levels. The leaders understood it literally: If they wanted a sign, Jesus would give it to them. If they were to destroy the Temple (to desecrate or destroy the Temple would have been a capital offense in both Roman and Jewish law), Jesus would restore it in just three days. Their reaction is expected: "What! . . . It has taken forty-six years to build this Temple" (2:20). Herod began building it in 20/19 BC and actually did not complete it until 64 AD, so it was still in the process of construction as Jesus was speaking (cf. note on 2:20). Still, they had asked for a sign, and that would certainly be one! In giving such an enigmatic response, Jesus was hardly answering their request. Rather, he was confirming their rejection. Whitacre (1999:83) points out that Jesus was testing their hearts, and he contrasts them to Nathanael, who listened to Jesus and waited until he understood. The leaders, who were not seeking truth, jumped to conclusions.

From Jesus' perspective, the enigmatic saying is a prophecy of the destruction of his bodily "temple" and his resurrection after "three days" (2:21). This explanation is meant to ensure that the reader understands what Jesus meant. It is also further proof that John understood the event of the cleansing of the Temple in one sense as a further "sign" pointing to Jesus' death and resurrection. What was hinted at there is made explicit here: all that Jesus said and did points to the Cross. This is the heart of John's theology. The world has rejected the revelation of God in Jesus (1:10-11), but God loves the world more than it hates him (3:16), and he has sent his one and only Son to be the sacrifice for sin (1:29; 3:16). This first Passover anticipates the last Passover, when Jesus' "temple" will be destroyed but raised three days later. That will be the final and true revelation of his glory.

Finally, from the disciples' perspective, the saying produces confusion and is not understood until "after he was raised from the dead," when they "remembered" the saying and "believed" (2:22). This is part of John's "misunderstanding" theme (Carson [1982] notes 30 examples of this), used by him to point out that the true personhood of Christ can only be understood in light of the reality of the Resurrection. Note that for the second time (with 2:11) the disciples "believed." This is in contrast to the leaders and is part of John's emphasis on faith-decision; every person who encounters Christ is brought to decision. Note also that they believe two things: (1) "the Scriptures," part of the Johannine theme of scriptural witness to the Christ-event (cf. 5:39, 46); and (2) "what Jesus had said," which shows that the disciples, unlike the leaders, were at all times seeking truth. They were confused but kept this in the back of their minds, and when the passion events corrected their misunderstanding, they were ready to believe. "Remembering" is an important motif in Scripture. Twice the disciples "remember" here (2:17, 22). In John's Gospel, memory comes from recollecting Jesus' teaching, and the remembrance initiates faith (2:22; 15:20; 16:4).

◆   ## 3. Inadequate faith based on signs (2:23-25)

[23]Because of the miraculous signs Jesus did in Jerusalem at the Passover celebration, many began to trust in him. [24]But Jesus didn't trust them, because he knew human nature. [25]No one needed to tell him what mankind is really like.

NOTES

2:23 *many began to trust in him.* There is a difference of opinion as to the significance of this scene. Some (e.g., Godet, Hendriksen, Carson, Comfort, Witherington) believe it speaks of a "spurious" faith, while others (Morris, Whitacre) take it as an "immature" but genuine faith. It is probably best to take a middle position (Bultmann, Brown, Beasley-Murray, Burge, Keener) that this was a "first step" toward true faith. It was incomplete but still moving in the right direction.

COMMENTARY

This short section functions similarly to 2:11 in that it concludes the previous section but is linked even more closely to what follows. It sums up the events "at the Passover celebration" when Jesus cleared the Temple, and it also tells us that he did other "miraculous signs" (note the plural) at that time. As 2:11 ended with the disciples believing in him, we now learn that many people began to trust in him (same Gr. verb as "believed" in 2:11) as a result of these other miracles. It is common to find a series of miracles summarized in the Gospels (cf. Matt 4:23-24; 9:35; Mark 3:10-11), and here the emphasis is not on the sign-miracles but on the reaction to the sign-miracles. The difficulty comes in the next verse, for although they "believed" in Jesus, he didn't "trust" in them. It is again the same Greek word (*pisteuō* [TG4100, ZG4409]), but it has double meaning. The construction indicates that Jesus did not "entrust himself" to them, but it also means he "didn't trust them." His reason is found in 2:25; he knew "what mankind is really like"—namely, that their faith was not truly complete. Since miracles are "signs" that point to Jesus, the "faith" that they generate is a good first step, but it is incomplete. In a sense, the "many" here are like the second and third "soils" in the parable of the sower (Mark 4:1-20); they seem to have an exciting belief in Jesus, yet when troubles or the temptations of pleasure come, they fall away. In fact, that is exactly what happens in 6:60-66, when a group of Jesus' "disciples" complained and then "turned away and deserted him."

There are two antitheses going on in these verses. First, the people's burgeoning faith is contrasted with the unbelief of the Jewish religious leaders. Second, the people's signs-based faith is contrasted with the true faith of the disciples. In the latter case, the message of this Gospel is that true faith centers on Jesus' person and not just his works. Their belief had more to do with their astonishment at the spectacular than with a real commitment to him. True faith must come from Jesus' words as well as his works. John notes two levels of discipleship: partial faith (here) and full faith (2:11). There is an important parallel in Christian ministry today. We often speak of two groups in the church—seekers and believers—but actually there are three: seekers, quasi-believers, and full believers. It is often said that as much as 85 percent of the people in the church attend services but do very little in the way of giving or working for the Lord. That 85 percent parallels the "many" here; they seem to believe but do not exemplify the "fruit" of conversion (15:1-8). Like Jesus, we dare not "trust" that they are true believers. Some are, but many are not. It is our task to challenge these "many" and bring them to full faith in Christ.

♦   ## 4. Jesus speaks to Nicodemus about regeneration (3:1-15)

There was a man named Nicodemus, a Jewish religious leader who was a Pharisee. ²After dark one evening, he came to speak with Jesus. "Rabbi," he said, "we all know that God has sent you to teach us. Your miraculous signs are evidence that God is with you."

³Jesus replied, "I tell you the truth, unless you are born again,* you cannot see the Kingdom of God."

⁴"What do you mean?" exclaimed Nicodemus. "How can an old man go back into his mother's womb and be born again?"

⁵Jesus replied, "I assure you, no one can enter the Kingdom of God without being born of water and the Spirit.* ⁶Humans can reproduce only human life, but the Holy Spirit gives birth to spiritual life.* ⁷So don't be surprised when I say, 'You* must be born again.' ⁸The wind blows wherever it wants. Just as you can hear the wind but can't tell where it comes from or where it is going, so you can't explain how people are born of the Spirit."

⁹"How are these things possible?" Nicodemus asked.

¹⁰Jesus replied, "You are a respected Jewish teacher, and yet you don't understand these things? ¹¹I assure you, we tell you what we know and have seen, and yet you won't believe our testimony. ¹²But if you don't believe me when I tell you about earthly things, how can you possibly believe if I tell you about heavenly things? ¹³No one has ever gone to heaven and returned. But the Son of Man* has come down from heaven. ¹⁴And as Moses lifted up the bronze snake on a pole in the wilderness, so the Son of Man must be lifted up, ¹⁵so that everyone who believes in him will have eternal life.*

3:3 Or *born from above;* also in 3:7.   3:5 Or *and spirit.* The Greek word for *Spirit* can also be translated *wind;* see 3:8.   3:6 Greek *what is born of the Spirit is spirit.*   3:7 The Greek word for *you* is plural; also in 3:12.   3:13 Some manuscripts add *who lives in heaven.* "Son of Man" is a title Jesus used for himself.   3:15 Or *everyone who believes will have eternal life in him.*

NOTES

3:3 *Kingdom of God.* This is not a usual Johannine expression (only in 3:3, 5 in John; cf. also 18:36). It means "God reigns." In the OT, the Kingdom referred first to God as the true King over Israel (1 Sam 12:12; Zeph 3:15) and indeed over all creation (Ps 24:10; Isa 6:5; 66:1). At the same time, the people longed for a future Kingdom at the Day of the Lord, in which their enemies would be destroyed and a messianic deliverer would liberate his people (Isa 9:2-7; Zech 9:9-17; 14:1-11; Mal 4:5). John tends to replace "kingdom" language with that of "life" or "eternal life."

3:5 *water and the Spirit.* Carson (1991:191-195) lists six possible understandings of this expression: (1) It refers to natural birth and spiritual birth (so Pamment 1983), but there is no evidence in ancient writings for "water" as a reference to natural birth. (2) "Water" is Christian baptism, which is effected through the Spirit, but this would have little relevance for the time of Jesus (for some [e.g., Bultmann] this means it was added by a later editor). (3) "Water" could refer to John's baptism, and Jesus is saying it is not enough without rebirth by the Spirit, but this does not fit with Nicodemus, who was hardly a follower of the Baptist. (4) This might refer to the water-purification rites of Qumran and Judaism in general as inadequate compared to Spirit-birth, but there is no contrast between water and Spirit here. (5) "Water" might refer to Torah or Jewish tradition, but this is never connected to birth imagery, so the idea of "born anew" through Torah is doubtful. (6) The best option is to see "and" as meaning "that is" and to take "water" as a symbol of the Spirit—thus, "born of water, namely the Spirit" (for epexegetical *kai,* see BDF § 442/9). This fits 7:38-39, where water is identified as the Spirit, and it also fits Jewish understanding, as stated above.

Comfort said, "The 'water' signifies the cleansing and life-imparting action of the Spirit. This is substantiated by 7:37-39, where the Spirit is likened to flowing waters, and by Ezekiel 36:25-27, where the cleansing and regeneration of Israel are associated" (1994:55).

3:11 we know. The "we" has been variously interpreted as Jesus and the disciples (Westcott, Godet, Morris, Burge), Jesus and John the Baptist (Hoskyns), Jesus and God (Chrysostom *Homilies on John*, 3:11), a plural of majesty, Jesus and the Spirit (Bengel), or a sardonic echoing of the "we know" used by Nicodemus in 3:2 (Beasley-Murray, Carson). Many critics believe it reflects debates in John's day between church and synagogue (Brown, Schnackenburg, Bruce, Barrett, Witherington), but that explanation is unnecessary. Certainly John would be aware of its relevance for his own time, but that does not mean it does not go back to Jesus' situation. Since both Jesus and the Spirit are present in the immediate context, the "we" may well represent the Godhead.

3:13 No one has ever gone to heaven. In the Gr., the perfect tense "has ascended" is somewhat problematic, for it seems to imply that Jesus at some time in the past went up to heaven—yet his ascension did not happen until the end of his life. Some believe it applies only to others and so no one in the past has ever done so (Bernard). Others again take this as a post-Resurrection saying read back into Jesus' life (Brown). It can also be taken as elliptical—"No one has ever ascended into heaven and remained there [and thus is able to speak of heavenly realities] but only the one who has descended from heaven [is able to do so]" (Carson, Köstenberger). Another solution is to note that the perfect tense normally stresses present results and in John is virtually equivalent to a present tense; the emphasis is, "No one at any time ascends to heaven—only Jesus," so it is "a state resulting from a fact" (so Godet). Either of these latter two are possible. The truth is both past and present: no one has ever ascended, then or now, except the Son of Man.

Son of Man. Several ancient mss add "who lives in heaven" to "Son of Man" (A 038 044 050 f[1,13] 𝔐). Some scholars prefer this on the grounds that it produces a more difficult reading. Still, the shorter reading has stronger ms support (𝔓66 𝔓75 B L W[s] 083 086 cop), and "who lives in heaven" was probably added later to reflect the Christological emphases of its time (cf. Metzger 1994:174).

3:15 everyone who believes in him will have eternal life. This can also be rendered as "everyone who believes will have eternal life in him" (cf. NLT mg). The ms evidence on this is divided (cf. Comfort 2007:[John 3:15]).

COMMENTARY

Nicodemus was evidently one of the "many" people referred to in 2:23. Jesus' dialog with him is his response to those with an inadequate faith, demonstrating that Jesus knew what Nicodemus was really like (2:25). This is a major theme concerning the salvation encounters in the rest of the book. Jesus will show the same depth of insight into the heart of the Samaritan woman in the next chapter. Nicodemus was one of the Pharisees described in 1:19, 24; in fact, he was a "leader" among them, most likely a member of the Sanhedrin (1:19). John chronicles his progressive conversion from confused seeker (3:1-15) to secret follower (7:50-51) to public witness (19:39). In his first encounter, Nicodemus came to see Jesus "after dark one evening," possibly because he wanted to avoid being seen by his fellow leaders in light of their opposition to Jesus (cf. 19:38) or because he wanted some uninterrupted time with Jesus. Yet there is a deeper meaning because "night" (*nuktos* [TG3571, ZG3816]) was used by John to typify spiritual darkness (1:5; 3:2; 9:4; 11:10; 13:30). Jesus certainly did not "trust" Nicodemus.

Nicodemus's opening compliment (3:2b) shows that he was one of the "many" of 2:23, for he centered on Jesus' sign-miracles, calling Jesus "rabbi" and saying, "We all know that God has sent you." We must remember that Nicodemus was a leading Pharisee and thus a distinguished "rabbi" in his own right. To say Jesus had come from God was high praise indeed, for it virtually made Jesus a special envoy, an inspired teacher set apart from others. Famous rabbis were often credited with miracles (cf. Schnackenburg). Note that Nicodemus states, "we all know," indicating that he was representing others who were quietly searching (perhaps Joseph of Arimathea [19:38] was another). For this group of leaders, the miracles Jesus had done provided evidence that God was with him. In light of the questions the Baptist had been asked by the delegation from the Sanhedrin (1:19-22), this identification could have some kind of messianic link. They were searching for truth but had not yet found it.

Jesus provided that truth for Nicodemus (in Gr., it is introduced by the second double *amēn* [TG281, ZG297] saying; see note on 1:51), but rather than answering Nicodemus's implied question, Jesus instead wrenched him out of his comfortable rabbinic categories by beginning with the statement, "unless you are born again." There is a play on words here in that "again" (*anōthen* [TG509, ZG540]) also means "from above." There must be a heaven-sent new birth (cf. 1:13) in order for Nicodemus to see who Jesus is and enter the Kingdom. It is this rebirth alone that allows one to "see the kingdom of God." Nicodemus had not connected the dots! He did not realize that Jesus had indeed come from God. Jesus was the King of Israel (1:49), who had brought the Kingdom of God to earth. When Nicodemus heard "kingdom," he would have thought of the Jewish national hope for God's future intervention, but Jesus was redefining the concept. In 18:36, he told Pilate, "My Kingdom is not an earthly kingdom," meaning it is a heavenly reality. Nicodemus could see it only if he experienced the heaven-sent new birth. The Jews thought they automatically had a part in the Kingdom because they were the children of Abraham, the covenant people (cf. 8:33, 39). Jesus said they could enter it only if they had a new birth.

Christ taught that the Kingdom was both imminent (Mark 1:15) and already here (Matt 12:28; Luke 11:20)—he had inaugurated it. Yet it was still to be consummated at his second coming (Luke 17:20-22; 21:31). We are in the Kingdom age but continue to long for it to be finalized in world history. In John, "Kingdom" teaching coalesces into the concept of "eternal life," which is also both present and future— that is, we have life now (3:16; 5:24) and still will be resurrected at the last day (5:28-29; 6:39-40). Oliver and van Aarle (1991:390-395) believe that "the kingdom of God" in John is equivalent to God's household, in which God is the father (patron) and the saints are his family (clients), who are given a place in his household (as in 14:2-6, 23).

Nicodemus misunderstood Jesus' talk concerning entrance into the Kingdom. He interpreted the spiritual "born again" (or "born from above") as "physically birthed a second time" and asked, "How can an old man go back into his mother's womb and be born again?" All his neat categories had been bypassed as he continued to think from an earthly perspective. He was trying to get Jesus to admit that what he said was absurd. Jesus clarified the concept of being "born again" further, emphasizing it with another double *amēn* [TG281, ZG297] (cf. 3:3): to "enter the Kingdom of God," one must be "born of water and the Spirit." To understand this, we refer to 7:38-39, where John says "the living water" is "the Spirit." The meaning, then, is "born of water, namely the Spirit" (cf. note on 3:5). Nicodemus had the Old Testament background to understand this, though he failed to do so. First, though the idea of rebirth is not common in the Old Testament, the theme of Israel as "the children of God" should have made it possible to understand birth imagery (so Brown). Second, water as spiritual cleansing is connected with the coming of the Spirit in Ezekiel 36:25-28: "I will sprinkle clean water on you, and . . . put a new spirit in you." This prepares for the "valley of dry bones" in Ezekiel 37, in which the dead are brought back to life (so Carson, Comfort). Clearly, what Jesus was saying was that the Kingdom can only come via "birth from above," namely a new birth from the Spirit that provides spiritual cleansing (cf. Belleville 1980).

Nicodemus's confusion must have been obvious, for Jesus clarified the new birth further, centering on the contrast between flesh and spirit (3:6): "Humans [flesh] can reproduce only human life, but the Holy Spirit gives birth to spiritual life." As long as Nicodemus remained on the earthly plane (as in 3:4), he could never go beyond this life. Only when he turned to the Spirit ("from above," 3:3) could he find spiritual life. There was no reason to be "surprised" when Jesus demanded, "You must be born again." As stated above, the Old Testament background should have made Nicodemus aware of the teaching. Note that new birth is a divine necessity (*dei* [TG1163, ZG1256], "must"); without it, there is no possibility of entering into the Kingdom. Also, the plural "you" shows that Jesus included all humanity in this need. Nicodemus's problem was that he, as a leading teacher, was still trying to control the process whereby one enters into the Kingdom. So Jesus used another illustration. Everyone knows you cannot control the wind; it "blows wherever it wants." A person can "hear the wind" but cannot tell either its origin or its destination (in an ultimate sense, not even with modern technology). Here Jesus was using another play on words, for the Greek word for "wind" is the same as for "spirit" (*pneuma* [TG4151, ZG4460]). For the ancients, the wind was the breath of God (so Brown). Moreover, it was the "breath from the four winds" of God that brought the dry bones of Ezekiel 37 to life. The Spirit is like the wind, and the voice of the Spirit is like the sound of the wind—you hear it but cannot control or truly understand it. Jesus' point was that the Spirit controls the process of salvation—*we* don't. We experience its effects via the Spirit rather than the flesh. We believe but do not actively control any aspect of it. Moreover, the natural person cannot understand those who are "born of the Spirit." The power of the Spirit within the believer is a mysterious force, and the resultant status of those who have become God's children (1:12) cannot be comprehended apart from the Spirit.

Nicodemus, still confused, asked, "How are these things possible?" (3:9). Jesus' words went against the grain of everything he had been taught, from the covenant privileges of Israel to the place of faithful adherence to the Torah. He had always believed that devotion to God and obedience to his commands were sufficient. Jesus had burst all these categories. In fact, this is the last time Nicodemus speaks in this section. The rest is all Jesus' words, for he did not treat this response as an honest search for truth but charged that it was in essence a refusal to accept the truth he should have understood. Jesus took the offensive, saying that since Nicodemus was a "respected Jewish teacher," he should have understood these things. There was nothing Jesus said that was incomprehensible to a person with a knowledge of the Old Testament. Nicodemus's problem was not ignorance but unbelief. Jesus told him "what we know and have seen" (3:11)—namely, the deep truths of spiritual salvation. The "we" probably refers to Jesus and the Spirit, thus referring to divine knowledge of these realities. The problem is that Nicodemus "won't believe our testimony." The same unbelief later charged to the Jews (5:41-47; 8:23-24, 45) was also true of Nicodemus.

Jesus then said, "If you don't believe me when I tell you about earthly things, how can you possibly believe if I tell you about heavenly things?" (3:12). The key issue in this discourse is that Jesus spoke from a heavenly perspective, while Nicodemus understood things only from an earthly perspective (3:12). At first glance, one would think that Jesus was referring to the earthly setting (Morris) or to the illustrations, such as physical birth, water, and wind (Westcott, Hoskyns)—but Nicodemus was hardly refusing to believe those things. In fact, that is exactly where his mind had been. Therefore, the "earthly" must relate to Jesus' teaching about salvation through "birth from above" because it involves the conversion of earthly beings. Even though it is a heavenly reality, it takes place on earth (Hendriksen, Beasley-Murray, Witherington). The "heavenly" realities then are the apocalyptic truths about the coming Kingdom and the heavenly world that Jesus both came from and was going to. That is the subject of 3:13-14. Jesus' first statement ("No one has ever gone to heaven") is puzzling in light of Enoch, who was translated to heaven (Gen 5:24), and Elijah, who went up to heaven in a fiery chariot in a whirlwind (2 Kgs 2:11). Also, Jewish tradition said that Moses was taken up to heaven at his death (so Brown, Whitacre). Jesus, in a sense, was denying all of this. The NLT's rendering, "gone to heaven and returned," provides part of the answer. Jesus was saying that only he had access to heaven and had brought heaven to earth (cf. 1:51). Carson says, "Jesus insists that no one has ascended to heaven in such a way as to return to talk about heavenly things" (1991:200-201).

But Jesus had "come down from heaven." Heaven is his origin and therefore his home. No one else can speak of heavenly realities except the Son of Man. This is an important dimension of John's "Son of Man" sayings. He is not only the representative human but also the God-man whose glory centers on the fact that he is a heavenly being who came from heaven and thus speaks of heavenly truths (cf. also 1:51). This introduces the "ascent-descent" imagery in John. Jesus "has come down" or "descended" from heaven (3:31; 6:33, 50, 51, 58); at his death and resurrection, he would "ascend" back to his Father (6:62; 13:3; 16:5; 20:17).

Jesus then alluded to another Old Testament image, which Nicodemus should have recognized. According to Numbers 21:4-9, Moses "lifted up the bronze snake on a pole in the wilderness" (3:14). Israel had grumbled against God, so God sent poisonous snakes that killed many of them. When the people repented, God had Moses put a bronze snake on a pole, and whoever looked at it lived. The incident became an illustration of the life God gives to those who repent and believe. Jesus centered on the image of the snake being "lifted up" and used double meaning to connect this with the divine necessity (*dei* [TG1163, ZG1256]; cf. 3:7) of the Son of Man being "lifted up," which connotes the exaltation and glory of Jesus (the verb is used in this way in Acts 2:33; Phil 2:9). This is the first of the three "lifted up" sayings (with 8:28; 12:32-34) in John. Where the Synoptics contain three passion predictions (Mark 8:31; 9:31; 10:33-34 and parallels), John has instead the three "lifted up" sayings, which are in effect passion predictions centering on the Cross as Jesus' exaltation. In other words, when Jesus is "lifted up" on the cross, he will be "lifted up" in glory. Hollis (1989:476-477) thinks the use of the Hebrew *nasa'* [TH5375, ZH5951] in Genesis 40 and Isaiah 52:13 provides the background. While the Greek *hupsoō* [TG5312, ZG5738] does not normally connote the idea of death, it carries that symbolic thrust (cf. Gen 40:19) in those Old Testament passages. Jesus' humiliation is at the same time his exaltation. In fact, his glory demands the Crucifixion, for that is the divinely necessary plan, the only possible basis for salvation.

This salvific purpose is made clear in 3:15; as a result of the Cross, "Everyone who believes in him will have eternal life." Through faith-decision, we are given a new authority as God's children (1:12), and we see his glory (2:11). Apart from his being "lifted up," there would be no belief. This is the first time in John that "eternal life" appears, and it too is a major theme (17 times in John and 6 times in 1 John). It refers not only to future life in eternity, but in John's Gospel it is a present possession that belongs to the believer now. It is indeed a life after death (cf. Dan 12:2 as background), but it is also a present reality—the life that infuses the child of God at the time of the new birth.

◆   ## 5. Life and light confront the world (3:16-21)

16"For God loved the world so much that he gave his one and only Son, so that everyone who believes in him will not perish but have eternal life. 17God sent his Son into the world not to judge the world, but to save the world through him.

18"There is no judgment against anyone who believes in him. But anyone who does not believe in him has already been judged for not believing in God's one and only Son. 19And the judgment is based on this fact: God's light came into the world, but people loved the darkness more than the light, for their actions were evil. 20All who do evil hate the light and refuse to go near it for fear their sins will be exposed. 21But those who do what is right come to the light so others can see that they are doing what God wants.*"

3:21 Or *can see God at work in what he is doing.*

NOTES

3:16 God loved. "Love" is a major theme in John, with three related terms occurring 116 times in his writings (56 in the Gospel). In John, the two main verbs, *agapaō* [TG25, ZG26] and *phileō* [TG5368, ZG5797], are synonymous (though he uses *agapaō* 36 times and *phileō* only 13). As Brown points out (1966:498), both verbs are used for the love of the Father for the Son, for Jesus' love for the disciples, for Jesus' love for Lazarus, for the beloved disciple, and for Christians as beloved. For John, it is a deep focused love that unites the Godhead and the believers into a single family and also launches their mission to the world. For an excellent discussion on the love of God, see Carson (2000). The third term in this group is *agapē* [TG26, ZG27], a noun for "love" that occurs 7 times in John's Gospel.

3:17 sent his Son. For an excellent argument for the synonymous use of the two Greek words for "sending" in John (and a history of the debate), see Köstenberger (1998a:97-106). Cf. note on 1:6.

not to judge. The statement that Christ came not to condemn but to save is also found in 12:47, but it appears to contradict what is said in 5:22 ("absolute authority to judge"), 5:30 ("I judge as God tells me"), and 9:39 ("I entered this world to render judgment"). At first glance, it appears to be an absolute contradiction, but when one considers the contexts, the statements can be reconciled. The solution is in 8:15-16, which says, "I do not judge anyone," and yet, "if I did, my judgment would be correct." Jesus did not enter this world to judge, but his coming caused every person to encounter the challenge to make a faith-decision. Those who put their faith in him were saved, but Christ became judge to those who rejected him.

3:19 people loved the darkness. Whitacre (1999:93) brings out that John especially has in mind the Jewish opponents. They believe that they know God's ways, but they are living a lie, for their rejection of Jesus and opposition to him are evil deeds that stem from the evil one, as Jesus says in 8:44.

COMMENTARY

Virtually all scholars (e.g., Westcott, Tenney, Bruce, Morris, Blomberg, Keener) recognize this section as John's own commentary, which provides a theological summary of the implications of the first three chapters. Tenney (1960:352-362) wrote the classic article on this and found 59 such "footnotes" added by John, occurring in nearly every chapter (except 13:31–17:26), with ten types: explanatory notes, time/place, custom, author, recollection, situations, summaries, identification, knowledge of Jesus, and theological commentary. This passage encompasses both summary and theological commentary. In ancient writing, there were no quotation marks to signify the end of a quote, so decisions about where quotations end are often difficult. The key here is that "Son of Man" is used only on the lips of Jesus in John, so 3:15 is probably part of Jesus' words. In 3:16-21, the tone changes, and there are three terms found only in editorial sections in John—"one and only" (3:16, 18), "believes in him [lit., his name]" (3:18), and "do what is right" (3:21).

As John sums up the implications of chapters 1–3, he begins with what is today one of the best known verses in the Bible. The words "God loved the world so much" tell us that the Cross was a loving act on the part of God (cf. Rom 5:8), whose deep love for the very world that rejected him (1:10) led to his great gift to mankind. Gundry and Howell (1999) translate this "This is how much God loved the world, with the result that he gave . . ." The world does not love God (5:42), but God loves the world "so much" that he gave "his one and only Son" to be a sacrifice on the cross. Interestingly, this is the only place in John that speaks of God's love for the world (his love for the disciples is featured more), but it is at the heart of his message, for the entire mission theme flows from this (cf. "Major Themes" in the Introduction). This message is explained perfectly in 1 John 4:8 ("God is love") and 1 John 4:9 ("God showed how much he loved us by sending his one and only Son into the world so that we might have eternal life through him"). The first passage shows God's character, the second his resultant action. The twin ideas of God giving (3:16) and sending (3:17) his Son refer both to the Incarnation and the Cross. Still, the only way to experience this gift is via a faith-decision (cf. Rom 3:21–4:25, where "faith" appears 18 times). The gift is then defined further—eternal life. Here for the first time the idea is expressed both ways—"not perish but have eternal life" (cf. 5:24; 6:39; 10:28; 12:25). This hardly means that none will die—rather, that none will experience the "second death" (Rev 2:11; 20:6), eternal punishment in the lake of fire. Note there are only two final states—eternal life and eternal punishment. There is no other possibility.

For the first time, we are told that God sent his Son. John the Baptist was "sent" as God's envoy (1:6; 3:28), but Jesus is the true envoy or agent of God "sent" to the world (this is said 41 times in John; see van der Merwe [1997:354-357] and Anderson [1999:36-40] for detailed studies of Christ as divine agent in John). A "sent one" builds on the Jewish idea of the *shaliach* (cf. TDNT 1.414-420), a representative or ambassador who is the very voice of the sender. At the same time, it emphasizes the dependence of Jesus upon the Sender, another major Johannine theme. Köstenberger (1998a:96, 107) shows how often "send" is paired with Father-Son terminology (3:16-17; 5:23, 30, 36; 10:36; 12:49) and how frequently they occur in contexts of controversy (5:30, 36, 43; 7:16; 8:14) and witness (1:6-8; 5:30-39; 8:18). Thus, it is at the heart of the mission theme. This also fits the theme of Jesus as the "living revealer" of God (cf. commentary on 1:10-18) quite well. As the Sent One, Jesus' mission was not judgment, for God "does not want anyone to be destroyed" (2 Pet 3:9; cf. 1:4, 7, 9). Thompson (2001:126-127, building on Harvey 1987) asserts that a juridical term is behind the idea of sending, which also is linked to (1) the unity of the work of the Father and Son (5:17-18; 10:29-30); (2) the obedience, even subordination, of the Son to the Father; and (3) the call to honor the Son as well as the Father (5:23).

This is also the first time "save" appears, and it is clearly synonymous with "have eternal life" in 3:16. The idea is to be rescued from death. There are two sides to the offer of eternal life—salvation and judgment. The judgment side is developed in 3:18. For those who do come to faith, there is no condemnation. They stand before God justified (Rom 3:21-26), declared right with God in his courtroom. The unbeliever, on the other hand, "has already been judged" at the moment he or she rejected God's "one and only Son." This is not the Great White Throne Judgment at the end of history (Rev 20:11-15) but the condemnation that typifies those who refuse to come to Christ. Here God is the judge. Note the centrality of "believe"; it is found three times in this verse. Every person is brought to a faith-decision as a result of the "true light" of Christ (1:9; 8:12). The decision to accept or reject Christ's offer determines one's destiny.

The process of light encountering darkness is traced in 3:19-21, and condemnation is explained in 3:19-20 as a judicial verdict ("the judgment is based on this fact"). God has condemned unbelievers, and his decision is just because they have rejected the Light. Jesus, the Light of the World (8:12), the Light that shines in the darkness (1:5) and encounters every person (1:9), came into the world (the world of mankind, not just believers), but "people loved the darkness more than the light" (3:19). The world has made an emphatic choice. Note the progression between 3:16 and 3:19: God loved the world, but the people of the world loved darkness. This is easily demonstrated in the world today. Night scenes dominate; cities like Las Vegas come alive at night. The reason people love darkness is that their actions are "evil" (3:19). Evil is the action side of darkness. The priorities of the people of the world have no place for God or Christ. They do not just prefer darkness; they "hate the light" and "refuse to go near it" for an obvious reason: "Their sins will be exposed." When the light shines in the darkness, it cannot be "extinguished" (1:5), and evil is always "exposed." The darkness of any sin city is always cloaked in artificial light (the red-light district, the neon lights of Las Vegas). The light of Christ removes this pretense, however; it exposes darkness for what it is. Those who reject the Light are guilty, and God's verdict of condemnation is just. As Witherington says (1995:103), "This is a portrait of humanity, with a guilty conscience and yet not prepared to give up its sin."

In contrast, "those who do what is right" are drawn to the Light (3:21). Note the emphasis on their action; it is assumed that they love the Light, so they "come" to it and "do" it. In Romans 12:2, Paul says that the person with a "transformed" or renewed mind literally "proves" that the will of God is "good and pleasing and perfect"; the idea is similar. The person of light wants "others [to] see that they are doing what God wants." They become witnesses to the value of following the will of God. The Greek text adds another nuance. They want people to see that everything they do is done "in God"—that is, through his strength. They are not trying to show off but to help others realize that only a God-centered life is worth living. This is a critical lesson for believers who are living a divided life, serving themselves as they try to serve God. There is no greater sorrow than a Christian living half in darkness, half in light.

◆   ## 6. John the Baptist exalts Jesus (3:22-30)

22Then Jesus and his disciples left Jerusalem and went into the Judean countryside. Jesus spent some time with them there, baptizing people.

23At this time John the Baptist was baptizing at Aenon, near Salim, because there was plenty of water there; and people kept coming to him for baptism. 24(This was before John was thrown into prison.) 25A debate broke out between John's disciples and a certain Jew* over ceremonial cleansing. 26So John's disciples came to him and said, "Rabbi, the man you met on the other side of the Jordan River, the one

you identified as the Messiah, is also baptizing people. And everybody is going to
him instead of coming to us."

[27]John replied, "No one can receive anything unless God gives it from heaven.
[28]You yourselves know how plainly I told
you, 'I am not the Messiah. I am only here

to prepare the way for him.' [29]It is the
bridegroom who marries the bride, and
the best man is simply glad to stand with
him and hear his vows. Therefore, I am
filled with joy at his success. [30]He must
become greater and greater, and I must
become less and less.

3:25 Some manuscripts read *some Jews.*

NOTES

3:23 *Aenon, near Salim.* Some see a symbolic aspect in John's ministry at the "springs"
(the meaning of "Aenon") that produce "peace" (the meaning of "Salim"). This may be
present, but the place names are primarily geographical.

3:24 *before John was thrown into prison.* The Evangelist wanted us to know that this event
took place "before John was thrown into prison." Carson (1991:210) points out that the
writer's purpose may have been to clarify that this event took place before the events
recorded in the synoptic Gospels. Mark 1:14 tells us that Jesus' Galilean preaching ministry
began after John was imprisoned, and the original readers could have seen a conflict with
John's dating and that of the Synoptics. The Evangelist was clarifying a potential discrepancy.

3:25 *a certain Jew.* Some ancient mss read the plural "some Jews" ($\mathfrak{P}$66 $\aleph$* 038 f[1,13] ite syr[c]
cop); however, the singular has equal support ($\mathfrak{P}$75 $\aleph$[2] A B L W[s] 037 044 070 086), and it is
the more difficult reading, since John prefers plurals. In other words, later copyists probably
switched to the plural in keeping with John's regular practice. The singular is more likely.

COMMENTARY

For the final time, John the Baptist bears witness concerning Jesus (cf. 1:6, 15, 19,
29, 36). Carson (1991:208-209) points out that this is the fourth successive passage
to show how Jesus was surpassing Judaism. In 2:1-12, the purification rites of
Judaism were surpassed by the new wine of Jesus; in 2:13-25, the Temple was dis-
placed by the Messiah, who became the ultimate mediator between God and man;
in 3:1-21, the new birth in the Spirit displaces Jewish rites as the only way to salvation. Now Jesus surpasses John's baptism as God's final envoy.

First, we see Jesus and his disciples leaving Jerusalem and going to the "Judean
countryside," where they minister and baptize people (3:22). Only here in the Gospels are we told that Jesus and his disciples engaged in baptism. This is clarified in
4:2, which adds that only his disciples did so. This was natural, for some of the disciples had been followers of the Baptist and would continue that "baptism of repentance" for a time. The picture is of an unhurried time in which Jesus got to know his
disciples better (so Morris). Nearby, "at Aenon, near Salim" (possibly a site in Samaria where there were plenty of springs), the Baptist was also engaged in his ministry of
baptism, and it was quite successful. It could well be that he had been forced to move
north from Judea because of persecution from Herod and the Jewish leaders. Jesus
then would probably have been in the northern part of Judea, not far from him.

A controversy emerged (3:25) when John's disciples began to debate a Jew about
"ceremonial cleansing," possibly Jewish rites of purification, like the washing of
hands (Mark 7:1-5) or the Qumran practice of daily washings. It could also have

included debate over the merits of John's baptism versus that of Jesus (so Beasley-Murray, Whitacre). This is viable because when John's disciples came to him, they did not discuss the debate but reported how Jesus was also practicing baptism and, more importantly, how "everybody is going to him instead of coming to us" (3:26). The "certain Jew" then is one who was leaning toward Jesus, and they were clearly upset. Notice that John's disciples called Jesus "the one *you* identified as the Messiah." They were not believers, and so there was jealousy and worry. They were being eclipsed. They did not want to accept the fact that John predicted that very thing (1:15, 30).

John responded by elaborating on his earlier prediction (3:27-30). He began with an aphorism, or general truth, that "no one can receive anything unless God gives it from heaven" (3:27). This applied to both Jesus and himself. God had given each the ministry he intended. John rejoiced in his ministry of preparing for the Messiah. His disciples should have also been happy. (Note how relevant this is to many today who are unhappy with their lot in life!) John reminded his disciples of his previous statement that he was not the Messiah (1:20) but the forerunner, the one who would clear the way (1:23). This is a remarkable testimony of one whose ministry was about to end, yet who was perfectly content with what God had for him.

To drive the point home, John the Baptist used the illustration of the best man (3:29, lit., "the friend of the bridegroom"). In Jewish weddings, his duty was to oversee most of the wedding details and lead the procession that brought the bride to the groom's home for the ceremony. While the groom was the focus, the best man was "simply glad to stand with him." Behind this is also the imagery of Israel as the bride of Yahweh (Isa 62:4-5; Hos 2:16-20) and the church as the bride of Christ (Eph 5:25-27; Rev 21:2, 9). John the Baptist had handed God's people over to the Messiah and was thrilled to do so. He concluded by clarifying what he meant when he said Jesus was the "greater" one who would surpass him (1:15, 30): God's sovereign will is that Christ "become greater and greater," while John becomes "less and less." Neyrey and Rohrbaugh (2001:467-468, 482-483) say that John's declaration fits the cultural idea of the "limited good" that mediates the feelings of pain and loss and solves the problem of envy among his followers. He was not just content but overjoyed with his diminished role because God had determined that it be so. The divine plan is everything, and he was privileged just to serve.

◆   ## 7. The glory of the Son (3:31-36)

³¹"He has come from above and is greater than anyone else. We are of the earth, and we speak of earthly things, but he has come from heaven and is greater than anyone else.* ³²He testifies about what he has seen and heard, but how few believe what he tells them! ³³Anyone who accepts his testimony can affirm that God is true. ³⁴For he is sent by God. He speaks God's words, for God gives him the Spirit without limit. ³⁵The Father loves his Son and has put everything into his hands. ³⁶And anyone who believes in God's Son has eternal life. Anyone who doesn't obey the Son will never experience eternal life but remains under God's angry judgment."

3:31 Some manuscripts omit *and is greater than anyone else.*

NOTES

3:31-36 It is commonly believed (e.g., Morris, Beasley-Murray, Carson, Michaels, Whitacre, Keener) that this is the reflection of the Evangelist because these verses seem to weave together many of the themes from the chapter (as is the case with 3:16-21). Though not quite as evident here, this is still quite viable, for the verses go beyond the theme that the Baptist was addressing in 3:27-30 and include one of the typical statements of the book: "Anyone who believes in God's Son has eternal life" (3:36).

3:31 *and is greater than anyone else.* This is omitted in some ancient mss ($\mathfrak{P}$75 $\aleph$* D, as well as all Old Latin versions and some Syriac and Coptic versions). The UBS committee placed it in brackets because it is uncertain whether later scribes might have deleted it as redundant or added it due to inattention (Metzger 1994:175). However, it is present in a number of mss and should be considered authentic (cf. further discussion in Comfort 2007:[John 3:31]).

3:34 *God gives him the Spirit without limit.* It is possible to construe this with Jesus as the subject, "He (Jesus) gives the Spirit without limit." Since Jesus is filled with the Spirit, he then becomes "the distributor of the Spirit" (so Burge 1987:55). However, this does not make as much sense in this context, in which God is both sender and giver.

3:36 *obey the Son.* Note the emphasis on obedience here. This is another theme in John, appearing 29 times in the book; belief must lead to obedience, the ethical result of true faith. The person who does not bear fruit for God has not truly been converted (15:1-8).

COMMENTARY

Loader (1984:191-192) states that this section contains all of the five major characteristics of John's Christology: Jesus as the Son of the Father, coming from and returning to the Father, sent by the Father, given all things by the Father, and revealing the Father. As such, Loader concludes that the section introduces the "central structure" of John's Christology. The exaltation and glory of Christ has been a major theme of this chapter, and the Baptist highlighted it by testifying that Jesus would become "greater and greater." This section tells why Jesus is greater, beginning with the fact that Jesus "has come from heaven" (lit., "comes from above"; cf. 1:51; 3:12-13). The Greek word for Jesus' origin here is *anōthen* [TG509, ZG540] (from above, again), the same word used in the phrase "born again" or, "born from above" in 3:3. The basis of heavenly rebirth is the heavenly one, and thus he is indeed "greater than anyone else" (lit., "above all") and is the source of divine revelation as the Word of God (1:1-18). In contrast, the earthly person can only "speak of earthly things." This especially refers to John the Baptist but also includes the earthly perspective of Nicodemus. The Baptist (and the OT prophets before him) could speak of earthly situations and call the nation to repentance; they could prophesy, but they had no access to heavenly secrets and no control over "birth from above." The One from above has "seen and heard" these heavenly truths firsthand (3:32) and has "testified" of them, but "few believe what he tells them." The people of the world reject these truths (1:10-11). The most important witness that the world will ever hear spoke, and he was greeted with unbelief.

Those who "accepted" (1:12) the witness—namely, Jesus' followers (the tense of the verb points back to their conversion)—"can affirm that God is true" (3:33). It is God who has sent his Son and provided the plan of salvation; so, while Christ is truth (14:6), so is God. "Affirm" (*sphragizō* [TG4972, ZG5381]) is a legal term for sealing a legal document or certifying that it is a true, valid document. In the ancient world, the seal authenticated a legal decision (so Godet, Morris, Michaels); thus "anyone who accepts his testimony" becomes a legal witness to the truth of God and his divine revelation in Jesus (on the "witness" theme, see 5:31-47; 8:13-18). Since Jesus is the Word, or living voice, of God, to authenticate God is to authenticate Jesus as the one who "is sent by God" and "speaks God's words." Jesus is the divinely sent herald or ambassador from heaven and, as the *shaliach* (cf. TDNT 1.414-420; *m. Berakhot* 5:5), speaks with the voice of God. Moreover, God "gives him the Spirit without limit" (or measure). A later rabbi said that the Spirit rested on the prophets according to the "measure" of each one's assignment (*Leviticus Rabbah* 15:2). There is no measure or limit to Jesus' calling and no limit to the Spirit that descended on him (1:32-33). Note the Trinitarian tenor of this passage: God has sent his Son and given to him the limitless Spirit. Moreover, because "the Father loves his Son" (cf. 5:20; 10:17; 15:9; for Christ's love of the Father, see 14:31), he has "put everything into his hands." This goes back to the Word as Creator (1:3-4); Jesus the Creator is cosmic Lord over "everything." This implies the conferral of universal power and authority on Jesus (so Schnackenburg).

As in 3:19-21, there are only two responses a person can have to Jesus: unbelief (loving darkness) or belief (coming to the Light). Verse 3:36, with its emphasis on the response to Christ, provides a fitting climax both to this section and to chapter 3 as a whole. It corresponds, in fact, to the primary message of the book (20:31, "these are written so that you may continue to believe"; cf. 3:18; 5:24, 29; 6:47). As stated often, John's is an encounter Gospel, calling readers to a faith-decision that will determine their destiny. Jesus has authority to give life (5:21, 26) and to pronounce final judgment (5:22, 27). Every person has to make a choice to believe or to reject God. Those who believe have "eternal life" as a present possession (it is theirs now, as well as at the final resurrection), but those who disobey remain under God's "angry judgment." This is the only place in John where the word *orgē* [TG3709, ZG3973] (wrath) is used, but it is in keeping with the recurring theme of judgment. God is both loving and just (these are the two foci of his holiness), and these two attributes are interdependent. The God who loves is also the God whose righteousness demands justice, and that judgment involves wrath on all who spurn his offer of salvation and disobey.

◆   ## 8. Jesus converts the Samaritan woman (4:1-42)

Jesus* knew the Pharisees had heard that he was baptizing and making more disciples than John ²(though Jesus himself didn't baptize them—his disciples did). ³So he left Judea and returned to Galilee.

⁴He had to go through Samaria on the way. ⁵Eventually he came to the Samaritan village of Sychar, near the field that Jacob gave to his son Joseph. ⁶Jacob's well was there; and Jesus, tired from the long walk, sat wearily beside the well about noontime. ⁷Soon a Samaritan woman came to draw water, and Jesus said to her, "Please give me a drink." ⁸He was alone at the time because his disciples had gone into the village to buy some food.

⁹The woman was surprised, for Jews refuse to have anything to do with Samaritans.* She said to Jesus, "You are a Jew, and I am a Samaritan woman. Why are you asking me for a drink?"

¹⁰Jesus replied, "If you only knew the gift God has for you and who you are speaking to, you would ask me, and I would give you living water."

¹¹"But sir, you don't have a rope or a bucket," she said, "and this well is very deep. Where would you get this living water? ¹²And besides, do you think you're greater than our ancestor Jacob, who gave us this well? How can you offer better water than he and his sons and his animals enjoyed?"

¹³Jesus replied, "Anyone who drinks this water will soon become thirsty again. ¹⁴But those who drink the water I give will never be thirsty again. It becomes a fresh, bubbling spring within them, giving them eternal life."

¹⁵"Please, sir," the woman said, "give me this water! Then I'll never be thirsty again, and I won't have to come here to get water."

¹⁶"Go and get your husband," Jesus told her.

¹⁷"I don't have a husband," the woman replied.

Jesus said, "You're right! You don't have a husband—¹⁸for you have had five husbands, and you aren't even married to the man you're living with now. You certainly spoke the truth!"

¹⁹"Sir," the woman said, "you must be a prophet. ²⁰So tell me, why is it that you Jews insist that Jerusalem is the only place of worship, while we Samaritans claim it is here at Mount Gerizim,* where our ancestors worshiped?"

²¹Jesus replied, "Believe me, dear woman, the time is coming when it will no longer matter whether you worship the Father on this mountain or in Jerusalem. ²²You Samaritans know very little about the one you worship, while we Jews know all about him, for salvation comes through the Jews. ²³But the time is coming—indeed it's here now—when true worshipers will worship the Father in spirit and in truth. The Father is looking for those who will worship him that way. ²⁴For God is Spirit, so those who worship him must worship in spirit and in truth."

²⁵The woman said, "I know the Messiah is coming—the one who is called Christ. When he comes, he will explain everything to us."

²⁶Then Jesus told her, "I AM the Messiah!"*

²⁷Just then his disciples came back. They were shocked to find him talking to a woman, but none of them had the nerve to ask, "What do you want with her?" or "Why are you talking to her?" ²⁸The woman left her water jar beside the well and ran back to the village, telling everyone, ²⁹"Come and see a man who told me everything I ever did! Could he possibly be the Messiah?" ³⁰So the people came streaming from the village to see him.

³¹Meanwhile, the disciples were urging Jesus, "Rabbi, eat something."

³²But Jesus replied, "I have a kind of food you know nothing about."

³³"Did someone bring him food while we were gone?" the disciples asked each other.

³⁴Then Jesus explained: "My nourishment comes from doing the will of God, who sent me, and from finishing his work. ³⁵You know the saying, 'Four months between planting and harvest.' But I say, wake up and look around. The fields are already ripe* for harvest. ³⁶The harvesters are paid good wages, and the fruit they harvest is people brought to eternal life. What joy awaits both the planter and the harvester alike! ³⁷You know the saying, 'One plants and another harvests.' And it's true. ³⁸I sent you to harvest where you didn't plant; others had already done the work, and now you will get to gather the harvest."

³⁹Many Samaritans from the village believed in Jesus because the woman had

said, "He told me everything I ever did!"
40When they came out to see him, they
begged him to stay in their village. So
he stayed for two days, 41long enough
for many more to hear his message and

believe. 42Then they said to the woman,
"Now we believe, not just because of what
you told us, but because we have heard
him ourselves. Now we know that he is
indeed the Savior of the world."

4:1 Some manuscripts read *The Lord.*   4:9 Some manuscripts omit this sentence.   4:20 Greek *on this mountain.*   4:26 Or *"The 'I AM' is here";* or *"I am the LORD";* Greek reads *"I am, the one speaking to you."* See Exod 3:14.   4:35 Greek *white.*

NOTES

4:1 *Jesus.* While good mss read "Jesus" ($\mathfrak{P}$66* ℵ D 038 086), equally good mss read "Lord" ($\mathfrak{P}$66ᶜ $\mathfrak{P}$75 A B C L Wˢ 083). Most likely "Jesus" was changed to "Lord" by scribes (such as the corrector of $\mathfrak{P}$66) because they wanted to alleviate the awkwardness of repeating Jesus' name twice.

4:4 *Samaria.* The animosity between Jews and Samaritans had been developing for centuries. When the Assyrians conquered Israel in 722 BC (2 Kgs 17), they left only a small number of Jews there and deported hundreds of pagans to live there. The resulting inter-marriage produced half-Jews who became the Samaritans. When the Jews returned from exile under Ezra and Nehemiah, they demanded that the people divorce their pagan spouses and return to the pure faith. The Samaritans refused and often sent letters to the Persians, accusing the Jewish people of sedition. Then around 400 BC, the Samaritans erected their own temple on Mt. Gerizim, which had been the center of the Jewish religion before Shiloh served this function (Deut 27; cf. Josh 8:30-35; 1 Sam 1:9). In 128 BC, John Hyrcanus, the Jewish king, destroyed the Samaritan temple, and that sealed the hatred between the two peoples. At the time of Christ, the animosity continued to be very strong.

4:5 *Samaritan village of Sychar.* We do not know for certain where Sychar was. We do know Jacob's well, for it is well attested (cf. Dalman 1935:212-216), but the identification of Sychar is uncertain. Some believe it is the modern town of Askar, east of Mounts Gerizim and Ebal (so Barrett, Carson), but because the remains on the site have only been dated to medieval times, many doubt it (so Brown, who prefers Shechem). But Shechem was destroyed by John Hyrcanus before 107 BC, so perhaps placing Sychar just east of Mounts Gerizim and Ebal is best (so Köstenberger).

4:7 *Jesus said to her.* He broke several taboos in speaking to this woman: (1) The religious taboo—Samaritans accepted only the Pentateuch as canon and would not worship in Jeru-salem, believing Mt. Gerizim to be the true holy site. In fact, several years earlier some Sa-maritans had scattered human bones (ritually unclean) in the courtyard of the Jerusalem Temple, further inflaming the animosity. (2) The sexual taboo—men were not supposed to associate with women. This was held more strictly in Judea than in Galilee, but to start a conversation with a female stranger at a well was pretty much unheard of anywhere. In fact, Jesus was risking ritual defilement by talking with a Samaritan woman. (3) The ethnic taboo—as stated above, Jews and Samaritans had no dealings with each other. The Synop-tics show how Jesus' compassion led him to ignore such things, as when he healed the woman with the hemorrhage and raised the little girl from the dead (Mark 5:21-43 and parallels). When there were physical or spiritual needs at hand, social and religious expec-tations became unimportant.

4:9 *Jews refuse to have anything to do with Samaritans.* Some mss (ℵ* D itᵃ,ᵇ,ᵉ,ʲ copᶠᵃʸ) omit this clause, probably because it seems clumsy and unnecessary. However, the ms evi-dence for its inclusion is too strong to ignore ($\mathfrak{P}$63 $\mathfrak{P}$66 $\mathfrak{P}$75 $\mathfrak{P}$76 ℵ¹ A B C L Wˢ et al.).

4:10 *the gift God has for you.* Schnackenburg (1980:426) says the "gift" was "a compre-hensive term for everything that God bestows on man for his salvation," such as the Torah for the Jews, the Holy Spirit for the church, as well as righteousness and the grace of God (Paul's emphases).

4:14 *the water I give.* Bruce points out (1983:105) that the rabbis compared the law to refreshing water. Jesus offered water superior not only to Jacob's well but also to the "legal religion of Jews and Samaritans alike."

4:18 *five husbands.* There are several symbolic interpretations of the five husbands—for instance, that the woman represents Samaria, who held that only the five books of Moses were canonical, or that this reflects 2 Kgs 17:24-25, where false gods were brought into Samaria by pagans from five cities. This would mean that Samaria considered Yahweh to be her husband but that she had no husband because her worship was impure. However, while there were five cities, the list of their gods in 2 Kgs 17:30-31 mentions seven gods. Moreover, this would not fit the Samaria of Jesus' day, which was strictly monotheistic. Finally, there is no hint of such a meaning in the context of John 4. This is simply the number of husbands she had been married to—it has no further symbolic meaning.

4:20 *So tell me.* It is possible that the woman was not so much interested in the theological issue as she was in steering the discussion away from the dangerous topic of her immoral life (so Morris). While this is viable, the flavor of Jesus' prophetic status seems to infuse what she says.

4:24 *God is Spirit.* The KJV has "God is a Spirit," but that is clearly wrong. First, the indefinite article is not mandated by the Gr. (cf. 1:1 on this), and even more, it could hardly mean "God is one of the spirits" in this context.

4:23-24 *in spirit and in truth.* There are two major issues regarding the interpretation of "in spirit and in truth." This first involves whether it has (1) an external force, in which *pneuma* [TG4151, ZG4460] refers to the Holy Spirit and the phrase can be taken as "the Spirit of truth" (so Barrett, Schnackenburg, Brown, Michaels, Burge, Thompson [2001:214], Keener); or (2) an internal force pointing to spiritual worship in one's spirit or with the whole heart (so Hendriksen, Morris, Whitacre, Blomberg, Köstenberger). But is only an "either-or" approach viable, or is there a "both-and" option? In the context of John, the latter is more likely. The Spirit is certainly connoted, for it is the Spirit that makes worship possible. At the same time, worship is to be an inner, spiritual act. The second issue is whether "spirit and truth" should be considered separate items (Barrett, Comfort) or one single entity (Carson). The former could be favored by the importance of both in John, but Carson correctly notes that both are governed by a single preposition and should be taken together. Since "God is spirit" worship must be a spiritual act; since "God is Spirit" worship must be in the Holy Spirit.

4:26 *I AM the Messiah!* Several (e.g., Brown, Carson) note that Jesus gives an unqualified affirmation of his messianic office to a Samaritan here in John, when he refused to do so in a Jewish setting in the synoptic Gospels (cf. Mark 1:44; 5:43; 7:36; 8:30; 9:9 and parallels). The reason for the so-called "messianic secret" in the Synoptics is that the Jews expected a military conqueror rather than a suffering Servant as Messiah and thus would have misunderstood the implications of such a claim—this was true even of Jesus' disciples! Jesus did not want his messianic work bandied about in such a setting. However, to the Gentiles (Mark 5:19) and Samaritans who did not have such a misunderstanding, he spoke more freely.

4:27 *They were shocked to find him talking to a woman.* This reflects the Jewish prejudices against both Samaritans and women (cf. note on 4:7). Rabbis were not allowed to have anything to do with women apart from their wives, for such contact was thought to detract from their study of Torah and bring evil upon them (cf. Strack and Billerbeck 2.438). In addition, some considered it inappropriate for women to study Torah at all (*m. Sotah* 3:4). Here, the disciples did not have the courage to question Jesus regarding his motive or purpose in conversing with the woman. He was their rabbi and Messiah. They had to wait and trust his reasons, even though they were skeptical.

4:28 *left her water jar.* Other possible explanations are that she left the water jar there so Jesus could get a drink (Hendriksen) or that the scene symbolizes that such a jar is unnecessary in light of the living water Jesus had provided (Brown). Both seem to go beyond the scene itself. The simpler explanation is that she left the jar in her haste to tell the townspeople about Jesus (Bruce).

4:38 *I sent you to harvest.* Many (e.g., Brown, Schnackenburg) believe this refers not so much to the mission of Jesus as to the later post-Resurrection mission to the Samaritans in Acts 8, referring especially to the success of Philip in Samaria. While John would have understood the relevance of this for that later event (he was sent with Peter to investigate it, Acts 8:14-17), there is no need to doubt the historical trustworthiness of this scene. Brown, in spite of his view regarding the focus of the verses, accepts a historical nucleus for this section (1966:183). It is better to say that the Samaritan harvest really occurred but also had added relevance for the early church in light of the events of Acts 8.

COMMENTARY

This is the third of the salvation dramas (1:35-51; 3:1-15); it shows Jesus again taking the initiative (cf. 1:43) in reaching out. Note how this develops chapter 3. There, he was reaching out (though in a slightly different way, for Nicodemus came to him) to a Jewish leader—here, to a despised, sinful woman among the despised Samaritans. Equally relevant is her positive reaction and the absence of any such response from Nicodemus at this stage. Moreover, this is a central section for John's mission theme, as it contains the first major discourse on mission (4:31-38). The Samaritan mission launches God's mission to the world.

The scene opens with Jesus traveling from Jerusalem to Galilee (4:3) and deliberately passing through Samaria on the way. He left because of the controversy that was brewing when "the Pharisees had heard" that Jesus was performing more baptisms than John (4:1). Most likely this means that opposition was about to break out because the Pharisees were focusing on Jesus. The Baptist had been in Aenon in the southern part of Samaria (3:23), quite possibly due to persecution. Jesus decided this was not the time for such conflict; he "left Judea and returned to Galilee" (4:3).

On the way to Galilee, Jesus stopped in Samaria because God led him to do so (4:4; *dei* [TG1163, ZG1256], referring to a divine necessity, cf. 3:7, 14, 30). It is clear in these chapters that everything occurs as part of the divine plan. Jesus could have gone by another route up through the valley east of the Jordan and avoided Samaria. Josephus tells us that the Samaritan route was the normal way to travel from Judea to Galilee (*Antiquities* 20.118), but some, like the Pharisees, preferred to travel up the east side of the Jordan River (in Gentile countryside) and then cross back over to Galilee. Again, it was not a geographic necessity but God's will that led Jesus to Samaria. As he passed through, he came to the village of Sychar near Jacob's well. There is no Old Testament evidence for this well, but the tradition regarding its location continues to our day and is probably correct. The well today is probably much the same as it was in Jesus' time, about 100 feet deep and seven feet in diameter. "The field that Jacob gave to his son Joseph" is mentioned in Genesis 48:22 and has an interesting history. The Hebrews brought Joseph's bones and buried them there after conquering Canaan (Josh 24:32).

When Jesus arrived there, it was noon, one of the hottest times of the day (4:6). Tired from the long trip, he sat beside the well to rest. The disciples had "gone into the village to buy some food," so Jesus was there by himself (4:8). At first glance, the purchase of food in Samaria could be thought unusual, since the Samaritans were considered unclean by strict Jews; but Galileans were not as legalistic, and travelers going through Samaria either had to carry a lot of provisions or buy food there. As Jesus waited for the disciples to return, a woman came to the well, which was unusual because most women came in groups, either in the morning or at dusk when it was cooler. This was certainly because she was known as an immoral woman (4:18) and would have been shunned by the others (cf. Burge); she came when she could be alone.

Jesus initiated the conversation, startling the woman (4:7). His request for a drink from the well was carefully calculated. Her reply (4:9) shows the distance between the two groups, centering not only on a Jew speaking to a woman but on a Jew asking for water from a Samaritan, for the Jews were very careful about eating or drinking with certain people. The principle was, "To share a meal is to share a life" (DJG 796-797), and Jesus often got into trouble for eating with disreputable people (Matt 9:11; 11:19; Luke 15:2; 19:7). John explained to his readers that "Jews refuse to have anything to do with Samaritans" (4:9). The verb literally means, "Jews do not use utensils (cups of water in this case)" with Samaritans, since that would make them ritually unclean (so Daube 1956:373-382). Jesus had a higher purpose in the request, preparing her for his next offer, though he would have willingly drunk the unclean drink if she had given it to him.

Jesus began, "If you only knew the gift God has for you and who you are speaking to" (4:10). This gift of God is the eternal life that results from faith (3:16, 36); it is also the gift of the Holy Spirit (3:5; 7:38-39). Jesus offered, "Ask me and I [will] give you living water." She had come seeking water from the well; he offered the Water of Life from God. For the people of his day, "living water" was water that came from fresh bubbling springs (like the pool of Bethesda in 5:2). Barrett (1978:233-234) shows that the idea of (living) water meant many things in the Old Testament and Judaism—not only Torah and the Spirit but also wisdom, God as the fountain of life, and the divine Word. This is especially so because "it is in the waterless spaces of the east that the value of water is most clearly apparent." In Jeremiah 2:13, God is "the fountain of living water," and Isaiah 12:3 speaks of drinking "deeply from the fountain of salvation." Zechariah 14:8 promises that in the day of the Lord, "life-giving waters will flow out from Jerusalem." "Living water" typifies the life-giving power of God and the presence of the Holy Spirit. This can come only from Jesus, God's Messiah and Son. As such, this symbol anticipates Revelation 21–22, which speaks of the river of the water of life coming to God's people from the throne of God and the Lamb, and of God becoming the Temple in the New Jerusalem (so Comfort).

Like Nicodemus, the Samaritan woman thought only on the earthly plane. She said, "But sir, you don't have a rope or a bucket . . . and this well is very deep" (4:11).

Indeed, the well was over 100 feet deep. She, of course, was thinking of a bubbling spring. This would fit Jacob's well since it was supplied by an underground spring. Then she went on the offensive—"Do you think you're greater than our ancestor Jacob?" Her words can also be translated, "You don't really think you're better, do you?" She looked at Jesus and saw an average-looking person who said outrageous things. How could such a one provide "better water" than Jacob had for his sons and cattle? Since there is no Old Testament mention of Jacob and the well, she was speaking from tradition. Still, her tone shows she was skeptical and unbelieving at this point.

Jesus explained the point further (4:13-14) so as to clear up her misconception, pointing out that as refreshing as Jacob's well was, those who drank from it would "become thirsty again," while those who accepted his water would "never be thirsty again." The earthly well is inadequate compared to the heavenly water Jesus makes available. While the well water is drawn with a bucket, the heavenly water is "a fresh, bubbling spring." The Greek verb underlying "bubbling" is very strong, picturing a geyser leaping up. The Old Testament promises behind this are plentiful (cf. Isa 49:10; 55:1-3). Some Samaritans believed that "water shall flow from [the Messiah's] buckets" (so Bruce, Carson).

The woman, not understanding Jesus, asked for this water so that she would never have to be thirsty or come to the well again (4:15). She exhibited no awareness of the spiritual reality Jesus was addressing. Then Jesus made an abrupt change of direction—but again it was carefully calculated, for it forced her to come face to face not only with who she was (she already knew that) but with who he was. He began by asking her to get her husband, leading her to admit that she was not married. She probably thought that would end the discussion, but Jesus was digging ever more deeply into her true spiritual condition. Before she could drink the living water, she had to come to grips with her moral condition.

Jesus' omniscient response (cf. his supernatural knowledge about Nathanael, 1:47-49) shocked her. Her five marriages probably included several divorces. Judaism did not prohibit divorce but generally allowed only two or three marriages for women (so Schnackenburg). If this was true of the Samaritans, she was immoral for the number of her husbands as well as for her current living arrangement. Jesus encountered her with the basic problem that was keeping her from the living water. Though she still could not deal with her own situation, Jesus' revelation of her true condition caused her to rethink who he was, and she said, "You must be a prophet" (4:19). There are two possibilities: (1) he was an inspired prophet who had been given special insight from God (cf. Luke 7:39); or (2) he was "the prophet," probably the "prophet like Moses" alluded to in 1:21. Since this was the one messianic figure from the Pentateuch, the Samaritans took this as the primary messianic prophecy. Most likely, there is double meaning here, with the woman intending the first but the Evangelist hinting at the second.

Since Jesus was a prophet, she thought he might be able to answer the major issue between the Samaritans and the Jews; it was the question as to whether Yahweh should be worshiped in Jerusalem or on Mt. Gerizim. The latter was visible while they talked. The Samaritans believed that God's true command to Israel in Deuteronomy 27:4-8 was to build an altar at Mt. Gerizim rather than Mt. Ebal after they entered the Promised Land (as the Samaritan version of the Pentateuch reads). Moreover, Shechem was the place where Abraham erected an altar when he entered the land (Gen 12:6-7). On this basis, the Samaritans argued that they had priority of place over Jerusalem, which did not become a religious center until after the Pentateuchal period.

The first part of Jesus' answer would also have startled her, for he gave a prophetic revelation regarding the future "time" when neither place would be the center of worship. While this could point to the destruction of Jerusalem by the Romans and the radical decentralizing of Jewish worship that followed, it is better to see it as pointing toward the coming of the Kingdom. But this is not so much a reference to the Eschaton as it is to the new era of salvation inaugurated by Jesus' death and resurrection. The "time" or "hour" in John always refers to the Cross (cf. note on 2:4). When that time comes, access to the Father will be direct, and neither Jerusalem nor Mt. Gerizim will be important. Since God will become in a new way the Father of his people (the relationship expressed in 1:14, 18 will be extended to his children), there will be a direct access to God (cf. 16:23), and the indirect way through the centers of worship will no longer be needed. Still, to answer her question, Jesus clarified his message further by saying that, as opposed to the Samaritans, "we Jews know all about [the one we worship]" (4:22). In effect, he was saying that the Samaritan religion was wrong, and the Jews had a superior knowledge of God. The Samaritan belief system was historically conditioned and wrongly based, and so their worship was inadequate. The reason was that "salvation comes through the Jews." This encompassed both God's plan of salvation and the Messiah through whom it would come. God had revealed himself to the Jews through the law (or Pentateuch), the prophets, and the writings, not just the Pentateuch, and they were the true path through which God would bring about his salvation. Jesus the Messiah was a Jew.

The key point comes in 4:23-24. Jesus had just said "salvation comes through the Jews"—something that was already a reality, for the Messiah had come—but he then switched to the present tense to clarify and emphasize the reality: "The time is coming—indeed it's here now." The "time" or hour, as we have seen (2:4; 4:21), refers to the divinely appointed time of Jesus' passion. The point here is that the new age to be inaugurated at the coming of the Messiah has now arrived. There is an already/not-yet tension in this: the coming Kingdom has already arrived but has not yet been consummated. There are three stages involved—the Incarnation, the death, and the Parousia (second coming) of Christ, with the first two emphasized here. John 4:23b-24 forms an ABA pattern, with "worship in spirit and in truth" (4:23b, 24b) framing "God is Spirit" (4:24a).

"God is Spirit" is the first of three times John defines God in his writings ("God is light" and "God is love" in 1 John 1:5, 4:8). This states that God is not material and should not be worshiped in a material way (e.g., in Jerusalem or Mt. Gerizim) in the new age. This "expresses the transcendence and holiness of God" (Schnackenburg 1990:1.438) and means that God is "life-giving and unknowable to human beings unless he chooses to reveal himself (cf. 1:18)" (Carson 1991:225). Since God is Spirit, there is only one way to worship that is acceptable to him—"in spirit and in truth." There is double meaning in this. In one sense, it refers to a worship that centers on the whole inner being of the person, deeply spiritual and wholehearted. In another sense, such worship is only made possible by the power of the Spirit. The new birth is "from above" (3:3), and Jesus is "from above" (3:31); true worship has a heavenly component and occurs only when one is seeking and thinking "about the things of heaven" (Col 3:1-2). Moreover, it is both in spirit and truth that "true worshipers" worship: first in the Spirit, who is truth (as Christ is truth, 14:6), and then in genuine, real worship. Those in the Spirit truly worship with all their heart, soul, mind, and strength. Note also the divine necessity (*dei* [TG1163, ZG1256], "must," 4:24; cf. 3:7, 14, 30; 4:4, 20) of worship. Thompson (2001:214-215) believes this culminates the emphasis in chapters 3–4, which is the centrality of the work of the Spirit and of the individual as recipient of the life-giving Spirit. Worship then is intertwined with the gift of the Spirit.

Finally, the woman has begun to realize that Jesus is more than a "prophet" (4:19). Jesus' deep explanation of worship triggered a thought, so she explored the possibility of the coming "Messiah," who will "explain everything" (4:25). This fits the Samaritan messianic beliefs. They normally did not use the term "Messiah" but spoke of a *taheb* or "restorer" who would be the new Moses (Deut 18:15-18) and restore true worship by teaching and revealing the final truths of God. She had not yet identified this one with Jesus but had a dim awareness that something extraordinary was happening. Jesus confirmed this when he replied, "I AM the Messiah." There is tremendous emphasis in John on the "I am" sayings, for the Greek phrase found in John (*egō eimi* [TG1473/1510, ZG1609/1639], "I am") reflects Exodus 3:14, where God reveals that the meaning of the new covenant name he has revealed to Moses, Yahweh, is, "I AM WHO I AM" (cf. also Isa 41:4; 43:10-13, 25; 45:18-19; 48:12; 52:6; and the discussion on 8:58). Thus, the "I am" sayings (such as this one) in effect mean, "I, Yahweh, am the Messiah" (cf. Ridderbos, Keener, Whitacre). Jesus is the true and only *taheb*, who alone can "explain everything" and provide the living water.

When one is thus gripped by Jesus, it is impossible to keep quiet. Such encounters always result in witness. The woman was so excited that she "left her water jar beside the well and ran back to the village." There are three things that show the state of her mind. Water jars were important utensils and would not be left sitting unless a great emergency occurred. Also, she was vilified by the community and had come at noon to get water so that she wouldn't have to face the other women. Finally, women did not normally talk to men in this way. In fact, women could not be official witnesses of anything. If a robbery occurred and was witnessed only by women, the thief could not be prosecuted because women could not provide official testimony (cf. *m. Rosh HaShanah* 1:8). (Maccini 1994:40-44 believes that such restrictions did not apply to Samaria, but it is difficult to see how they would accept the word of a woman who was known to be immoral). Still, what the Samaritan woman had experienced in talking to Jesus gave her a sense of urgency that surmounted these barriers. Jesus' incredible revelation regarding her private life had shaken her to the core, so she quickly went back to town and invited everyone to "Come and see a man who told me everything I ever did!" Her tentative conclusion was, "Could he possibly be the Messiah?" (4:29). She clearly hoped that this might be true. The result was that "people came streaming from the village to see him" (4:30). The impression is that large numbers of villagers flocked to see Jesus. Even though this woman was undoubtedly held in contempt for her immoral lifestyle, her witness sparked great curiosity, and the people came to see Jesus for themselves. We hear nothing more of the woman in the story, but the pattern is so close to that of 1:35-50 (the conversion of Andrew and Philip is implied in their actions) that the Evangelist likely intends us to see that she became a believer, along with the majority of the village.

As the villagers were on their way to see Jesus, the disciples asked Jesus if he wanted to eat. The minds of the disciples were entirely on food (the earthly perspective once more). Jesus had a vastly superior meal to the one they were offering, and he wanted them to understand what really matters, so he said, "I have a kind of food you know nothing about" (4:32). The idea of living water or spiritual food that Jesus had offered the woman was the farthest thing from their minds. Naturally, they understood Jesus in a material way (cf. Nicodemus in 3:4, 9 and the woman in 4:11, 15) and asked each other, "Did someone bring him food while we were gone?" One could say they were "spiritually challenged" individuals. Jesus' comment about their ignorance of his spiritual food reflects the fact that the disciples were still in their spiritual infancy. They had not been with Jesus long, and they lacked understanding. Sadly, this misunderstanding lasted throughout their time with Jesus (cf. Carson 1982).

While Jesus refused to explain the living water to the woman, he did not leave his disciples in the dark. He told them that his food was "doing the will of God, who sent me, and . . . finishing his work" (4:34). Behind this concept is Deuteronomy 8:3, "People do not live by bread alone; rather, we live by every word that comes from the mouth of the LORD." The people had grumbled about the manna in the wilderness, but Moses pointed them to what really matters. Jesus wanted his disciples to learn a similar lesson. The concept of the "will of God" in the New Testament is supremely ethical, dealing with every aspect of life and centering on the Christ-centered walk, as in Romans 12:2, where transformed Christians show how "good and pleasing and perfect" the will of God is by their lives. In John, a major purpose of Jesus is to "do the will of God" (5:30; 6:38), and those who center on God's will have the guarantee of eternal life (6:39, 40). God hears their prayers (9:31). "Finishing [God's] work" (4:34) is also connected to Jesus' "hour" (cf. note on 2:4) of destiny, including his passion (cf. the similar Gr. term for "finish" in 19:30, spoken from the cross—*teleō* [TG5055, ZG5464]; cf. *teleiō* [TG5048, ZG5457]) and the time of salvation that would result. That time had begun (4:23), and the evangelization of the Samaritans was part of this work.

Jesus then introduced his mission theology (4:35-36), beginning with an observation: "Four months between planting and harvest" (4:35; for the authenticity of this saying, see Ensor 2000). Some have taken this as a temporal reference, meaning they were passing through Samaria in January or February, four months before the May harvest. It is equally likely that this is simply a proverb, as the introductory "You know the saying" also introduces a proverb in Matthew 16:2 (so Brown). Although there is no record of such a proverb from that time, the pithy style would fit such. Either way, Jesus' point is that farmers normally wait four months from planting to harvest. Then when he says, "Wake up and look around," he moves from the natural harvest to the spiritual harvest. The command to "wake up" is a call for spiritual vigilance, also used in Revelation 3:2-3 and 16:15 of the need to overcome spiritual lethargy. Jesus asked his disciples to be vigilant for the harvest of souls God was giving them. In the narrative, this has special relevance to the Samaritan mission, for the townspeople were on their way there as Jesus was talking (4:30). They were the "fields" that were "ripe for harvest," as in the parallel Matthew 9:37-38, which says, "Pray to the Lord who is in charge of the harvest . . . to send more workers into his fields."

A four-month period separates the work of the "planter" from that of the "harvester," but Jesus' point is that in the harvest of souls, there is often no period between the two. The disciples were clearly the harvesters who are "paid good wages" in that they would reap a crop of souls for "eternal life." They had just returned from purchasing food, but Jesus told them they not only had a much better meal awaiting them but also a terrific harvest to participate in. This is a powerful metaphor. Any of us would jump at the opportunity to earn a lot of money for a certain harvest. How much more should we want to participate in an eternal harvest! It is difficult to know who the "planters" are. It could be John the Baptist who had been ministering nearby in Aenon (3:23, so Robinson), or it could be all the prophets leading up to and including the Baptist (Lindars, Bruce, Carson, Köstenberger). The planter could even be Jesus, who had planted spiritual seed in the woman in 4:7-26, and the woman, who had planted the seed in the villagers (Witherington). It could be argued that Jesus placed himself with the disciples as harvesters, but Jesus could well be both planter and harvester. The Father may even be the sower, with Jesus and the disciples as the harvesters (Whitacre). It is difficult to know for certain. The main point, though, is found in the proverb: "One plants and another harvests" (4:37), and "joy" (4:36) awaits them both. This seems to allude to Amos 9:13, which speaks of the coming time of restoration: " 'The time will come,' says the LORD, 'when the grain and grapes will grow faster than they can be harvested.' " According to Isaiah 65:21-22, God's people will "eat the fruit of their own vineyards" and "enjoy their hard-won gains." Both of these passages refer to the final Kingdom that God will establish for his people.

Jesus was saying that the expected messianic age had arrived, and it would be a time of incredible harvest. Schnackenburg (1980:450) summarizes it well: "The mission becomes an eschatological event: Jesus gathers the people of God, to lead it to the Kingdom of God, and sends out his disciples to help with this work or to continue it." The Samaritans were the crop, and the disciples were invited to the harvest; Jesus *sent* them to harvest. There is no mention in John of a previous mission, but the Synoptics mention several at the start of Jesus' ministry (e.g., Matt 4:23-25; Mark 1:38-39). This scene could simply summarize the disciples' involvement in ministry in the first three chapters of John. They were "sent ones" (cf. 17:18; 20:21), just like Jesus (3:17, 34) and the Baptist (1:6). Though they did not plant, they joined in the harvest so that all could rejoice in the crop. This is an important message for mission. All success in ministry occurs on the basis of the work of those who have prepared the ground before. Those who reap the harvest of souls build on the work of the many who have witnessed beforehand. When a person witnesses and is rebuffed, they have not been defeated. Their witness is faithful obedience in the eyes of God and may well be another link in a chain of conviction that will later produce a conversion.

The harvest promised in 4:35 comes to fruition in 4:39-42. The Samaritan woman is one of the links in the chain of the conversion of many villagers. They "believed in Jesus because [of what] the woman had said" (4:39). Her witness brought many to Jesus. This chain may have continued even up to the time when Philip evangelized the Samaritans in Acts 8. It is very possible that he came to this region and that the "ready acceptance" of his message was a result of this early mission (so Carson). The Samaritan woman functioned like Andrew and Philip in 1:35-50, bringing others to Jesus. The villagers were not content just to hear her testimony, however; they wanted to hear Jesus for themselves. They invited Jesus to their village, and he stayed two days. Note how much more open they were than Nicodemus was. They "hear his message and believe" (4:41). Note also how their faith was centered on his words and not just his miraculous signs (contra those of 2:23-24). This culminates in their confession of Jesus as "Savior of the world."

This concludes not just the story of the Samaritan mission but the whole of 1:35-4:42. The "one and only Son" sent by God to provide salvation for mankind (3:16-17) alone removes the sin of the world (1:29). The one who has become the living Word and provided the living water (1:1, 18; 4:10), the one who has shed the light of God on every person (1:4, 7, 8) is indeed the "Savior of the world" (also 1 John 4:14). This would especially be true for the Samaritans who recognized that their *taheb* (cf. commentary on 4:19) was also the Jewish Messiah and, therefore, the only Messiah for the whole world.

◆   ## 9. Healing and conversion in Cana (4:43-54)

43At the end of the two days, Jesus went on to Galilee. 44He himself had said that a prophet is not honored in his own hometown. 45Yet the Galileans welcomed him, for they had been in Jerusalem at the Passover celebration and had seen everything he did there.

46As he traveled through Galilee, he came to Cana, where he had turned the water into wine. There was a government official in nearby Capernaum whose son was very sick. [47]When he heard that Jesus had come from Judea to Galilee, he went and begged Jesus to come to Capernaum to heal his son, who was about to die.

[48]Jesus asked, "Will you never believe in me unless you see miraculous signs and wonders?"

[49]The official pleaded, "Lord, please come now before my little boy dies."

[50]Then Jesus told him, "Go back home. Your son will live!" And the man believed what Jesus said and started home.

[51]While the man was on his way, some of his servants met him with the news that his son was alive and well. [52]He asked them when the boy had begun to get better, and they replied, "Yesterday afternoon at one o'clock his fever suddenly disappeared!" [53]Then the father realized that that was the very time Jesus had told him, "Your son will live." And he and his entire household believed in Jesus. [54]This was the second miraculous sign Jesus did in Galilee after coming from Judea.

NOTES

4:44 *a prophet is not honored in his own hometown.* At first glance, this statement appears to contradict 4:45, for it says prophets are not honored, while 4:45 says "the Galileans welcomed him." Several solutions have been suggested: (1) His "own hometown" is Judea since he was born in Bethlehem of Judea, so that he had no honor there but was made welcome in Galilee (Origen, Westcott, Hoskyns, Sanders, Lindars). John, however, emphasized Jesus' Galilean roots (1:46; 2:1; 7:41-42) and said nothing of his Judean birth. (2) It was added by a later redactor (Brown). This explanation is unnecessary in light of the flow of the text; there is no true contradiction. (3) The lack of honor comes from this world as a whole, and Jesus' "homeland" is heaven (Lightfoot, Morris). Yet while this is certainly true in John as a whole, there is no indication this is the meaning here, and if true, it could even necessitate the idea that Jesus is not honored in heaven, his "homeland." The earth/heaven distinction is not in the immediate context. (4) His "own country" is "Jewish soil" (both Galilee and Judea, so Carson, Blomberg, Burge, Köstenberger), and the contrast is between true reception (1:11) and an ironic, apparent reception (4:45; see commentary below). This is probably the best interpretation since it fits the context better than the others.

4:46 *government official in nearby Capernaum whose son was very sick.* Many have thought this to be a variant of the similar miracle reported in Matt 8:5-13, in which Jesus healed a centurion's slave, but the differences outweigh the similarities. This man was a royal official, not a centurion, and the one healed was his son, not his slave. The illness here is a fever; there it is paralysis. The centurion's faith is strong, while the official's is inadequate. Moreover, the actual wording is not close enough to support the view (so Hoskyns) that they are the same story in different guises.

COMMENTARY

This story frames the section (2:1–4:54) with miracles that occur in Cana. After the wedding feast at Cana in Galilee (2:1-11), Jesus had returned to Jerusalem for Passover (2:13–3:15) and then on his return to Galilee, stopped in Samaria at the village of Sychar for two days (4:40). Then he finished his journey to Galilee (4:43-45), where he would encounter the local official. There seems to be a contrast between 4:44, which is Jesus' saying that prophets have no honor in their "own hometown" (in Mark 6:4 this refers to Nazareth, but here to Judea and Galilee as a whole), and 4:45, which says "the Galileans welcomed him." The negative statement of 4:44 repeats the theme that Jesus' own people rejected him (1:11), and this carries into the episode in Cana, where Jesus derided the Galilean demand for miraculous signs (4:48). The solution is found in 2:23-25, where Jesus refused to "trust" in the inadequate faith of those who focused only on his signs. True faith must be grounded in who he is and not just what he does. Carson correctly notes (1991:236), "*Therefore when he arrived, the Galileans welcomed him—not as the Messiah, but because they had seen all that he had done at the Passover Feast in Jerusalem.*" They were like Nicodemus, thrilled with his power but not understanding his person. In that sense, their welcome was halfhearted and inadequate.

As Jesus came to Cana, he met "a government official" from Capernaum (4:46). The Greek (*basilikos* [TG937A, ZG997]) indicates a "royal official," probably a member of Herod's court—perhaps Chuza, Herod's "business manager" (Luke 8:3), or Herod's "childhood companion," Menaen (Acts 13:1). Herod Antipas was actually tetrarch of Galilee rather than king, but he was popularly called king (cf. Mark 6:14). The official had apparently heard about Jesus' earlier miracle in Cana (4:46), as well as of the events in Jerusalem (4:45), and so traveled to Cana from Capernaum (about 16 miles) to ask Jesus to return with him and heal his son, who was close to death (4:47). Jesus' response was harsh, but it must be noted that he was addressing the Galilean people as a whole and not just the official. Still, the official demonstrated only a desperate hope that a miracle might save his son—not true faith in Jesus. Unlike the centurion in Matthew 8:8, he thought Jesus could only heal if he came to the boy; there was no faith in Jesus' healing word. As in 2:23-25, Jesus denounced those who only believe when they "see miraculous signs and wonders." Wonderment centered on the sensational will never suffice for genuine faith in the "Savior of the world" (4:42). This was also a call to the official to find true faith.

The father was not put off by Jesus' harsh tone; he repeated his plea for Jesus to come with him to Capernaum (4:49). All he cared about at this point was his son. Jesus made a call for faith when he replied, "Go back home. Your son will live." The man's focus finally shifted to Jesus, and "the man believed what Jesus said." His faith became properly centered on the power of Jesus' words, and he started home. This is the key to a burgeoning faith, one that combines belief with response. The royal official proved the reality of his belief by beginning the journey back to Capernaum. Before he arrived, however, the good news came: "Some of his servants met him with the news that his son was alive and well." The startling part is the news that the boy "had begun to get better . . . yesterday afternoon at one o'clock" (cf. note on 1:39 regarding ancient timekeeping), the very moment when Jesus had told him, "Your son will live." As a result, "he and his entire household believed in Jesus" (4:53).

Note the progression of faith: he had an inadequate faith based only on miraculous signs (4:48); then a preliminary faith in Jesus' words (4:50); and finally a full-fledged faith that included his whole family, probably his slaves as well (in the ancient world, a family generally followed the patriarch's faith). Jesus had shown himself to have power over life (cf. 5:21; 11:25), and this led to full-fledged faith.

Note also the different types of faith to this point: The disciples believed when they saw Jesus' glory (2:11), but many others believed only on the basis of signs (2:23); the Samaritans believed on the basis of his words (4:39-42), but many Galileans believed only on the basis of signs and wonders (4:48). Finally, the official and his house came to faith on the basis of Jesus' works and his words. John concludes by pointing out that "this was the second miraculous sign Jesus did in Galilee." There were other signs (2:23), but this is the second in Galilee.

There is also a message here based on geography. Both miracles occurred just after Jesus left Judea and arrived in Galilee (2:1; 4:54), perhaps indicating that Judea was not as favored as Jesus' opponents thought (so Whitacre). The power of God was moving out from Judea to Samaria and Galilee—then to the world (3:16; 4:42).

◆ **B. Jesus and the Feasts of the Jews—Conflict and Fulfillment (5:1–10:42)**

1. Jesus heals a lame man on the Sabbath (5:1-15)

Afterward Jesus returned to Jerusalem for one of the Jewish holy days. ²Inside the city, near the Sheep Gate, was the pool of Bethesda,* with five covered porches. ³Crowds of sick people—blind, lame, or paralyzed—lay on the porches.* ⁵One of the men lying there had been sick for thirty-eight years. ⁶When Jesus saw him and knew he had been ill for a long time, he asked him, "Would you like to get well?"

⁷"I can't, sir," the sick man said, "for I have no one to put me into the pool when the water bubbles up. Someone else always gets there ahead of me."

⁸Jesus told him, "Stand up, pick up your mat, and walk!"

⁹Instantly, the man was healed! He rolled up his sleeping mat and began walking!

But this miracle happened on the Sabbath, ¹⁰so the Jewish leaders objected. They said to the man who was cured, "You can't work on the Sabbath! The law doesn't allow you to carry that sleeping mat!"

¹¹But he replied, "The man who healed me told me, 'Pick up your mat and walk.'"

¹²"Who said such a thing as that?" they demanded.

¹³The man didn't know, for Jesus had disappeared into the crowd. ¹⁴But afterward Jesus found him in the Temple and told him, "Now you are well; so stop sinning, or something even worse may happen to you." ¹⁵Then the man went and told the Jewish leaders that it was Jesus who had healed him.

5:2 Other manuscripts read *Beth-zatha;* still others read *Bethsaida.*   5:3 Some manuscripts add an expanded conclusion to verse 3 and all of verse 4: *waiting for a certain movement of the water, 4for an angel of the Lord came from time to time and stirred up the water. And the first person to step in after the water was stirred was healed of whatever disease he had.*

N O T E S

5:2 Bethesda. The mss tradition is somewhat confused, with three names: Beth-zatha (ℵ L 33 Eusebius); Bethsaida (𝔓66 𝔓75 B Wˢ); and Bethesda (A C 038 078 f¹,¹³ 𝔐). The ms evidence is difficult, with all three having good support; however, the copper scroll at Qumran (3Q15) has given added support to Bethesda, with the meaning "house of the two springs." Some scholars think this is likely the original reading (cf. Barrett, Brown).

5:3b-4 *lay on the porches.* The KJV, on the basis of the TR, adds material to v. 3a, "waiting for a certain movement of the water, for an angel of the Lord came from time to time and stirred up the water. And the first person to step in after the water was stirred was healed of whatever disease he had" (cf. NLT mg). This gloss, however, is missing from the oldest mss—as follows: omit 5:3b (𝔓66 𝔓75 ℵ A* B C* L T cop); and omit 5:4 (𝔓66 𝔓75 ℵ B C* D T Wˢ 33 cop). Several other mss have marks indicating that the scribes considered it doubtful (S 039 041 047 1079 2174 syrʰ). As a result, it is nearly unanimous among scholars that this was added later to the text. At the same time, it probably reflects an ancient tradition and is hinted at in the man's response to Jesus in 5:7. It is probably a genuine tradition but was not written by John.

5:14 *stop sinning, or something even worse may happen.* Carson (1991:245-246) discusses attempts to avoid saying the man's illness was not the result of sin: (1) "Stop sinning" only implies that the man was not chosen due to his moral perfection; nothing more is meant; (2) elsewhere illness and death occur for the glory of God, not due to sin (9:3; 11:4); (3) as in Luke 13:1-5 (the murder of Galileans and those on whom the tower of Siloam fell), terrible events are not always due to personal sin. But such is not the case here: (1) Much suffering in Scripture is due to specific sins (Acts 5:1-11; 1 Cor 11:30); (2) here "something even worse" is tied together with "stop sinning," implying that the earlier illness was the result of sin; (3) Luke 13:1-5 does not address the suffering individual and so is irrelevant for this issue; (4) according to Scripture, the Fall has produced all suffering, and so it makes sense that some suffering will be specifically linked to sin; (5) in this context it is possible, indeed likely, that Jesus chose this invalid because his illness was tied to a specific sin.

COMMENTARY

Beginning with chapter 5, Jesus is seen interacting with four principal Jewish holy days or feasts: Sabbath (ch 5), Passover (ch 6), Tabernacles (ch 7–9), and Dedication/Hanukkah (ch 10). There are two themes. The main one is conflict, as the opposition intensifies and Jesus challenges the Jewish people with who he really is. The second is fulfillment, as each feast is replaced with the reality of Jesus as God's Son and envoy, sent to provide the only basis for eternal life. In the midst of this, the Christological emphasis on Jesus as God's envoy (ch 5), Bread of Life (ch 6), giver of the Spirit (ch 7), Light of the World (ch 8), giver of sight (ch 9), gate, and Good Shepherd (ch 10) grows steadily.

The geography of this section is difficult. Jesus returned to Jerusalem (5:1), went back to Galilee (6:1), then back to Jerusalem in 7:10, where he seemingly remained until his death. The Galilean ministry of the Synoptics, in which Jesus' first trip to Jerusalem comes at his passion, is not recounted in John. The best explanation for this and the numerous trips to Jerusalem John records (2:13; 5:1; 7:10) is that he was deliberately trying to supplement the synoptic Gospels (cf. "Literary Style" in the Introduction) and show another side of Jesus' ministry, namely his extensive ministry in Judea. Blomberg is largely correct when he says (1987:169), "A strong case can be made for the view that John describes the ministry of Jesus almost entirely in chronological order (though omitting numerous episodes), whereas the Synoptics are more topical in their structure, especially for Jesus' Galilean and Perean ministries."

As chapter 5 opens, we see Jesus going down to Jerusalem for "one of the Jewish holy days." This holy day is unidentified. In spite of attempts to link it with Purim or Passover or the Day of Atonement, it is intentionally left unnamed as the emphasis here is on the Sabbath, not a particular feast (though some Jews considered the Sabbath an official festival). When he arrived, he went to "the pool of Bethesda" near "the Sheep Gate." This gate was a small opening on the north wall northeast of the Temple through which sacrificial animals were brought. The pool itself has been excavated near St. Anne's Church on the northeastern side of the old city. "Bethesda" is a transliteration from the Hebrew, meaning "house of outpouring." It apparently was a pair of pools with four "covered porches" or colonnades surrounding it and a fifth between the pools. When Jesus arrived, there were "crowds of sick people" lying on the porches. The added verses (5:3b-4; see note) that crept into the KJV were certainly not part of the original text but are probably historically correct in terms of first-century Jewish tradition. The many sick and crippled people were present because of a tradition related to the periodic bubbling of the pool, which held that an angel periodically stirred up the pool, offering healing to the first person to reach the water.

When Jesus arrived, he met a man who had been crippled for 38 years (5:5). This does not mean he had been at the pool for all that time but probably indicates that he had come regularly for many years. When Jesus saw him, he supernaturally "knew" that the man had been ill for a long time. In John, Jesus' omniscience has been demonstrated before (1:47-48; 2:25; 4:17-19, 29, 39) and once again is center stage. As in all of the encounters thus far, Jesus elicits a response, "Would you like to get well?" This question seems rather silly—of course he would! But Jesus wanted him to get involved in the process.

The man's situation was hopeless. He had no one to help him reach the water when it was stirred up; he could only lie there in abject sorrow. His deep-seated desire for wholeness is seen in the fact that he apparently came regularly in spite of the futility of it all. Someone else always beat him to the pool, but he still came in the hope that someone would show up to help him. Judging from his response to Jesus, he hoped Jesus might be that man to help him get to the pool. Indeed, help had arrived, but not the kind he expected.

Jesus' command must have shocked him: "Stand up, pick up your mat, and walk!" (5:8). One can only imagine his feelings as he felt the healing power of God flow through his emaciated body. His crippling disease was not just taken away; his muscles were given back their strength. The healing was total (so Barrett, Whitacre). The "mat" would have been a light, straw-filled sleeping mattress of the type used by the poor. He was able to get up that instant, roll up his mattress, and walk around. What excitement and surprise it must have caused! The healing was done apart from the pool, and it was not an angel but the Son of God who was at work.

This healing, however, raised a problem: It was the Sabbath, and the religious leaders were scandalized that their oral tradition had been breached. The Torah said that one could not work on the Sabbath, and the Pharisees had developed elaborate rules as to what constituted work. Their determination was that work on the Sabbath was allowable only in life-threatening situations, so Jesus was breaking the law. Furthermore, the man was carrying his mat, and that was also work. The rabbis had developed 39 classes of prohibited work, the last of which was carrying anything from place to place (*m. Shabbat* 7:2; 10:5). The man was in trouble because he had been healed!

The man was in a bind now, and three elements of the unfolding situation show he was insensitive to the spiritual reality of the scene: First, he said that he was told to carry his mat by the one who had healed him (5:11). In so doing, he was shifting the blame from himself to Jesus and showing himself to be not only weak but self-serving. Second, when the authorities demanded to know who "said such a thing as that," he showed that he had not even bothered to learn the name of the one who had healed him. He was so self-centered that he was not even interested in the healer, unlike the crowds (who were enamored with Jesus whenever they just witnessed a miracle, let alone experienced one) and the leaders who turned their attention to Jesus. In the meantime, "Jesus had disappeared into the crowd," obviously not wanting to start another controversy. This was a common practice of his (6:15; 8:59; Mark 7:33; 8:23).

The third and final element is the most unfortunate of them all, one that is quite ironic (5:14-15)—the man reported Jesus to the authorities! Jesus' compassion had led him to find the man, to whom he said: "Now you are well; so stop sinning, or something even worse may happen to you" (5:14). It is common in healing miracles for physical transformation to lead to spiritual transformation. In many miracle stories, the verb *sōzō* [TG4982, ZG5392] has this double meaning, indicating both to "heal" and "save" (cf. Mark 5:34; 6:56; 10:52; and parallels). Jesus challenged the man to get right with God lest he face divine judgment for sin, which is far worse than simple illness. This was more than a moral challenge. Jesus offered the man life from above (3:3, 5; so Whitacre). He had shown a glimmer of faith when he responded to Jesus' command by getting up and carrying his mat. Now he had to make the second step and turn from sin to God. He had to choose between life and judgment. There was no middle ground. This is the key message of the book—light or darkness, life or judgment. We must all make the same choice as this man, and that choice will determine whether we receive eternal life or face eternal death. Sadly, this man made the wrong choice. Rather than respond to Jesus, he "went and told the Jewish leaders that it was Jesus who had healed him." He betrayed Jesus to his enemies. This does not mean the man was another Judas; he acted in ignorance—but ignorance in this book is tantamount to rejection (cf. 1:10). Metzner (1999:179-180, 190-191) shows that this man, who never came to faith, represents Jewish unbelief. Unlike the man born blind (9:17, 25, 30-33, 36-38), he showed no movement from spiritual dullness to belief. He failed to respond to Jesus' offer and so provided the worst example yet of those encountered by Jesus. This was no studied rejection. He simply remained in ignorance and thus in unbelief (see Moloney, Keener, Köstenberger).

◆   ## 2. Conflict over Jesus' claim to be the Son of God (5:16-30)

16So the Jewish leaders began harassing* Jesus for breaking the Sabbath rules. 17But Jesus replied, "My Father is always working, and so am I." 18So the Jewish leaders tried all the harder to find a way to kill him. For he not only broke the Sabbath, he called God his Father, thereby making himself equal with God.

19So Jesus explained, "I tell you the truth, the Son can do nothing by himself. He does only what he sees the Father doing. Whatever the Father does, the Son also does. 20For the Father loves the Son and shows him everything he is doing. In fact, the Father will show him how to do even greater works than healing this man. Then you will truly be astonished. 21For just as the Father gives life to those he raises from the dead, so the Son gives life to anyone he wants. 22In addition, the Father judges no one. Instead, he has given the Son absolute authority to judge, 23so that everyone will honor the Son, just as they honor the Father. Anyone who does not honor the Son is certainly not honoring the Father who sent him.

24"I tell you the truth, those who listen to my message and believe in God who sent me have eternal life. They will never be condemned for their sins, but they have already passed from death into life. 25"And I assure you that the time is coming, indeed it's here now, when the dead will hear my voice—the voice of the Son of God. And those who listen will live. 26The Father has life in himself, and he has granted that same life-giving power to his Son. 27And he has given him authority to judge everyone because he is the Son of Man.* 28Don't be so surprised! Indeed, the time is coming when all the dead in their graves will hear the voice of God's Son, 29and they will rise again. Those who have done good will rise to experience eternal life, and those who have continued in evil will rise to experience judgment. 30I can do nothing on my own. I judge as God tells me. Therefore, my judgment is just, because I carry out the will of the one who sent me, not my own will.

5:27 "Son of Man" is a title Jesus used for himself.

NOTES

5:17 Jesus replied. This is the only place in John (with 5:19) where "replied" (or "explained") is in the middle voice, suggesting a legal setting in which one is giving a defense against charges (so Brown, Morris, Michaels, Whitacre).

My Father. This begins a remarkable run in the use of patēr [TG3962, ZG4252] (father), which occurs 9 times in 5:17-26. John has a remarkable predilection for using "father" language to highlight the intimate relation between Jesus and God. Of the 414 uses of patēr in the NT, John contains 136 of them. Jesus calls God his Father 100 times in John versus 3 times in Mark, 4 in Luke, and 31 in Matthew (EDNT 3.53). There are two emphases in this title in John. First, it partakes of the "Abba" theme, a term rarely used in Jewish prayers because it is a family term, expressing a deep intimacy and a sense of sonship (DJG 619). This usage stressed the unique unity and love between Jesus and God. Second, it has a polemical connotation in chs 5-8, where it leads to Jewish opposition due to Jesus' claim to the special status of Son of God—the only revelation of the transcendent God (DJG 274).

5:18 equal with God. While the equality is strongly emphasized, the context also stresses Jesus' subordination to the Father. Jesus does what he sees the Father doing (5:19), and his authority is given by God (5:21, 22). The two aspects, equality and subordination, are interdependent aspects of Jesus as the God-man. As God, he is equal to the Father; as a human being incarnate in this world, he is subordinate to the Father (cf. Keener 1999).

5:19-30 Blomberg (2001:112-113) sees a chiastic pattern here with salvation (5:24-25) as the central point: thesis (the Son doing what the Father does, 5:19-20a, 30); right and wrong ways to be "astonished" or "surprised" (5:20b, 28-29); illustrations about life and judgment (5:21-22, 26-27a); the purpose for God's actions (5:23, 27b); salvation (5:24-25).

5:20 *the Father loves the Son.* This is the only place in John where *phileō* [TG5368, ZG5797] is used for the love between the Son and the Father (elsewhere *agapaō* [TG25, ZG26] is used). While some think there is a difference of meaning, with *phileō* [TG5368, ZG5797] here indicating "a more strongly affective love" (Schnackenburg, Whitacre), it is more likely that the two verbs are synonymous in meaning in John (Brown, Bruce).

5:27 *Son of Man.* This is the only place in the NT where "Son of Man" appears without the definite article, and many have interpreted this as "mortal" or "human" after the use of "son of man" in Ezekiel (an expression for his mortality). The idea is that Jesus can judge human beings because he himself is human. However, definite predicate nouns coming before the verb regularly lack the article—this is the case here. Additionally, the "someone like a son of man" in Dan 7:13 is also anarthrous, and this is an allusion to that passage (Bruce, Morris, Carson, Michaels, Whitacre).

COMMENTARY

As a result of the lame man's testimony, the leaders "began harassing Jesus for breaking the Sabbath rules" (5:16). The verb may indicate that this is not the first time Jesus had done so, possibly reflecting the many Sabbath violations recorded in the Synoptics. At any rate, the "persecution" (the verb behind "harassing") began. This is the first time in John's Gospel that actual persecution is mentioned (cf. 7:1, 19-20, 25-26, 30, 32, 44, 45; 8:37, 40, 59; 11:8, 53, 57). To the charge of Sabbath violation, Jesus responded simply, "My Father is always working, and so am I." To modern readers, this is a simple response that says that Jesus was doing his Father's work. In a Jewish context, it meant a great deal more; it implied equality with God. The rabbis taught that only God can work on the Sabbath, alluding to the creative nature of God as part of his ceaseless activity in the world (*Exodus Rabbah* 30:6, so Barrett). At issue is the statement in Genesis 2:2 that God "rested from all his work" on the seventh day. But if he ceases working every Sabbath, how does the universe continue running? Therefore, God must work on the Sabbath. But then does he break his own law, becoming a Sabbath breaker? No, because as God he alone is exempt from this rule. Jesus' claim to work as well is tantamount to a claim to be God's equal. Moreover, he made his claim even more clear by stating that God was his Father. The Jews addressed God as "our Father" in their synagogue prayers, but Jesus "appeared to be claiming God as 'his own Father' in an exceptional, if not exclusive sense" (Bruce 1983:127). This was blasphemy to the leaders, so they tried "all the harder to find a way to kill him" (5:18). This is also the first time that their resolve to execute Jesus is mentioned.

The rest of this section (5:19-30) clarifies the right of Jesus to claim equality with God. Jesus' response is that the power of life and judgment belong only to God, yet they have been turned over to the Son. Jesus addresses two aspects of this reality: realized eschatology in 5:19-24 (i.e., these powers are his now), and final eschatology in 5:25-30 (i.e., he controls the final judgment, so Brown). In 5:19, we have what Lightfoot calls a "defense of Christian monotheism": Jesus does not act independently of the Father but rather is at all times dependent on him. He is equal yet in his incarnate state "does only what he sees the Father doing." While some (e.g., Dodd) call this a hidden parable, it is better to see this as an illustration built on the idea of a son as an apprentice learning his father's trade—something Jesus did when he was apprenticed to his stepfather Joseph, learning to become the village carpenter at Nazareth (so Beasley-Murray, Carson). Here, Jesus viewed himself as the ultimate apprentice to his true Father. Jesus is at one and the same time the one and only God (1:14, 18) and submissive as his Son. Both are critical to a proper understanding of the second member of the Trinity.

Verses 19-23 develop this thesis via four consecutive *gar* [TG1063, ZG1142] ("for") clauses. The first (5:19b) explains that sonship demands unity of action: "Whatever the Father does, the Son also does." The emphasis here is on the unity of the Father and the Son in terms of action. As Westcott says (1881:85), "His action is not only coincident but coextensive with the action of the Father . . . not in imitation, but in virtue of His sameness of nature." He is at the same time one with the Father and dependent on the Father. Thompson (2001:69-72) develops the uniqueness of the filial relationship between Jesus and God: John never uses "son" (*huios* [TG5207, ZG5626]) of the disciples—only "child" (*teknon* [TG5043, ZG5451]). In every aspect the Father and the Son are inseperable. She notes two points: (1) God's actions are uniquely concentrated toward and through the Son; (2) God's activity is all-embracing with respect to the Son, especially in terms of life-giving power. At the same time, the Son's submission to the Father is also highlighted. There is an ontological unity and yet a functional subordination within the Godhead (cf. commentary on 3:17; note on 14:28).

The second "for" clause (5:20) states that this union of action is grounded in the love of the Father. As a result of that depth of love, God "shows him everything he is doing." In other words, the sharing between Father and Son is absolute, with nothing held back. In 5:19, Jesus "sees" what the Father is doing, and here the flip side is stressed, with the Father showing everything he is doing. This reciprocal knowledge is based on reciprocal love. Here we see the basis of the omniscience Jesus had demonstrated several times (1:42, 47-48; 4:18). In fact, Jesus adds that the revelation from the Father will enable him to do even "greater works" than the healing of the lame man. Probably this points to the next two verses, which describe how the Father will give the Son authority over life and judgment. The greatest miracle of all is the gift of eternal life (cf. 14:12). The purpose of this (*hina* [TG2443, ZG2671], "in order that") is so they can "truly be astonished," noting the many times the people marvel at the knowledge and power of God in Jesus (3:7; 4:27; 5:28; 7:15, 21). The surprise and wonder they feel are a step toward faith and are part of encountering God in Jesus.

The other two *gar* [TG1063, ZG1142] (for) clauses that explain the unity of Father and Son provide two illustrations of the "work" they share (5:21-23)—namely, authority to give life and to judge. As stated above, the Father "shows" all things, and the Son "sees" them and then "does" them. Here the Father "gives life" via resurrection, and the Son "gives life to anyone he wants." The raising of the dead was considered the special provenance of God (1 Sam 2:6; 2 Kgs 5:7), and later Judaism believed this power would not even be given to the Messiah (*b. Ta'anit*; *The Eighteen Benedictions*; cf. Köstenberger 2004:187). Elijah is the sole exception (1 Kgs 17:17-24) but only because God chose him to be such. Jesus transcends Elijah because he shares the divine power of life and gives it to "anyone he wants," a reference to divine sovereignty over life. This gift is both spiritual life now and final resurrection.

The final *gar* [TG1063, ZG1142] clause in 5:22 ("In addition," NLT) goes beyond the idea of 5:21, that Jesus has God's power in giving life. Here, Jesus makes the surprising statement, "The Father judges no one" but instead "has given the Son absolute authority to judge." Throughout the Old Testament and in Judaism, Yahweh alone is the final Judge. Jesus is saying that the power of life and judgment has now been passed to him, the Son (cf. the note on 3:17 regarding the possible contradiction with that verse). This hardly means that God ceases to be the final Judge, for according to Revelation 20:11-15, God is on the white throne at the final judgment. Rather, he has shared that authority with Jesus, who became the earthly Judge of all in his ministry and who will share in the final judgment. The purpose of this is that the Son may have the same "honor" (*timaō* [TG5091, ZG5506]) as the Father. While the Son is dependent on the Father (5:19-20), he is also equal to the Father in authority over life and judgment (5:21-22); they have equal honor and glory. To honor the Father is to honor the Son; to refuse the Son is to refuse the Father. This becomes a major facet of Jesus' teaching in John: one cannot believe or honor God without believing in and honoring Jesus (5:38, 43-44; 7:16-17; 8:19, 28, 42, 47; 10:38; 14:1), and the Son is the only path to God (14:6). As Carson brings out (1991:255), there is a salvation-historical progression here. Abraham, Moses, and David honored God with their lives, but now the final stage in the history of redemption has arrived. To try to honor God while rejecting his Son (as many Jews did at that time) is now a logical impossibility. The Messiah has come; he is the focus of the divine plan, the only one worthy of worship.

Jesus concludes the first half of his retort with another double *amēn* [TG281, ZG297] saying (5:24, "I tell you the truth," see note on 1:51) leading to a solemn, critical truth: if Jesus is indeed one with God (5:19-23), then "eternal life" can come only as a result of listening to and believing in him. Like 3:16, 31ff, this sums up themes introduced earlier. This is the Johannine Gospel in embryo, and it builds on the implications of 5:21-23. Since Jesus (as the Sent One; cf. note on 3:17) is God's "premiere agent in the world" (Burge), he has divine power over life and judgment; so the only way to participate in life and avoid judgment is to hear and believe. In John, hearing Jesus' word is a critical step to believing in him, as seen in 1:37, 40 (the Baptist's disciples hear and follow) and 4:42 (the Samaritan villagers hear and believe, cf. also 6:63, 68). When Jesus encounters people with the claims of God, a faith-decision is the natural result. Those who respond "have eternal life" and "will never be condemned for their sins" (5:24). Note once more the already/not-yet tension of John. Eternal life is a present possession here; the believers have already "passed from death into life," though they have not yet begun their final life in eternity. The process is presented as a change of realms in which the believer has moved from one realm to the other. This concept is also utilized in Romans 5:12–6:11, in which death is personified as an evil force that reigns over mankind, while the believer is united to the death of Christ and therefore changes realms to live a new life in Christ. We who were dead in sin have now found life in Christ.

The second half of the passage (5:25-30) repeats the themes of life and judgment. The already/not-yet tension is again apparent in "the time is coming, indeed it's here now" (so Carson), which repeats the idea from 4:23. The new Kingdom age has arrived in Christ, and the spiritually "dead will hear (his) voice" and "live." The afterlife the Jews anticipated has already become a reality, and eternal life is a present possession as well as a future certainty for those who believe. Apart from Christ, all people are already dead in sin, and the only hope for life is his life-giving word (6:63, 68; 10:3, 16, 27; 11:43). The life of the final resurrection is available in the here and now for those who listen and believe. Note once more that faith comes by hearing (as in 5:24 above). Jesus alone has the words that call forth life.

The basis for this power is seen in 5:26-27, which restates Jesus' authority to give life and to judge (cf. 5:21-23). Both stem from the Father. First, the Father has "life in himself" (5:26) and so grants the Son the authority to have "life in himself" (the same exact language is repeated in the Gr.). This is more than just "life-giving power." The Father and the Son possess life; it is internal to their being and inherent in who they are. The functional aspect (the power to give life) flows out of the ontological (they are life). Thompson (1999:20-21) says this verse is the key to the Johannine idea of the Father–Son relationship; the Father, who gives life, passes this authority on to his Son. Second, "the authority to judge" has also been passed from the Father to the Son (cf. 5:22). The positive side (give life) and the negative side (pronounce judgment) are closely intertwined and depend on the faith-decision. Jesus came to save, not to judge (3:17), but his coming forces an encounter with God and demands a faith-decision. That decision determines whether we face judgment or find life. This power to judge belongs to God but has been passed to the Son "because he is the Son of Man." This is most likely a reference to Daniel 7:13-14, where the "someone like a son of man" is given "authority, honor, and sovereignty over all the nations of the world." Jesus has dominion over this world and therefore is given power to judge by God. Carson (1991:257) sees three strands coming together here: Jesus is the apocalyptic Son of Man, who is given dominion over this world; he is fully human and one with humanity, so has complete understanding; and he is the revelation of God (the living voice) and so judges those who reject that revelation.

This life and judgment is not just present but also future (5:28-29). For this reason, Jesus added, "Don't be so surprised"—the same thing he said to Nicodemus (3:7). Such divine truths are difficult to comprehend and produce amazement, but anyone who comes to know Jesus will not be surprised that he has such power. Jesus' hearers had difficulty comprehending his power to give life and judge in the present, so he turned to a subject they were familiar with—final judgment and everlasting life. He controls that as well and stated that "the time is coming when all the dead in their graves will hear the voice of God's Son." (Note the absence of "it's here now" [5:25] in Jesus' clarified reference to the Eschaton, or "end" of world history, here.) This is a clear reference to the Parousia, when he will "come down from heaven with a commanding shout" (1 Thess 4:16). Then all mankind will be divided into two groups (cf. the parable of the wheat and the weeds in Matt 13:24-29, 36-43)—those who have "done good" and those who "continued in evil." The one will inherit "eternal life"; the other "will rise to experience judgment." Ridderbos (1997:201) speaks of this as an "apocalyptic compensation" for people's reactions in the "now" of 5:25 but argues even more strongly for an inseparable union between the present state and the future reality. In 3:21, those who "do what is right" joyfully come to the Light; here they find their reward, eternal life. They have resurrection life now (cf. Rom 6:4-5), as well as the promise of everlasting life in the future. Those who prefer evil are under indictment now (5:22-24) and will rise to everlasting judgment (5:29; cf. Rev 20:11-15).

Concluding this section, Jesus returns in 5:30 to the theme of his dependence on the Father introduced in 5:19-20 (especially regarding his authority to judge) and switches back to the first person "I" of verses 19 and 24 for emphasis. In verses 19-20 he "sees" the Father; here he hears the Father; both mean he submits to his Father's will. It is not his own power, but judgment occurs only "as God tells" him. It is his Father's decision, passed on to the Son, so his hearers can be assured of complete justice. It is also his Father's voice ("as God tells me") and his Father's will ("I carry out the will of the one who sent me"). Jesus is the divine envoy and herald of God. He does not act on his own. He conveys the decisions of God, and his judgment, therefore, is completely righteous and just (the double meaning of *dikaia* [TG1342, ZG1465] in 5:30). His judgment is "righteous" in the sense that it proceeds from the very character of God; it is "just" in the sense that it reflects divine justice in this world.

◆   ### 3. Witness and unbelief (5:31-47)

31"If I were to testify on my own behalf, my testimony would not be valid. 32But someone else is also testifying about me, and I assure you that everything he says about me is true. 33In fact, you sent investigators to listen to John the Baptist, and his testimony about me was true. 34Of course, I have no need of human witnesses, but I say these things so you might be saved. 35John was like a burning and shining lamp, and you were excited for a while about his message. 36But I have a greater witness than John—my teachings and my miracles. The Father gave me these works to accomplish, and they prove that he sent me. 37And the Father who sent me has testified about me himself. You have never heard his voice or seen him face to face, 38and you do not have his message in your hearts, because you do not believe me—the one he sent to you.

39"You search the Scriptures because

you think they give you eternal life. But the Scriptures point to me! ⁴⁰Yet you refuse to come to me to receive this life.

⁴¹"Your approval means nothing to me, ⁴²because I know you don't have God's love within you. ⁴³For I have come to you in my Father's name, and you have rejected me. Yet if others come in their own name, you gladly welcome them. ⁴⁴No wonder you can't believe! For you gladly honor each other, but you don't care about the honor that comes from the one who alone is God.*

⁴⁵"Yet it isn't I who will accuse you before the Father. Moses will accuse you! Yes, Moses, in whom you put your hopes. ⁴⁶If you really believed Moses, you would believe me, because he wrote about me. ⁴⁷But since you don't believe what he wrote, how will you believe what I say?"

5:44 Some manuscripts read *from the only One.*

NOTES

5:37 *the Father who sent me has testified.* Some think the witness of the Father is direct and specific, perhaps at Jesus' baptism (but John does not record the voice of testimony at the Baptism in 1:32-33) or at Sinai and the giving of the Law (due to 5:37 and 39, but the context is insufficient for this). It is best to see the Father's testimony as indirect or general—evident in Jesus' incarnation, life, and ministry as well as in scriptural fulfillment (so Beasley-Murray, Köstenberger).

5:39 *You search the Scriptures.* The verb could be imperative, "search the Scriptures" (KJV) or indicative, "you are searching the Scriptures." Most opt for the indicative, for as Dodd points out (1953a:329), it would be unnecessary for Jesus to urge the Jews to study their Scriptures since they had been doing so.

5:42 *God's love.* Lit., "The love of God." This is definitely an objective genitive (denoting the people's love for God) rather than a subjective genitive (indicating God's love for them). John 3:16 tells us "God loved the world so much," but the problem here is that people have not returned that love.

5:44 *the one who alone is God.* Some mss have "the only One" ($\mathfrak{P}$66 $\mathfrak{P}$75 B W itᵃ,ᵇ copˢᵃ,ᵇᵒ,ᵃᶜʰ) rather than "the only God" ($\aleph$ A D L 063 0210ᵛⁱᵈ f¹,¹³ 33 itᵉ syr 𝔐). While there are good mss behind both, it is possible the original term "God" was omitted in later copies due to transcriptional oversight, with the nomen sacrum for *theos* [ᵀᴳ2316, ᶻᴳ2536] being accidentally omitted (so Metzger 1994:180). Comfort, however, argues for the shorter reading on the basis that the title "the only One" has the earliest support ($\mathfrak{P}$66 $\mathfrak{P}$75 B) and was an apt title for God in this context. Furthermore, scribes would be more inclined to add "God" than delete it (2007:[John 5:44]).

COMMENTARY

The idea of witness or testimony appears often in this Gospel (cf. 1:7). Boice (1970:24) points out that 60 percent of the New Testament occurrences of the verb for "witness" (*martureō* [ᵀᴳ3140, ᶻᴳ3455]) occur in John's writings (47 of 77 times, with 33 in his Gospel). Boice links the theme closely with that of divine revelation. Witness refers to official, objective testimony to the truthfulness of God's revelation in Jesus.

Jesus begins in 5:31 by saying that if he were to witness on his own behalf, his "testimony would not be valid." Jesus was following the rabbinic principle that no one can testify for themselves (*m. Ketubbot* 2:9, so Brown). This is a common sense statement that simply means a person's own testimony on his behalf cannot be trusted in a court of law (cf. 8:18 for the seeming contradiction there). Deuteronomy 17:6 (cf. Deut 19:15) states that in a capital case (note that in 5:18, they were plotting to kill Jesus), two or three witnesses are needed to convict a person. As Schnackenburg brings out (1980:2.120), "Jewish legal procedure is not based on the interrogation of the accused but on the examination of witnesses." Jesus realized that his claims of equality with God were not legally sufficient on their own. His point was that if they did not want to accept his word for it, he had four more to back it up. This passage first presents the witnesses (5:31-40) and then the unbelief of the Jews in rejecting these witnesses (5:41-47).

In reality there is only one true witness, the Father, and the others are expressions of that one ultimate testimony. Jesus spoke of another witness (5:32, "someone else") who was completely qualified to speak, and his testimony would be completely valid. This, of course, is the Father, whose testimony doesn't appear until 5:37. As Whitacre says (1999:36), "only God, and those whom he uses, can testify to God." There are four sets of witnesses.

The Testimony of John the Baptist (5:33-35). Jesus reminded his opponents of the earlier time when the Sanhedrin sent a team to investigate John (1:19-28), and then Jesus told them "his testimony about me was true." According to 1:6-7, John the Baptist was sent as God's envoy to testify about the "light"; the Baptist later proclaimed Jesus as the "Lamb of God" and "the Chosen One of God" (1:29, 33-34). Then he added to that testimony that his ministry was a preparation for the Messiah, Jesus, and that he rejoiced at the privilege (3:27-30). Still, Jesus added, "I have no need of human witnesses." He and the Father are one (5:17, 19; 10:30), and since he has power over life and judgment, he needs no human confirmation to know who he is. But those on earth did need such confirmation, especially Jesus' opponents. Therefore, Jesus provided official testimony "so you might be saved"— that is, so that those who are open to such witness might realize its truth, believe, and be saved (the result of divine love, 3:16-17).

John the Baptist is an especially relevant testimony because although he was not the light (1:8-9), he was "like a burning and shining lamp" (5:35), possibly an echo of Psalm 132:17-18, which promised that God had "prepared a lamp for [his] anointed" one (NASB) and would "clothe his enemies with shame." The Baptist was that lamp, and his opponents would indeed know shame. That the Jewish people had been "excited for a while about his message" may indicate that he was in prison at this time or was perhaps already dead. The problem was that the excitement was short lived and did not fulfill the Baptist's major purpose, faith in the true Messiah. The people joyfully listened for a while, but they were unwilling to find the permanent joy of turning to Jesus.

The Testimony of Jesus' Works (5:36). In the final analysis, John's witness, though extremely helpful, was insufficient for Jesus, for he had "a greater witness than John," namely his works—that is, his teaching and miracles. The reason his works were such a powerful witness is that the Father gave them to him. They were signs (2:11; 4:54) pointing to the divine reality behind them, and God was the indwelling presence who performed these works in Jesus (cf. 14:10). They were greater than

Moses's accomplishments and beyond anything Elijah or Elisha did. Therefore, they provided proof that God had sent Jesus as his divine envoy and Son.

The Testimony of God Himself (5:37-38). Jesus returned to the witness that is behind all the others (5:32)—namely, "the Father who sent" him. This witness is general, for God does not speak until 12:28. It could refer to the internal witness of God in the hearts of people (1 John 5:9-10), or it may go beyond that (while including it) to the Father's witness at Jesus' baptism (so Bruce, Blomberg), but it is probably more general, namely through Jesus' words and works, through God's presence in Jesus' life, and through Scripture (5:39-40).

The results of this witness among the Jews were disheartening. First, they had "never heard his voice," as Moses had at Sinai (Exod 33:11), or as the prophets and especially Jesus had. The Greek text has "never at any time," indicating that the people refused God's voice in Moses, the prophets, and Jesus. Second, they had never "seen him face to face" (lit., "seen his form"), which means they had refused to see God in Jesus (1:18; 14:9), so they stood guilty before God. They had both seen and heard God when they encountered Jesus, but they rejected the witness. Third, they did "not have his message in [their] hearts." Jesus is the Word of God (1:1-18), the living revealer of the Father, but they refused his message. Moses received the Ten Commandments on Sinai; Joshua studied the "Book of Instruction" (Josh 1:8); and the psalmist hid God's word in his heart (Ps 119:11). In contrast, the people of Jesus' day rejected that Word of God in Jesus; their hearts were closed to the truth. The reason was that they did not believe in the one whom God sent. The witness of God was all around them and is still open to those with the eyes of faith, but these people closed their hearts to it and rejected the true witness.

The Testimony of the Scriptures (5:39-40). The final witness should have made the difference, for these were people who searched the Scriptures, thinking they provided "eternal life." The verb "search" is particularly strong, a rabbinic term for professional study and exposition of the law (so Ridderbos). The scribes and Pharisees went to great pains to understand the Scriptures deeply and developed an oral tradition to help people contemporize the law into their daily practice. Yet they missed the boat, for they failed to realize that "the Scriptures point [lit., 'testify'] to [Jesus]!" They sought "eternal life" in the wrong place, for the Messiah—the only basis for life—had come in fulfillment of the Scriptures, and they rejected him. Salvation is not to be found in the words of Scripture themselves but only in the one about whom the Scriptures testify. This is a critical emphasis of both Jesus and the early church, seen in the vast number of fulfillment passages in the New Testament. Jesus fulfilled Old Testament prophecy, which pointed to him as God's Messiah. The basic problem of the people was unbelief: "You refuse to come to me to receive this life" (5:40). The leaders preferred their love for minutia to the broad sweep of scriptural witness to Jesus.

Jesus' Condemnation of Their Unbelief (5:41-47). Once Jesus had presented his evidence, he took the offensive, declaring them guilty of unbelief. He began by saying, "Your approval means nothing to me." He had need neither of "human witnesses"

(5:34) nor of human approval or glory—in this case, praise or esteem from people. He had received all the approval he needed from the Father, and further praise was unnecessary. This was especially true because he knew "human nature" (2:24-25) and therefore realized his opponents didn't have the love of God in them. Naturally, they believed they loved God; in fact, their entire oral tradition was geared toward remaining in a right relationship with God. Their rejection of Jesus, however, proved that they did not truly love God. As Hendriksen says, "Had there been this love in their hearts, they would of course have accepted the Father's testimony concerning his Son" (1953:210). The proof of this lack of true love is the fact that "I have come to you in my Father's name, and you have rejected me" (5:43). He was not only the divine envoy ("sent me" in 5:23, 24, 30, 36, 38) but also the one and only Son (1:14, 18; 3:16; 5:18-19), yet they refused to accept him (1:11-12).

In contrast, they freely welcomed the many messianic pretenders of the era (5:43). It is estimated that there had been as many as 64 claimants around this time (cf. Morris), and they all had their followers. It is ironic that the claimant with one of the smallest groups of adherents (the only groups of disciples mentioned numbered 12, 72 [Luke 10], 120 [Acts 1], and 500 [1 Cor 15]) is the one true Messiah. The worldly self-centeredness of the false messiahs struck a responsive chord in many people's hearts. Therefore, it is "no wonder [they] can't believe," for like the false messiahs they sought "honor [from] each other" rather than from God (cf. 12:43). Their whole life was a constant striving for human attention rather than pleasing God. They served a false God, mankind, but as Jesus said, one cannot "serve two masters" (Luke 16:13). As believers today, we also must ask to what extent we seek honor for ourselves rather than seeking glory only for (and from) God.

Jesus then presented Moses, the prosecuting attorney who would accuse them "before the Father" (5:45). Jesus is the Judge (5:22, 30; 9:39), and he will not need to bring the charges, for that role will be assumed by the one most qualified of all, the very Moses who gave Israel the Torah. To Israel, Moses was the very savior who had freed them from the Egyptians and given them the law by which they stayed right with God. Jesus was saying that they had fooled themselves, for Moses would be the very one to bring evidence against them. Salvation for Israel centered on four things: the law, the land, the Temple, and the covenant. Moses was responsible for giving them the law, bringing them to the land, and establishing worship in the Tabernacle (Israel's first Temple structure). If they had really "believed Moses," though, they would have believed in Jesus because he "wrote about [Jesus]" in Deuteronomy 18:15, the prophecy of the final messianic prophet (cf. 1:21; 4:19 and commentary). The Jewish people prided themselves on the centrality of Scripture, particularly the Torah, in their lives. Yet they were rejecting the very one Moses had prophesied about. Thus, they rejected Moses's writings when they rejected Jesus. No wonder they could not accept Jesus' words; they had rejected the words of Moses himself. Thus, Moses will stand up against them in the final judgment and accuse them of unbelief.

◆   4. Jesus feeds five thousand (6:1-15)

After this, Jesus crossed over to the far side of the Sea of Galilee, also known as the Sea of Tiberias. ²A huge crowd kept following him wherever he went, because they saw his miraculous signs as he healed the sick. ³Then Jesus climbed a hill and sat down with his disciples around him. ⁴(It was nearly time for the Jewish Passover celebration.) ⁵Jesus soon saw a huge crowd of people coming to look for him. Turning to Philip, he asked, "Where can we buy bread to feed all these people?" ⁶He was testing Philip, for he already knew what he was going to do.

⁷Philip replied, "Even if we worked for months, we wouldn't have enough money* to feed them!"

⁸Then Andrew, Simon Peter's brother, spoke up. ⁹"There's a young boy here with five barley loaves and two fish. But what good is that with this huge crowd?"

¹⁰"Tell everyone to sit down," Jesus said. So they all sat down on the grassy slopes. (The men alone numbered about 5,000.) ¹¹Then Jesus took the loaves, gave thanks to God, and distributed them to the people. Afterward he did the same with the fish. And they all ate as much as they wanted. ¹²After everyone was full, Jesus told his disciples, "Now gather the leftovers, so that nothing is wasted." ¹³So they picked up the pieces and filled twelve baskets with scraps left by the people who had eaten from the five barley loaves.

¹⁴When the people saw him* do this miraculous sign, they exclaimed, "Surely, he is the Prophet we have been expecting!"* ¹⁵When Jesus saw that they were ready to force him to be their king, he slipped away into the hills by himself.

6:7 Greek *Two hundred denarii would not be enough.* A denarius was equivalent to a laborer's full day's wage.
6:14a Some manuscripts read *Jesus.*   6:14b See Deut 18:15, 18; Mal 4:5-6.

NOTES

6:1 *Sea of Tiberias.* This is another name for the Sea of Galilee. This name was borrowed from the town of that name erected by Herod and dedicated about AD 20 to the Emperor Tiberias. The name was probably attached to the lake after the time of Jesus and was used by John for clarity here and in 21:1 (its only occurrences in the NT).

6:3 *climbed a hill.* Some see symbolism in the mountain mentioned here, perhaps seeing Jesus as fulfilling the work of Moses, who ascended Sinai (so Schnackenburg). While Matthew emphasized mountain scenes (cf. Matt 5:1; 17:1; 24:3; 28:16), John did not, and it is doubtful whether there is any typology here.

6:11 *gave thanks to God, and distributed them to the people.* It is common to see eucharistic overtones because the language here is so similar to the prayer and distribution of the elements at the Last Supper (cf. Mark 14:22; 1 Cor 11:23, so Brown, Perkins, Schnackenburg, Michaels). However, every detail here fits the Jewish meal liturgy, and John gave very little attention to the meal on the night of the Last Supper. Thus, there is no evidence that there are eucharistic connotations here. As Witherington says (1995:152), "We are to think of a hearty repast, perhaps even a depiction of the messianic banquet, when many would come from the east and west and eat with Messiah (cf. Luke 14:15-24)"—but no Eucharist.

6:14 *sign.* Other mss read "signs" ($\mathfrak{P}$75 B 091 it^a), but this may be a scribal assimilation to 2:23; 6:2 (so Metzger 1994:181). In spite of the quality of witnesses behind the plural, the majority of mss support the singular and include early and diverse witnesses.

6:15 *force him to be their king.* Many scholars have seen John's portrayal of the feeding of the 5,000 as an independent story with many fictional elements, such as naming Philip and Andrew and especially including the final scene where the people try to make Jesus the conquering king. The Synoptics move directly into the walking on the water scene, after Jesus dismisses the disciples and the crowds and goes off by himself to pray (Mark 6:44-46 and parallels). However, these details are not mutually exclusive. When Jesus sent the crowds home, it is easy to surmise that a group of nationalists refused to go and demanded that Jesus begin the messianic rebellion. Also, the messianic fervor can be seen in Mark's picture of the people's and Herod's reactions, wondering if Jesus might be Elijah or the Baptist returned from the dead (Mark 6:14-16). The accounts can be harmonized and do not contradict one another (cf. Bernard, Morris, Carson). Blomberg (2001:120; so also Pryor 1992:31) takes this scene as a sign of historicity: "It fits the rising nationalistic fervor of first-century Israel, cuts against the grain of Johannine redaction in treating Jesus as a merely political king, and embarrassingly portrays Jesus as having to run away from the crowds, as it were."

COMMENTARY

This is the fourth sign-miracle and is the only miracle found in all four Gospels (the walking on the water is missing in Luke). This is probably due to the depth of its theology. It reproduces not only the manna in the wilderness (Exod 16) but also the multiplication of loaves in 2 Kings 4:38-44, which describes how Elisha fed 100 people with 20 loaves of bread. Notice that Elisha multiplied the bread fivefold (a loaf is enough for one person), while Jesus multiplied it 1,000 times (a fact that would have been noticed by the early church). This was truly a messianic miracle pointing forward to the messianic banquet. The abundance of wine in the Cana miracle also pointed to the messianic banquet (2:1-11).

The scene is set in 6:1-4. Jesus was back in Galilee (ch 5 is set in Jerusalem) and crosses to "the far side of the Sea of Galilee," the east side opposite Capernaum and the Jewish villages. This "rapid oscillation" of geographical movement (in ch 7 Jesus goes back to Jerusalem) fits John's style, for he did the same thing in 1:19–4:54 (so Carson). Once more, a "huge crowd" followed him, and as in 2:23-25, their faith was inadequate, centered only on his sign-miracles. Their faith was insufficient because they were only enamored with the spectacular and just wanted to see more. In the meantime, Jesus wanted to be alone with his disciples, so he climbed a hill to be with them. This may well refer to the "hill country" of the region, probably the area known today as the Golan Heights (so Carson). John tells us this occurred about the "time for the Jewish Passover celebration" (6:4), the second Passover mentioned in John (cf. 2:13; 13:1). His purpose is theological rather than chronological. The key to the Passover is the death of the sacrificial lamb for the people, and Jesus is to be the "Lamb of God who takes away the sin of the world" (1:29). This fulfillment theme will dominate the chapter.

As Jesus settled down to enjoy his time with the disciples, he saw a "huge crowd" approaching (6:5). He decided to use this as an opportunity to "test" (*peirazō* [TG3985, ZG4279]) his disciples, a term often used of temptation but here used neutrally of a general test (in Jas 1:2-3, like here, it is a test of faith; cf. 1 Pet 1:6-7). He asked Philip (the Synoptics have Jesus ask the disciples in general, while John specifies which one is asked) how they were going to feed so large a crowd. Philip, like Nicodemus and the Samaritan woman before him, was thinking entirely on the earthly plane, so he replied that it would take 200 denarii to buy enough food (cf. Mark 6:37). Since a denarius was the wage for a single day's work for the average laborer, he was saying that it would take eight month's pay to buy enough food. Of course, Jesus was thinking on a higher plane and was preparing them for the miracle to follow. Andrew spoke up (6:8-9), pointing to a boy in the crowd with "five barley loaves and two fish." Barley loaves were the food of the poor, and this detail prepares for the great miracle to follow. It was also barley loaves that Elisha used in 2 Kings 4:42 (the term for "young boy" is also found there). Jesus here was fulfilling the Elijah/Elisha tradition (as is often seen in the Gospels, e.g., Luke 4:25-27; 7:16; 9:8, 19). The two fish were probably pieces of dried or pickled fish used to give the bread flavor.

Jesus took charge (6:10), telling everyone to sit down on "the grassy slopes" in preparation for the meal. Mark 6:39 tells us the grass is green, and this fits the time of Passover in early spring (so Westcott). This was a huge crowd; as only the men were numbered (cf. Matt 14:21), the 5,000 could easily have been 10,000 or more. Jesus then blessed the food by giving "thanks to God" for it, becoming in effect the head of the family there. Barrett (1978:276) relates the common blessing: "Blessed are thou, O Lord our God, King of the universe, who bringest forth bread from the earth." The synoptic Gospels tell us the disciples distributed the food, while John stays centered on Jesus. He was entirely in charge. The miracle was extravagant, as the people "ate as much as they wanted" to the extent that "everyone was full" (6:11-12). The food for the poor had been turned into a lavish banquet, and they all literally stuffed themselves (the abundance is akin to that of the Cana miracle in ch 2). God's supply is boundless, and he provides beyond anyone's expectation. As Burge points out (2000:194), Jesus was deliberately "fulfilling and re-creating images from Israel's sacred past," underscoring the reality that he is "the provider of food, the source of life for these people."

The incredible bounty of the miracle is seen also in the gathering up of the leftovers. Gathering up the leftovers is a Jewish custom, not so much cleaning up the environment as making sure nothing is wasted (Carson calls this "an ethical note of social responsibility"). There are 12 baskets gathered, presumably one for each of the disciples; the "basket" is a small wicker basket of the type used for carrying provisions when traveling. This makes the point that there is far more left after everyone has been filled than before they started. The fact that there are 12 baskets left after the feeding of the 5,000 (perhaps symbolic of the restoration of the 12 tribes in the 12 disciples, so Borchert, Köstenberger) and seven left after the feeding of the 4,000 (perhaps symbolic of God's perfect work) may be significant (cf. Matt 15:38), for these were certainly important numbers for the early church. But the face value of these statements is quite significant in itself—the numbers probably show simply that God was in control, giving graciously to his people.

As before, the people were overwhelmed by "this miraculous sign" (6:14), but they drew a similar conclusion to that of the Sanhedrin delegation with regard to the Baptist in 1:21, thinking that Jesus was the "prophet like Moses." It is interesting that they centered on the Mosaic Prophet rather than the Messiah, but there is some evidence that segments of Judaism linked the Prophet with the Messiah. This could be signified here with the added "we have been expecting" (lit., "who is to come into the world"), showing they were thinking of the coming Messiah. This would make sense in light of the connection of the multiplication of loaves with the manna that fell in the wilderness in Moses's time (cf. 6:31). The problem, however, is that this was a political cry, and Jesus realized that their true desire was "to force him to be their king." In other words, they wanted Jesus to destroy the Romans and usher in the Kingdom they had been longing for. The Jewish people (and the disciples too) had no idea of a suffering Messiah; they expected only a political Messiah who would conquer their enemies. For them, Isaiah 53 referred to the nation's sufferings, not the coming Messiah. Thus, if Jesus would not go along, they were perfectly willing to "force" him to do so—that is, start a revolt and place him at the head of it by force if necessary. His response was to "[slip] away into the hills by himself"; Jesus knew he was not to be an earthly king, so he withdrew privately.

◆   ## 5. Jesus walks on water (6:16-21)

[16]That evening Jesus' disciples went down to the shore to wait for him. [17]But as darkness fell and Jesus still hadn't come back, they got into the boat and headed across the lake toward Capernaum. [18]Soon a gale swept down upon them, and the sea grew very rough. [19]They had rowed three or four miles* when suddenly they saw Jesus walking on the water toward the boat. They were terrified, [20]but he called out to them, "Don't be afraid. I am here!*" [21]Then they were eager to let him in the boat, and immediately they arrived at their destination!

6:19 Greek *25 or 30 stadia* [4.6 or 5.5 kilometers].   **6:20** Or *The 'I AM' is here;* Greek reads *I am.* See Exod 3:14.

NOTES

6:19 *walking on the water.* Many have said (e.g., Schleiermacher) that Jesus was not walking on the water but on the shore by the sea. Note that this same phrase (*epi tēs thalassēs* [TG2281, ZG2498]) is used with that meaning in 21:1, but the context here does not make this possible. They had rowed several miles onto the sea when Jesus came, and that could hardly allow a scene on shore. If the disciples had stayed near the shore the whole way and saw Jesus there (so Bernard), it is hard to see why they would be so afraid. As Barrett says (1978:281), "There can be little doubt that both Mark and John . . . intended to record a miracle." Whitacre notes there are three ways to view this miracle: (1) a suspension of natural law; (2) Jesus was using nature to accomplish his purposes; (3) a unique supernatural event happened. Any of the three is possible; the main thing is that God was bending the laws of nature to his will.

COMMENTARY

At first glance, it looks as if this story is out of place, for it seemingly interrupts the progression from the multiplication of the bread miracle to Jesus' presentation of himself as the Bread of Life. It actually fits very well, for it identifies Jesus as the divine provider. In a sense, the feeding miracle undergirds the "Bread of Life" aspect of 6:35, and the walking on the water undergirds the "I AM" aspect of 6:35. In Mark 6:45, Jesus made his disciples get into the boat and head across the lake. Here, John records, they went "to the shore to wait for him," and when he didn't come "as darkness fell," they started across the lake. The Sea of Galilee is 13 miles long and seven miles across at the widest part. They were headed across the northern tip, probably about a five-mile journey. On the eastern shore, the lake is ringed by mountains, and often the wind whips through the passes and causes terrible storms with waves several feet high. One of these storms caught the disciples on the way across, and it was a particularly severe one.

They left at about dusk, and Mark tells us (6:48) that Jesus came to them at 3 A.M. They had been rowing for their lives for nine hours, and John said they had only gone three or four miles (6:19), a distance that would normally take only about an hour to row. They were naturally at the end of their strength and filled with terror when suddenly they "saw Jesus walking on the water toward the boat." There are several miracles here. Mark also tells us Jesus was praying up in the hills when he "saw that they were in serious trouble" (6:48). How could he see three or more miles away through a storm? How could he walk to them not just on water but through that same storm? Stilling the storm may have actually been one of the lesser miracles!

Jesus reached them, calmed their fears, and made the key pronouncement: "I am here" (or better, "The I AM is here," or, "I, Yahweh, am here"). Certainly, by itself the phrase means simply, "It's me," but in the context of John with all the absolute uses of *egō eimi* [TG1473/1510, ZG1609/1639] (8:24, 28, 58; 13:19; 18:5), as well as predicated forms like "I am the bread of life" (6:35), it means much more. Brown (1966:536) sees the primary background for its use in Isaiah 43:10, 25; 47:8, 10; 51:12; Hosea 13:4; and Joel 2:27 for "God and God alone" (e.g., Isa 43:10, "to know me, believe in me, and understand that I alone am God"). I would add Exodus 3:13-15, where God gave Moses his covenant name at the burning bush and defined it as, "I AM WHO I AM."

Then comes the third miracle (or fourth, if one includes seeing a great distance through the storm): they let him into the boat, "and immediately they arrived at their destination" (6:21). Notice that the actual stilling of the storm is not mentioned here; instead, they arrived at the shore at once, implying a further miracle. Perhaps the stilling was not mentioned so that the whole emphasis would be on Jesus and who he is rather than on what he did. "Jesus comes to them as the 'I am,' the divine provider, and swiftly takes them to shore—the goal of their journey" (Comfort 1994:71).

◆   ## 6. Jesus, the Bread of Life (6:22-58)

22The next day the crowd that had stayed on the far shore saw that the disciples had taken the only boat, and they realized Jesus had not gone with them. 23Several boats from Tiberias landed near the place where the Lord had blessed the bread and the people had eaten. 24So when the crowd saw that neither Jesus nor his disciples were there, they got into the boats and went across to Capernaum to look for him. ²⁵They found him on the other side of the lake and asked, "Rabbi, when did you get here?"

²⁶Jesus replied, "I tell you the truth, you want to be with me because I fed you, not because you understood the miraculous signs. ²⁷But don't be so concerned about perishable things like food. Spend your energy seeking the eternal life that the Son of Man* can give you. For God the Father has given me the seal of his approval."

²⁸They replied, "We want to perform God's works, too. What should we do?"

²⁹Jesus told them, "This is the only work God wants from you: Believe in the one he has sent."

³⁰They answered, "Show us a miraculous sign if you want us to believe in you. What can you do? ³¹After all, our ancestors ate manna while they journeyed through the wilderness! The Scriptures say, 'Moses gave them bread from heaven to eat.'*"

³²Jesus said, "I tell you the truth, Moses didn't give you bread from heaven. My Father did. And now he offers you the true bread from heaven. ³³The true bread of God is the one who comes down from heaven and gives life to the world."

³⁴"Sir," they said, "give us that bread every day."

³⁵Jesus replied, "I am the bread of life. Whoever comes to me will never be hungry again. Whoever believes in me will never be thirsty. ³⁶But you haven't believed in me even though you have seen me. ³⁷However, those the Father has given me will come to me, and I will never reject them. ³⁸For I have come down from heaven to do the will of God who sent me, not to do my own will. ³⁹And this is the will of God, that I should not lose even one of all those he has given me, but that I should raise them up at the last day. ⁴⁰For it is my Father's will that all who see his Son and believe in him should have eternal life. I will raise them up at the last day."

⁴¹Then the people* began to murmur in disagreement because he had said, "I am the bread that came down from heaven." ⁴²They said, "Isn't this Jesus, the son of Joseph? We know his father and mother. How can he say, 'I came down from heaven'?"

⁴³But Jesus replied, "Stop complaining about what I said. ⁴⁴For no one can come to me unless the Father who sent me draws them to me, and at the last day I will raise them up. ⁴⁵As it is written in the Scriptures,* 'They will all be taught by God.' Everyone who listens to the Father and learns from him comes to me. ⁴⁶(Not that anyone has ever seen the Father; only I, who was sent from God, have seen him.)

⁴⁷"I tell you the truth, anyone who believes has eternal life. ⁴⁸Yes, I am the bread of life! ⁴⁹Your ancestors ate manna in the wilderness, but they all died. ⁵⁰Anyone who eats the bread from heaven, however, will never die. ⁵¹I am the living bread that came down from heaven. Anyone who eats this bread will live forever; and this bread, which I will offer so the world may live, is my flesh."

⁵²Then the people began arguing with each other about what he meant. "How can this man give us his flesh to eat?" they asked.

⁵³So Jesus said again, "I tell you the truth, unless you eat the flesh of the Son of Man and drink his blood, you cannot have eternal life within you. ⁵⁴But anyone who eats my flesh and drinks my blood has eternal life, and I will raise that person at the last day. ⁵⁵For my flesh is true food, and my blood is true drink. ⁵⁶Anyone who eats my flesh and drinks my blood remains in me, and I in him. ⁵⁷I live because of the living Father who sent me; in the same way, anyone who feeds on me will live because of me. ⁵⁸I am the true bread that came down from heaven. Anyone who eats this bread will not die as your ancestors did (even though they ate the manna) but will live forever."

6:27 "Son of Man" is a title Jesus used for himself.   **6:31** Exod 16:4; Ps 78:24.   **6:41** Greek *Jewish people;* also in 6:52.   **6:45** Greek *in the prophets.* Isa 54:13.

NOTES

6:27 *the seal of his approval.* Some (Westcott, Hoskyns, Morris) read this as a Jewish metaphor for Jesus as the acceptable sacrifice, "sealed" as the perfect victim. This is unlikely; the more frequent use of "seal" is preferable (cf. commentary on 6:27).

6:33 *the one who comes down from heaven.* The descent-ascent motif is very important in John (cf. Köstenberger 1998a:121-130). Jesus is the one who has "come down from heaven," and he will soon return there. This begins in 1:9; 3:19 with the Light coming into the world and forcing division so that the blind are given sight and "those who think they see" are shown to be blind (9:39). The two ideas together begin in 1:51 with the idea of the angels ascending and descending on Jesus, with the thrust that Jesus has united heaven and earth. Then in 3:13 they occur for the first time as a reference to Jesus as the glorified Son of Man. According to Köstenberger (1998a:126), ascent-descent is part of a "journey theme" with Jesus' fourth trip to Jerusalem presented as a journey back to the Father via the cross. His descent centers on his mission to call the world to God, and it will be met with controversy and widespread rejection. His ascent back to God is a return to glory and vindication.

6:36-40 Brown (1966:275-276, following Léon-Dufour), finds a chiasm here:
  A. seeing and not believing (6:36)
    B. not driving out what the Father has given (6:37)
      C. I have come down from heaven (6:38)
    B'. losing nothing of what he has given (6:39)
  A'. looking and believing (6:40)

6:37 *those the Father has given me will come to me.* Arminian theology accepts the doctrine of predestination but asserts that it occurs on the basis of foreknowledge (Rom 8:29; 1 Pet 1:2)—that is, God knew beforehand who would respond to the Spirit's convicting power via faith-decision, and he chose them. On predestination according to foreknowledge, see Osborne 2003:221-222.

6:39 *I should not lose even one.* Arminians accept the security of the believer but believe it is conditional rather than unconditional—that is, God keeps believers secure, but we are responsible to avail ourselves of his power. In John, there are not only the examples of 6:60-66 and 17:12 but the warning passage of 15:1-6, stating that if those who are in Jesus quit bearing fruit, they will be "thrown away . . . wither . . . [and be] gathered into a pile to be burned." Outside John, Arminians appeal to such passages as Heb 6:4-6; 10:26-31; Jas 5:19-20; 2 Pet 2:20-21; 1 John 5:16. In other words, they believe that God keeps us secure but that there is a real danger of rejecting his security and turning our backs on Christ. As Witherington says, "God's role in the relationship is incomparably greater than the human one, but the fact remains that God does not and will not save a person without the positive human response, called faith, to the divine leading and drawing" (1995:158).

at the last day. It is strange that so many higher critics separate John's realized eschatology (the present gift of eternal life) from his final eschatology (the final resurrection), as if they were somehow contradictory. Both are found clearly in his Gospel (for final eschatology, see 5:28-29; 14:2-3; 21:22-23, as well as 6:39-40, 44, 54) and are interdependent. Future security is the natural extension of present protection. The God who watches over us now will continue to do so until "the last day."

6:51 *this bread . . . is my flesh.* This is similar to the words of institution at the Last Supper (Mark 14:22, "This is my body") and appears eucharistic at first glance. However, it probably was not intended as such by Jesus since he said it long before the Last Supper and used "flesh" rather than "body." The arguments for a eucharistic connotation (e.g., "flesh" is the more primitive form of "body") are usually linked to the view that this is a later addition rather than a record of the actual words of Jesus, but this explanation is unnecessary (against a sacramental interpretation see Morris, Carson, Ridderbos, Burge, Blomberg,

Keener, Köstenberger). As Kysar points out (1986:108-109), it is possible that sacramental overtones were originally present, but there is little evidence for such in the text here and even less evidence of eucharistic allusions elsewhere in John.

6:56 *remains in me, and I in him.* The theme of "abiding" or "remaining in" occurs in many ways in John and is translated variously by the NLT. The Gr. *menō* [TG3306, ZG3531] (abide) occurs, for example, in 5:38; 6:27; 14:10; 14:17; 15:4, 5, 7; 15:9-10. In these contexts it primarily characterizes the relationship between the Father, Son, Spirit, and believer.

COMMENTARY

The theme of this section is Jesus' demand that everyone experience a total encounter with him as the Bread of Life. The event occurs at Passover (6:4) and is preceded by two nature miracles that prepare for his claim to be the living bread that must be consumed by all who believe. The first, the multiplication of loaves (6:1-14), establishes him as the giver of manna who satisfies the multitudes. The Exodus typology is foremost, as seen in the mention of Passover (6:4) and the crowds' exclamation of him as the "prophet like Moses" (6:14). The second establishes him as the "I am" (6:20)—that is, the Bread of Life is Yahweh himself. It supports the sign of the feeding by establishing Jesus' divine status and helping presence (so Schnackenburg). In the Exodus story, God gave the manna to the people, and here the God-man does the same. This prepares for the claim itself (6:35), after which Jesus demands that he be consumed completely (6:53-58) by anyone who wants eternal life. Jesus has been presented as life-giver and judge (ch 5) and now anchors this in the facts that he alone can provide life and that he forces all to a decision, resulting in the judgment of all who refuse to believe.

In 5:21-29, Jesus described himself as the life-giver as a result of his relationship with his Father; those who come to him in faith will find eternal life. This discourse expands on both these elements of that seminal speech in chapter 5. Jesus gives life because he is the Bread of Life, and people find that life only by consuming him totally. While it is common to consider this an artificially constructed sermon in several stages of redaction (e.g., Bultmann, Schnackenburg) by different authors, it is more and more common to see this as a well-constructed unity (e.g., Borgen, Lindars, Carson, Ridderbos, Blomberg). The organization of the discourse is much debated. Perhaps the best approach is to see this as a Jewish midrashic homily, an idea developed especially by Borgen (1965:59-98) and basically accepted by many others (Brown, Barrett, Schnackenburg, Ridderbos). This is valid because 6:59 labels the passage as a synagogue address. Thus, I take 6:22-24 as the setting of the discourse; 6:25-29 as the introduction, centering on the work that produces life; 6:30-34 as the central Pentateuchal citation on bread from heaven; 6:35-50 as a midrashic homily on Jesus as the Bread of Life; and 6:51-58 on the consequent need to consume his flesh and his blood. There is some question regarding where the synagogue address begins. Since many synagogue messages involved dialog such as is found throughout this passage, it is likely that the discourse begins with the first question in 6:25. The hint of the text is that the entire dialog takes place in the synagogue.

Setting for the Discourse (6:22-24). The synagogue setting reintroduces the crowd and tells us the audience for the discourse. They were still on the shore where the miracle occurred and opposite to where Jesus and the disciples had gone. They suddenly realize two things—the boat was gone with the disciples, and Jesus did not go with the disciples but was also gone. Fortunately for them, just at that moment some boats from the town of Tiberias (cf. note on 6:1) south of Capernaum arrived, and they obtained a ride over to Capernaum. The boats may well have come for the people or been driven ashore by the storm; whichever, they came just in time to take the crowd "across to Capernaum to look for" Jesus. Capernaum was Jesus' headquarters for his Galilean ministry (Mark 1:21; 9:33); he had probably moved there from Nazareth after his messianic ministry began. The feeding miracle had captured the crowd's attention, and they, like the "many" in 2:23 and Nicodemus in 3:1-2, wanted to know more about Jesus.

The Work That Produces Life (6:25-29). When the crowd finally found Jesus, they called him "Rabbi," a far cry from the king they wanted to crown the day before, though this acknowledged him as a teacher. Still, their reaction to his teaching in the ensuing verses will show the irony of their depiction of him. Their question asks both "when" he arrived and how long he had been there. There is a certain challenge implicit in it—how could he have left them back in Tiberias like that? Jesus refused to answer their question (as often in John), and instead his response is quite negative and fits with 2:24-25—he did not believe in them, for he knew their hearts. This is another double *amēn* [TG281, ZG297] saying—"I tell you the truth"—indicating a serious and important truth. He pointed to the fact that their interest was entirely earthly, centering on the "food" they received, rather than heavenly, centering on the significance of the "signs." This does not mean they failed to see the miracle, for they called him the messianic Prophet and tried to make him the kingly Messiah (6:14-15), but they misunderstood the true significance of the sign (and we must remember the meaning of "sign")—namely, that it pointed to Jesus not as a miracle worker but as the Bread of Life. A true sign demands an encounter with Jesus, and that is exactly the topic of 6:35-50.

Their problem was their consuming interest in "perishable things like food" (6:27). The message here is similar to Jesus' challenge of the Samaritan woman. He told her that the water she offered would only make her thirst again, while the "living water" he offered would be a "fresh, bubbling spring," yielding "eternal life" (4:13-14). In similar fashion, he told the crowd that they should stop seeking perishable food but instead go after "the eternal life that the Son of Man can give you." That is the only thing worthy of their "energy." Literally, this says that they should "work for the food" that produces eternal life. It is interesting that eternal life is both work (our part) and gift (Christ's part), concepts often thought of as opposing one another (so Whitacre). Here is another paradox: faith is not a work (Eph 2:8-9), but the only work God will allow is the act of faith (6:29).

This challenge is as valid today as in Jesus' time. Too many Christians, let alone unbelievers, are wasting their time pursuing only the temporary "treasures here on earth" and ignoring the "treasures in heaven" (Matt 6:19-21). The only source of real value is the Son of Man, the one who united heaven and earth (1:51; 3:13) and was appointed by God as Savior (3:17; 4:42) and judge (5:27). The reason Christ can do this is that his Father has placed "the seal of his approval" on him, which could refer to his incarnation or baptism but probably is meant more generally (the aorist verb translated "has given . . . the seal" is global, referring to Jesus' ministry as a whole). Christ bears God's royal seal and so is his official agent or envoy (cf. the "sent one" passages; e.g., 3:17, 34; 5:23-24, 36, 38, as well as 6:29, 38 below).

The crowd picked up on the idea of working for eternal life and asked how they could "perform God's works" as well—that is, those deeds God requires for salvation (6:28). As usual, they misunderstood and thought of earning something from God, entirely ignoring the major truth that eternal life is a divine gift rather than something to be earned. They were, in effect, asking Jesus to give them a grocery list of things they could do. Again, this is a common error today, as people attend church and become active in its work, hoping to buy or earn their way into heaven. Jesus' response went directly to the point: The only work God requires is faith! Eternal life is not something that can be earned by works.

Jesus is the heaven-sent envoy from God (cf. 6:27), and he alone is the source of salvation. People can find eternal life only by believing in him. As Carson brings out (1991:285), this is indistinguishable from Paul, who says that a person is "made right with God through faith and not by obeying the law" (Rom 3:28).

Bread from Heaven (6:30-34). Jesus had spoken with authority greater than what the crowd was used to (cf. Mark 1:21-22), so they asked for an authenticating sign in order to "believe in" him (Keener [2003:676] notes how this reiterates 2:18). He declared himself greater than Moses, who was also sent from God (5:45-47), and they had already wondered whether he might be the messianic Prophet predicted by Moses (6:14). They asked for further proof. It is amazing that the feeding miracle, linked as it is to the manna in the wilderness, would not suffice (let alone all the other sign-miracles). Moses did not control the manna but received it as a gift from God (Exod 16:4-5, 15-16), but Jesus did control the second, great manna gift. The key, of course, is that they had not understood the "sign" itself and so wanted more. The manna perished in the wilderness and the bread Jesus provided sufficed for only one meal, so they sat asking for a greater "miraculous sign." They perhaps desired a heavenly portent like that mentioned in Matthew 12:38 and 16:1 but, more likely, another manna miracle, for they went on to talk about the manna in the wilderness that their ancestors ate. This expectation is exemplified in *Midrash Rabbah on Ecclesiastes* 1:9: "As the former redeemer caused manna to descend . . . so will the later Redeemer [the Messiah] cause manna to descend" (so Whitacre). The concluding "What can you do?" is taken by Derrett (1993:143) as an allusion to Isaiah 45:9 (LXX), where the pot (Israel) asks a similar question of the potter (God). Israel, in Isaiah 45:9, is also guilty of unbelief; in this sense, the unbelief of Israel directed at Jesus is equivalent to their unbelief against God in Isaiah.

It is commonly agreed that the quotation in 6:31b is the center of this section

("Moses gave them bread from heaven to eat") and directly prepares for Jesus' self-assertion in 6:35. There is no single Old Testament passage corresponding to this quote. It is probably an amalgamation of Exodus 16:4, Nehemiah 9:15, and Psalm 78:24-25. The idea of "bread from heaven" has a double meaning: both the manna from heaven in Exodus and the new heavenly reality Jesus has introduced (1:51; 3:13, 31). The crowd understood only the former, but the latter is inferred in the larger context. Jesus responded with his customary "I tell you the truth" for an important message. First, he corrected their misinterpretation of Scripture regarding Moses and the manna (a common rabbinic technique): "Moses didn't give you the bread from heaven. My Father did" (again, see Exod 16:4-5, 15-16). Second, in the Greek Jesus says, "My Father does" (present tense), implying that the gift of manna is an ongoing gift, now given through God's Son (as in the feeding miracle). This becomes the basis for 6:33, when Jesus will identify himself as that heavenly gift. Third, the manna in the wilderness is earthly and perishable like the "food" of 6:27. The Father's gift is "the true bread from heaven" (note the switch to the new heavenly reality noted above) that will never cease.

In 6:33, Jesus explicitly identifies "the true bread of God" (the point of 6:32) as himself: "the one who comes down from heaven and gives life to the world" (6:33). Note the two emphases of this section—Jesus provides the bread (6:27, 33), and he is the bread (6:33, 35). This sums up several themes in John thus far. First, he is the one who "comes down" from heaven, as implied in the prologue (the Word "with God" in 1:1, 2 who becomes incarnate in 1:14) and stated explicitly in 1:51; 3:13, 31. This will be a major theme in this discourse (7 occurences, cf. 6:38, 41, 42, 50, 51, 58). Jesus' true origin was heaven, and God has "sent" him from there to earth as his official representative. Second, Jesus as the provider of life has also been a key motif, beginning with the prologue (1:4, "the Word gave life") and occurring often elsewhere (3:15, 16, 36; 4:14; 5:21, 24, 26, 29, 39-40; 6:27). It too will become a dominating theme in this discourse (6:35, 40, 47, 48, 51, 53, 54). Third, the focus shifts from the Jews to "the world," a concept also seen in the prologue (1:9, 10) and later chapters (1:29; 3:16, 17, 19; 4:42; 6:14). It is emphasized again in 6:51 ("so the world may live"). The message of the fourth Gospel is that salvation comes for Jew and Gentile alike on the basis of faith rather than pedigree (cf. Rom 3:21-4:25). It is clear that Jesus' claim here is thematic for the rest of the Bread of Life discourse. The crowd missed the fact that Jesus declared himself to be the living bread and believed he was offering them the miraculous sign they requested in 6:30. Like the Samaritan woman (4:15), they asked Jesus to give them "that bread every day," expecting him to expand on the manna of Exodus and give them the life they sought. "Every day" (*pantote* [TG3842, ZG4121]) could mean they wanted it regularly repeated (Lenski, Schnackenburg), but more likely it means they thought of a heavenly once-for-all gift that would be with them always (Barrett, Morris). They still did not understand that it could only come from faith in Jesus.

Jesus as the Bread of Life (6:35-40). Jesus had stated fairly clearly that he was the bread from heaven in 6:33; now he states it decisively: "I am the bread of life." The whole chapter thus far has pointed to this proclamation, and everything following is a clarification of its significance. This is the first of seven "I am" statements, all highly theological—the Light of the World (8:12), the gate (10:7, 9), the Good Shepherd (10:11, 14), the resurrection and the life (11:25), the way, truth, and life (14:6), and the true Vine (15:5). These seven descriptions fill out the significance of the absolute "I am" statements (cf. commentary on 6:20) and define the person and mission of the divine Son (on the historicity of these sayings, see Blomberg 2001:124). This first one presents him as the only food that can provide eternal life ("of life" is an objective genitive, "the bread that produces life"). The two statements that follow tell how people can find this life. To have this eternal food, we must "come" and "believe." The two terms are virtual synonyms—coming to Jesus is believing. The subject of consuming this bread does not come until 6:51ff. The idea of coming/believing, therefore, has priority over the idea of eating/drinking (so Carson). The only way to find life is to believe in Jesus (3:16; 5:24). In a sense, this combines the bread metaphor ("never be hungry again") with the living water metaphor of 4:14 ("never be thirsty again") and prepares for the image of eating Jesus' flesh and drinking his blood in 6:53-56. This same idea is found again in 7:37, where the "thirsty" must "come."

This passage defines the divine and the human sides of salvation. In that sense, it combines the Arminian and the Calvinist systems. The human side is to "come" and "believe," and the divine side is that God "draws" the believers to Jesus (6:44), gives them to him (6:37, 39), and keeps them secure (6:40, 44). The problem with the crowd was that they refused to believe even though they had seen what he said and did. This is the same unbelief seen in 1:11; 3:19-20; and especially 5:38, 46-47. They had seen the sign of the feeding miracle and still asked for more (6:30). They had heard Jesus explaining who he was and still failed to understand or accept his words.

In 6:37-40, Jesus stated why they had not found faith—they were not of God. This is one of the great passages of Scripture on the sovereignty of God in salvation. The reality that the majority of Jesus' countrymen rejected God's plan of salvation and turned their backs on Jesus did not discourage him, for God was still in charge. In fact, "those the Father has given [Jesus] will come to [him]" (6:37). There is a two-way street here. Jesus brings people to God, but they already belong to God and are God's gift to Jesus. The doctrine behind this is called predestination, the view that God has chosen believers from before the foundation of the world, and they will come to Jesus. The point is that God is very aware of those who refuse to believe, and it does not damage his plan at all. The elect will come, and God's purpose will be shown. Moreover, following predestination, Jesus alluded to the security of the believer: "I will never reject them" means that Jesus will preserve his followers. They belong to God, are given to Jesus, and Jesus not only accepts them but also watches over them.

This new sovereign power in salvation is anchored in the will of God (6:38-40). Christ already spoke of the will of God in 4:34, where he said his food (similar imagery to this passage) is "doing the will of God," which he defined as his mission to gather a harvest of souls. Here also he states that he came down from heaven to "do the will of God who sent me" (6:38). Jesus was "sent" as God's sovereignly appointed envoy, a major emphasis in this section (cf. 6:27, 29, 39, 44, 57); as such, his origin is heavenly, and he has descended to earth (cf. note on 6:33) for the sole purpose of obeying his Father's will rather than his own (cf. 5:30). His mission is an act of obedience, and it is the result of complete unity between Father and Son. God guarantees that Jesus "should not lose even one of all those he has given me." This tells how Jesus will preserve his followers. Note the progression—God gives them in 6:37 and protects them in 6:39 (this is elaborated further in 6:44). This is realized eschatology, as God ensures the present security of all Jesus' true followers. Yet there is also a final eschatology, as Jesus will "raise them up at the last day." Their ultimate future is also guaranteed.

Verse 40 summarizes the themes stated in 6:35-39. "All who see his Son and believe in him" (cf. 6:35) "have eternal life" in the present (cf. 6:37, 39a) and the guaranteed promise of final resurrection "at the last day" (cf. 6:39b). We again see both sides of the salvation debate—human decision ("see/believe") and sovereign protection ("my Father's will"). Note the exceptions in 6:60-66 (the apostasy of "many of his disciples") and 17:12 ("not one was lost, except the one headed for destruction"). The question is whether these were true followers of Christ. For Judas, the answer is "no," but for the disciples in 6:60-66, the answer is "possibly" (cf. comments on 2:23-25). The final balance between the security and responsibility of the believer, between divine sovereignty and the will of the individual, is a mystery and will remain so until we enter eternity. Still, John's Gospel is the perfect book for working out the debate between Arminianism and Calvinism, for both sides are present here and must be held in tension.

Debate with the Jews (6:41-46). The debate with the crowd in the synagogue continued, as they began to "murmur in disagreement" because Jesus had identified himself as the bread from heaven. This is similar to 5:17-18, where the leaders plotted to kill him because he had made himself equal with God. The language of murmuring against Jesus may allude to the wilderness murmurings against God (Exod 15:24; 16:2, 7; 17:3), which were seen as unbelief (Ps 105:24-25, LXX) and disobedience toward God (Isa 30:12). They ignored his claim to be the life-giver and centered only on his assertion that he had descended from heaven. Their opposition flowed out of their knowledge of Jesus' humble origins as "the son of Joseph." Since they knew his parents, they could hardly accept his claim to come from heaven. It may well be that Jesus' family moved to Capernaum with him (so Carson), and thus his parents were well known (if Joseph lived this long). This was a common objection to Jesus' claims (cf. Mark 6:3; Luke 4:22) and showed the people's ignorance of him. As always, they focused only on the earthly and ignored the heavenly.

Jesus responded by repeating what he had just said in 6:37 but with one very important difference. Their complaints should cease (6:43) because they could never find God that way (as their ancestors had proven). In fact, they could only find life if they came in God's way. In 6:37, believers were "given" to Jesus by God, and here we see that they were drawn by God, and only then could they come to

Jesus. Once more, salvation is sovereignly controlled by God, and only those brought to faith by God can come. This is a reference to the convicting power of the Spirit, but it goes beyond that to describe the whole process of salvation. Calvinists have called this "irresistible grace," and Morris (1995:371) argues that the drawing power of God is always successful. This might go too far, however, for in 12:32 Jesus says he will "draw everyone to [himself]," and he was hardly teaching universalism. Still, 6:44 refers to God's control of salvation and to the security of the believer, for Jesus also repeats the promise that he will raise them at the last day (cf. 6:39, 40). Jesus was saying that a person's rejection of him was a rejection of God's drawing, and that would mean death for them.

Jesus anchored his assertion regarding God's drawing his chosen in a free translation of Isaiah 54:13: "They will all be taught by God" (6:45). This is one of the new covenant passages (cf. Isa 42:6; 54:10; Jer 31:31-34; Ezek 36:26) in which God promises a glorious future for Zion. At that time, his people will find a new, direct, internal relationship with him. Jesus was saying that his followers constitute that new community and fulfill the prophecies to that effect. The "all" includes the world (6:14, 33, NASB) as a whole, Jew and Gentile. Applying this to his Jewish listeners, he once more centered on the basis of their unbelief: only those who listen and learn can come to Jesus (6:45). There have now been four synonymous metaphors for conversion—"see" and "believe" in 6:40, as well as "listen" and "learn" here. All the senses are involved—the eyes, the heart, the ears, and the mind. Conversion is a total process in which God captures and involves the whole person in a holistic change from the earthly to the heavenly. The Jewish people had been unwilling, and they rejected the divine call at every level. To clarify the means by which God teaches, Jesus then added that he is the only path to knowing God. Repeating the message of 1:18 and 5:37, he stated that no one but him has ever seen the Father. He is the only revelatory means of seeing God or finding salvation; it is Jesus who reveals God (1:18; 14:6-7).

Summary on the Bread of Life (6:47-50). For the seventh time, Jesus uses the double *amēn* [TG281, ZG297] ("I tell you the truth") to highlight a significant saying (6:47). The saying summarizes a major theme (found in 3:15, 16, 36; 5:24; 6:35, 40) that only those who come to faith in Jesus have eternal life. Faith is the only possible approach, for Jesus is truly the only "bread" that can bring one to "life." This is the reason the Jewish listeners had no access to the life from God—they had no faith. Salvation is not based on one's religious pedigree or good works or relation to the law. It is based entirely on one's relationship to "the bread of life." Jesus returned to the issue of the "manna in the wilderness" that has dominated the chapter (6:31-32) since the feeding miracle and its fulfillment of the manna. Like all "perishable things" (6:27), manna kept the Israelites alive for a while, but it was unable to sustain life forever, so all who ate it eventually "died" (6:49). There is only one path to everlasting life—namely, to "[eat] the bread from heaven" (6:50). This prepares the reader especially for the following section in which Jesus will deepen his demands as to what eating means. Manna, like all food, could only sustain life for a short period. The message is the same today as it was then: Watch your diet closely. Be careful what you eat! A truly healthy diet in the heavenly sense must center upon true soul food—the Bread of Life.

Eating the Flesh and Drinking the Blood of the Son of Man (6:51-58). This is a much-debated section, primarily in regard to the sacramental overtones of this passage. It must be said, however, that there is little evidence that Jesus would have intended this in a sacramental way; the language is just not there. Most who take it that way think it an addition by the later church, but this is erroneous. Christ's purpose here was to culminate his insistence on encountering him as God's envoy by saying here that it must be a total encounter. There are actually three emphases in the passage (in order of importance): (1) Primarily, it anchors the teaching of the discourse as a whole—namely, that one must consume Jesus, the Bread of Life, completely to be his true follower. Halfhearted commitment is not enough (cf. esp. 6:53-56). (2) This points forward to Jesus' death, when he would yield his "flesh" for the world (6:51) and become "the Lamb of God who takes away the sin of the world" (1:29). (3) John and his readers would likely see sacramental significance in the imagery, and so it may well be present but secondary. In 6:48, Jesus summed up the discourse by affirming himself again as "the bread of life" (cf. 6:35), and here he addresses two other critical aspects of what this means (6:51a-b) and then provides a new aspect of its meaning (6:51c). Jesus slightly alters the key phrase and calls himself "the living bread," paralleling 4:10 where he offers the Samaritan woman "living water." This is the sixth of seven times in this chapter that Jesus is described as coming down from heaven (6:33, 38, 41, 42, 50, 51, 58), further emphasizing the important theme that his true origin is heaven. The salvation he has brought is "from above" (3:3, NLT mg), not of the earth. Further, what is at stake is eternal life, not just earthly nourishment (cf. 6:27, 33, 35, 40, 47, 48, 53, 54, 57, 58). It is clear that the primary message of this discourse is that the only path to eternal life is to partake of the Bread of Life because that alone is heavenly rather than earthly in origin and so provides eternal rather than temporal life.

Jesus added the new truth, stating, "This bread, which I will offer so the world may live, is my flesh." This becomes the theme for this final section of the discourse. It refers to Jesus' passion. The "Word [that] became flesh" (1:14, NLT mg) will give his "flesh" on the cross "so the world may live." In 6:33 Jesus said, "The true bread . . . gives life to the world," and now he speaks to how that will come to pass. The great paradox of Christianity is that life comes through death. Jesus died so that we may live, and we live by dying to this world (Rom 6:4-6). Moreover, the Greek says that Jesus dies "for (*huper* [TG5228, ZG5642]) the life of the world," and this preposition probably signifies substitutionary atonement—that Jesus is a vicarious sacrifice "for" the world. It is used in this way in the eucharistic saying of Mark 14:24 ("This is my blood . . . poured out as a sacrifice *for many*"), and the preposition is found in sacrificial contexts throughout John's Gospel (10:11, 15; 11:50-52; 15:13; 17:19; so Barrett). Our "life" has its basis in Jesus' atoning sacrifice, and we appropriate it by faith—that is, by eating the bread, by trusting in his fleshly sacrifice that atones for our sin.

This led to further debate (6:52), as the people in the synagogue started arguing sharply (stronger than the "murmur" in 6:41) over how Jesus could "give us his flesh to eat," reminiscent of Israel's striving with Moses (so Schnackenburg, Borchert). Again, they were thinking from an earthly perspective and could not understand the heavenly reality. As John Chrysostom points out (*Homilies on John* 46.2), "When questioning concerning the 'how' comes in, there comes in with it unbelief." Jesus' response develops significantly what he meant when he spoke of the need to "[eat] the bread from heaven" (6:50). As another solemn truth (note the double *amēn* [TG281, ZG297]; cf. 6:47), this is especially important. In fact, 6:53-56 form the climax of this narrative. He shocked them to the core of their being when he said they must "eat the flesh of the Son of Man and drink his blood." The first half may well go back to the Passover Lamb of 1:29. The Torah said that after the sacrifice, the lamb was to be wholly consumed, every part (Exod 12:9-10). Also, "flesh and blood" is a Jewish idiom for the whole person (so Brown). Jesus' point was that the encounter must be total, but by adding "drink his blood," Jesus invoked a strange and scandalous (even repulsive) element that deepened the point. God had forbidden the Jews to drink blood (Gen 9:4; Lev 7:26-27). The early church was concerned enough about this that the Jerusalem council asked Gentiles Christians (who had no such rule) to respect Jewish sensitivities and not drink blood in their presence (Acts 15:28-29). Since blood signifies violent death in Scripture (so Carson), Jesus' comment was a clear reference to his death on the cross. Jesus used very strong metaphors to say that only the one who wholly surrenders to Jesus and his death "has eternal life." Secondarily, Christians who read this would certainly think of the Lord's Supper. Jesus, however, did not intend a sacramental reading. This statement does not point forward to the Lord's Supper; rather, the Lord's Supper draws significance from its truth about the necessity of Jesus' death.

To make certain they understood his message, Jesus clarified that his flesh and blood were "true food" and "true drink" (6:55). This means that his flesh and blood really are what food is meant to be; they are archetypal food in its truest sense (so Barrett). Food and drink sustain life, but Jesus' flesh and blood provide everlasting life. This is because anyone who partakes of Jesus wholly "remains in him," and he remains in them. This is called "mutual indwelling" and is another key theme in John's writings (cf. 14:20; 15:4-7; 1 John 2:24; 3:24; 4:15). The Father and the Son share completely in this way (10:38; 14:20; 17:11, 21), and when we become one with the Son, we share in that union. This produces a dynamic day-by-day union and fellowship with the Son that will always be at work in us.

All of this is dependent on the relationship between the Father and the Son and the relationship of both to life (as in ch 5). God is "the living Father," the one who is life and who gives life. He is also the Father who "sent" Jesus as his official envoy (cf. 6:29, 38, 39, 44). Therefore, Jesus lives because of him (6:57)—that is, Jesus finds his source of life and mission from his Father. This goes back to 1:14: "The Word became human and made his home among us." The incarnate God-man draws his life from the Father but has also been given authority over that life in his mission (5:21, 25-26), so in turn he becomes the source of life for anyone who feeds on him. Since Jesus is the Bread of Life (6:35), the only way to have eternal life is to "eat" that bread—that is, encounter him wholly and come to faith. Note the progression: the "living Father" is the source of life for Jesus, and Jesus is the source of life for us. This is because Jesus is "the true bread . . . from heaven," a title that combines the idea that he is "the bread of life" (6:35, 48) with the idea that he has "come down from heaven" (6:33, 38, 41, 42, 51).

The message of the Bread of Life discourse is simple and yet the most important truth in human history: eternal life is available only to those who partake of Jesus by coming to faith in him.

◆   ## 7. Division among Jesus' disciples (6:59-71)

[59]He said these things while he was teaching in the synagogue in Capernaum. [60]Many of his disciples said, "This is very hard to understand. How can anyone accept it?"

[61]Jesus was aware that his disciples were complaining, so he said to them, "Does this offend you? [62]Then what will you think if you see the Son of Man ascend to heaven again? [63]The Spirit alone gives eternal life. Human effort accomplishes nothing. And the very words I have spoken to you are spirit and life. [64]But some of you do not believe me." (For Jesus knew from the beginning which ones didn't believe, and he knew who would betray him.) [65]Then he said, "That is why I said that people can't come to me unless the Father gives them to me."

[66]At this point many of his disciples turned away and deserted him. [67]Then Jesus turned to the Twelve and asked, "Are you also going to leave?"

[68]Simon Peter replied, "Lord, to whom would we go? You have the words that give eternal life. [69]We believe, and we know you are the Holy One of God.*"

[70]Then Jesus said, "I chose the twelve of you, but one is a devil." [71]He was speaking of Judas, son of Simon Iscariot, one of the Twelve, who would later betray him.

6:69 Other manuscripts read *you are the Christ, the Holy One of God;* still others read *you are the Christ, the Son of God;* and still others read *you are the Christ, the Son of the living God.*

NOTES

6:60 *hard to understand.* Carson (1991:300) points out four things that made it so hard: (1) they were more interested in food, politics, and miracles than in spiritual realities; (2) they were unwilling to surrender their own autonomy in order to come in faith; (3) they were offended by Jesus' claims to be greater than Moses and to have authority to give life; and (4) they were even more offended by the metaphors of eating his flesh and drinking his blood.

6:62 *what will you think.* The actual sentence is not finished; the "if" clause has no "then" clause, so Jesus could mean this in either a positive (you will be more convinced) or negative way (you will be more offended). This conditional clause is best understood as deliberately ambiguous and meant both ways. Those who have faith will be more persuaded; those who do not will be even more scandalized.

6:66 *turned away and deserted him.* The debate over the possibility of apostasy (cf. also note on 6:39) is in some ways a dangerous one. Calvinists stress the impossibility and so offer security to those who should not have it, and Arminians often stress the likelihood of it and produce a generation of neurotic Christians who think they have lost their salvation at the drop of a hat. The truth is in the middle. Members of the church will apostatize (15:1-6; Heb 6:4-6), and the only debate is whether those who do so were ever true believers or not. Calvinists and Arminians alike should use passages like this to warn the wavering "Christians" (we do not know whether they are true believers or not) in their church of a very real danger. The truth is that Arminians need to preach the security passages more, and Calvinists need to preach the warning passages more. Followers of both systems are spiritually truncated as a result of this lack of balance.

6:69 *Holy One of God.* Various mss differ regarding this title, with some reading "the Christ, the Holy One of God" ($\mathfrak{P}$66 cop^{sa,bo,ac2}), others "the Christ, the Son of God" (C^3 038 f^1 33 it^{a,c,e} syr^s), and still others "the Christ, the Son of the Living God" (038^c 0250 f^{13} syr^{p,h} $\mathfrak{M}$). It is generally agreed that the simpler "Holy One of God," supported by good mss ($\mathfrak{P}$75 $\aleph$ B C* D L W it^d), is original, with the other changes introduced by assimilation to Peter's confession at Caesarea Philippi in Matt 16:16.

COMMENTARY

This section has two parts: the first pertains to the unfaithful disciples who deserted Jesus (6:60-66), and the second to the faithful ones who remained loyal to him (6:67-71). Jesus' ministry caused division; as the living Revealer of the Father (cf. on "Word" in 1:1), he presented every person with the light of God (1:4, 7, 9; 3:18-21). In these encounters, here could be no neutrality; everyone becomes part of either darkness or light. All halfhearted disciples (2:23-25) eventually must make a final choice, and that is what happens in this passage. The hard sayings of Jesus in 6:22-58 (esp. 6:51-58) forced final choices, and many of his disciples departed.

The setting for all of this was a synagogue in Capernaum (6:24, 59). Many of the participants consisted of the wider circle of Jesus' "disciples," probably a group similar to that noted in 2:23-25—those who began to "trust in [Jesus]" even though he did not "trust in" them. They were similar to the plants in the rocky soil and the thorny ground in the parable of the sower (Mark 4:5-7, 16-19); as soon as troubles came, they wilted. These disciples found Jesus' teaching in this discourse not only "hard to understand" (6:60; lit., it is a "hard word") but also virtually impossible to accept.

The "complaining" of these disciples (6:61) parallels that of the Jews in 6:41-42 and the Israelites in the wilderness. Jesus confronted them with their own darkness by saying that if his words offended them, they would be even more disturbed when they saw "the Son of Man ascend to heaven again." The Cross and Resurrection are seen as a stumbling block or offense in John 16:1 (so also 1 Cor 1:23; Gal 5:11; 1 Pet 2:8). Jesus often claimed that his true home was heaven and that he had descended from there (implying his preexistence, cf. 3:13; 6:33, 38, 41, 42, 50, 51, 58). Here he reversed that image, speaking of the time when he would "ascend" back to heaven. The problem is that John does not describe Jesus' ascension (only Luke does in Luke 24:50-52; Acts 1:9-11), so many believe this refers to Jesus' exaltation after his resurrection, as in the three "lifted up" sayings of 3:14; 8:28; 12:32 (cf. Beasley-Murray). Still, the Ascension is alluded to in 20:17, and it is best to take this as a reference to the whole complex of events seen in John as the time of Jesus' glory—cross, resurrection, ascension, exaltation (so Westcott, Bruce). For John, Jesus' humiliation was the first step in his exaltation.

Jesus then introduced the third member of the Trinity to the conversation (6:63; "Spirit" is not the human spirit here). God controls the gift of eternal life (3:16, 36; 5:21a, 24) and has passed that authority to the Son (5:21b, 28-29; 6:27, 33, 35, 39, 40, 44, 48, 50-51, 54, 57). This power to give life is inherent in the Spirit, who "alone gives eternal life." The Spirit of God giving life is a frequent Old Testament theme (Gen 1:2; Isa 11:2; 44:3; 61:1; Ezek 37:5-6, 9-10; Joel 2:28; Zech 4:6), as well as a New Testament emphasis (Rom 8:4; 1 Cor 15:45; 2 Cor 3:6; Gal 5:16; 6:8), and one central to John (3:5, 8; 7:37-39; 14:17). Here, the message is that it is the Spirit, not "human effort" (lit., "the flesh"), that provides eternal life. Jesus made this point throughout the "bread of life" discourse. Jesus' teaching is "spirit and life," meaning that Jesus' words are filled with the power of the Spirit and produce life in those who believe them (the verb "to be" is reproduced before "Spirit" and "life," thereby giving them separate emphases; so Godet). To believe Jesus' words is to believe in him, for his words are life (cf. 5:46-47).

Jesus "knew" who had rejected him "from the beginning." His offensive teaching simply brought to light the unbelief that for some of them was there from the beginning. To anchor this prescient knowledge, John added that Jesus also knew "who would later betray him"—namely Judas, a trusted member of the apostolic band. John probably intended to link these quasi-followers with Judas; desertion is a form of betrayal. This is an important message for quasi-followers of Christ today. Many attend church regularly and seem concerned about their spiritual state but are unwilling to do anything about it in the way of true commitment. Many will face the parallel (and terrifying) indictment of Matthew 7:21-23, where Jesus said, "I never knew you. Get away from me." Jesus connects this unbelief with his previous response to the unbelief of the Jews in 6:37, 44, that the only ones who can come are those who were given to him by the Father. In other words, God knew about them all along, and they were not among the elect. At that point, a group of them "turned away and deserted him" (6:66). It is clear that they found his teaching intolerable and were unwilling to make the sacrifice necessary to come to faith in him. Bruce says it well (1983:164): "What they wanted, he would not give; what he offered, they would not receive." This does not tell us whether or not all the disciples outside the Twelve deserted Jesus. They probably did not, for we know of the "seventy-two other disciples" in Luke 10:1 who formed a circle of followers. Probably only some of the wider group of followers deserted Jesus here.

After speaking with those disciples who deserted him, Jesus turned to the Twelve and asked, "Are you also going to leave?" (6:67). Jesus knew the hearts of the Twelve (2:24-25; 6:64b), but he wanted to challenge them regarding the level of their commitment. As usual, Peter spoke for the others. First, he admitted, "Lord, to whom would we go?" They certainly knew the other religious options, but unlike the rest of the disciples, they had the faith to accept Jesus' difficult teachings in 6:22-58. They had, in that sense, decided to consume Jesus and his teaching, so the other religious possibilities were not a true option. They did not want to turn to anything else, for they knew his words were indeed "spirit and life" (6:63). Second, Peter made two confessions: he said that Jesus' words alone offer "eternal life" and that Jesus is "the Holy One of God" (6:68-69). According to the Greek, Peter said they "have believed" and "have known," with the verbs in the perfect tense, signifying the disciples' state of being. Unlike the other disciples, they had been believing and knowing Christ; this is why they would not desert him.

The title "the Holy One of God" is found elsewhere only in Mark 1:24 and Luke 4:34, when a demon confesses this of Jesus. There is not much evidence for it as a messianic title, but that is probably its meaning here. In the Old Testament, this phrase is used often of God as one who is apart from all other gods, or of God's chosen leaders (Judg 13:7 [LXX, Vaticanus]; Ps 106:16) or priests (Lev 21:6-7). In John, the "Holy Father" (17:11) sets Jesus apart as his own (10:36). Peter was certainly recognizing Jesus as having been set apart by God as the chosen Messiah.

Lest Peter and the others should think too highly of themselves for remaining loyal to him, Jesus made it clear who was sovereign in the situation (6:70-71). According to 6:37-44, God is sovereign over the process of salvation, and Jesus is his official envoy, whom God made the life-giver. Therefore, the disciples had not just chosen him but he had chosen them (cf. 15:16, 19). In fact, Jesus was sovereignly aware of the one exception, Judas, the one "who would later betray him" (6:64). In 17:12, Jesus calls him "the one headed for destruction"; here he calls him "a devil," which could mean that he was demon possessed but more likely means that he was a tool of Satan who would be used to betray Jesus, as seen in 13:2, 27, when the devil first prompted Judas and then entered into him. Jesus knew Judas all along for what he was, but Jesus was is in control, not Judas or any of the Twelve.

◆   ## 8. Jesus at the Feast of Tabernacles (7:1-13)

After this, Jesus traveled around Galilee. He wanted to stay out of Judea, where the Jewish leaders were plotting his death. ²But soon it was time for the Jewish Festival of Shelters, ³and Jesus' brothers said to him, "Leave here and go to Judea, where your followers can see your miracles! ⁴You can't become famous if you hide like this! If you can do such wonderful things, show yourself to the world!" ⁵For even his brothers didn't believe in him.

⁶Jesus replied, "Now is not the right time for me to go, but you can go anytime. ⁷The world can't hate you, but it does hate me because I accuse it of doing evil. ⁸You go on. I'm not going* to this festival, be-cause my time has not yet come." ⁹After saying these things, Jesus remained in Galilee.

¹⁰But after his brothers left for the festival, Jesus also went, though secretly, staying out of public view. ¹¹The Jewish leaders tried to find him at the festival and kept asking if anyone had seen him. ¹²There was a lot of grumbling about him among the crowds. Some argued, "He's a good man," but others said, "He's nothing but a fraud who deceives the people." ¹³But no one had the courage to speak favorably about him in public, for they were afraid of getting in trouble with the Jewish leaders.

7:8 Some manuscripts read *not yet going.*

NOTES

7:3 *see your miracles!* Brown (1966:308) makes a very interesting comparison between the three requests made to Jesus in chs 6–7 and the three temptations by Satan in Matt 4:1-11; Luke 4:1-13. In 6:15, "to be their king" parallels Satan offering him the kingdoms of the world; in 6:31, the people asking for miraculous bread parallels turning the stones into bread; and in 7:3, asking for a display of miraculous power parallels showing power by jumping from the Temple's pinnacle.

7:6 *not the right time.* The normal term for "time" as the hour of Jesus' passion is *hōra* [TG5610, ZG6052] (as in 2:4; 7:30; 8:20), but the term here is *kairos* [TG2540, ZG2789] (season). Often *hōra* has the idea of chronological, successive time and *kairos* the idea of a period of time with an emphasis on its quality (e.g., opportune time or rainy time); but there is no evidence for that distinction in John. In fact, John uses *hōra* for the qualitative idea of the appropriate time for Jesus' passion. The key is John's use of synonyms (in this case *hōra* and *kairos*) throughout his Gospel for major ideas, like "know" or "see." With the different Gr. terms in 2:4 and 7:6, John is simply using a variety of terms for greater impact (so Brown, contra Beasley-Murray, Carson).

7:8 *I'm not going to this festival.* Ancient mss are divided between "not (*ouk* [TG3756, ZG4024]) going" (ℵ D it syrᶜ·ˢ copᵇᵒ) and "not yet (*oupō* [TG3768, ZG4037]) going" (𝔓66 𝔓75 B L T W 038 044 070 0105 0250 f¹·¹³ 𝔐 syrᵖ·ʰ copˢᵃ·ᵃᶜ²). Though the ms evidence is much stronger for the second reading, it is generally agreed that *oupō* is a scribal change intended to resolve the seeming inconsistency of Jesus saying he wasn't going in 7:8, when he does go in 7:10.

COMMENTARY

This is the third feast Jesus attended (Sabbath, ch 5; Passover, ch 6), and once more the major themes are Christological revelation and the conflict it engendered in the Jewish people. The opposition intensified, as there were four attempts to arrest Jesus. This was because Jesus' teaching about himself and his role deepened, as well. Once again, he revealed that he was the God-sent teacher (7:16-19), the one who had come from God (7:28-30); he also showed that he would be the source of the Holy Spirit (7:37-39) and the Light of the World (8:12). Then he went on the offensive and stated that even though they believed Abraham was their father (8:39), in reality their true father was the devil (8:44). He was clearly not trying to "win friends and influence people"! This is confrontation counseling from the outset. Neyrey (1996:111-115) notes how Jesus is on trial but reverses the situation and places the Jewish people on trial (cf. vv. 19, 24, 28-29, 33-34). At the same time, Jesus is seen fulfilling the imagery of the Festival of Shelters, particularly the water ceremony that occurred every morning (7:37-39; cf. *m. Sukkah* 4:1, 9-10) and the light ceremony that occurred every evening (8:12; cf. *m. Sukkah* 5:2-4). On the historicity of the material, Blomberg states (2001:140), "John is not monolithically representing response to Jesus as negative, even among the Jewish leadership, despite his redactional concerns to highlight Jesus' ultimate, widespread rejection. Historical concerns that depict a nuanced response despite growing opposition complement John's theological emphases rather than competing with them."

As a result of the controversies that occurred at the healing of the lame man (ch 5) and the Passover debate about Jesus as the Bread of Life (ch 6), Jesus stayed away from Judea, "where the Jewish leaders were plotting his death" (7:1). He restricted his mission to Galilee for a time (this period, perhaps a year long, dominates the synoptic Gospels, in which Jesus did not go to Jerusalem until Passion week). After a time, the Festival of Shelters (or Tabernacles or Booths) was approaching (about six months after the Passover events of ch 6, as it took place from 15 to 21 Tishri by the Jewish calendar—hence, early October). It was a harvest festival to celebrate the end of the harvest season after all the crops had been gathered in (Exod 23:16; Lev 23:33-43). Lasting for seven days, with an eighth "holy day" (Num 29:35) to conclude the celebration, it was one of the three great festivals (with Passover and Pentecost) that brought pilgrims to Jerusalem. The name "Shelters" (or Tabernacles) is associated especially with the wilderness wanderings, when the people of Israel all lived in tents and God also lived among them in a tent—the Tabernacle—watching over them. People would build leafy booths out of branches and dwell in them for the festival period. It was a joyous occasion, centered on thanksgiving to God. By the time of Christ it had also "become associated, specifically in connection with the daily solemn outpouring of water during this feast, with eschatological hopes (and 'the wells of salvation' predicted in them; cf. Zech 14:16ff; Isa 12:3)" (Ridderbos 1997:257).

Jesus' brothers (7:3; see note on 2:12) had not yet become disciples (7:5). So far as we know, they were not converted until Jesus' resurrection appearances (1 Cor 15:7). Two of them (James and Jude) became leaders in the church and later wrote New Testament books. They believed in his miracles (they had to; they had seen several) but not his claims. In the midst of their doubts, they wanted Jesus to go to Jerusalem for the feast to perform miracles for everyone to see. The expression "leave here" (7:3, Greek) may well imply more than a pilgrimage trip—probably an extended stay, perhaps even moving his ministry there (so Ridderbos; Schnackenburg doubts it implies a permanent move). They were especially interested in Jesus' "followers" (lit., "disciples"), probably those noted in 2:23 who needed more proof, and possibly also those in 6:66 who deserted him and returned to Judea. They urged him, "Show yourself to the world!" They wanted Jesus to boldly prove himself publicly. In this sense, they were acting similarly to Satan in the wilderness temptation of Matthew 4:1-11 and parallels. The miracles would then be intended to laud Jesus himself rather than to glorify God or help people. Their reasoning was quite logical; no one does such things in secret if they want a public ministry; this is a good example of the worldly "if you've got it, flaunt it" mentality today! It is interesting that John has "world" here. Likely his brothers meant by this the Jewish nation, but Jesus' ministry was for the whole world of mankind not just for the Jews (cf. 1:10; 3:16; 4:42; 6:51). Probably Jesus' brothers were challenging him for their own sakes as well. John tells us that they "didn't believe in him" (cf. Mark 3:21, 31-32; 6:4), so they were daring him in a sense to prove himself to them as well. They may have been genuinely searching at this point, but they went no further than his miracles. There is no evidence that they were willing to consider his claims regarding himself.

Jesus rejected their suggestion, saying, "Now is not the right time for me to go"

(7:6). In John, the "time" or "hour" refers to Jesus' death on the cross (cf. on 2:4 which uses similar language), so there is double meaning here. It was not the "right time" for Jesus to go; that "time," when it would come, would bring quite a different sign than they expected—namely, the cross. When Jesus went to Jerusalem in the way they wanted, the public demonstration would be one of messianic suffering. As for his brothers, they could "go anytime," but Jesus had to wait for his Father's will. They had no such restraints, for they were not following God's will. This is why the world hated Jesus, while it didn't hate his brothers. He accused it of doing evil, while his brothers were part of the world. The world hates the light because it is full of darkness at the core (3:19-20). Therefore, when darkness is "exposed" for what it is, it reacts with hatred (3:20). The idea of Jesus accusing (7:7) is a legal metaphor. It pictures him not only proving their guilt before the divine law court but also proving to the evildoers that they were guilty (cf. 16:8-11 on the Spirit "convict[ing] the world").

Jesus told his brothers to "go on" to Jerusalem for the festival, but he would not be going because his "time has not yet come" (7:8). The inconsistency of Jesus saying he wouldn't go and the fact that he did go (7:10) is obvious. The key is to realize that Jesus was saying that he wouldn't go until the Father designated that the time was right. He would not go in the way they wanted—that is, to provide public proof that he was the Messiah—but he would go in the way his Father wished, in private. He would not go with his brothers and do it the world's way. The term for "go on" in verses 8 and 10 is "ascend" (*anabainō* [TG305, ZG326]), so some (e.g., Carson) see this as a possible symbol of Jesus' later glorification, but that is not likely in this context (so Michaels, Köstenberger).

After waiting in Galilee a short time, Jesus went to the festival—but "secretly, staying out of public view" (7:10). It is uncertain whether he missed part of the festival, arriving in the middle of it (so Ridderbos), or if he arrived on time but worshiped privately, out of public view (I find this more likely). At the feast, the "Jewish leaders" were looking for Jesus, undoubtedly with hostile intent (cf. 5:18, where they plotted to kill him). They regularly asked people (imperfect tenses are used in the Gr., indicating their ongoing activity) whether they had seen "that man" (7:11, Gr.; intended pejoratively). In the meantime, the "crowds" or common people were also "grumbling" (the same term as the "murmuring" and "complaining" in 6:41, 43, 61) about him. Here it is not as negative as in chapter 6 but indicates debate over who and what he was; still, there was not a completely open discussion because they had no "courage to speak favorably about him in public" out of fear of the leaders (7:13). This was a serious situation, for the leaders were not only seeking Jesus but even censoring what people said. It was still the type of murmuring that occurred in the wilderness wanderings because there was no boldness to be open to the truth. The debate was not as deep as the questions asked of John the Baptist in 1:19-21. Some considered Jesus "a good man" and others "a fraud who deceives the people" (7:12). The latter became the basic Jewish attitude toward Jesus, as in the Talmudic passage that said he was executed because he was a sorcerer who led the people astray (*b. Sanhedrin* 43a; so Beasley-Murray).

◆   9. Conflict at the Feast (7:14–52)

¹⁴Then, midway through the festival, Jesus went up to the Temple and began to teach. ¹⁵The people* were surprised when they heard him. "How does he know so much when he hasn't been trained?" they asked.

¹⁶So Jesus told them, "My message is not my own; it comes from God who sent me. ¹⁷Anyone who wants to do the will of God will know whether my teaching is from God or is merely my own. ¹⁸Those who speak for themselves want glory only for themselves, but a person who seeks to honor the one who sent him speaks truth, not lies. ¹⁹Moses gave you the law, but none of you obeys it! In fact, you are trying to kill me."

²⁰The crowd replied, "You're demon possessed! Who's trying to kill you?"

²¹Jesus replied, "I did one miracle on the Sabbath, and you were amazed. ²²But you work on the Sabbath, too, when you obey Moses' law of circumcision. (Actually, this tradition of circumcision began with the patriarchs, long before the law of Moses.) ²³For if the correct time for circumcising your son falls on the Sabbath, you go ahead and do it so as not to break the law of Moses. So why should you be angry with me for healing a man on the Sabbath? ²⁴Look beneath the surface so you can judge correctly."

²⁵Some of the people who lived in Jerusalem started to ask each other, "Isn't this the man they are trying to kill? ²⁶But here he is, speaking in public, and they say nothing to him. Could our leaders possibly believe that he is the Messiah? ²⁷But how could he be? For we know where this man comes from. When the Messiah comes, he will simply appear; no one will know where he comes from."

²⁸While Jesus was teaching in the Temple, he called out, "Yes, you know me, and you know where I come from. But I'm not here on my own. The one who sent me is true, and you don't know him. ²⁹But I know him because I come from him, and he sent me to you." ³⁰Then the leaders tried to arrest him; but no one laid a hand on him, because his time* had not yet come.

³¹Many among the crowds at the Temple believed in him. "After all," they said, "would you expect the Messiah to do more miraculous signs than this man has done?"

³²When the Pharisees heard that the crowds were whispering such things, they and the leading priests sent Temple guards to arrest Jesus. ³³But Jesus told them, "I will be with you only a little longer. Then I will return to the one who sent me. ³⁴You will search for me but not find me. And you cannot go where I am going."

³⁵The Jewish leaders were puzzled by this statement. "Where is he planning to go?" they asked. "Is he thinking of leaving the country and going to the Jews in other lands?* Maybe he will even teach the Greeks! ³⁶What does he mean when he says, 'You will search for me but not find me,' and 'You cannot go where I am going'?"

³⁷On the last day, the climax of the festival, Jesus stood and shouted to the crowds, "Anyone who is thirsty may come to me! ³⁸Anyone who believes in me may come and drink! For the Scriptures declare, 'Rivers of living water will flow from his heart.'"* ³⁹(When he said "living water," he was speaking of the Spirit, who would be given to everyone believing in him. But the Spirit had not yet been given,* because Jesus had not yet entered into his glory.)

⁴⁰When the crowds heard him say this, some of them declared, "Surely this man is the Prophet we've been expecting."* ⁴¹Others said, "He is the Messiah." Still others said, "But he can't be! Will the Messiah come from Galilee? ⁴²For the Scriptures clearly state that the Messiah will be born of the royal line of David, in Bethlehem, the village where King David was born."* ⁴³So the crowd was divided about him. ⁴⁴Some even wanted him arrested, but no one laid a hand on him.

⁴⁵When the Temple guards returned without having arrested Jesus, the leading priests and Pharisees demanded, "Why didn't you bring him in?"

⁴⁶"We have never heard anyone speak like this!" the guards responded.

⁴⁷"Have you been led astray, too?" the Pharisees mocked. ⁴⁸"Is there a single one of us rulers or Pharisees who believes in him? ⁴⁹This foolish crowd follows him, but they are ignorant of the law. God's curse is on them!"

⁵⁰Then Nicodemus, the leader who had met with Jesus earlier, spoke up. ⁵¹"Is it legal to convict a man before he is given a hearing?" he asked.

⁵²They replied, "Are you from Galilee, too? Search the Scriptures and see for yourself—no prophet ever comes* from Galilee!"

7:15 Greek *Jewish people.*   7:30 Greek *his hour.*   7:35 Or *the Jews who live among the Greeks?*   7:37-38 Or *"Let anyone who is thirsty come to me and drink. ³⁸For the Scriptures declare, 'Rivers of living water will flow from the heart of anyone who believes in me.'"*   7:39 Some manuscripts read *But as yet there was no Spirit.* Still others read *But as yet there was no Holy Spirit.*   7:40 See Deut 18:15, 18; Mal 4:5-6.   7:42 See Mic 5:2. 7:52 Some manuscripts read *the prophet does not come.*

NOTES

7:18 *lies.* Schnackenburg points out that *adikia* [ᵀᴳ93, ᶻᴳ94] (normally indicating "evil, wickedness") includes "lies" or "falsehood" but is even more comprehensive than that (cf. 1 John 5:17), and it shows here that no one can accuse Jesus of any sin because he is God's envoy and in perfect harmony with him. "This is the irreducible claim of the true revealer, and the believer finds it authenticated (cf. 7:17)" (Schnackenburg 1982:133).

7:27 *When the Messiah comes.* Carson (1991:317) sees in this chapter three popularly held tests regarding how the Messiah could be identified: (1) he would appear suddenly and no one would know his origin (7:27); (2) he would perform incredible miraculous signs (7:31); and (3) he would be of the royal Davidic line, born in Bethlehem (7:42).

7:30 *his time had not yet come.* While it is common to interpret the "time" in John as primarily referring to the Cross, Beutler (1997:26-27) argues that it is much broader, referring to the Cross and the Resurrection, as well as to the sending of the Holy Spirit and Jesus' second coming. This is viable, but the major emphasis is still on the Cross as initiating these other events.

7:32 *Pharisees . . . leading priests.* It at first seems unusual that the Pharisees and Sadducees (the party of the leading priests, meaning the most powerful priestly families in charge of the Temple) acted together on anything, for they were political enemies. Thus, some scholars think this joint move is implausible (e.g., Bultmann, Barrett)—but this is probably shorthand for an official act of the Sanhedrin, which consisted of the Sadducees (in the majority), the Pharisees, and the elders (so Westcott, Schnackenburg, Kysar, Keener). There is no reason to think that these two groups never acted together.

7:34 *search for me but not find me.* Whitacre (1999:191) says this fulfills a prophetic and wisdom tradition found, for example, in Amos 8:12 (the days are coming when people will search for the word of the Lord and not find it) and Hos 5:3-6 (God has withdrawn, so his people will search but not find him). In Prov 1:28-31, Wisdom says that since the people hate knowledge and spurn her advice, "When they cry for help, I will not answer. Though they anxiously search for me, they will not find me." The nation of Jesus' day had the same unfaithful heart, and God had withdrawn from them.

7:35 *teach the Greeks!* When Jesus mentioned that the scribes and Pharisees "cross land and sea to make one convert" (Matt 23:15), he was not speaking of missions to the Gentiles but rather of going to the synagogues in Diaspora communities to convince Gentile God-fearers (Acts 10:2, 22, 35; 13:16, 26) to be circumcised so that they could become true proselytes. There is little evidence of any Jewish mission to the Gentiles (cf. McKnight 1991).

7:37 *the climax of the festival.* Many scholars (Bultmann, Sanders, Brown, Schnackenburg, Ridderbos, Whitacre) believe this would have been the seventh day because the eighth day is a late addition and a time of rest rather than activity. Yet at the same time, the eighth day is also a special day and a climax for the feast. Moreover, Jesus' pronouncement on this last day would have been especially forceful because the water and light ceremonies were not repeated, and he would be inserting himself as the climax and fulfillment of those ceremonies (so Hoskyns, Barrett, Lindars, Bruce, Beasley-Murray, Carson, Michaels, Blomberg, Köstenberger).

7:37-38 *Anyone who believes in me may come and drink! For the Scriptures declare, "Rivers of living water will flow from his heart."* This is certainly one of the more debated passages in John. There are two primary interpretations, and they center for the most part on whether or not one places a stop at the end of the Gr. text of 7:37, thus separating it from the phrase "anyone who believes," which occurs in the beginning of 7:38. This would read, "Let anyone who is thirsty come to me and drink. As the Scripture says, 'Rivers of living water will flow from the heart of *anyone who believes* in me.'" Moving the full stop into 7:38 results in the reading, "Let the thirsty *who believe* come and drink. As the Scripture says, 'Rivers of living water will flow from his [Christ's] heart.'" "Anyone who believes" can belong to either clause, so the true question is whether the believer or Christ is the place from which the Spirit is flowing (the "rivers of living water"; cf. 4:13-14; 7:39). The "believer" position is held by the eastern Fathers (e.g., Origen; in addition see Westcott, Lindars, Barrett, Fee 1978, Kysar, Morris, Carson, Ridderbos, Köstenberger, KJV, RSV, NASB, NIV, TNIV); the Christological position is held by the western Fathers (e.g., Tertullian; in addition see Dodd, Bultmann, Kilpatrick 1960, Brown, Schnackenburg, Bruce, Beasley-Murray, Comfort, Michaels, Meyken 1996, Whitacre, Marcus 1998, Burge, Blomberg, NRSV, NLT). Meyken (1996:163-166) thinks that "anyone who believes" belongs with 7:38 but that Jesus is still the referent. The problem is virtually insoluble in any final sense. If the believer is placed with 7:37, an interesting chiasm is produced, with the subjects (the thirsty and the believer) framing the verbs (come and drink). However, if the believer begins 7:38, it would also place the Scripture formula in the middle of the quote, modifying a participle, a pattern unique in John, and indeed, in the NT as a whole. Moreover, the thirsty would first drink and then give out the water to others, a possible but unlikely metaphor in this context (so Schnackenburg). Still, if Jesus were referring to himself, why would he say, "from *his* heart" (Fee, Carson)?

The answer, I believe, is in the context. Jesus saw himself fulfilling the water ceremony, and the entire context of chs 5–10 is Christological. It would be a strange interruption if he were making the believer, rather than himself, the source of the Holy Spirit, especially in light of 14:26; 16:7, where Christ sends the Spirit on his mission. The use of "his" fits Jesus' frequent use of "Son of Man" for himself. Therefore, the Christological interpretation fits best in the context.

COMMENTARY

Carson (1991:310) notes a pair of cycles in this section, each with three sections: the teaching of Jesus (7:14-24, 37-39), followed by debate and speculation (7:25-31, 40-44), leading to an attempt to arrest Jesus by the leaders (7:32-36, 45-52). This makes good sense of the passage and will be followed here.

Jesus, the Divinely Sent Teacher (7:14-24). Jesus likely spent the first part of the Festival privately worshiping his Father (7:10). Halfway through, in the midst of the tensions aroused by the leaders, he could no longer keep quiet. In the phrase "midway through the festival," Dodd sees a fulfillment of Malachi 3:1, ("The Lord you are seeking will suddenly come to his Temple") and states that "it is the Day of the Lord, which, according to Zech xiv, the Feast of Tabernacles foreshadows" (1953a:351). He sees in this scene a "manifestation of the eternal Logos, as life and light, to the world of humankind." This is somewhat overstated but still relevant. Jesus was indeed showing himself to the world but not in the way his brothers wanted (cf. 7:4). He came to them with words, not just works. The people were "surprised" (lit., "amazed") by the depth of his knowledge and asked how this was possible without proper training in rabbinic schools (7:15). One Talmudic passage (b. Sota 22b) says that a person who studies the Torah without formal rabbinic training is no better than the common people who know nothing. Such comments were often made about Jesus (Matt 13:54-56; Mark 1:22; Luke 2:47; 4:22) and the apostles (Acts 4:13).

Jesus quickly told them the source of his authority for his insights (7:16-19). Their idea of authority was merely rabbinic education; Jesus, however, delivered a message that came from God, who sent him. He was not self-taught, nor was he dependent on the interpretation of others (rabbis, like many scholars today, did little more than quote other rabbis' opinions). His message came directly from God and so was ultimate truth. Moreover, in contrast with the prophets, who periodically reinforced their words with the phrase, "Thus says the Lord," Jesus never had to say this, for he was the heaven-sent envoy, and all his words were and are God's truth. This, he says, is evident to "anyone who wants to do the will of God." This builds on 5:37-38, 41-44, where recognizing Jesus depends upon receiving God's word, seeking God's glory, and having love indwell us. Jesus lived entirely according to God's will and leading. It follows that anyone who truly walks the same road as Jesus will recognize that he is from God. Note that the criterion is not intellectual but ethical. It is not a state of knowledge but a way of living that makes the difference. This is similar to 3:21, where "those who *do what is right* come to the light" so it can be known that they "are *doing what God wants.*" It is living according to the will of God that truly matters.

If Jesus were self-taught (i.e., if his teaching were "merely [his] own"), he would be seeking only his own glory (7:17-18). That is simply natural law; the one who develops his own brand of truth seeks his own glory. That is not the case with Jesus; everything he said and did had only one goal—honoring the one who sent him. Thus, he not only "speaks truth, not lies"; he *is* the truth (14:6), meaning he is not only truth incarnate but can be trusted completely as the one who gave the words of God. Furthermore, Jesus declared that there was no unrighteousness in him— unlike the Jewish people who had rejected God's way of righteousness. Jesus then proved the unrighteousness of the Jews by showing how they transgressed their own law. On a previous visit to Jerusalem, the authorities had tried to arrest him on capital charges (5:18; 7:1), and they would do so again (7:32, 45; 8:59). Jesus challenged their obedience to the law of Moses, which was the basis of their religious education as well as of their civil law. In their desire to execute Jesus, they were guilty of the murder of a "righteous" man (7:19). Moses had actually been a witness to Jesus' true ministry and status before God (5:45-47), and now he was a witness to their violation of his law.

The response of the crowd to Jesus was, "You're demon possessed" (7:20)—a statement that effectively meant "you're crazy," as the two ideas were intertwined in the ancient world. Most in the crowd had no desire to kill Jesus and were unaware of the leaders' plans, so to them he was simply guilty of being delusional. Christ's response was to continue with the theme that they were guilty of breaking the law. He returned to the events that led to the capital charges, namely the miracle of healing the lame man on a Sabbath (5:1-15). They were "amazed" not so much at the miracle but at the fact that Jesus would break the oral tradition by healing on the Sabbath. Jesus reminded them that they too broke that tradition when they obeyed "Moses' law of circumcision," referring to the rule that a male child is to be circumcised on the eighth day, even if that day fell on the Sabbath (cf. Lev 12:3, as further developed in *m. Shabbat* 18:3; 19:1-3).

Jesus' point was that circumcision had precedence over the law since it "began with the patriarchs, long before the law of Moses." Therefore the "work" of circumcision is a higher good and valid as a Sabbath activity. Jesus was engaging in a double argument from the greater to the lesser. First, circumcision is greater than the tradition about working on the Sabbath; and second, since circumcision aids only a small part of the body and Jesus' miracle healed the whole body, it is greater than circumcision (so Brown 1966:318). They had no right to "be angry" at the miracle. It is important to realize that Jesus was not disparaging the Sabbath laws; rather, it should be understood that his doing the work of God was another exception, like circumcision. Jesus was doing the work of God in bringing God's saving presence to bear on a paralyzed man, so it was a valid activity. His opponents had been judging wrongly on the basis of a superficial use of the law, and they needed to stop judging in this way. Again, it was the earthly versus the heavenly perspective. They needed to see the situation from God's viewpoint. Then they would know that Jesus was not breaking the Sabbath but upholding its true purpose.

Debate over Jesus as the Messiah (7:25-31). The previous dialog probably centered on pilgrims to Jerusalem from Galilee and the Diaspora who didn't know about the authorities' desire to arrest Jesus (7:20). Now "the people who lived in Jerusalem" began asking questions. They were aware of the leaders' desire and so asked how a "wanted man" could have such a bold, public ministry without being arrested. This made them wonder if perhaps the leaders had studied the evidence further and now believed Jesus to be the Messiah (7:26). The authorities had never been tentative about arresting others, so maybe this meant they had been converted. They rejected this notion because they knew where Jesus came from (probably that he grew up in Nazareth and recently moved to Capernaum), while no one would know the origin of the Messiah. This does not mean that they were ignorant of Micah 5:2 and the Messiah's birth in Bethlehem. Rather, it refers to a popular belief, either that the Messiah would be hidden by God until the divinely appointed time for his manifestation (*1 Enoch* 48:6; *4 Ezra* 7:28; 13:51-52; *2 Baruch* 29:3) or, more likely, that he would be born normally but not recognized until he was made known by God (Justin Martyr *Dialogue with Trypho* 8). Since the local Jews had known about Jesus, they figured he could not be the Messiah. The irony, of course, is that they were right. Jesus did live a normal life until he began his messianic ministry, and that ministry is what the people had rejected.

Jesus, recognizing their faulty logic (perhaps another occasion of his omniscience; cf. 1:47-48; 4:17-18), gave his response (7:28-29). He began with what they did know—"where [he had] come from" (7:27-28), but even this concession is filled with irony ("You really think you know where I come from!"). The people were unaware of his true origins. Jesus not only came from God, but he also was not there on his own. His mission was God's mission. Dahms (1981:80-82) says this alludes to Isaiah 55:11, where it is said that God sends out his word and it prospers. The basic error of the crowds was that they thought Jesus' teaching was all his own idea and therefore false. In reality, "the one who sent [Jesus] is true" (7:28), just as Jesus himself is "true" (7:18, KJV). Jesus told these Jewish people that they didn't know the true God—the God of the Old Testament—who had sent him, though they claimed to. Only Jesus could truly know him (cf. 1:18a; Matt 11:27) because God is his origin and was the source of his mission. The Jewish people had always been proud of their covenant relationship; they bragged of their knowledge of God (Rom 2:17, 23), but Jesus exposed this as false pride by explaining his unique relationship to the Father—they did not know the true God, for they had rejected his Son. The way people relate to Jesus determines whether or not they truly know God. The Jews here had failed that test.

The division between the leaders and the people is starkly presented in 7:30-31. The leaders tried to arrest him, which was part of the ongoing plot to get rid of Jesus (5:18; 7:1). The attempt to arrest him was futile because "his time had not yet come." This is part of an ongoing theme regarding the "hour" of destiny, the time allotted by God as "the right time" (Gal 4:4) when the plan of salvation would be finalized at the Cross (cf. 2:4; 4:23; 7:6; 8:20; 12:23, 27; 13:1; 16:4, 32; 17:1). The point is that God was in control, not the leaders. They tried to arrest Jesus, but until the Father said, "It is time," their attempts would end in futility. "Many among the crowds at the Temple," however, "believed in him" (7:31). Certainly their faith centered on the "miraculous signs," just like those in 2:23-25, but it was still an important beginning. It was as yet an inadequate faith, but they realized that Jesus' deeds were worthy of the Messiah and so took a preliminary step of faith and became followers (cf. 7:27).

Attempt to Arrest Jesus (7:32–36). The Pharisees learned of the burgeoning faith of many in the crowds and so sent "Temple guards to arrest Jesus" (7:32). Since they acted together with the "leading priests," this is probably an arrest warrant issued by the Sanhedrin as a whole (cf. note on 1:19). The "Temple guards" were the police force of the Sanhedrin, primarily consisting of Levites whose duty was to maintain order in the Temple but who also kept general civic order in the city for the Sanhedrin. John did not tell us the outcome of this police action (cf. 7:45ff) but instead related further teaching at the Festival of Shelters. At the same time, this provides a proper reaction to Jesus' enemies. While there was "only a little longer" left for Jesus' earthly ministry, the Sanhedrin was not in charge. God was, and his plan would prevail. When it was finished, Jesus would return to the one who had sent him (7:33)—the God in heaven from whom Jesus descended in the first place (cf. 6:33, 38, 41, 42, 50, 51, 58). His coming death was not an end to his ministry but a new beginning. Jesus' statement that the leaders would search for him but not find him (7:34) has a double meaning referring not only to their search to arrest Jesus but also to their search for God and for eternal life (so Godet—the seeking is either inspired by hatred or a sign of repentance). Lenski says (1942:570), "This terrible seeking comes when the day of grace is past," alluding to Hebrews 3:15 and the warning from Psalm 95:7-8, "When you hear his voice, don't harden your hearts as Israel did when they rebelled." Because the nation was under divine judgment, they "cannot go where [Jesus is] going." Heaven will not be their destiny.

The Jewish leaders among the crowds once more failed to grasp what Jesus meant because of their earth-centered perspective (cf. 3:4, 9; 4:9, 11, 15; 5:7; 6:7, 25, 34, 52). They were "puzzled" and wondered if he was planning to leave Judea and go to the Diaspora communities throughout the Roman world (7:35). Hellenistic Jews in fact would be coming to see Jesus (12:20-36), so this was a real possibility. It is hard to know whether "teach the Greeks" means they thought he would actually go to the Gentiles or (more likely) minister to the Gentile proselytes (Carson) or Greek-speaking Jews (Witherington) in other lands, for there is too little evidence of actual Gentile mission among the Jews. As Bruce brings out (1983:180), the repetition of Jesus' words in 7:36 may hint at the later teaching of 8:21ff that it is sin and unbelief that made it impossible for them to go where he was heading.

Jesus Gives the Spirit (7:37-39). This begins the second cycle of this narrative (cf. the first paragraph of commentary on 7:14-52). It takes place "on the last day, the climax of the festival." This is the eighth day, a "holy day" and "solemn occasion" for the joyous festival (Lev 23:36; so Carson, Morris, Moloney; some like Brown, Schnackenburg, and Ridderbos believe it is the seventh and last day; the eighth day was a solemn assembly celebrating the seven-day feast). For the seven days previous, there was a particularly joyful water procession at dawn. This was a harvest festival, and all night long the revelers would celebrate the crops God had given them— wheat and barley as well as grapes and olives—but in the morning they thanked God for the rain that made the crops possible, drawing on Isaiah 12:3—"with joy you will drink deeply from the fountain [lit., 'waters'] of salvation." Every morning for the seven days, a priestly procession led by the high priest went down to the pool of Siloam and drew water in a golden pitcher. They went up to the Temple at the time of the morning sacrifices to the blowing of the shofar (or trumpet), as the pilgrims shook *lulabs*, or leafy branches, to symbolize the wilderness journey and held up a piece of citrus fruit (traditionally a citron or etrog) to symbolize the harvest (so Morris, Carson, Burge). They marched around the altar seven times, pouring the water into a funnel on the side of the altar, and it flowed about the base of the altar as the Temple choir sang the Hallel from Psalms 113-118.

Possibly in the morning (when it was symbolically appropriate), Jesus "stood and shouted to the crowds" that the thirsty believers could come and drink of him. Since Jesus was the divine envoy, he then became the source of the "waters of salvation" (Isa 12:3), fulfilling the symbolism of the water ceremony. This also continues the image of 4:10, 13-14 and 6:53-56, as Jesus both provides the living water and becomes the Water of Life from which the thirsty must drink to have eternal life (cf. 6:35). The joy that attended the feast was even more evident in what Jesus said. Here the Old Testament promise of the living water has finally been realized, and the final source of life that the Jewish people had always longed for had come to them. The messianic fulfillment had come, and the age of salvation had arrived. The two themes of Tabernacles—harvest and eschatological hope—are combined in Jesus.

The Scripture citation in 7:38 does not allude to any particular Old Testament passage but sums up a theme. If one were to posit the believer as the source of the "rivers of living water" (cf. note on 7:37-38), it would allude to Proverbs 18:4 ("Wisdom flows from the wise like a bubbling brook") and Isaiah 58:11 ("You will be like a well-watered garden, like an ever-flowing spring"). If the source is Christ, it would allude to Zechariah 14:8 ("On that day life-giving waters will flow out from Jerusalem," an important passage because it is connected with Tabernacles in Judaism), Ezekiel 47:9 ("Life will flourish wherever this water [from the new Temple] flows"), and Jesus as the fulfillment of the rock struck by Moses with the water gushing out (Exod 17:1-6; cf. Pss 78:16: 20; 105:40-41; Meyken [1996:167-174] goes so far as to suggest that Ps 78 is the primary referent). This is often taken as a type of Christ (e.g., 1 Cor 10:4). As I have argued in the note on 7:37-38, the latter is more likely— the living water here is flowing from Christ. Of course, it must be said that both views have a great deal in common in that Christ is the living water and sends out the Spirit in both (the first view holds that he sends out the Spirit through the believer). Nevertheless, one must choose, and Christ as the ultimate source best fits the Christological emphasis.

Water as a symbol for the Holy Spirit has already been discussed in 3:5, but John makes the connection absolutely clear here. Some rabbis linked the water-drawing ceremony with the promised Holy Spirit and even called the courtyard in the Temple "the house of the water-drawing" (y. Sukkah 5.1, 55a; Ruth Rabbah 4:8). It is also possible there is an allusion to Isaiah 12:3, "You will drink deeply from the fountain of salvation," with Jesus' innermost being as the "fountain of salvation" (some associated Isa 12:3 with the Festival of Shelters; so Marcus 1998). Jesus was fulfilling further prophecy by giving the Holy Spirit to those who would believe. John wants to make the time of this gift clear. It "had not yet been given" during Jesus' life and ministry, but it would be given after Jesus "entered into his glory." This in fact is the theme of the Farewell Discourse of chapters 14–17: "I must depart so the Spirit might come." It is the Spirit who would carry out Jesus' directive and make the final salvation available to all. Jesus made the gift possible; the Spirit is the operative force. This, of course, does not mean the Spirit did not yet exist, for we see the Spirit in the Old Testament as well as in Jesus' early ministry (1:32: 3:34). However, the age of the Spirit was yet to come and would begin with Jesus' exaltation and conferral of the Spirit upon his disciples (20:22).

Further Division and Unbelief (7:40-44). Now the crowds were asking the same questions that the Sanhedrin delegation asked the Baptist (1:19-22): is Jesus the expected "prophet like Moses" (cf. 6:14) or the Messiah? The Mosaic prophet would make sense in light of the manna imagery of chapter 6, and the imagery of the "rivers of living water" would recall the water from the rock of Exodus 17, adding more fuel to the "prophet like Moses" speculation. Many Jews separated the figures of the "prophet like Moses" and the Messiah (e.g., 1QS 9:11), and that was the case here. Some believe that Christians were the first to identify the two figures because Jesus fulfilled both expectations (so Bruce, Carson). The same doubts as those seen in 7:27 convinced other Jews that Jesus could not be the Messiah, for he was from Galilee rather than the royal birthplace of David, Bethlehem (in Judea), noted in Micah 5:2 as the birthplace of the Messiah. (The Davidic origins of the Messiah had been established in 2 Sam 7:12-16; Ps 89:3-4; and Isa 9:7). Here is further irony because Jesus' Davidic origin was commonly understood in the early church (Matt 2:4-5; Mark 12:35-37; Luke 2:4; Rom 1:3; 2 Tim 2:8); certainly John and his readers were aware of it as well.

The division of the crowd was caused by ignorance and unbelief. Wherever Jesus went, he caused division, for he encountered the darkness in every person (1:5, 9) and forced them to come to a faith-decision. Those who preferred darkness rejected that Light (3:19-20). So it was in this case as well. Once again, some joined the leaders in seeking his arrest, but once more "no one laid a hand on him" because the divinely appointed "hour" had not yet arrived (cf. 7:30; 8:20).

The Futility of the Leaders' Opposition (7:45-52). Leaving the crowds for the moment, John returned to the "leading priests and Pharisees" and the futile attempt of the Sanhedrin to arrest Jesus (cf. 7:11, 30, 32). The group of Temple police they had sent out to arrest Jesus (7:32) had returned empty-handed (7:45). It is clear that they were present for the dialog between Jesus and the crowds, but they were so caught up in the power of his teaching that they were unable to fulfill their assignment: "We have never heard anyone speak like this!" (7:46). This appears strange in light of modern police procedures, but these were Levites and not professional soldiers. The most amazing thing is that they had been gone for four days (7:14, 32, 37, so Whitacre), they were so caught up with Jesus' teaching. They must have recognized that Jesus' words were indeed "spirit and life" (6:63). This does not mean they were converted but rather that they were stirred to the depths of their beings.

The leaders reacted harshly, as one would expect, accusing them of being "led astray" like so many in Israel (7:47). Jesus had already been called a deceptive fraud (7:12), so it was natural that the leaders would think he had deceived their Temple guards. Their statement to the guards that none of the leaders believed in him was certainly an overstatement, for Nicodemus, one of them, did not share their unbelief (7:48, 50). The same division that occurred everywhere concerning Jesus probably also occurred among the leaders, although we have no evidence that any had yet become followers. John tells us of two at his death—Joseph of Arimathea and Nicodemus—but describes Joseph as a "secret disciple" due to fear of the other leaders (19:38). These two (and possibly a few others) were converted at some stage during Jesus' ministry. Certainly the pressure against speaking favorably about Jesus that the common people felt (7:13) was also felt by the leaders themselves. At any rate, the Pharisees were saying to the Levites that they, the Pharisees and leading priests, were the experts in the law, not them, so they should quit listening to this upstart, Jesus. Then they accused these Levitical police of becoming like the "foolish crowd" who followed Jesus. To do so was to be "ignorant of the law" and under "God's curse" (7:49). This corresponds to the Pharisaical attitude toward "the people of the land" (Heb. 'am ha'arets [TH5971A/776, ZH6639/824]), who did not know the law to the same scrupulous degree that the Pharisees did and so were regarded as under the covenant curses (Deut 27:26; Ps 119:21; Jer 11:3). They viewed these people as open to all kinds of trickery by false teachers.

In an ironic development, one of their own proved the leaders wrong by taking Jesus' side (7:50-52). Nicodemus, who had interacted with Jesus in 3:1-15, challenged them regarding the legality of convicting someone without a hearing. Nicodemus appears three times in John's Gospel—at first not as a believer (3:1-15) but in the end as a believer (19:39-42). At some time, he became a follower, and it may have been before this statement, but we do not know. As Michaels says (1989:142), he is here as a contrast with the Pharisees and as a "plea (unheeded) for fairness" rather than to signify a stage in his own spiritual progress.

In 7:49, the Jewish leaders implied they were experts on the law, so Nicodemus raised a point of law. There is no exact statement in rabbinic literature to this effect, but several texts demand a serious investigation regarding any illegality (e.g., Deut 1:16; 17:2-5; 19:15-19; cf. Exodus Rabbah 21:3). The Romans had the same rule (cf. Acts 25:16). The other leaders did not answer his query but derided him as an honorary Galilean (an obvious slur, in effect calling him a provincial nincompoop) and repeated their earlier attack on Jesus (cf. 7:41). In actuality, they were wrong in saying that no prophet came from Galilee, for Jonah and Nahum were from that province, and rabbis at that time said prophets had arisen from every tribe (b. Sukkah 27b). They most likely intended to refer only to the "prophet like Moses," but John was showing the extent of their rejection of Jesus. They were so opposed to him that they were not even thinking logically. Most importantly, as before, they remained ignorant that he was actually from heaven.

◆   ## 10. Excursus: the woman caught in adultery (7:53–8:11)

[The most ancient Greek manuscripts do not include John 7:53–8:11.]

CHAPTER 8

53Then the meeting broke up, and everybody went home.

Jesus returned to the Mount of Olives, 2but early the next morning he was back again at the Temple. A crowd soon gathered, and he sat down and taught them. ³As he was speaking, the teachers of religious law and the Pharisees brought a woman who had been caught in the act of adultery. They put her in front of the crowd.

⁴"Teacher," they said to Jesus, "this woman was caught in the act of adultery. ⁵The law of Moses says to stone her. What do you say?"

⁶They were trying to trap him into saying something they could use against him, but Jesus stooped down and wrote in the dust with his finger. ⁷They kept demanding an answer, so he stood up again and said, "All right, but let the one who has never sinned throw the first stone!" ⁸Then he stooped down again and wrote in the dust.

⁹When the accusers heard this, they slipped away one by one, beginning with the oldest, until only Jesus was left in the middle of the crowd with the woman. ¹⁰Then Jesus stood up again and said to the woman, "Where are your accusers? Didn't even one of them condemn you?"

¹¹"No, Lord," she said.

And Jesus said, "Neither do I. Go and sin no more."

NOTES

7:53–8:11 This passage is as close to a conclusive text-critical case as exists in the NT. Almost certainly this story was not originally part of John but was added by later scribes. It is missing from nearly all the early mss (e.g., 𝔓66 𝔓75 ℵ Aᵛⁱᵈ B Cᵛⁱᵈ L N T W 037 038 044 0141 0211 33). As for the mss A and C, though they both have lacunae in this portion of John, careful measurements show that it is unlikely that there was enough space in the original codices of either of these mss to contain the story (so Metzger 1994:187). No Greek Father commented on the passage before the twelfth century. It is also missing from many of the oldest mss in the versions (e.g., Old Latin, Syriac, Coptic). The only early Greek ms to include it is D, and it is notoriously expansive. Furthermore, the story is placed in several places in the Gospels by various later scribes—after Luke 21:38 or after John 7:36, 7:44, or 21:25. Finally, the language of the story is closer to the synoptic Gospels, esp. Luke (e.g., having "the teachers of religious law and the Pharisees" in 8:3, a phrase not found in John). This evidence shows that John never included this story in his Gospel; it was added later. Nonetheless, it is likely that this is a true story, an authentic piece of tradition from the apostles. Eusebius (*History* 39.16) mentions a similar story by Papias, and this story is found in the third century *Didascalia Apostolorum* (ch 7 [§2.24]). The story itself is like similar stories of attempts to trap Jesus, and his actions are in keeping with his responses elsewhere.

COMMENTARY

As the note on 7:53–8:11 points out, this story is not part of the canonical Gospel—that is, it was not written by John. Nevertheless, it is most likely a true story about Jesus. Thus, it is true but not canonical—so, how do we handle it in a teaching or preaching situation? I believe the best way is to rely on other biblical material on handling sexual sin in the church (e.g., 1 Cor 6:12-20; 1 Thess 4:1-8) and use this as an exemplary story to demonstrate how Jesus dealt with such sinners. Though it is not canonical, it is excellent illustrative material on an important issue. Let us briefly consider the story.

The setting (7:53–8:2) could fit the time of the Festival of Shelters (Whitacre) or the Passion Week (Carson). At any rate, Jesus was staying on the Mount of Olives (his home for Passion Week, cf. Luke 21:37), probably in Bethany at the foot of the mountain (Mark 11:11-12), and going to the Temple to teach every morning. The encounter with the teachers of religious law and Pharisees trying to trap him (8:3-6a) is similar to the Temple debates in Mark 11:27–12:24 (esp. 12:13, 15). It seems that the teachers of religious law and Pharisees had been laying in wait for Jesus. They had caught a woman in an adulterous liaison, probably the night before, and were just then bringing her to Jesus. Whitacre (1999:205-206) calls their treatment of her "callous and demeaning," noting that they must have held her incommunicado just for the opportunity to "trap" Jesus (there probably had been no trial for her as yet). Her humiliation and fear would have been incredible. These teachers asserted that the law of Moses says to stone such women (8:5), a rather hard-nosed statement; there is little evidence that they were seeking justice or truth. The law was fairly clear. Stoning was only demanded if a virgin engaged to be married committed adultery, and then both the man and the woman were to be stoned (Deut 22:23-24). In other types of adultery, death was prescribed, but the means was not specified (Deut 22:22). Such legalities were not the interest of the leaders, however; they wanted only to "trap [Jesus] into saying something they could use against him" (8:6). If he treated the law lightly, they could accuse him of disobeying it. If he enforced it, they could get him in trouble with the Romans, who did not allow the Jews to execute people (cf. note on 18:31). Moreover, there is some evidence that stoning was rarely done and was not very popular with the people (so Carson). These leaders were coldheartedly using the unfortunate woman to get at Jesus.

Jesus' reaction (8:6b-9) is noteworthy. Still sitting (cf. 8:2), he bent over and started writing in the dust. A great deal has been written regarding the message he may have left in the dust, perhaps Jeremiah 17:13 ("All who turn away from you . . . will be buried in the dust of the earth [lit., 'written in the dust']"—a view held by Augustine) or the sins of the accusers (suggested by Jerome) or the sentence Jesus would deliver (a Roman practice—to write down the sentence and then read it; see Brown for other conjectures). But in the final analysis, there is no way to know what he wrote. While he was writing, the leaders kept hounding Jesus for his answer, so he finally stood up and gave his response, "All right, but let the one who has never sinned throw the first stone." This was a brilliant riposte and in keeping with Matthew 7:1-5, "Do not judge others . . . [with a] log in your own eye." This would be in keeping with the first suggestion above regarding Jeremiah 17:13, for Jesus had shifted the focus from the woman to their own sins. Many (e.g., Lindars, Ridderbos) believe there may also be a reference to Deuteronomy 13:9 and 17:7, in which the official witnesses to the adultery were to cast the first stones. In other words, Jesus was saying, "Who is prepared to come forward as a witness against this woman, when he has the witness of God against himself?" (Schnackenburg).

Beginning with the oldest (in traditional Jewish deference to older people but possibly also because they were more aware of their sins), the people gathered there slipped away one by one until Jesus was alone with the woman. When Jesus said, "Didn't even one of them condemn you?" (8:10), he was hardly referring to the whole scene, for they had been condemning her for the entire time until that moment. Jesus meant "condemn" in the ultimate sense; all her accusers had left. When she answered, "No, Lord," he then delivered his sentence: "Neither do I" (7:11). Jesus had the God-given authority to judge (5:22, 30), and thus he had the authority to forgive (Mark 2:5-11; Luke 7:48-49). The experience of forgiveness, however, places a moral and spiritual responsibility on the individual, so Jesus added, "Go and sin no more." Here Jesus shows his knowledge of the woman's sins (7:11). She was undoubtedly guilty, but her life of sin had to end with this experience of God's forgiveness.

◆ ## 11. Jesus, the Light of the World (8:12-20)

¹²Jesus spoke to the people once more and said, "I am the light of the world. If you follow me, you won't have to walk in darkness, because you will have the light that leads to life."

¹³The Pharisees replied, "You are making those claims about yourself! Such testimony is not valid."

¹⁴Jesus told them, "These claims are valid even though I make them about myself. For I know where I came from and where I am going, but you don't know this about me. ¹⁵You judge me by human standards, but I do not judge anyone. ¹⁶And if I did, my judgment would be correct in every respect because I am not alone. The Father* who sent me is with me. ¹⁷Your own law says that if two people agree about something, their witness is accepted as fact.* ¹⁸I am one witness, and my Father who sent me is the other."

¹⁹"Where is your father?" they asked.

Jesus answered, "Since you don't know who I am, you don't know who my Father is. If you knew me, you would also know my Father." ²⁰Jesus made these statements while he was teaching in the section of the Temple known as the Treasury. But he was not arrested, because his time* had not yet come.

8:16 Some manuscripts read *The One.*   8:17 See Deut 19:15.   8:20 Greek *his hour.*

NOTES

8:14 ***These claims are valid.*** There is a seeming contradiction between 5:31 ("my testimony would not be valid") and Jesus' statement here. The reason for this is that Jesus was speaking from a different perspective on each occassion. Legally speaking, his self-witness would not be valid in a court of law, but spiritually speaking, it was valid because he was the Son of God who had came from heaven, speaking with the voice of God.

COMMENTARY

According to 7:37-39, the morning event of the Festival of Shelters (the water-drawing ceremony) was fulfilled by Jesus. According to 8:12, the evening event, the candle ceremony, was fulfilled when he "once more" (this is the second of three speeches in a chain of messages, together with 7:37-39 and 8:21ff) declared, "I am the light of the world." At dusk, the priests would light four huge lamps in the Court of Women in the Temple; these were quite tall and had to be reached by ladders. At the top, each stand held four golden bowls filled with oil, and the worn-out undergarments of the priests were used for the wicks (so Brown, Burge, Keener). Since this took place on the Temple mount, the highest point in the city, it is said that all of Jerusalem was lit from those lamps. There would be more dancing and joy through the night. Probably at the end of the festival (though John does not say), Jesus again stated that he is not just the light of Jerusalem but of the whole world. He was in the "Treasury," which is in the Court of Women, so he may have been standing beneath the golden bowls as he made his announcement.

The structure of 8:12 closely resembles the "living water" saying of 7:37-38, with three aspects—the claim, a reference to the believer who follows, and the results for those who adhere (so Ridderbos, Blomberg). As in the previous "I am" saying (6:35), Jesus portrays himself as fulfilling Yahweh imagery from the Old Testament, as well as the festival itself. At the Exodus, the special presence of God (or shekinah) was symbolized in the pillar of fire by night and the cloud by day (Exod 13:21-22; 14:24; Ps 78:14), and light became a symbol of the divine presence (cf. the theophany in Gen 15:17), God's salvation (Ps 27:1, "The LORD is my light and my salvation"; cf. Ps 44:3; Isa 60:19-20), and the deliverance of God's people (Judg 7:16; 15:4-5). Light was also symbolic of God's word (Ps 119:105) and Israel, which was called to be "a light to the Gentiles" (Isa 49:6; cf. Isa 9:2). This last point is especially relevant, for according to 1:4, 9, Jesus is the Word who sheds God's light on every person. Jesus saw himself as the divine light-bearer. He was the divine light that brought light into the darkness (1:5; 3:19-20) of the world.

We earlier noted that Zechariah 14:8 underlies the water ceremony (cf. on 7:37-38). In Zechariah 14:6-7, God promised that when the day of the Lord came it would be "continuous day . . . at evening time it will still be light." This had relevance for the light ceremony of this festival, as Jesus proclaimed that he was bringing a new light of God not only to the Jews but to the world—a new time of salvation. He went on to tell the people how they could find this salvation: "If you follow me, you won't have to walk in darkness" (cf. 1:5; 3:19-20; 12:35-36, 46). As stated in 1:11, Jesus' own people rejected him and chose the path of darkness. But if they would turn to him, they would "have the light that leads to life." Israel was delivered by following the pillar of fire. Jesus promised a much greater deliverance, an eternal salvation, to those who would follow the true Light.

The Pharisees raised a legal question (8:13) that is reminiscent of 5:31. Jesus was making "claims" about himself, and self-witness was legally invalid. Deuteronomy 19:15 demands two or three witnesses to validate any legal claim. Jesus here clarifies his statement of 5:31. While his testimony to himself was not valid in a court of law, this was not such a court, and he was not a normal witness. As the Son of God, he knew both his origin ("where I came from") and his final destination ("where I am going"). The Pharisees' judgment was faulty because once again they were thinking with an earthly rather than a heavenly perspective. They didn't know about Jesus and his true origin, not because they could not know but because they had rejected his light.

Jesus then contrasted his own divine judgment with their own "human standards" of judging—that is, their fleshly limitations (8:15-16). In 3:17 we are told that Jesus came not to judge but to save, and yet in 5:22, 30 he said he was called by his Father to judge. And here he again says that he does "not judge anyone." This is not a contradiction. Jesus did not mean that he never functioned as judge but rather that he could never make a superficial, human judgment the way his opponents did (so Carson, Whitacre). He clarified this in the next verse. "If I did" is equivalent to "when I judge"—in light of his God-given authority in 5:22, 30. When that happens, his judgment is "correct in every respect" because it is not based on "human standards" but is in complete union with the Father who sent him. Jesus' judgment is equivalent to God's decision. Putting it all together (3:17; 5:22, 30; 8:15-16), we understand that Jesus did not come to judge but to bring people to salvation; but his coming forced people to make a decision. For all those who rejected his offer of salvation, he became the God-appointed judge, and his decision is a divine decision. Also, in both cases (when he judges and when he does not), he is acting in union with God. When he does not judge, it means he does not do so on his own; when he does, he is acting as the agent of his Father (so Barrett, Blomberg). "I and the Father who sent me" is a Semitism denoting the unity between Father and Son and indicates "that Christ had now taken the place of Israel in relation to God (cf. 15:5)" (so Köstenberger 2004:255-256).

Jesus then returned to the argumentation of 5:31-40 and the law's demand (Deut 17:6; 19:15) for two witnesses (8:17-18). He is one, and his Father the other. He calls it "your own law" (8:17) because he is providing a new law—"the Torah of the Messiah," so to speak—and he is contrasting his new revelation with the legalistic Pharisaic brand of Torah interpretation. Also, at first glance this would not be a valid argument, for Jesus' self-witness would not be allowed (5:22), but Jesus' witness to himself transcends that rule because he is the divinely appointed envoy, the Son of God (note "Father who sent me" in 8:16, 18). The Pharisees' earthbound reaction was, "Where is your father?" (Philip will make a similar error in 14:8). They could not begin to understand or accept what Jesus had said since 5:17, that his Father is in heaven, the place of his own origin (the misunderstanding theme continues, see Carson 1982). Jesus responded as he had elsewhere: they neither knew him (5:37-38) nor God (7:28). This gets at the heart of Jewish self-identity as the covenant people who have identified themselves as the children of God. Jesus' point was that if they did not know the one sent by the Father, they could not know the sender either. One can only know the Father through "the one and only Son" (1:14, 18; 3:16).

John concludes this section by telling the reader that the dialog took place "in the section of the Temple known as the Treasury," the place in the Court of Women that contained 13 trumpet-shaped receptacles where people gave their offerings (cf. Mark 12:41-44). Since it was the place where the candle-lighting ceremony took place, it was a natural setting for this discourse (so Michaels). It was right in the open where multitudes could hear the give and take. The leaders still could not arrest him because, as before, "his time had not yet come" (cf. 7:30). Until the hour of destiny God had stipulated, Jesus' opponents were powerless.

◆   ## 12. Jesus warns the unbelievers (8:21-30)

²¹Later Jesus said to them again, "I am going away. You will search for me but will die in your sin. You cannot come where I am going."

²²The people* asked, "Is he planning to commit suicide? What does he mean, 'You cannot come where I am going'?"

²³Jesus continued, "You are from below; I am from above. You belong to this world; I do not. ²⁴That is why I said that you will die in your sins; for unless you believe that I AM who I claim to be,* you will die in your sins."

²⁵ "Who are you?" they demanded.

Jesus replied, "The one I have always claimed to be.* ²⁶I have much to say about you and much to condemn, but I won't. For I say only what I have heard from the one who sent me, and he is completely truthful." ²⁷But they still didn't understand that he was talking about his Father.

²⁸So Jesus said, "When you have lifted up the Son of Man on the cross, then you will understand that I AM he.* I do nothing on my own but say only what the Father taught me. ²⁹And the one who sent me is with me—he has not deserted me. For I always do what pleases him." ³⁰Then many who heard him say these things believed in him.

8:22 Greek *Jewish people;* also in 8:31, 48, 52, 57.   **8:24** Greek *unless you believe that I am.* See Exod 3:14. **8:25** Or *Why do I speak to you at all?*   **8:28** Greek *When you have lifted up the Son of Man, then you will know that I am.* "Son of Man" is a title Jesus used for himself.

NOTES

8:24 *believe that I AM.* Witherington (1995:175) reminds us that this "does not amount to a claim to be the heavenly Father, or to exhaust the Godhead" but is "a claim to divine status or eternal existence"; Jesus is divine yet still "dependent on the Father, and while on earth as his agent, in a subordinate role to him." This tension between equality and subordination defines the Christology of John (cf. also 5:18). Jesus is one with the Father in his being and yet subordinate to him in his incarnate state.

die in your sins. Interestingly, "sin" is singular in 8:21 (for the realm of sin) and plural in 8:24 (for the individual sins people commit). As in Rom 5:12 ("for everyone sinned"), every person both inherits the sin principle and participates in it by committing sins.

8:25 *The one I have always claimed to be.* The Gr. is difficult and has led to several interpretations: (1) it is an affirmation of what has been said, with respect to Jesus' personhood: "(I am) from the beginning what I tell you" (Miller 1980, Baesley-Murray, Michaels, so NLT); (2) it is an affirmation of his function: "(I am) what I have told you from the beginning" (Bruce, Beasley-Murray, Carson, Comfort, Michaels, Blomberg, RSV, NASB mg, Phillips, NIV, NJB); or (3) it is a question: "Why do I speak to you at all?" (Greek Fathers, NEB, NASB, NLT mg). The affirmation view best fits the Greek and the context. The two options for the affirmation (personhood and function) are very similar, but due to the high Christological content of the surrounding verses, personhood may be slightly preferable.

8:28 *When you have lifted up.* This is the only one of the three "lifted up" sayings that is in the active voice. The others (3:14; 12:32) have passive voices ("the Son of Man must be lifted up"). Here the emphasis is on Jewish guilt for putting Christ on the cross. Yet, as in the sermons in Acts (e.g., Acts 2:23, 36, 38; 3:13-19), their guilt should not lead to anti-Semitism. Instead, the message is a call to repentence: *You killed Jesus, but he died for your sins; therefore, repent.*

COMMENTARY

This third message in the series at the Festival of Shelters (cf. "once more" in 8:12, 21, pointing to a chain of messages—7:14ff; 8:12ff; 21ff) adds further material on

Jesus' divine origins and the terrible destiny of those who refuse to believe. In it, a series of oppositions is established between Jesus and the Jews: He is from above; they are from below. He is not from this world; they are of this world. His destiny is not theirs. His father is God; theirs is the devil (so Barrett, Carson). His first contrast centers on his destiny, repeating the message of 7:33-34. He would soon depart, and they would search for him (meaning they would continue to seek their Messiah, never accepting the fact that they had already met him)—but they could not go where he was going. On the surface, this could mean anything. In 7:35, they thought he was moving to another country. His departure, of course, would be at the Cross, when he became the atoning sacrifice for sin. They knew nothing of that, for they had rejected him. Therefore, they would "die in (their) sins" rather than experience that atoning sacrifice. This is why they could not accompany Jesus to his final destination—the Father in heaven. The only way to get there is through faith (3:16; 5:24, 38; 6:35, 47; 7:38). The disciples would be told something very similar (13:33, 36) but without the menacing danger. They were to remain on earth and follow Jesus later (14:2-4), while these opponents would never be able to go.

As always, the Jewish people failed to understand and this time asked if Jesus was planning suicide (8:22), thinking that when he said "you cannot come," he meant they would not want to join him in death. There is certainly irony here, for Jesus *was* referring to his death but not in the way they thought. He would surrender his life, but it would be in the "hour" of destiny (NLT, "time," 8:20; cf. 2:4; 7:30) established by God's plan of salvation, not in some suicidal act. Then Jesus gave the second contrast—they are "from below," he "from above" (8:23). In the same way that salvation is "from above" (3:3, NLT mg), Jesus is "from above." "From below" does not mean the realm of Satan but rather this earthly sphere (so Comfort). Jesus and they were from two different realms—that of God and that of sinful mankind. The gap could not be bridged except by Jesus himself (1:51; 14:6); now he has descended to the lower realm and "opened up a way—indeed, himself constituting the way—by which others may ascend there too" (Bruce 1983:192).

Because they had chosen to belong to the realm of sinful humanity, they would "die in (their) sins" (8:24). They would not only die physically but spiritually in an eternal death. The noun for "sin" only occurs once before this (1:29, "the Lamb of God who takes away [your] sin") but is found three times in 8:21 and 24, emphasizing the terrible danger they were in. "Sin" is in absolute opposition to the holiness of God and is the primary barrier between mankind and God. To "die in your sins" is to die without any hope of reconciliation with God. There are only two options: have their sins forgiven via the Lamb's atoning sacrifice or face God's wrath in eternal punishment (3:36). The only way to life is stated clearly by Jesus: unless you believe that I am who I claim to be (8:28), with double meaning also implying "that I am Yahweh" (cf. commentary on 6:19-21). There are three occurrences of the absolute "I am" in this chapter (8:24, 28, 58; cf. 13:19; 18:5-6). Jesus deliberately makes the phrase ambiguous to provide multiple levels of meaning. At one level is the translation here: they must believe the claims he has made in the preceding context—to be the Bread of Life, the one who descended from heaven, and the Light of the World. At another level is the immediate context: believe that I am the one soon to ascend to my Father at the appointed hour for my death. At the third level is the major theme, the deity of Christ. This was not understood by the crowd and leaders, but since they eventually tried to stone Jesus (for blasphemy), they must have begun to catch on to this nuance. The disciples did not begin to understand this until Thomas's proclamation in 20:28: "My Lord and my God."

It was natural that the crowd responded to this with "Who are you?" (8:25). Jesus responded by reiterating his previous teaching regarding himself—"The one I have always claimed to be." He wanted them to understand that he had been telling them who he was from the beginning. Their problem was that they had not been listening, and what they had understood they had rejected. Therefore, Jesus went on, having much to say, primarily in the area of judgment due to their unbelief (5:45-47; 6:26-27, 41-42, 52; 7:7, 34). It was no use, though—they were on a completely different wavelength. He reiterated that the source of his teaching was "the one who sent me." (For Jesus doing what he "sees" his Father doing, see 5:19; for his saying what he hears from the Father, see 5:30; 8:26, 40; for both seeing and hearing, see 3:32.) As expected, the crowd still did not get it. They failed to realize that Jesus was "talking about his Father" (8:27), even though he had used the phrase "the one who sent me" of his Father so often.

As they continued to fail to recognize that God the Father had sent Jesus, so they also failed to recognize that Jesus was the Messiah. Jesus had already told them of his approaching departure (8:21), and in 8:28a he tells them that at that time they will finally understand who he is. Note the great irony in the fact that when the Jews crucify Jesus, they are actually "lifting him up" to glory (so Köstenberger, following Bultmann). This is the second of three sayings in John about the Son of Man being "lifted up" (with 3:14; 12:32); these sayings are John's equivalent to the Synoptic passion predictions. As stated in the commentary on 3:14, the double meaning is powerful: When Jesus is "lifted up" on the cross, he will be "lifted up" in glory. The cross is his throne, his time of exaltation. In this sense, the Cross, Resurrection, and Ascension become one event in salvation history. Therefore, it is at that time that the Jews finally "will understand that I AM he." This hardly means mass conversion, although after Pentecost there were 3,000 conversions (Acts 2:41). The national revival will not occur until the Lord returns (cf. comment on Rom 11:25-32 in Osborne 2003).

Finally, Jesus repeats (8:28b) what he has often said—that he does nothing on his own (5:19, 30; 6:38; 7:16, 28; 8:16). He had the absolute knowledge that everything he did was from God. He spoke only what he had "heard" from God, and now he states that he does only what his Father has taught him. What he says and does is absolute truth because his Father is "truthful" (8:26). This was the basis of his confidence. His opponents wanted to kill him (5:18; 7:1, 19), and many of his followers had deserted him (6:60-66). He was soon to die the most horrible death imaginable. Yet still he was supremely at peace with it all. Why? Because "the one who sent me is with me—he has not deserted me" (8:29). When even his closest followers and friends deserted him, he said, "The time is coming—indeed it's here now—when you will be scattered . . . leaving me alone. Yet I am not alone because the Father is with me" (16:32). There is a lesson in this for us. When we face our own trials and troubles, we need to be aware of God's presence with us. As Paul says in Romans 8:31, "If God is for us, who can ever be against us?" (cf. 8:31-39). The result is that "many" of his hearers "believed in him." In 2:23, many who saw his deeds put their faith in him, and that faith turned out to be immature. Here, many who heard his words found faith, and perhaps that faith would be stronger (cf. 4:41 for the discussion of word-based faith). As stated before, John's theme is that it is important to see Jesus' deeds *and* hear his words in coming to faith.

◆   ## 13. The children of Abraham and the children of the devil (8:31-59)

31Jesus said to the people who believed in him, "You are truly my disciples if you remain faithful to my teachings. 32And you will know the truth, and the truth will set you free."

33"But we are descendants of Abraham," they said. "We have never been slaves to anyone. What do you mean, 'You will be set free'?"

34Jesus replied, "I tell you the truth, everyone who sins is a slave of sin. 35A slave is not a permanent member of the family, but a son is part of the family forever. 36So if the Son sets you free, you are truly free. 37Yes, I realize that you are descendants of Abraham. And yet some of you are trying to kill me because there's no room in your hearts for my message. 38I am telling you what I saw when I was with my Father. But you are following the advice of your father."

39"Our father is Abraham!" they declared.

"No," Jesus replied, "for if you were really the children of Abraham, you would follow his example.* 40Instead, you are trying to kill me because I told you the truth, which I heard from God. Abraham never did such a thing. 41No, you are imitating your real father."

They replied, "We aren't illegitimate children! God himself is our true Father."

42Jesus told them, "If God were your Father, you would love me, because I have come to you from God. I am not here on my own, but he sent me. 43Why can't you understand what I am saying? It's because you can't even hear me! 44For you are the children of your father the devil, and you love to do the evil things he does. He was a murderer from the beginning. He has always hated the truth, because there is no truth in him. When he lies, it is consistent with his character; for he is a liar and the father of lies. 45So when I tell the truth, you just naturally don't believe me! 46Which of you can truthfully accuse me of sin? And since I am telling you the truth, why don't you believe me? 47Anyone who belongs to God listens gladly to the words of God. But you don't listen because you don't belong to God."

48The people retorted, "You Samaritan devil! Didn't we say all along that you were possessed by a demon?"

49"No," Jesus said, "I have no demon in me. For I honor my Father—and you dishonor me. 50And though I have no wish to glorify myself, God is going to glorify me. He is the true judge. 51I tell you the truth, anyone who obeys my teaching will never die!"

52The people said, "Now we know you are possessed by a demon. Even Abraham and the prophets died, but you say, 'Anyone who obeys my teaching will never die!' ⁵³Are you greater than our father Abraham? He died, and so did the prophets. Who do you think you are?"

⁵⁴Jesus answered, "If I want glory for myself, it doesn't count. But it is my Father who will glorify me. You say, 'He is our God,*' ⁵⁵but you don't even know him. I know him. If I said otherwise, I would be as great a liar as you! But I do know him and obey him. ⁵⁶Your father Abraham re-joiced as he looked forward to my coming. He saw it and was glad."

⁵⁷The people said, "You aren't even fifty years old. How can you say you have seen Abraham?*"

⁵⁸Jesus answered, "I tell you the truth, before Abraham was even born, I AM!*"

⁵⁹At that point they picked up stones to throw at him. But Jesus was hidden from them and left the Temple.

8:39 Some manuscripts read *if you are really the children of Abraham, follow his example.* **8:54** Some manuscripts read *your God.* **8:57** Some manuscripts read *How can you say Abraham has seen you?* **8:58** Or *before Abraham was even born, I have always been alive; Greek reads before Abraham was, I am.* See Exod 3:14.

NOTES

8:31 *Jesus said to the people who believed in him.* These people—apparently those who came to faith in 8:30—seem to be described later as "slave[s] of sin" (8:34), trying to kill him (8:37a, 40), hardened to his message (8:37b), children of the devil (8:44), unbelievers (8:45-47), and liars (8:55). Several explanations have been offered (cf. Beasley-Murray, Carson): (1) There is a distinction in Greek between "believe in" (actual believers, 8:30) and "believe" with the dative (quasi-believers, 8:31)—but this does not fit, since the former is also used of halfhearted faith in 2:23 and the latter of true faith in 5:24. These two constructions are virtually synonymous, and are accordingly translated in the NLT. (2) The faith in 8:30 and 31 was false faith, and Jesus exposed it in 8:31-59—but in Johannine theology, word-based faith, such as that in 8:30-31, is a strong faith. (3) These are Judaizing Christians who demanded that all Christians follow the law of Moses—but this does not fit the context, for this debate did not occur in Jesus' day. (4) These are genuine believers, but the polemic is addressing a problem in the time of John rather than Jesus—possible, but such a manufactured situation is unnecessary in this context. (5) Jesus is addressing a crowd in which some have been converted (8:30-31) but many opponents still remain. It is the latter that Jesus is addressing in this discourse. These could be the immature believers of 2:23-25, but the language of this passage does not fit their situation. This last view is the best for the context here.

8:36 *truly free.* Hendriksen (1953:54) says that there are two levels of freedom in Christ—first freedom from slavery to sin and second freedom plus sonship—that is, in Christ alone the emancipated slave is also adopted as God's own child, rejoicing in the glorious freedom of sonship (cf. 2 Cor 3:17; Gal 4:6, 7). This is more than John intended but is nevertheless true theologically.

8:56 *rejoiced as he looked forward to my coming.* Some scholars (Lindars, Haenchen) believe this refers to Abraham in paradise watching the events of Jesus' life unfold. This is possible, given Jesus' use of Abraham in paradise in the parable of the rich man and Lazarus (Luke 16:19-31), but in light of the past tenses of the verbs here it is unlikely.

COMMENTARY

This dramatic dialog is the culmination of the conflict between Jesus and the Jews in chapters 5–8. It consists of three parts: the Jewish claim to be descendants of Abraham (8:31-41a); Jesus' countercharge that their true father is the devil (8:41b-47); and Jesus' claim to deity (8:48-59).

The Jewish Claim to Be Descendants of Abraham (8:31–41a). Jesus addressed those who came to faith in 8:30 and defined true "disciples" as those who "remain faithful to my teachings" (lit., "remain in my word"). The verb "remain" (*menō* [TG3306, ZG3531]) is a key term in John (40 occurences compared to a total of 12 in the Synoptics) that connotes a permanent relationship with God, an enduring, abiding faith, and an indwelling presence (so Brown 1966:510-511). The idea here is a complete commitment and an abiding faithfulness to Jesus' teaching. Those who are sold out to his word in this way "know the truth"—that is, they can discern the true way to live and are committed to living that way (cf. Heb 5:14). "Truth" here is Jesus' revelation of the Father, but it is dynamic, changing lives (cf. 8:36), as well as propositional, establishing doctrines. This kind of truth "will set you free"—that is, it will free you from sin (8:34; cf. Ps 119:45). As Whitacre says (1999:219), "to know Jesus is to be liberated from all error and evil, for it is to know God himself, who is truth and purity and life." This is an important message for the church in our time, when half-hearted commitment is so common. Jesus made it clear in his teaching: "Anyone who puts a hand to the plow and then looks back is not fit for the Kingdom of God" (Luke 9:62). Those who play games with Jesus and his word are not truly "disciples," and we must question whether or not they were true believers. Those who think Jesus meant that we are "free" to pursue whatever dreams we want are sadly mistaken. Rather, we are free to follow God.

The crowd once more failed to understand Jesus and centered on his use of "set you free" (8:33), interpreting it as freedom from enslavement by other nations. Since they had maintained their national identity throughout their subjugation to Assyria, Babylon, Persia, Greece, and Rome (conveniently ignoring their enslavement by Egypt), they centered on the Abrahamic covenant and said, "We have never been slaves." Their point was that in spite of political dominance, they had never been truly controlled by the others. As Carson says (1991:349, following Barrett), "compare Mark 2:17, where the Jews are convinced they are whole and therefore need no physician—just as they are convinced they are free and therefore need no liberation (cf. also 9:40-41)." The people challenged Jesus' statement that they needed to be "set free." The importance of Jesus' response is seen in his solemn double *amēn* [TG281, ZG297] introduction, rendered "I tell you the truth" in the NLT (8:34; cf. 1:51; 5:19, 24, 25; 6:26, 32, 47, 53). He corrected their mistaken political understanding and made it clear that he was speaking of spiritual and moral enslavement instead. The true slave is "everyone who sins" (8:34) because sinners sell themselves to a vicious taskmaster. Paul used the same image in Romans 6:6-7, 14, 16-23, telling us that everyone is a slave of something, either of sin or of righteousness. Only Christ can set us free from the one to follow the other. For Jesus and Paul (Rom 6:1-14), sin is a conquering power that takes people captive and then controls their lives.

Jesus then developed this metaphor into an illustration contrasting the status of the slave with that of the son (8:35-36). The purpose was to make his Jewish hearers aware of their misperception. They thought of themselves as children of Abraham (8:33, 39), but in reality they were slaves of sin (8:34). In fact, many think Jesus was quoting an existing parable here (Dodd, Lindars, Bruce). In the ancient world, the nuclear family didn't only consist of husband, wife, and children but also included one's slaves. A slave, however, was never "a permanent member of the family" because he or she could be sold to someone else or could earn his or her freedom. (In Judaism a slave was to be given freedom after six years in the "sabbatical year" [Deut 15:12-14], but this was probably not observed that often. In the Greco-Roman world, manumission occurred more frequently than one would think, many were freed even before they reached 30 [ABD 6.71].) A son, however, was "part of the family forever" (8:35). He would always be a part of the family, even after death. Jesus was obviously contrasting his Jewish hearers (slaves to sin) with himself (the Son of God). He descended from heaven and came directly from God, while they had rejected God's Son and chosen the path of sin. He offered hope, however. These slaves could be freed from their bondage—but in this case, that freedom could only be purchased by the Son. In the ancient household, a son could, when he became an adult, free a slave. Jesus had been given that authority from God (3:35), and he was the only path to freedom. When he frees people, they "are truly free"—the power of sin has been broken once and for all. Paul speaks of Christians' "old selves," which have been nullified by the Cross (Rom 6:6), and the liberation that has brought us into a new realm, that of Christ and the Spirit.

Jesus then specified the true status of his Jewish listeners (8:37-38). Yes, they "are descendants of Abraham" in terms of lineage, but that was not the whole truth, for they were not Abraham's children (8:39). They did not qualify spiritually—that is, they were Jews outwardly but not inwardly (Rom 2:28-29; cf. Jer 9:25-26). There were two problems: First, some were trying to kill Jesus, which was the ultimate proof that they had rejected God's path and had turned against his divinely sent envoy. Second, there was no room in their hearts for Jesus' message—further proof that they had turned their backs on God's truth. As stated in 8:31, the true disciple remains faithful to Jesus' message. Their actions were proof positive that they qualified as Abraham's descendants only physically and were not his children spiritually. Jesus could prove that he was one with his Father because he had given the revelation he saw when he was with his Father. His message had its origin in heavenly reality and came from the Father. In contrast, they were "following the advice of (their) father" (8:38), later identified as the devil (8:44). They were enslaved to sin just like their true father, and that is why they had no access to God or heaven.

Jesus' hearers misunderstood his point about "the advice of [their] father" and so claimed, "Our father is Abraham" (8:39), going back to their physical lineage. The spiritual problem remained, so Jesus repeated the point he had just made. If their father was truly Abraham, they would "follow his example." When my wife taught first grade, she could tell which children belonged to which parents within the first minute of meeting them. The children were the image of their parents. That was Jesus' point; the Jewish people's actions showed who their true parent was, and it was not Abraham. Again, the proof was their desire to kill Jesus. This showed that they had completely rejected the truth. In other words, their actions proved their true heritage. To reject the Son is to reject the Father. To refuse Jesus' truth is to refuse God's truth, and in this refusal, they were no longer the covenant people of God. Abraham never rejected God's message or tried to kill God's messengers (as at Sodom and Gomorrah), so this proved they were in actuality imitating their real father, the devil, not Abraham.

Jesus' Countercharge: Children of the Devil (8:41b-47). Again, the Jews misunderstood Jesus' point (8:41b), saying, "We aren't illegitimate children! God himself is our true Father." They claimed their lineage from Abraham and their inherited good relationship with God. But they had not been listening, for Jesus called both into question. Behind this could well be the conflict between the Jews and the Samaritans as to who were the actual children of Abraham. The fact that the Samaritans were the result of the Assyrian occupation of Israel and the forced interbreeding of the Jews who remained in the land after the Exile with pagans brought in by the Assyrians caused the Jews to regard the Samaritans as half-breeds. Also, there is some evidence that the Samaritans believed the Jews descended from Cain rather than Seth and that Cain was the result of the seduction of Eve by Satan (so Bruce). Both regarded each other as "illegitimate." It is also possible that the Jews were asserting that Jesus was an illegitimate son born out of wedlock and therefore contrasting themselves to Jesus (so Brown, Lindars contra Ridderbos, Borchert). In any case, the focus is their claim to be the legitimate children of God (cf. Exod 4:22; Deut 32:6; Isa 64:8; Jer 3:4; Mal 2:10); they believed that they had not committed spiritual adultery ("illegitimate" in the Greek is "children of fornication") but had remained true to God. Keener (2003:759) calls this another case of irony; they claim to have descended from God when they do not have the Spirit.

Jesus' retort (8:42) repeats the point of 8:37. If God were truly their father, they would love his Son. Jesus had been "sent" by him, and therefore the reception of God's envoy was a sign of love for God. As stated so often in chapters 5–8, Jesus had come to this earth from heaven (6:33, 38, 51, 58; 7:28; 8:14, 23) and had been sent from God (5:36, 38; 6:29, 57; 7:29, 33; 8:16-17). Since the Father and Son are one, to love one is to love the other. At the same time, to hate one is to hate the other. Their attitude toward Jesus showed that God was not their father. In frustrated indignation, he first asked, "Why can't you understand what I am saying?" and then tells them why. "It's because you can't even hear me!" Their ears had been stopped, first by unbelief and then by an outside force, their father, Satan. As Morris says (1995:463), "They are so wrapped up in their preconceptions that they cannot perceive the truth. It repels them."

Jesus spelled out clearly what he had been hinting at all along (8:44). Their true father was neither Abraham (8:39) nor God (8:41) but rather the devil—"You are the children of your father the devil." They were slaves of sin (8:34) and children of Satan. Their true paternity was revealed, as Jesus confronted them at the deepest level. There are three ways in which their kinship to the devil was manifest: (1) They loved the same kind of evil deeds he does. There is a double emphasis on their desires and the resultant deeds. Satan's basic desire is to set himself up as god, and this has led him to oppose God at every level. They followed in his footsteps and turned their backs on the God of their fathers by rejecting his Son. (2) They sought to kill Jesus, following the one who "was a murderer from the beginning." The "beginning" is a reference to Satan's seduction of Adam and Eve (cf. 1 John 3:8, 15), leading to their expulsion from Eden and the introduction of death to mankind (cf. Rom 5:12-14). The death of Jesus was ultimately attributable to Satan (13:2, 27). (3) By rejecting God's truth in Jesus, they had followed the one who "has always hated the truth, because there is no truth in him." Satan's chief characteristic is deception (Rev 12:9; 20:3, 8, 10); he does not overpower people so much as lead them astray via lies. In fact, lying is at the heart of "his character; for he is a liar and the father of lies." We expect lies from him; there will never be truth in anything he says or does. All lies (for instance, those spoken by the leaders about Jesus) have their origin with Satan. There was a book written a few years ago that said the average American speaks 600 lies a day, most of them things like, "I'm fine" or "You look great." Indeed, the natural man lives with lies every moment of the day—the only place for truth is in Christ.

Since the people followed "the father of lies," they naturally didn't believe Jesus when he told the truth. In fact, the Greek says that "because" he spoke truth they didn't believe. The truth of God in Jesus was so repugnant to them that they automatically rejected it. It is the greatest tragedy imaginable for anyone to reach that state. It is as close to the unpardonable sin (Mark 3:28-29; Heb 6:4-6) as one can get. As Köstenberger says (2004:267), "Hence, unbelief is shown to be rooted ultimately in people's subjection to satanic lies and deception rather than merely lack of comprehension or human choice."

Jesus then asked two questions centering on their charges: (1) "Which of you can truthfully accuse me of sin?" (8:46). Jesus knew that they thought him to be a Sabbath-breaker and blasphemer (5:18), a messianic pretender (6:41-42; 7:27, 41-42, 52), a false teacher (7:47), and demon possessed (7:20; 8:48). His question was a legal one: on what grounds could they accuse him and make it stand? Jesus dared them to convict him of sin. (2) "Why don't you believe me?" (8:46). The answer to the first question (i.e., they could not convict him of sin) should lead to a proper response to the second (they should put their trust in him). He was the only one actually telling them the truth, and yet they rejected it. Of course, Jesus himself had already answered this—it was because they followed their father, the devil. Only the one "who belongs to God" can "[listen] gladly to the words of God" (8:47). This goes back to 6:35-44; God had given some to Jesus, and they rejoiced in the truth. But generally the Jews refused to listen because they didn't belong to God—a point made throughout this discourse. They had rejected the Son and so were no longer the children of God. One could virtually say that they had switched fathers!

Jesus' Claim to Be Deity (8:48-59). The Jewish reaction to Jesus' charge that they were the children of the devil proves the truthfulness of his accusation. They already had accused him of being demon possessed (7:20; cf. 10:20), and now they add the charge that he was a Samaritan. It is possible that this is linked with Jesus' time in

Samaria and his positive reception there (so Keener, Köstenberger). The Jews thought that the Samaritans were heretics, and Samaria was also a major source of sorcerers like Simon Magus (Acts 8:9-24). The charge in 8:48 combined ideas of heresy, blasphemous claims, and sorcery, as well as being closely connected to being demon possessed (so Schnackenburg). In a sense, they were turning the tables on Jesus: "You say we don't descend from Abraham; we say you don't either—you come from the Samaritans. You say we're the children of the devil; we say you're demon possessed." As in Mark 3:20-30, Jesus denied the charges and returned to the theme of his honoring and glorifying God (cf. 7:18). A heretic or a demon-possessed individual would never seek to honor God, but Jesus always did (the verb is present tense pointing to an ongoing activity). In contrast, they continually dishonored Jesus, God's Son, and therefore dishonored God the Father. At the same time, Jesus never sought his own glory (again, 7:18)—further proof that he was not what they claimed. As a result of his perfect orientation toward God, Jesus would be glorified by the Father. This, in fact, is the theme of the Philippian hymn (Phil 2:6-11): Jesus sought humility and left the glory up to God. Since God is the "true judge" (8:50), that glory (cf. 1:14; 2:11 for this theme in John) is both certain and right. The fact that the Jewish people had rejected Jesus and sought to kill him was inconsequential; God's pleasure in him was all that mattered.

Using another double *amēn* [TG281, ZG297] saying (8:51, "I tell you the truth"; see note on 1:51), Jesus pointed to a critical truth: "Anyone who obeys my teaching will never die." Note that the emphasis in this saying has moved from believing (as in 5:24) to its result: "obeys my teaching." Of course, obedience is inherent in "listen to my message" in 5:24; in the Bible, to hear is to obey. Literally, Jesus challenges his hearers to "keep" his teaching, which involves not only obedience but also maintaining its priority in the church and in our personal lives. Those who base their lives on Jesus' teaching will have eternal life (cf. 6:39-40, 47, 50-51, 58). Still hearing Jesus at the superficial level (cf. 8:19, 22, 33, 39, 41, 48), the people interpreted "never die" as living on this earth forever. They were astonished, for "even Abraham and the prophets died" (8:52)—and that in spite of their faithful obedience to God. How then could Jesus say that those who obeyed his teaching would never die? Such blasphemy could only come from a demonic delusion. Was he making himself greater than Abraham? They concluded with the question, "Who do you think you are?" (8:53). Note the irony—the one who, more that anyone who ever lived, does not seek his own glory (7:18; 8:49-50) is the one they accused of magnifying himself.

Jesus once again reiterated the points he had been making all along (8:54-56). This short paragraph could well be called a summary of the main points in the discourses of chapters 5–8: (1) Jesus did not seek his own glory or do anything on his own (5:19, 30; 6:38, 57; 7:16, 18, 28; 8:16, 26, 28, 42, 50). Every aspect of his existence was in conscious union with the Father and had as its goal the glory of the father. (2) All his glory comes from the Father (5:23; 6:27; 8:50). Because Jesus is completely oriented to God's glory, God gives him glory (cf. 12:28; 17:1-5), but not the glory the Jews understood. The glory of Jesus was in being lifted up on the cross (3:14; 8:28; 12:32). (3) The people didn't really know God, even though they claimed he was their God (5:37-38, 42; 7:28; 8:19, 47). This is the heart of the conflict and repeats a frequent Old Testament theme (Isa 1:3; Jer 2:8; 4:22; Hos 4:1). They had rejected Jesus because he did not fit their conception of the Messiah; they did not realize that he was more than Messiah—he was the Son of God. Therefore, they did not know the true God. (4) Jesus both knew God and obeyed him (5:19; 6:46; 7:28-29; 8:29). There is only one path to God (14:6) and only one way to know God—through the one and only Son who knows him utterly and completely (1:18).

Then Jesus returned to the subject of Abraham (8:56), whom they had claimed as their father (8:33, 39). They thought they were related to him, but Jesus had a far greater right to speak, for Abraham "rejoiced as he looked forward to [Jesus'] coming" (8:56). There is some question as to which event in Abraham's life this rejoicing refers. Most agree that Jesus is building on Genesis 15:17-21 (Abraham's vision of the covenant ceremony). Jewish rabbis differed in their interpretation of Genesis 15, some saying it referred to this age and the age to come (Akiba) while others restricted it to this world (Johanan ben Zakkai). Literally, this says that Abraham rejoiced "to see my day," and for Judaism this most likely referred to "the Day of the LORD," with Jesus making the Day of Yahweh his day. It is sometimes debated whether the "day" refers to Jesus' life and ministry or to the events of the last days, but actually this is a moot point since Jesus' life and ministry inaugurated the last days. Mainly, it points to the Incarnation as the dawning of the final age (so Carson, Ridderbos, Morris, Köstenberger).

The response of the crowd is interesting (8:57) and once more is firmly anchored in a worldly perspective, "You aren't even fifty years old." Jesus was probably 33 or 34, so this is a round number. M. J. Edwards (1994:451-454) argues that John had in mind the year of Jubilee, possibly building on the 50-year cycles of the book of Jubilees. The people's statement would in this light be an unconscious prophecy of Jesus as lord over history and lead into Jesus' response in 8:58. Abraham had been dead for nearly 2,000 years, so they were aghast at Jesus' statement. Jesus' answer (the third double *amēn* [TG281, ZG297] saying in this chapter, cf. 8:34, 51) is one of the better known sayings in John: "Before Abraham was even born, I AM!" The absolute *egō eimi* [TG1473/1510, ZG1609/1639] here is the clearest example yet (cf. 8:24, 28; 13:19; 18:5-6) of the proclamation, "I am Yahweh," seen in its Isaianic background (cf. Isa 41:4; 43;10-13, 25; 45:18-19; 48:12; 52:6) as a divine self-disclosure. Jesus was saying in effect, "Before Abraham was even born, I, Yahweh, was there." Thus, this is a claim not only of divinity but also of pre-existence. Jesus, as part of the divine Godhead, was in existence long before Abraham. Hoskyns (1947:349) says, "The contrast is between the existence initiated by birth and an absolute existence. . . . The Being of the Son is continuous, irrespective of all time (Chrysostom [*Homilies on John*])." The emphasis is not just on Jesus' personhood but on what he means for salvation, in keeping with Exodus 3:14-15

(Yahweh as the faithful God of the covenant) and Isaiah 43:11-13; 46:4; 48:12 (so Beasley-Murray). The point is that Jesus was not acting as a mere messianic figure; he is the Word, the divine Revelation, God himself. The various categories bandied about throughout the Festival of Shelters (wonder-worker, prophet, Messiah) were transcended by Jesus, who claimed to be the living water, the light of the world, and the "I am" (so Dodd, Whitacre).

The Jews tried to stone him for blasphemy (8:59), showing they understood his claim (cf. 5:18; 10:31). They were unable to do so, however, because Jesus "was hidden from them and left the Temple." This hints at a miracle: the Son of God hid himself from them because his hour of destiny had not yet arrived (cf. 7:30, 44; 8:20). Jesus' departure from the Temple in this scene is his last appearance at the Temple in John's account. It is possible that there is symbolic meaning in this, picturing the shekinah presence of God abandoning the Temple (so Schnackenburg, Carson). As such, Jesus would be symbolically proclaiming divine judgment on the Temple (as in the Olivet Discourse; cf. Mark 13 and parallels). "Jesus left Jerusalem behind, abandoning the beloved city to its own spiritual ruin (cf. Matt 23:37-39; Luke 13:34-35). Subsequently, his task was to call his believers out from Judaism, even as a shepherd calls his sheep to leave the fold for lush, green pastures" (Comfort 1994:86-87).

◆   14. Jesus heals a man born blind (9:1-41)

As Jesus was walking along, he saw a man who had been blind from birth. ²"Rabbi," his disciples asked him, "why was this man born blind? Was it because of his own sins or his parents' sins?"

³"It was not because of his sins or his parents' sins," Jesus answered. "This happened so the power of God could be seen in him. ⁴We must quickly carry out the tasks assigned us by the one who sent us.* The night is coming, and then no one can work. ⁵But while I am here in the world, I am the light of the world."

⁶Then he spit on the ground, made mud with the saliva, and spread the mud over the blind man's eyes. ⁷He told him, "Go wash yourself in the pool of Siloam" (Siloam means "sent"). So the man went and washed and came back seeing!

⁸His neighbors and others who knew him as a blind beggar asked each other, "Isn't this the man who used to sit and beg?" ⁹Some said he was, and others said, "No, he just looks like him!"

But the beggar kept saying, "Yes, I am the same one!"

¹⁰They asked, "Who healed you? What happened?"

¹¹He told them, "The man they call Jesus made mud and spread it over my eyes and told me, 'Go to the pool of Siloam and wash yourself.' So I went and washed, and now I can see!"

¹²"Where is he now?" they asked.

"I don't know," he replied.

¹³Then they took the man who had been blind to the Pharisees, ¹⁴because it was on the Sabbath that Jesus had made the mud and healed him. ¹⁵The Pharisees asked the man all about it. So he told them, "He put the mud over my eyes, and when I washed it away, I could see!"

¹⁶Some of the Pharisees said, "This man Jesus is not from God, for he is working on the Sabbath." Others said, "But how could an ordinary sinner do such miraculous signs?" So there was a deep division of opinion among them.

¹⁷Then the Pharisees again questioned the man who had been blind and demanded, "What's your opinion about this man who healed you?"

The man replied, "I think he must be a prophet."

¹⁸The Jewish leaders still refused to believe the man had been blind and could now see, so they called in his parents. ¹⁹They asked them, "Is this your son? Was he born blind? If so, how can he now see?"

²⁰His parents replied, "We know this is our son and that he was born blind, ²¹but we don't know how he can see or who healed him. Ask him. He is old enough to speak for himself." ²²His parents said this because they were afraid of the Jewish leaders, who had announced that anyone saying Jesus was the Messiah would be expelled from the synagogue. ²³That's why they said, "He is old enough. Ask him."

²⁴So for the second time they called in the man who had been blind and told him, "God should get the glory for this,* because we know this man Jesus is a sinner."

²⁵"I don't know whether he is a sinner," the man replied. "But I know this: I was blind, and now I can see!"

²⁶"But what did he do?" they asked. "How did he heal you?"

²⁷"Look!" the man exclaimed. "I told you once. Didn't you listen? Why do you want to hear it again? Do you want to become his disciples, too?"

²⁸Then they cursed him and said, "You are his disciple, but we are disciples of Moses! ²⁹We know God spoke to Moses, but we don't even know where this man comes from."

³⁰"Why, that's very strange!" the man replied. "He healed my eyes, and yet you don't know where he comes from? ³¹We know that God doesn't listen to sinners, but he is ready to hear those who worship him and do his will. ³²Ever since the world began, no one has been able to open the eyes of someone born blind. ³³If this man were not from God, he couldn't have done it."

³⁴"You were born a total sinner!" they answered. "Are you trying to teach us?" And they threw him out of the synagogue.

³⁵When Jesus heard what had happened, he found the man and asked, "Do you believe in the Son of Man?*"

³⁶The man answered, "Who is he, sir? I want to believe in him."

³⁷"You have seen him," Jesus said, "and he is speaking to you!"

³⁸"Yes, Lord, I believe!" the man said. And he worshiped Jesus.

³⁹Then Jesus told him,* "I entered this world to render judgment—to give sight to the blind and to show those who think they see* that they are blind."

⁴⁰Some Pharisees who were standing nearby heard him and asked, "Are you saying we're blind?"

⁴¹"If you were blind, you wouldn't be guilty," Jesus replied. "But you remain guilty because you claim you can see.

9:4 Other manuscripts read *I must quickly carry out the tasks assigned me by the one who sent me;* still others read *We must quickly carry out the tasks assigned us by the one who sent me.*   **9:24** Or *Give glory to God, not to Jesus;* Greek reads *Give glory to God.*   **9:35** Some manuscripts read *the Son of God?* "Son of Man" is a title Jesus used for himself.   **9:38-39a** Some manuscripts do not include *"Yes, Lord, I believe!" the man said. And he worshiped Jesus. Then Jesus told him.*   **9:39b** Greek *those who see.*

NOTES

9:1-41 This story has been a favorite for scholars trying to recover the "life-setting" of John's Gospel in his community (Bultmann, Haenchen, Martyn). For instance, when it says the man's parents were afraid of being "expelled from the synagogue," higher critics see this as fitting John's own time, when Christians had been expelled from synagogues (from the mid-80s on). This interpretation, however, is unnecessary. It simply means that the parents would be placed under the ban, and it does not have to stem from a later historical situation. There is nothing in the story that does not fit into the period of Jesus' life (cf. note on 9:22).

9:2 *Was it because of his own sins or his parents' sins?* The suffering of children due to their parents' sins is found in Exod 20:5; Deut 5:9. The possibility of a child sinning in the womb is discussed in *Genesis Rabbah* 63:6 in terms of Jacob and Esau struggling in the womb (Gen 25:22) on the basis of Ps 58:3, "These wicked people are born sinners; even from birth [lit., 'from the womb'] they have lied and gone their own way."

9:3 *This happened so the power of God could be seen in him.* The Gr. *hina* [TG2443, ZG2671] (so that), as rendered here, indicates that the man's blindness did not occur because of sin but for the sake of God's power being shown. The phrase "This happened" does not appear in the Greek but is supplied by the NLT (cf. NIV) for clarity. But there is another way to understand this—namely, to connect the purpose clause to what follows: "So that the power of God may be seen in him, we must quickly carry out the tasks . . ." (so Poirier 1996, Burge). If this were correct, Jesus would not be saying that God allowed the man to be blind for a higher purpose but simply would be saying why they must act quickly. This view is quite possible but perhaps not quite as likely because the context seems to indicate that Jesus was answering their question as to the reason for the man's blindness. It is also possible that this is linked with Jesus' time in Samaria and his positive reception there (see Köstenberger).

9:4 *We must . . . us.* Some mss have "me" in place of "us" here. "Me" is supported by B D 070 (it^d) syr^pal cop^sa geo^1; this was most likely the original reading. The mss that have "us" (𝔓66 𝔓75 ℵ* cop^bo) appear to have made the change to better match the opening "we." The same is true of those that replace the opening "we" with "I" (ℵ^1 A C Θ Ψ f^1.13 33 𝔐). Cf. NLT mg.

9:7 *Go wash yourself.* Some scholars (e.g., Cullmann, Brown) believe the washing of the eyes is symbolic of baptism as a salvific act; however, there is no evidence in the text for such an interpretation (cf. Schnackenburg, Carson).

9:14 *because it was on the Sabbath.* The NLT makes the Sabbath the reason why the people took the man to the Pharisees. Actually, the Sabbath is the reason the Pharisees use to condemn Jesus. By making clay he was working on the Sabbath, and further, he was not supposed to heal a person on the Sabbath unless it was a life-threatening illness.

9:16 *Some of the Pharisees said, . . . Others said.* The division of the Pharisees on this issue follows generally the party lines of the Pharisees. Some (the school of Shammai, the more conservative branch) followed the letter of the law—Jesus' working on the Sabbath made him a sinner. Others (the school of Hillel, less conservative) followed the spirit of the law and considered the facts of the case—Jesus had performed a good work (so Bruce).

9:22 *expelled from the synagogue.* Carson (1991:369-370) shows how many (e.g., Barrett, Martyn) explain this as anachronistic, pointing to a late-first-century date. The verb occurs only in John in the NT, and seems to reflect the rewriting (c. AD 85–90) of the Twelfth Benediction (from the Eighteen Benedictions that Jews recited three times a day), which excluded Christian Jews from the synagogue. The ban in Jesus' day allowed participation in religious exercises, so it is argued that the later date is best. However, there are good reasons to doubt this scenario: (1) Luke 12:8-9 gives corroborative evidence that a test of Christian heresy involving expulsion from the synagogue did indeed occur during Jesus' life. (2) There is evidence of excommunication before the time of Jesus, as in the first century BC (*m. Ta'anith* 3:8), and Paul was expelled (Acts 13:50) long before AD 85–90. (3) There is considerable debate regarding the rewritten Twelfth Benediction, and the wording could have been aimed at other Jewish sectarians and not Christians. (4) Horbury (1982) argues convincingly that a ban against heresy existed long before 85 AD and that the reworked Twelfth Benediction actually reinforced it with the intent of preventing Christians and others from serving as officers in the synagogue. (5) John's literal statement in 9:22 that the Jews "had announced" (*ēdē . . . sunetetheinto*) about putting these people out of the synagogue recognizes that this practice predated Jesus. (6) The idea of confessing Jesus as Messiah makes perfect sense during his lifetime. In short, the evidence supports the historical veracity of this story.

9:31 *We know.* The man had almost joined the ranks of the followers of Jesus. At this stage, he may well have been a partial believer like those in 2:23-25. Earlier he had said that Jesus was "a prophet" (9:17), and here he said that Jesus had come "from God" (9:33). His faith continued to develop.

9:35 *Son of Man.* This is a strange title here, and one would expect more simply "Son" or "Son of God." In fact, several later mss have "Son of God" (A L 038 044 070 0250 𝔐 f[1,13] it[mss] syr[p,h]). But there is excellent support for "Son of Man" (𝔓66 𝔓75 ℵ B D W it[d] syr[s] cop), and "Son of Man" is the more difficult reading (i.e., it is more likely that it would have been changed). Thus, it is probably the original reading.

9:38-39a *"Yes, Lord, I believe!" the man said. And he worshiped Jesus. Then Jesus told him.* Some ancient mss (𝔓75 ℵ* W it[b] cop[ac2,sa MS]) have not included this section. It is possible that the words may have been added later on the basis of baptismal liturgy. Brown (1966:380-381) suggests that "the words were an addition stemming from the association of John 9 with the baptismal liturgy and catechesis." Porter (1967) affirms the same. But it is also possible that the words are original due to the weight of evidence in favor of their inclusion (𝔓66 A B C D 𝔐). Metzger (1994:195) argues that the words were accidentally omitted or that perhaps the omission was the result of an editorial omission made to unify the teaching in 9:37, 39.

9:39 *I entered this world to render judgment.* Many quote Bultmann here (1971:341-342): "This is the paradox of the revelation, that in order to bring grace it must also give offence, and so can turn to judgment. In order to be grace it must uncover sin; he who resists this binds himself to his sin, and so through the revelation sin for the first time becomes definitive."

9:41 *If you were blind, you wouldn't be guilty.* This can be understood three ways: (1) if you realized you were blind, you could come to me in faith and have your guilt removed (Whitacre); (2) if you were in complete darkness and had no light at all, you would not be guilty of the sin of unbelief, for you would have acted in ignorance (Morris, Carson); or (3) if you were only physically blind, that would not be a sin and not keep you from being healed (Ridderbos). The first is attractive but has to read more into the language than is viable. The third does not quite fit the symbolic cast of 9:39-41. The second is the most viable.

C O M M E N T A R Y

Jesus had fulfilled the major events of the Festival of Shelters by declaring himself "the light of the world" (8:12) and by shedding his light on the Jewish crowds. Next, he demonstrated this light by healing a blind man and showing that the Pharisees were blind (9:39-41). What Jesus said of himself in chapter 8 is shown to be true by his miracle in this passage. The healing of the blind had never occurred before (9:32), so for the Jews, this should have been proof positive that the Messiah had indeed arrived.

This is a brilliantly written story; it centers on a series of interrogations (9:8-12, 13-17, 18-23, 24-34) sandwiched between an opening and a closing (9:1-7, 35-41, see Schnackenburg, Beasley-Murray, Burge). The movement in the story is quite explicit: the man begins blind and proceeds to physical sight and then to spiritual sight; in contrast, the Pharisees claim to have spiritual sight and by the end are shown to be blind. There is a subtheme, as well—the importance of taking a public stand for Jesus (cf. Luke 12:8). The parents and then the man himself were called upon to publicly side either with Jesus or the leaders. There was no middle ground. It is interesting that, like the Samaritan woman, the man was never named; the emphasis is more on the symbolism of the story and the spiritual nuances than on the individuals involved.

The Healing of the Man (9:1-7). At some time between the Festival of Shelters (in the fall) and Hanukkah (10:22ff), Jesus was walking along and saw a man who had been "blind from birth." Most likely, part of the dialog here was not recorded, for the disciples' question to Jesus is based on knowing that the man's condition was from birth. They wanted to know if his blindness was his own fault or the result of his parents' sin. This is certainly a common belief, then as well as now. Some rabbis even said that a child in the womb could already be involved in sin (*Genesis Rabbah* 63:6). While some suffering is the result of sin, the Bible is clear that there are many reasons for suffering—examples include the trials of Job and Paul's thorn in the flesh (2 Cor 12:7-9), which he considered a sign of God's grace, allowing him to boast in his weakness and exalt "the power of Christ" at work in him. Something similar to Paul's situation was at work here. As Jesus said, "This happened so the power of God [lit., 'the works of God'] could be seen in him." The cause was not as important as the purpose. This concept is paralleled in Exodus 9:16 (God's rationale for dealing harshly with Pharaoh) and Luke 13:1-5 (it is not the degree of sinfulness but the fact of repentance that matters—so Blomberg). Jesus' "work" is the Father's "work" (5:17, 19), and the goal is always the glory of the Father. So it was in this instance. This was the time of God's work; therefore Jesus said, "we (Jesus and the disciples) must quickly carry out the tasks assigned us by the one who sent [*me*]" (see note on 9:4). Note the switch from plural "we" to singular "me." While the disciples worked with him, the task they engaged in was his. The disciples (and we readers) have the privilege of assisting Jesus in his work.

The reason they must do so "quickly" (lit., "while it is day") is that "the night is coming" when "no one can work" (9:4). "Day" refers to the time when Jesus was with them on earth, and the "night" refers to a time of darkness when he would be taken from them. The "light of the world" was with them now (cf. 12:35-36, "Walk in the light while you can, so the darkness will not overtake you"), but the night was coming (cf. 13:30, Judas leaves at night; 20:1, the women come to the tomb while it is still dark). The "night" refers not so much to the period after the Spirit is poured out (who is, in a sense, the continuing presence of Jesus with his disciples) but rather to the time between the Cross and the coming of the Spirit (so Carson). During that time, they did not work but rather experienced the resurrection appearances (the first 40 days, Acts 1:3) and then waited in the upper room and at the Temple, rejoicing during the other ten days before Pentecost (50 days after Passover, cf. Luke 24:53; Acts 1:13-14). Still, during the time before his departure, Jesus continued to be "the light of the world," and his followers rejoiced in the day he brings. This is the theme of the chapter, as the "Light" brings "light" to the man born blind.

The actual process of this healing is very strange to the modern mind. The idea of Jesus spitting on the ground, making a mud pack of it (the clay is associated by the early Fathers with the creation of mankind from dust, Gen 2:7 [Irenaeus *Heresies* 15.2]), and putting the pack on the man's eyes is repugnant to most of us. Similar miracles utilizing spittle occur at Mark 7:33 (a deaf and dumb man) and 8:23 (a blind man). In the ancient world, the spittle of a holy man was viewed as having healing powers (*t. Sanhedrin* 12:10), and Jesus was accommodating himself to the level of the man's faith. He told the man to wash the mud off his eyes at the pool of Siloam (cf. 2 Kgs 5:10-14, Naaman washing in the Jordan to cure his leprosy), southwest of the city by the valley of Hinnom. John brought out the meaning of the name Siloam, "sent" (from the Heb. *shiloakh* [TH7971, ZH8938]), undoubtedly emphasizing that Jesus was doing the work of God as the sent one, God's envoy (stressed throughout chs 5–8), and possibly also creating a wordplay with Jesus "sending" the man to the pool.

Interrogation by the Neighbors (9:8-12). The blind man was probably a fixture in the community, possibly begging in the same place for years. Therefore, many people knew him by sight, and when he walked by as a normal, seeing person, they were shocked, with some recognizing the formerly blind beggar but others convinced that he only looked like the blind man. To everyone who asked, he kept repeating, "Yes, I am the same one!" Next they asked the natural follow-up question: "Who healed you? What happened?" So far, the story seems similar to that of the crippled man in chapter 5, who was also asked about who healed him. But the crippled man had appeared dimwitted and said in effect, "Beats me!" The healed blind man was far more aware of the situation (as we will see throughout the story); he answered his questioners, "The man they call Jesus," and then gave a synopsis of what had occurred. As the story progresses, we see his understanding develop (so Bruce). However, when asked where Jesus was, he could not answer. Most likely, the people he was speaking with wanted to meet Jesus rather than attack him.

Interrogation by the Pharisees (9:13-17). The neighbors probably "took the man who had been blind to the Pharisees" because the Pharisees were the religious experts and would know what to make of the extraordinary event. They did not expect that the Pharisees would be so hard on the man. Those who ask why they went to the Pharisees, rather than to the scribes and the priests, ask a question that cannot be answered. The reason may simply be that the Pharisees were there. Also, there was no need to take such an issue to the priests, for no ritual uncleanness would be involved. Scribes could have been involved, but many of them were Pharisees, and John never mentions the scribes, probably because in his day (after the destruction of Jerusalem) all scribes were Pharisees (so Carson).

The trouble starts with the fact that the healing took place on the Sabbath (9:14)—the same situation as the healing in 5:1-15. The Pharisees had developed a series of oral traditions regarding what constituted work prohibited on the Sabbath. Jesus had broken three of the rules: (1) healing was only allowed on the Sabbath in a life-threatening situation; (2) some rabbis believed that anointing the eyes on the Sabbath was wrong; and (3) kneading was disallowed, and making a mud poultice was a type of kneading (so Beasley-Murray, Blomberg). When the Pharisees heard the man recount his story to this effect, the result was division, as usual (9:16; cf. 6:60-71; 7:12-13, 30-31, 40-44; 10:19-21). The reaction of some was what one would expect: Jesus was not "from God" (*para theou*, cf. this phrase in the Gr. of 1:6 regarding the Baptist), for he was working on the Sabbath. He must be a false prophet, for he did not keep the Torah. Yet others were not so sure. An "ordinary sinner" could hardly perform "such miraculous signs," they stated. He had not just performed any miracle (Deut 13:1-5 warned of false prophets doing miracles)—he had healed a blind man, one blind from birth.

The Pharisees came back to the healed man a second time and asked for his "opinion about this man who healed" him (9:17). In 5:15, the crippled man who had been healed reported Jesus to the authorities. Here, the reaction was just the opposite. He confessed, "I think he must be a prophet." His spiritual development is evident here. At first, he only knew of his healer as "the man they call Jesus." He had obviously been reflecting on the implications of this and was now ready to acknowledge him as a prophet. He had not yet understood Jesus as *the* prophet (i.e., the "prophet like Moses"; cf. 1:21; 6:14), but he probably saw him in the Elijah/Elisha mold—a miracle-working prophet (cf. the Samaritan woman in 4:19). Several (Carson, Keener, Köstenberger) note how the man becomes a model disciple as he progresses in his understanding of Jesus as healer (9:11), then prophet (9:17), one to be followed (9:27), one from God (9:33), and finally, the Lord to be worshiped (9:38).

Interrogation of the Parents by the Pharisees (9:18-23). The Pharisees are now "the Jewish leaders," because they represent the apostate nation (a Johannine theme, see 1:11). They were still hopelessly divided, but the majority were certain that no true God-sent miracle could have occurred. They needed more evidence, so they decided to question the man's parents, perhaps hoping to find that he himself was a fraud. This now has the look of a legal investigation, but not one handled responsibly. They were not looking for truth but rather for evidence to support the position they had already decided on—that Jesus (and the man) must be guilty. They asked the parents if he had really been blind from birth, expecting to hear that it was not so. The only thing they were sure of was that no actual miracle could have taken place, so if he was indeed blind from birth, "how can he now see?"

The parents refused to be used in this way (9:20-21), undoubtedly sensing the negative intention of the Pharisees. They were willing to affirm the basic facts—he was indeed their son and he was indeed born blind. They were not willing to go beyond that. They had no idea how he was healed or who did it. They demanded, "Ask him. He is old enough." A child became an adult at age 13 and could then be legally interrogated. The ball was back in the court of the leaders, and their ploy had failed to work. John then explains why the man's parents were so cautious. They were "afraid of the Jewish leaders" because the word had gone out that they had threatened to use the ban on "anyone saying Jesus was the Messiah" (9:22). As Whitacre says (1999:243), "This scene is full of tragedy, for these parents are not allowed to give thanks to God for the great thing he has done for their son. They must have agonized over the blindness and begging he was forced into. Now he has been miraculously healed, and they must put aside the overwhelming parental joy and knuckle under to the goons from the committee for the investigation of un-Jewish activity, as it were."

A Second Interrogation of the Man (9:24-34). The attack intensified, as the leaders virtually required the man to repent, commanding him to "give glory to God" (9:24, NLT mg). They meant that as long as he acknowledged Jesus, he could not acknowledge God. They could no longer doubt that he had been blind and that now he could see. Thus, they changed their strategy. The one thing they were certain of was that "this man Jesus is a sinner" (9:24)—their conclusion after the debates in chapters 5–8. Their statement, "Give glory to God" is virtually equivalent to "tell the whole truth" in the sense of a formal oath when testifying (cf. Josh 7:19; 1 Sam 6:5, so Westcott, Kysar). They demanded that the healed man admit Jesus was not a prophet. The man's reply was curt; he knew only one thing: he was blind and now he could see.

The Pharisees' frustration is apparent. They had to go back to the beginning: "How did he heal you?" (9:26). The formerly blind man seems to have realized the lack of honest searching on their part and so went on the offensive, saying, "Didn't you listen?" He had had it with their double-edged questions and realized they were not searching for what had really happened. He then turned to biting irony: "Do you want to become his disciples, too?" He wanted to expose their lack of desire to know the truth. At this, they showed their true colors, as they began to curse him (9:28). This does not refer to profanity but to calling down the covenant curses for blasphemy (cf. Lev 24:10-16; Num 15:30). This is a key to the whole debate between Jesus and the Jews. They were "disciples of Moses," while in their view anyone who followed Jesus was his disciple and could not follow Moses. They had artificially set up an absolute dichotomy between Jesus and Moses; to believe in one meant rejecting the other. They believed that God revealed his law to Moses (Num 12:8) and viewed Jesus as a contrary upstart. But in this attitude they were actually rejecting Moses because they had rejected the one Moses wrote about. Witherington (1995:184) says, "This, of course, is precisely the problem—not knowing Jesus' origins and destiny leads to inevitable misunderstanding of Jesus and his work."

The man's sarcasm against the leaders increased, as he said, "Why, that's very strange!" (9:30). He found the unbelief of the leaders rather remarkable in light of the simple fact that Jesus healed the blind. That is the one thing their radical skepticism was unable to answer. How could they say they "don't know where this man comes from"? It should have been rather obvious since none of them could heal the blind. God must have had a very special relationship with this Jesus. The one area in which the healed man was in agreement with the leaders was the fact that "God doesn't listen to sinners" (cf. 9:24), but that was as far as it went. He went on to say that God *does* "hear those who worship him and do his will" (9:31). The point is that only a godly man could do such a thing, especially since the particular miracle, the healing of the blind, had never occurred before. His logic was impeccable. Such a miracle could not mean anything other than that Jesus was indeed "from God." A false prophet could perform some miracles, but not this one.

Stymied in their attempt to get the man to turn against Jesus, the leaders turned against him (9:34). They had been upstaged by his arguments and so reacted viscerally, in a sense saying, "You have no right to teach us." As Pharisees, they looked down on anyone without proper training, let alone a former beggar. They returned to the mistaken logic of 9:2; since he was born blind, he must have been "born a total sinner." Before, they had said that sin brought physical blindness; now they claimed his sin had brought spiritual blindness. They were wrong again (so Burge). He was accused of the same thing as Jesus (9:24)—being a sinner. They also proved once more that they were unteachable and completely closed to the truth. As will be stated explicitly in 9:40-41, the truly blind ones were the Jewish leaders.

Conclusion: True Sight versus Blindness (9:35-38). The movement observable throughout this narrative now comes to full fruition. It is quite apparent that two things were happening: The man was moving step by step from physical sight to spiritual sight, and at the same time the Pharisees were descending further and further into complete spiritual blindness. Light was conquering darkness (1:5). The Pharisees were doing everything they could to prove that Jesus was a false prophet. Their efforts had come to naught; they had evicted this man from the synagogue, and now Jesus approached him again. Jesus often encountered people directly (1:43, 47; 4:7; 5:6) as he does here. We should remember that the man was sent to wash the mud pack off his eyes while still blind (9:7) and had not seen Jesus' face until this moment. Jesus' direct challenge to him must have seemed abrupt and come as something of a shock. Yet it was the perfect question in light of his developing understanding. When Jesus asked, "Do you believe in the Son of Man?" (9:35) the man was ready.

Why do we find the "Son of Man" title here? "Son of God" is more frequent in John and would make more sense (cf. note on 9:35). However, Jesus as "the Son of Man" in John is the one who brings life and judgment (1:51; 3:13-14; 5:26-27; 8:28; esp. 6:27, "[seek] the eternal life that the Son of Man can give you"). It is the Son of Man who rewards the man's belief with life here and then brings judgment upon the blind Pharisees in 9:39-41. As Son of Man, Jesus unites heaven and earth (1:51), provides salvation via the Cross (8:28), and discloses divine truth to the world. Obviously, the man could not understand much of this, but the reader is expected to see the larger picture. In 3:14-15, the lifting up of the Son of Man is a call to believe in him and have eternal life. This story acts out that same challenge. The man responded immediately, saying, "I want to believe in him." He had no idea who this "Son of Man" was, but he knew God had done something astounding in his life, and he wanted to believe. (Contrast this with the crowd's "Who is this Son of Man?" in 12:34, where they do not want to believe.)

As with the Samaritan woman (4:26), Jesus told the healed man that the one he was seeking was indeed the very one he was seeing (a second miracle of coming to sight!) and speaking with (9:37). The Pharisees looked and saw a false prophet they despised, while the man was now looking on the face of the very Son of Man who brings eternal life. The man did not hesitate at all but immediately cried out, "Yes, Lord, I believe!" (9:38). Then he prostrated himself before Jesus in worship. What a moment! The first time he actually saw Jesus, he found out he was also looking upon the face of the Son of Man. Though he worshiped, the man surely did not recognize Jesus as God himself at this stage (cf. Thomas in 20:28); he was worshiping the God who acted in Jesus (so Schnackenburg, Beasley-Murray). Yet at the same time, such obeisance in the Bible is indicative of a theophany (cf. Gen 18:2; Judg 13:15-22), so the man was symbolically recognizing more than he realized (so Brown, Carson).

Jesus gave life to the man but then explained to him the other side of his mission as Son of Man: rendering judgment, which in this story means "to give sight to the blind and to show those who think they see that they are blind" (9:39). This was in actuality the "moral of the story," helping the healed man "to grasp that the miracle that opened his eyes, and the ensuing debate with the religious authorities, constituted an acted parable about sight and blindness in the spiritual realm" (Carson 1991:377). The growing openness of the man to truth and the developing rejection of the leaders is the story in a nutshell. Brown (1966:377) shows how three times the man had confessed his ignorance (9:12, 25, 36), while three other times the Pharisees bragged of how much they knew (9:16, 24, 29). Jesus' statement in 9:39 might well contain an allusion to Isaiah 6:10, which he quotes in 12:40: "The Lord has blinded their eyes and hardened their hearts." As with Pharaoh, God may well judge those who turn a blind eye to him by making them even more blind. The message is quite clear: Those of us who acknowledge our blindness and turn to Christ in belief will receive sight, but those who go on pretending they know the truth will descend further and further into darkness and be rendered blind by God. We must choose between Jesus and self, between light and darkness, between life and death.

Jesus was speaking loud enough for the crowds as well as for the man himself. Some Pharisees heard him and asked the natural question, "Are you saying we're blind?" They had just enough perception to realize Jesus was speaking of spiritual blindness (they would not have asked if they were thinking of physical blindness) but not enough to catch the true meaning of what he had just said. Jesus' response was indirect yet powerful. He began by saying that if they were completely in darkness and failed to understand spiritual realities, they would not have sinned in acting as they did (cf. Rom 5:13). They could not have been blamed for acting in ignorance (Morris 1995:497). The problem was that they claimed they saw spiritual realities, and so their guilt remained. "In contrast to the man who had received his double sight, the Pharisees had sight but no light. They were spiritually blind, though they thought they were enlightened" (Comfort 1994:92). The light of God had shone upon them in the person of his Son, Jesus, and their arrogant assumption of their law had led them to reject that light. They stood before God completely guilty of the primary sin of unbelief.

It is common to see this as synonymous with the unpardonable sin of blasphemy against the Spirit (Mark 3:29 and parallels; so Barrett, Sanders, Carson), but that goes beyond the language here. It is better to see this as serious rejection but not irredeemable (so Bruce, Kysar). This is a warning to all who think they have the answers and ignore the clear demands of Jesus in the Word of God. There is only one way to eternal salvation, and that is through the atoning sacrifice of Christ, not the self-righteous efforts of any person or religious movement.

◆ 15. The Good Shepherd and his sheep (10:1-21)

"I tell you the truth, anyone who sneaks over the wall of a sheepfold, rather than going through the gate, must surely be a thief and a robber! ²But the one who enters through the gate is the shepherd of the sheep. ³The gatekeeper opens the gate for him, and the sheep recognize his voice and come to him. He calls his own sheep by name and leads them out. ⁴After he has gathered his own flock, he walks ahead of them, and they follow him because they know his voice. ⁵They won't follow a stranger; they will run from him because they don't know his voice."

⁶Those who heard Jesus use this illustration didn't understand what he meant, ⁷so he explained it to them: "I tell you the truth, I am the gate for the sheep. ⁸All who came before me* were thieves and robbers. But the true sheep did not listen to them. ⁹Yes, I am the gate. Those who come in through me will be saved.* They will come and go freely and will find good pastures. ¹⁰The thief's purpose is to steal and kill and destroy. My purpose is to give them a rich and satisfying life.

¹¹"I am the good shepherd. The good shepherd sacrifices his life for the sheep. ¹²A hired hand will run when he sees a wolf coming. He will abandon the sheep because they don't belong to him and he isn't their shepherd. And so the wolf attacks them and scatters the flock. ¹³The hired hand runs away because he's working only for the money and doesn't really care about the sheep.

¹⁴"I am the good shepherd; I know my own sheep, and they know me, ¹⁵just as my Father knows me and I know the Father. So I sacrifice my life for the sheep. ¹⁶I have other sheep, too, that are not in this sheepfold. I must bring them also. They will listen to my voice, and there will be one flock with one shepherd.

¹⁷"The Father loves me because I sacrifice my life so I may take it back again. ¹⁸No one can take my life from me. I sacrifice it voluntarily. For I have the authority to lay it down when I want to and also to take it up again. For this is what my Father has commanded."

¹⁹When he said these things, the people* were again divided in their opinions about him. ²⁰Some said, "He's demon possessed and out of his mind. Why listen to a man like that?" ²¹Others said, "This doesn't sound like a man possessed by a demon! Can a demon open the eyes of the blind?"

10:8 Some manuscripts do not include *before me.*   10:9 Or *will find safety.*   10:19 Greek *Jewish people;* also in 10:24, 31.

NOTES

10:1-21 Burge (2000:286) provides three reasons why this passage should not be exclusively tied to ch 9: (1) There is an abrupt change from "light" to "shepherd," so we could be in a new setting. (2) In the Hanukkah address of 10:26-27, Jesus returned to the topic of sheep, assuming the same audience as 10:1-21. (3) Ezekiel 34 (with its shepherd imagery) plays an important role in the Hanukkah Festival and further ties the sections together. Therefore, it is safe to say that 10:1-21 is a transition that concludes ch 9 and at the same time prepares for the Hanukkah passage of 10:22ff.

10:6 *illustration.* The term *paroimia* [TG3942, ZG4231] ("illustration"; used also in 16:25, 29) is similar to the synoptic *parabolē* [TG3850, ZG4130] ("parable"; this term is never used in John) and indicates a highly figurative or cryptic saying (called in Judaism a *mashal*) intended to bring hearers to a greater understanding of spiritual truth upon further reflection. The difference between this and the synoptic parables is that the latter contain a plot or story, while this is an extended metaphor or allegory in which each detail has meaning (cf. also 15:1-6).

10:8 *All who came before me.* Several mss omit "before me" ($\mathfrak{P}$45^vid $\mathfrak{P}$75 ℵ* 036 037 𝔐); it is possible that these words were added to clarify a terse sentence. In other mss, however, the "all" is also omitted (D it^b,d Vulgate^MSS), and it seems both omissions were attempts to soften the strong condemnation of the leaders here (cf. Beasley-Murray); the phrase is likely original.

10:14 *I know my own sheep.* Bruce points out (1983:227) that "know" occurs four times in 10:14-15, always in the present tense with a gnomic or timeless force. The special knowledge of the Father and the Son in eternity is extended to embrace the new relationship between Jesus and the believer.

COMMENTARY

In chapter 9, the Jewish authorities oppose Jesus utterly and appear not only blind to the truth of God in him but also threaten anyone who would become his follower. The chapter ends with the verdict that their sin remains (9:41). In John 10, we see Jesus expand on that verdict, as he continues to address them and reveal that they are false shepherds, thieves and robbers, and hired hands who care nothing for the flock of God. In contrast, Jesus is the Good Shepherd and the gate to God's sheepfold.

Jesus' message here is expressed in the form of an extended metaphor or "illustration" (10:6), using shepherding as a means of teaching these ideas. It builds on Ezekiel 34, where God tells Ezekiel to "prophesy against the shepherds, the leaders of Israel" (Ezek 34:2). They had forsaken their flock, so God said he himself would shepherd his people and "set over them one shepherd, my servant David. He will feed them and be a shepherd to them" (Ezek 34:23). It is generally agreed that this is a messianic promise, and Jesus saw himself fulfilling that prophecy as the Good Shepherd (10:11). The illustration itself is found in 10:1-5 and is then developed via two extensive explanations: that of the gate in 10:7-10 and that of the shepherd in 10:11-16. Links with the Festival of Shelters (chs 7–9) continue, as Jesus is not only water and light (7:38; 8:12) but also the messianic shepherd. While it was often said that only the Torah could be the true shepherd, light, and water (2 *Baruch* 77:11-16), Jesus was saying that in reality he is the true Word (so Blomberg). Neyrey (2001:278-281), building on Hellenistic-Jewish rhetorical practices, thinks that the major emphasis is on the "noble death" of the shepherd (10:11, 15, 17-18); the thrust would then be the courageous death of the "noble (*kalos* [TG2570, ZG2819]) shepherd," which becomes a victory that benefits the people of God.

Illustration: the Shepherd and the Sheep (10:1-5). Jesus prefaced this teaching with "I tell you the truth," highlighting a particularly important saying (cf. 1:51; 8:58). It is thought by some that Jesus was using two separate illustrations in 10:1-3a and 10:3b-5, but such a division is somewhat artificial; it is best to see this as a single parable. There is no plot, so it is not a parable as in the Synoptics; in fact, there are no parables as such in John.

The basis of Jesus' illustration is the sheepfold of the first century, an enclosure, often built at the foot of a hill with walls on the three sides and a small opening with a gate for entering and leaving. The image of the fold here envisions a large enclosure, probably housing several flocks, for an under-shepherd is mentioned (10:3; cf. "gatekeeper," NLT). This assistant would man the gate to protect the sheep and keep them from escaping. Bailey (1993:3-6) says that the scene is early morning in a Palestinian village, with the inhabitants (who only had a few sheep each) rounding their sheep up together under a single shepherd and sending them into the countryside to graze. The danger was always that a "thief" or "robber" (virtual synonyms here) would sneak over the wall and either steal the sheep or kill them in order to bankrupt the owners (10:10). The walls were usually not more than waist high because their purpose was to keep the sheep in and predators out rather than to stop thieves. It was the job of the "gatekeeper" to prevent robbers. On the other hand, a shepherd entered properly through the gate, and both the gatekeeper and the sheep knew him. This was how one could tell the true shepherd from the false; he entered properly and never snuck into the enclosure another way.

This scene has a great deal of Old Testament background behind it. God is often depicted as Israel's shepherd (Gen 48:15; Pss 28:9, 80:1; Isa 40:11; Mic 5:4), who leads his people to safety and protects them (Ps 23; Ezek 34:11-16). In contrast, the leaders are false shepherds who take the milk and wool for themselves and butcher the sheep for themselves (Ezek 34:3; cf. Isa 56:11; Jer 23:1-4). As a result, the flock has been "scattered without a shepherd" (Ezek 34:5; cf. Matt 9:36; Mark 6:34). Obviously, Jesus had in mind the Jewish authorities who had opposed the work of God and tried to steal his flock. This closely resembles false teachers or cult leaders in our own day, who superimpose their own "endless discussion of myths and spiritual pedigrees" (1 Tim 1:4) over biblical truth. Jesus is the only true shepherd of God's flock, and anyone who develops a messiah complex or claims to dictate all truth is moving in a very dangerous direction. There are too many so-called Christian leaders whose methods and message are not centered on God or his Word. In our age, as in much of modern history, Christians need to use a great deal of discernment (Heb 5:14) in living the Christian life and choosing the proper place of worship.

The true shepherd also has a very deep relationship with his flock (10:3b-5). He calls them by name, and they follow him out of the sheepfold because they know his voice. In Jesus' day (as today), a shepherd would often assign each sheep a certain name or call (sometimes a certain note on a flute) and teach it to them. This would enable him to call any one back if it started to wander away (so Carson, Bailey, Keener). In the Near East, they would also precede their sheep and keep the animals following through their distinctive calls. Obviously, a stranger could not do this since the sheep would neither know a stranger's voice nor respond to his leading. Jesus' illustration here has Numbers 27:16-17 as its Old Testament background: Moses asked God for a new shepherd for the community; that person was Joshua (the Heb. form of the name "Jesus"). This is an important picture of the true Christian community/flock: Jesus knows each and every one individually and calls that person to himself (divine sovereignty, cf. 6:36-40), and his sheep are so attuned to the Master's voice that they both follow him implicitly and immediately recognize a false message (human responsibility, cf. 6:35; 9:35-38). It is also the critical responsibility of all who are "under-shepherds" (1 Pet 5:2-4) to teach God's flock to recognize the difference between truth and error.

Explanation regarding the Gate (10:6-10). As always, the people failed to understand Jesus' point (cf. 8:19, 22, 27 33, 41, 52, 57; 9:40-41), so he explained it further in two stages—first the gate (10:7-10) and then the shepherd (10:11-18). "I am the gate for the sheep," is the third "I am" saying (cf. 6:35; 8:12) and indicates Jesus as the only way into God's community. In 10:2, he described himself as the shepherd who entered the gate; here he describes himself as the gate itself. In the open field at night, shepherds often built a makeshift pen with piled rocks and thorns on the top of the rocks to keep out the wild animals. The shepherd would then sleep across the opening of the pen, becoming in effect the "gate" for the sheep (so Whitacre, Blomberg). As such, Jesus is quite distinct from the thieving Jewish leaders (10:8) "who came before" him. This refers not to the prophets and great leaders of the Old Testament but to the authorities of Jesus' day (linked with the false shepherds as in Ezek 34); they are derided in such passages as Mark 12:38-40 and Matthew 23:1-36 for their pride and for doing such things as "cheat[ing] widows out of their property" (i.e., cheating them out of their meager life's savings). The leading priests actually became quite wealthy through their control of the Temple proceedings. In addition, Jesus may have intended the messianic pretenders of his own day, who led insurrections and caused great suffering (so Barrett, Beasley-Murray, Carson).

In contrast to the leaders who pretended to bring the people to God, Jesus is the true "gate" to salvation, the only way by which anyone "will be saved" (10:9; cf. 6:53; 8:24; 14:6). Köstenberger (2004:303) speaks of the ancient (Greco-Roman and Jewish) concept of entering heaven via a gate, a picture that fits this passage well. Jesus as the "gate to heaven" would also fit the emphasis of 1:51. Those who seek another door to salvation will face the wrath of final judgment, but those who come to God by him will "go freely and will find good pastures"—words that picture the sheep being led by the Good Shepherd to lush pasturelands (cf. Ps 23; Rev 7:17). Once more, he is quite distinct from the false shepherds, who "steal and kill and destroy"—a picture that stems from Ezekiel 34:2-3 ("feed yourselves instead of your flocks . . . and butcher the best animals") and fits such recent false messiahs as Jim Jones and David Koresh. In contrast, under Jesus there will be "a rich and satisfying life" (lit., they will "have life and have it completely"). In every area there will be an abundance of divine provisions. This goes beyond the idea of eternal life to the daily needs of God's flock. The sheep who come to Jesus find themselves members of a new flock or community, and they are recipients of an incredible outpouring of spiritual blessings.

Explanation regarding the Shepherd (10:11-18). The second set of explanations (10:11-18, consisting of two parts: 10:11-13 and 10:14-18) flows out of the second "I am" saying here (10:11)—"the good shepherd," meaning the noble, worthy, ideal shepherd (so Lindars). This is certainly one of the most beautiful and well-known descriptions of Jesus, reminding us of Psalm 23 and the kind of God who "lets me rest in green meadows" and "leads me beside peaceful streams," who prepares "a feast for me in the presence of my enemies" (Ps 23:2, 5; cf. Gen 49:24; 2 Sam 5:2; Ps 78:52 on Yahweh as the shepherd of Israel). In contrast to the evil shepherds of Israel, the Good Shepherd sacrifices his life for the sheep (10:11). This is an important passage, for it demonstrates Jesus' awareness of the fact that he would die as an atoning sacrifice for mankind (cf. 1:29; 6:51; 10:15; 11:50-52; 18:14), an idea connected to the prophecy of Isaiah 53:10 that said the Suffering Servant's life would be "an offering for sin." Jesus laid down his life "for" or "on behalf of" (*huper* [TG5228, ZG5642]) God's sheep. Shepherds often faced dangerous predators (cf. David's statement in 1 Sam 17:34-37), but many were not willing to lose their lives in the process. None deliberately sacrificed themselves for their sheep; only Jesus gave himself as part of a divine purpose.

In contrast, the leaders were like "a hired hand" who would run away at the sight of a wolf (10:12). The hired hand had no pride or care of ownership. The Mishnah said that he must defend the sheep if one wolf came but not if two came (so Morris), but the hired hands Jesus addressed ran at the first sign of danger. This echoes Ezekiel 34:8 ("You abandoned my flock and left them to be attacked by every wild animal"), and like the hireling here, they simply cared nothing for God's flock. In Acts 20:28-29, Paul warns the Ephesian elders of the "false teachers, like vicious wolves," who "will come in among you after I leave, not sparing the flock." Churches must choose their leaders carefully and make certain their choices are not based on charisma but on their walk with God and on the centrality of scriptural truth in their ministries.

The second section (10:14-18) begins with the repetition of "I am the good shepherd" and then goes into another aspect of 10:3-5, namely the extraordinary relationship between Jesus and his flock that is the direct result of his atoning sacrifice (emphasized further in 10:15, 17, 18). The mutual indwelling of 6:56 becomes mutual knowledge in 10:14, "I know my own sheep, and they know me." In 10:3-4, the shepherd calls his sheep by name, and they know his voice. This develops that image further and carries over to the mutual indwelling in 15:4, 5, 7—that is, the basis of the fruitful Christian life. This mutual knowledge between the shepherd and his sheep is itself grounded in the mutual knowledge between Jesus and the Father. The depth of Jesus' knowledge of his Father is especially prominent in 1:18—"the one and only Son is himself God and is near to the Father's heart. He has revealed [Greek, 'made him known'] God to us" (cf. also 17:21-23). The intimacy between Jesus and his Father is translated into a similar intimacy between Jesus and his flock. As God knew his people in the Old Testament (e.g., Pss 7:9; 139:23; Jer 1:5) and the New Testament (1 Cor 8:3; Gal 4:9) so his Son knows his followers. The proof of this knowledge is that he sacrifices his "life for the sheep," repeating 10:11. Without that sacrifice, there could be no intimacy, for sin would be an ultimate barrier to knowing Christ.

The "sheepfold" Jesus has been talking about in this passage is Judaism. In 10:16, he tells the people that he has "other sheep, too, that are not in this sheepfold"; this must refer to the Gentiles, also known by Jesus (10:14) but who were yet to come into the Kingdom. These are the "children of God scattered around the world," who will be brought together and united with the Jewish believers (11:52; cf. 17:20-23). Jesus' statement that he "must bring them also" indicated that the Gentile mission was a divine necessity. The coming of Gentiles into the people of God has a strong basis in the Old Testament, beginning with the covenant promise to Abraham that "all the families on earth will be blessed through you" (Gen 12:3; cf. 18:18; 22:18; 26:4; 28:14) and continuing in God's charge to Israel that he would make them "a light to the Gentiles" (Isa 49:6; cf. 42:6). It has always been God's plan to bring Jew and Gentile into his larger fold, and his choice of Israel as the covenant people is to bring about the procession of the nations to Zion (Isa 2:2-4; 11:10, 12; 14:1; 56:6-7; 60:3). John emphasized this in his emphasis on Jesus as "the Savior of the world" (4:42) and the "light of the world" (8:12). The love of God (3:16) and the mission of both Jesus and the disciples (17:18; 20:21) was to the "world."

The result of Jesus' work was to be "one flock with one shepherd" (10:16). Jesus would be the *one* shepherd (distinguishing him from the other so-called shepherds of Israel), uniting his people. "This indicates that the oneness will be between two groups of sheep (Jew and Gentile) and between them and the Shepherd. In other words, the oneness of the sheep is related to their oneness with the Shepherd" (Comfort 1994:95-96). The theme of unity in the church is especially stressed in 17:20-23 ("I pray that they will all be one, just as you and I are one"). Yet there is a twofold theme in this chapter: purity and unity. Purity is seen in the images of the thieves and robbers and the hired hands, the false teachers who will try to destroy the church. The church in every age must find the balance between purity and unity, between those times when heretics are deceiving the flock and those times when we must agree to disagree over issues that should not divide the church. In doing so, we have to distinguish between cardinal doctrines, which must lead to church discipline (doctrines such as the Trinity, the deity of Christ, and substitutionary atonement), and non-cardinal doctrines, which should not split the church but be handled within unity (issues like the rapture debate, Calvinism versus Arminianism, and the charismatic debate; see Osborne 1991:311-314). For instance, the doctrine of the Holy Spirit is cardinal, but the issue of the gifts of the Spirit is not; the return of Christ is cardinal, but the millennial debate is not.

Everything is anchored in the Father's love (10:17). Salvation was made possible because "God loved the world so much" (3:16), and Jesus' mission flowed out of

God's love for him. As Morris says (1995:512), "the meaning here is that the death of Jesus is the will of God for him. And because he is in perfect harmony with the will of God he goes forward to that death." The Father's perfect love is linked with his Son's perfect union with the divine plan, salvation flowing out of his "sacrifice" on the cross. Yet the wonderful truth is that Jesus laid down his life in order to take it up again. His death and the resurrection are a single event in salvation history. Death is the path to life, both for Jesus and for us. Jesus' death also constituted his being "lifted up" to glory (3:14; 8:28; 12:32). Moreover, his death was his time of destiny (2:4; 7:30; 8:20) and was under God's control; therefore, no one could take his life (10:18)—he would only die when he "voluntarily" gave himself up to the divine plan. The Father had given his Son "authority" to die when he wanted and also to rise from the dead at the proper moment. These two themes are central: Jesus' absolute authority and his perfect obedience in fulfilling "what my Father has commanded." In one sense, it was the Jewish authorities who demanded his death, and he was nailed to the cross by Roman command, but in the deeper, ultimate sense, it was Jesus' authority and God's command that actually led to the Cross.

Division among the Jews (10:19-21). As often before, the Jews were divided in their reaction to Jesus (cf. 6:52; 7:25-27, 40-43). Some believed that anyone who could speak of himself in such a way must be "demon possessed and out of his mind" (10:20). People in the ancient world linked insanity and demon possession, so once they decided Jesus' statements were lunacy, it was natural to attribute them to demon possession. This is the same charge as in 7:20; 8:48, 52 and also in Mark 3:20-30. It made it easier for them to dismiss what he said. However, clearer heads assessed the evidence, pointing out that no demon could "open the eyes of the blind" (cf. 9:16, 32 for this same conclusion). Jesus' works showed that his words had to be considered with the utmost care. Still, it must be noted that this second group was still unwilling to come to belief.

◆ ## 16. Jesus at the Feast of Dedication claims to be the Son of God (10:22-42)

²²It was now winter, and Jesus was in Jerusalem at the time of Hanukkah, the Festival of Dedication. ²³He was in the Temple, walking through the section known as Solomon's Colonnade. ²⁴The people surrounded him and asked, "How long are you going to keep us in suspense? If you are the Messiah, tell us plainly."

²⁵Jesus replied, "I have already told you, and you don't believe me. The proof is the work I do in my Father's name. ²⁶But you don't believe me because you are not my sheep. ²⁷My sheep listen to my voice; I know them, and they follow me. ²⁸I give them eternal life, and they will never perish. No one can snatch them away from me, ²⁹for my Father has given them to me, and he is more powerful than anyone else.* No one can snatch them from the Father's hand. ³⁰The Father and I are one."

³¹Once again the people picked up stones to kill him. ³²Jesus said, "At my Father's direction I have done many good works. For which one are you going to stone me?"

³³They replied, "We're stoning you not

for any good work, but for blasphemy! You, a mere man, claim to be God."

34Jesus replied, "It is written in your own Scriptures* that God said to certain leaders of the people, 'I say, you are gods!'* 35And you know that the Scriptures cannot be altered. So if those people who received God's message were called 'gods,' 36why do you call it blasphemy when I say, 'I am the Son of God'? After all, the Father set me apart and sent me into the world. 37Don't believe me unless I carry out my Father's work. 38But if I do his work, believe in the evidence of the miraculous works I have done, even if you don't believe me. Then you will know and understand that the Father is in me, and I am in the Father."

39Once again they tried to arrest him, but he got away and left them. 40He went beyond the Jordan River near the place where John was first baptizing and stayed there awhile. 41And many followed him. "John didn't perform miraculous signs," they remarked to one another, "but everything he said about this man has come true." 42And many who were there believed in Jesus.

10:29 Other manuscripts read for *what my Father has given me is more powerful than anything;* still others read for *regarding that which my Father has given me, he is greater than all.*   10:34a Greek *your own law.* 10:34b Ps 82:6.

NOTES

10:22 *Hanukkah, the Festival of Dedication.* "Hanukkah" is supplied by the NLT for clarity. The Gr. is *ta enkainia* [TG1456, ZG1589] (lit., "renewal"). Comfort says of this (1994:98), "This is key to an interpretation . . . that Jesus had come to provide a complete spiritual renewal for the people of God, wherein he became the spiritual reality of all that they cherished."

10:24 *How long are you going to keep us in suspense?* This question can also be translated as "How long are you going to annoy us?" implying opposition, but the context favors the NLT's rendering, which implies a sincere desire to learn Jesus' true self-image. The opposition and rejection does not come until the next scene.

10:27-30 *My sheep listen to my voice.* Michaels (1989:186-187) develops the parallels between this and 10:14-16. Both are revelatory "I sayings" in which the speaker is the Shepherd/Son with three features in common: (1) the mutual knowledge of the shepherd and the sheep; (2) the shepherd giving life to the sheep; and (3) the shepherd's ministry to the sheep.

10:28 *they will never perish.* For the Arminian response, see the note on 6:39.

away from me. Lit., "out of my hand."

10:29 *my Father has given them to me.* There are several different variations involving the relative pronoun in the Greek of this verse. Thus it could be (literally), "my Father who has given me" (cf. NLT, NIV, NASB) or "what my Father has given me" (NRSV) or even "regarding that which my Father has given me" (NJB), depending on whether the pronouns are masculine, neuter, or a combination. See Comfort 2007:[John 10:29] for further discussion of the issues.

10:30 *The Father and I are one.* Since the word "one" (*hen* [TG1520, ZG1651]) is neuter rather than masculine, it is common today to see this as a functional unity of will and purpose rather than an ontological unity of person (Bruce, Ridderbos, Witherington, Michaels, Burge). But the statement must also imply a unity of essence (so Carson, Morris, Moloney, Köstenberger). While it is not a metaphysical statement, it clearly places Jesus with God and goes beyond action, in accord with "the Word was God" (1:1) and "the unique One, who is himself God" (1:18; cf. Morris). As Barrett says (1978:382), "The oneness of Father and Son is a oneness of love and obedience even while it is a oneness of essence."

10:32 *good works.* As in 10:11, "good" is the term *kala* [TG2570, ZG2819], emphasizing that these works were "noble, beautiful, fine" (so Beasley-Murray, Carson). Jesus was asserting that his divine origin was shown in the "noble works" of God.

10:33 *blasphemy.* This has often been seen as problematic because the Mishnah (*m. Sanhedrin* 7.5) clearly says that people do not become blasphemers unless they pronounce the name of God (the tetragrammaton *yhwh* [TH3068, ZH3378]) itself. Therefore, some doubt the authenticity of John 10:33 and the surrounding verses. However, the Mishnah was not codified until about AD 200, and there is some doubt as to whether it describes the situation before AD 70, especially for the Sadducees. Furthermore, there is much evidence that a charge of blasphemy was decisive at Jesus' trial (Bock 2000). The verse should be accepted as authentic.

10:34 *you are gods.* There is considerable debate regarding the identity of those called "gods" in Ps 82: (1) They could be corrupt judges of Israel who have denigrated their office, but it is difficult to think of them as receiving "God's message." (2) It could refer to Israel itself, who had received the law yet had been unjust in treating the poor (a frequent charge from prophets like Jeremiah or Amos). (3) It could be angelic powers who had abused their God-given authority. This third, while possible for the Psalm itself, does not seem likely here, for there is no hint whatsoever in the context of angels. In light of their reception of God's word, Israel is the best understanding (so Beasley-Murray, Whitacre).

10:40 *the place where John was first baptizing.* As in 1:28, the exact location for this is debated. Some (Schnackenburg, Brown, Beasley-Murray) suggest "Bethany beyond the Jordan" in Perea (1:28-34). Others (Carson, Riesner 1987, Köstenberger) look to Batanea, northeast of Judea in the tetrarchy of Philip and farther from Jerusalem. This latter is the more likely (see note on 1:28) because it is farther removed from Jesus' troubles in Judea.

10:41 *John didn't perform miraculous signs.* Plummer (1981:230) makes the interesting point that this provides indirect evidence for the veracity of the miracle stories. John was viewed as the first prophet in four centuries and as the fulfillment of Elijah's ministry, yet in all those years of enthusiastic response, no miracles were attributed to him. Instead, all traditions attribute miracles to Jesus. It is unlikely that these traditions would simultaneously be correct regarding John and incorrect regarding Jesus.

COMMENTARY

This section recounts the last of the four festivals that Jesus is seen fulfilling in John (cf. Sabbath [ch 5], Passover [ch 6], Tabernacles [chs 7-9]) and represents the culmination of the debates between Jesus and the Jews. The central theme is the identity of Jesus, especially the question of whether he is actually the Messiah (10:24) and the "Son of God" (10:36). The Festival of Dedication, or Hanukkah, is the only extrabiblical feast in the Jewish calendar. It stemmed from the events of 167-164 BC, when the Seleucid king Antiochus Epiphanes outlawed the Jewish religion and tried to force Hellenistic religion on the land. Soldiers went from village to village forcing the people to sacrifice pigs on pagan altars (cf. 1 Macc 1:41-50). An elderly priest, Mattathias, revolted, and a group gathered around him and his sons, fighting a guerilla war against the Seleucid armies (1 Macc 2:15ff). After a series of battles under the leadership of his son Judas (called "the Maccabee" or "the Hammer," 1 Macc 3:1), they liberated Jerusalem on 25 Kislev (= November/December) 164 and rededicated the Temple (cf. 1 Macc 4:36ff). The eight-day celebration that ensued is also called the "Festival of Lights" due to the lighting of lamps in the homes and the legend of the miracle of the oil lamp (*b. Shabbat* 21b); it became Hanukkah, or the Festival of Dedication.

Jesus was still carrying out his ministry in the Temple, and John tells us it was winter (10:22). John would not need to tell his readers this since they would have been aware of the season of the feast, so some (e.g., Beasley-Murray) think the word has symbolic overtones—like "night" in 3:2; 9:4; 13:30—so that it refers to the cold spiritual climate in Israel. It is more likely an explanation as to why Jesus was walking through "the section known as Solomon's Colonnade," a section on the east that rested on pre-Herodian stone believed to go back to Solomon's Temple (so Michaels). The cold winter winds forced rabbis to seek the shelter of the colonnaded porch rather than the open courtyard. While he was walking there, some Jews challenged Jesus to stop keeping them "in suspense" and declare plainly whether or not he was the Messiah (10:24). At this stage, there was not an antagonistic air; it seems to be the result of all the debates over Jesus' true identity in chapters 5–9. They wanted him to settle the issue once and for all. To this point, Jesus had not explicitly stated that he was the Messiah in Jerusalem (the only one he told was the Samaritan woman, 4:26), spending most of his time telling them he was the divine envoy and the Son of God. We seldom realize the incredibly political nature of messianic expectations in the first century, which were centered on a nationalistic hope with military overtones (cf. on 6:15). Moreover, the Jewish people had already rejected the witnesses to who and what he was (5:31-47; 8:14-18). In light of the situation, Jesus' reluctance is understandable. Still, they wanted a plain answer.

Jesus' response was unequivocal: "I have already told you, and you don't believe me" (10:25). This does not mean that Jesus had told them "plainly" but that he had told them sufficiently. It is rather clear, when we read the dialogs of chapters 5–10 thus far and consider the sign-miracles, that Jesus was communicating his identity to the people in every way possible—he is the "Son" of the Father and the heaven-sent envoy of God. Every time, they greeted his message with unbelief (cf. 5:45-47; 6:36, 64; 7:48; 8:24, 45-46). As Jesus said, his "work" made it very clear and provided more than sufficient "proof" (in 5:36 the works provide an official "witness") of his identity as the Messiah. Still they rejected him. The reason for this was that they were not his sheep (10:26). This goes back to 6:35-44; the sovereign God had not drawn them, and they had not "come," so they were not his sheep. Three stages are mentioned of Jesus' sheep: they "listen" or hear his call, Jesus "knows" them, and they "follow" him in response (10:3-4, 8, 14-16). The Jewish people did not have the eyes of faith and so could not catch the implications of his works and his words.

Then follows one of the most beautiful statements on the security of the believer in the Bible (10:28-29). Jesus gives eternal life to the sheep who hear and follow him—the ultimate culmination of the "rich and satisfying life" the shepherd gives the sheep (10:10). In John, eternal life is characterized as both a present possession (3:15-16, 36; 5:24; 6:40, 47, 51, 54, 58; 20:31) and a future promise (5:28-29; 14:2-3). This means that the sheep "will never die" (8:51, 52; 11:26) and "never perish."

For God's sheep, death is still "the last enemy" (1 Cor 15:26), but at the same time it is also a step upward to our heavenly destiny. This security has nothing to do with our own effort but is rather centered on the power of Christ (cf. 6:37-40; 1 Pet 1:5)—"no one can snatch them away from" him, neither the thief nor the wolf (10:1, 8, 10, 12). The idea of sheep being snatched away (cf. 6:15) is a violent one and pictures an enemy tearing us away from Christ (cf. 10:12). Paul developed this idea further in Romans 8:31-39, where he said, "nothing can ever separate us" from the love of God and Christ. The love and enabling presence and power of God keep the believer secure. Jesus holds us in his hand (10:28), and the Father's "hand" is superimposed over Christ's hand (10:29) so that we have a double security! Jesus made it clear that everything he did was based on the Father and flowed from the Father (5:19, 30; 7:16, 28; 8:16, 29, 42). God's strength guarantees the security of the sheep, for he is "more powerful than anyone else" (10:29). The predatory leaders of Jesus' day and the false teachers of John's day could not steal the sheep, for God was watching over them.

The reason that the Father and the Son work in such union for the security of the sheep is that "the Father and [Jesus] are one" (10:30). Michaels (1989:187) sees this as the culmination of a syllogism:

If:
no one can snatch them away from me (10:28; lit., "out of my hand")
and
no one can snatch them out of my Father's hand (10:29)
then
I and the Father are one (10:30).

This is one of the high points in John's Gospel concerning the deity of Christ. As stated in the note on 10:30, this is primarily a statement of the unity between God and Jesus, with the word "one" pointing first to a unity of work (as in 5:18-30), then to a unity of purpose and will (as in 17:11, where the unity between believers parallels the unity of Jesus and God), and therefore to a deeper unity of essence between the Father and the Son. The Jews would not have tried to stone Jesus for blasphemy (10:31) if Jesus had meant only that he had the same purpose as God (so Hoskyns, Morris). In fact, they stated directly their belief that he had claimed to be God (10:33). But we should not forget the immediate context either: Jesus was emphasizing that in protecting his sheep, he and the Father act together in complete unity. To belong to Jesus, then, is to belong to God.

Jesus as Son of God (10:31-38). The fact that the hearers picked up stones to execute Jesus for blasphemy (10:31; cf. Lev 24:16) shows that they perceived that he was making himself equal with God (cf. 5:18; 8:59). Technically, stoning was illegal, for the Roman government reserved the right of capital punishment for itself. While disallowed, it did happen (e.g., Acts 7:54-8:1, the stoning of Stephen); but note Jesus' control. He did not flinch, even though he was in mortal danger. Rather, he continued the discussion, pointing to the "many good works" that came at his

"Father's direction" (10:32). Note again the emphasis that all he did was in accordance with his Father's will, in that sense providing proof of the veracity of his statement in 10:30. The sign-miracles were pointers to the reality of the unity between Father and Son—could he have performed such wondrous works if he were a false prophet? Instead, they proved the opposite: that he was sent from God and was one with him. Ignoring the evidence of his "good works," the Jews directly accused him of blasphemy and defined it—"You, a mere man, claim to be God." They considered his works to be irrelevant in light of his claim—a claim that constituted blasphemy and demanded stoning.

Jesus' response (10:34-36) was a rabbinic argument stemming from their "own law" (10:34, NLT mg), language that does not constitute a rejection of the Old Testament ("law" here refers to the whole OT canon, not just the Torah) but was rather a challenge to their understanding of the law (cf. also 8:17). Jesus then quoted Psalm 82:6, where it says of the people of Israel, "I say, you are gods." The full text says, "I say, 'You are gods; you are all children of the Most High. But you will die like mere mortals and fall like every other ruler.'" The context is the oppression of the poor by Israel and the judgment they were to receive for their unjust decisions. They had "received God's message" on Sinai and were called God's "firstborn son" (Exod 4:22), yet fell due to worshiping the golden calf. Jesus argued from the lesser to the greater: If they could be called "gods" (Heb. *'elohim* [TH430, ZH466]), how could anyone object to Jesus being called "the Son of God"? Since "the Scriptures cannot be altered" (10:35) and they were called "gods," then even more rightly could Jesus call himself "Son of God." They had only received the law, while it is Jesus whom the Father "set . . . apart" (*hagiazō* [TG37, ZG39]); he had been consecrated to and sent upon his mission by God. Of course, Israel was also consecrated and sent, so this did not so much emphasize Jesus' unique status as it explained why he was not guilty of blasphemy (so Ridderbos). He could validly call himself "Son of God." Of course, Jesus' challengers didn't even begin to understand the deeper implications of his reasoning.

Having proven his right to label himself "Son of God," Jesus turned to the reasons why they should believe in him (10:37-38). He made the same point as in 10:25 (cf. 5:36): If they would not believe because of his words, they should believe because of his works, for the works showed that he was carrying out his Father's work. They point beyond Jesus to the one who sent him, and even more to the fact that he is his Father's Son. The Jews greeted his earlier claim in 10:25 with unbelief and an attempt to stone him, but he appealed to the same evidence once more. In 2:23-25, we observe that a sign-based belief is only a partial belief, but in 5:36, the works are offered as legal testimony that should lead to belief, for they substantiate Jesus' words. Belief is the proper response because Jesus' works are "evidence" for the validity of his words. They show his unity with the Father—specifically, that they act in concert. The purpose was that the Jews might "know and understand" (10:38) the mutual union between Father and Son. The formula, "the Father is in me, and I am in the Father," occurs again in 14:10-11 and 17:21 and is the basis for the unity between believers and Jesus/the Spirit (6:56; 14:20; 15:5, 7; cf. 1 John 2:24; 3:24; 4:15) as well as the internal unity of the church (17:20-23). The knowledge of this complete intimacy between these two members of the Godhead is at the heart of true faith.

Rejection and Departure (10:39-42). Once more they tried to arrest Jesus, undoubtedly to try him for a capital offense (cf. 5:18; 7:30, 32; 8:37, 40, 59; 10:31), but he slipped away (his "time" had not yet arrived, cf. 7:30; 8:20) and went beyond the Jordan River to the place where the Baptist had ministered—Bethany (1:28, different from the Bethany near Jerusalem where Lazarus lived; Aenon near Salim [3:23] is not across the Jordan). He stayed there awhile, though as can be seen from 11:1, his time there was short. It is difficult to know how long Jesus stayed there, but the implication is several days at least. Both Judea and Galilee had become hotbeds of opposition, and this brief respite provided a transition to the final events that would begin with the raising of Lazarus (ch 11). This mention of John the Baptist is also significant for two other reasons: it provides an *inclusio* with the beginning of Jesus' ministry in the witness of the Baptist (1:28-29), and it highlights his ministry as a fulfillment of the ministry of his forerunner, John the Baptist (so Schnackenburg, Sanders, Morris, Burge).

Many followed Jesus to the Transjordan (10:41, showing his public popularity had not diminished), and they commented on the significance of John. The fact that he "didn't perform miraculous signs" showed that he fulfilled the ministry of Elijah only in the sense of messianic forerunner (Mal 4:5); Jesus, however, did fulfill the miraculous ministry of Elijah (and Elisha). As John had said, "He must become greater and greater, and I must become less and less" (3:30). Yet this was also his significance, for everything he said about Jesus had come true (10:41). He was the faithful witness (5:36, the nearest previous mention of John), and he fulfilled his mission perfectly (cf. "sent" in 1:6). As a result of reflection on John's witness to Jesus, "many who were there believed in Jesus." While those in Judea, where Jesus should have been welcomed, rejected him, many "in the wilderness where John had called for a 'highway' for Jesus" were prepared to make a decision (Ridderbos 1997:379).

◆　**C. Final Events: The Raising of Lazarus and the Beginning of Jesus' Passion (11:1–12:50)**
　　1. Jesus raises Lazarus from the dead (11:1-57)

A man named Lazarus was sick. He lived in Bethany with his sisters, Mary and Martha. ²This is the Mary who later poured the expensive perfume on the Lord's feet and wiped them with her hair.* Her brother, Lazarus, was sick. ³So the two sisters sent a message to Jesus telling him, "Lord, your dear friend is very sick."

⁴But when Jesus heard about it he said, "Lazarus's sickness will not end in death. No, it happened for the glory of God so that the Son of God will receive glory from this." ⁵So although Jesus loved Martha, Mary, and Lazarus, ⁶he stayed where he was for the next two days. ⁷Finally, he said to his disciples, "Let's go back to Judea."

[8]But his disciples objected. "Rabbi," they said, "only a few days ago the people* in Judea were trying to stone you. Are you going there again?"

[9]Jesus replied, "There are twelve hours of daylight every day. During the day people can walk safely. They can see because they have the light of this world. [10]But at night there is danger of stumbling because they have no light." [11]Then he said, "Our friend Lazarus has fallen asleep, but now I will go and wake him up."

[12]The disciples said, "Lord, if he is sleeping, he will soon get better!" [13]They thought Jesus meant Lazarus was simply sleeping, but Jesus meant Lazarus had died.

[14]So he told them plainly, "Lazarus is dead. [15]And for your sakes, I'm glad I wasn't there, for now you will really believe. Come, let's go see him."

[16]Thomas, nicknamed the Twin,* said to his fellow disciples, "Let's go, too—and die with Jesus."

[17]When Jesus arrived at Bethany, he was told that Lazarus had already been in his grave for four days. [18]Bethany was only a few miles* down the road from Jerusalem, [19]and many of the people had come to console Martha and Mary in their loss. [20]When Martha got word that Jesus was coming, she went to meet him. But Mary stayed in the house. [21]Martha said to Jesus, "Lord, if only you had been here, my brother would not have died. [22]But even now I know that God will give you whatever you ask."

[23]Jesus told her, "Your brother will rise again."

[24]"Yes," Martha said, "he will rise when everyone else rises, at the last day."

[25]Jesus told her, "I am the resurrection and the life.* Anyone who believes in me will live, even after dying. [26]Everyone who lives in me and believes in me will never ever die. Do you believe this, Martha?"

[27]"Yes, Lord," she told him. "I have always believed you are the Messiah, the Son of God, the one who has come into the world from God." [28]Then she returned to Mary. She called Mary aside from the mourners and told her, "The Teacher is here and wants to see you." [29]So Mary immediately went to him.

[30]Jesus had stayed outside the village, at the place where Martha met him. [31]When the people who were at the house consoling Mary saw her leave so hastily, they assumed she was going to Lazarus's grave to weep. So they followed her there. [32]When Mary arrived and saw Jesus, she fell at his feet and said, "Lord, if only you had been here, my brother would not have died."

[33]When Jesus saw her weeping and saw the other people wailing with her, a deep anger welled up within him,* and he was deeply troubled. [34]"Where have you put him?" he asked them.

They told him, "Lord, come and see." [35]Then Jesus wept. [36]The people who were standing nearby said, "See how much he loved him!" [37]But some said, "This man healed a blind man. Couldn't he have kept Lazarus from dying?"

[38]Jesus was still angry as he arrived at the tomb, a cave with a stone rolled across its entrance. [39]"Roll the stone aside," Jesus told them.

But Martha, the dead man's sister, protested, "Lord, he has been dead for four days. The smell will be terrible."

[40]Jesus responded, "Didn't I tell you that you would see God's glory if you believe?" [41]So they rolled the stone aside. Then Jesus looked up to heaven and said, "Father, thank you for hearing me. [42]You always hear me, but I said it out loud for the sake of all these people standing here, so that they will believe you sent me." [43]Then Jesus shouted, "Lazarus, come out!" [44]And the dead man came out, his hands and feet bound in graveclothes, his face wrapped in a headcloth. Jesus told them, "Unwrap him and let him go!"

[45]Many of the people who were with Mary believed in Jesus when they saw this happen. [46]But some went to the Pharisees

and told them what Jesus had done. [47]Then the leading priests and Pharisees called the high council* together. "What are we going to do?" they asked each other. "This man certainly performs many miraculous signs. [48]If we allow him to go on like this, soon everyone will believe in him. Then the Roman army will come and destroy both our Temple* and our nation."

[49]Caiaphas, who was high priest at that time,* said, "You don't know what you're talking about! [50]You don't realize that it's better for you that one man should die for the people than for the whole nation to be destroyed."

[51]He did not say this on his own; as high priest at that time he was led to prophesy that Jesus would die for the entire nation. [52]And not only for that nation, but to bring together and unite all the children of God scattered around the world.

[53]So from that time on, the Jewish leaders began to plot Jesus' death. [54]As a result, Jesus stopped his public ministry among the people and left Jerusalem. He went to a place near the wilderness, to the village of Ephraim, and stayed there with his disciples.

[55]It was now almost time for the Jewish Passover celebration, and many people from all over the country arrived in Jerusalem several days early so they could go through the purification ceremony before Passover began. [56]They kept looking for Jesus, but as they stood around in the Temple, they said to each other, "What do you think? He won't come for Passover, will he?" [57]Meanwhile, the leading priests and Pharisees had publicly ordered that anyone seeing Jesus must report it immediately so they could arrest him.

11:2 This incident is recorded in chapter 12.   **11:8** Greek *Jewish people;* also in 11:19, 31, 33, 36, 45, 54.   **11:16** Greek *Thomas, who was called Didymus.*   **11:18** Greek *was about 15 stadia* [about 2.8 kilometers].   **11:25** Some manuscripts do not include *and the life.*   **11:33** Or *he was angry in his spirit.*   **11:47** Greek *the Sanhedrin.*   **11:48** Or *our position;* Greek reads *our place.*   **11:49** Greek *that year;* also in 11:51.

NOTES

11:2 *This is the Mary who later poured the expensive perfume on the Lord's feet.* It is difficult to know why John relates this at this point. Perhaps he simply wanted to point forward to a key event, but it does seem to presuppose that John expected his readers to know of this event. Thus, it is likely that many (but not all) of the intended audience were Christians who had already heard of it (contra Carson) and that John wished to explain who these women were. Also, as Witherington points out (1995:200), this is evidence that some of Jesus' followers were well off. Not only did she have very expensive perfume, but they took care of many Jews who had come to mourn Lazarus (11:19, 45) and later held a banquet for many of them (12:1-2). The tomb with a rolling stone also indicates wealth. Probably Jesus and his disciples often stayed in their home when visiting Jerusalem. This indicates that Jesus ministered to the upper class as well as the outcasts.

11:3 *Lord.* It is generally agreed that by saying "Lord," the sisters were not recognizing his universal lordship but rather were showing themselves as disciples of their rabbi/master. It was a title with greater weight than "sir" (cf. 4:19 for "sir") but less than a reference to deity.

11:9 *twelve hours.* People of the ancient world did not calculate time as exactly as today, for they did not have clocks like we do. Day and night were calculated at 12 hours each. The actual length of daylight in Palestine varied from 9 hours 48 minutes to 14 hours 12 minutes (so Morris).

11:16 *Thomas, nicknamed the Twin.* The Heb. for "twin" (*toa'mim* [TH8380, ZH9339] or cf. the Aramaic *t'oma'*) sounds like the Gr. for "Thomas," and sometimes a Jewish man who was a twin or descended from one was given the name "Thomas." It may be that the added "Didymus" (cf. NLT mg) was used as a reminder of the Semitic origin and meaning of his name (so Michaels).

11:19 *come to console.* There were three stages to the mourning rituals: For the first seven days, the family stayed at home, receiving condolences and leaving only to visit the tomb; then for 30 days they did not participate in feast days or leave town. After that, they returned to normal life (McCane 2000:174-175).

11:25 *the resurrection and the life.* It is debated whether "resurrection" and "life" are synonyms (in the sense that resurrection is further explained by life; so Bultmann, Schnackenburg) or complementary ideas (with physical resurrection extending into eternal life; so Dodd, Brown, Carson). The latter is better, seen in 11:25b-26, which explains how the two relate to each other.

11:27 *I have always believed.* This is in the perfect tense, emphasizing her state of being. Martha was affirming that belief defined her life.

11:28 *called Mary aside.* Some have read theological meaning into the secrecy surrounding Martha and Mary's interaction with Jesus—for instance Barrett (1978:398), who takes these verses as "marks of the secrecy which is characteristic of the miracle narratives in Mark." This is too allegorical and does not fit Johannine themes. It is best to take this as simply part of the local color of the story.

11:38 *a cave with a stone rolled across its entrance.* This cave became an important place of pilgrimage, and in the fourth century, Christians had a church erected over it called "the Lazareion." While we cannot be sure of the authenticity of the cave as shown today, it is of the same style as the one described here.

11:39 *Roll the stone aside.* Wilcox (1977:131-132) thinks that this prayer at the rolling away of the stone deliberately echoes the "stone" imagery of Ps 118:22 ("The stone that the builders rejected has now become the cornerstone") and is an "early Christian 'stone' midrash." While difficult to prove, the idea is an interesting possibility. At the same time, the statement foreshadows the greater rolling away of the stone at the resurrection of Jesus (20:1; Mark 16:3-4).

11:42 *You always hear me.* This special privilege would be passed on to the disciples, as power in prayer was given to them in 14:12-14; 15:7, 16; 16:24. In fact, every aspect here would be handed over to the disciples, who would become "sent ones" in 17:18; 20:21 after receiving the Spirit (20:22). This is indeed the mission theology of John (cf. "The Holy Spirit" and "Mission" in the Introduction).

11:45-54 It is common today to think that this is John's version of the Sanhedrin trial found in the Synoptics (Bultmann, Schnackenburg, Lindars). But the historical details of this meeting before Jesus was arrested fit closely with what we know of legal procedures at the time (cf. Blomberg 2001), and a close reading of Mark 14:1-2 (two days before Passover) indicates that the chief priests and scribes were putting into action a decision that had already been made. There is no good reason to doubt the historicity of this event.

11:49 *at that time.* Lit., "that year." While according to the OT, high priests held the office all their lives (Num 35:25), the Romans used to replace Jewish high priests as they saw fit, though not every year. Some (e.g., Bultmann) have taken "that year" to indicate that John ignorantly read pagan customs (changing the high priesthood every year) into the Jewish situation. It is more likely that "that year" refers not to the timing of Caiaphas's reign but to "that *fateful* year in which Christ died" (Brown 1966:440, italics his).

11:51 *led to prophesy.* In general, the high priest was occasionally linked to prophetic gifts. Josephus (*Wars* 1.68-69) attributes prophecy to John Hyrcanus (high priest from 135–104 BC) and describes a revelation given to the high priest Jaddua when Alexander the Great visited Jerusalem (*Antiquities* 11.327, 333-334).

11:52 *bring together.* Lit., "gather"; a word found also in 11:47, when the Sanhedrin gathered together. Blomberg (2001:173-174) thinks the paragraph (11:47-53) is framed by the two "gatherings," thus determining a central contrast in the paragraph between "the gathering of the mighty to maintain a rule of violence versus the gathering of humanity united by one who is a powerless victim."

11:55 *Passover.* This is an important note in dating Jesus' death. Since Jesus began ministering in the forty-sixth year of the ongoing construction of Herod's temple (AD 27–28, see on 2:20), and this was the third Passover/second year from then, Jesus probably died in 30 AD (cf. Carson). This also means that Jesus had a ministry lasting a little over two years (depending on how much time elapsed between his baptism and the first Passover in 2:13).

COMMENTARY

There has always been reluctance on the part of certain scholars to accept the historicity of this miracle, for it is not only the most spectacular of the miracle stories, engendering incredible publicity, but it also appears only in John. While some like Bultmann reject it out of anti-supernatural bias, others believe the evidence for it is too scanty, thinking it a development of the parable of the rich man and Lazarus in Luke 16. But it is difficult to see why so developed a story would grow out of a parable that is so very different in substance. And there are good reasons for accepting the historicity of this account: The incredible detail and lifelike portrayal is historically plausible and fits a first-century setting. Also, as stated in the Introduction, John is quite trustworthy in his handling of his sources throughout his Gospel. Furthermore, there are two other passages that make reference to Jesus raising the dead (Matt 11:5; Luke 7:22) and two other accounts of him raising dead people—Jairus's daughter (Mark 5:22ff) and the son of the widow of Nain (Luke 7:11ff). There is insufficient reason for refusing to keep this among the historical stories (cf. Morris, Carson, Blomberg 2001, Keener).

This is a beautiful story, not just about Jesus' power to raise the dead, but also about the loving relationship Jesus had with his friends. It is the seventh sign-miracle (see commentary on 2:1-12) and the culmination of the series, demonstrating in a powerful way Jesus' authority to give life (5:21, 25-26). There is also deep-seated irony in this story, for Jesus' giving life to Lazarus precipitates the events that lead to his own death (cf. 11:45-54).

The Death of Lazarus (11:1-16). Jesus' retreat lasted only a short time because his friend Lazarus became seriously ill. Lazarus is not mentioned elsewhere in the New Testament, although Mary and Martha appear also in Luke 10:38-42. Martha was probably the older sister (she is described as the hostess in Luke 10), but Mary appears to have been the better known, for she is the one noted here for anointing Jesus' feet (11:2; cf. 12:1-8). They were not authority figures or official witnesses like the disciples but are presented as ordinary believers and friends of Jesus and thus accessible models for the Christian community at large (so Michaels). The village where they lived, Bethany, is about two miles from Jerusalem on the road to Jericho. This is not the same Bethany as the one that was across the Jordan (cf. 1:28), the place where Jesus was resting and ministering when he heard about Lazarus (10:40). So Jesus would have traveled from Bethany, across the Jordan, to Bethany, the suburb of Jerusalem. These three siblings were quite close to Jesus, as seen in their message,

"Lord, your dear friend [lit., 'the one you love'] is very sick." The fact that they did not name him but just said "your dear friend" shows how close they were. Note that they refrained from asking Jesus to come. They were well aware of the serious danger to him if he should come. Perhaps they hoped he would heal Lazarus at a distance, as he had the official's son in 4:50-52. Like Mary in 2:5, they simply trusted Jesus to do what was right. He would, but hardly in the way they expected.

Jesus responded very strangely, prophesying that Lazarus's illness would not end in death but that the final result would be "for the glory of God" (11:4; cf. his response here to his comment about the blind man in 9:3). The glory of God was the major goal of Jesus' life, and everything he did was meant to bring his Father glory (12:28; 14:13; 17:1, 4). The glory of God meant also the glory of Jesus, for the mutual union between the Father and the Son (10:38; 14:10, 11, 20; 17:21) means a reciprocity of glory. Carson brings out (1991:406) that the glory of God in John is "not the praise that is God's due but his revelation, his self-disclosure" that comes primarily via the Son. The glory of one is the glory of both. The raising of Lazarus would reveal the glory of the Father in the Son. Yet the glory of the raising of Lazarus was but a preparation for the true glory to be demonstrated in the dying and rising of Jesus himself.

Then comes an even stranger aspect of the story. After telling the messengers everything would be all right, he stayed there in Bethany, in Transjordan (Perea) an extra two days (11:5-6). He dearly loved all three (naming Martha first may mean she was the oldest of the three), and yet he stayed put, almost as if he was enjoying his R & R too much to leave just yet. In fact, Lazarus must have died shortly after the messengers left to see Jesus: the journey took about a day, and in 11:17, we learn that Lazarus had been dead for four days when they arrived (one day for the messengers to come, two days that Jesus remained there, and a fourth day for Jesus to travel to Bethany). This hints at omniscience on Jesus' part (cf. 1:48; 4:18). He knew the whole situation. There may have been two reasons for the delay: (1) it heightened the miracle, showing even more powerfully that he is "the resurrection and the life" (so Carson, Burge); and (2) it showed that Jesus was waiting for God's timing. Jesus knew that when he left, the "time" would arrive for the Passion events to begin (cf. 7:30; 8:20). Jesus waited for his Father to signal that the time had come (so Morris, Ridderbos, Köstenberger). Only then did he tell his disciples that they would be returning to Judea (11:7).

The emphasis on Judea rather than Bethany shows that his major emphasis was on the events soon to transpire and not just on the imminent miracle. The disciples were very aware of the danger of returning; after all, that was the reason they had left—after the Jews had tried to stone Jesus (10:31, 39). The disciples had realized they were in grave danger as well. In a short while, Thomas would say, "Let's go, too— and die with Jesus" (11:16). They could not believe he wanted to go there again.

Christ's response (11:9-10) reiterated the point he made in 9:4, that night was coming so they had to work while it was still day. The metaphor is quite simple: it is easier to walk during the daytime, when "the light of this world" helps you to see obstacles and not stumble over them. The spiritual thrust is also clear: Jesus, "the light of the world" (8:12), was illuminating this world of darkness with the light of God (1:4, 5, 9). There was only a short time left before the darkness took over and he faced the Cross. Therefore, he had no time to remain in hiding but had to go confront the powers of darkness (cf. 12:30-31). He had to perform the work of his Father while the "twelve hours" of his life and ministry lasted. That night was almost there, and he had to use every minute of the remaining time he had. The same was true for his disciples: The Light was with them for only a short time, and they had to follow that Light while they could. To "walk safely," they had to follow the Light, and that meant a return to Judea. Ironically, there was no "danger of stumbling" so long as they followed Jesus into danger!

When Jesus told them, "Our friend Lazarus has fallen asleep" (11:11), he expected the disciples to understand the phrase "wake him up" as indicating Jesus' intention to raise him from the dead. After all, they had seen Jesus raise people from the dead before. The disciples, however, completely missed his point and took it literally, figuring "he will soon get better" (11:12). This can be taken as an indication of their obtuseness and stupidity (so Calvin) or as a natural misunderstanding in light either of the fact that they were thinking about illness or the fact that sleep and waking up were not really used in the ancient world as euphemisms for death and resurrection (so Bruce, Carson). The latter is more likely since John thought he needed to explain to the readers that Jesus was speaking of death (11:13). At any rate, they believed this was a sign that Lazarus was getting better. This type of literal misunderstanding occurs often in John (e.g., 3:4, 9; 4:33; 6:7-9) and always leads to further teaching on the issue—in this case, teaching on Jesus as the resurrection and the life (11:25).

Jesus then told the disciples directly that Lazarus was dead (11:14). What followed must have been confusing to the disciples. Jesus was "glad" that he wasn't there when Lazarus was dying. This perhaps sounds startling to us, as well—but as with the blindness of the man in 9:3, there were larger issues involved. Jesus wanted them to know that God was orchestrating the scene "for your sakes" (11:15). First, it was happening "for the glory of God" (11:4) and, second, so the disciples would "really believe" (11:15; cf. 11:42, 45, 48). If Jesus had been there, it would have been a healing miracle, but now he was about to demonstrate his authority to give life, an event that would strengthen the disciples' faith. Jesus did not mean that the disciples had no faith but that their young faith needed to develop further. Thomas, not understanding, was thinking only of the danger they all faced. He told the others that it was time to go "and die with Jesus" (11:16; though some [e.g., Zahn; and Köstenberger calls it "possible"] think "die with him" refers to Lazarus—a view rejected by most). He had tremendous courage and certainly exemplified Jesus' dictum in Mark 8:34 to his would-be followers—"You must turn from your selfish ways, take up your cross, and follow me." Thomas had great earnestness but lacked understanding, a characteristic that continues in other scenes (14:5; 20:24-29). He was not really "doubting Thomas" (for this see comments on 20:24-29), for his courage and willingness to go with Jesus all the way were his primary characteristics.

Jesus, the Resurrection and the Life (11:17-27). After a few days' journey, they arrived at Bethany on the outskirts of Jerusalem (cf. 11:1). At that time they were told that Lazarus had been in the grave for four days (the Jews usually buried a person the same day he died). This was significant and possibly a major reason why Jesus waited for two days before leaving (11:6). The rabbis believed that the soul lingered near the grave for three days, hoping to re-enter the body, but as decomposition became evident, the soul would depart (*Leviticus Rabbah* 18:1; *Ecclesiastes Rabbah* 12:6). In the oral law, if a body needed to be identified, it had to happen within three days (so Michaels; note cautions in Keener). Thus, this would be an especially dramatic raising from the dead.

The fact that Bethany was "only a few miles" (lit., "15 stadia," about 2.8 kilometers or 1.7 miles) from Jerusalem meant that the mourners who came to "console Martha and Mary" were primarily from Jerusalem. The fact that there were many visitors may well indicate that they were a prominent family (so Carson). At the same time, it also hints that the "time" (2:4; 7:30; 8:20) of Jesus' destiny had nearly arrived, for he had come virtually to Jerusalem. Mourning was a serious duty within Judaism. There was a great deal of weeping and loud exclamations, and grief was shown quite openly by all concerned (cf. 11:33). As he was nearing Bethany, word came that he was close, and Martha rushed to see him. This was a slight breach of custom, for the family usually stayed at home and sat *shiva*, waiting for people to arrive, which is exactly what Mary did. The picture also fits the story in Luke 10:38-42, with Martha busy bustling about, while Mary sat at Jesus' feet. Keener (2003:843) says Martha was showing Jesus "great respect" by rushing out to meet him.

Martha's statement to Jesus ("Lord, if only you had been here, my brother would not have died," 11:21) may sound like a rebuke, but she would have known that Lazarus died shortly after the messengers had been sent. It probably represents her sorrow and sincere belief that Jesus could have done something if only he had been there. When she added, "even now I know that God will give you whatever you ask," it sounds like full-blown faith, but her insufficient faith leads to a challenge by Jesus in 11:39-40. Several scholars think she looked at Jesus as merely an intermediary with God (Westcott, Brown, Whitacre, Ridderbos); however, that is a little too strong. Her response was not a literal misunderstanding like Nicodemus, the Samaritan woman, or the Jews. There is a definite faith component—not fully developed to be sure, but still present (so Barrett, Carson, Burge, Köstenberger). She did not go so far as to say that he could still raise Lazarus from the dead, but there was an indistinct hope that God through Jesus could still do something.

Jesus drew out the limit of her faith by affirming, "Your brother will rise again" (11:23). Martha could not have been thinking of Lazarus's resurrection that same day because she affirmed her belief in the resurrection "at the last day." This was a major debate between the Pharisees and the Sadducees, who denied any possibility of afterlife (cf. Mark 12:18-27; Acts 23:6-10); the majority of Jews sided with the Pharisees. Later, after the destruction of Jerusalem, belief in the resurrection and afterlife became the official Jewish view. Martha was looking forward to that distant day and did not understand that Jesus was promising more than she thought, possibly because Lazarus had been dead four days (cf. on 11:17).

The keynote for the entire story is sounded in 11:25, when Jesus utters his fifth "I am" saying with a predicate (6:35; 8:12; 10:7, 14)—"I am the resurrection and the life." A major theme in John is Jesus' authority to give life, both eternal life in the present (5:21, 24, 25; 6:27, 33) and the resurrection of the body in the future (5:28, 29; 6:39-40, 44). Martha had not understood the key truth that Jesus is life itself; she needed to deepen her partial realization regarding the afterlife to a personal faith in the one who gives it. The key is belief. The one who comes to a faith-decision "will live, even after dying." This is the physical resurrection. Death has no hold on the one who believes. Though it is "the last enemy" (1 Cor 15:26a), its destiny is "to be destroyed" (1 Cor 15:26b). The one who lives and believes in Jesus "will never ever die." This is the spiritual resurrection; eternal life is the believer's destiny. Jesus is life and controls life; the only way to participate in his life is via faith (note Rom 3:21–4:25, where "faith", *pistin* [TG4102, ZG4411], occurs 18 times).

Jesus' challenge ("Do you believe this, Martha?") was an invitation that went beyond raising Lazarus from the dead. He asked Martha to believe in the power that not only can raise the dead but also can give eternal life. The raising of Lazarus was in this sense a prophetic action (like those performed by Jeremiah or Ezekiel) signifying the new life that God, in Jesus, offers to anyone who believes (cf. 6:35-44). When Martha responded, "Yes, Lord," she was taking a step of saving faith. Note her language, confessing Jesus as "Messiah, the Son of God," the very titles used in 20:30-31 as a definition of true faith. She had taken an important step, bringing "faith" to its fullest development to this point in John's Gospel. Like Andrew, she confessed him as Messiah (1:41); like Nathanael, she confessed him as Son of God (1:49, so Bruce). She also confessed him as "the one who has come into the world from God" (11:27; cf. 7:28-29; 8:29, 42).

Jesus' Outrage at the Power of Death (11:28-37). Martha and Mary were apparently trying to keep the presence of Jesus quiet, possibly because of the danger to him in Judea (so Sanders) but probably mostly in order to have some time of privacy with him (so Carson). Martha went out to him privately and then came back to Mary, calling her aside and telling her, "The Teacher is here and wants to see you." It is interesting that she used the title "teacher" after calling him "Lord" in 11:21, 27, but those were contexts of confession, while here she returned to the term (= Rabbi) they used most frequently for Jesus. The great affection they felt for Jesus can be seen in the fact that Mary "immediately went to him" (lit., "arose quickly and went"). The attempt at privacy was short lived. The Jewish friends who were there to console her believed she was headed for the tomb and therefore followed her out in order to comfort her there. When she saw Jesus, she repeated the same message as Martha in 11:21 ("If only you had been here, my brother would not have died") but omitted any confession of faith. For this reason, some have seen this as a rebuke (Schnackenburg 1982:333 calls her "a complaining woman"), but it must be noted that she "fell at his feet," indicating reverence. Thus, she too is best characterized by grief rather than rebuke—she was pouring out her heart to Jesus. She had the same faith in Jesus' power to heal that Martha did.

Jesus' reaction was quite surprising. Most translations have watered down the verbs (e.g., NIV, "deeply moved in spirit and troubled"), but the first verb (*embrimaomai* [TG1690, ZG1839]; 11:33) always speaks of deep-seated anger and does not connote mere emotional upheaval (cf. the excellent discussion in Beasley-Murray, contra Lindars, Morris, Köstenberger [who see this more as excitement than anger]). The second term, rendered "deeply troubled," is used of Jesus' state of mind when he faced the Passion (12:27; 13:21; cf. 14:1). But what was Jesus very angry about and deeply troubled by? There are three possibilities: (1) anger that they were forcing a miracle on him, leading to a response similar to 2:4 (Barrett); (2) anger at lack of faith in their excessive mourning (Schnackenburg, Comfort, Keener); (3) anger at the power of sin and death in this world. The first is unlikely because Jesus fully intended to perform a miracle all along (Westcott, Brown, Burge). The second could fit here but not in 11:38 where the verb is repeated. The third is the best answer, although overtones of the second are certainly present, at least in this scene (so Carson, Whitacre). Jesus was overcome with the scene and its futility, with the terrible specter of death hanging over God's people and the fact that the mourners were overcome with it rather than trusting in the one who is life itself. This is a critical message for us all. Christ has overcome death, and we need to live in light of that fact.

Christ then asked, "Where have you put him?" (11:34). Upon being shown the tomb, he wept. Paul says that believers should "not grieve like people who have no hope," (1 Thess 4:13) and that is Jesus' example here. The verb does not denote the same wailing of the mourners in 11:31 and 33 but a more gentle form of weeping. Here we see the two sides of Jesus' nature—his justice and his love as seen in wrath and grief. Carson (1991:416) says, "Those who follow Jesus as his disciples today do well to learn the same tension—that grief and compassion without outrage reduce to mere sentiment, while outrage without grief hardens into self-righteous arrogance and irascibility." Jesus knew he was about to raise Lazarus from the dead, and he still wept, undoubtedly for the same reason—that his loved ones and followers still had to suffer the horrible pangs of death. The onlookers were split in their feelings. Some were overcome by the depth of his love for Lazarus; others were upset that the same one who could heal the blind had not kept Lazarus from dying. Both sides were partly right (he did love Lazarus and could have healed him) but mainly wrong; they realized neither Jesus' true intention nor his power over death.

Lazarus Raised from the Dead (11:38-44). Jesus was again burning with anger (11:38) as he arrived at the tomb—he would confront and overcome the powers of evil. His work in raising Lazarus was that of the conquering Messiah defeating the powers of sin and death. The cave Lazarus was buried in, with a stone rolled over the entrance, anticipated the burial cave of Jesus (19:41; 20:1) and demonstrated the social prominence of the family—only the wealthy could afford such a tomb. It was a "rolling stone" type of tomb, with the stone rolled back to allow access (so Burge). When Jesus commanded them to "roll the stone aside," there was still no awareness or faith, and Martha, ever the practical one (cf. Luke 10:38-42), objected because Lazarus had been decomposing for four days in the tomb and the smell would be terrible (11:39). While Egyptians used extensive embalming techniques, the Jews did not, so decomposition would have been extensive by then. In fact, all the burial spices and perfumes used to anoint the dead (cf. 19:39-40; Mark 16:1) were intended to counter the smell.

Martha still did not understand Jesus' intentions, in spite of the dialog in 11:21-27. So Jesus repeated his challenge: "Didn't I tell you that you would see God's glory if you believe?" (11:40). In 9:3, Jesus said the man was born blind "so the power of God could be seen in him," and this is similar. The glory of God is often linked to miracles as a sign of the shekinah presence of God (cf. 2:11; for the death and Resurrection as "glory," see 12:41; 17:5) and is also seen as the reason for this miracle in 11:4. The promises of 11:23-26 are summed up as "glory." Yet to see that glory, Martha and the others needed the same faith that the disciples showed in 2:11. The glory would be shown no matter the faith, but it would be perceived and appropriated only via faith. Without faith they would not benefit from God's great deed.

After they rolled away the stone, Jesus lifted his face to heaven in prayer (11:41). The gesture of looking to heaven is itself a symbol of the contents of the prayer since it signifies dependence on heavenly power. Interestingly, this is the only mention of a prayer before any of Jesus' miracles in the Gospels, and Jesus himself stated that he was doing this for the benefit of the hearers (11:42). He wanted them to know that everything he did only happened because he was completely dependent on the Father (5:19, 30; 7:16, 28; 8:16, 29, 42). As is characteristic of his prayers (the only exception is the cry of dereliction on the cross, Mark 15:34 and parallels), he began with "Father," the title for God he used throughout this Gospel and the one that most thoroughly acknowledges Jesus' special relationship to God. He then showed that the decision to raise Lazarus had already been made, so that now Jesus merely thanked God for listening to his previous prayer. In fact, God always hears Jesus. The Old Testament teaches that God hears the righteous (e.g., Pss 34:15; 145:19), and Jesus is perfectly righteous. As R. H. Fuller says (*Interpreting the Miracles*, 107-108, cited in Whitacre 1999:290), "Jesus lives in constant prayer and communication with the Father. When he engages in vocal prayer, he is not entering, as we do, from a state of non-praying into prayer. He is only giving overt expression to what is the ground and base of his life all along." The resurrection of Lazarus was proof that Jesus' claim of a special relationship with God was true. In Jesus' prayer he stated that on account of this, the bystanders should indeed believe that God had sent him (11:42). There could be no better proof that Jesus was indeed God's envoy (cf. on 3:17). It is insufficient to believe in Jesus as a wonder-worker or even as a prophet. He is the one sent from heaven by God.

Having prayed, Jesus cried out, "Lazarus, come out!" (11:43). It has often been said that if Jesus had not specified Lazarus, all the dead would have emerged from every grave, for Jesus' authority was such that in the last days, all the dead would hear his voice and rise again (5:28-29). And the last days were indeed here. We now see why Jesus did not heal Lazarus before he died; God's will was to use him to show that Jesus was indeed "the resurrection and the life." At Jesus' command, Lazarus emerged "bound in graveclothes, his face wrapped in a headcloth." The Jews buried their dead by placing the corpse on a long wide cloth with the feet at one end. Then the cloth would be drawn over the head to cover the body, where it would be tied together at the ankles, with the arms secured to the body with linen strips and the face bound with a headcloth over the face to hide its discoloration (so Sanders, Beasley-Murray). Needless to say, Lazarus could do little but shuffle to the opening, so Jesus said, "Unwrap him and let him go!" (11:44). (One wishes John had described the scene with its hysteria and joy, as well as the aftermath at the family's home in Bethany, but those details must await their telling in eternity.) Here we see another parallel with the Resurrection story, for Jesus left the "linen wrappings" and the head cloth "folded up and lying apart from the other wrappings" (20:5, 7). The difference was that Lazarus would die again, while Jesus conquered death forever at his resurrection (so Beasley-Murray).

The Decision to Kill Jesus (11:45-54). Once again the Jews were divided (cf. 6:64; 7:12-13; 10:19-21), with many of the mourners believing but others reporting the events to the leaders (11:45-46). Jesus' miraculous signs always galvanized the crowds and forced them to take sides. This is the heart of John's Gospel, in which Jesus' deeds and words encounter every person and force each to a decision, either belief or rejection. There are no neutral people in John, and that is also true in this story. In our ministries, we must warn the "seekers" that so long as they try to remain neutral, they are in the process of rejecting Christ. This was especially true in the case of the raising of Lazarus on account of its impressive and public nature.

This caused the authorities to call a meeting of the Sanhedrin (11:47), though it is possible it was more unofficial, judging from the tone (so Brown). As stated earlier (cf. 1:19), the Sanhedrin was the Jewish high council into whose hands the Romans had placed authority for civil and religious affairs. It was made up of 70 Jewish leaders— some chief priests (the extended family of the high priest and other temple officials, all of them Sadducees, who dominated at this time), some Pharisees (lay leaders and experts of law), and some elders (the landed aristocracy)—with the high priest leading it. They had intended to kill Jesus earlier (5:18), had thoroughly muddled attempts to arrest him (7:32, 45), and had been outclassed by a formerly blind beggar (ch 9).

Now a true crisis had arrived that threatened the very future of the nation, and a final decision about Jesus had to be made. Jesus' many miraculous signs had made the people flock after him, and if things continued, everyone would soon believe in him (11:48). There could be no more indecisive leadership; they had to act firmly. If they were to fail at this point, the Roman army would "come and destroy both [their] Temple and [their] nation" (11:48). Since many of the first-century rebellions were messianic in nature, the leader's fear was that the fervor that people were showing toward Jesus would be interpreted as another anti-Roman rebellion. Note that there was no consideration that he might actually be the Messiah. They had already hardened their hearts and were no longer open to the truth (cf. 5:41-47; 7:27, 47-49; 8:48-59; 10:33). Also, note the centrality of "our" (first in the Greek for emphasis). While at one level, they seemed to be concerned for the nation, they were actually more concerned for their own positions. They acted as if the nation and Temple were their own possession (so Westcott).

Then Caiaphas, "high priest at that time" (lit., "that year"), took over (11:49-50). Caiaphas reigned for quite a length of time (AD 18–36), taking office shortly after his father-in-law Annas had held it (AD 6–15; Annas appears in 18:12-24). By Jewish law a high priest reigned for life, but the Romans controlled the reins of government, even the high priesthood, and frequently would replace a high priest who had fallen out of favor. To the Jewish people, however, such a person would still be considered a high priest (e.g., Annas in 18:12-24). As head of the Sanhedrin, it was natural for Caiaphas to speak up. He began with a blast at his own colleagues, accusing them of ignorance. His tone fits Josephus's charge that the Sadducees were wild and barbarous toward each other (*Wars* 2.166). Self-interest controlled his statement: "It's better for you"; the national interest took second place. "The portrait here of Caiaphas as a blunt, cynical, and self-serving figure is only confirmed by what Josephus says about the Sadducees as leaders in general" (Witherington 1995:205). Still, as Beasley-Murray says (1987:196-197, building on Daube, *Collaboration with Tyranny in Rabbinic Law*), there may have been precedent for this type of statement. Building on 2 Samuel 20:1, where a troublemaker, Sheba, was surrendered to Joab during a revolt, it may have been deemed viable to give up a named individual to save the lives of the people. Still, however, self-interest prevailed with Caiaphas.

Caiaphas didn't realize the significance of what he said. John tells us that "one man should die for the people" (11:50) was actually an unconscious prophecy. The language used here is interesting: "As high priest at that time he was led to prophesy" (11:51). In the Old Testament, the high priest was God's spokesman and often declared the will of God, which he ascertained by means of the Urim and Thummim (cf. Exod 28:30; Deut 33:8; Ezra 2:63), even at times given a prophetic voice by God (cf. Bruce, Schnackenburg). This was the case here, but Caiaphas did not realize it. First, he prophesied that "Jesus would die for (*huper* [TG5228, ZG5642]) the entire nation," referring to a substitutionary or atoning sacrifice in which he died in their place. This is emphasized more often in John than in the Synoptics (cf. 1:29; 6:51; 10:11, 15; 11:50-52; 15:13; 17:19). Note that John uses only "nation" and omits "people" from 11:50. Whitacre (1999:297) points out that the term "people" was not used often in classical Greek but is found 2,000 times in the Septuagint in reference to the covenant people, Israel. This shift in wording could signify that the Jews were no longer the "people" but had become only another "nation" (so also Westcott).

Second, Caiaphas prophesied that Jesus would "unite all the children of God scattered around the world." This, of course, goes beyond the scattered Jewish communities of the Diaspora to embrace the Gentile mission. As in 6:51, Jesus would die "so the world may live." This develops further the idea of the Good Shepherd sacrificing his life not only for his sheep but also for those "not in this sheepfold" (10:15-16). These groups constituted "the children of God" (11:52) because they had been drawn to or given to Jesus by the Father (6:37, 44), and they would be gathered into one church (cf. 10:16, "one flock with one shepherd"; 17:11, 20-23). Throughout this Gospel, the object of God's mission was "the world" as the object of his love (3:16), and the Jewish people had been part of the world (1:10-11). Christ had "come into the world" (11:27) to be "the Savior of the world" (4:42) and "the light of the world" (8:12). The whole world of mankind was (and is) the object of the divine mission, and Jew and Gentile would become one in Christ (cf. Eph 2:11-22).

The final decision was made to seek the death of Christ (11:53). The string of decisions to eliminate the troublemaker (5:18; 7:30, 32; 8:59; 10:31) had entered its final stage. The resurrection of Lazarus was the climactic catalyst (Blomberg) because it made Jesus more popular than ever, and the leaders felt they dare delay no longer. The news undoubtedly spread quickly, so Jesus halted his public ministry and "left Jerusalem." In light of what we read in 7:30 and 8:20, this was not because he was afraid but because "his time had not yet come." God, not the Sanhedrin, would determine the exact hour, and Jesus alone had "authority" to surrender his life (10:17-18). He took his disciples to a village called Ephraim, a small town near Bethel, 12 to 15 miles northeast of Jerusalem (so Brown, Barrett, Carson). He wanted to be away from the furor of Jerusalem but close enough to return in a few days for his final Passover.

Opening Events as Passover Approaches (11:55-57). Events were now escalating to that most decisive moment in human history when the Son of God was to be "lifted up" to the cross and glory (3:14; 8:28; 12:32). We now come to the third and final Passover mentioned in this Gospel (2:13; 6:4). It is the most important of all of history's Passover festivals, when the imagery associated with it (the blood freeing God's people from death) was finally fulfilled once and for all (cf. Heb 9:28). Lazarus had probably been raised a couple of weeks before Passover (see note on 12:1), and at this time pilgrims were arriving from everywhere for the festival. Jerusalem would swell from a population of about 70,000 to over 200,000 (Reinhardt [1995:262-263] estimates as many as a million), and people would be camping everywhere. In an obvious hyperbole, Josephus mentions 2,700,000 people at a single Passover just before the onset of the final war (*Wars* 6.422-425). The reason the people came early was to undergo "the purification ceremony." To offer the paschal lambs, the men had to go through seven days of purification (Num 9:6-12; 2 Chr 30:17-19; see also Josephus *Wars* 1.229).

During these days, Jesus was the hot topic. The pilgrims looked everywhere for him, figuring that, with the danger, he would not dare to come. The major area of discussion was the Temple, both because it was the focus of all the Passover activity and because it was where Jesus taught when he was in Jerusalem (7:14, 28; 8:20; 10:23). The tone of the discussion indicates they were "well-disposed towards him" (Schnackenburg). In contrast, the authorities had not only put out an arrest warrant but warned the people that they had better report any sighting of him.

◆   **2. Jesus anointed at Bethany (12:1-11)**

Six days before the Passover celebration began, Jesus arrived in Bethany, the home of Lazarus—the man he had raised from the dead. ²A dinner was prepared in Jesus' honor. Martha served, and Lazarus was among those who ate* with him. ³Then Mary took a twelve-ounce jar* of expensive perfume made from essence of nard, and she anointed Jesus' feet with it, wiping his feet with her hair. The house was filled with the fragrance.

⁴But Judas Iscariot, the disciple who would soon betray him, said, ⁵"That perfume was worth a year's wages.* It should have been sold and the money given to the poor." ⁶Not that he cared for the poor—he was a thief, and since he was in charge of the disciples' money, he often stole some for himself.

⁷Jesus replied, "Leave her alone. She did this in preparation for my burial. ⁸You will always have the poor among you, but you will not always have me."

⁹When all the people* heard of Jesus' arrival, they flocked to see him and also to see Lazarus, the man Jesus had raised from the dead. ¹⁰Then the leading priests decided to kill Lazarus, too, ¹¹for it was because of him that many of the people had deserted them* and believed in Jesus.

12:2 Or *who reclined.* **12:3** Greek *took 1 litra* [327 grams]. **12:5** Greek *worth 300 denarii.* A denarius was equivalent to a laborer's full day's wage. **12:9** Greek *Jewish people*; also in 12:11. **12:11** Or *had deserted their traditions*; Greek reads *had deserted.*

NOTES

12:1-11 There are two issues related to this account that need to be addressed: (1) harmonizing the Gospel accounts and (2) the chronology of the event. As to the first issue, some think this story appears in all four Gospels. Luke's account (7:36-50), however, is clearly a separate event, for the details are quite different (a dinner at the home of a Pharisee; an alabaster jar of perfume; an immoral woman, who has been forgiven by Jesus and who anoints Jesus' feet with her tears and then the perfume; the issue of being touched by a disreputable woman). The story in Matt 26:6-13 and Mark 14:3-9 has some interesting differences (the home of Simon the leper, an unnamed woman who breaks the jar and anoints Jesus' head), but the similarities are far greater, and as the discussion below will show, the differences can be reasonably harmonized. These are the same account, so historically Jesus was anointed twice—first, the one in Luke and second the one reported in the other three Gospels.

As to the second issue, the story in Matthew and Mark occurs after the Triumphal Entry, while the one here in John occurs before that event. However, this is only a problem if we demand that the Gospels follow a strictly chronological pattern. Actually, this is a modern development, and ancient historians did not do so. It has long been realized that the Gospel writers often arranged their material topically, especially the Synoptics (cf. Blomberg 1987). It is generally agreed that John probably has the correct order (he tends to have a more chronological arrangement, so Coakley 1988) and that Matthew and Mark place it where they do in order to contrast the woman's worshipful act with Judas's betrayal (cf. Carson, Blomberg 2001, Keener).

12:1 *Passover.* For the major chronological debate over the dating of the Last Supper and Passover, see the note on 13:1.

12:2 *A dinner was prepared.* John gives the impression that this meal was in Lazarus's home, but Matt 26:6 tells us it was in the home of Simon the leper. Some have said he was the father of the three siblings, but that cannot be known. The whole village could have been celebrating the event in Simon's home, or (perhaps more likely) it could have been a private banquet there. There is no contradiction either way.

12:7 *She did this in preparation for my burial.* This is difficult Greek and can be translated several ways (cf. Carson 1991:429-430): (1) "Let her alone so she can keep it [the perfume] for the day of my burial," but she has already poured it all out onto Jesus; (2) she has "done this [i.e., saved the perfume] for the day of my burial," a definite possibility; (3) an imperative: "let her keep it [the perfume] for the day of my burial," but this does not quite fit the Greek; or (4) "let her keep the credit for having poured this [perfume] out for the day of my burial," but this adds too much to the actual Greek. On the whole, the second is preferable.

12:8 *you will not always have me.* Ridderbos sees this as a major theme in John's Gospel: the Cross as the ultimate separation between the earthly and the heavenly. At the moment of his death, the manifestation of his glory in the flesh would be over. John "presents it as the break between faith and unbelief, a separation realized in relation to this end, as that comes most radically and exemplarily to expression in the contrast between Mary and Judas" (1997:418-420).

12:10 *kill Lazarus.* For the historical trustworthiness of the plot to kill Lazarus, see Blomberg (2001:178).

COMMENTARY

It was Saturday evening, six days before Passover. At least a week had passed since Lazarus was raised from the dead, and Jesus had been with his disciples in the village of Ephraim—a 3-4 hour walk away (11:54). Jesus' hour, the divinely chosen time of destiny, had arrived (2:4; 7:30; 8:20), so Jesus and his apostolic band came back to Bethany (on the slopes of the Mount of Olives, two miles from Jerusalem) to stay with his friends at Lazarus's home. The scene was set, and history's greatest Passover sacrifice, the "Lamb of God who takes away the sin of the world" (1:29), was making himself ready. At the evening meal, Jesus was the celebrated guest, with Lazarus, whom he had raised from the dead, as host or another honored guest. The latter is more likely, for the people there were probably celebrating the recent miraculous event. Martha, in keeping with her domestic instincts (cf. Luke 10:40), was serving the guests. They would have been following the normal custom at formal meals: eating while reclining on couches (cf. 13:23, 25).

The same Mary who had sat at Jesus' feet in Luke 10:39 took "a twelve-ounce jar (Gr., *litra*) of expensive perfume made from essence of nard" (12:3). The plant comes from the mountains of northern India, and this was pure nard, a very expensive perfume indeed (cf. 12:5)—either a family heirloom or a sign of the family's wealth. Taking this precious perfume, she anointed Jesus. While Matthew and Mark relate that she anointed Jesus' head, John centers on the feet. Most likely she anointed both (cf. Blomberg 2001). Since they were reclining, she would have anointed his head and then walked down to his feet. Moreover, she used all the perfume (in Mark 14:3, she broke the jar, possibly the seal at the top), an incredibly lavish and devotional act. It must have run down his head and onto his robe as well as dripped off his feet. No wonder "the house was filled with the fragrance" (in Mark 14:9, this is a sign that the whole world will hear of her act). When she wiped his feet with her hair (cf. Luke 7:38), this was almost scandalous, since only a husband was supposed to view a woman's hair. "Mary is acting with abandon, extravagant abandon, hoping that the close circle of friends will understand" (Burge 2000:339). John centers on Jesus' feet both to show Mary's servanthood (only slaves washed feet) and because feet signified the destiny of a person (for background sources see Coakley 1988). In Matthew and Mark, the anointing of the head was a messianic act; here, the anointing of the feet stressed that he was anointed for his death (lavish amounts were used there as well—75 pounds of myrrh and aloes in 19:39). Giblin (1992:563-564) calls Mary's act a "prophetic action" in which the anointing pointed to his burial and the wiping off to his resurrection. While this latter aspect is perhaps too allegorical, her act was an unconscious prophecy on her part.

Judas spoke up for the rest of the disciples (12:4-5; the person is unnamed in Matt and Mark) and uttered what most of them were probably thinking—that it would have been far better to sell the perfume and give the proceeds to the poor. We must remember that the rest of the disciples did not yet know Judas's true character, and he probably often spoke up like this. As the treasurer of the group, he would have been looked up to as a leader. In the early church, it was the pastors who were also the church treasurers. It is hard to know how Judas knew the value of the perfume. At any rate, the "year's wages" (lit., "300 denarii," with a denarius the daily wage of the average worker) is an unbelievable sum, enough to take care of an entire family for a year! In light of the incredible expense of the perfume, we can see that Judas had a point. It is always difficult to measure devotion versus need. This type of issue is present every time a church is built—how much goes for worship and how much for ministry? How much is spent on the building's beauty and how much reserved for practicality?

John is clear, however, that Judas was not interested in the poor (12:6). He was a thief who carried the money purse for the apostolic band and often "stole some for himself." Money was also one of the major reasons why he would betray Jesus. While according to Mark 14:11, the priests gave him money; according to Matthew 26:15, he demanded the money. The actual money purse was probably a box (the word was also used for a case to hold a flute or reed, so Brown) that held monetary gifts from people like the women patrons who traveled with the group (Luke 8:2-3). It paid for the needs of the group and was used to give alms to the poor. Judas would often take what he wanted from it.

Jesus defended Mary's action as a preliminary gift for his burial (12:7-8). Such an extravagant amount would have been acceptable for a funeral (cf. 19:39; the 75 pounds of spices), so why wasn't it also perfectly fine to give this to him while he was still alive and could enjoy her gift of love (so Bruce)? It is certainly doubtful that she understood this. For her, it was an act of love. It was common in the ancient world to wash the feet of especially important guests, to say in effect, "We are your humble servants." In fact, that is exactly what Jesus did at the Last Supper, when he washed the disciples' feet (13:1-20). Jesus was saying that Mary was giving an unconscious prophecy (like Caiaphas did in 11:50). Jesus then added, "You will always have the poor among you." There was Jewish precedent in the idea that caring for the dead has priority over almsgiving (*b. Sukkah* 49b; so Morris, Whitacre). There was only a short time left to show love to Jesus. The sentiment is similar to the metaphor the Baptist used in 3:29, regarding the joy that the friend of the bridegroom has when hearing the voice of the groom. Devotion to Jesus has priority over everything.

Word of Jesus' arrival spread quickly (12:9), and a large crowd gathered to see him and Lazarus, probably from the surrounding villages, as well as from Jerusalem itself. They had both become celebrities, and Lazarus was attracting almost as much attention as Jesus. As many point out (Bruce, Carson), Lazarus had likely been kept sequestered by his sisters since the great event, so this was the first occasion people had to see him. The authorities were now doubly alarmed (12:10-11). They had lost many former followers who "deserted them and believed in Jesus" (12:11) because of what happened to Lazarus. The peoples' loyalty had shifted from the leaders to Jesus, but even worse, they accepted him as their Messiah. Lazarus had therefore become almost as great a threat as Jesus had. Amazingly, the leading priests decided to eliminate Lazarus too. It is hard to know whether the rest of the Sanhedrin agreed with them. There is no evidence anything ever came of this. Note the irony, however: Jesus had raised Lazarus from the grave, and now they wanted to return him to it. There could be no stronger proof of their utter depravity than this. As Keener says (2003:866), "Jesus went to Judea, risking his life to give life to Lazarus; now Lazarus's new life may cost him his life."

◆   3. Jesus' triumphal entry (12:12-19)

¹²The next day, the news that Jesus was on the way to Jerusalem swept through the city. A large crowd of Passover visitors ¹³took palm branches and went down the road to meet him. They shouted,

"Praise God!*
Blessings on the one who comes in the name of the LORD!
Hail to the King of Israel!"*

¹⁴Jesus found a young donkey and rode on it, fulfilling the prophecy that said:

¹⁵"Don't be afraid, people of Jerusalem.*
Look, your King is coming,
    riding on a donkey's colt."*

¹⁶His disciples didn't understand at the time that this was a fulfillment of prophecy. But after Jesus entered into his glory, they remembered what had happened and realized that these things had been written about him. ¹⁷Many in the crowd had seen Jesus call Lazarus from the tomb, raising him from the dead, and they were telling others* about it. ¹⁸That was the reason so many went out to meet him—because they had heard about this miraculous sign. ¹⁹Then the Pharisees said to each other, "There's nothing we can do. Look, everyone* has gone after him!"

12:13a Greek *Hosanna*, an exclamation of praise adapted from a Hebrew expression that means "save now." 12:13b Ps 118:25-26; Zeph 3:15.   12:15a Greek *daughter of Zion*.   12:15b Zech 9:9.   12:17 Greek *were testifying*.   12:19 Greek *the world*.

NOTES

12:13 *Praise God!* Lit., "Hosanna" or "save now" (cf. NLT mg). At the Festival of Shelters (cf. 7:37), the Temple choir would sing the Hallel (Pss 113–118) every morning, and when they reached the "Hosanna" of 118:25 ("Please save us," NLT), the people would wave the *lulab* (branches of willow and myrtle tied with palm) and repeat the cry three times (so

Beasley-Murray). So this was connected in the minds of the people with the palm branches, and it was a natural thing to do when many believed their conquering king was coming. The Hallel psalms were used in Sabbath worship and at festivals, including the Passover celebration, which, at this point in Jesus' life, was just a week away. Psalm 118 is a natural passage for the pilgrims in procession to Jerusalem (Ps 118:27, "with boughs in hand, join in the festal procession," NIV cf. NJPS, NJB). *Hosanna* is the transliteration of the Aramaic (the Heb. would be *hoshi'ah-na'*) and in Ps 118:25, LXX it is translated as a prayer, "Save now." Its force here is debated. Most believe that in the first century it had become a cry of praise (Brown, Barrett, Carson, Ridderbos, Köstenberger), though a few would retain the prayer form from Ps 118 as a cry for the Kingdom to arrive (Pope 1988, Keener).

12:15 *Look, your King is coming, riding on a donkey's colt.* Carson (1991:433-434) notes three points regarding the Zech 9:9 quote: (1) this was associated with the cessation of war, showing Jesus could not be a Zealot (as some have said); (2) this would produce a worldwide reign of the gentle King (cf. Ps 72:8; alluded to in Zech 9:10); (3) this was associated with the blood of God's covenant that brings relief for prisoners (cf. 1:29, 34; 3:5; 6:35-38; 8:31-34), connected with Passover and the death of the Servant-King. There is evidence the passage was considered messianic in Jesus' day or shortly thereafter (*Genesis Rabbah* 75:6, *b. Sanhedrin* 98a, so Köstenberger, Keener), and Jesus' act fits the mode of an eschatological prophet implying a royal claim. Clearly, Jesus saw himself as the royal Messiah (so J. Collins 1995:206).

12:19 *There's nothing we can do.* It is interesting to contrast the attitudes of the three major parties of the last half of the first century (the Zealots appeared later but had their roots in Jesus' day). The Sadducees believed in complete cooperation with the Romans; the Pharisees believed in tolerance—it was an oppressive thing that had to be endured; the Zealots believed it was an insult to the God of Israel and that any recognition of Rome constituted high treason against God (so Bruce).

COMMENTARY

Jesus openly declared who he was by entering Jerusalem on a donkey in direct fulfillment of Zechariah 9:9 (see note on 12:15). The Synoptics (Mark 11:1-7 and parallels) tell of the elaborate preparations Jesus made for the occasion and the deliberate nature of the whole scene; he was in a sense throwing down the gauntlet. Yet, by riding a donkey rather than a warhorse, he was also making a declaration that he was not the kind of Messiah they were expecting; he had come to bring peace, not a sword. The "next day" (12:12) indicates Sunday, one week before the Resurrection. As Jesus left for Jerusalem, the news galvanized the city. A huge crowd of "Passover visitors" (see commentary on 11:55-57) poured out to see the sight (others were also part of the crowd, see 12:17). They waved palm branches to welcome Jesus. It used to be debated whether this was a sign from the Festival of Shelters rather than Passover (actually, the palms were used at both feasts), but recently it has become more clear that it signified messianic fervor. Palm branches had long been used to welcome conquerors and celebrate military victories (1 Macc 13:51; Josephus *Wars* 7.100-102), and the Jews wanted Jesus to conquer the Romans for them.

The titles they used for Jesus (12:13) were also messianic. The first thing they shouted was "Praise God!" (lit., "Hosanna"). It used to be thought that this was a prayer, "O Lord, save," which is its meaning in Aramaic, but recent studies have shown that it was a cry of acclamation (such as "hooray") or praise to God (see note on 12:13). Since the titles were generally taken from Psalm 118, "praise God" may have been the meaning as well, in which it could have some aspect of meaning from 118:25, "Please, LORD, please save us. Please, LORD, please give us success." The psalm celebrated pilgrims coming to Jerusalem and was particularly apt for this Passover celebration. Then the people called down divine blessing on "the one who comes in the name of the LORD," from Psalm 118:26, a passage the Jews understood messianically (seen in the midrash on Ps 118 [*Midrash Tehillim* 244a], so Beasley-Murray). They wanted God to particularly bless their hoped-for liberator. Some (e.g., Michaels), however, think the crowd was not citing Scripture but uttering a spontaneous cry. The following cry, "Hail to the King of Israel" (cf. 1:49; 18:33, 37, 39; 19:19, 21), does not come from Psalm 118 but was a concluding ascription for their Davidic conqueror. It is most likely that the crowd's words were a combination of words from Psalm 118 and their own messianic cry. The reason the people were there is rather obvious. They could almost see the gathering battle.

Jesus quickly dashed their hopes (12:14-15). He was not riding a warhorse (cf. 1 Kgs 4:26; Isa 31:1-3 for the association with military conquest) but a donkey, signifying peace (remember Matt 21:1-7 and the elaborate preparations Jesus made to do this very thing). However, the people were likely looking to him as the conquering Messiah, for the imagery (even the donkey) was often seen in royal processions (e.g., Solomon in 1 Kgs 1:33, 38, 44). It was actually a dangerous situation; the crowd was a tinderbox ready to explode into a full-scale messianic riot. Jesus was alleviating pressure, as well as correcting their misunderstanding. John tells us this was still, however, prophetic fulfillment of Zechariah 9:9, a passage also understood messianically in the first century. Actually, two Old Testament passages are combined in John 12:15, for "don't be afraid" does not come from Zechariah but from Zephaniah 3:16 (Brown) or Isaiah 40:9 (Carson). The Zephaniah passage would fit the "King of Israel" ascription above, for that occurs in Zephaniah 3:15, and that passage was written to show Israel that Yahweh was in their midst as king (though not in a nationalistic sense) and would deliver them. There is also a universal aspect in Zephaniah, as people will be gathered from all over the earth (3:9-10). This matches a similar theme in Zechariah and is explicitly stated in 12:19.

Zechariah 9 has a similar thrust to Zephaniah 3:9ff, promising a lowly king who will deliver his people from their oppressors and "bring peace to the nations," establishing his rule "from sea to sea" (9:10). So, Jesus' entry on the donkey was a prophetic act to counter the nationalistic messiah the Jews wanted. Jesus was saying the universal kingship would be established only by his death. John remarks that at that time they did not understand this prophecy until "after Jesus entered into his glory" (12:16). This should probably be understood in light of 14:26, where Jesus says the Spirit will "remind you of everything I have told you," including things they had not previously understood. The mention of "glory" is significant and once more emphasizes the Passion as Jesus' time of "glory." It was the glorified Lord and his Spirit who gave them the deeper understanding (as is also the case with us). Incidentally, John was always careful to tell when the disciples' understanding came later (cf. 2:22, where Jesus said he would raise up the temple of his body in three days), further proof of his historical trustworthiness.

The triumphal entry is framed by two passages (12:9-11, 17-19) that contrast belief (Jews—12:11; the whole world—12:19) with the leaders' rejection of Jesus. Added to the pilgrims in the crowd who had come for the feast (12:12) is another group of people: those who had "seen Jesus call Lazarus from the tomb" (12:17). Those who had seen the raising of Lazarus "were telling others about it" (lit., "bearing witness"), probably telling them that such a person could certainly deliver the Jewish people from the Romans. Thus continues the important theme of witness in the Gospel (cf. on 1:27; 3:26; 5:31ff; 8:13ff). In fact, it was their witness that led to the large crowds and their enthusiasm in the first place (12:18). In 12:18 the raising of Lazarus is called a "sign"—the seventh and last of the "miraculous signs" that to an extent control chapters 2-12 (see commentary on 2:1-12). The Pharisees were distraught at seeing their careful plan to take Jesus away quietly go up in smoke. They were helpless and could do nothing. Their last statement (12:19, cf. NLT mg) is another great example of double meaning. They were hardly acknowledging the universal impact of Jesus; even his disciples had no idea about this. They meant instead that pilgrims from all around the Jewish world had flocked after Jesus in the Triumphal Entry. The Evangelist John saw a great deal more significance, and this builds on the universal implications of the Zephaniah 3:16 and Zechariah 9:9 passages above. Like Caiaphas in 11:50, the Pharisees said far more than they realized; indeed the whole world *would* go after Jesus (12:19). For John, the Triumphal Entry both corrected the false understandings of the Jews (and the disciples) and prepared for an explosion of the gospel throughout the world.

◆   ## 4. Jesus predicts his death (12:20-36)

20Some Greeks who had come to Jerusalem for the Passover celebration 21paid a visit to Philip, who was from Bethsaida in Galilee. They said, "Sir, we want to meet Jesus." 22Philip told Andrew about it, and they went together to ask Jesus.

23Jesus replied, "Now the time has come for the Son of Man* to enter into his glory. 24I tell you the truth, unless a kernel of wheat is planted in the soil and dies, it remains alone. But its death will produce many new kernels—a plentiful harvest of new lives. 25Those who love their life in this world will lose it. Those who care nothing for their life in this world will keep it for eternity. 26Anyone who wants to be my disciple must follow me, because my servants must be where I am. And the Father will honor anyone who serves me.

27"Now my soul is deeply troubled. Should I pray, 'Father, save me from this hour'? But this is the very reason I came! 28Father, bring glory to your name."

Then a voice spoke from heaven, saying, "I have already brought glory to my name, and I will do so again." 29When the crowd heard the voice, some thought it was thunder, while others declared an angel had spoken to him.

30Then Jesus told them, "The voice was for your benefit, not mine. 31The time for judging this world has come, when Satan, the ruler of this world, will be cast out. 32And when I am lifted up from the earth,

I will draw everyone to myself." ³³He said this to indicate how he was going to die.
³⁴The crowd responded, "We understood from Scripture* that the Messiah would live forever. How can you say the Son of Man will die? Just who is this Son of Man, anyway?"
³⁵Jesus replied, "My light will shine for you just a little longer. Walk in the light while you can, so the darkness will not overtake you. Those who walk in the darkness cannot see where they are going. ³⁶Put your trust in the light while there is still time; then you will become children of the light."
After saying these things, Jesus went away and was hidden from them.

12:23 "Son of Man" is a title Jesus used for himself.   12:34 Greek *from the law.*

NOTES

12:21 *we want to meet Jesus.* Some (e.g., Bruce, Carson) believe this was a couple of days after the Triumphal Entry, and so the second cleansing of the Temple (Mark 11:15-17) had occurred, in which Jesus expelled the traders to make the Temple "a house of prayer for all nations" (Isa 56:7). The Greeks may have been curious to see if he had them especially in mind.

12:23 *enter into his glory.* Ridderbos (1997:428-429) states that the glorification of the Son of Man was only now "really" beginning and sees this defined in light of the "descent-ascent schema" of 3:13. The heavenly glory of Jesus (his ascent to heaven) centered on the finalization of his ascent from earth via the Cross.

12:27 *my soul is deeply troubled.* A similar passage is found in Heb 5:7-10, also a meditation on Gethsemane. It tells how Jesus "offered prayers and pleadings, with a loud cry and tears, to the one who could rescue him from death." God heard his prayers, and as a result "he learned obedience from the things he suffered." In this and other passages on Jesus' "troubled" heart (e.g., 11:33, 38; 13:21), Beutler (1978:35-37) thinks Pss 42–43 (David's laments) are echoed.

'Father, save me from this hour'? While most take this as part of the question (NIV, NRSV, NJB, NLT and most commentators), some believe it is an actual prayer like the Gethsemane prayer (cf. Luke 22:42a) and should be read, "What should I pray? Father, save me from this hour! But no—this is the very reason I came" (so Carson, Witherington, Whitacre, Burge). The parallel with the Gethsemane prayer makes this a very attractive possibility. Either way, it shows that Jesus was rejecting his natural inclination to be delivered from his terrible destiny.

12:28 *a voice spoke from heaven.* This is the only time in John's Gospel that God speaks audibly, although God speaks twice in the Synoptics (at the Baptism and at the Transfiguration).

12:34 *We understood from Scripture that the Messiah would live forever.* Most likely "the Scripture" here (lit., "the law") refers not only to the written law but to the oral law. Therefore, this statement probably derives from three sources: (1) OT passages on the eternal reign of God's earthly Kingdom (Ps 89:36 on his eternal dynasty; Isa 9:7 and Ezek 37:25 on the eternal Davidic line; Dan 7:14 on the eternal dominion of the one like a son of man); (2) intertestamental passages on the eternal reign of the Messiah (*1 Enoch* 49:2; *Psalms of Solomon* 17:4); and (3) Targumic passages on the eternal reign (e.g., *Targum Isaiah* 9:5). Scholars debate which of these are primary, but the crowd was speaking generally, and their belief was anchored in all three.

12:34 *the Son of Man.* There has been considerable discussion of whether or not first-century Jews would have understood the Son of Man as a messianic figure since there is not much Jewish material that would make such an identification certain. Probably the crowd's identification was not based so much on the Son of Man title but rather on the fact that Jesus called himself Son of God and claimed to be the Messiah. Given that time of messianic foment, such a link is easy to understand. Chilton (1980:177-178) thinks that on the basis of Targum Isaiah 53:13 (which identifies the Messiah with the exalted "Servant"), the crowd understood at some level that Jesus was speaking of the Messiah with his "lifted up" language.

COMMENTARY

There are five sections in this unique story: (1) the introduction (12:20-22), in which some Gentiles (Greeks) are brought to Jesus; (2) the arrival of the "time" and its significance (12:23-26)—death as the lot of Jesus and the focus of his disciples; (3) the Father testifying to the glory that will arise from Jesus' Passion (12:27-30); (4) the meaning of Jesus' work as a whole—this is the time of judgment and salvation (12:31-33); and (5) the fact that light was going to be there only a little longer (12:34-36). The theme of Jesus' impending death dominates, but within this there is an emphasis on true discipleship and the necessity of encountering Jesus while there is time.

Among the pilgrims who had come for Passover were many "Greeks" (12:20). These could possibly have been Greek-speaking Jews, but the Greek term used here normally refers to those of non-Jewish birth (Gentiles, proselytes or God-fearers). Thus the statement of the Pharisees that "everyone" (12:19) had flocked after Jesus was already coming to pass! Many Hellenists would certainly have come "for the Passover celebration" to worship God and discover more about the Jewish religion. In the book of Acts, God-fearers like Cornelius form a major source for early converts (Acts 10:2, 22, 35; 13:16, 26; cf. also Luke 7:1-5). They worshiped Yahweh and were drawn to the Jewish life but were not yet willing to undergo circumcision and become full proselytes. They were allowed in the court of the Gentiles and could participate in the festivities there but could not enter the inner courts on penalty of death.

Naturally, they were very curious about this Jesus and wanted to know more (12:21). Their desire to meet him (lit., "see" him) may have salvific significance in light of the importance of the verbs for "see" in the Johannine theme of salvation-encounter (see "Literary Style" in the Introduction). Like anyone wanting to meet a famous person, they were probably afraid to try by themselves. They probably came to Philip because, like Andrew, he was from Bethsaida (1:44), a village on the northeast corner of the Sea of Galilee and officially in Gaulanitis. It was near the Ten Cities (Decapolis), and some of these Greeks may have been from that area. They could also have been drawn to Philip because of his Greek name. At any rate, they asked him to introduce them to Jesus, and so he, along with Andrew, took them to see his Lord.

Jesus' response (12:23) seems to ignore them, but in the larger picture it provides the core of the salvation they sought. Moreover, Jesus may well have been saying that with them, the procession of the nations to Zion that had been prophesied in Isaiah (e.g., Isa 60) had begun. This may well have been the crucial "signal" to Jesus that his hour had finally arrived (so Carson). The time was here, fulfilling the expectation of much of this Gospel regarding Jesus' hour of destiny, when God's plan of salvation would culminate (2:4; 7:6, 8, 30; 8:20). That hour was the hour of his death, spoken of first as his entering into his glory. John 12:23ff is one of the key Son of Man passages (along with 1:51) associated with heavenly glory and the salvation he would provide. For the Son of Man, suffering was the path to glory; in fact, here suffering *is* glory! As in Isaiah 52:13, Jesus, the Servant of Yahweh, "will prosper; he will be highly exalted" in the midst of his suffering (12:24-25). The idea of the suffering Servant dominates this section (so Carson, Blomberg).

Jesus used a short parable (12:24) about a kernel of wheat to teach this, beginning with another double *amēn* [TG281, ZG297] ("I tell you the truth"; cf. 1:51; 5:24; 6:26) to highlight its importance. It is similar to a couple of the Synoptic parables, like the parable of the Sower (Mark 4:1-20) and the two short seed parables of Mark 4:26-32. Jesus had utilized harvest imagery before to stress the importance of his mission (4:35-38). Now he used it to emphasize the event that made the mission possible—his death. This agricultural image is very apt, centering as it does on the necessity of the grain dying before it can produce a harvest. When it does die, it produces "many new kernels—a plentiful harvest of new lives." The contrast is between remaining alone and "bearing much fruit" (a literal rendering of 12:24). If Jesus had not died on the cross, his life would have affected no one but himself—but his death has affected the whole world. As Whitacre points out (1999:310), this harvest is not only "the fruit of evangelism" but also means that "through his death fruit will be produced in the lives of his followers."

This discipleship theme is developed in 12:25-26, a passage reminiscent of Jesus' teaching following his first passion prediction in Mark (Mark 8:31-38). In terms of loving and hating life (12:25), there are five Synoptic passages on the same theme (Matt 10:39; 16:25; Mark 8:35; Luke 9:24; 17:33). This idea is the natural follow-up to 12:24 and could be called an "intermezzo," applying the thrust of that teaching to the disciples (Ridderbos, Köstenberger). The same process of life via death exemplified in Jesus must be seen in his disciples. There is an antithetical dualism in the two contrasts: the destroyed life (= loving the world/self) and the preserved life (= hating the world/self). The disciple who loves the world and its things (cf. 3:19; 12:43) will lose both in the end. The disciple who focuses on self rather than Jesus will end up with nothing. Jesus said it very well in Mark 8:34: "If any of you wants to be my follower, you must turn from your selfish ways, take up your cross, and follow me." Taking up the cross was a very specific metaphor; when the Romans made Jesus or anyone else bear their cross to the place of execution, they were giving them a message: "You are already dead!" To take up the cross is to count yourself dead to the things of this world. That person will "keep (his life) for eternity" (12:25). The disciples must become like the master; death is the path to life.

Therefore, the disciple must truly "follow" Jesus—that is, center on him rather than on oneself (12:26). When Jesus says, "my servants must be where I am," it must be remembered that he was on his way to the cross: As the Cross is the basis of Jesus' glorification, our "death" becomes the basis of our living for him (so Carson). Discipleship is based on servanthood in John; thus, it is natural that "the

Father will honor anyone who serves" Jesus. As several have pointed out (e.g., Schnackenburg, Ridderbos), the context is the continuation of Jesus' mission. The life of the disciple is a continuous reliving of the life and ministry of Jesus (also a major theme of Acts), meaning that like him, we focus entirely on the work of God and bringing the world to an encounter with the promise of life in Christ. Only then will there be reward.

Jesus then had a Gethsemane-type experience. In fact, it has often been thought that John reworked the synoptic Gethsemane story here (Schnackenburg, Lindars), though that is very unlikely in light of the significant differences in the accounts. Gethsemane was hardly the only time Jesus struggled with his impending death. As he spoke of it here, he stopped and said, "Now my soul is deeply troubled" (12:27), reflecting the deep-seated (the "soul" was the deepest part of the self) agony of heart he felt. The "now"-ness of the "time" (12:23) was upon him, and he experienced great distress (cf. Mark 14:34, "My soul is crushed with grief to the point of death"). He questioned whether he should ask the Father to "save (him) from this hour." This is similar to the Gethsemane prayer, "Abba, Father, . . . everything is possible for you. Please take this cup of suffering away from me" (Mark 14:36a). Yet the possibility was no sooner mentioned than rejected (cf. Mark 14:36b, "Yet I want your will to be done, not mine"). Jesus realized that his coming death was the "very reason" he had come (12:27). The importance of this statement cannot be overstated. The purpose of the Incarnation was his death (Phil 2:6-8); Christmas, from the start, meant the Cross. At every turn, Jesus was centered upon his Father's will (5:19; 6:37; 8:29, 38; 14:31), and that was never more true than in his Passion. The glory of God would only be complete with his death as the basis of the divine gift of salvation, so he cried, "Father, bring glory to your name" (12:28). His lifelong purpose was to glorify the name of God (7:18; 8:49), and this brought that goal to its culmination. As Jesus brings glory to God, God brings glory to him. That is a dominant theme in John.

The Father's response was immediate and powerful (12:28), centering on the descent-ascent motif in John. "I have already brought glory to my name" refers to the Incarnation and ministry of Jesus on earth. Jesus had descended (*katabainō* [TG2597, ZG2849]) from heaven (3:13, 31; 6:38, 42, 50, 51, 58) and is the one who united heaven and earth (1:51). Thus, he is the man of glory (1:14; 2:10-11; cf. Isa 35:1-2; Joel 3:18). The glory of Christ had been manifested in his revelation of divine truths and in his performance of divine deeds. At the same time, the Father would glorify himself again. The future glory of the Christ would be seen in his ascent (*anabainō* [TG305, ZG326]) to heaven (3:13; 6:62; 20:17), when he would reclaim his preexistent glory. In John, the Passion events are regularly called the glory of Jesus (7:39; 13:31-32; 17:1, 5, 24). They encompass his death (as in the "lifted up" theme of 3:14; 8:28; 12:32), as well as his resurrection and ascension into glory. Beasley-Murray (1987:212) calls this "an end which is the beginning of glory." Jesus glorifies the Father (12:28a) as the Father glorifies Jesus (12:28b), and both aspects culminated in the Cross.

The message of God at first glance seems to have been meant primarily for Jesus, not the bystanders. The crowd could not tell what had occurred (12:29, similar to Christ's message to Paul on the Damascus road, Acts 22:9) but thought it either had thundered (which shows the power of the voice) or that perhaps an angel had spoken. Their response is not surprising; thunder is often associated with heavenly voices (2 Sam 22:14; Ps 18:13; Rev 6:1; 10:3-4; 14:2), and angels often spoke for God (so Keener). Jesus replied, "The voice was for your benefit, not mine" (12:30). This statement is probably a Semitic contrast (so Tasker)—that is, "more for your sake than mine." Obviously the message was of comfort to Jesus, but he didn't need it as much as they did. God was giving Jesus another "seal of his approval" (cf. 6:27), but the crowd needed to understand its significance. Jesus was giving them an opportunity to respond. Like Jesus' prayer at the raising of Lazarus (11:41-42), "it was a bridge between Jesus and heaven, an unusually concrete example of 'heaven open . . .' (1:51) and a reminder that Jesus was acting not on his own, but always and only on his Father's initiative" (Michaels 1989:226-227). Such a supernatural portent does not happen every day, and it should have made them think carefully about their response. Even if they did not understand the words, they knew the voice was of heavenly origin (as the ancients thought regarding thunder), and so they ought to have listened and responded with zeal.

To make it absolutely clear, Jesus spelled out the implications (12:31-32). The "time" had arrived (12:23), and Jesus' death was imminent (12:24). Yet at the same time, this was his hour of glory (12:28). Clearly, it was the turning point of the ages, that "right time" (Gal 4:4) that all the promises of the Old Testament had prepared for. Two implications flow out of this.

First, it was "the time for judging this world" (12:31). John tells us that Jesus came to save the world rather than to judge it (3:17; 8:15) but that at the same time he became its judge (8:16; 9:39). In fact, God had made Jesus judge over the world (3:35-36; 5:22-23, 29-30). The reason is that, as the living revealer (the "Word") of God, he encounters every person at the deepest part of their being and forces them to a decision. That decision determines their destiny. For those who believe, he becomes Savior (4:42), but for those who reject him, he becomes judge. The world is characterized by rejection and rebellion (1:10), and so it is judged. This is the great irony: at the Cross, Jew and Gentile united in judging Jesus, while in reality they were being judged by Jesus!

In fact, it was far more than just the world that was being judged. At the Cross "Satan, the ruler of this world, will be cast out" (12:31b). Satan is called "ruler [or prince] of this world" in 14:30;16:11, and elsewhere he is called "commander of the powers of the air" (Eph 2:2, NLT mg), "god of this world" (2 Cor 4:4), and "great dragon—the ancient serpent" (Rev 12:9; cf. 20:2). The name Satan means "accuser" or "adversary." He led the great rebellion against God and was cast out of heaven (Rev 12:4, 7-9). He possessed Judas (13:27; Luke 22:3) and helped bring about the Cross, thus participating in his own defeat. Kovacs (1995:236-238) calls the Cross a "cosmic battle," which became the final victory over Satan (*1 Enoch* 1:3-4; *4 Ezra* 13:26ff). The book of Revelation makes it clear that the final defeat of Satan will not be at the battle of Armageddon but has already taken place at the Cross (Rev 5:5, 6; 12:11; 13:8); Armageddon is nothing more than the last act of rebellion by an already defeated foe. Probably at the very moment Christ died on the Cross, he told the demonic forces that they had lost (1 Pet 3:19) and then disarmed them, leading them in his victory procession (cf. Col 2:15 and note the imagery of a Roman triumph).

In short, Satan is still in power in this world, but his authority is only in this world, which is actually the prison he has been "cast" into (cf. 2 Pet 2:4; Jude 1:6). When we say that Satan is the "ruler of this world," he rules only his prison block. In fact, Witherington (1995:224) believes this passage is describing not Satan "cast out" of heaven but rather Satan removed from his role as "ruler of this world." There is, in a sense, a tension between the already (1 John 5:4-5; Rev 12:11) and the not-yet (1 John 5:19; Rev 13:7) with respect to our struggle against Satan. Tying this together is the adverb "now" (12:31; lit., "now is the time . . . now the ruler will be cast out"), emphasizing that these end time events have already begun (so Carson). The age between the advents is a time for the progressive unfolding of the defeat of Satan, as well as of the glory of Christ.

Second, the arrival of his "time" meant that it was time for Jesus to be "lifted up from the earth" (12:32), the third of the three "lifted up" sayings in John (with 3:14; 8:28; see note on 8:28). This metaphor means that as Jesus was lifted up on the Cross, he was lifted up into glory. This same verb is used in Isaiah 52:13 (LXX) where the Servant of Yahweh is called "highly exalted" (cf. Phil 2:9); for John, the Cross was Jesus' throne, his place of exaltation. When that happened, he would "draw everyone to" himself. The image is often used of a dragnet drawing in the fish "destined to be caught. And so it is for all the believers who have been captivated by Jesus and drawn to him" (Comfort 1994:110). This goes back to 6:44, where the Father "draws" to Jesus all he has given to him (6:37) and who come to him (6:35, 44). Yet there is also a difference, for the Father "draws" only those who come, while Jesus will draw "everyone." This is similar to the universal salvific will passages of 1:4, 7, 9, where Jesus as the Word "gives light to everyone." As the "light of the world" (9:5), Jesus enlightens every person, encountering them with the truth and reality of God. This work of Jesus will be carried on after his ascent by the Holy Spirit, who will "convict the world of its sin, and of God's righteousness, and of the coming judgment" (16:8; cf. 8-11). Moreover, "everyone" means all without distinction, Jew as well as Gentile, constituting the "one flock" of 10:16; cf. 11:52; 17:20-23. To make sure no reader would misunderstand the meaning of "lifted up," John added that by "lifted up," Christ was signifying "how he was going to die" (12:33).

The crowd finally understood something—that Jesus was speaking of his death (12:34)—but they were confused about what he said. In this context he does not say that the Son of Man must be lifted up (he says this in 3:14), only that the Son of Man would be glorified (cf. 12:23). Moreover, they were seeing this in light of their messianic expectations and wondered how he could say that the eternal Messiah would die. If he is eternal, then how could he die? Also, they expected the Messiah to be a victorious conqueror, not a Suffering Servant (they didn't understand the Servant Songs of Isaiah to be messianic). Therefore they asked, "Just who is this Son of Man, anyway?" This does not mean they failed to grasp that Jesus was calling himself the Son of Man. (This title could be taken as equivalent to "human" or "mortal" and did not demand extraordinary faith or comprehension; see note on 1:51.) Rather, they wanted to know what kind of Messiah Jesus claimed to be. The kind he seemed to be describing was not the Messiah they understood or could accept.

Jesus virtually ignored their question (12:35-36). This is his last encounter with the crowds in John, and his reply centers on their response to the light (cf. 9:4; 11:9-10). Verse 35 seems to be a short parable on a person traveling at sunset, who must hurry lest the darkness overtake him and he lose his way. It is a parable of crisis, similar to those in Matthew 24–25 (so Lindars, Blomberg). This is the time of spiritual conflict, in which the "ruler of this world" (12:31) is operating. In the light, the darkness has been overcome (1:5), but those who refuse the light and prefer darkness (3:19-20) are in incredible danger of losing their way to God and therefore of suffering eternal darkness. The idea of darkness overtaking a person (12:35) reverses 1:5 (the same verb), where the light overtakes the darkness. Those who "walk in the darkness" cannot see their way. They think they are headed in the right direction but are on the way to destruction. They must "put [their] trust in the light while there is still time" (12:36). The darkness had already gained mastery over many of the leaders, but Jesus did not want this to happen to the crowds. The only answer was a faith-decision. Jesus, the Light, would only be with them a little longer (mere days at this time), so they would not have many more chances. If they responded, they would become "children of the light." The Essenes of Qumran called themselves "the sons of light" and called outsiders "the sons of darkness." Jesus was using this language to describe his followers in contrast to those who reject him. "Child of" was a Semitic idiom pointing to a person's primary characteristic; their primary characteristic would be "light." As Jesus is the Light, so they would be "of the light."

This was a very fitting way for Jesus to end his public ministry, with a call for all who heard to leave the realm of darkness and come to the light. There is a type of *inclusio* in this, with the prologue centering on light encountering everyone (1:3-5, 7, 9) and Jesus' ministry ending with a call to become "children of the light." At this time, Jesus left and hid himself from them (12:36; cf. 8:59); in this, he was both symbolizing God's judgment on those who rejected him and awaiting the final "hour" that God had established. He had been warning them, and now the time was up.

◆   ## 5. The unbelief of the people (12:37-50)

37But despite all the miraculous signs Jesus had done, most of the people still did not believe in him. 38This is exactly what Isaiah the prophet had predicted:

"LORD, who has believed our
    message?
To whom has the LORD revealed
    his powerful arm?"*

³⁹But the people couldn't believe, for as Isaiah also said,

⁴⁰"The Lord has blinded their eyes
  and hardened their hearts—
so that their eyes cannot see,
  and their hearts cannot understand,
and they cannot turn to me
  and have me heal them."*

⁴¹Isaiah was referring to Jesus when he said this, because he saw the future and spoke of the Messiah's glory. ⁴²Many people did believe in him, however, including some of the Jewish leaders. But they wouldn't admit it for fear that the Pharisees would expel them from the synagogue. ⁴³For they loved human praise more than the praise of God.

12:38 Isa 53:1.   12:40 Isa 6:10.

⁴⁴Jesus shouted to the crowds, "If you trust me, you are trusting not only me, but also God who sent me. ⁴⁵For when you see me, you are seeing the one who sent me. ⁴⁶I have come as a light to shine in this dark world, so that all who put their trust in me will no longer remain in the dark. ⁴⁷I will not judge those who hear me but don't obey me, for I have come to save the world and not to judge it. ⁴⁸But all who reject me and my message will be judged on the day of judgment by the truth I have spoken. ⁴⁹I don't speak on my own authority. The Father who sent me has commanded me what to say and how to say it. ⁵⁰And I know his commands lead to eternal life; so I say whatever the Father tells me to say."

NOTES

12:38 This is exactly. In actuality, the Gr. introduces the Scripture fulfillment formula with *hina* [ᵀᴳ2443, ᶻᴳ2671] (so that): "so that the word of Isaiah might be fulfilled"; many have asked how strongly the *hina* should be interpreted. Did God cause Jewish unbelief "for the purpose" of fulfilling Scripture (so Hendriksen, Carson, Ridderbos)? Or should it be seen more simply as a fulfillment formula (Brown)? The answer may be best expressed by Bruce (1983:271), who calls it a "Hebraic fashion of expressing result as though it were purpose." In the context of John, there is perfect symmetry of divine sovereignty and human responsibility, so it goes too far to take a double predestination approach: John was not saying that God predestined the Jews to unbelief. Rather, the two sides worked together in a way similar to Pharaoh, who hardened his heart as God was hardening it (cf. Osborne 2003 on Rom 9:16-18, 22).

12:44-50 Whitacre (1999:324) sums up the Johannine themes present here: faith (12:44-45), Jesus the "sent one" (12:44-45, 49), light versus darkness (12:46), judging (12:47-48), saving the world (12:47), not speaking on his own (12:49), and eternal life (12:50).

12:49 I don't speak on my own authority. Jesus' subordination to the Father is not the whole of who Jesus is but relates entirely to his earthly mission. We could call it a functional subordination (see note on 14:28). It must be balanced by the ontological oneness between Jesus and God in 1:1, 18; 10:30. Jesus is the God-man, both subordinate and equal with God.

COMMENTARY

Scriptural Proof of Unbelief (12:37-43). Keener (2003:882) states that 12:37-43 provides a theological summation of responses to Jesus and 12:44-50 gives Jesus' reaction to a series of representative responses. Another way to look at it is to consider 37-43 an Old Testament fulfillment interpretation of Jewish rejection and 44-50 Jesus' personal response to that rejection. The "signs" section of John (chs 2–12) ends on the same note of unbelief that preceded it (1:11). Even with the incredible sign-miracles, the people refused to put their faith in Jesus. This situation remained a quandary for the early church such that Paul addresses it in Romans 9–11: If Jesus was indeed the Messiah sent from heaven, then why had so few Jews been won to him? In Romans, the question is whether God had been faithful to his promises (Rom 9:6, 14). Here, the question is which Old Testament prophecies made it possible to understand the phenomenon. Yet this demonstrates that the same hardness of heart that met Jesus' ministry continued after his death and resurrection. The majority of Jewish people remained closed to the gospel. They were like the ancient Israelites to whom Moses spoke in Deuteronomy 29:2-4: "You have seen with your own eyes . . . all the great tests of strength, the miraculous signs, and the amazing wonders. But to this day the Lord has not given you minds that understand, nor eyes that see, nor ears that hear."

The message here is that this salvation-historical tragedy is in itself a fulfillment of prophecy. John centers on two passages from Isaiah, probably because the same apostasy in the land occurred in Isaiah's day. First, he quoted the Greek version of Isaiah 53:1 (12:38), found in the fourth of the Servant songs (52:13–53:12, with 52:13 alluded to in 12:32). This song states that while the Servant is exalted by God (52:13, used in 12:32), the nations were appalled that he was disfigured and rejected. Verse 53:1 asks the natural question, "Who has believed our message? To whom has the Lord revealed his powerful arm?" God had previously shown himself in mighty deeds like the Exodus and the deliverances through the judges or David, but when he did so through one who was "despised and rejected—a man of sorrows" (Isa 53:3), the people reacted in disbelief. Jesus, the Suffering Servant, faced the disbelief prophesied in Isaiah. The Isaiah passage also sums up the impact of the words ("message") and deeds ("powerful arm") of Jesus. The Israel of Jesus' day was just like the Israel of Isaiah's day. Both rejected the clear message of God. The rejection would only become more intense when Jesus manifestly became the Suffering Servant in his Passion!

The second passage cited is Isaiah 6:10 (12:39-40); this is the major passage cited in the New Testament on Jewish unbelief (Mark 4:10-12; Acts 28:26-27; Rom 11:8). Isaiah had perhaps the most amazing, and at the same time the most appalling, commissioning service in all of human history. He had seen a vision of God on his throne and yet had been told he was to be sent on a mission of inevitable failure. God wanted him to preach to a people who would not listen to or accept his message. In fact, God was going to use him to *cause* that very rejection! John altered the sequence of the lines in Isaiah to apply it especially to Jesus. In Isaiah, the order is heart, then ears and then eyes. John dropped the reference to the ears and reversed the order—eyes and then hearts—because he centered on the "miraculous signs" the people had seen in Jesus and their effect on the people's hearts (12:37). Jesus was reliving the ministry of Isaiah. Through his sign-miracles, their eyes had been blinded so they could not see, and their hearts had been hardened so that they could not understand.

Note that God would no longer allow them to repent—"They cannot turn to me and have me heal them." This is what is normally called a "judicial hardening" of the people. Yet it was not just a cold, calculated act. Burge (2000:348) calls it "a judicial hardening that settles on a people who are already guilty." We must remember that throughout John, the divine and the human are intertwined; sovereignty and responsibility are interdependent. The people had been guilty of unbelief, and God was hardening them. The exact logical relationship is a mystery that will not be fully understood until we get to heaven (though too many theologians believe they have it all figured out). Divine sovereignty is primary, but human responsibility is equally important, in Romans 9-11 as well as here. Köstenberger calls it "unambiguously predestinarian and yet compatibilist, including elements of human responsibility as well" (2004:391).

John explained that Isaiah was referring to Jesus "because he saw the future and spoke of the Messiah's glory" (12:41). Of course, Isaiah saw the glory of Yahweh, but as Jesus and God are one (1:1, 18; 10:30), Isaiah saw Jesus' glory in a typological sense. How does this relate to a context of judicial hardening? The glory of God and of Jesus are not just seen in the salvation of the faithful but also in the judgment of the enemies of God. The exalted Jesus is also Judge of all, and that is his glory as well. This theme is especially developed in the book of Revelation (e.g., the "hallelujah" choruses of 19:1-5 that celebrate the destruction of the evildoers).

Yet not all were guilty of unbelief, for even some of the Jewish leaders put their faith in him (12:42). Behind this is the assumption that even more of the common people had become followers. John wants us to understand that the rejection was not universal, even among the leaders. Even the group most active in opposing Jesus and plotting his death had some converts; however, they never spoke up "for fear that the Pharisees would expel them from the synagogue," as they had expelled the man healed from blindness (9:34; cf. 9:22). They are described well in 12:43: "They loved human praise more than the praise of God." One whom we have already met, Nicodemus (3:1-15; 7:50-51), revealed himself only after the death of Jesus (19:39). Another was Joseph of Arimathea, described directly as "a secret disciple of Jesus (because he feared the Jewish leaders)" (19:38). Undoubtedly, there were several others. There is no reason to think that they were not true believers; they were merely weak believers without the courage of their convictions, like all too many today. This goes back to 2:23-25. One could almost say there are several levels of faith in John, and it is impossible (and not in John's interest) to say which level separates the true from the false believer. Suffice it to say that every so-called "believer" must continually examine his or her faith and make certain it is vibrant and growing. The danger of losing it all in eternity is too great. Those who "trusted" in 2:23-25 thought they were all right, but Jesus knew better, and their true colors were shown in 6:60-66. Others will not find out until the last judgment, when Jesus will say, "I never knew you. Get away from me" (Matt 7:23). Therefore, those with a weak faith are in serious danger. For such "closet Christians," like those mentioned in 12:42-43, there is spiritual danger, and they could come under the indictment of 12:47-48 (commented on below).

Final Charge to Believe (12:44-50). We do not know at what point or where Jesus delivered this final charge, but it neatly summarizes his message thus far. Thus it is the perfect final paragraph for drawing together Jesus' message to the people (and John's message to his readers). At the outset, Jesus centers on two of his major motifs—belief and God as the one who sent him (12:44-45). For belief, he also uses the twin concepts of trusting and seeing: to trust/see Jesus constitutes trusting/seeing the one who sent him. Since he was God's envoy or agent, and since he would be with them only a while longer, the only proper response was faith (cf. Matt 10:40-42; Mark 9:37). Jesus as the Sent One is central to the portrait of Christ and his mission in John (cf. Introduction and 3:17). Endemic to it is the fact that in everything Jesus centers on his Father: He does the work of his Father and is one with the Father. Therefore, faith in him constitutes faith in God. He is the voice of God and the presence of God, the only path to God (14:6), so we cannot believe in God without believing in Christ.

Then in 12:46, Jesus turns once more to the imagery of light vs. darkness (cf. 9:4; 11:9-10; 12:35-36). Since one may "see" (12:45) the Father in the Son, he is naturally the "light" who reveals God. As "the light of the world" (8:12), he shines in this dark world to illuminate or expose its sin and rebellion (1:4-5, 9; 3:19-21). The purpose, however, is redemptive rather than punitive, for salvation rather than judgment (so 3:17). The light shines so that people can put their trust in Jesus and therefore overcome and leave the darkness (cf. 1:5).

For those who reject the light, however, Jesus is also judge (12:47-48), another primary theme in John (cf. 5:22-23, 30; 9:39). Two groups are described here: The first consists of those "who hear me but don't obey me," namely those with inadequate faith (2:23-25; probably those closet Christians of 12:42-43). Jesus says he "will not judge" them. This does not mean that there will be no judgment, for clearly such people will bring judgment down on themselves (3:19-20; 6:60-66). Rather, Jesus came to bring them salvation rather than judgment (repeating 3:17). He works with them to produce repentance and a belief that is put to work in obedience. James 2:17 says "faith by itself isn't enough. Unless it produces good deeds, it is dead and useless"; without the obedience that results, there is no faith in the first place. The second group is made up of those who reject Jesus and his teaching and "will be judged on the day of judgment." This builds on 5:41-47, where the words of Moses will be their judge, for they have rejected God's truth. Here, the "truth I have spoken" will be their accuser at the judgment day.

Jesus ends on the note with which he began this final charge (12:44-45)— namely, his subordination to his Father (12:49-50). The central point here is the Father's "commands," which are behind everything Jesus says and does. His commands are the "authority" behind Jesus' words. Here, the Father commands Jesus' words, and in 14:31, he commands Jesus' deeds, especially the Passion events. The commands of God determine Jesus' mission as a whole (Brown 1966:504). This may be reminiscent of the "prophet like Moses" of Deuteronomy 18:18-19: "I will put my words in his mouth, and he will tell the people everything I command him." This is fulfilled in Jesus, the final prophet (so Brown, Whitacre). The point is that

Jesus' teaching has no origin in human ideas but stems from God entirely, so it has absolute authority. Since "his commands lead to eternal life," and Jesus is one with him, it is the words of Jesus that alone are eternal life (5:24; 8:51).

◆ IV. The Last Supper and Farewell Discourse (13:1–17:26)
   A. Jesus Washes His Disciples' Feet (13:1-17)

Before the Passover celebration, Jesus knew that his hour had come to leave this world and return to his Father. He had loved his disciples during his ministry on earth, and now he loved them to the very end.* ²It was time for supper, and the devil had already prompted Judas,* son of Simon Iscariot, to betray Jesus. ³Jesus knew that the Father had given him authority over everything and that he had come from God and would return to God. ⁴So he got up from the table, took off his robe, wrapped a towel around his waist, ⁵and poured water into a basin. Then he began to wash the disciples' feet, drying them with the towel he had around him.

⁶When Jesus came to Simon Peter, Peter said to him, "Lord, are you going to wash my feet?"

⁷Jesus replied, "You don't understand now what I am doing, but someday you will."

⁸"No," Peter protested, "you will never ever wash my feet!"

Jesus replied, "Unless I wash you, you won't belong to me."

⁹Simon Peter exclaimed, "Then wash my hands and head as well, Lord, not just my feet!"

¹⁰Jesus replied, "A person who has bathed all over does not need to wash, except for the feet,* to be entirely clean. And you disciples are clean, but not all of you." ¹¹For Jesus knew who would betray him. That is what he meant when he said, "Not all of you are clean."

¹²After washing their feet, he put on his robe again and sat down and asked, "Do you understand what I was doing? ¹³You call me 'Teacher' and 'Lord,' and you are right, because that's what I am. ¹⁴And since I, your Lord and Teacher, have washed your feet, you ought to wash each other's feet. ¹⁵I have given you an example to follow. Do as I have done to you. ¹⁶I tell you the truth, slaves are not greater than their master. Nor is the messenger more important than the one who sends the message. ¹⁷Now that you know these things, God will bless you for doing them.

13:1 Or *he showed them the full extent of his love.*   13:2 Or *the devil had already intended for Judas.*
13:10 Some manuscripts do not include *except for the feet.*

NOTES
13:1 *Before the Passover celebration.* Critics are divided on the chronology of the Last Supper. Many scholars (Lindars, Schnackenburg, Kysar, Michaels) believe John places the Last Supper one day earlier than the synoptic Gospels do. (For example, Mark 14:12 places it on "the first day of the Festival of Unleavened Bread [= Passover], when the Passover lamb is sacrificed"; this differs from John's timing here: "Before the Passover.") Their idea is that John wanted to make a theological point by showing Jesus' crucifixion coinciding with the time when the Passover lambs were slaughtered (a Thursday that particular year). Such scholars see this timing corroborated by John's calling the day of the Crucifixion the "day of preparation" for the Passover (19:14, 31, 42; cf. 18:28), indicating Thursday. Several solutions have been suggested to explain the differences in chronology: (1) Jeremias (1966) thinks the Last Supper was not a Passover meal but another of the preparatory meals, perhaps a *Kiddush*

("prayer") meal or a *Habburah* ("fellowship") meal. The details, however, clearly reflect Passover imagery. (2) Jaubert (1965) posits that John followed a sectarian solar calendar rather than the lunar calendar of the Pharisees and so placed it a day earlier, essentially calling the same day by a different name (so also Keener). However, there is no evidence for this, and the sacrifices in the Temple were offered on the official day (Thursday), so this theory is unlikely. (3) Witherington (1995:231) believes this was not a Passover meal but a Greco-Roman banquet celebrated sometime during Passion week (in fact he takes the farewell address of 13–17 as not a single address but a composite of messages delivered on several occasions during the week). This is possible but unnecessary. (4) It is best to follow those (Morris, Carson, Ridderbos, Burge, Blomberg, Köstenberger) who point out that "the day of preparation" on which Christ was crucified actually refers to the day before the "special Sabbath"— namely, the Sabbath (Saturday) of Passover week, rather than Friday. Therefore, John and the Synoptics are in agreement that the Last Supper was on Thursday night and the Crucifixion on Friday, which would have been the day of preparation for the Sabbath.

He had loved his disciples. Dodd (1953a:398) provides an interesting statistic: In chs 2–12, words for "life" (50 times) and "light" (32 times) predominate over words for "love" (12 times—I am adding the *philos* [TG5384, ZG5813] word group to this statistic). In chs 13–17, however, words for "love" (37 times) predominate over "life" (6 times) and "light" (no occurence). Jesus' love and concern for his disciples control this section.

13:2 the devil had already prompted Judas. There is a text-critical question as to whether the text has the genitive *Iouda* [TG2455, ZG2683], in which it is the heart "of Judas" (A D K 28 33 𝔐), or the nominative *Ioudas* [TG2455, ZG2683], in which Satan decides "in his own heart" to do it (𝔓66 ℵ B L W 044 070). The nominative, as the more difficult reading, is probably the original (cf. discussion in Comfort 2007:[John 13:2b]), but this does not mean Satan made the decision himself. Rather, Satan and Judas formed a conspiracy of evil (so Carson).

13:10 bathed all over. This has often been seen as a reference to water baptism, but that hardly fits the context, which shows no awareness of such a theology. This is spiritual cleansing rather than baptism.

except for the feet. This phrase is missing in a few mss (ℵ D Origen), and this is preferred by several scholars (e.g., Bultmann, Hoskyns, Lindars, Barrett, Brown, Beasley-Murray, Burge) on the grounds that the bath is complete and so the context makes the added material superfluous. The vast majority of mss, however, include the phrase, and this makes perfect sense in the context (as the interpretation above demonstrates). Therefore, it is likely that the phrase is original (so Westcott, Bruce, Morris, Michaels, Carson).

COMMENTARY

John gives us a rather unique portrait of the events preceding Jesus' arrest. The synoptic Gospels provide an extensive presentation of the Last Supper, including Jesus' elaborate preparations, the predictions of the betrayal of Judas and the desertion of the other disciples, and especially the words of institution over the bread and the wine, followed by the group's movement to Gethsemane. John, probably aware of the Synoptic tradition (cf. the Introduction), decided to supplement their presentation with his own portrayal. The two central themes are found in 13:1— Jesus' preparation of himself and his disciples for his departure from this world and his deep love for his disciples. The unique aspects are the washing of the disciples' feet (13:1-20), the farewell discourse (13:31–16:33), and his high priestly prayer (17:1-26). The focus has shifted from the crowds to Jesus' disciples. Jesus never again addresses the Jewish people in John but instead turns inward to prepare the disciples for the humanly terrible, yet spiritually wonderful, events to come. Lombard and Oliver (1991:367-369) argue that 13:1-38 is in effect an introductory section preparing for the major themes of Jesus' farewell discourse. Within this scheme, the Last Supper becomes a "working supper" in which Jesus was trying to accomplish a great many things, such as to exemplify humble service in leadership, point to his betrayer, and launch his disciples into their future ministries.

The opening of chapter 13 places the time just "before the Passover" meal began and states that Jesus was aware of two things. First, he knew "his hour had come." When he left Ephraim and came back to Bethany (11:54; 12:1), he knew the time had arrived, and this was corroborated when the Greeks came seeking him (12:23). This was the hour "to leave this world and return to his Father." The world is the place of rebellion and rejection, but it is also the object of God's redeeming love (3:16). He descended from heaven to this world (3:13) but was now about to ascend back to heaven; he had entered the final phase of his life on earth, and his attention was riveted on his disciples, to prepare them for the terrible process by which the "hour" would unfold. Second, his focus on his followers was controlled by love; he loved them to the very end. There is double meaning in "to the very end"; the end refers to both time (to the end of his life) and degree (to the uttermost, absolutely, so Morris, Ridderbos, Keener, Köstenberger). The theme of Jesus' love for his own dominates the section. Hultgren (1982:542-544) thinks this scene entails Jesus' offer of "eschatological hospitality" to his disciples and so tells them that they are welcome in his Father's house (cf. 14:2ff).

It was "time for supper" (13:2), probably meaning supper had just been served (so Barrett, Carson). John wants us to understand that "the devil had already prompted" Judas's betrayal. The spiritual war already acknowledged in 12:31 was now in full sway—the betrayal was not simply engineered by Judas for the money (12:6; 13:27-30) but had been planned by Satan all along. In the midst of this cosmic war, however, Jesus "knew" two things (13:3): he had power and authority from God "over everything," and he was soon to return to his heavenly origin. There was no question as to how the battle would turn out, for Jesus knew he was Lord of all. The Cross was not an isolated skirmish but the central act in the greatest cosmic drama history would ever know. The outcome was already settled. God was in charge, not Satan, and he had given all authority to his Son. Moreover, this was the time of the great return in which Jesus would ascend to that heavenly home from which he had come in the first place (cf. 3:13).

To show his deep love for his disciples, and in light of his knowledge that the time of destiny had arrived, Jesus decided to perform a symbolic act that would help his disciples understand what his sovereign authority meant and why he was surrendering his life (13:4-5). We must understand that this was a sovereign act and one at the heart of true leadership; that is, Jesus showed them that to follow his example, their authority had to be exercised via servanthood (for the foot washing as a "model of humility," see Keener 2003:904-907). To understand the significance of washing another's feet, remember what the Baptist said: "I'm not even worthy to be his slave and untie the straps of his sandal" (1:27). Only a slave would wash the feet of a guest; in fact, some Jews believed it should only be Gentile slaves, not Jewish ones, since the task was so menial (*Mekilta* on Exodus 21:2). Still, wives would wash their husbands' feet, children their parents', and disciples their teachers' (so Barrett, Edwards). When Jesus "took off his robe, wrapped a towel around his waist, and poured water into a basin," the disciples were aghast. Jesus was reversing the social order!

Imagine the scene. As it was a formal meal, the disciples would have been reclining on couches or mats, probably in a U-shape radiating out from Jesus with the heads facing inward. When Jesus wrapped the towel around him, he took on the menial dress of a slave. This was anchored further when he began washing their feet, thereby demonstrating that the one who was God deliberately took on "the humble position of a slave" (Phil 2:6-7; cf. Luke 22:27, "I am among you as one who serves"). There may be a link to Mark 10:44-45, "whoever wants to be first among you must be the slave of everyone else," perhaps with a connection to Jesus' death as "a ransom for many" (Mark 10:45), the moment culminating Jesus' life of servanthood (so Barrett, Edwards). Remember that one of those whose feet Jesus washed was Judas himself. This was a model of unbelievable love, to wash the feet of the very one who would send him to his death!

Peter's protest (13:6) was very understandable; the others were probably in stunned silence. Disciples were expected to serve their rabbis, never vice versa. They all must have been in shock. Peter's query, "Lord, are you going to wash my feet?" must have been filled with incredulity. In the Greek, "you" and "my" are side-by-side for emphasis: "You mean *you* . . . *my* feet?" Jesus' response addressed them all: they didn't understand then, but they would later. Usually this type of comment refers to the time after Jesus' resurrection (2:22; 12:16); here it probably means after the Spirit had come to illumine their spiritual minds (14:26). Peter still could not comprehend the reason for Jesus' incomprehensible act and so again protested (13:8), this time even more strongly: "You will never ever wash my feet!" As Whitacre says (1999:329): "In Peter's response we see the pride and self-will that is at the heart of all sin and that is the very thing for which the Cross will atone and bring healing. Peter is working from a worldly point of view, and not for the first time (cf. Matt 16:22ff)."

This time Jesus' reply was equally forceful: "Unless I wash you, you won't belong to me" (lit., "you will have no part with me"). The language of having a "part" means to have a share in his inheritance (cf. Rom 8:17; Eph 3:6; 1 Pet 1:4). This was more than just a physical service; there was double meaning in "wash," referring to not just physical but spiritual cleansing. Washing is the result of the cleansing of the Cross. Without accepting the cleansing Jesus offered, there could be no sharing in his Kingdom and community. Peter, in his typical exuberance, then went to the opposite extreme: "Then wash my hands and head as well!" (13:9). If that was the necessary requirement for acceptance by Jesus, Peter wanted more than just his feet washed—Peter remains an example of discipleship characterized by lots of heart and little head knowledge.

Jesus clarified his point further, and this is critical to understanding the footwashing scene: "A person who has bathed all over does not need to wash, except for the feet, to be entirely clean" (13:10). The picture is of a person attending a feast, who bathes at home and then at his arrival only has to clean his feet (due to the dusty road) to be wholly clean at the table (so Morris). His point was that the disciples were wholly clean because they had believed in Jesus. All they needed was to take care of their individual sins (so Thomas 1991:124-125); however, not all the disciples were clean. Judas had his feet washed, but he experienced only outward and not inward cleansing. He remained covered by the far more serious dirt of sin. Moreover, his was a filthy presence among the disciples, and his departure was part of the cleansing of the group (so Whitacre).

When the foot washing ended, Jesus donned his robe once more and returned to his mat to teach them further about the significance of what he had done (13:12). There was no way the disciples could understand it, especially since the meaning of the event was so intimately tied to Jesus' coming death. This is another thing they would not comprehend until after Jesus' death and resurrection. They had no idea of a suffering Messiah, as seen in the fact that when Jesus was later arrested, Peter drew his sword and struck a man (18:10), undoubtedly thinking that the angelic hosts would arrive and the conquering Messiah, Jesus, would finally reveal who he really was. By washing the disciples' feet, Jesus had just shown that he was truly the Servant of Yahweh, but even more that he was the servant of all (Luke 22:27). Finally, he had shown that this is the way God expects his servants to act toward others. This is the subject of 13:13-17.

Jesus began with what they did understand—namely, his authority, affirming that he was indeed their teacher, or rabbi, and their Lord (13:13). Disciples regularly addressed their rabbis as "teacher/rabbi" and "lord" (Aramaic, *mari*), a title of respect (cf. Strack-Billerbeck 2.558). Jesus meant more than they realized, however, for he is cosmic Lord of the universe. The first to realize this was Thomas, who in 20:28 called Jesus "my Lord and my God" (see notes on 20:24-29). Then it became part of Christian confession—"Jesus Christ is Lord" (Phil 2:11; cf. 1 Cor 16:22). Once more, this was beyond their ken at this time, but they understood it dimly. Jesus was beginning where they were, with his identity as the authoritative Messiah. Then he moved into the area of their confusion, that the "Lord" washed their feet. Two aspects are critical: first the extent to which that act made them a family, and then the extent to which it was to guide their lives. As Ridderbos says (1997:463), "He has washed their feet to portray to them the nature of the fellowship that not only unites them with him but must also be the permanent measure and source of their mutual relations when he has gone from them." If they were bound to Christ, they had to be bound to each other via acts of service and humility. Michaels (1989:241) calls this a "triangular statement" in that Jesus' action was meant to result in a new set of "disciple to disciple" relations (for other triangular statements, cf. 13:34; 15:12; 17:11, 20-23).

The footwashing was an example, a pattern or model for their future action, not only for their relations with each other but in their future ministries (13:15). Jesus' self-sacrificial love, as exemplified in washing their feet, was to be the mainstay of the way they conducted themselves when they became leaders in the church. Leadership without servanthood is against God's will. Jesus' command in 13:15 has been interpreted in various ways in the history of the church. Many groups have taken this command literally and have virtually turned foot washing into a sacrament, observing it regularly, often as part of the eucharistic service. There is no evidence for this practice in the early church. The only other time it is mentioned (1 Tim 5:10, NLT mg) concerns a qualification for ministry in the order of widows. Foot washing was not practiced as a Christian rite in the patristic period. It would seem, then, that while it is good to have a footwashing ceremony on occasion as a reminder, such a rite is not required for the church.

Jesus closed with another double *amēn* [TG281, ZG297] (13:16), highlighting an important saying (see note on 1:51): "Slaves are not greater than their master," nor the messenger greater than the sender (cf. Matt 10:24-25; Luke 6:40). Here, a shift begins from focus on Jesus as the one sent (3:17, 34; 5:36, 38) to Jesus as the one who sends. He would now be sending the disciples to continue his mission (17:18; 20:21). His mission had been characterized by self-sacrificial love and self-surrender (so Ridderbos), and why should they think that this was beneath them? True leaders are called to serve their flock, not lord it over them (cf. 1 Pet 5:3). The key was that God would bless them *only* if they continued in these acts of service (13:17). This has been a huge problem for Christian leaders in the past, and it is equally problematic today. All too few have a servant's heart. In fact, I recall speaking with a group once about having a pastor's seminar on leadership—when I said they should begin with servanthood, the general response I received was "Why?"

◆   B. Jesus Predicts His Betrayal (13:18-30)

18"I am not saying these things to all of you; I know the ones I have chosen. But this fulfills the Scripture that says, 'The one who eats my food has turned against me.'* 19I tell you this beforehand, so that when it happens you will believe that I AM the Messiah.* 20I tell you the truth, anyone who welcomes my messenger is welcoming me, and anyone who welcomes me is welcoming the Father who sent me."

21Now Jesus was deeply troubled,* and he exclaimed, "I tell you the truth, one of you will betray me!"

22The disciples looked at each other, wondering whom he could mean. 23The disciple Jesus loved was sitting next to Jesus at the table.* 24Simon Peter motioned to him to ask, "Who's he talking about?" 25So that disciple leaned over to Jesus and asked, "Lord, who is it?"

26Jesus responded, "It is the one to whom I give the bread I dip in the bowl." And when he had dipped it, he gave it to Judas, son of Simon Iscariot. 27When Judas had eaten the bread, Satan entered into him. Then Jesus told him, "Hurry and do what you're going to do." 28None of the others at the table knew what Jesus meant. 29Since Judas was their treasurer, some thought Jesus was telling him to go and pay for the food or to give some money to the poor. 30So Judas left at once, going out into the night.

13:18 Ps 41:9.   13:19 Or that the 'I AM' has come; or that I am the LORD; Greek reads that I am. See Exod 3:14.
13:21 Greek was troubled in his spirit.   13:23 Greek was reclining on Jesus' bosom. The "disciple Jesus loved" was probably John.

NOTES

13:18 *this fulfills the Scripture.* The early church generally understood Judas' betrayal in terms of scriptural fulfillment. Matthew 27:9 uses Zech 11:12-13 to explain the 30 pieces of silver, and Peter in Acts 1:20 cites Pss 69:25 and 109:8 to explain the betrayal.

turned against me. The actual image is "lifted up his heel against me," one of the worst insults imaginable, even today.

13:23 *The disciple Jesus loved.* It has at times been suggested that this refers to Lazarus since he is the only male disciple (the pronoun is masculine) described as "loved" by Jesus (11:3, 5, 36). It is clear, however, that the Twelve were the ones with Jesus at the Last Supper, so this is unlikely. Others have taken this to be a reference to a literary figure—the ideal disciple—rather than an actual person. This is too disjunctive; there is no reason that the beloved disciple cannot be both an actual person and a model for the ideal disciple.

sitting next to Jesus. Lit., "in the bosom of Jesus" (cf. NLT mg), the same wording as 1:18 ("near to the Father's heart," or, "in the bosom of the father"). This indicates that the beloved disciple enjoyed relationship with Jesus similar to that which Jesus had with the Father (so Beasley-Murray, Whitacre).

13:29 *go and pay for the food.* Many have used this to support a meal before the Passover since at this time on a festival night shops would not have been open. This was a Thursday night, however, and shops were open for supplies in light of their being closed Friday and Saturday. Moreover, the food purchases would have been for the meals for that whole Passover (including the Festival of Unleavened Bread, called the *hagigah* meals) week. Also, giving gifts to the poor on Passover eve was customary; the Temple gates were open from midnight on so that beggars could congregate there.

COMMENTARY

We now return to the scene of the Last Supper that parallels the Synoptics—the betrayal of Judas (Mark 14:18-21 and parallels). Here it is a much longer scene. Jesus had already warned them repeatedly (6:70; 12:24; cf. also the synoptic passion predictions), even in this scene (13:10). In promising that God would bless his disciples (13:17), Jesus clarified that he was not speaking of "all" the disciples. He had "chosen" the Twelve, including Judas (6:70), but had been aware of his betrayer from the start. It is difficult to know why he allowed Judas to operate as he had; probably it was fulfillment of prophecy, as he went on to say, citing Psalm 41:9, "The one who eats my food has turned against me." According to the Psalm, David as the righteous sufferer experienced the betrayal of a close friend—and all while he was ill and being persecuted by his enemies. This is not an explicit messianic passage but was applied typologically by Jesus (that is, Jesus was reliving/fulfilling the experience of David). Carson makes two points (1991:470): first, from such passages as 2 Samuel 7:12-16 and Psalm 2, we see that David was a type of the future Messiah so that Jesus the Messiah fulfilled many aspects of his life; second, one of the major Davidic themes picked up in the New Testament is his suffering (e.g., Ps 22 later in the Passion events), leading to David as a type of the suffering Messiah. Judas, then, was the antitype of David's treacherous friend. The point is that God and Jesus were well aware of Judas's intention, indicating that they were in complete control.

The point of his prophecy (13:19) was not just to prepare the disciples beforehand for what was going to happen (he certainly knew they would be confused) but to help them even more afterwards. Then they would realize he had known all about it; they would understand he is indeed the "I AM" (in the Greek this is another of the absolute "I am" passages, cf. 8:24, 28, 58), Yahweh himself (cf. Exod 3:14; Isa 41:4; 43:10). Jesus was well aware of the difficulties that were ahead for the disciples. Such hints as those he gave here were intended to provide a foundation for them to center upon in the times of confusion and reflection to follow. In fact, the entire farewell discourse that begins in 13:31 has that purpose.

Jesus now makes his second "I tell you the truth" statement in this discourse (13:20; cf. 13:16; see note on 1:51), with much the same message as the first. Jesus was ready to be taken from them and was in the process of passing the baton to them. They were to replicate his servant heart (13:16), but they would also have the same authority as he did. A slave is like his master, and an agent like the one who sends him (13:16), so accepting these agents would mean accepting their two senders, Jesus and his Father (13:20; see 17:18; 20:21). Jesus was elevating the status of the disciples and giving them the same significance that he has. Jesus is one with the Father as the "I AM," and now we see a oneness between him and his followers (cf. 15:5, "those who remain in me, and I in them"). They were to take up the banner of his mission, and thus they would constitute his presence in the world. This is very similar to the mission discourse of Matthew 10:40-42, where Jesus also said that the reception of his disciples constituted reception of him and the Father.

After this brief excursus on the mission of the disciples, Jesus expressed his deep sorrow that one of them would betray him (13:21). For the third time (after the death of Lazarus in 11:33 and at the realization that the "time" had arrived in 12:27), Jesus was "deeply troubled." This time his heart broke more over the sin of Judas than over his own approaching death. As Whitacre (1999:334) says, "In his anguish we see revealed the effects of our sin on the heart of God from the first rebellion in the garden right up to the most recent sin you and I have committed today."

Again we see the lack of understanding on the part of the disciples (13:22). They were surprised and shocked at these words (though it is difficult to see why, in light of the number of times Jesus had hinted at this very thing—6:64, 70-71; 12:24; 13:10-11, 18). In the Synoptic accounts they look at each other and ask, "Am I the one?" (Mark 14:19 and parallels). John expanded the scene in order to introduce the beloved disciple. We are told that he was "reclining on Jesus' bosom" (13:23, NLT mg), which means that he was in one of the places of honor to the right of Jesus (the primary place of honor was on the left—perhaps Judas, 13:26; cf. Mark 10:37), since a guest would recline with his left elbow on the cushion and his head therefore near the person on his left (so Ridderbos). There is no evidence that there was any required seating pattern for the disciples or that social protocol was followed here. At any rate, Peter had put his foot in his mouth once already (13:6-9) and was probably leery of doing so again, so he motioned to the beloved disciple and asked, "Who's he talking about?" It was the beloved disciple who asked, "Lord, who is it?"

Calling one disciple "the disciple Jesus loved" does not mean Jesus failed to love all of them (13:1) but that there was a special relationship between them. Therefore, it seems likely that he was one of the inner circle (Peter, James, and John), and since Peter is named here, he must have been one of the two brothers. They were cousins of Jesus (see note on 19:26), and of the two, John is the most likely. He is named in every Gospel except this one. He did not call himself "the disciple Jesus loved" out of pride but undoubtedly out of a sense of awe at the grace of God in Jesus. This disciple appears often (19:26; 20:2; 21:7, 20), usually in scenes with Peter (another point favoring John, for they were close). In these scenes, the beloved disciple always seems to triumph, and so some have thought there was a sense of rivalry between them. Few have pursued this, however, because closer reflection actually shows that Peter and the beloved disciple triumphed together. In a sense, the beloved disciple is the archetypal disciple showing the difference Christ can make in a person willing to follow him all the way (cf. Köstenberger 1998a:154-161).

When the beloved disciple asked who it was, Jesus responded with a symbolic act (13:26), telling them the betrayer was the one to whom he would give a piece of bread dipped in the bowl. At the Passover meal, the bowl probably was the *haroseth*, which consisted of a fruit paste made from dates, raisins, and sour wine; at an earlier part of the meal, bitter herbs would have been dipped in the sauce (so Bruce). A supreme irony, the act of passing a choice morsel to Judas honored him as a favorite. It was a demonstration that, with regard to Judas as well, Jesus "loved [him] to the very end" (13:1). Jesus must have said this quietly so that only the beloved disciple heard, for no one seemed to understand. When Jesus gave the morsel to Judas, however, "Satan entered into him" and possessed him completely (13:27). The evil union was complete, a terrible copy of the supreme oneness between Jesus and his followers (6:56; 15:4; 1 John 2:24; 3:24). Judas was hardened, assuming a terrible resolve to carry out his evil deed, and Jesus, knowing the hour had arrived, said, "Hurry and do what you're going to do." The climax of the ages had come.

The rest of Jesus' companions seem to have remained in stunned silence, not knowing what was happening (13:28). It is hard to know why the beloved disciple did nothing, for he certainly had heard what Jesus said. Perhaps he was in shock (cf. also 20:9-10, when he does this again). Since Judas was the treasurer (cf. also 12:6), the disciples assumed that when Jesus told him to "do what you're going to do," he was telling Judas to go buy more food or to give money to the poor. The supplies would have been for the week of festival meals, and almsgiving was expected at Passover time (cf. note on 13:29). With this, Judas headed out "into the night," ("night" symbolizing sin; cf. "dark" in 3:2). As Hendriksen says (1953:250), "night outside; night also in the heart of Judas."

◆   C. The Farewell Discourse (13:31–17:26)
      1. The first discourse (13:31–14:31)

[31]As soon as Judas left the room, Jesus said, "The time has come for the Son of Man* to enter into his glory, and God will be glorified because of him. [32]And since God receives glory because of the Son,* he will soon give glory to the Son. [33]Dear chil-

dren, I will be with you only a little longer. And as I told the Jewish leaders, you will search for me, but you can't come where I am going. ³⁴So now I am giving you a new commandment: Love each other. Just as I have loved you, you should love each other. ³⁵Your love for one another will prove to the world that you are my disciples."

³⁶Simon Peter asked, "Lord, where are you going?"

And Jesus replied, "You can't go with me now, but you will follow me later."

³⁷"But why can't I come now, Lord?" he asked. "I'm ready to die for you."

³⁸Jesus answered, "Die for me? I tell you the truth, Peter—before the rooster crows tomorrow morning, you will deny three times that you even know me.

CHAPTER 14

"Don't let your hearts be troubled. Trust in God, and trust also in me. ²There is more than enough room in my Father's home.* If this were not so, would I have told you that I am going to prepare a place for you?* ³When everything is ready, I will come and get you, so that you will always be with me where I am. ⁴And you know the way to where I am going."

⁵"No, we don't know, Lord," Thomas said. "We have no idea where you are going, so how can we know the way?"

⁶Jesus told him, "I am the way, the truth, and the life. No one can come to the Father except through me. ⁷If you had really known me, you would know who my Father is.* From now on, you do know him and have seen him!"

⁸Philip said, "Lord, show us the Father, and we will be satisfied."

⁹Jesus replied, "Have I been with you all this time, Philip, and yet you still don't know who I am? Anyone who has seen me has seen the Father! So why are you asking me to show him to you? ¹⁰Don't you believe that I am in the Father and the Father is in me? The words I speak are not my own, but my Father who lives in me does his work through me. ¹¹Just believe

that I am in the Father and the Father is in me. Or at least believe because of the work you have seen me do.

¹²"I tell you the truth, anyone who believes in me will do the same works I have done, and even greater works, because I am going to be with the Father. ¹³You can ask for anything in my name, and I will do it, so that the Son can bring glory to the Father. ¹⁴Yes, ask me for anything in my name, and I will do it!

¹⁵"If you love me, obey* my commandments. ¹⁶And I will ask the Father, and he will give you another Advocate,* who will never leave you. ¹⁷He is the Holy Spirit, who leads into all truth. The world cannot receive him, because it isn't looking for him and doesn't recognize him. But you know him, because he lives with you now and later will be in you.* ¹⁸No, I will not abandon you as orphans—I will come to you. ¹⁹Soon the world will no longer see me, but you will see me. Since I live, you also will live. ²⁰When I am raised to life again, you will know that I am in my Father, and you are in me, and I am in you. ²¹Those who accept my commandments and obey them are the ones who love me. And because they love me, my Father will love them. And I will love them and reveal myself to each of them."

²²Judas (not Judas Iscariot, but the other disciple with that name) said to him, "Lord, why are you going to reveal yourself only to us and not to the world at large?"

²³Jesus replied, "All who love me will do what I say. My Father will love them, and we will come and make our home with each of them. ²⁴Anyone who doesn't love me will not obey me. And remember, my words are not my own. What I am telling you is from the Father who sent me. ²⁵I am telling you these things now while I am still with you. ²⁶But when the Father sends the Advocate as my representative—that is, the Holy Spirit—he will teach you everything and will remind you of everything I have told you.

²⁷"I am leaving you with a gift—peace of mind and heart. And the peace I give is a gift the world cannot give. So don't be troubled or afraid. ²⁸Remember what I told you: I am going away, but I will come back to you again. If you really loved me, you would be happy that I am going to the Father, who is greater than I am. ²⁹I have told you these things before they happen so that when they do happen, you will believe.

³⁰"I don't have much more time to talk to you, because the ruler of this world approaches. He has no power over me, ³¹but I will do what the Father requires of me, so that the world will know that I love the Father. Come, let's be going.

13:31 "Son of Man" is a title Jesus used for himself. 13:32 Some manuscripts omit *And since God receives glory because of the Son.* 14:2a Or *There are many rooms in my Father's house.* 14:2b Or *If this were not so, I would have told you that I am going to prepare a place for you.* Some manuscripts read *If this were not so, I would have told you. I am going to prepare a place for you.* 14:7 Some manuscripts read *If you have really known me, you will know who my Father is.* 14:15 Other manuscripts read *you will obey;* still others read *you should obey.* 14:16 Or *Comforter,* or *Encourager,* or *Counselor.* Greek reads *Paraclete;* also in 14:26. 14:17 Some manuscripts read *and is in you.*

NOTES

13:32 *And since God receives glory because of the Son.* This clause is missing in many early mss (𝔓66 ℵ* B C* D L W), but the clause could have been omitted due to homoioteleuton (a visual error by a scribe) or perhaps because it was thought to be redundant. Metzger (1994:206) says, "There is a logical connection rightly expressed between the earlier and subsequent glorification, and the step-parallelism is characteristically Johannine."

13:34 *Love each other.* Strangely, some scholars believe this to be an inferior brand of love because it does not include love for outsiders. This is indeed an odd sentiment because love for the world is so essential to John (1:10; 3:16, 19-20; 1 John 4:9). It is clear that all three aspects of love—for God, the world, and fellow believers—are equally essential in John's Gospel. Also, as noted in the commentary on 13:13, this verse again shows what may be called a "triangular statement" of love in that Jesus' love for the disciples should bring about love between each of them (Michaels 1989:273; cf. 15:12; 17:11).

14:1 *Trust in God.* There are several translation possibilities in light of the fact that the verbs can be indicative or imperative: (1) "You are trusting in God and trusting in me" (both indicatives); but this is unlikely because they are in fact failing to trust in Christ. (2) "You are trusting in God; now trust in me" (the second switches to imperative), but the context doesn't really support a statement that they are in fact trusting God. (3) "Trust in God, and trust in me" (both imperatives), which better fits a context where Jesus was commanding them to trust as the only antidote to fear (so Carson, Beasley-Murray, Burge contra Brown, who prefers indicative/imperative).

14:2 *room.* The KJV "mansions" stems from the influence of William Tyndale, who in the fourteenth century followed the Latin Vulgate's *mansiones.*

would I have told you that . . . ? Although "that" (*hoti* [ᵀᴳ3754, ᶻᴳ4022]) is missing in several witnesses (𝔓66* C²ᵛⁱᵈ 038 𝔐—so the KJV, NIV), it was probably omitted by later copyists as superfluous (cf. Metzger 1994:206) and does belong in the text. As such, it could either introduce a question (as in the NLT reading above) or a causal idea ("If it were not so, I would have warned you, because I am going to prepare a place for you"). The question is problematic because there is no record that Jesus had told them any such thing yet. The causal is even more difficult, however: why would Jesus "warn" them about such a thing? It is best to take the question and presuppose that Jesus had indeed told them previously (there are certainly many sayings not recorded in the Gospels).

14:3 *I will come.* Some scholars (e.g., Gundry 1967; Keener 2003:932-939) think this refers to Jesus' coming via the Holy Spirit and the new fellowship the believers would enjoy with Jesus through the Spirit. This is quite possible, for in 14:23, Jesus is likely referring to the Spirit's coming when he says that he and the Father will "come and make our home with" the disciples (this and 14:2 are the only uses of *monē* [TG3438, ZG3665], "room" in John). Also, 14:18 says, "I will not abandon you as orphans—I will come to you," a definite reference to the Spirit (cf. 14:16-17). Comfort (1994:123-126) interprets this section with respect to Jesus' coming to the disciples after his resurrection and giving them the Spirit. As such, the believers will be able, through the Spirit, to live in God the Father, and both God the Father and the Son will be able live in the believers. He argues that the context of John 14–16 and 20 points to Jesus' coming in resurrection to impart the Spirit into the disciples (20:22) so that God and the believers can mutually indwell each other. Thus, when Jesus said that there are many rooms in the Father's house, he was speaking of preparing the way for the believers to live in him (Jesus) and thereby also to live in the Father. Kangas (2000:27-29) takes this one step further and argues that the "home" is the church, the body of Christ, in which both God and his people dwell together. The imagery of "Father's house" and "many rooms," however, strongly favors a reference to Jesus' return at the end of the age. It is possible that there is a double meaning here, in which there might be the return of Christ in the Spirit as the first stage of the final coming (cf. Barrett 1978:457 who says "the theme of 'going and coming' is constantly repeated in the future communion of Jesus with his disciples"; see also Westcott and Witherington for this idea). The primary referent, however, is to Jesus' second coming (so Segovia 1985, Beasley-Murray, Michaels, Carson, Burge, Köstenberger). There is a development of the image from Jesus' second coming and preparation of a home in heaven for them in 14:2-3 to Jesus' coming and dwelling with them via the Holy Spirit in 14:18, 23.

14:7 *If you had really known me.* There are two mss readings—one a condition contrary to fact (entailing a rebuke as in the NLT; supported by A B C D¹ L 038 044 f¹,¹³ 𝔐 and accepted by NASB, NIV, Westcott, Brown, Hendriksen, Morris), the other a condition of fact (entailing a real condition with a promise [cf. NLT mg]; supported by 𝔓66 ℵ D* W and accepted by UBS, NJB, Beasley-Murray, Michaels, Carson, Ridderbos, Köstenberger). The ms evidence is virtually even, but the context seems to support the second, more positive view, as in the latter half of the verse ("from now on, you do know him"). A rebuke would fit 14:9, but the context of 14:7 is more positive. The contrary to fact could be an assimilation to 8:19—"If you had known me, you would have known my Father too."

14:16 *Advocate.* The meaning of *paraklētos* [TG3875, ZG4156] is very disputed: it is translated "Comforter" in the KJV; "Helper" in the NASB, Phillips; "Counselor" in the NIV; and "Advocate" in the NRSV, NJB, REB, NLT. The problem is that no single translation will truly suffice, for the work of the Spirit in these five passages is too broad for any one term (cf. the excellent discussions in Brown 1970:1135-1143; Keener 2003:953-964). The Paraclete teaches, reveals, and guides the believers and witnesses to, convicts, and prosecutes the unbelievers. "Comforter" does not fit at all, and "Helper" (Köstenberger—"helping presence") does not describe Jesus' work in the world. "Counselor" can fit the Spirit as guide, strength, and help to the disciples (so Carson) but again does not fit his work in the world. "Advocate" fits the general meaning of the term best, for in the first century it meant "one called upon for support . . . assistance" (BAGD), thus "a legal advisor or helper or advocate" (EDNT 28). Yet in this context it does not completely fit since it referred to an intercessor or defense attorney, while the Paraclete functions like a prosecuting attorney in 16:8-11. Still, "Advocate" catches the nuances of the term better than other words and is probably the best English equivalent (cf. Witherington). Johnston (1970) argues (probably rightly) that, on the whole, the Paraclete is the "representative" of God. Jesus was the first representative, envoy, or agent, and the Holy Spirit is another one. Several (Burge, Keener) also suggest a background in wisdom literature; building on Jesus as personified Wisdom, the Spirit is also the presence of God (and Jesus) in this world.

14:17 *the Holy Spirit, who leads into all truth.* There may be some polemical intention here (so Beasley-Murray) with the Spirit of truth in contrast with the lying spirit of the devil (8:44), fitting the Passion events as the defeat of Satan (12:31; 14:30; 16:11). Jewish writings normally used "Spirit of truth" in contrast to "the spirit of error" (*Testament of Judah* 20:1-5; 1QS 3:18-21). While John's Gospel does not contain this dualism (so Carson), the battle between Christ and Satan in this section makes some connection likely.

he lives with you now and later will be in you. There is grammatical ambiguity and a text critical question as to whether these two verbs were orignally in the present or future tense. The best support is for the NLT reading—present tense for "lives" and future tense for "will be" (cf. Comfort 2007:[John 14:17]).

14:18 *I will come to you.* Bultmann (1971:617-618) believes this is a more developed version of Christian doctrine in which Jesus' resurrection and second coming have been "demythologized" and collapsed into the coming of the Spirit. This explanation is certainly unnecessary, for the teaching of the early church never wavered regarding the expectation of Christ's later return. There is simply no evidence for such a development.

14:28 *the Father, who is greater than I am.* This statement has caused great controversy. The fourth century heretic Arius (followed by modern Arians like the Jehovah's Witnesses) said that this implies that Jesus is not divine. Yet John's emphasis on the oneness between Jesus and the Father is the strongest in the NT (1:1, 18; 8:58; 10:30; 20:28). At the same time, Jesus clearly deferred to his Father on numerous occasions (3:17; 4:34; 5:19, 30, 36; 6:38; 7:16, 33; 8:29; 12:27, 49). How do we reconcile the seeming contradiction? Only by allowing each aspect to define the other. It is clear that Jesus is divine (1:1, 18; 10:30; the "I Am" passages), and it is also clear that he also placed himself under his Father on occasion (4:34; 5:19-30; 6:38; 8:29; 12:48-49). Two solutions suggest themselves: (1) he is one with the Father and yet in his incarnation was under the Father; and (2) he was subordinate to his Father's will in his mission on earth (so Westcott, Michaels, Whitacre). Both aspects are correct and help us to understand this complex issue. Godet has an excellent remark: "Our passage breathes, in him who thus speaks, the most lively feeling of his participation in divinity. God alone can compare himself with God" (1969:289). Barrett adds, "The Father is God sending and commanding, the Son is God sent and obedient" (1978:468). At the same time, it must be stated that the Father-Son relationship exists within the Godhead and is an eternal relationship. There is ontological equality and functional subordination.

COMMENTARY

Suppose you had not been feeling well and finally visited a doctor. After tests, he called you in and told you that you had less than 24 hours to live. That evening, you only had a short time to tell your children the news, sum up everything you had been trying to teach them, and launch them into life without you. That is precisely the purpose of Jesus' farewell discourse in 13:31–17:26. Jesus was preparing his disciples for the unbelievably difficult days ahead and for their mission to come afterwards. He also wanted to tell them why the approaching difficulties must come. The basic theme is, "I must depart so the Spirit might come." Rahner (2000:76-80) thinks the tension between Jesus' fast approaching departure and the coming of the Paraclete to finish his mission is the key to the whole discourse. Jesus was about to finish his course, the way to the new era of salvation. The Spirit would take over and bring God's plan to completion.

The form of speech Jesus chose—the farewell discourse—is found often in the Old Testament (e.g., Jacob in Gen 47:29–49:33; Moses in Deut 32; Joshua in Josh

23–24; Samuel in 1 Sam 12; and David in 1 Chr 28–29). The similarities with these speeches are not surprising, as each of these great men comforted his followers in the face of his impending death and predicted what the future would bring (so Brown, Whitacre). While Jesus followed this pattern, he also transcended it because his was the death of the Messiah and Son of God. Most importantly, none of the others returned after they departed. Jesus is the only one who came back from the grave (so Carson). Primarily, Jesus provided a unique look at the Spirit as God's "Paraclete" in this speech (see note on 14:16; cf. 14:25-26; 15:26; 16:7-15) and gave seven all-embracing prayer promises (14:13, 14; 15:7, 16; 16:23, 24, 26).

There are three parts to the farewell speech (13:31–17:26): the first discourse (13:31-14:31), consisting of teaching and four dialogs with disciples—Peter (13:36), Thomas (14:5), Philip (14:8), and Judas (not Iscariot, 14:22); the second discourse (15:1–16:33), consisting entirely of Jesus' elaboration on the themes in the first discourse; and the third, the high priestly prayer (17:1-26), centering on Jesus' concern for glorifying his Father and for his followers.

Many critical scholars (e.g., Segovia 1985; for a survey of the literature, see Klauck 1996) think this was not one continuous speech but rather involves duplicated material (with chs 14 and 15–16 being two versions of the same material) or is an edited piece containing several levels of redaction by more than one author. Brown (1970:582-583) lists six details that call for this conclusion: (1) 14:30-31 ("Come, let's be going") is a natural conclusion, yet Jesus continued speaking; (2) sections contradict each other (e.g., 13:36; 16:5); (3) there are many duplications (e.g., 14:28 = 16:5-7; 14:1 = 16:6; 14:16, 26 = 15:26, 16:7; 14:12 = 16:10; 14:30 = 16:11, 12); (4) some material matches Synoptic parallels closely (e.g., 15:1–16:4 = Matt 10:17-25); (5) some material (e.g., 15:1-6) has little connection with the theme of Jesus' departure; and (6) the variety of theological expression is hard to explain in a single discourse. The whole, however, is constructed very carefully and does not really contain evidence of clumsy compiling. Blomberg (2001:197) finds evidence of a chiastic arrangement (A = 14:1-31; B = 15:1-17; B′ = 15:16–16:4; A′ = 16:5-33), indicating both thoughtful construction and a unified discourse (for chiasm behind 13:31–17:26, see Keener 2003:895). This runs counter to the idea that we are observing duplications and misplaced material in the speech (in which case, one would have to wonder about the competence of later editors). The greatest difficulty for viewing the passage as one speech is 14:31. Carson (1991:479) notes two plausible scenarios: (1) Jesus and the disciples did not leave the upper room until 17:26; the statement of 14:31 then would be an original desire to go, but the conversation continued for a while before they actually left. By including 14:31, John was showing that Jesus' love for them was so great that he had to go over his points again. (2) They could have left after 14:31 and continued their conversation in the streets of the city on the way to Gethsemane. Some believe chapters 15–17 were uttered in the Temple (giving rise to the vine imagery in 15:1ff and the high priestly prayer of 17) on the way (so Westcott, Burge). Either is possible and both supply a valid explanation for 14:31 (I prefer the second overall). In short, there are valid reasons for asserting that Jesus uttered this discourse as it stands.

Glory, Love, and Betrayal (13:31-38). There is debate as to whether this section belongs more with the section on the Last Supper (due to the prediction of Peter's betrayal, 13:36-38) or to the farewell discourse (due to the emphasis on glory and love, 13:31-35). Actually, it is a transition and belongs to both, but the themes of 13:31-35 are so intertwined with chapters 14-17 that I have placed it with the farewell discourse. In fact, the themes introduced here (glory, departure, love) are found in reverse order in ensuing chapters (love—15:1-16:4a; departure—16:4b-33; glory—17:1-26), forming a chiasm (so Westcott, Michaels, Whitacre). In 12:23 Jesus said, "Now the time has come for the Son of Man to enter into his glory." After Judas left on his terrible errand, Jesus reiterated that truth. A dominant theme of John is that the Cross would be Jesus' time of glory when he was "lifted up" to exaltation (3:14; 8:28; 12:32). This is the supreme paradox: the most horrifying event in human history was also the most glorious! The "Son of Man" title is used in the full sense of Daniel 7:13-14, that of dominion and glory (cf. on 1:51). Note also that the glory of the Son also means the glory of the Father. In the supreme manifestation of the Father's love, when he gave his Son to die for us (Rom 5:8), the greatness and goodness of God was completely revealed. It is interesting that the three verbs related to "glory" in 13:31-32 are aorists; this might mean the event is viewed as a complete whole (so Morris, Burge), or perhaps the aorist here is an equivalent to the Hebrew niphal stem for "glorify," which speaks of God revealing his splendid acts (cf. Isa 49:3 of God displaying his splendor to Israel), meaning that God shows his splendor in Jesus' act of obedience on the cross (so Carson).

Since Jesus and his Father are one, the reverse is true (13:32). Not only is the Father glorified in Jesus, but also God "will soon give glory to the Son." The combination of the future tense with "soon" emphasizes the imminence of the Cross. In reality, Jesus would be dead in less than 24 hours. If the discourse occurred near midnight, it would be completed 15 hours later! In this cataclysmic event, Jesus glorified God by being obedient to his will, and God would glorify Jesus by making the Cross the final cosmic victory over Satan and the moment of Jesus' supreme triumph.

Then Jesus switched to another of the major themes: his departure (13:33). He began with "dear children" (used only here in John but found seven times in 1 John) to show them the depth of his love and to continue his role from the Passover meal as family head of the apostolic band (a common metaphor for the rabbi-disciple relationship). The Father-Son relationship is reproduced in Jesus' relationship with his followers (as also the loving unity of Father and Son in 15:4, 9; 17:21-22). The message that Jesus was going soon to a place where they could not find him had been conveyed twice to the Jewish leaders (7:34; 8:21). Now Jesus wanted his disciples to know it as well—but the difference was huge. His opponents had little hope of ever "going" to meet Jesus in heaven (few of them ever converted, though see Acts 6:7), but the separation from his "children" would be only temporary. Jesus was "going to prepare a place for [them]" (14:2) and "will come back to" them (14:28), both in the Holy Spirit and at his second coming.

The third theme of the discourse is introduced in 13:34-35, as Jesus gave them "a new commandment" to "love each other." The importance of this is seen the common name "Maundy Thursday" for the anniversary of the Last Supper, reflecting the Latin Vulgate's *mandatum novum* (new commandment); the early church considered this command an essential component of the Last Supper. In John, love is one of three great gifts along with "peace" (14:27) and "joy" (15:11, so Bruce). The command to love was hardly new, as in the Old Testament the people were told to love God (Deut 6:5) and their neighbors (Lev 19:18), commandments summarized in Jesus' well-known teaching of Mark 12:29-31. It was "new" because it was grounded in two things: God's love for Jesus and Jesus' love for them, and the fact that he had brought them the new covenant. Hartin (1991:347) says it was new in the sense that Jesus had become the paradigm of sacrificial love, and the disciples thus had a new model to follow. It is also possible that "new commandment" was built upon the "new covenant" in Jesus' eucharistic words ("new covenant . . . confirmed with my blood," 1 Cor 11:25, so Lindars, Carson).

Newness characterizes every aspect of the kingdom reality. The new age has indeed begun, and now there is a new depth to the community love that characterizes the church. Moreover, this new love has been modeled in the love shown by Christ in both the Incarnation and the Cross: "Just as I have loved you, you should love each other." As the disciples experience divine love, they participate in it also via their love for one another. The New Testament message is clear—we cannot truly love Christ without loving each other. Moreover, this love is at the heart of the church's mission (cf. 17:20-23), for their mutual love is what will "prove to the world that you are my disciples." Throughout history the love of the community—both external love for the unsaved and internal love for the brotherhood (cf. Gal 6:10)—has been an essential component of Christian outreach. On the other hand, dissension in the community has always constituted a major barrier to the spread of the Gospel.

Peter (again probably speaking for the rest of the disciples) was rather confused by Jesus' whole train of thought to this point. Ignoring the love command, he focused on what he thought was the key issue—"Lord, where are you going?" (13:36). Like the Jews of 7:35; 8:21-22, he could not comprehend Jesus' prophecy about his departure, though he did realize that death was involved (13:37). Jesus' response was quite different than his statement to the Jews in 7:34; he told Peter he could not come then but would follow him later. "Follow" is an essential component of discipleship in John (1:43; 8:12; 10:4, 27; 12:26; 21:19-22), and this probably applies to *imitatio Christi*—that is, the disciple following Jesus all the way, even unto death (cf. Mark 8:34). Only Jesus' death could make it possible to follow him into the presence of God, though Peter would "follow" him later (21:18-19).

Peter protested that he wanted to follow Jesus, even if it meant dying for him. He was probably thinking of the final eschatological war, for soon after this he drew his sword and did battle against the infidels, probably expecting the angelic hosts to appear (cf. on 18:10). Jesus, who knows everyone's heart (2:25), was fully aware of the truth. Far from dying for Jesus, Peter would "deny three times" that he knew Christ, "before the rooster crows" (13:38). Peter's love was misdirected, for he did not realize how weak he really was. Jesus, with his omniscience, knew better. This prophecy is found in all four Gospels and emphasizes at a deep level the discipleship failure that is part of our own spiritual weakness and sin.

Jesus, the Way to the Father (14:1-14). There are two parts to this section of the discourse—Jesus preparing a place in his Father's house for the disciples (14:1-4), and Jesus as the only way to the Father (14:5-14). It is clear from Peter's questions that the disciples were deeply upset by the dialog. Jesus had also been very "troubled" by his impending destiny on the cross (12:27; 13:21). The disciples should have been comforting Jesus at this desperate hour, but they could not understand his words, let alone find it in themselves to comfort him. Then Jesus turned to them and said, "Don't let your hearts be troubled" (14:1). I've heard many sermons saying that it is a sin to have a troubled heart, but if that were true, Jesus would not be sinless! He had a troubled heart (11:33; 12:27; 13:21)—here he was saying that we don't have to allow our troubled hearts to consume us. The disciples were deeply anxious regarding Jesus' imminent departure and his prophecy of their coming desertion (cf. 13:38; Mark 14:27-31). This was understandable, but Jesus wanted them to know that they did not have to continue in this state. His answer was simple: "Trust in God, and trust also in me." The only possible antidote to worry is faith and prayer (cf. Phil 4:6-7), for with God, all trials will turn out for the best (Rom 8:28; Jas 1:2-4; 1 Pet 1:6-7). This was even more the case for Jesus himself since the Passion would be the turning point of all history. This prepares for the emphasis on believing prayer in 14:12-14; 15:7, 16; 16:23, 24, 26; now Jesus as well as the Father is to be the object of the disciples' trust.

Jesus' death would also be the turning point for the future destiny of the disciples. After his death, Jesus would return to his Father in heaven, for he was going away specifically to "prepare a place" for them (14:2-3). This was a major reason for them to trust in him—he was securing them a place in heaven. The image in 14:2 (cf. NLT mg) is of a large house (but not a "mansion," [contra KJV], which was based on the Latin [the Vulgate] *mansiones*, which meant a "stopover place"; cf. Brown, Carson, Köstenberger) with many rooms for his followers, possibly reflecting the idea of the Temple as a multiroom house (so Blomberg). This is a metaphor for heaven; thus, Christ was going to heaven to prepare a place for his followers. In light of the following material in 14:15-29 about Jesus' coming back to the disciples in resurrection via the Holy Spirit (cf. notes on 14:2-3), it is certainly possible that there is a double meaning with respect to his coming—with the coming of the Spirit anticipating the final coming. Still, I take the primary meaning of 14:3 to center on the Second Coming. Thus, Jesus was promising them a "room" prepared in heaven. The picture is of Jesus going home to heaven and there readying dwelling places in his Father's heavenly "home" (14:2) and then going back to get the disciples and take them home to spend eternity with him (14:3; "so that you will always be with me where I am"). The path to his going home is the Cross, Resurrection, and Ascension. The path to his disciples joining him is their own resurrection, as Paul says in 2 Corinthians 5:1—"when this earthly tent we live in is taken down . . . we will have a house in heaven." Paul's reference is to Jesus' second coming, with the "house" here paralleling the "city" of Revelation 21. In both places, the image is that of the disciples dwelling with the Father and the Son for all eternity. The goal is that the believers "will always be with" Jesus, experiencing an eternity of joy in his presence. Since the disciples had been Jesus' followers and had listened to his teaching, they should have known his way to the Father (14:4).

We will see in the very next verse that they seemingly knew nothing of the sort. They actually did "know the way," even though they didn't realize it, for they knew Jesus, and he is the "way" (14:6). Still, Thomas demurred, saying, "We have no idea where you are going, so how can we know the way?" (14:5). Thomas, though a committed disciple, seems to be filled with doubts and questions throughout John (cf. 11:16; 20:24-25). Yet he did the right thing and brought his uncertainty to Jesus (a good lesson for us all!). Again, the disciples were thinking on the earthly plane, while Jesus was speaking of heavenly realities. This is the third of four passages (with 5:28-29; 6:39-40; 21:22) centering on a final eschatology (the end of the age) rather than a realized perspective (the present situation), and the disciples were completely confused. Like the Jewish authorities (7:35-36), they seemed to be wondering what earthly place he was planning to move to.

Jesus' reaction (14:6) was quite different from his denunciation of the ignorance of the authorities (8:14b-21). Since the disciples were faithful and were honestly seeking the truth, Jesus responded with another "I am" saying, pointing to his identity with Yahweh and his resultant characteristics (14:6; see commentary on 6:16-19). Schnackenburg (1982:64-65) calls this "a unique statement that has lost none of its sovereign power" and says it is "a culminating point in Johannine theology, in particular his doctrine of salvation as centered entirely in Jesus Christ." As a response to Thomas's query regarding "the way," the central point is Jesus as "the way," and the other two clarify why he is the only "way." It is best to translate Jesus' words as "I am the way—namely, the truth and the life" (or "true and living way," perhaps even "the way to truth and life," though more likely they all three refer to Jesus). The idea of "the way" was at the heart of early Christian consciousness (they called themselves "the Way" [Acts 9:2; 19:9, 23] and at the earliest stage considered themselves the messianic sect of the Jews), derived from Isaiah 40:3 (cf. Mark 1:2-3). As Jesus and his disciples were on the road to Jerusalem in Mark, they were said to be "on the way" (cf. the Greek of Mark 9:33, 34; 10:17, 32, 52). There, it was "on the way" to Jesus' destiny in Jerusalem; here, it is "the way" to the Father. As Keener says (2003:940-941), Jesus is "the way of righteousness and wisdom" as well as to life in God.

As "the way," Jesus is also "the truth" and "the life." He is "truth" because he is the living revealer, the very voice and revelation of God. As the incarnate shekinah, the "Word" is "grace and truth," defined as "unfailing love and faithfulness" (1:14). Also, in Jesus is "life" (1:4), and God has granted him "life-giving power" (5:26) so that he bestows life on whomever he wants (5:21). Only by believing in Jesus can eternal life be found (3:15, 16, 36; 5:24). Jesus is the truth-teller and the life-giver, but even more, he *is* truth and life. For this reason, "no one can come to the Father except through" him. To many people this idea is highly offensive, and the Christian message is oppressive because it dares to say that Jesus is the only way to eternal life; others take an inclusive approach and say anyone who lives up to the "light" God provides them will get to heaven. But why would God go to so much trouble as to have his Son assume human flesh and die on the cross for our sins if he knew there were already many ways to eternal life? In truth, sin is an eternal force (called "total depravity") that makes it impossible for people to come to God on their own merits or by their own religious beliefs. The atoning sacrifice of Christ is the only path to God that *could in any way* suffice to atone for sin. Therefore, he is indeed the only way to God and to eternal life.

Jesus concluded this with a statement of fact and a promise. In spite of their constant misunderstandings, the disciples "have really known" Jesus. On that basis, they could be assured that they would know his Father (cf. note on 14:7). They had progressively grown in their knowledge and had recognized him as Messiah, King of Israel, and Son of God (1:41, 49). Therefore, they could be assured that they were also coming to know the Father. After all, Jesus is the *shaliach*, the official representative agent or envoy of God (see notes on 1:6; 3:17); he is the representative of the Father and one with the Father (5:19; 10:30). To know him is to know the Father. Moreover, to know and see the Son is to share full community with the Father (so Schnackenburg).

Philip makes a natural request coming out of this: "Lord, show us the Father, and we will be satisfied" (14:8). This could hardly betray a desire to physically look on the face of God, for 1:18 tells us "no one has ever seen God." Most likely, Philip wanted the type of vision that Isaiah was privileged to experience. Perhaps like Moses he desired to see the glory of God (Exod 33:18). Still, he failed to understand that in Jesus he had indeed looked on the glory of God. In fact, this was exactly the point Jesus made (14:9): How could Philip have spent so much time with him and not known who he really was? They had spent so much time with Jesus that they should have realized the truth: "Anyone who has seen me has seen the Father!" (14:9). Jesus turned to the language of belief (14:10); they didn't know because they had not yet come to faith regarding Jesus' true identity. They believed he was the Messiah, even the Son of God, but they had not yet perceived his true relationship with the Father. The mutual indwelling of Jesus and the Father has already been stated in 10:38 and is explored further in 14:11, 20; 17:21-23. Jesus' point was that if they had this depth of faith and knowledge of Jesus as one with the Father as well as Messiah, they should have no trouble understanding that to see him is to see God. Not only that, but Jesus' words are also the words of the "Father who lives in" him (cf. 8:28; 12:49). He does nothing on his own, but instead, everything he does is the Father working through him. In John, Jesus' works are more than his miracles; all his words and deeds are the work of the indwelling Father through him (for his works, see 5:17, 19; 9:3-4; 14:31; for his words, see 12:49).

In 14:10, Jesus challenged Philip to "believe"—but this is not saving faith as elsewhere in John. Rather, it is illuminating faith, the Spirit-given ability to see and understand truth. Jesus told them how they could find such faith (14:11). First, even if they couldn't comprehend the key truth regarding the mutual indwelling of Father and Son, they could accept it by faith on the basis of Jesus' teaching. Then, if they could not attain faith based simply on his teaching, they should believe on the basis of Jesus' "work," his miracles (called "signs" throughout, meaning they point to the true nature of Jesus) and other incredible deeds. In 5:36-40, Jesus told the Jewish people that "the Father gave me these works to accomplish, and they prove that he sent me." He was telling the disciples the same thing. It would be best if their faith was grounded entirely in Jesus, but if they needed more concrete evidence, then they could remember his "work."

Jesus expanded on the implications of faith for the disciples (14:12). It is an appropriating faith: Those who have come to that illumination regarding the true nature of Jesus via the Spirit will have incredible spiritual power. Jesus defined this two ways. First, they will be able to "do the same works I have done"—in one sense another reference to miracles. In other words, the power to do miracles is available to the church and is appropriated by faith. At the same time, the "works" are wider and include a life of piety and prayer. James says it correctly, "Unless [faith] produces good deeds, it is dead and useless" (Jas 2:14-17). Works cannot save us, but works are the necessary fruit of any true salvation. Second, Jesus goes beyond this: those who have faith will even perform "greater works" (cf. 1:50; 5:20). What can be greater than the raising of Lazarus or the multiplication of the loaves? There have been many answers, such as doing even more works than Jesus did. But the best view is that this refers to life in the Spirit—i.e., experiencing the reality of the new life under Christ, namely the post-Resurrection power (Beasley-Murray, Carson, Whitacre). This, of course, is true, for Jesus clarifies it with "because I am going to be with the Father," referring to the period after his work was done, and he ascended to the Father. That would introduce the age of the Spirit. Köstenberger (1998a:171-175) says the "greater" probably is meant eschatologically as a reference to the new age in salvation-history inaugurated by Jesus. Yet the text also says "greater *works*" (14:12), and the greatest miracle of them all is not the raising of the dead to earthly life but the bestowal of eternal life upon the unsaved. Jesus made salvation possible through his death, and in the age of the Spirit, his disciples would participate in the mission to the lost (cf. 20:21-23, so Westcott, Bruce, Schnackenburg, Ridderbos). Thus the "greater works" are both the new power of the Spirit and the resultant privilege of mission produced by the Spirit (so Keener).

As part of the "greater works" of the new age inaugurated by Christ's passion, there is a new prayer power (14:13-14). This exhibits an A-B-A pattern, as the two prayer promises frame the purpose, "so that the Son can bring glory to the Father" (14:13b). Christ sought to bring glory to the Father throughout his earthly ministry (7:18; 13:31; 17:4), and by answering prayer, he would continue to do so in heaven. In this sense, through prayer we participate in the glory of the Godhead! On the surface, these prayer promises are extraordinary, saying "ask me for anything . . . and

I will do it." Yet to assume we can get anything we want through prayer is not just an error but a dangerous theology. If that were true, we would be in control of God (as seen in prosperity preaching).

In reality, the key is "in my name" (also in 14:26; 15:16; 16:23, 24, 26). This is not a magical formula with which we close our prayers (nowhere in the NT does it come at the end of a prayer). Instead, it is the true perspective of prayer. In the ancient world, the person's name defined who they were, the essence of their being. Parents would give their children the name they hoped would shape their lives. For instance, the angel told Mary to name her son "Jesus, for he will save his people from their sins" (Matt 1:21) (the name "Jesus" (Heb., *yehoshua'* [TH3091, ZH3397] or *yeshua'* [TH3442, ZH3800] originally meant "Yahweh saves"). To pray in Jesus' "name" means to pray in union with who he is (note the indwelling motif in 14:10, 11), reflecting a life and prayers that are in accordance with his will (see Whitacre, Keener). Prayers that center on what we want without considering God's will are not answered (Jas 4:3). This new prayer power was proof positive that the Kingdom had arrived, and it is mentioned often in John's writing (15:7, 16; 16:23, 24, 26; 1 John 3:22; 5:14-15 [which adds "anything that pleases him"]).

The Coming Paraclete, the Holy Spirit (14:15-31). These final three sections (14: 15-21, 22-24, 25-31) of the first discourse (13:31–14:31) develop four themes. The three persons of the Godhead (the Spirit [or, Paraclete], the Son, and the Father) are developed in the first two sections, and in the third section, where Jesus speaks of his departure, the idea of peace is developed as the natural result of understanding the work of the Godhead. Yet the Paraclete (for the meaning of this, see note on 14:16) dominates, and the other sections clarify his presence further.

The necessary responsibility of the believer in light of the "greater works" and prayer power of 14:12-14 is love and obedience. This provides a transition to 14:16ff, for it is also the necessary qualification for experiencing the Holy Spirit. The phrase, "if you love," does not really question the disciples' love for Jesus but rather uses their love for him as a springboard to their need to obey him (so Ridderbos). They must demonstrate their love in obedience. The connection between love and obedience is frequent (14:15, 21, 23; 15:14; 1 John 5:3) and implies its converse: to disobey means we do not love Christ. His commands include understanding and accepting the whole of his teaching, followed by a desire to live our lives on the basis of that teaching with its ethical/spiritual requirements. Love must naturally lead to obedience.

The responsibility of a disciple is to love and obey. Jesus promised that if his disciples obeyed, he would "ask the Father, and he [would] give [them] another Advocate (*paraklētos* [TG3875, ZG4156]; 14:16)"—that is, the Holy Spirit. It is the Spirit who will enable the believer to have power in prayer and to obey the commands of the Lord. This is the first of five passages dealing with the ministry of the Holy Spirit as Paraclete (this Greek word now appears in many English dictionaries since no single translation does it justice; see note on 14:16), and the first thing we must notice is that he is "*another* Advocate," meaning that Jesus was the first one. Everything the

Spirit is described as doing in these passages Jesus had already done, so the Spirit continues the work of Jesus on earth. Also, the Spirit is given by the Father here. Twice he was sent by the Father (14:16, 26) and twice by the Son (15:26; 16:7). This continues the mission theme in John (cf. "Major Themes" in the Introduction)—the Father sends the Son to the world, and both Father and Son send the Spirit. Like Jesus, the Advocate's ministry is both to the believer and the unbeliever; both are addressed in 14:16-17.

Jesus then defines the Advocate as the Spirit of truth, or "the Holy Spirit, who leads into all truth" (14:17; cf. 15:26; 16:13), meaning one both characterized by truth and proclaiming truth. In his ministry to both the saved and the unsaved, the Spirit communicates divine truth, as did Jesus (8:32, 40, 45-46; 14:6). He comes first to the world, which "cannot receive him" (the same as Jesus, cf. 1:10). The "world" in John is controlled by sin and rebellion, and thus rejection of Jesus and the Spirit is to be expected, for "it isn't looking for him and doesn't recognize him." The world is spiritually blind—the natural result of total depravity (note that it "*cannot* receive him").

In contrast, the disciples do "know him," for they have spiritual sight. Not only that but the Spirit, like Jesus, lives with them now (14:17). The movement from the present "lives with you" to the future "will be in you" has occasioned much discussion. The Spirit had not yet been given to the disciples (7:39; that will occur in 20:22), so in what sense was the Spirit *with* them and in what sense would the Spirit be *in* them? Did he live with them? The difference is that the Spirit was with them throughout Jesus' ministry—in the person of Jesus. After Jesus' resurrection, the Spirit would indwell them.

The disciples were feeling isolated and alone in their fear, so Jesus said, "I will not abandon you as orphans," a term sometimes used in secular Greek of disciples when their teacher died (Plato *Phaedrus* 116a). While Jesus would leave them to ascend to his Father, he would not leave them alone (cf. Josh 1:5, "I will not fail you or abandon you"). In Jesus statement, "I will come to you," (14:18) there is ambiguity as to whether he meant he would come back to them in his resurrection appearances, in the coming of the Spirit at Pentecost, or at the Parousia, his second coming. Some believe it is his coming in the person of the Spirit since this section is bracketed by passages on the Paraclete (14:16-17, 25-26). Others take it as the Parousia on the basis of 14:2-3. The most likely and the simplest answer is that Jesus was telling them he would come back to them in his resurrection appearances. At that time, the world would no longer see him, but the disciples would "see" him (14:19; there are no appearances to unbelievers except to his brothers, cf. 1 Cor 15:7). The language is too personal and specific ("see me") to fit the coming of the Spirit (so Beasley-Murray, Carson, Borchert contra Bruce, Köstenberger). Not only that but Jesus' next statement promised that he would be the firstfruits and guarantee of their own future resurrection—"Since I live, you also will live" (14:19; so Sanders, Morris). Yet there could also be double meaning here, for this may also indicate a new spiritual life that will be inaugurated by the events of the Resurrection (so Barrett, Whitacre).

The new spiritual life is clarified further in 14:20. "When" is literally "on that day," an apocalyptic phrase used throughout the Old Testament (especially in the prophets) to refer to the coming Kingdom of God. Here it refers to the Resurrection as an apocalyptic, world-changing event. Then they "will know," meaning not just intellectual apprehension but the participation of the whole person in the new age that Christ was about to introduce. Their new life would involve a depth of union that they never could have imagined. This threefold progression is truly one of the remarkable truths in Scripture; it is conveyed via the "indwelling" motif: as (1) Jesus indwells the Father, (2) believers indwell Jesus, and (3) Jesus indwells them. The principle is clear—the union within the Godhead is reflected in the mutual union we have with Jesus! This is explored even more deeply in 17:20-23. Here there is a double union—the Paraclete indwells us (14:17), and Jesus indwells us (14:20).

The central command of this section is to "accept my commandments and obey them"; this is connected with experiencing the love of Jesus (14:21; cf. 14:15, 23). Once more, it is impossible to love him truly without living on the basis of his teaching. The new relationship with Jesus, inaugurated by the new eon that was established by the Resurrection events, demands a new level of adherence to his precepts. Note also that while there is a union of essence (14:20), there is also a union of love (14:21), for when we love Jesus and obey him, we will experience the love of both the Father and the Son. There is a oneness between the Father and the Son, and this is mirrored by the oneness between Jesus and us (so Carson). Moreover, Jesus would "reveal [himself] to each of them." This manifestation of himself would begin with the resurrection appearances but would move beyond them to "his progressive self-revelation after his departure," as seen in the switch to referencing disciples in the third person ("they"), showing that Jesus here includes future believers (Ridderbos 1997:507). It is likely that this progressive revelation of himself includes all the levels of this chapter—his resurrection appearances (14:18), the coming of the Spirit (14:16), and his Parousia (14:3), where the final revelation of himself will occur.

The Coming of the Father and the Son (14:22-24). The other Judas was "Judas son of James," a member of the Twelve mentioned in Luke 6:16; Acts 1:13. He is probably the same person as Thaddeus in the list of the Twelve in Matthew 10:3 (= Mark 3:18). This is the only other place he is mentioned in the New Testament. When Jesus said he would "reveal" himself, Judas was confused, probably thinking of some kind of theophany (so Brown). Judas wondered why it would be a private manifestation to them alone rather than a public manifestation that would show the whole world his glory.

Jesus responded by contrasting the reactions of his followers and the world. Jesus would reveal himself to "all who love me" and "do what I say" (14:23). This is the third time obedience is stressed as the key response of the true believer (cf. 14:15, 21). A life molded by Jesus' teaching is proof positive that one loves him. These are the ones who experience God's love and to whom Jesus promised that he and the Father would "come and make our home with each of them" (14:23). While Jesus was preparing a future "home" (*monē* [TG3438, ZG3665], 14:2) in heaven, he and the Father would also make a present "home" (14:23) in the life of the believer. This takes place through the Spirit, called both the "Spirit of God" (Rom 8:9a, 14; 1 Cor 6:11) and the "Spirit of Christ" (Rom 8:9b; Phil 1:19; 1 Pet 1:11). As the Spirit indwells the Christian (14:17), he is the presence of the Father and the Son. At the same time, it can also be said that the triune Godhead dwells within the believer! In a very real sense, this is a touch of heaven, an anticipation of the final reality expressed in Revelation 21:3—"Look, God's home is now among his people! He will live with them, and they will be his people." The world, by contrast, neither loves nor obeys Christ (14:24). That is why he reveals himself only to his own. To anchor both truths (14:23 and 14:24a), Jesus reminded them that his teaching was not his own but came directly from God. He wanted his disciples to understand the eternal truths embodied in them.

Jesus Speaks of His Departure (14:25-31). Jesus' departure was on his mind at this point. He wanted his disciples to know that even though they could enjoy his physical presence and audible teaching only a little longer (14:25), the Spirit was soon going to take his place. As the "Advocate," the Spirit would carry on Jesus' guiding presence in their lives. In fact, in the same way that Jesus was the "representative" of the Father (cf. note on 14:16), the Spirit is the "representative" of Jesus (lit., "send in my name"). The disciples could rely on him in the same way they relied on Jesus. The purpose of the Spirit in this sense was to "teach" and "remind" (probably intended as synonyms, so Schnackenburg) them of "everything" Jesus had told them. John twice mentions that the disciples did not understand certain sayings until after the Resurrection (2:22; 12:16) and that their later understanding was provided by the Spirit. A good example of this would be the inspiration of the Spirit in the writing of the Gospels themselves: the Spirit guided the sacred Evangelists and helped them to understand the words of Jesus as they wrote. This does not refer to new revelation from the risen Lord but rather to correct understanding of what the historical Jesus said (so Burge 1987:210-221). This promise was primarily given to the disciples themselves in the first century but still relates to later believers in the sense that the Spirit helps us to remember passages when we need them.

Jesus concluded the first half of his discourse with the promise of peace (14:27). The Hebrew *shalom* [TH7965, ZH8934] (peace) was the traditional "good-bye," but Jesus' intent went far beyond that. Here it was "a benediction full of grace and power" (Ridderbos 1997:511). In the Old Testament, peace was associated with God's gift of salvation (Ps 29:11; Isa 57:19) and was a major messianic promise for the last days (Isa 9:6; 52:7; Ezek 37:26; Zech 9:10). Peace was also the blessing the disciples would receive again when Jesus had risen (20:19, 21, 26). In the midst of the tumult and fear that the disciples were undergoing, Jesus promised a messianic peace that was beyond human understanding (cf. Phil 4:7). It is a prime characteristic of the new order that Christ introduced (so Hoskyns, Beasley-Murray) and, as such, is a peace "the world cannot give" (14:27). The world's peace is always a facade and is upheld only by military prowess (e.g., the Cold War or *Pax Romana* [the "Roman peace"], which were maintained by violence). There are never any lasting results. Only Christ can both provide inward peace and guarantee it for eternity. So as in 14:1, he told them they didn't need to "be troubled or afraid." The triune Godhead was watching over them and would be indwelling them.

After comforting his disciples, Jesus pointed out their failures. They had forgotten and failed to understand his repeated message: "I am going away, but I will come back to you again" (14:28). He had told them about his coming departure even more often than John records. The Synoptics have three Passion predictions, and Luke records several others. Between the Gospels, Jesus had told them 10 to 12 times that he would die and rise again. Yet as the women went to the empty tomb, they expected only a corpse (cf. Mark 16:1-2 and parallels), and even the Twelve initially showed strong doubts on the whole (Luke 24:11). Jesus' statement, "if you really loved me" (14:28), implies that they did not (a contrary-to-fact condition in Greek). Jesus wasn't really saying that they did not love him at all but rather that their love had not led to understanding and a greater concern for what was best for him rather than for themselves. They were still in denial (a common reaction to tragedy).

When Christians lose a loved one, it is natural that they vacillate between grief at the loss (11:35; Phil 2:27) and joy that the departed are with the Lord. Jesus asked that their love for him produce happiness since he would be with his heavenly Father. Then he added that his Father "is greater than I am" (14:28), meaning that God was in complete control of the situation (on Jesus' subordination to the Father, see notes on 5:19-30; 8:29; 12:49-50) and his will was being accomplished. If the disciples were truly trusting God and concerned for his will, they would rejoice as they saw the events taking place exactly as he had ordained. If they truly loved Jesus, they would rejoice that he was returning to his true home. Also, Jesus told them (14:29) that he had related these things concerning the future so that their faith would be strengthened when the events came to pass (cf. 13:19; 16:4).

Since Jesus was near the end of his life, he told them he had little time left to talk with them (14:30), for "the ruler of this world approaches," implying that Judas, possessed by Satan, was approaching. In this Gospel, the death of Jesus is clearly portrayed as a cosmic war (also 6:70; 12:31; 13:27; 16:11). Satan led Jesus to the Cross and precipitated his own defeat, certainly one of the greatest tactical errors in history! Yet what else could Satan do? He had been cast out of heaven and knew his time was short (Rev 12:12). His final defeat was certain, and he knew it. Even in the end times, God will allow the Antichrist to martyr the saints (Rev 13:7), yet each death will be another defeat for Satan (Rev 12:11). Jesus added, "He has no power over me." There is a legal connotation here: the devil can make no charge against Jesus (so Beasley-Murray). Also, the statement shows that Satan is not in control—God is.

Rather than giving in to Satan, Jesus was actually doing "what the Father requires" (14:31). Satan only ever seems to be winning; in reality, even he can do only what God allows (Rev 13:5-8; 17:17). Jesus loves the Father and obeys him (the supreme example for us, cf. 14:15, 21, 23). The Cross was an act of divine obedience, not a victory for Satan. In the final analysis, the world would know of Jesus' love for the Father (14:31), not of Satan's act. At this point, Jesus said, "Come, let's be going," signifying the end of the dialog. At this point Jesus was either simply indicating his desire to leave (something which may not have happened until the end of chapter 16), or he and the disciples actually were leaving and he continued their conversation in the streets of the city on the way to Gethsemane (cf. Carson 1991:479). What is clear is that Jesus knew it was time to meet his destiny.

◆   ## 2. The second discourse (15:1–16:33)

"I am the true grapevine, and my Father is the gardener. [2]He cuts off every branch of mine that doesn't produce fruit, and he prunes the branches that do bear fruit so they will produce even more. [3]You have already been pruned and purified by the message I have given you. [4]Remain in me, and I will remain in you. For a branch cannot produce fruit if it is severed from the vine, and you cannot be fruitful unless you remain in me.

[5]"Yes, I am the vine; you are the branches. Those who remain in me, and I in them, will produce much fruit. For apart from me you can do nothing. [6]Anyone who does not remain in me is thrown away like a useless branch and withers. Such branches are gathered into a pile to be burned. [7]But if you remain in me and my words remain in you, you may ask for anything you want, and it will be granted! [8]When you produce much fruit, you are my true disciples. This brings great glory to my Father.

[9]"I have loved you even as the Father has loved me. Remain in my love. [10]When you obey my commandments, you remain in my love, just as I obey my Father's commandments and remain in his love. [11]I have told you these things so that you will be filled with my joy. Yes, your joy will overflow! [12]This is my commandment: Love each other in the same way I have loved you. [13]There is no greater love than to lay down one's life for one's friends. [14]You are my friends if you do what I command. [15]I no longer call you slaves, because a master doesn't confide in his slaves. Now you are my friends, since I have told you everything the Father told me. [16]You didn't choose me. I chose you. I appointed you to go and produce lasting fruit, so that the Father will give you whatever you ask for, using my name. [17]This is my command: Love each other.

[18]"If the world hates you, remember that it hated me first. [19]The world would love you as one of its own if you belonged to it, but you are no longer part of the world. I chose you to come out of the world, so it hates you. [20]Do you remember what I told you? 'A slave is not greater than the master.' Since they persecuted me, naturally they will persecute you. And if they had listened to me, they would listen to you. [21]They will do all this to you because of me, for they have rejected the One who sent me. [22]They would not be guilty if I had not come and spoken to them. But now they have no excuse for their sin. [23]Anyone who hates me also hates my Father. [24]If I hadn't done such miraculous signs among them that no one else could do, they would not be guilty. But as it is, they have seen everything I did, yet they still hate me and my Father. [25]This fulfills what is written in their Scriptures:* 'They hated me without cause.'

[26]"But I will send you the Advocate*— the Spirit of truth. He will come to you from the Father and will testify all about me. [27]And you must also testify about me because you have been with me from the beginning of my ministry.

CHAPTER 16

"I have told you these things so that you won't abandon your faith. ²For you will be expelled from the synagogues, and the time is coming when those who kill you will think they are doing a holy service for God. ³This is because they have never known the Father or me. ⁴Yes, I'm telling you these things now, so that when they happen, you will remember my warning. I didn't tell you earlier because I was going to be with you for a while longer.

⁵"But now I am going away to the One who sent me, and not one of you is asking where I am going. ⁶Instead, you grieve because of what I've told you. ⁷But in fact, it is best for you that I go away, because if I don't, the Advocate* won't come. If I do go away, then I will send him to you. ⁸And when he comes, he will convict the world of its sin, and of God's righteousness, and of the coming judgment. ⁹The world's sin is that it refuses to believe in me. ¹⁰Righteousness is available because I go to the Father, and you will see me no more. ¹¹Judgment will come because the ruler of this world has already been judged.

¹²"There is so much more I want to tell you, but you can't bear it now. ¹³When the Spirit of truth comes, he will guide you into all truth. He will not speak on his own but will tell you what he has heard. He will tell you about the future. ¹⁴He will bring me glory by telling you whatever he receives from me. ¹⁵All that belongs to the Father is mine; this is why I said, 'The Spirit will tell you whatever he receives from me.'

¹⁶"In a little while you won't see me anymore. But a little while after that, you will see me again."

¹⁷Some of the disciples asked each other, "What does he mean when he says, 'In a little while you won't see me, but then you will see me,' and 'I am going to the Father'? ¹⁸And what does he mean by 'a little while'? We don't understand."

¹⁹Jesus realized they wanted to ask him about it, so he said, "Are you asking yourselves what I meant? I said in a little while you won't see me, but a little while after that you will see me again. ²⁰I tell you the truth, you will weep and mourn over what is going to happen to me, but the world will rejoice. You will grieve, but your grief will suddenly turn to wonderful joy. ²¹It will be like a woman suffering the pains of labor. When her child is born, her anguish gives way to joy because she has brought a new baby into the world. ²²So you have sorrow now, but I will see you again; then you will rejoice, and no one can rob you of that joy. ²³At that time you won't need to ask me for anything. I tell you the truth, you will ask the Father directly, and he will grant your request because you use my name. ²⁴You haven't done this before. Ask, using my name, and you will receive, and you will have abundant joy.

²⁵"I have spoken of these matters in figures of speech, but soon I will stop speaking figuratively and will tell you plainly all about the Father. ²⁶Then you will ask in my name. I'm not saying I will ask the Father on your behalf, ²⁷for the Father himself loves you dearly because you love me and believe that I came from God.* ²⁸Yes, I came from the Father into the world, and now I will leave the world and return to the Father."

²⁹Then his disciples said, "At last you are speaking plainly and not figuratively. ³⁰Now we understand that you know everything, and there's no need to question you. From this we believe that you came from God."

³¹Jesus asked, "Do you finally believe? ³²But the time is coming—indeed it's here now—when you will be scattered, each one going his own way, leaving me alone. Yet I am not alone because the Father is with me. ³³I have told you all this so that you may have peace in me. Here on earth you will have many trials and sorrows. But take heart, because I have overcome the world."

15:25 Greek *in their law*. Pss 35:19; 69:4.   **15:26** Or *Comforter*, or *Encourager*, or *Counselor*. Greek reads *Paraclete*.   **16:7** Or *Comforter*, or *Encourager*, or *Counselor*. Greek reads *Paraclete*.   **16:27** Some manuscripts read *from the Father*.

NOTES

15:1-17 There are almost as many outlines of this section as there are scholars. Bruce, Schnackenburg, and Witherington see it as 15:1-11, 12-17; Bultmann, Michaels, Carson, and Ridderbos as 15:1-8, 9-16 (17); Brown and Whitacre as 15:1-6, 7-17; Burge as 15:1-8, 9-11, 12-17. One key decision is whether 15:7-8 belongs with the illustration or as part of the explanation. It seems to me that the themes of remaining and bearing fruit begin the interpretation and belong with the latter category. Also, 15:9-17 breaks naturally into two parts and with the inclusion of 15:7-8, we have a three-part explanation of the extended metaphor—15:1-8, 9-11, 12-17. This seems to be the most natural breakdown of the passage.

15:1-6 It is common to interpret the vine *mashal* (see note on 10:6) in a sacramental way as eucharistic (so Brown, Barrett), due to its setting in the Last Supper scene and the use of "vine" in the Synoptic Last Supper accounts ("I will not drink again of the fruit of the vine until that day . . ." [NIV]). But it is far more likely that the vine symbol represents Israel, and Christ is showing that the new community, the true Israel, must be found in him (as discussed in the commentary below).

15:2-3 *cuts off . . . prunes . . . purified.* There is a strong play on words in the Gr., in which the heavenly Gardener "cuts off" (*airei* [TG142, ZG149]) the dead branches and "prunes" (*kathairei* [TG2508, ZG2748]) the fruitful ones, while the disciples are already "purified" (*katharoi* [TG2513, ZG2754]) (cf. Bruce, Carson). Note the similar sound of the final two syllables of each word. The emphasis is on the contrast between the removal of dead branches/disciples and the pruning/purification of the faithful disciples. The purification process is not explained here but probably would be the trials of life that God uses to help the believer grow in faith (cf. Heb 12:6-11; Jas 1:2-4; 1 Pet 1:6-7).

15:4 *Remain in me.* There may be a slight conditional force in this ("if you remain . . . I will remain"). This is represented in the NLT ("Remain in me, and I will remain in you"). In this sense, the disciples' perseverance in Jesus would be "the occasional cause, not the ultimate cause, of Jesus remaining in the believer (cf. 8:31-32; 15:9-11)" (Carson 1991:516).

15:7-17 Some scholars (Brown, Whitacre) think this passage is a chiasm, with teaching (15:7, 17) and answered prayer (15:7, 16) framing the section, and joy (15:11) in the center. Some of the parallels are difficult to maintain, however, and the threefold outline here seems better.

15:13 *lay down one's life for one's friends.* Some critics have called this a lesser passage than Rom 5:8, for surely dying for one's enemies is greater than dying for one's friends. Yet that is hardly the point. As Morris says (1995:599), "He is in the midst of friends and is speaking only of friends. With respect to them he is saying that one cannot have greater love than to die for them."

15:20 *if they had listened to me, they would listen to you.* This can be interpreted two ways: negatively—"if they had listened to me (which they haven't), they would listen to you (which they won't)" (so Brown, Whitacre, Burge, Köstenberger); or positively—"if they listened to me (some did), they will listen to you (some will)" (so Barrett, Schnackenburg, Comfort, Carson). The question is the relationship between the negative "since they persecuted me" statement to the parallel "if they had listened" statement. A case can be made for the positive as providing the two sides of ministry: persecution and positive response to the Gospel. This would be favored by Jesus' prayer for "all who will ever believe in me through their message" (17:20). The immediate context (15:18-25), however, is completely negative and thus this statement would fit parallels in Isa 6:10 (where Isaiah is told to "harden the hearts of these people . . . plug their ears and shut their eyes") and Ezek 3:7 ("the people of Israel won't listen to you any more than they listen to me"). The disciples would be persecuted, and their message would be rejected, just as Jesus was.

15:26 *the Spirit of truth.* The emphasis here is on the Spirit as a person, seen in the masculine "he" (*ekeinos* [TG1565, ZG1697]) following "Spirit." Carson (1991:528-529) speaks of the "procession" of the Spirit from the Father and of the Trinitarian basis of this passage. The Spirit comes from the Father and is sent by the Son on his mission; the Godhead is acting together in unity in responding to the world's opposition.

15:27 *you have been with me from the beginning of my ministry.* This verse has its primary application with the historical disciples (so Carson, Whitacre). Since they were eyewitnesses from the start (cf. Luke 1:2; Acts 1:21-22; 2 Pet 1:16), they were the divinely chosen witnesses. For the early church, historical proof of the accounts was extremely critical. Moreover, this concern for verifiable history on the part of the early church is important to us in an age when many critical scholars are dismissing the verifiability of the Gospel accounts. Still, it is also valid for us to contextualize this as a promise that the Spirit will continue to empower our witness today.

16:1 *abandon your faith.* The verb *skandalizō* [TG4624, ZG4997] means to "stumble" or "go astray." It is used in 6:61 of those disciples who were offended and then fell away (6:66). It also appears in Mark 14:27 in Jesus' use of the language of apostasy to predict that upon his arrest the disciples would all "desert" him.

16:2 *the time is coming.* This is a semitechnical phrase in John (4:21, 23; 5:25, 28; 16:25, 32) for the eschatological last days, which had arrived. It was the time of true worship (4:23) and the time of messianic salvation (5:25) and final revelation (16:25; cf. "soon," NLT). Persecution (16:2, 32) is also part of the last days.

16:8 *convict the world.* The verb in the NT is always used of proving someone a sinner so as to call them to repentance (TDNT 2.473-474), but it can mean to "expose" sin (so Brown, Hoskyns, Beasley-Murray, Derrett 1999, Whitacre), to "convince" people of their sinfulness (Bruce), to "convict" of being wrong (Westcott, Kysar), or to prove them guilty of sin (Carson, Barrett, Schnackenburg, Ridderbos, Burge). In 3:20, the verb is used of exposing evil deeds, and in 8:46 of accusing Jesus of sin. The context here is decidedly forensic, and so this last option is best. The Spirit is proving both to the world itself and to the judgment seat of God that the world is guilty.

16:9-11 *that . . . because . . . because.* All three clauses have the Paraclete convicting the world, but the contents of the conviction use a *hoti* [TG3754, ZG4022] clause that can be translated "that" or "because" and therefore may give either the contents of the conviction or the reason for it. Scholars are divided, with some saying it gives the substance of the charge ("that," so Brown, Morris) and others the basis of it ("because," so Barrett, Carson). In the forensic context of this passage, the three better express the cause of the charge than its substance.

16:10 *Righteousness.* This is the most difficult content of the three *hoti* clauses (see note on 16:9-11) to specify. There are several options: (1) in a legal context it could be "justice," showing that Jesus was innocent and just (Brown, Whitacre); (2) it could be demonstrating Jesus' righteousness in light of his exaltation and return to the Father (Hoskyns, Bruce, Beasley-Murray, Comfort, Witherington, Burge, Keener, Köstenberger); (3) to continue the centrality of the world in the three clauses, it means convicting the world of its lack of righteousness (Carson, Blomberg); (4) it could refer to the "justification" of believers, as they suffer for the Lord (Barrett). Of these, the second is the most natural in light of the whole context. The world is convicted of three things—its sin, Christ's righteousness (in light of its condemnation of him), and its coming judgment.

16:13 *into all truth.* Carson (1991:539-540) makes a strong case for understanding this as "in all truth," pointing out that Jesus had already revealed all truth in himself (14:6). This "suggests an exploration of truth already principally disclosed," and the Spirit guides the believer into the implications of those truths.

16:16 *a little while . . . a little while.* Some believe the first refers to the interval between Jesus' death and resurrection and the second time, between his resurrection and second coming (Barrett, Bruce), but it is more likely they refer, respectively, to the time before his death and the time between his death and resurrection because the context refers to the joy of seeing Jesus again (16:21-24), undoubtedly at the resurrection appearances (Michaels, Witherington, Burge).

16:19 *Jesus realized.* As in 1:47; 2:24; 6:61, Jesus was almost supernaturally aware of what his disciples were saying and thinking. His knowledge of people and their thoughts was further proof of his heavenly origin.

16:21 *brought a new baby into the world.* Some have seen a reference to Gen 3:16 and 4:1, and so to a new creation theme with Jesus as the new Adam. This is hardly the stress here; that idea has a stronger association with the Day of the Lord. The emphasis here is on Jesus' death and resurrection. In one sense, Jesus brought about a new creation (cf. 1:1), but there is no new Adam theme here.

16:23 *At that time.* This phrase is lit. "in that day," and in both the OT (Isa 2:11, 17; 3:6, 18; Hos 2:16, 18) and NT (Mark 13:11, 17, 19, 32; Acts 2:18; 2 Tim 1:12, 18; 4:8; Heb 8:10; Rev 9:6), it refers to the Day of the Lord when the present world order will be overthrown. Here it is used in an inaugurated sense of the beginning of those last days.

won't need to ask me for anything. Scholars are divided as to whether this concludes 16:17-22 (Westcott, Bultmann, Hoskyns, Brown, Barrett, Morris, Beasley-Murray) or introduces 16:23-24 (Bernard, Bruce, Carson). The verb "ask" here probably means they will no longer need to ask him any questions (as in 16:17-19) rather than prayer requests, so the first option is better.

16:31 *Do you finally believe?* Some (Michaels, NIV) make this a positive statement, "You believe at last," on the basis that the context shows genuine faith on the part of the disciples. It is better to take this as a question, indicating Jesus' doubt regarding the degree of their faith since there is more a tone of rebuke in the context (Barrett, Witherington, Burge, NRSV, NLT—Carson keeps the exclamation but sees it as sarcastic).

16:32 *you will be scattered.* Ridderbos (1997:545) believes this alludes not just to Zech 13:7 but also to 1 Kgs 22:17, which mentions not only the sheep scattered but also includes the command, "send them home in peace." Thus after the battle, the enemy will stop pursuing, and the scattered army will be able to return in peace. Jesus would bear the full burden of the world's hostility, as the disciples returned to their homes. This is possible, but it must be stated that, if so, it came true only after the Resurrection.

you will be scattered. . . . Yet I am not alone because the Father is with me. There are two problems here: (1) John never mentions the desertion of the disciples (cf. Mark 14:50-52 and parallels), so it is best to take this as a piece of tradition embedded in John to warn later followers against such failures (so Brown). (2) How do we reconcile Jesus' statement here with the cry of dereliction in Mark 15:34 and parallels: "My God, my God, why have you abandoned me?" Some (Brown, Kysar) believe John would never use such a saying in light of this; others (Hoskyns, Barrett, Lindars) that he corrects a false understanding of that cry. It is better to say that the two statements relate two separate aspects of Jesus' experience of the Cross: he was conscious of his Father's presence but for that terrible moment expressed his deep agony via Ps 22:1, the cry of dereliction (so Beasley-Murray, Carson, Borchert, Köstenberger).

COMMENTARY

The farewell discourse is organized in two cycles, a Hebraic method of writing that goes over the same material twice, adding further clarification (this method is central in Heb 8–10, 1 John, and the book of Revelation). Jesus went over the material in 13:31–14:31 a second time, building on several themes like the necessity of love in the community (13:34-35 // 15:17), the coming of another Paraclete (14:15-17, 26 // 15:26; 16:7-15), spiritual warfare (14:30 // 16:11), and the prayer promises (14:13-14 // 15:7, 16; 16:23). At the same time, he added further nuances. In the first half, he centered on his need to depart so that the Spirit could come. In this cycle he centers more on the disciples, who would have to remain in him and bear fruit, and the fact that they would endure persecution as he did.

The Vine and the Branches (15:1-6). At the outset, Jesus made the disciples aware of their need to "remain in him" if they were to bear fruit for God. He used a powerful extended metaphor (not a parable, for there is no plot) or allegory (every detail carries meaning, cf. 10:6) like the one on the Good Shepherd in 10:1-5. Also, in the same way that he explained the metaphor in 10:7-18, he explained the implications of the Vine in terms of three aspects—15:7-8 on remaining and bearing fruit, 15:9-11 on love and joy in Jesus, and 15:12-17 on loving one another.

This is the last of the seven "I am" sayings in John (cf. 6:35; 8:12; 10:7, 11; 11:25; 14:6). The illustration of the Vine has background in the use of a vine for Israel in the Old Testament (Ps 80:8-18; Isa 5:1-7; 27:2; Jer 2:21; 5:10; Ezek 15; 17:1-6; Hos 10:1) and intertestamental period (Sir 24:17-21; 2 Baruch 39:7). As Burge brings out (1994:392), the idea is that Israel's "holy space" is in the land God has given her. In these passages, the vine metaphor is usually negative, centering on divine judgment on the nation for its unfaithfulness to God (so Pryor). Jesus used it more positively but still with negative overtones.

It is possible that Jesus, on the way from the upper room with his disciples, was standing on the Temple grounds looking up at the Holy Place where, at the entrance above the linen curtain, there was a large grapevine (with some clusters the "height of a man," so Josephus Antiquities 15.395) of pure gold, symbolizing Israel (so Burge). In a further fulfillment theme (similar to the feasts in chs 5–10), Jesus identified himself as "the true grapevine," replacing Israel as God's true vineyard. Consider what Jeremiah 2:21 says about the vine (Israel): "I [God] was the one who planted you, choosing a vine of the purest stock—the very best. How did you grow into this corrupt wild vine?" The nation was no longer fit to be the source of the covenant people of God; Jesus became the only way (14:6). The "sacred space" in which God's people must now dwell is Jesus. Earlier, he replaced the Temple (ch 2), the Passover (ch 6), the Festival of Shelters (chs 7–8), and now he replaces the land (so Burge 1994:393-394). As Ridderbos says (1997:515), Jesus "applies to himself the redemptive-historical description of the people of God. He thus becomes the one who represents or embodies the people." Now a personal relationship with Jesus defines God's people, and so the disciples constitute the new Israel. Building on the background in which Wisdom is planted among the people of God and produces fruit (Sir 24:17-21), Witherington (1995:255-257) sees Jesus as the Wisdom of God, "the authentic source of nourishment, strength, and empowerment for ministry." Moreover, the "Father is the gardener" (15:1), the one who controls the vineyard and decides which branches are to remain on the vine. Isaiah 5:2 speaks of the gardener as the one who "plowed the land, cleared its stones, and planted it with the best vines."

There are two kinds of branches—fruit-bearing ones and those that fail to produce fruit—but it is important to realize that both types of branches are "in me" (that is, originally part of the vine). Here Jesus was utilizing the ancient practice of viticulture as an illustration. Dead branches were removed, and fruitful branches were trimmed so that they would be even more productive. In one sense, this summarizes chapter 13, as the "dead branch," Judas, was cut off and the good branches, the disciples, were pruned (so Whitacre). Fruitless branches are cut off, a strong image elaborated in 15:6. It connotes the idea that they are useless and have ceased to be living branches. The good branches are then pruned so they will "produce even more" (15:2). Brown (1970:675) gives the background: The removal of dead branches occurred in February–March, and at times the vines resembled "stalks bereft of branches." The pruning occurred in spring and then a second time in August (so Keener) after the vine developed leaves, and the gardener would press off the little shoots so that the main fruit-bearing branches would get all the moisture. The meaning of removing the dead branches is explored in 15:6; however, the thrust of the act of pruning by the heavenly gardener should be explored here. Obviously, it refers to growth in the new life in Christ, and the idea of producing more fruit sums up all the qualities of discipleship in John—increased faith, prayer, obedience, love, mission, ministry—all that brings glory to God (15:8). The process of pruning probably refers to the difficulties in life, the trials that make the believer "strong in character" and "ready for anything" (Jas 1:2-4, TLB).

Jesus then applied the allegory to the disciples (15:3-4), saying first that they "have already been pruned and purified" by his teaching. Jesus had been developing them spiritually throughout his ministry with them, and they were already bearing fruit. There may also be a reference to Jesus' earlier teaching during the Last Supper (the setting for this discourse, cf. 13:10, "you disciples are clean"), which in a sense finalized the cleansing process by preparing them for Jesus' true destiny. Since they were clean, they needed to continue in that state, and there was only one way to do so: "Remain in me, and I will remain in you" (15:4). Mutual indwelling is the key concept in this section of the discourse (15:4, 5, 6, 7, 9, 10) and continues the theme from 14:16, 20, 23. The life of the believer is to be lived entirely in union with Jesus and in dependence on his presence. All branches have life only to the extent that they are attached to the vine, and fruitfulness is completely dependent on life-giving sap from the vine. Jesus could not be more clear. The extent to which the disciples relied on themselves was the extent to which they would fail (cf. the discipleship failure motif in Mark [6:52; 8:14-21; 9:14-29]). The only way to a fruitful life is to dwell entirely in Christ and the Spirit. As said by Paul (Eph 2:8-10) and James (2:14-26), works cannot produce faith, but faith must produce works. The believer is totally responsible to continually draw sustenance and life from union with Jesus.

Returning to the metaphor, Jesus repeated the theme: "Yes, I am the vine; you are the branches" (15:5). The thrust is clear. Only by remaining in Jesus is there any possibility of fruit-bearing, "for apart from me you can do nothing." In the new life after Jesus had departed and the Spirit had come, the disciples must absolutely rely on Jesus in every area of life. Hartin (1991:347) says this is the heart of the new ethics Jesus introduced; as the model of self-sacrificial love, Jesus becomes one with the members of his community and makes it possible for them to exemplify the same love. The alternative is fearful indeed. Those branches that cease to "remain" and bear fruit will be "thrown away like a useless branch," withering and being "gathered into a pile to be burned" (15:6). This expands the image in 15:2. This is a very serious warning since it implies fiery judgment; and as it is tied in closely with the issue of the security of the believer according to John (cf. 6:37-40; 10:27-29), it is quite controversial. The Arminian theologian takes this as a warning against the apostasy of a believer (note "every branch *of mine*" in 15:2); note that they refuse to "remain in" Christ. Westcott (1881:217) says the unfruitful branches are true branches "in Christ," and several (Brown, Whitacre) suggest that this echoes Old Testament passages on the fate of apostate Israel (Ezek 15:4-6; 19:12), as well as Matthew's parable of the weeds (13:30). Witherington (1995:258) says, "This being cut off is not seen as happening to those who have never been a part of the authentic vine but to those who 'do not remain in me.' This of course presupposes that at one point they were authentically joined to Jesus but did not stay the course because of pressures and problems created by a hostile world" (cf. Keener 2003:1000-1002).

The Calvinist says that these are not true disciples, even though they were part of the church (so Hendriksen, Blomberg, Köstenberger; Michaels takes this as a reference to Judas who was never a believer; Comfort and Hawley [1994] apply 1 John 2:19: "These people left our churches, but they never really belonged with us"). Some also suggest that these were perhaps the Jews who were once in God's vine but refused to remain when Christ came (so Carson). Others say that the cutting off and burning are simply viticultural images that stress the need to remain in the vine without implying the apostasy of true believers (Morris, Ridderbos). The latter interpretation is unlikely, for if the pruning is meant to be applied, so is the cutting off. Also, the Jewish interpretation is unlikely, for Jesus says "in me," not "in God." Thus, the two most likely are the views that true believers can apostatize or that the apostates are part of the church, though not of the elect. While in my opinion, "in me" favors true believers, both are possible, and the issue must be decided not just on this text but on a study of the security and warning passages throughout Scripture (cf. Osborne 2003 on Rom 8:28, 29-30, and 10:21). In reality, there is a mediating position. The warning to the church is very real here as well as in passages like Hebrews 6:4-6 and 10:26-31, and it should be preached as such in our churches, for we do not know who is a true believer and who is not. In a sense, the debate occurs *after* someone apostatizes—that is, was the person a believer before (we thought so) or not? In other words, both sides should preach security in security passages (e.g., 6:35-44; 10:27-29) and warning in warning passages such as this one.

The Implications of the Illustration (15:7-17). There are three parts to the explanation of the extended metaphor of 15:1-6; they are reflections on remaining and
bearing fruit (15:7-8), love and joy in Jesus (15:9-11), and loving one another
(15:12-17). The idea of remaining in God or Christ has been shown to be new covenant language from the Old Testament, in which remaining leads to a new heart
and the presence of the Spirit in an individual, leading to obedience (so Carson,
Blomberg). In 15:4, believers dwelling in Christ received the promise that Christ
would dwell in them. Here the promise is that his words would dwell in them, a reference back to the Spirit who would remind them of his teaching (14:26). This
leads to a further all-embracing promise of a new power in prayer (cf. 14:13-14).
The implication is that when we truly center our lives in him, and when his teachings are in control of us (= the obedience of 14:15, 21, 23), we will truly be "in [his]
name" (14:13)—that is, in union with him.

Our prayer life will thus reflect that union, and so we can "ask for anything" and
"it will be granted." The implication, as in 14:13-14, is that we will not ask self-
centered requests. Our prayer life will be concerned more for the glory of God (the
"thou-petitions" of the Lord's prayer, Matt 6:9-10) than for our own needs (the "we-
petitions," Matt 6:11-13, which come after the God-centered requests). Prayer,
along with Christ answering such prayers, is a major type of fruit-bearing and is a
hallmark of true discipleship. Every disciple is defined by the quality of fruit they
produce.

The goal of a disciple is to remain in Jesus and bear much fruit for him (15:8, cf.
4-5). "Christians were chosen for this and appointed for this. It is God's design and
economy that each believer should live in union with his Son and be fruitful (i.e.,
express the effect of that union in daily life)" (Comfort 1994:133-134). One of the
primary means by which this fruitful life is accomplished is to depend upon Christ
to the extent that all needs are placed before him in prayer. This, in fact, is the meaning of the first we-petition in the Lord's prayer, "Give us today the food we need"
(Matt 6:11). The prayer is not equivalent to, "Gimme, gimme!" but rather, "Lord, I
surrender my needs to you." Producing much fruit, moreover, "brings great glory
to" God. In 14:13, Jesus already said he answered prayer in order to glorify his
Father. This is expanded here into every kind of fruit-bearing. It is all a product of
Christ indwelling the believer, and so the purpose of every kind of fruitfulness is to
glorify God. As the Westminster Confession says, we have been created to "glorify
God and enjoy him forever." Glorifying God is the great privilege and joy of the
disciple.

The second part of Jesus' amplification of the vine and branches illustration
focuses on the love and joy the believer experiences in Jesus (15:9-11). Throughout
the farewell discourse, the relationship between Jesus and the disciples reflects the
relationship between Jesus and the Father. This is especially the case in experiencing
Jesus' love. The love he has for us is the outgrowth of the love he shares with his
Father. This is beyond understanding. The depth of that love cannot be expressed in
human language. It can only be experienced. The Greek (*ēgapēsa* [TG25, ZG26], "loved";

aorist tense) expresses the completeness of God's love for his Son and connotes an eternal love that existed even before time began (so Carson). The depth of that eternal love is now experienced by Jesus' followers. As Romans 5:8 says, "God showed his great love for us by sending Christ to die for us while we were still sinners." This love continues throughout our lives. Yet to experience its depths, we are responsible to "remain in (his) love." Love must be experienced to be complete. The self-centered believer is like a self-centered spouse—they are loved but remain unaware of it. It is a terrible tragedy to be loved by Christ and yet not respond to it.

Remaining in Christ's love is further defined as obedience to his commands (15:10). Moreover, obedience, like love, is built upon the relationship between God and Christ. His obedience to his Father is the basis and model for our obedience, a major emphasis in John (4:34; 5:17, 19-20; 6:38; 8:29; 10:18; 12:49-50), especially in this section (14:15, 21, 23, 31). Jesus' love is the ground of obedience, and our love for him is the wellspring from which our obedience flows. Like Jesus, as we obey, we "remain in [God's] love" (15:10). This does not mean that when we fail to obey, he stops loving us (Rom 8:31-39); rather, disobedience keeps us from experiencing his love. Further, the purpose for this teaching is joy—he wants us to be filled with joy and for that joy to "overflow" (15:11). Jesus had given his disciples messianic "peace" (14:27) and now offered them messianic "joy," a promise that would culminate in the upper room appearance to them (20:19-20). In fact, all three of the messianic gifts—love, peace, joy—are now available to Jesus' followers. With this, even our trials can be greeted with "great joy" (Jas 1:2); we may not have happiness, for trials are painful (Heb 12:11), but we have joy because Christ is in control.

The third implication of the vine illustration that Jesus discusses is the love that believers share with one another (15:12-17). This completes the three stages of love: love between the Father and the Son leads to love between Jesus and the disciples (15:9-10), and now his love for us must be reflected in our love for one another (15:12). Michaels (1989:273) sees in this the same triangular pattern as in 13:34; Jesus loves each believer, and that love must lead to his followers loving one another. Our relationships with each other are part of our relationships with Christ. This is true at every level—husband–wife (1 Pet 3:7), parent–child (Eph 6:1-4), or Christian–government (Rom 13:1-2; 1 Pet 2:13), as well as in areas like forgiveness (Matt 6:14-15) or social concern (Jas 2:13). We cannot truly experience the love of Christ without loving one another. These all tie together: Love for God and Jesus demands obedience, and obedience includes the "new commandment" of 13:34-35 to love each other (so Carson). This love then will involve even laying down our lives for our friends (15:13), an extension of God's love as demonstrated in Christ's death (Rom 5:8; 1 John 3:16). The model is Jesus, who would lay down his life for them just hours after delivering this address. As we emulate Christ's love, we too may someday be required to give our lives for others (as many missionaries have done). God's Word is clear on this: godly suffering is a special sharing with Christ (Phil 3:10), and God will use it redemptively (the blood of the martyrs is the seed of the church).

Jesus then gave his disciples an entirely new status and relationship with him. In a sense, this was their graduation ceremony. They were no longer just disciples but friends (15:14-15). First, his friends are those who obey him. This is not really a condition, as if every act of disobedience destroys that friendship. Rather, it flows out of what he had been saying. Love and obedience are deeply intertwined (14:15, 21, 23); it is when we obey that we experience the depth of his love (15:10). Nothing can separate us from Christ's love (Rom 8:35), but as we live according to his precepts, we know a special intimacy with him. The slave/master terminology was often used of the relationship between a rabbi and his disciples. Also, "slave" (*doulos* [TG1401, ZG1528]) and related words are used throughout the New Testament to describe the relationship between the believer and God (cf. John 13:16; 15:20). It means that we belong to God and are part of his family (a slave was a member of the household in the first century). Jesus was not saying that this metaphor no longer applied but rather that his relationship with his followers was changing. They were now "friends" (for background on this see Keener 2003:1006-1011) and not just "slaves" (cf. 20:17 where they become "brothers"). A slave owner does not "confide" in his slave but demands unquestioning adherence. Jesus, however, shared everything his Father had told him (as emphasized throughout this discourse). This would be continued even more in the ministry of the Paraclete (14:26; 16:13-15). The disciples now enjoyed a special status as "friends of God," a concept the Jewish people reserved primarily for the great leaders of the past, like Abraham and Moses (cf. TDNT 9.168).

The relationship is completely dependent on Christ, not them: "You didn't choose me. I chose you" (15:16). This also makes even more apparent the incredible privilege of being one of the chosen (so Ridderbos). Jesus' followers are truly the special people in this world. Moreover, they were not just chosen but "appointed" or "set apart" (*ethēka* [TG5087, ZG5502]) from the rest of humanity. This is often used for appointment to ministry (Gen 17:5; Num 8:10; 27:18; Acts 13:47; 1 Tim 1:12), and the specific ministry here is to "produce lasting fruit," certainly pointing generally to the fruitful Christian life (Schnackenburg) but specifically referring to the missionary mandate to reach the world for Christ (Westcott, Bernard, Barrett, Beasley-Murray, Carson, Köstenberger). The most enduring fruit there can be is converts. When we are engaged in mission, God also grants us our requests in prayer (cf. 14:13, 14; 15:7). Prayer might be called the lubricating fluid for the engine of fruit-bearing. It channels the presence of God into our mission and ensures his power in our task. Concluding this section, then, is the reiteration of the command to "love each other" (15:17), thus framing this section with the necessity of brotherly love (cf. 15:12). Love in the community is necessary to the success of the Christian mission.

The Hatred of the World (15:18–16:4a). The title of this section could easily be that of Bonhoeffer's classic work, *The Cost of Discipleship*. Jesus passed his ministry on to his disciples, and with it came the opposition of the world. This also serves as a kind of summary of John's theology of the "world" as a place of rebellion and rejection. Keener (2003:1017-1018) points out the apocalyptic background—that is, the hostility of the world of evil to its confrontation by the Spirit through the church (cp. 16:7-11). The contents can be presented as a kind of syllogism:

Major premise: The world hates Jesus.
Minor premise: Jesus loves and indwells the disciples.
Conclusion: The world hates his disciples.

The section thus has an A-B-A pattern as well: opposition (15:18-25), mission (15:26-27), opposition (16:1-4). While Jesus will be with us in a special way on our mission, the world will hate us. The first part centers on four conditional clauses (15:18-21). They are all concrete conditions presupposing the reality of the premises. "If the world hates you," Jesus said, it should be almost expected, for it hated Jesus first. In 1:10-11, the Jewish people are implied to be part of the world. Here it is explicit. The Jewish opponents of Jesus and his disciples are labeled "the world." Since the disciples were one with Jesus and part of his mission to the world, they would face the same opposition he did. While 15:18 speaks of what will happen (the world will hate you), 15:19 speaks of why. The world would accept the disciples "if [they] belonged to it," but instead they belong to the light and so "are no longer part of the world." Darkness hates light (3:19-20). The disciples are God's special people, the chosen ones, so they should not be unduly shocked when the world wants nothing to do with them. They simply do not belong to it. Peter puts it another way—we are "temporary residents and foreigners" here (1 Pet 2:11; cf. 1 Pet 1:1, 17). As Comfort and Hawley say (1994:250), "A Christian's distinction and separation from the world constitutes his sanctification, a sanctification not of his own choosing, but of the Lord's. This holy separation arouses the animosity of those from whom we are separate and distinct."

Jesus had just told them, in the context of the foot washing, that "slaves are not greater than their master" (13:16). There, the emphasis was the necessity of a servant heart; here, it was the necessity of sharing their Master's suffering (15:20). As they became more Christlike, they would face the same persecution he had. In fact, their message would be treated the same way (cf. note on 15:20). They were ambassadors of the Word of God and so were in direct opposition to the world. In the same way that the people of this world had rejected Jesus' message, they would reject the preaching of the disciples. Yet the true reason for this rejection was not the disciples or their message but rather the One who sent them (15:21). Jesus would send them on their mission, as he was sent by his Father (17:18; 20:21). It is "because of" Jesus that they would be hated, and in reality he was rejected because they rejected the One who sent him. The Jewish people claimed to know God, but they proved their true ignorance when they rejected his Son. In the same way that there are three stages of union—Father, Son, believers—there are the same three stages of rejection.

The guilt of the world and the Jewish people is explored in 15:22-25. The basis of the world's problem is willful ignorance, which equals rejection. Jesus had come with words (15:22) and works (15:24), and they had rejected both. As he said here, their guilt would not be so clear if he had never spoken to them (15:22), but since he had come, they "have no excuse for their sin." They had met the Son of God, and they had rejected God's final revelation. Instead of accepting the divine offer of salvation, they had responded to the Son with hatred (15:23). As Ridderbos says (1997:525), "This hatred is the human 'no' to the divine 'yes' expressed in the mission of his Son." In hating the Son, they had by extension hated the Father as well, and this after they had not only heard his words but also seen his works (15:24). So they were doubly without excuse. Remember that in John, Jesus' words and his works are the "signs" that point to the reality of Jesus and call people to salvation; yet even the world's hatred is part of God's larger purpose and was planned for in Scripture. John points out that it "fulfills what is written in their Scriptures. 'They hated me without cause'" (15:25). This is found in Psalms 35:19 and 69:4 (more likely the latter is the source here since it is quoted so often in the NT). In those psalms, David grieves over the number of enemies who oppose him; in John, Jesus is seen as the Davidic Messiah, suffering the same fate as David. In light of this parallel, Jewish guilt becomes all the more evident, for they had turned against their own Messiah "without cause."

Jesus' mission to the world was to be continued by the Paraclete and the disciples. That is the theme of 15:26-27 (in fact, it is also the primary theme of the farewell discourse). These are not two independent witnesses but one. The Spirit empowers and indwells the community of saints, and he inspires their witness (so Bultmann, Brown, Barrett; cf. Matt 10:20; Acts 5:32, 6:10). Once more, the origin of the Paraclete is stressed: "I will send you the Advocate. . . . He will come to you from the Father." The Father sent the Son, and the Father and Son together would send the Spirit. The mission to the world is a heavenly one, and the entire Godhead is involved. In fact, in the legal setting of the world's opposition, the "Advocate" would "testify" on behalf of Jesus. As "the Spirit of truth" (cf. 14:17; 16:13), the Paraclete ensures that the world hears what is absolutely true of Jesus. There will be no avoiding the light as it shines forth (1:5). In the Spirit's witness, the world's encounter with Jesus will continue unabated. This will take place primarily through the witness of the disciples (though not entirely, for the Spirit works in many ways, cf. 16:8-11), who had been with Jesus from the beginning. Jesus commanded the disciples to bear witness (the verb is an imperative). They were Jesus' chosen envoys from the start, and so it was their calling to continue his witness to the world. It was not only *their* calling—it is the task of every Christian to proclaim the truth of Jesus Christ to a lost world.

As the disciples engaged in mission through the presence of the Spirit (15:26-27), they should expect fierce opposition (16:1-4). Jesus covered this issue generally in 15:18-25 but here described specific trials they would undergo. The great danger was not just discouragement due to hard times but abandoning the faith—apostasy. He had already presented this danger in the vine and branches illustration (cf. 15:2, 6), and it was demonstrated in the case of Judas. Moreover, the entire Epistle to the

Hebrews is devoted to this problem, showing that it was a very real danger in the early church as well as today (see commentary on 15:6 for the theological issue). The first specific trial is expulsion from the synagogue (16:2), which happened to the man born blind (9:34; cf. 9:22; 12:42; for the historical issue see note on 9:22). Jesus warned of this in the Synoptics as well (Matt 10:17; Mark 13:9; Luke 21:12), and it was more than just being removed from synagogue membership. It meant being put under the ban and cut off from the Jewish community itself.

Second, they would not only be killed, but their murderers would "think they are doing a holy service for God" (16:2). In Mark 13:12, Jesus warned, "A brother will betray his brother to death, a father will betray his own child, and children will rebel against their parents and cause them to be killed." This began with Jesus, when Caiaphas said, "It's better for you that one man should die for the people than for the whole nation to be destroyed" (11:50). Since Christians came to be viewed as heretics by the Jews, it was thought that killing them was serving God (*Numbers Rabbah* 21 [191a]; *m. Sanhedrin* 9:6; so Beasley-Murray). It was thought that so long as there was blasphemy in the land, the Messiah would not come. Paul himself undoubtedly believed that arresting Christians, putting them in prison, and having them killed (Acts 8:3; 9:1; 26:10) was an act of piety on his part. As seen throughout Acts, the Jews, rather than the Romans, were the primary source of persecution in the early years of the church. The saddest aspect is that Christians, who have been the brunt of such religious persecution so often, have all too frequently been the instigators of the same kind of slaughter "in the name of Christ," as in the Crusades or the Jewish pogroms.

The reason for such rabid hatred is that "they have never known the Father or me" (16:3; cf. 15:21). This has been an emphasis since 1:10-11. Christ is the only path to knowing the Father (14:6-7, 9-10), so when one rejects the Son, one is rejecting the Father as well. As in 1:10, the failure to know means more than ignorance and connotes deliberate rejection of the truth. In 16:4 Jesus reiterates the point he made in 16:1. He was "telling [them] these things now" so that when the persecution began, the disciples would "remember" his "warning" not to "abandon [their] faith." They would then realize that Jesus had known all along what would happen and that he is sovereign over all such events. "When they happen" is literally "when their hour comes," and it is connected to the "hour" theology in John (see commentary on 2:4). The "hour" of their trial was instigated by Jesus' "hour" (so Carson).

The Work of the Paraclete (16:4b-15). Beginning in 16:4b (cf. Brown, Carson), Jesus moves to discuss his imminent departure. Jesus did not tell them about their difficult future ahead of time because he was with them and could watch over them. As his departure was at hand, they needed to know about both the future difficulties the world would bring (15:18-16:4) and the work of the Paraclete in this world (16:5-15). The last part of 16:5 ("not one of you is asking where I am going") is difficult in light of 13:36 (Peter asks, "Lord, where are you going?") and 14:5 (Thomas says, "We have no idea where you are going"). This has led many scholars (e.g., Brown, Schnackenburg) to consider this verse an addition by a later editor, who, possibly out of reverence for the tradition, did not correct the discrepancy it created. Yet there is a simpler understanding, seen in the present tense, "is asking." Jesus was concerned that the disciples were no longer asking questions about his departure, and he wanted them to be personally involved in the discussion once again (so Barrett, Blomberg, Keener). They were so filled with grief about his imminent passion (16:6) that they had failed to realize that it was more of a beginning than an end (so Burge). They were so concerned for their needs that they were not thinking of the larger picture—God's purpose in the events.

Therefore, Jesus clarified the eternal picture behind these events, and he did so from their perspective. He returned to the major theme of the farewell discourse and told them that unless he went away, "the Advocate won't come" (16:7) and God's plan would not be completed. It was the Cross that had to inaugurate the end times, and only then would the age of the Spirit begin (cf. 7:39). This was for the disciples' good, for then they would find their destinies as well. In fact, this was Peter's answer to the discouragement caused by persecution. He asked his readers to reflect upon the fact that they were living in the age of salvation (1 Pet 1:3-12), the time the prophets longed to see (1 Pet 1:10-12), thereby putting their persecution in proper perspective. The time the prophets longed for is indeed the age of the Spirit (Isa 11:1-2; 32:15; 42:1; 44:3; Ezek 37:14; 39:29; Joel 2:28).

Jesus elaborated on this by bringing to completion everything he had said regarding the work of the Paraclete in the world (16:8-11) and the church (16:12-15). First, he would "convict the world," a strong legal concept presupposing a courtroom scene—meaning to "prove the world guilty." The Paraclete is a prosecuting attorney providing irrefutable evidence of guilt (Keener, Köstenberger). Carson adds a further important point (1979:547-566; 1991:536-537) that the Paraclete is not pictured here arguing the case before God, the judge, but is rather "shaming the world and convincing it of its own guilt, thus calling it to repentance." The courtroom is the court of the mind, and the Spirit would convict through the witness of the disciples, as well as through the going forth of the gospel in diverse ways.

There are three areas in which the Spirit's convicting power operates (16:9-11). First, the world is convicted of "sin" because "it refuses to believe in me." The basic sin is unbelief. If they believed, they would find the light (3:18-21) and eternal life (3:16; 5:24). As a result of unbelief, the world lives in sin. Jewish opponents had accused Jesus of being a sinner (9:16, 24), when in reality they were steeped in sin and unbelief (5:47; 6:64; 7:48; 8:24; 9:41; 15:22).

Second, the world is convicted of "righteousness." The world condemned Jesus and put him on the cross as a blasphemer, but God demonstrated his innocence and true righteousness by raising him and taking him home to heaven. Beasley-Murray (1987:282) says it well: "The lifting up of Jesus on the cross, which in the world's eyes was the demonstration of Jesus' unrighteousness, was none other than the means of his exaltation to heaven by the Father; it was at once God's reversal of the verdict of men . . . the justification of Jesus thus is the vindication of his righteousness in life and his entrance upon *righteousness in glory* with the Father (cf.

12:23; 13:31-32; 17:1, 5; 1 Tim 3:16)." The disciples would "see [Jesus] no more" (16:10) because they would depend on the Paraclete, who would strengthen their witness. They would not see Jesus physically but would see him through the Paraclete (so Brown), who mediates his presence in the world and makes the righteousness of Jesus evident in the world as a convicting force.

Third, through the Paraclete the world stands convicted of judgment "because the ruler of this world has already been judged" (16:11). The world judged Jesus but is now judged by Jesus. Its judgment had been proven false (cf. 7:24; 8:16). In his passion, Jesus confronted and defeated "the ruler of this world" (12:31; 14:30), and the world shares his defeat the same way the saints share Christ's victory. This must be understood on the spiritual plane; Satan is still "god of this world" (2 Cor 4:4) but is defeated by those who "put on all of God's armor" (Eph 6:10-17). This is inaugurated eschatology at its best: Satan still has a hold on this world (Eph 6:12; 1 John 5:19), but his power has been broken, and the process of his demise has begun, to be completed at the eschaton (Rev 20:7-10).

Then Jesus turned to the work of the Paraclete among his followers (16:12-15). He told them he would like to say more, but he could not because they "can't bear it now." They were so beaten down with grief and worry that they simply were unable to hear any more. This is similar to 13:7, when Jesus said "you don't understand now," meaning it would become clear later. As Ridderbos says (1997:535), "Only the overpowering surprise of seeing him again after his resurrection will explain the riddle—partly in the light of the Scriptures (cf. 20:9) and above all through the assistance of the Spirit." Complete understanding of what Jesus had said would be provided by the Paraclete; this full understanding was promised to come after the Resurrection via the Spirit (2:22; 12:16; 13:7; 14:26).

It is the "Spirit of truth" who will "guide you into all truth" (16:13). This builds on 14:26 and the work of the Paraclete in teaching and reminding them of "everything I have told you." There is Old Testament background to the Spirit as guide (Ps 143:10; Isa 63:14, LXX; cf. Ps 25:4-5), and the idea is that the Spirit would continue the work of Jesus in leading the disciples to a full understanding of the divine truths. Comfort (1994:137) thinks John follows the classical meaning of the Greek *eis* [TG1519, ZG1650] as "into" used dynamically to mean the Spirit "penetrates" into the sphere of ultimate truth and guides the disciples into their destiny, the truth of Christ. This means that those who are guided will pattern their lives after the teaching (the verb means "guided on the way" and is connected with Jesus as the "way" [14:6]). Moreover, the Spirit guides entirely in accordance with Jesus' teaching, revealing not "his own" message but only "what he has heard" from Jesus. This is the process of divine revelation: In the same way that Jesus revealed only what he heard from the Father (3:34; 5:19; 7:16-17; 8:26, 28; 12:47-50; 14:10; 15:15), so the Spirit passes on what he has been given by Jesus. The disciples received these truths and passed them on via teaching and preaching.

Next, the Paraclete "will tell you about the future." This could be the immediate future—referring to the death, resurrection, and ascension of Jesus (so Whitacre)—

but much of that would happen before the Spirit was given (20:22). Or, this could be final eschatology, referring to apocalyptic predictions of the final events of human history, as in the book of Revelation (so Bernard, Johnston); however, there is little in this context to suggest such a switch of focus. Additionally, this could refer to the gift of prophecy, referring to Spirit-inspired prophets who guide the church (Burge). This could certainly be part of the meaning but can hardly constitute the whole. Most likely the statement refers in a comprehensive way to the Spirit guiding the church into the future, building on all that Jesus had said and done (so Brown, Beasley-Murray, Ridderbos, Keener, Köstenberger). "This includes the Paraclete's own witness to Jesus, his ministry to the world (16:8-11) primarily through the church (15:26-27), the pattern of life and obedience under the inbreaking kingdom, up to and including the consumation" (Carson 1991:540).

The purpose of the Spirit's work is to bring glory to Jesus (16:14-15), just as the Son had sought always to glorify the Father (7:18; 13:31; 14:13; 17:4). The way the Spirit does this is to guide the disciples into a full understanding of Jesus' teaching (repeating the point of 16:13a). As the Father's work is completed in the Son's work (5:19-20), so Jesus' work is completed in the Spirit's ministry. By the literal phrase "what is mine" ("all that belongs to the Father," NLT), John refers both to Jesus' words and his works—what he said and did. As Bruce says (1983:321), "Since the Father has given him 'all things' (13:3), what the Spirit discloses to the disciples is 'everything the Father has.'" The Spirit not only makes the Son known but also makes known the Father, who is revealed in the Son. In other words, the Spirit discloses the triune Godhead.

Sadness Turned to Joy (16:16-28). Jesus promised the disciples that, although his departure was imminent, "a little while after that, you will see me again." Many scholars see in this a triple schema in which Jesus simultaneously predicts his resurrection appearances, the coming of the Spirit, and his second coming (so Bruce; Brown; while Barrett takes it as Resurrection and Parousia). Certainly all three have been in the larger context, with the coming of the Spirit in 14:16, 26; the resurrection appearances in 14:18, and the Parousia in 14:2-3. In the context of 16:16-21, however, we must narrow it (as also in 14:18) to his resurrection appearances. In 7:33 and 13:33, "a little longer" meant the short time before Jesus' death. Here it means the short time between his death and his appearances. Shortly, they would not see him because he would die on the cross (and they would desert him, though this is not meant here), but shortly after that he would appear to them again as the risen Lord. As always, the disciples were completely befuddled (16:17-18), understanding neither "you won't/will see me" nor "a little while." They had no cognitive categories for the kind of Messiah who would die and rise again, and the thought that this incomprehensible event was soon to take place was too much for them.

The emphasis is on Jesus' knowledge (16:19): he fully "realized" their perplexity regarding his prophecy of his death and resurrection and so dispelled their confusion. Using another double *amēn* [TG281, ZG297] saying (16:20; see note on 1:51) to emphasize the importance of his message, he predicted once more the great turning point in human history, this time stating it from the disciples' vantage point and organizing it along the lines of his statements in 16:16 and 19. After the first "little while" (his death), the disciples would "weep and mourn" while "the world will rejoice" (16:20). At that time, their ignorance of what Jesus had been saying to them would cause them horrible grief. Not realizing that this would be the single greatest event ever to occur on planet Earth and the center of God's plan of salvation, they would weep and mourn as at a funeral (note the women in Mark 16:1, going to anoint a corpse!). At the same time the world, also not understanding the import of God's great victory on the cross, would rejoice at their having disposed of this troublemaker—seemingly once and for all. However, after the second "little while," Jesus would appear to them in glory, and their "grief will suddenly turn to wonderful joy." Then the incredible victory God accomplished in Christ would suddenly become clear to them.

To illustrate the sorrow turning to joy, Jesus used the imagery of birth pangs (16:21). This is obviously a perfect illustration of intense pain turning to wonderful joy, and it was used often in the Old Testament (Isa 26:17-21; 66:7-14; Jer 13:21; Mic 4:9-10) and New Testament (Mark 13:8) of the sufferings of God's people and of God's promised deliverance. In Isaiah 26:16-21, the phrase "a little while" is used, and the promise of resurrection from the dead is emphasized. In Isaiah 66:14, the statement "Your heart will rejoice" occurs. The Isaianic promise of salvation through suffering, along with the joy of experiencing divine deliverance, is at the heart of what Jesus was saying. The emphasis is on the divine initiative. He is the one to make the "new baby" (= eternal salvation) possible. In 16:22, Jesus applied this directly to the disciples, who would "sorrow" briefly and yet turn to joy when Jesus saw them again. Then no one would be able to rob them of their joy (16:22); it would never go away, for Jesus' resurrection is an eternal event and the "first of a great harvest" (1 Cor 15:20; cf. 1 Cor 15:23), guaranteeing their own resurrection. In it, Jesus ushered in the new age of joy and peace. It must be remembered by all of us that we live in this age of joy, so it is even more incumbent upon us that we greet each trouble we encounter with joy (cf. Jas 1:2; 1 Pet 1:6).

For the fourth time, Jesus promised them a new power in prayer (16:23-24; cf. 14:13-14; 15:7, 16), but this time it is linked to the new age that would begin after the Resurrection. Actually, there are two promises here, for first Jesus told them they would have a new understanding. When he said, "at that time [namely, when the new age arrives] you won't need to ask me for anything" (16:23), he was concluding the section on knowledge from 16:16-22. The disciples had shown a nearly complete lack of understanding in their questions (e.g., 16:17-19). Soon they would no longer need to address their questions to Jesus, for as the new dispensation began, they would have the Holy Spirit to give them understanding. Second, they would also have a new source of power in prayer. For the second time, he began with a double *amēn* [TG281, ZG297] to highlight its importance (cf. 16:20). According to 16:23a, they would no longer need to go to Jesus for information because they would have the Spirit. Now in 16:23b he said that they would no longer need to go to him in prayer because they would have direct access to the Father. This is, in a sense, the promise of a deeper intimacy with God (so Brown). Their union with Christ (15:4, 7) would produce a new union with the Father (14:20, 23).

Jesus is the key. They will ask "using my name," and the Father will "grant your request because you use my name" (16:23-24). Jesus' name is the basis of both the prayer and the answer to the prayer. As Brown says (1966:734), "Since Jesus dwells in the Christians, their petitions are in Jesus' name; since the Father is one with Jesus, the petitions He grants are granted in Jesus' name." Moreover, this promise is a sign of the new era; the disciples "haven't done this before" (16:24; i.e., they haven't prayed directly to the Father like this; this type of prayer is a gift for the new age). After the Cross and Resurrection inaugurate the new eschatological order, they will ask and receive, thereby experiencing "abundant joy." This is the joy now experienced by each believer; this prayer power is ours. It is easy to take our situation for granted. Carson (1991:546) thinks this association of prayer and joy compresses themes from chapter 15: "If that joy is part of the matrix of consistent obedience (15:11), that obedience, that remaining in Jesus (15:4) and his love (15:9) and his word (8:31), is the matrix out of which fruit-bearing springs, the fruit bearing that is the direct consequence of prayer (15:7, 8)."

Jesus had been speaking enigmatically "in figures of speech" (16:25)—those elusive illustrations in his farewell speech that were so hard to understand—but the days of obscure truths were almost over. Soon he would tell them plainly about the Father. The problem was not with the illustrations but with the deeper mysteries they represented. Jesus was promising them that in the period of the Spirit about to be introduced, these mysteries would finally be "plainly" understood. He also meant that his final address was almost finished, and the ensuing events would usher in the new era. This is the opposite of Mark 4:10-12, 33-34, where Jesus spoke plainly to the disciples and addressed the others "in parables." Mark shows that Jesus did not want the leaders to understand all his teachings because they had rejected God's offer of salvation. But Jesus did want the disciples to understand, and what remained obscure before his death and resurrection would be clear afterwards. Jesus had told them again and again of his departure and exaltation, but they could not comprehend it. Only after these events took place and the Spirit had arrived could they realize these things (cf. 2:22; 12:16; 14:26). So it is with us; we are living in the new age of understanding, but like the disciples, we need the Spirit to comprehend these truths fully.

The final of the seven all-embracing prayer promises then comes in 16:26 (cf. 14:13-14; 15:7, 16; 16:23, 24). The new relationship with the Father produces a new depth of asking and receiving. Previously, Jesus said he would answer their prayers directly (14:13, 14). Now he said they did not need his intercession, for "the Father himself loves you dearly." This does not mean that the believer no longer needs Jesus' intercessory work (mentioned in Rom 8:34; Heb 7:25; 1 John 2:1) but rather that by that work, Jesus produces a whole new intimacy between God and his children (see Brown, Köstenberger). That love produced a direct line to God, a whole new access to him (cf. Heb 10:19-20). We still pray "in [Jesus'] name" (i.e., in union with him), but the new relationship he has produced for us with God (Eph 2:6, "seated us with him in the heavenly realms") gives us the kind of efficacious prayer never before thought possible (cf. Jas 5:16b). The Father loves his Son (17:23-26) and so loves the Son's followers "because you love me and believe that I came from God" (16:27). There is a three-way relationship between the Father, the Son, and the believers. Jesus concluded his point about their relationship to the Father by reminding them of the descent-ascent basis of his mission: he "came from the Father" (descent—3:13, 31; 6:33, 50, 51, 58) and was now ready to "leave the world and return to the Father" (ascent—6:62; 20:17). The idea of his departing and returning to the Father is a major theme of the farewell discourse (13:33, 36; 14:2, 19-20, 28; 16:5, 16, 17, 19).

Jesus Predicts the Disciples' Desertion of Him (16:29-33). Jesus promised to speak plainly and predicted that the disciples would come to a new understanding (16:23a, 25). The disciples wanted badly to understand, and they seem to at first, saying "At last you are speaking plainly," and boasting, "Now we understand" (16:29-30). Their confession that Jesus "came from God" is similar to Peter's confession in 6:69 that Jesus is "the Holy One of God"; they were growing in their faith. They recognized that the crisis was coming to a head (though they had no clue as to what it would entail), and they wanted Jesus to know that they were finally with him and would be loyal to the end. But they still did not realize how little they truly knew. Jesus had said, "At that time [after the Resurrection] you won't need to ask me" (16:23), but they claimed this for the present as well: "You know everything, and there's no need to question you" (16:30). The confidence of their affirmation itself reveals their continuing misunderstanding; in one sense, they were completely faithful and wanted to understand, but in another sense they spoke out of ignorance and were full of a false bravado.

Jesus' response was to shatter their falsely based confidence (16:31-32). He asked them with a tinge of sarcasm, "Do you finally believe?" He did not doubt the degree of faith they had but wanted to bring them back to reality. Their faith was very real but incomplete; they had to realize where they actually stood—they were still in process as they had been all along. The situation here echoes 13:37-38, where Peter earlier showed the same bravado ("I'm ready to die for you"), and Jesus predicted his coming failure. Now he predicts a similar failure for all the disciples. The "time" (lit., "hour") when his destiny would be realized (2:4; 7:30; 8:20) is a major theme in John, and Jesus was saying that it had arrived. One of the events of that divinely appointed hour would be the desertion of his followers, when they would "be scattered, each one going his own way, leaving [Jesus] alone" (16:32). As in the Synoptics (Mark 14:27 and parallels), Jesus was alluding to Zechariah 13:7 ("strike down the shepherd, and the sheep will be scattered"), a passage on the apostasy of Israel. The disciples would completely fail Jesus and leave him all alone (the one exception being John; cf. 19:25-27). In the same way that Paul could never quite forgive himself for persecuting the church, the disciples had to live the rest of their lives knowing that while their Lord was suffering on the cross, they had cowered behind closed doors.

Jesus would not be completely deserted however: "Yet I am not alone because the Father is with me" (16:32). In 8:28-29, Jesus said, "when you have lifted up the Son of Man on the cross, then you will understand that I AM he. . . . And the one who sent me is with me—he has not deserted me." This was about to come to pass; even though his closest followers would desert him, his Father would not. Still, though the disciples would desert him, Jesus would not desert them. In fact, he was telling them this not to reject them or even to rebuke them but rather "so that you may have peace in me" (16:33). The discourse proper (13:31–16:33) ends on a note of encouragement. The reason is that the love of Jesus and his Father can and would overcome the personal failures of the disciples. They would be given the strength to transcend their "trials and sorrows" on this earth. In the midst of troubles and difficulties, they would have "peace," not because life is easy but because Christ was with them. Notice it is "peace in me," not a peaceful life, that was promised. The basis of this promised peace is, "I have overcome the world" (cf. 1:5). Christ was victorious not only over the world but also over "the ruler of this world" (12:31; 14:30). Satan and this world were conquered at the Cross; the true battle is over. But Satan, and the world with him, is filled with rage because his time is short (Rev 12:12). Still, in the midst of our personal battles, we must also "take heart" and be aware that we are on the winning side and can also be victorious by depending on God and Christ (Jas 4:7-8; 1 Pet 5:6-9).

◆   ### 3. The farewell prayer of Jesus (17:1-26)

After saying all these things, Jesus looked up to heaven and said, "Father, the hour has come. Glorify your Son so he can give glory back to you. [2]For you have given him authority over everyone. He gives eternal life to each one you have given him. [3]And this is the way to have eternal life—to know you, the only true God, and Jesus Christ, the one you sent to earth. [4]I brought glory to you here on earth by completing the work you gave me to do. [5]Now, Father, bring me into the glory we shared before the world began.

[6]"I have revealed you* to the ones you gave me from this world. They were always yours. You gave them to me, and they have kept your word. [7]Now they know that everything I have is a gift from you, [8]for I have passed on to them the message you gave me. They accepted it and know that I came from you, and they believe you sent me.

[9]"My prayer is not for the world, but for those you have given me, because they belong to you. [10]All who are mine belong to you, and you have given them to me, so they bring me glory. [11]Now I am departing from the world; they are staying in this world, but I am coming to you. Holy Father, you have given me your name;* now protect them by the power of your name so that they will be united just as we are. [12]During my time here, I protected them by the power of the name you gave me.* I guarded them so that not one was lost, except the one headed for destruction, as the Scriptures foretold.

[13]"Now I am coming to you. I told them many things while I was with them in this world so they would be filled with my joy.

¹⁴I have given them your word. And the world hates them because they do not belong to the world, just as I do not belong to the world. ¹⁵I'm not asking you to take them out of the world, but to keep them safe from the evil one. ¹⁶They do not belong to this world any more than I do. ¹⁷Make them holy by your truth; teach them your word, which is truth. ¹⁸Just as you sent me into the world, I am sending them into the world. ¹⁹And I give myself as a holy sacrifice for them so they can be made holy by your truth.

²⁰I am praying not only for these disciples but also for all who will ever believe in me through their message. ²¹I pray that they will all be one, just as you and I are one—as you are in me, Father, and I am in you. And may they be in us so that the world will believe you sent me.

²²I have given them the glory you gave me, so they may be one as we are one. ²³I am in them and you are in me. May they experience such perfect unity that the world will know that you sent me and that you love them as much as you love me. ²⁴Father, I want these whom you have given me to be with me where I am. Then they can see all the glory you gave me because you loved me even before the world began!

²⁵O righteous Father, the world doesn't know you, but I do; and these disciples know you sent me. ²⁶I have revealed you to them, and I will continue to do so. Then your love for me will be in them, and I will be in them."

17:6 Greek *have revealed your name*; also in 17:26.   17:11 Some manuscripts read *you have given me these [disciples]*.   17:12 Some manuscripts read *I protected those you gave me, by the power of your name*.

NOTES

17:1-26 The outline I use, which topically divides Jesus' prayer into four sections (17:1-5, 6-19, 20-23, 24-26), is also utilized by Schnackenburg, Morris, Carson, Comfort, Whitacre, and Köstenberger. Yet there is another possibility, used by Brown, Burge, and Blomberg: three sections (17:1-8 [personal prayer], 17:9-19 [disciples], 17:20-26 [future followers]), with each section containing parallel themes—each begins with the basic request (17:1, 9, 20), followed by a theme of glory (17:1-5, 10, 22), an address to the Father (17:5, 11, 21), an emphasis on disciples given to Jesus by the Father (17:2, 9, 24), and Jesus revealing the Father to his disciples (17:6, 14, 26).

17:3 *the way to have eternal life.* Many have believed this to be a parenthetical verse, perhaps a midrashic exposition of 17:2 by John himself (Barrett, Schnackenburg, Witherington, Blomberg), but it flows naturally from 17:2 and is better seen as Jesus' own commentary on the meaning of eternal life (so Carson, Whitacre).

17:4 *completing the work.* It is common among scholars to believe that 17:4 refers to the work Jesus had completed up to this point and to include the future work on the cross in 17:5, but that is not the best way to understand the statement. As Burge says (2000:463), "It is best to see this finished work as including the hour of glorification in which Jesus is now engaged. This work includes his death, resurrection, and return to the Father, as much as it includes the revelation of the Father to the world."

17:4-8 Michaels (1989:294) understands 17:4-8 (apart from 17:5) not as a series of requests but as a summary of Jesus' earthly mission, "a kind of last report to the Father of what Jesus has done on earth in the course of his ministry."

17:11 *you have given me your name.* Some mss (D¹ cop^sa) replace the dative relative pronoun *hō* [^TG3739, ^ZG4005] with the accusative (of the same) *hous*, thus changing the meaning of the phrase to "you have given me these [disciples]." The better mss ($\mathfrak{P}$60 $\mathfrak{P}$66^vid $\mathfrak{P}$107 ℵ A B C et al.) have the dative—thus, the reading found here.

by the power of your name. Scholars are divided as to whether it should be instrumental ("*by* your name"), intimating that his powerful name is the means of protecting his people (so Bultmann, Bruce, Köstenberger) or locative (*"in* your name"), making this a prayer that God keep them faithful to his name (so Schnackenburg, Lindars, Beasley-Murray, Carson, Ridderbos). It may be that both are correct (so Brown, Keener), but of the two, the instrumental may be favored as the power that protects the disciples. While they are certainly kept "in his name," the emphasis is on the power that provides the protection.

17:12 *by the power of the name you gave me.* The same textual variation as that found in 17:11 with the dative and the accusative occurs again here, and for the reasons stated in the note above, the preferred reading is the dative *hō* [TG3739, ZG4005] and the reading found here.

17:13 *I told them many things while I was with them in this world.* There are three possible interpretations of the "many things": Jesus' teaching throughout his time with his disciples, the farewell discourse itself, or the prayer of ch 17 in particular. The most likely is the second, for Jesus throughout this discourse had been preparing the disciples for his final departure from this world.

17:23 *that you love them.* Does this mean that the world will know of God's love for itself (Bernard) or for the community of disciples (Brown)? God's love for the world is expressed in 3:16, but according to 15:19, the world hates the disciples, and in 17:9, Christ says he is not praying for the world. Moreover, throughout John, the love of God and Christ for the believer is manifest. Therefore, the love of God for believers is the more likely meaning here.

17:25-26 *the world doesn't know you.* The verbs in these verses are aorist and probably sum up the past situation (so Westcott, Whitacre)—"the world hasn't known you, but I have." Also, the difficult syntax (*kai . . . de . . . kai* [TG2532/1161, ZG2779/1254]) is probably best understood this way: "*Although* the world hasn't known you, *yet* I have known you, *and* these have come to know you sent me" (so Beasley-Murray).

COMMENTARY

This has often been called "the high priestly prayer" on the grounds that Jesus was interceding for his disciples. Yet some (Westcott, Hoskyns, Witherington, Keener) prefer to call it "the prayer of consecration" due to Jesus' dedication of himself to God in 17:1, 19. Both aspects are present in the prayer. Jesus was concerned for the glory of God, for his final righteous deeds, and for his disciples.

Jesus concluded his farewell discourse with this powerful "high priestly prayer," a feature that is congruent with Old Testament and Jewish parallels (Gen 49; Deut 32–33; *Jubilees* 22; *4 Ezra* 8; *2 Baruch* 48) but is at the same time unique because it was uttered by the "one and only Son," the incarnate Word of God (1:14). This is the longest prayer of Jesus in the Gospels, and it is also the deepest theologically. Though Jesus was praying from the perspective of this world, he was also praying from the perspective of the eternal realm, as if he was already with the Father (17:11, lit., "I am no longer in this world," so Brown, Whitacre). It is linked thematically with the rest of the discourse and indeed functions almost as a summary of the fourth Gospel as a whole, addressing Jesus' obedience to and glorification of his Father, Jesus as the revelation of God, his death and resurrection as glory, the choosing of the disciples and their mission to the world, their unity as modeled on the unity of the Godhead, and their destiny to be in the presence of Jesus and God (so Carson, cf. Black 1988). At the same time, this is more than a prayer—it was also meant as final teaching and preparation for the disciples so that they could understand the true significance of the Passion events (so Beasley-Murray). There is a very interesting parallel between this and the Lord's Prayer in Matthew 6:9-13 (so Blomberg following Walker 1982), with only one element ("forgive us our sins") omitted:

> Our Father in heaven // "looked up to heaven. . . Father" (17:1a)
> Your name be kept holy // "give glory back to you" (17:1b)
> Your Kingdom come // "gives eternal life" (= "kingdom" in John) (17:2)
> Your will be done on earth // "on earth by completing the work" (17:4)
> Give us today the food we need // "All who are mine belong to you" (17:10)
> Don't let us yield to temptation // "protect them by the power of your name" (17:11)
> Rescue us from the evil one // "keep them safe from the evil one" (17:15)

Jesus' prayer can be outlined topically as prayer for his own glory (17:1-5), for the disciples (17:6-19), for the unity of the church (17:20-23), and for the perfection of the believers (17:24-26). In the discussion below this outline is followed.

Prayer for His Glorification (17:1-5). As in 11:41, Jesus began his prayer by looking "up to heaven," a natural thing to do since heaven was his home. A basic Jewish prayer posture was to raise one's hands and look up to heaven, acknowledging total dependence on the Father (cf. Ps 123:1, "I lift my eyes to you, O God, enthroned in heaven"). Jesus began every prayer but one (Mark 15:34, the cry of dereliction) with "Father" (cf. 11:41; 12:27); behind this is a special filial relationship (the "Abba" theme is probably present, connoting a deep intimacy between them, see note on 5:17). The "hour has come" brings the culmination of this major theme (found also in 2:4; 7:30; 8:20). Jesus' hour is already said to have arrived in 12:23, 27, 31; 13:1 because the "hour" refers to the whole time of Jesus' glory and so starts at the beginning of Passion week.

Note that Jesus does not bring a grocery list of requests like most of us do. His prayer for himself is very simple in 17:1-5 and is stated in 17:1, "Glorify your Son so he can give glory back to you." Jesus asked his Father to fulfill his promise and the imagery of all the "lifted up" passages (3:14; 8:28; 12:32)—namely, to turn the shame of the Cross (lifted up on the cross) to glory (lifted up to glory). John is unique in his constant emphasis on the Cross as the time of Jesus' exaltation. "Glory" means "praise, honor, veneration." God was elevating Jesus on the cross to the place of honor (so Burge; Carson—"clothed in splendor"). Yet even here, Jesus' main concern was not for himself but for his Father, that his glory might bring glory to God. The glory theme of the whole Gospel culminates here. The glory shown in his sign-miracles (2:11; 11:4, 40) was but a foretaste of this glory. As Jesus is glorified by God (5:44; 8:54), he glorifies God in himself (7:18; 13:31-32).

The basis of Jesus' glory is the "authority" God has given him (17:2). The "authority over everyone" (lit., "over all flesh") is similar to "all authority in heaven and on earth" in the great commission (Matt 28:18) and means universal, cosmic author-

ity. This undoubtedly refers especially to the authority over life and judgment that
God gave Jesus (5:21-23; cf. Dan 7:14). There is a strong grammatical symmetry
between 17:1-2, as the references to both Jesus' glory and his authority are followed
by purpose clauses (so Carson, Burge). Jesus sought glory so that he could return
that glory to his Father, and he received authority so that he could bestow eternal
life on his followers. In fact, the two verses are intimately bound together, for Jesus'
glory is especially seen in his power to bestow life. Certainly he has authority "over
everyone"—the unsaved as well as the saved—but his power over the unbeliever is
seen in judgment, while the saved experience his redemptive power. Moreover, the
gift of life necessitated his death on the cross, and the Cross was his moment of
glory, especially because it is the atoning sacrifice that brings life. Note also the
emphasis on divine election (17:2); these are those the Father has "given" the Son
(cf. 6:37, 39; 17:6, 9, 24).

Jesus expanded on the meaning of this new creation, which the Cross made possible (17:3). The "way" to eternal life is "to know you, the only true God," and the
Son, "Jesus Christ," who was "sent to earth." As elsewhere in John, knowledge is
synonymous with belief and indicates salvific knowledge. As Hendriksen says
(1953:350), this "refers not to merely abstract knowledge but to joyful *acknowledge-
ment* of his sovereignty, glad *acceptance* of his love, and infinite *fellowship* with his
person." The phrase, "the only true God," emphasizes the fact that he alone is God
(cf. 1 Thess 1:9, 1 John 5:20), the only source of eternal life. To know God, moreover, is to know "Jesus Christ"—unusual on Jesus' lips but not unprecedented in
Scripture (cf. the Heb. of 2 Sam 7:20, where David calls himself "David" in his
prayer). Since Jesus is the only "way" (14:6), people must have saving knowledge of
him in order to have eternal life. We cannot know the Sender without knowing his
Sent One (1:18; 14:7).

Then Jesus returned to the theme of glory (17:4-5), reversing the order from his
statement in 17:1. First, he reflected on the earthly glory he brought to the Father "by
completing the work" that the Father gave him to do. Every moment of his life from
the Incarnation onward had been a moment of glory (1:14, "we have seen his glory"),
and Jesus' "work" refers not only to his miraculous works but to all of God's work that
he had been sent to accomplish. As he said in 5:17, "My Father is always working, and
so am I," and in 5:19, "Whatever the Father does, the Son also does." The work God
gave Jesus was primarily the work of salvation, and it implicitly included the Cross
and the Resurrection, when that work would indeed be completed. Verse 5 moves
from Jesus' earthly work of glory to the preincarnate glory he shared with the Father.
Jesus was asking that this glory be reinstated to him in his exaltation after his earthly
work was done. This indicates that the Incarnation to some extent involved a forfei-
ture of that glory (so Haenchen, Carson, cf. 6:62; Phil 2:6-7). During his life, he did
possess "glory," but that was the glory of the incarnate Son (1:14; 2:11; 8:50, 54), a
glory given by the Father and recognized by his followers. After his exaltation, he
returned to the complete glory of the Godhead, a glory that is beyond human experience and knowledge, entailing his transcendence over the world (so Schnackenburg).

Prayer for His Disciples (17:6-19). Jesus' glorious work is intimately connected to his disciples, so it was natural that he should address their situation. He began by praying about why the disciples needed his intervention as they faced their life without him. First, they were the ones God gave him from the world. This divine gift was part of their election (6:37, 39; 10:29), as God chose them out of the world (they were formerly estranged and without hope, like the Gentiles in Eph 2:12) to be his possession (Titus 2:14; 1 Pet 2:9). This is why Jesus adds, "They were always yours,"—they had been chosen before the creation of the world (Eph 1:4). As his own possession, God then "gave" these chosen ones to Jesus (the idea of God giving occurs 12 times in this chapter) so that they now belonged to him. Because of this, Jesus "revealed" God (lit., "your name") to them—that is, progressively brought them to a greater awareness of God in their lives. This is John's encounter theology at its best. To meet Jesus is to meet God, and when he speaks, it is with the voice of God. Thus, he reveals God in all he says and does. Keener (2003:1056) links this with the Jewish belief that God's name would not be fully revealed (sanctified) until the coming age, so this is part of John's realized eschatology—the final age has begun. As a result, the disciples "kept your word"—that is, obeyed God's commands (cf. 14:15, 21, 23)—just as Jesus obeyed (8:55; 14:31; 15:10). This hardly means they were paragons of obedience—we have seen their failures all too often—but they had committed themselves to his word and sought to follow his commands.

The centrality of God's gift continues in 17:7-8. In 17:3, the disciples are said to "know" God, and here they "know" (the perfect tense here indicates a continuing state of knowledge, so Carson) that every aspect of Christ's life is a divine "gift" (17:7). They recognized the basic fact of Jesus' message, that at every level he was tied to the Father. This is another reflection of Jesus' subordination to God while on earth, but it also means that behind every single thing Jesus says and does is the authority of God. This is the great mystery—Jesus is at the same time one with God (10:30) and completely dependent on God. This is at heart the mystery of the Incarnation. The primary area in which this is true is Jesus' teaching. God gave the message to Jesus, and he passed it on to the disciples (17:8). Moreover, the disciples "accepted" that message and believed that God had indeed "sent" Jesus. This is another aspect of their obedience (17:6). This is the path we all must follow—belief, acceptance, obedience. We are at least as imperfect as the disciples, but again God has chosen us as his own and given us to Jesus—we are jars of clay with God's treasures within (cf. 2 Cor 4).

As imperfect, yet divinely chosen, instruments, the disciples desperately needed Christ's intercession, so he prayed especially for them (17:9). When Jesus said, "My prayer is not for the world," he hardly meant that he would never pray for the world. The world is the object of divine love (3:16) and Jesus' salvific work (4:42)—indeed, of the mission of the triune Godhead (cf. "Mission" in the Introduction)—but the disciples are the true people of God, those chosen from the world to "belong to" God and to be given to Jesus (17:9b-10; cf. 17:6). They are the ones who most need the divine protection and power. Literally, 17:10 says "All that is mine is yours, and all that is yours is mine," very similar to the words of the father to the prodigal son in Luke 15:31, and this implies that the disciples are participants in Jesus' relationship with the Father and have all they could ever need, similar to the idea of Matthew 6:11: "Give us today the food we need" (so Blomberg). Moreover, they are the ones who "bring [Jesus] glory" (17:10), just as the Father does. They perceived his "glory" (2:11) and worshiped him as "the Holy One of God" (6:69), and they would proclaim his name in the world as his sent ones (17:18; 20:21).

Finally, the disciples needed prayer because they were "staying in this world" while Jesus departed to the Father (17:11a). He had already told them of the terrible opposition they would experience (15:18–16:4), and they would have to face it without their Lord there to undergird them. In fact, Jesus was actually saying, "I am no more in the world." While he was speaking to them, in his heart he was already with the Father (so Schnackenburg). Their hour of terrible isolation was already in process. Of course, he had already told them he would be back for them (14:2-3) and would send the Spirit to them in their time of need (14:16-17), but they would still be without him in their imminent troubles.

Jesus addressed his prayer to his "Holy Father," a title found only here but reflecting Jewish prayers to God, the Holy One (cf. Isa 49:7; 54:5; Hos 11:9; Hab 1:12; 1 John 2:20; Rev 16:5). Holiness is the key characteristic of God, and his whole being flows out of it. Here, the title prepares for Jesus' prayer that the Father "make [the disciples] holy" (17:17), as Jesus would give himself as a "holy sacrifice for them" (17:19). He prayed that God's holiness might radiate through his sacrifice on the cross and through the life of holiness that would result for the disciples. The basis of the prayer is "the name" God had given Jesus, which was God's own name. In the Bible, the "name" of God is the means by which he reveals himself to his people. As God, Jesus partook of God's holy name and is the final revelation of God. This is further reflected in the phrase, "as we are one" (17:22; cf. 10:30). Jesus asked that the very holy name he shared with God would now protect the disciples by its power (17:11; lit., "keep them in your name"). The disciples would not be left alone. They would have the Spirit and the powerful name of God watching over them. Their lacking strength would be undergirded by the very power and might of God (cf. Eph 1:19-20). The goal of Jesus' prayer was unity—"that they will be united just as we are" (17:11). This prepares for the major teaching in 17:20-23 and builds on the earlier statements of 10:16 and 11:52. Unity in the church is a fragile state that is often disrupted by self-centered leaders, as proven by most of the Epistles in the New Testament that address fractured churches. In this sense, the prayer for protection may have in mind not so much the danger of persecution from without but the danger of schism from within; the disciples needed protection from themselves and the human tendency toward conflict.

Jesus then reflected on his past protection of his followers (17:12). Up to this time, he had been there to protect them, but he was soon departing, so they would need his Father's power behind them. In fact, "not one was lost" except Judas, who was "headed for destruction" (lit., "the son of perdition") in accordance with prophecy. In this case, "son of" refers to Judas's divinely appointed destiny—damnation and destruction. The "Scriptures" probably refers to Psalm 41:9, "Even my best friend, the one I trusted completely, the one who shared my food, has turned against me." Jesus had used this of Judas (13:18). There are a few passages cited by New Testament writers as fulfilled in the life of Judas: Psalms 69:25 and 109:8 in Acts 1:20; Zechariah 11:12-13 in Matthew 27:9-10. This is Jewish typology at its best: the events in the Old Testament are analogous with and ultimately fulfilled in the life of Jesus. The point here is that Jesus' power had always been sufficient; even though Judas did betray him, Jesus knew about it all along, and his power was sufficient even there (cf. 6:64, 70-71; 13:10-11, 21, 26-27).

Jesus' departure to the Father was imminent; soon he would be "coming" home to the Father (17:13). He turned from reflecting on his past protection of his disciples to his past teaching of them, particularly in the farewell discourse beginning at 13:31. Interestingly, six of the seven occurrences of the Greek noun for "joy" (*chara* [TG5479, ZG5915]) in John occur in this discourse, with the list culminating in 17:13 (15:11; 16:20, 21, 22, 24). There Jesus said his teaching was intended to impart his joy to them—so "your joy will overflow" (15:11)—promising them that their grief at his departure would be turned to joy in all its fullness (16:20-24). The basis of this joy was not only communion with Jesus but the fact that he had "given them" God's "word" (17:14)—that is, the truth about God and his plans for the world. Here is the basic problem: because the world is darkness and therefore hates the light (3:19-21), the world by necessity hates Jesus and therefore his disciples (15:18–16:4); this is because the disciples no more belong to this world than Jesus does. The difference is that Jesus understood this while his followers did not (the same problem Christians have today). All who belong to God are "temporary residents and foreigners" (1 Pet 2:11; cf. 1 Pet 1:1, 17) who have been chosen out of this world (15:19) and do not belong to it.

Since they were no longer a part of this world but understood this only partially, they needed God's protection (17:15; cf. 17:11b). At the same time, it was God's will that they remain in this world. This is the classic definition of holiness; as in the modern proverb, "We are apart from this world and yet a part of this world." Jesus was not asking God to remove them from the world; they would become the next stage of God's mission to the world (17:18; 20:21). Rather, Jesus prayed that his Father would "keep them safe from the evil one," possibly in a reflection of the Lord's prayer (Matt 6:13; cf. discussion above). Christ had conquered the "ruler of this world" (12:31; 14:30; 16:11), but Satan is still the "god of this world" (2 Cor 4:4; cf. 1 John 5:19) and so seeks to sift the disciples like wheat (Luke 22:31) and "devour" (1 Pet 5:8) Jesus' followers. They would only be victorious by focusing on Jesus (Rev 12:11), so Jesus asked his Father to protect them against Satan. Again, the reason is that "they do not belong to this world" (17:16; cf. 17:14). The world is controlled by Satan, so to be victorious over the world means to conquer Satan as well. Carson concludes (1991:565), "But if the Christian pilgrimage is inherently perilous, the safety that only God himself can provide is assured, as certainly as the prayers of God's own Son will be answered."

When God protects his people, he does so by sanctifying them, making them holy (17:17). The "Holy Father" (17:11) enables his chosen followers to share his holiness. In the Old Testament, this concept is often used of consecrating or setting apart people for God's service (Witherington takes this as the meaning here), whether the nation as a whole (Exod 19:6) or a priest (Exod 28:41) or prophet (Jer 1:5). Those sanctified are in a sense sacred vessels in God's sanctuary. Following the holiness code (Lev 11:44; 19:2; 20:26), the command is "You must be holy because I am holy" (1 Pet 1:16). It may well be that the emphasis is both on the sphere of holiness (i.e., *in* the truth) and the means by which it takes place (*by* your truth, 17:17; cf. 17:12). Since Jesus is "truth" (14:6), holiness takes place in union with him and his word (i.e., in obedience to his teaching). As Jesus was set apart and sent into the world (10:36) so are the disciples (17:18). Therefore, the process occurs as Jesus asks the Father to "teach them [his] word, which is truth" (17:17). There are three stages in this: Jesus leads them into truth (14:6); then the Spirit of truth leads them into truth (14:17; 15:26; 16:13); and finally they live by the truth of the Word and obey it (8:32; 14:15, 21, 23). Holiness is more than just being set apart from the world; it is more about being set apart for God—that is, thinking as God would have us think and living as God would have us live.

Holiness also involves mission (17:18). A further transfer from Christ to his followers occurs here: Earlier it was glory (17:1-5), then name (17:6-11), unity (17:11), and the life of holiness (17:17). Jesus transfers his mission to his followers: "As you sent me into the world, I am sending them into the world" (17:18). The sending of the disciples is actually stated in the aorist tense in Greek, meaning that their mission began when Jesus chose them, though it would attain its peak at Pentecost. So, they too were "sent ones" (see commentary on 3:17), God's agents or envoys to the world. This prepares for the more fully developed theology of mission in 20:21-23 and builds on the divinely ordained three stages: Jesus' mission to the world as sent by God in 3:17, 34, and throughout John; the Spirit as sent into the world in 14:16-17, 26; 16:7-8; and the completion of the process when the disciples are sent out in mission (17:18; 20:21; cf. Köstenberger 1998a). Carrying on the ministry of Jesus in the world, they were to be his voice and presence in the world as the Spirit of Christ indwelt and empowered them.

Finally, Jesus turns from the sanctification of his followers to the sanctification of himself, saying literally, "For them I sanctify myself" (17:19). Elsewhere it is said that God has set Jesus apart for his mission (10:36), but here Jesus sets himself apart. His mission centers on his sacrificial death, thus the NLT translation, "I give myself as a holy sacrifice for them." He was consecrating himself as a sacrifice (cf. Exod 13:2; Deut 15:19, 21) and thus saw his death as a sacrifice for their salvation. This parallels his saying at the Last Supper, "This is my body, which is given for you" (Luke 22:19, so Hoskyns, Beasley-Murray, Whitacre), and evokes the image of atonement (Köstenberger). The process by which the disciples were to be made holy was built on Jesus' own sanctifying work. The process by which we give ourselves over to God follows Jesus' supreme example and is made possible only by his supreme sacrifice. Jesus' death is the only thing that could make a world mission possible, as seen in 10:15-16, 18 (lay down his life), 12:24 (the seed dying), and 12:32 (lifted up to draw all people to himself).

Prayer for the Unity of the Future Church (17:20-26). In this section, Jesus extended his prayer from the present disciples to all future believers. He sent his disciples on mission in 17:18; here he brought before the Lord all those who would respond to their mission. There are two criteria: they believe not just in Jesus but in who he is (Johannine faith), and they believe "through their message"—that is, as a result of the Johannine "chain of revelation" (Father to Son, to Spirit, to disciples, to the world; cf. commentary on 17:18). His prayer repeats the request of 17:11— the unity of the church as built on the unity of the Godhead (17:21). A couple of years ago, I spent a long weekend in Denver with about 20 other scholars and Christian leaders, trying to work out a policy statement (unpublished) on racial and denominational reconciliation. On the latter, the Lord led us to center on John 17:21-23, and this was our core statement:

> The unity of the church (mentioned three times in this passage) is a reflection of and witness to the unity of the Godhead in heaven (found twice), and the very mission of the church is at stake (found twice). The unity of the church is not an option but a mandate, and a fractured church (too often the case) is an abomination in the eyes of the Lord!

The unity of the church is a union of love (13:34-35; 15:12, 17; 1 John 3:11) but it cannot be simply reduced to love. The key is in the power of God and the Spirit: It is a horizontal unity (among ourselves) made possible by a vertical unity (the indwelling union with the Father and the Son; cf. 6:56; 15:4-7; 1 John 2:24; 3:24; 4:15). Christ emphasized, "May they be in us" (17:21); unity cannot be achieved until we are one with God and Christ. Only then can we be "one" with each other. It is a dynamic union, involving a strong sense of community (10:16; 15:5, 6; cf. 1 Cor 12:12-26; Eph 4:3-6; 1 Tim 3:15). Further, it is a unity built on the truth of the Word (17:17); since the people of God live by the same eternal truths, they must overcome their differences (even theological) and find a deeper unity (cf. the discussion of unity and purity at 10:16).

The basis of oneness among the believers is the oneness between the Father and the Son, which is the major Christological theme of John's Gospel (e.g., 1:1, 18; 5:17, 19; 10:27-30, 38; 14:10, 11, 20; 17:11, 21-23; see Staton 1997). If the Son does everything on the basis of his unity with the Father, how much more are we dependent on that same unity! As Ridderbos says (1997:561), "The dominant thought of Jesus' prayer is that the church's unity may be controlled by, and find its criterion in, its unity with the Father and the Son, that is, in Jesus' coming into the world and his work in the world in keeping his unity with the Father." Kysar (2001:374-375) goes even further, calling the church a new household in which the believers share in the communion and relationship of the triune Godhead. The purpose of it all is "so the world will believe you sent me" (i.e., rest their faith on the fact that Jesus is the Sent One, the final revealer of the Father). The church, empowered by the Spirit (15:26, 27), is a witness to the reality of God in Jesus. In this sense, there are four dimensions to this unity—God with Jesus, the Godhead with the believer, believers with one another, and a united mission to the world (cf. the excellent charts in Schnackenburg and Whitacre).

Next, this unity consists of a shared "glory" (17:22). God has showered his glory on Christ (1:14; 8:50, 54; 11:4; 12:28; 17:5, 24), and now Christ was sharing that glory with his followers. He bore the glory of God, and now the church is the glory-bearer. The shekinah glory of God first moved from the mountain to the Tabernacle and dwelt among the people of God shortly after the Exodus (Exod 24:16; 40:34). In Jesus, that shekinah glory became incarnate (1:14), and now the glory was passing to Jesus' followers as they were indwelt by him (so Burge). This glory demands unity—"so they may be one as we are one" (17:22). To have the glory of God, we must exemplify the unity of God. Obviously, this is not meant in an absolutist sense, otherwise all the dissenting denominations and church traditions (e.g., Reformed vs. dispensational vs. charismatic; Arminian vs. Calvinist; high church vs. low church) would be entirely emptied of the glory of God. It does, however, mean that the church's glory is diminished and is not what it could be and should be.

Thus the need is for "perfect unity," the complete oneness between different factions in the church that can only come from Christ—"I am in them and you are in me" (17:23). The mutual indwelling of the Godhead with us can overcome the many differences—temperament, theological outlook, worship style, etc.—that tend to fracture the church. When we are one with the Son, who is one with the Father, we can rise above petty conflicts to attain a higher, perfect unity. Then the world will know not only the nature of Christ but also the love of God for his own— "You love them as much as you love me." In Revelation 3:9, we read Christ's promise to the beleaguered saints at Philadelphia that he would make their persecutors "come and bow down at your feet. They will acknowledge that you are the ones I love." As Keener notes (2003:1061), "The way believers treat one another is an essential component of proclaiming Jesus to the world . . . the same kind of witness concerning Jesus' origin as the raising of Lazarus." (Both 11:42 and 17:23 present actions as testimonies "that [God] sent [Jesus].")

Jesus turned from the present to the future, asking his Father for two things for "these whom you have given me" (17:24; referring back to their election in 6:37, 39). First, he prayed that his disciples might be "where I am," which could mean he wanted them to be beside him as he was going through the terrible events to come. They were clearly not with him through the Passion events, however, and the context here does not really support this reading. Most likely, Jesus wanted them with him in his final glory in heaven. In 12:26, Jesus told his disciples and the Greeks that "my servants must be where I am." Then in 14:2-3 he said he was going to heaven to prepare a place for them and would return for them so that they would always be with him. The prayer of 17:24 is toward the fulfillment of that promise. While in this world the disciples would experience constant trouble and opposition, but they would be in union with the Godhead now and have the promise of eternal life in heaven afterward.

Second, Jesus prayed that the disciples might "see all the glory you gave me because you loved me even before the world began," (17:24b) a reference back to 17:5, where Jesus asked to be restored to "the glory we shared before the world began." As Comfort says (1994:146), "Jesus lifted the veil to give us a glimpse of his eternal, preincarnate relationship with the Father." Jesus' glory, resulting from the Father's love for him, was observable from the start (1:14; cf. 2 Cor 3:18; 4:6), seen even in the first miracle at Cana (2:11) and culminating in the Lazarus miracle (11:4, 40) and even moreso in the Cross and Resurrection as a "lifting up" to glory (3:14; 8:28; 12:32). That was Jesus' glory shining through his incarnate state, but as no one has ever seen God (1:18), so no one has ever seen Jesus' true celestial glory. That will await the eschaton and eternity, when we will "see him as he really is" (1 John 3:2). This passage promises the reality of that future hope. Throughout eternity, we will see and share in his final glory.

Finally, the prayer concludes with a summary of the themes in Jesus' prayer and a further promise (17:25-26). It begins with "righteous Father" because every aspect of the prayer (the gift of Jesus to the world, the mission to the world, the condemnation of the world) was the result of God's righteous acts. This is also the foundation for Jesus' appeal here (so Köstenberger). First, Jesus summed up the situation of the world: it "doesn't know" God (17:25; cf. 1:10-11; 7:28; 8:19, 55). The ignorance and rejection of the world is overcome by the fact that Jesus does indeed know God and therefore has made him known (1:18). As Jesus has revealed the Father to the disciples, this enabled them to know that God had sent him. Note that Jesus did not say they came to know the Father (which they did) but rather that they recognized the mission that the Father had "sent" Jesus to accomplish—namely, to reveal God to the world. Within the parameter of this mission, Jesus promised that he would continue to reveal God to them, undoubtedly through the Paraclete (14:26; 16:12-15). This is the process of revelation: from the Father to the Son to the Spirit to the church, which is then enabled to reveal God to the world (cf. 20:20-23).

There is a twofold goal in this continuing revelation: First, that "your love for me will be in them" (17:26)—an incredible promise. The love of the Father for the Son is an eternal force, deeper than any human being can ever know, and this love will be both experienced by us and lived out among us. The love of the Father can be known to us only via the Son, who demonstrated that love on the Cross (Rom 5:8). We experience divine love on the basis of the mutual indwelling of the Son in us and us in him (15:4-7). Moreover, this provides the basis for the community love that so characterizes the farewell discourse (13:34-35; 15:12, 17). Love for one another is a reflection of experiencing God's love in ourselves, and in fact it is impossible without the enabling power of that deeper love. As we experience his wondrous love, it drives us ever more deeply into a living relationship with him and makes it possible for us to love each other. The second goal/promise of Jesus' revelation is that "I will be in them," summarizing not just the mutual indwelling theme but the central theme of Scripture, the promise of Exodus 25:8 (cf. 2 Chr 6:18; Ezek 48:35) to be fulfilled in the new heaven and the new earth: "God's home is now among his people! He will live with them, and they will be his people. God himself will be with them" (Rev 21:3). Jesus inaugurated the fulfillment of this promise by dwelling within the believer (6:56; 15:4; 17:23; 1 John 2:24; 3:24; 4:15) as a foretaste of the final reality to come. This was his final comment before his arrest—that his deepest desire is to love and indwell his followers!

◆ V. The Arrest, Trial, and Passion of Jesus (18:1–19:42)
   A. The Arrest of Jesus (18:1-11)

After saying these things, Jesus crossed the Kidron Valley with his disciples and entered a grove of olive trees. ²Judas, the betrayer, knew this place, because Jesus had often gone there with his disciples. ³The leading priests and Pharisees had given Judas a contingent of Roman soldiers and Temple guards to accompany him. Now with blazing torches, lanterns, and weapons, they arrived at the olive grove.

⁴Jesus fully realized all that was going to happen to him, so he stepped forward to meet them. "Who are you looking for?" he asked.

⁵"Jesus the Nazarene,"* they replied.

"I AM he,"* Jesus said. (Judas, who be-

trayed him, was standing with them.) ⁶As Jesus said "I AM he," they all drew back and fell to the ground! ⁷Once more he asked them, "Who are you looking for?"

And again they replied, "Jesus the Nazarene."

⁸"I told you that I AM he," Jesus said. "And since I am the one you want, let these others go." ⁹He did this to fulfill his own statement: "I did not lose a single one of those you have given me."*

¹⁰Then Simon Peter drew a sword and slashed off the right ear of Malchus, the high priest's slave. ¹¹But Jesus said to Peter, "Put your sword back into its sheath. Shall I not drink from the cup of suffering the Father has given me?"

18:5a Or *Jesus of Nazareth;* also in 18:7.   18:5b Or *"The 'I AM' is here";* or *"I am the LORD";* Greek reads *I am;* also in 18:6, 8. See Exod 3:14.   18:9 See John 6:39 and 17:12.

NOTES

18:1 *Jesus crossed the Kidron Valley.* This parallels David's flight from Absalom across this valley (2 Sam 15:23) after having been betrayed by Ahithophel, who later hung himself (2 Sam 17:23). John may have seen parallels between the stories (so Westcott, Brown, Whitacre). See Blomberg 2001:228-230; Keener 2003:1070-1073 for a defense of the historicity of the scene.

18:6 *they all drew back and fell to the ground.* Ridderbos (1997:576) brings out another possible nuance: "These actions . . . convey the transcendent ('eschatological,' cf. 8:28) character of the confrontation between Jesus and the power of darkness that came out against him (cf. 14:30; 12:31)." He sees a parallel between this and Pss 27:1-3; 56:7-10, in which God triumphs over his enemies.

COMMENTARY

John's Presentation of Jesus' Passion. The order of the Passion events is the same in all four Gospels and covers the chronology of the events, though the details differ somewhat. John shares many details with the Synoptics, like the movement of Jesus with his disciples to the Mount of Olives, his betrayal by Judas and subsequent arrest, his trials before the high priest and Pilate, Pilate's assumption of innocence and desire to release Jesus rather than Barabbas, the insistence of the crowd that Jesus be crucified, Pilate's acquiescence, the Crucifixion between two criminals, the dividing of Jesus' garments and offer of wine, and the death and burial of Jesus.

Yet John's portrayal is unique in many of its details. As Burge brings out (2000:486), he omits many aspects (the betrayal with a kiss, the Gethsemane prayer, the sleepiness of the disciples, the healing of the servant's ear, Simon of Cyrene carrying the cross, the mocking crowds, Jesus' cry from the cross) and adds many others (Roman soldiers and Temple guards falling to the ground, the conversations with Annas and Pilate, the emphasis on the inscription on the cross, the details on the dividing of the garments, Jesus giving his mother, Mary, to the beloved disciple, the breaking of the two criminals' legs, Jesus being pierced with the spear, and Nicodemus being at the burial). In short, John constructs a rather unique portrayal of the Passion events, centering upon Jesus' sovereign control of the chaos surrounding him. As seen throughout the Gospel (e.g., in the "lifted up" sayings of 3:14; 8:28; 12:32), all of Jesus' life has led to this moment. John presents quite a different portrait of Jesus' crucifixion. Gone is the horror of putting to death the Son of God (Matthew and Mark) or the death of the innocent, righteous martyr with its worshipful atmosphere (Luke). Instead, the Cross is Jesus' exaltation, the culmination of his glory. "The overall impression of the arrest scene is of a divine Jesus who overwhelms his supposedly powerful adversary by a mere repetition of the divine name" (Witherington 1995:285).

Interestingly, there is more space given here to the role of both the Romans and the Jews (a fact critical scholars often ignore when they assume the ahistorical nature of John's portrait). Only John mentions the Roman cohort at the arrest (18:3), and Pilate is given a much expanded role. Still, the primary thrust is the Jewish demand for Jesus' death (in Greek, "the Jews" is found 22 times in chs 18–19). This, however, is not anti-Semitism (a charge often made of late); in fact, both Roman and Jewish guilt are stressed in John. The emphasis is upon the rejection of Jesus by the world as a whole, Jew and Gentile alike. This is a Johannine theme found throughout his Gospel.

The Arrest of Jesus (18:1-11). After Jesus finished giving his farewell address ("after saying these things"), he led his followers east out of Jerusalem and "crossed the Kidron Valley," a wadi or dry riverbed, which flows only in the rainy winter season and empties into the Dead Sea. To the east of the Kidron Valley is the Mount of Olives, and Jesus took his disciples to "a grove of olive trees" there, called "Gethsemane" in the Synoptics (Mark 14:32). They entered the grove there and did not exit until Jesus went out to meet those who had come to arrest him (18:4). John omitted the scene of Jesus praying there (Mark 14:32-42 and parallels), probably to center upon the arrest itself. Instead, the scene shifts to Judas, who knew Jesus would be in Gethsemane, "because Jesus had often gone there with his disciples" (18:2). Luke 21:37 and 22:39 tell us Jesus spent each night of the Passion week on the Mount of Olives, possibly at this very spot. The Jewish law said that all pilgrims were to remain in the vicinity of Jerusalem during Passover, an area that included the olive grove but not Bethany, where Jesus had been staying at the start of the week (12:1; cf. Mark 11:12; 14:3). It is likely that the grove had walls around it, and perhaps a supporter allowed Jesus and his disciples to use it (so Carson). At any rate, Judas knew exactly where to lead the troops.

Since Judas had agreed to betray his Lord (Mark 14:10-11), the Sanhedrin (the governing council made up of "the leading priests and Pharisees") sent with him a contingent of troops made up of Temple guards. John alone tells us that a detachment of Roman soldiers also accompanied them (on the historicity of this see Giblin 1984:217). The Greek term indicates a "cohort"—in theory a thousand soldiers and usually at least 600. The term could also refer to a "maniple" of 200 soldiers. This seems an overly large number for such a task, but we do know that their "commanding officer" was present (18:12), and the Romans would want to make certain no riot developed with all the volatile pilgrims present (so Carson, Blomberg, Köstenberger, contra Keener who thinks these are Jewish guards rather than Roman). So it was a fairly sizable group, carrying "weapons" (at least swords and possibly spears as well; Mark 14:48 mentions "swords and clubs") to keep the peace (so Bruce 1980:8-9). It is a fair guess that a maniple of 200 accompanied Judas (note that 470 soldiers guarded Paul on his trip to Caesarea in Acts 23:23). They also brought torches and lanterns because it was late at night.

The next event (18:4-9) is recorded only in John's Gospel, and its historicity is doubted by many because it is so supernatural. First, Jesus is once more omniscient (cf. 1:42, 47; 13:1) in that he "fully realized all that was going to happen to him" (18:4). The theme is his complete authority over all the events, including his death and resurrection (10:18), reminiscent of his supernatural knowledge in 13:1, 3 (so Michaels). Jesus took the initiative and went out of the grove to meet his fate head on. When he asked whom they wanted, they answered, "Jesus the Nazarene" (18:5). It was common then either to use one's father's name, "Jesus bar-Joseph (son of Joseph)," or one's hometown, as here. Jesus' response, "I AM he" (*egō eimi* [TG1473/1510, ZG1609/1639]), seems innocuous at first since "he" can be presupposed—but in John it has far deeper connotations, seen in the "I am" sayings (6:35; 8:12; 10:7, 11; 11:25; 14:6; 15:1) and especially the absolute "I AM" statements (6:20; 8:24, 28, 58; 13:19), where it is the equivalent of "Yahweh."

The results bear this out. As Jesus said this, the whole arresting party "drew back and fell to the ground!" (18:6). Jesus' words had some extraordinary power, and John drew attention to this by repeating that the response of the soldiers occurred at the moment Jesus said "*egō eimi* [TG1473/1510, ZG1609/1639]." While it is possible that this indicates nothing more than the soldiers clumsily falling over one another due to surprise at Jesus' boldness (so Carson, Blomberg), it is far more likely that John was creating an ironic scene of theophany—that is, a manifestation of God. People often fell to the ground when confronted with God's manifest presence (Judg 13:20-21; Ezek 1:28; Acts 9:4; Rev 1:17), and so it is here (so Brown, Lindars, Barrett, Kysar, Burge, Keener, Köstenberger). Schnackenburg adds the idea of the powerlessness of God's enemies when confronted by his presence (2 Kgs 1:9-14; Isa 11:4), and

Giblin (1984:219) goes so far as to say that the "falling back" is symbolic of those who reject Jesus and are non-disciples (cf. 6:66). This does not mean that the soldiers understood what was happening; that is the irony of the scene. Soldiers do not fall to the ground; their very life is at stake in remaining upright in the midst of battle. As they picked themselves up, they undoubtedly asked something like, "What happened? An earthquake perhaps?" They were in the presence of deity.

Their consternation was heightened by the fact that Jesus had to repeat his question (18:7-8). This time Jesus' control of the situation led him to virtually command that they allow his disciples to go free. Their acquiescence is not stated but presupposed, and in its place is a statement on the fulfillment of Jesus' own prophetic words, "I did not lose a single one of those you have given me." This refers back to 17:12 (cf. 6:39; 10:28) and shows that Jesus' own words had the same authority as Scripture. Judas is not mentioned (though he was among the others) because he was not one of the elect "given" to Jesus but rather was "headed for destruction" (17:12). Earlier, the promise of protection and deliverance related to final salvation, but here it is extended to protection from harm. Jesus, the Good Shepherd, both watches over and protects his sheep from the wolves (10:3, 12) and lays down his life for them (10:11, 15).

The Synoptics tell the story of the disciple drawing his sword (Mark 14:46-47 and parallels), but it is John who tells us the disciple was Peter and the servant was Malchus (18:10-11). While it used to be thought that John's addition of the names is proof of a later developing tradition (so Bultmann), it is more and more being seen as a sign of an eyewitness account (so Witherington). The sword (*machaira* [TG3162, ZG3479]) may have been a long knife hidden in Peter's clothing. It is not hard to imagine why Peter may have acted so brashly. Peter and the other disciples still failed to understand Jesus' teaching regarding a suffering Messiah, and Peter probably expected the armies of heaven to appear and begin the final war. Instead, his clumsy thrust just cut off the right ear of Malchus (though some think he intended to do just this), and Jesus told him to put the sword back in its sheath. Luke tells us that Jesus healed the ear (22:51), and Matthew has Jesus adding, "Those who use the sword will die by the sword" (26:52). John, however, centers on Jesus' sense of destiny—"Shall I not drink from the cup of suffering the Father has given me?" (18:11; cf. his Gethsemane prayer in Mark 14:36 and parallels). The "cup" as a symbol of suffering/wrath is found in Psalm 75:8, Isaiah 51:17, 22, Jeremiah 25:15, and Mark 10:38. Jesus had embraced the divine will and wanted to complete his calling, while Peter had unwittingly placed himself against God's will.

◆   ## B. Jesus' Trial before Annas and Peter's Denials (18:12-27)

[12]So the soldiers, their commanding officer, and the Temple guards arrested Jesus and tied him up. [13]First they took him to Annas, the father-in-law of Caiaphas, the high priest at that time.* [14]Caiaphas was the one who had told the other Jewish leaders, "It's better that one man should die for the people."

¹⁵Simon Peter followed Jesus, as did another of the disciples. That other disciple was acquainted with the high priest, so he was allowed to enter the high priest's courtyard with Jesus. ¹⁶Peter had to stay outside the gate. Then the disciple who knew the high priest spoke to the woman watching at the gate, and she let Peter in. ¹⁷The woman asked Peter, "You're not one of that man's disciples, are you?"

"No," he said, "I am not."

¹⁸Because it was cold, the household servants and the guards had made a charcoal fire. They stood around it, warming themselves, and Peter stood with them, warming himself.

¹⁹Inside, the high priest began asking Jesus about his followers and what he had been teaching them. ²⁰Jesus replied, "Everyone knows what I teach. I have preached regularly in the synagogues and the Temple, where the people* gather. I have not spoken in secret. ²¹Why are you asking me this question? Ask those who heard me. They know what I said."

²²Then one of the Temple guards standing nearby slapped Jesus across the face. "Is that the way to answer the high priest?" he demanded.

²³Jesus replied, "If I said anything wrong, you must prove it. But if I'm speaking the truth, why are you beating me?"

²⁴Then Annas bound Jesus and sent him to Caiaphas, the high priest.

²⁵Meanwhile, as Simon Peter was standing by the fire warming himself, they asked him again, "You're not one of his disciples, are you?"

He denied it, saying, "No, I am not."

²⁶But one of the household slaves of the high priest, a relative of the man whose ear Peter had cut off, asked, "Didn't I see you out there in the olive grove with Jesus?" ²⁷Again Peter denied it. And immediately a rooster crowed.

18:13 Greek *that year.* 18:20 Greek *Jewish people;* also in 18:38.

NOTES

18:12-14 It has been common to deny the historicity of the Sanhedrin trial (found in the Synoptics; John centers on a preliminary hearing) on the grounds that the Sanhedrin tractate of the Mishnah (AD 200) says there could not be a nighttime trial and that such trials had to last two days. Carson (1991:574-575) provides a viable response: (1) Many Mishnaic rules never had the force of obeyed law but were theoretical in nature. (2) There is a lot of evidence that legal rules could be breached if there was an emergency situation, such as would have been the case if Jesus was indeed arrested the night before Passover began. (3) The Gospel accounts point to certain irregularities that would naturally arise in the heat of the moment. (4) Many scholars think much of the Mishnah relates more to the post-70 AD situation rather than the time of Jesus, so we cannot be certain that such rules held sway at the earlier time. One thing is clear: The authorities wanted to execute Jesus for blasphemy. Moreover, the volatile Passover time would indeed have frightened them due to the excitable pilgrims, so the nighttime trial makes perfect sense (cf. Keener 2003:1084-1089).

18:15 *another of the disciples.* This person has normally been thought to be the "disciple Jesus loved"—that is, John. The problem with this identification is that "acquainted" (*gnōstos* [TG1110, ZG1196]) points to a close friend (Barrett, Brown, Carson, Keener), and there is a very real question as to how a lowly Galilean fisherman like John could have been a close friend of the aristocratic high priest. Perhaps it was someone at the level of a Nicodemus or a Joseph of Arimathea. (Michaels understands this "other disciple" as a resident of Jerusalem who had become a believer.) However, there are good reasons for assuming it was John. Such people as Nicodemus are regularly named; even Malchus is named (18:10). The only other unnamed disciple is the beloved disciple, and he, like this disciple, is always connected in some way with Peter (13:23-26; 20:1-10; 21:7-8, 18-24). Also, fishermen were not always at the bottom end of the social scale. John's father Zebedee had servants (Mark

1:20) and may have been the head of a thriving fishing trade and perhaps even of the priests in Jerusalem. Moreover, if Jesus and John were cousins (so Brown), then Mary's priestly contacts in Jerusalem (Luke 1:36-45) may have been available to John (so Burge).

18:17 *The woman asked Peter.* The fact that the Gospels differ regarding who challenged Peter in the three denials has caused many to doubt the historical worth of the stories, but as several point out (e.g., Morris, Blomberg), it was probably a group of servants peppering Peter with questions, and the order is not critical. Also, in John it occurs in the courtyard of Annas, while in the Synoptics it is at Caiaphas's palace. Some have proposed as a solution that the residence of these two men was virtually the same, with both residing in separate wings of the old Hasmonean palace (so Morris), but even if this was not the case, the two accounts are easily harmonized, as John places the last two denials (in 18:25-27) after Jesus has been sent to Caiaphas.

COMMENTARY

In the next two scenes (18:12-27; 18:28–19:16), John is at his dramatic best; in both he has interspersed scenes for dramatic effect. In this first scene, he placed Jesus' interrogation by the high priest Annas next to the three denials by Peter for the sake of contrast. Jesus was still in sovereign control in giving himself over to the authorities, while Peter lost all control in his desire to save himself, thus contrasting "the faithlessness of the disciple with the fearlessness of the master" (so Beasley-Murray). The trial at night was a necessity, for the leaders were afraid that Jesus might start a riot by appealing to the volatile pilgrims, thereby bringing down the wrath of Rome on the nation. Moreover, Pilate sat to hear cases shortly after dawn, and they needed to have Jesus on the cross early so he would be dead before nightfall, when the corpses had to be taken down from the crosses due to the Passover festival. They had to find legal evidence to present to Pilate before dawn.

Jesus Taken to Annas (18:12-14). John alone tells us of a preliminary hearing before Annas. The soldiers (Romans and Temple police) arrested Jesus and took him to Annas, probably for an informal interrogation to gather evidence that Caiaphas could use later that night. The Roman detachment, having ensured there would be no riot, probably returned to the headquarters at the Fortress of Antonia on the Temple mount. Annas had been high priest (AD 6–15) and was succeeded by his son-in-law Caiaphas, who held office until AD 36/37. According to Jewish thought, a high priest held office for life (Num 35:25), but the Romans took upon themselves power over the priesthood and felt free to switch high priests as they saw fit. Pilate's predecessor Gratus had made the switch, but Annas was still considered a high priest by the people. Moreover, five of his sons at one time or another held the office of high priest, so he was in a sense the patriarch of the high priesthood. Thus, there is no "historical difficulty" with his role in this scene (so Barrett). John reminds the reader of Caiaphas's inadvertent prophecy ("It's better for you that one man should die for the people," 11:50), not only to identify Caiaphas but also to remind the reader of the events to come and God's control of them. Even Caiaphas was a tool of God and witnessed once more to the substitutionary nature ("for the people") of Jesus' coming death.

Peter's First Denial (18:15-18). John does not tell us of the desertion of the disciples (cf. Mark 14:50-52 and parallels), but he does center on Peter's failure, set in
contrast with the sovereign splendor of Jesus. The purpose, as in all four Gospels, is
to show the extent to which Jesus faced these terrible hours alone. Even his closest
disciples failed him utterly. The "other disciple" (only in John and probably identical with the beloved disciple, see note on 18:15) "was acquainted with" the high
priest and so was able to get Peter access to the courtyard. Peter was forced to stand
"outside the gate" until that disciple "spoke to the woman watching at the gate,"
enabling Peter to get inside. The fact that a woman was guarding the gate is interesting in light of the expectation that a male would be guarding the gate of the high
priest, especially if the supposition is true that Annas and Caiaphas both lived in the
Hasmonean palace on the west hill of the city (so Zahn, Plummer, Köstenberger).
Yet such was fairly common (cf. Acts 12:13).

The woman challenged Peter, "You're not one of [Jesus'] disciples, are you?" She
knew the other disciple (John) and assumed that Peter was a disciple as well. Like
the other disciples, Peter was still afraid of being arrested, so he lied, "I am not." At
this point, we must remember that while Peter did fail Jesus, he and John were the
only ones brave enough to come this far. The rest were hiding behind closed doors
(20:19). It was a cold night, so everyone was standing by the fire, warming themselves. The mention of a "charcoal fire" (*anthrakia* [TG439, ZG471]) is a historical touch
in keeping with John's inclination toward adding such authentic eyewitness details.
This was an unusual scene, for it was seldom that such things would happen at
night—but these were extraordinary times!

Jesus Interrogated by Annas (18:19-24). John did not narrate the main trial before
Caiaphas and the Sanhedrin; rather, he focused on the preliminary interrogation by
the former high priest Annas, still called high priest (see *m. Horayot* 3:1-4 for this practice). He questioned Jesus regarding two things—"his followers and what he had been
teaching them." In an actual trial setting, a Jewish judge would not do this but instead
would interrogate witnesses to see if two or more would substantiate the charges. So,
this was an unofficial query. He obviously was looking for evidence of a conspiracy
and of seditious teaching. The leaders had for a long time assumed Jesus' guilt and did
not seek the truth but rather evidence to use against Jesus. This was undoubtedly Annas's intention as well. He was hoping to catch Jesus in a blasphemous claim as to who
he thought he was and what he hoped to accomplish with his movement. Then Annas
himself could become a key witness against Jesus at the upcoming trial.

Jesus' response was fairly curt (18:20-21). He did not answer about his disciples
but centered on his own teaching, saying that he had never taught secretly (the normal approach of an insurrectionist—Jesus would be crucified between two of them)
but openly in synagogues and the Temple. In fact, he had been teaching in the Temple all week (Luke 21:37). He did not provide one set of teachings for the public and
another for his followers. His message was public record and could be determined
easily. In short, Jesus said that Annas should have already known his teachings.
Then he went on the offensive and demanded that Annas question witnesses, which

is what he should have been doing in an official investigation (Roman courts inter-rogated the accused, but Jewish procedure centered on witnesses). Anyone could tell him what he wanted to know.

When the officials heard Jesus challenging Annas legally, they saw it as disrespect; so one of the Temple guards struck him in the face (18:22). Jesus' reaction was quite different from that of Paul when he was rebuked for insolence in Acts 23:4-5. Paul took the expected tack of humility and deference (so Brown) by apologizing. Paul, however, had called the high priest a "whitewashed wall" (cf. NLT, "corrupt hypo-crite"), while Jesus had said nothing wrong. Jesus responded here by asking them to specify a reason for striking him. He had spoken "the truth" rather than anything wrong. Throughout the fourth Gospel, there has been stress on witness to the truth (1:7; 5:31-40; 8:13-18). Jesus was demanding that proper witnesses be consulted regarding the charges, knowing that he would be exonerated. There was nothing more to be said, and the gambit had not succeeded. Annas terminated the examina-tion and sent him "bound" to his son-in-law Caiaphas for the formal trial. He had been bound at his arrest (18:12) and had probably been unbound for his interroga-tion. This was probably repeated before Caiaphas as well. By telling us that Jesus was sent to Caiaphas, John shows he was aware of the major trial described in the Synop-tics (Mark 14:53-65 and parallels) and had decided not to describe it, possibly expecting his readers to know about it (so Burge, Blomberg). It is also possible that John (as a witness to the trial before Annas) decided to provide only testimony of the trial he himself witnessed, which adds credence to the historicity of the account.

Peter's Second and Third Denials (18:25-27). Back at the charcoal fire in the court-yard, it seemed everyone ("they," indicating servants and Temple police) was accusing Peter of being Jesus' disciple. Once again, Peter denied any connection with Jesus. The final challenge came from "a relative" of Malchus, "whose ear Peter had cut off" (18:10, only in John). He had seen the event occur in the olive grove and recognized Peter. For the final time, Peter denied any knowledge of Jesus, and then "a rooster crowed," showing that Jesus' prophecy (13:38) had indeed been fulfilled. John's ac-count is much more sparse than the Synoptics. There is no series of oaths when Peter denied Jesus the third time, nor are there any bitter tears when he realized he had ful-filled Jesus' prophecy. John wanted to center on the contrast between Peter and Jesus, so he kept the narration simple. This was likely the worst moment in Peter's life, but there was hope for the future, for Peter would be reinstated (cf. 21:15-17). If there is hope for him, there is also hope for all of us when we fail in similar ways.

◆ ## C. Jesus' Trial before Pilate (18:28–19:16a)

28 Jesus' trial before Caiaphas ended in the early hours of the morning. Then he was taken to the headquarters of the Roman governor.* His accusers didn't go inside because it would defile them, and they wouldn't be allowed to celebrate the Passover. 29 So Pilate, the governor, went out to them and asked, "What is your charge against this man?"

30 "We wouldn't have handed him over

to you if he weren't a criminal!" they retorted.

³¹"Then take him away and judge him by your own law," Pilate told them.

"Only the Romans are permitted to execute someone," the Jewish leaders replied. ³²(This fulfilled Jesus' prediction about the way he would die.*)

³³Then Pilate went back into his headquarters and called for Jesus to be brought to him. "Are you the king of the Jews?" he asked him.

³⁴Jesus replied, "Is this your own question, or did others tell you about me?"

³⁵"Am I a Jew?" Pilate retorted. "Your own people and their leading priests brought you to me for trial. Why? What have you done?"

³⁶Jesus answered, "My Kingdom is not an earthly kingdom. If it were, my followers would fight to keep me from being handed over to the Jewish leaders. But my Kingdom is not of this world."

³⁷Pilate said, "So you are a king?"

Jesus responded, "You say I am a king. Actually, I was born and came into the world to testify to the truth. All who love the truth recognize that what I say is true."

³⁸"What is truth?" Pilate asked. Then he went out again to the people and told them, "He is not guilty of any crime. ³⁹But you have a custom of asking me to release one prisoner each year at Passover. Would you like me to release this 'King of the Jews'?"

⁴⁰But they shouted back, "No! Not this man. We want Barabbas!" (Barabbas was a revolutionary.)

CHAPTER 19

Then Pilate had Jesus flogged with a lead-tipped whip. ²The soldiers wove a crown of thorns and put it on his head, and they put a purple robe on him. ³"Hail! King of the Jews!" they mocked, as they slapped him across the face.

⁴Pilate went outside again and said to the people, "I am going to bring him out to you now, but understand clearly that I find him not guilty." ⁵Then Jesus came out wearing the crown of thorns and the purple robe. And Pilate said, "Look, here is the man!"

⁶When they saw him, the leading priests and Temple guards began shouting, "Crucify him! Crucify him!"

"Take him yourselves and crucify him," Pilate said. "I find him not guilty."

⁷The Jewish leaders replied, "By our law he ought to die because he called himself the Son of God."

⁸When Pilate heard this, he was more frightened than ever. ⁹He took Jesus back into the headquarters* again and asked him, "Where are you from?" But Jesus gave no answer. ¹⁰"Why don't you talk to me?" Pilate demanded. "Don't you realize that I have the power to release you or crucify you?"

¹¹Then Jesus said, "You would have no power over me at all unless it were given to you from above. So the one who handed me over to you has the greater sin."

¹²Then Pilate tried to release him, but the Jewish leaders shouted, "If you release this man, you are no 'friend of Caesar.'* Anyone who declares himself a king is a rebel against Caesar."

¹³When they said this, Pilate brought Jesus out to them again. Then Pilate sat down on the judgment seat on the platform that is called the Stone Pavement (in Hebrew, *Gabbatha*). ¹⁴It was now about noon on the day of preparation for the Passover. And Pilate said to the people,* "Look, here is your king!"

¹⁵"Away with him," they yelled. "Away with him! Crucify him!"

"What? Crucify your king?" Pilate asked.

"We have no king but Caesar," the leading priests shouted back.

¹⁶Then Pilate turned Jesus over to them to be crucified.

18:28 Greek *to the Praetorium;* also in 18:33.   18:32 See John 12:32-33.   19:9 Greek *the Praetorium.*
19:12 "Friend of Caesar" is a technical term that refers to an ally of the emperor.   19:14 Greek *Jewish people;* also in 19:20.

NOTES

18:28–19:16 While most of the material here is unique to John, and while the insider information is often questioned because it seems private to Jesus and Pilate, this is insufficient reason to doubt its historical worth (contra Bultmann, Haenchen). It holds together well, and the details could have come from the risen Lord himself or from servants who were present (so Carson). In short, while not ultimately provable, the story as a whole is plausible and trustworthy (so Schlatter, Dodd, Brown). It is certainly true that this is a highly theological narrative, but that does not mean it is therefore ahistorical (so Ridderbos).

18:31 *Only the Romans are permitted to execute someone.* There is considerable debate regarding this, as many (Winter 1974, Barrett) think the Sanhedrin did have the right to mete out capital punishment, as seen in the stoning of Stephen (Acts 7:57-58), including the right to execute a Gentile that entered the inner sanctuary of the Temple. The stoning of Stephen, however, was mob action, and the right to execute those who transgressed the sacred precincts was a Roman exception intended as a concession to the Jews (so Bruce, Sherwin-White, Blomberg, Keener). Most scholars think the situation here is historically correct.

18:36 *not of this world.* It is possible to see double meaning in "world," with the surface meaning to Pilate being "not an earthly kingdom" but with the deeper theological overtones of having "no part in the sinful rebellious world"; this view probably reads too much into the context.

18:37 *to testify to the truth.* Throughout the fourth Gospel, the idea of Jesus bearing testimony to what he had heard from the Father is quite frequent (3:11-12; 8:28, 38; 12:49; 14:10; 17:8). As such, he had come to destroy falsehood, especially the "father of lies" (8:44).

18:39 *release one prisoner each year.* The so-called "paschal amnesty" has been often doubted (e.g., Bultmann) because there is no definite external evidence from Roman or Jewish sources that it had ever occurred. There is one Mishnaic passage, *Pesahim* 8:6 [*b. Pesahim* 91a], that mentions "one who has received a promise to be released from prison" in a list of those who might not be able to participate in the Passover celebration. It seems likely that this is talking about a Roman court situation since there would not be such doubt regarding the release if a Jewish court were involved. This may be a reference to the paschal amnesty (so Beasley-Murray, Carson). Also, Josephus (*Antiquities* 20.209) and Livy (*History* 5.13) attest to analogous Roman practices. Most modern critical scholars think that such a gesture of goodwill on the part of the Romans makes good sense and generally accept the likelihood of the event (so Brown, Lindars, Barrett, Schnackenburg, Keener).

19:1 *had Jesus flogged.* At first glance, this seems to contradict Mark and Matthew, which say Jesus was scourged after the sentencing (Matt 27:26; Mark 15:15); however, this is answered by recognizing two different beatings—the first a less severe one at this point of the trial (cf. Luke 23:16) and the second a severe scourging just before they took Jesus away to be crucified.

19:5 *here is the man!* There are several options for the connotation of "the man": the emphasis could be on the Son of Man, as in 8:28—"When you have lifted up the Son of Man on the cross, then you will understand that I AM he"—or perhaps it is on Jesus as the last Adam, as in Rom 5:12-21; 1 Cor 15:45. Probably it is best to see Jesus in his true humanity as the God-man, the Word become flesh (cf. Brown, Whitacre).

19:7 *he called himself the Son of God.* Brown (1995:534-544) notes five possibilities behind the Jewish charge of blasphemy: (1) He called himself Messiah, but there were many messianic aspirants in the first century. (2) He called himself Son of God; Brown doubts Jesus used the title, but it is certainly part of the solution. (3) He claimed to be Son of Man and to come on the clouds of heaven (Mark 14:62), but this is not enough to constitute blasphemy in and of itself. (4) Some claimed he said he'd destroy the Temple, but this was not linked with a charge of blasphemy. (5) He was a false prophet and as such deceived the people, but this was not centrally addressed in the trial. Bock (2000:234-236) moves toward a solution: (1) Blasphemy per se was an inappropriate use of the divine name, but there were also acts of blasphemy, such as idolatry or disrespect toward God. (2) Only a few were allowed to approach the Holy God; even the archangel Michael is never depicted as seated before God; so for Jesus to claim to be "seated in the place of power at God's right hand" (Mark 14:62) would have been blasphemous. (3) This was not a capital trial but a hearing before the Sanhedrin in order to gain material to use before Pilate. (4) Sources for information regarding this trial were plentiful: Joseph of Arimathea, Nicodemus. (5) There were two levels of blasphemy: Jesus' claim to possess comprehensive authority from God (the "Son of God" title would function here), and his claim to be the future judge of the Jewish leaders themselves (a violation of Exod 22:28 on not cursing God's leaders). This latter would also be used as a sociopolitical challenge to Rome's authority.

For Pilate, there would be two, perhaps three connotations: (1) The emperor was also called "son of God," and so this continued their charge of sedition. (2) In a Greco-Roman context, this could also place Jesus in the category of "divine man"—a term used of people so filled with virtue and wisdom that they were seen to be virtually "divine." (3) For centuries nations had deified their emperors (e.g., Egypt, Cyrus in Persia), and in Rome, Julius Caesar and Augustus were deified after their deaths (it became "the imperial cult" by the time Revelation was written). Tiberias allowed a temple to be built in his name in 25 AD but said to the Senate, "I am a mere mortal, and divine honors belong only to Augustus, the real savior of mankind" (Tacitus, *Annals* 4.37-38). It is conceivable that Pilate saw an implicit claim to deity, but the most likely option is the second, based on Jesus' role in society.

19:13 *Pilate sat down.* There has long been a debate regarding whether the verb is intransitive ("Pilate sat down") or transitive ("Pilate sat Jesus down on the judge's seat"). Some scholars (Lightfoot, Haenchen, Meeks, Barrett) have argued that the verb could be transitive and that Pilate placed Jesus on his tribunal (probably on another chair beside himself). If so, he would be making another contemptuous reference (to the Jews) regarding Jesus' kingship. If this were so, it would also hint that as the Jewish people cried for his crucifixion, Jesus faced them as their judge. Most recent scholars (Brown, Beasley-Murray, Carson, Ridderbos, Burge, Köstenberger) find this interesting but not likely, for here the *bēma* [TG968, ZG1037] was certainly the judgment seat itself. While Jesus was certainly seen (and mocked) as King throughout the arrest and trial, he was not considered as judge, and Pilate's sitting him on a seat beside his *bēma* would not communicate this strongly enough to make the proposed contemptuous reference. Moreover, the judgment seat was the sign of Pilate's office, and for Pilate to misuse it in this way was not very likely.

19:14 *about noon.* Lit., "the sixth hour." This creates a discrepancy with Mark 15:25 and 15:33, which tell us that Jesus was crucified at the "third hour" (= 9 A.M.) and that darkness started at the sixth hour. Some ancient mss (e.g., the corrector of Sinaiticus) harmonized John with Mark by changing the time to the third hour. Some scholars (e.g., Westcott) think John was using the Roman method of marking time (which began with midnight), thus making this 6 A.M. Neither is likely. The answer is probably to be seen in the way the ancients told time. Rather than hours and minutes, they thought in terms of "watches," with the nighttime and daytime consisting of four three-hour watches. Most likely the verdict and placing of Jesus on the cross occurred at some time between 9 A.M. and noon, and so in noting the "hour" of an event, one writer (e.g., John) could easily have rounded the time up to "*about* noon", while another (e.g., Mark) rounded it down to 9 A.M. (so Morris, Carson, Burge, Blomberg).

COMMENTARY

In John, this trial scene is handled in a way opposite that of the previous "trial." John shortened the Sanhedrin trial (18:19-24) by omitting the scene before Caiaphas, but he expanded the trial before Pilate (18:28–19:16a) with a great deal of material not found in the Synoptics. As such, this text presents a dramatic seven-scene masterpiece. It is common to think of this as chiastic, with 19:1-3 being the central scene (so Brown, Whitacre, Burge, Blomberg, Keener).

A. Outside: the Jews demand Jesus' death (18:28-32)
  B. Inside: Pilate questions Jesus about his kingship (18:33-38a)
    C. Outside: Pilate finds Jesus not guilty (18:38b-40)
      D. Inside: The soldiers scourge Jesus (19:1-3)
    C'. Outside: Pilate finds Jesus not guilty (19:4-8)
  B'. Inside: Pilate talks with Jesus about power (19:9-11)
A'. Outside: The Jews obtain Jesus' death (19:12-16a)

The contrasts in the scene are stark. Inside there is more and more a sense of peace, as Jesus remains incredibly calm, and Pilate finds him innocent. Outside there is more and more clamor and chaos, as the Jewish people call for Jesus' death. As before, the primary thrust is Jesus' sovereign authority. It is clear who the true king is and who is really in charge. Pilate is weak and vacillating, while Jesus is in solitary splendor as he gives himself over to his destiny. It is also clear that this is a legal farce—the Jews brought him to Pilate on the basis of his alleged political aspirations, while throughout it is clear that their actual grievance was his claim to unity with the Father (so Ridderbos).

Outside: The Jews Demand Jesus' Death (18:28-32). Because Pontius Pilate heard cases shortly after dawn, they had to get Jesus there "in the early hours of the morning." After the Sanhedrin had condemned Jesus and gathered the evidence they needed to demand his death, they then took him to Pilate's headquarters (*praitōrion* [TG4232, ZG4550], the residence of the governor). The Romans did not allow provincial courts the right to execute prisoners. They, in fact, called their own rule *ius gladii*, "the law of the sword." Thus, the Jewish authorities could not execute Jesus on their own but had to ask the Romans to do it for them. Pilate actually ruled the province from Herod's palace in Caesarea but would come down to Jerusalem with a detachment of soldiers for every Jewish feast because that was when riots were most likely to break out. While there, he would stay either in Herod's palace on the West Hill or at the Tower of Antonia, a Hasmonean castle used by a Roman cohort during festivals and just east of the Temple (we do not know which castle). Pilate was "prefect" of Judea and had ruled for four years (his rule was AD 26–37). He was known for his total contempt of Jewish ways and for his brutal repression of dissent (cf. Luke 13:1). At the same time, he was in a difficult spot. Every governor of Judea had failed because they walked a tightrope of Roman expectations and Jewish sensitivities that were nearly impossible for them to understand. Still, Pilate never showed any desire to understand.

The Jewish contingent stopped at the door of the palace lest they become ritually impure and be unable to take part in the Passover ceremonies (18:28b). The Passover celebration began that evening, and the Jews could not take a chance of being ritually defiled. It is not that Gentiles by nature were unclean but that there were many causes of defilement in a Gentile house, like yeast (Bruce) or road dust from foreign lands or even the presence of Pilate's wife (Matt 27:19) since Gentile women did not observe levitical rules regarding menstruation. Also, Gentiles were thought to bury the bodies of aborted fetuses in their homes or flush them into their sewers, thereby rendering any Jewish person unclean by being in contact with a corpse (a seven-day defilement, see Brown, Carson). So the Jews stayed outside. Since the Passover meal was eaten the night before, the Jews present were concerned about the *hagigah* meal celebrated the morning of Passover day (see the note on 13:1), which would have been shortly after this trial. This began the seven-day celebration of the Festival of Unleavened Bread, which started the day after Passover (they were considered a single feast and together called Passover). Each of the festive meals was a "Passover" meal. Any defilement whatsoever, whether one-day or seven-day, would prohibit full participation in the festival.

Throughout the trial, Pilate had to go outside into the courtyard to meet with the Jews. It is this which gives the scene its movement inside and outside. Some scholars (e.g., Haenchen) have thought this historically unlikely since Pilate would never lower himself to go to meet the Jewish authorities, but Brown comments (1966: 859), "How can one be so sure? Were there never moments when Pilate, like other politicians, had to swallow his pride in order to avert worse trouble?" The scene as a whole is very plausible in light of Jewish sensitivities and the type of politics at play during Passover.

Since Roman soldiers had been involved in the arrest, Pilate knew the Jews would be coming and so was prepared. First, he asked a formal question as to their "charge against this man" (18:29). This caused great consternation, and their reply at first glance seems rather insolent: "We wouldn't have handed him over to you if he weren't a criminal!" (18:30). Yet remember that Pilate had sent a detachment of soldiers, possibly indicating a preliminary agreement between Pilate and the Sanhedrin, leading the authorities to expect Pilate to rubber-stamp their judgment and order the execution (so Beasley-Murray, Carson). When Pilate began another formal trial, they were nonplussed.

Since they had no formal charge, Pilate sarcastically told them to "judge him by your own law" (18:31). He was certainly aware of the trial that they had just finished but wanted to show his contempt for them and his desire to demonstrate their impotence, thus humiliating them (so Schnackenburg). This forced the Jews to state their true desire to see Jesus killed at the outset, thereby highlighting their guilt: "Only the Romans are permitted to execute someone" (18:31). They wanted Jesus dead (decided long before, cf. 5:18; 7:19; 8:40, 59; 10:31; 11:50) and wanted it now, irrespective of a fair trial. The Jews could have requested to kill Jesus themselves, probably by stoning or strangling, but they "probably want him crucified (19:6, 15) not only because it was a particularly brutal and painful form of death, but because it would signify that Jesus is accursed by God (Deut 21:23, cf. Gal 3:13)" (Whitacre 1999:439). John saw this as a fulfillment of Jesus' prophecy that he would be "lifted up from the earth" (12:32; cf. 3:14; 8:28). God was in sovereign control even over Jesus' opponents.

Inside: Pilate Questions Jesus about His Kingship (18:33–38a). After listening to the Jewish authorities, Pilate returned to Jesus and asked him the key question, "Are you the king of the Jews?" (18:33). This was certainly the charge that the Sanhedrin had given Pilate in order to make Jesus appear as a threat to Rome (cf. Luke 23:2). There had been no king in Judea since Herod the Great, and while false messiahs had appeared, claiming to be in the Davidic line, Jesus hardly had the appearance or demeanor of such. Several insurrectionists had been arrested recently (e.g., Barabbas and the two who would be crucified with Jesus), and the differences between Jesus and them were apparent. Pilate needed to probe Jesus and find out his claims regarding himself.

In the Synoptic accounts, Jesus responded, "You have said it" (Mark 15:2 and parallels). John records this at 18:37 and inserts a lengthy section in which Jesus clarifies the true meaning of his kingship. Jesus' response here (18:34) shows his awareness of the political repercussions. If the question came from Pilate himself, then Jesus could probe whether he was perceived as a political threat or whether there might be some interest on Pilate's part; then Jesus could instruct him more deeply. If the question came from the Jewish leaders (as Jesus suspected), then it was an antagonistic question and stemmed from a deep misunderstanding of the nature of Jesus' kingship. Pilate's response shows great irritation: "Am I a Jew?" (it begins with *mēti* [TG3385, ZG3614] in Greek and can be translated, "I am not a Jew, am I?") He made it clear that he had no personal interest in the issue. The charge came entirely from the Jewish people and the leading priests. They turned Jesus over to Pilate, and he wanted to find out why: "What have you done?" (18:35). Like all Romans, he was mystified at the whole scenario. Jesus obviously was not a military man, an insurrectionist. How could he have the Jewish authorities so inflamed?

Jesus clarified the nature of his royal office (18:36). He did not directly answer Pilate's question about what he had done but instead told Pilate in negative fashion who he was. This was a very astute answer. It not only removed the charges that Jesus was a threat to Rome but challenged Pilate (and John's readers) with the otherworldly character of Jesus' "kingdom" (this verse is the last time the term appears in John, cf. 3:3, 5). Earlier, Jesus defined his origin as "from above" rather than from this world (8:23; cf. 3:31), and in the same way he defined his kingship for Pilate as "not of this world." "Kingdom" here refers to his kingly reign. While this term rarely occurs in John (contra the Synoptics), Beasley-Murray (1987:330) rightly notes that "the whole Gospel is concerned with the kingship of God in Jesus." In one sense,

Jesus was saying his kingship was no threat to Pilate; in another sense, he was revealing to Pilate a whole other realm of reality he knew nothing about. Jesus also
wanted to protect his followers (cf. 18:8) and added, "If it were, my followers would
fight to keep me from being handed over" (18:36). Of course, Peter did just that
(18:10-11), but Jesus told him to put away his sword. He wanted Pilate to realize
that he led no band of insurrectionists against Rome. Jesus' rule was at a different
level; his Kingdom is not of this world, though it is at work in this world. It functions on the spiritual rather than the political plane.

Pilate recognized that Jesus was nonetheless making some kind of royal claim, so
he probed further (18:37): "So you are a king?" Jesus' answer was somewhat vague
and could be translated, "King is your word, not mine" (so Dodd, Bruce, Whitacre).
It could also be more positive, basically affirming the reality of it (so Beasley-
Murray, Carson). Ambiguity seems more likely in this context. Jesus did not want to
play the political game. He had affirmed his kingly role but did not want the label.
Instead, he wanted to go more deeply into his true purpose and mission. Then Jesus
stated the true purpose of his incarnation: "to testify to [lit., "bear witness to"] the
truth." Jesus' Kingdom is a kingdom of truth. Here we find another of the major
themes of the book, noted first in 1:14 where the incarnate shekinah, the Word
made flesh, was (literally) "full of grace and truth," meaning "full of [God's] unfailing love and faithfulness." Jesus is truth (14:6), and his revelation of the Father is
truth itself (8:31-32, 40; 17:17), made known to us by the Spirit of truth (14:17;
16:13-14). Burge says it well (2000:501): "It is reality lived out in divine light, which
by virtue of its spiritual link with God is thereby *genuinely* truthful and honest"
(italics his).

Finally, Jesus gave Pilate a chance to respond. This is an area that a Hellenist like
Pilate could relate to—namely, the issue of "truth." Jesus said, "All who love the
truth [hint—do you love the truth, Pilate?] recognize that what I say is true"
(18:37). The positions were reversed; Jesus became the interlocutor, and Pilate was
challenged to choose truth over falsehood. Unfortunately, Pilate rejected the invitation. His curt, "What is truth?" was in effect a dismissal of Jesus' offer. He knew that
Jesus posed no threat to Rome and that the charges of the Sanhedrin against Jesus
were invalid. At the same time, he wanted no more of Jesus' message of truth than
they did and so sadly joined the legion of unbelievers. His reply is justly famous, for
it is the heart-cry of all seekers of truth. With it, John asked his readers to search their
hearts for an openness to "truth," especially the truth of Jesus.

Outside: Pilate Finds Jesus Not Guilty (18:38b–40). Having made his decision, Pilate left Jesus in his inner room and went outside to the courtyard to give the Jews
his verdict: "He is not guilty of any crime" (by which Pilate meant no crime against
Rome). Pilate simply did not care about Jewish matters. That was for the Sanhedrin
to decide. Jesus' aspirations in a religious sense were of no concern to him (as a
Roman judge). It is helpful to realize that at this point Luke tells us that the crowd
shouted that Jesus had fomented problems everywhere, giving Pilate an excuse to
send Jesus on to Herod (Luke 23:5-12). John omits this, instead centering on Pilate

and the crowds. Pilate could easily have dismissed the charges and released Jesus, but here his personal weakness and vacillation are revealed. Due to past defeats by the Jews (he was forced to back down on more than one occasion), he was unwilling to take the high road. To assuage the crowds, Pilate tried another tack and invoked the custom of releasing "one prisoner each year at Passover" (18:39), a custom used by the Romans as a gesture of goodwill. He hoped the people would allow him to make Jesus that prisoner. On the basis of passages like Matthew 27:20 (the leaders persuade the crowd to ask for Barabbas rather than Jesus), it seems the people were allowed to choose the prisoner to be released, so Pilate could not just decide to release Jesus.

When he asked the people whether he should release Jesus, he could not help but throw out one more barb to the Jewish leaders and say, "Would you like me to release this 'King of the Jews'?" (18:39). On his part, there is a definite tinge of sarcasm and contempt; he presented it as if he agreed with the title and thought Jesus an apt king of this rabble. At the same time, John and his readers could see another unconscious prophecy similar to Caiaphas in 11:50-52. Jesus was indeed the "King of the Jews," and his own people were demanding the death of their royal Messiah! Yet Pilate's plan backfired, for he had underestimated the resolve of Jesus' enemies. The crowd shouted back, "No! Not this man. We want Barabbas" (18:40). Barabbas was an insurrectionist (*lēstēs* [TG3027, ZG3334]) who had committed murder—possibly the leader of the two who would be crucified with Jesus. He could have been the leader of the rebellion mentioned in Luke 23:18-19, 25 (so Comfort and Hawley). This may have been another strategic error on Pilate's part; to the Romans, Barabbas was a murderous terrorist, but to many Jews he may have been a folk hero, an ancient Robin Hood. The irony of the scene is very great, especially if the variant scribal reading in Matthew 27:16 (cf. NLT mg) is correct and Barabbas's name was "Jesus Barabbas": the crowd was choosing between two men named "Jesus" (a name meaning "God saves"), with both being "the son of the father" (the meaning of "Bar Abbas"). The types of salvation the two offered were quite different, however: temporal deliverance by the sword versus eternal deliverance by a Savior (so Whitacre).

Inside: The Soldiers Scourge Jesus (19:1-3). From the modern perspective, it is difficult to understand why Pilate would try to release Jesus and then immediately have him beaten. The solution is found in the parallel passage in Luke 23:16: "I will have him flogged, and then I will release him." That was clearly the intent here as well. This was a second ploy to appease the Jews; he hoped that the flogging would satisfy their desire to see Jesus punished. There were three kinds of beatings: the *fustigatio*, a less severe form for light offences; the *flagellatio*, a severe beating for hardened criminals; and the *verberatio*, the most severe, in which the victim was beaten by a succession of soldiers, often with a scourge, a whip with several leather thongs with pieces of metal or bone tied on the end (so Sherwin-White, Beasley-Murray, Carson, Keener). A scourging could break a person's back, strip his skin off, and leave him with his entrails exposed, often killing the person (Josephus *War*

612). It is unlikely that the third type occurred here, for Pilate hoped to release him, and such a flogging would leave him unable to continue the trial. Most likely this was the least severe kind, intended both to appease the Jews and provide a lesson to Jesus to be more circumspect in the future.

As was typical in such situations, the prisoner was made the butt of cruel jokes by the soldiers. Since Jesus had been charged as "king of the Jews," the soldiers gave him mock homage, undoubtedly laughing raucously as they inflicted one painful humiliation after another. They wove thorns together to make a crown, probably imitating the radiant corona worn by rulers, appearing on many coins from that time. The thorns may have come from the type of thornbushes mentioned in Isaiah 34:13 or the date palm, which had much longer thorns, up to 12 inches in length (cf. Hart 1952:70-74). If the latter, there is further irony since the same palm tree yielded the branches used to hail Jesus as king just five days earlier. Then they dressed Jesus in a mock robe of royal purple (probably an officer's cloak, perhaps a deep red similar to purple [few soldiers could afford purple]), the color worn by emperors. A number of times (imperfect tense) they mimicked the "Ave Caesar" cry (so Brown), but instead of bowing before Jesus in submission, they struck him in the face to show their contempt. Once again, however, they did more than they thought, for they were truly addressing the "King of all kings and Lord of all lords" (Rev 19:16).

Outside: Pilate Again Finds Jesus Not Guilty (19:4-8). Still convinced that Jesus was innocent and probably believing he had suffered enough, Pilate returned outside once more to talk sense into the rabble, telling them he was bringing out a man he found "not guilty." When he brought Jesus out in his pathetic robe and crown of thorns, it was not to parade the prisoner in all his misery but to make the people realize that Jesus had been punished enough. When he said, "Look, here is the man," he was not saying this out of contempt for Jesus but to show that he was no threat and should be released. Jesus must have presented a sorry sight with his beaten face and the blood oozing from the thorns. (Surely the people would see this pathetic sight and find some compassion for him!) Once more we have an unconscious prophecy (cf. 11:50-52; 18:33; 19:2-3). Jesus is in reality "the Man," the incarnate shekinah, the Word become flesh (1:14).

The priests and Temple guards, not listening to Pilate, led the cry: "Crucify him! Crucify him!" (19:6). There was to be no mercy for Jesus. Their cry also shows that their charge against Jesus involved sedition against Rome because crucifixion was used primarily for enemies of the state. This angered Pilate, who knew Jesus was not such, so he responded, "Take him yourselves and crucify him." He knew they could not do so (cf. 18:31b) but was filled with disgust that they refused to accept his verdict. Since Pilate did not have the courage of his convictions (i.e., to release Jesus), he resorted to legalities, but they were not working. This goaded the Jewish authorities into revealing the true nature of their charges. They realized the political charge would not work, for Pilate had said three times that he rejected their arguments. They turned to the true religious nature of their demand for Jesus' death: "By our law he ought to die because he called himself the Son of God" (19:7). By Roman law he might be innocent, but by Jewish law he had to die!

This was actually the verdict of the Sanhedrin trial in the Synoptics (Matt 26:62-66 and parallels). The charge was blasphemy against the name of God (Lev 24:16, "Anyone who blasphemes the Name of the LORD must be stoned to death"). Later this was narrowed to uttering the divine name "Yahweh" (*m. Sanhedrin* 7:5; the tetragrammaton was regarded as too sacred to be pronounced by human beings), but in the first century it was interpreted more broadly. While the title "Son of God" could be used for celestial beings (Gen 6:2; Ps 29:1, NLT mg) or kings (2 Sam 7:14; Ps 2:7) or the Messiah (4Q174 1:10-11), Jesus' opponents rightly saw that he used it to make himself equal with God (5:17-18; 10:30, 33-37).

Pilate's response ("more frightened than ever," 19:8) seems strange in light of his obvious disdain for the Jewish leaders. Part of the explanation is the fact that while Pilate was predominantly interested in Roman issues, he was still obligated by his office to keep the Jewish peace as well, and that involved sensitivity to Jewish religious interests. Pilate had never truly cared for that aspect of his office, but he would be held accountable for it by Rome; that may have frightened him somewhat. Still, while this may be part of it, it is clear in the context that his fear was directed to the title "Son of God" ("When Pilate heard *this,* he was more frightened"). As a Roman, he may have been startled by the "Son of God" title, thinking that if Jesus was indeed a "divine man" (cf. note on 19:7), he might be a messenger from the gods or even a god come down in human form. Pilate "was superstitious enough to be fearful of getting on the wrong side of the gods" (Witherington 1995:293), especially since he had just had Jesus flogged! Note also that his wife had warned him about Jesus because of a nightmare she'd had (Matt 27:19). This would heighten his fear (so Schnackenburg, Beasley-Murray, Blomberg).

Inside: Pilate Talks with Jesus about Power (19:9-11). Pilate's first question shows his superstitious fear—"Where are you from?" He wanted to make certain Jesus was not a heavenly being. He was both surprised and angered when Jesus was silent. For the early Christians, this would remind them of Isaiah 53:7 ("as a sheep is silent before the shearers, he did not open his mouth"). Jesus had already answered Pilate, in part, when he said his Kingdom was not of this world (18:36), and there was no use in explaining further. For Pilate, however, this was insolence, for accused criminals were required to respond. He reminded Jesus that he had absolute power to release Jesus or crucify him.

Jesus reminded Pilate of a higher truth: he would have no power "unless it were given to [him] from above" (19:11). This was meant by Jesus as a claim that God was the true source of Pilate's authority. Jesus is "from above" (3:31; cf. 3:3), and all authority stems from that realm. There may also be a hint that the Father had given that authority over to Jesus, so Jesus rather than Pilate controlled the outcome here. Pilate, however, undoubtedly interpreted it to mean that Rome had the true power. Jesus added, "The one who handed me over to you has the greater sin" (19:11).

Pilate was sinning by not having the courage to release Jesus; God had given him the authority to do the right thing, but he had not done so. Yet there was another who was more guilty. There is some question as to the identity of this individual. Judas seems a good candidate since he did "betray" Jesus or hand him over (6:71; 13:21; 18:2)—but he had disappeared from the scene by this time, and he did not personally hand Jesus over to Pilate. A better option is Caiaphas, the high priest over those who actually "handed over" Jesus (18:30, 35). He presided over the Sanhedrin and its decision.

In what sense was Caiaphas (who probably stands for the Jewish leaders as a whole) more guilty than Pilate? It was in the fact that Jesus came to be the Jewish Messiah spoken of in their own Scriptures, and they rejected him with impunity. Moreover, Caiaphas spearheaded all the events that led to Jesus' trial before Pilate. At this point, it is critical to understand the exact nature of Jewish guilt because misuse of it has led to tragedy—for example, the erroneous labeling of modern Jews as "Christ-killers," and other libelous ideas leading to the pogroms and the Holocaust. The book of Acts makes it clear that the recognition of this guilt by the early church did not lead to anti-Semitism even against the Jews of Jesus' generation but rather to an evangelistic invitation. In the sermons of Acts, the message is, "You put Christ on the cross, and he died for you, so believe in him and find salvation" (cf. 2:36-39; 3:15-19; 13:27-31, 38-40).

Outside: The Jews Obtain Jesus' Death (19:12–16a). For a final time, Pilate tried to free Jesus, but again the leaders stopped him. All along he realized that Jesus had done nothing that threatened Roman rule; however, he was up against an implacable foe. Finally, they brought up the most serious point of all (for Pilate): "If you release this man, you are no 'friend of Caesar.'" Pilate was under the protection of Sejanus (the chief administrator of the empire under the emperor Tiberius), who actually got him his position as prefect of Judea. The historian Tacitus (*Annals* 6.8) said that any friend of Sejanus was a friend of Caesar (Witherington, Köstenberger), and later under Vespasian, "friend of Caesar" became virtually a technical term for close companions of the emperor. Pilate may have been a member of just such a group (Bammel 1952). In AD 31, Tiberius became convinced that Sejanus was a threat and had him executed along with relatives and friends. Pilate would have been left on his own after that and indeed would have had reason to be afraid. If this trial were in AD 32 or 33 (as some believe), his fear here would have been quite justified. But even in AD 30, it was a serious threat; thus, it hit Pilate close to home. To be labeled "no friend of Caesar" (the Jews had already sent a couple of delegations to Rome to denounce Pilate) could mean the end of his career. When the leaders added, "Anyone who declares himself a king is a rebel against Caesar" (19:12), they lifted the argument to a much higher level. Pilate did not want to be accused of pardoning an enemy of Rome. There are several ironic aspects: Pilate was called "no friend of Caesar" by the primary group in the Empire who were no friends of Caesar, and Jesus, the true King of kings, was finally arraigned to die on the charge that he called himself king.

The fact that Jesus posed no threat to Rome no longer mattered. Pilate's career was at stake, so Jesus had to go. As is so often the case, politics won out over truth. Pilate finally brought Jesus outside to face his accusers as he delivered the verdict (19:13). He sat on the *bēma* [TG968, ZG1037], or judge's seat. John emphasizes this scene by telling us the area was called "Stone Pavement," or in Hebrew, "Gabbatha" (its meaning is disputed but could be "high place" or "hill"; cf. Josephus *War* 5.2.1). Such a paved area with stones has recently been found in the Tower of Antonia, but it is now recognized to be from the time of Hadrian. Instead, it is likely that John references a raised area at the governor's residence, Herod the Great's former palace (the same site for the scene as in the Synoptics; so Keener, Köstenberger). John emphasized this because it is the climactic scene, not just in the trial but in the Passion event as a whole. Here God's will was accomplished; he had allowed human depravity to come full circle in order to provide the final solution for sin, the atoning sacrifice of his Son. Next, John tells us it was "about noon" (lit., "the sixth hour") on the "day of preparation" for the Passover events. If this were the day before Passover, it would be the time when the lambs were slaughtered, a powerful symbol for Jesus as the true Paschal Lamb (so Grigsby 1982), but that is unlikely (for the chronological issue, see note on 13:1). Rather, the day is Friday, the time of preparing for the Sabbath of Passover Week (the start of the Festival of Unleavened Bread). John's purpose is simply to highlight this moment by emphasizing both the place and the date on which it occurred.

Instead of making a formal decision, Pilate, one last time, showed his disdain for the Jewish leaders by proclaiming, "Look, here is your king!" (19:14b). As Hendriksen says (1953:421), "It was born of sullen resentment. Such is your king, O Jews, shackled, weak, defenseless, bloody, sentenced to a horrible death, *at your own request!*" Yet there is also another unconscious testimony (11:50-52; 18:33, 37, 39; 19:5). They were actually crucifying not just their king but the king of the ages. The response of the crowd was tumultuous: " 'Away with him,' they yelled. 'Away with him! Crucify him!' " (19:15). Pilate said one last time in mockery, "What? Crucify your king?" The final retort by the leading priests is telling: "We have no king but Caesar." Thus they denied the biblical injunction that God alone is King (cf. Judg 8:23; 1 Sam 8:7; 10:19). In effect, they were denying not just the royal office of the Messiah but God himself; at the same time, they were rejecting the antipathy that much of Judaism harbored toward Roman rule (though the leading priests were already pro-Roman for the most part).

Then in complete capitulation, Pilate handed Jesus over for crucifixion (19:16a). As with the Synoptics, John does not record the actual sentence but implies it. Note that John said he handed Jesus over to "them," which in the context would be the Jews. While this was not technically correct, it does fit the theme of Jewish guilt (so Brown, Schnackenburg, Comfort, Ridderbos; contra Lindars, Carson, who take it to be the soldiers). Pilate allowed the Jewish authorities to have their way and turned Jesus over to the soldiers to prepare him for crucifixion.

◆   ## D. The Crucifixion of Jesus (19:16b-37)

So they took Jesus away. [17]Carrying the cross by himself, he went to the place called Place of the Skull (in Hebrew, *Golgotha*). [18]There they nailed him to the cross. Two others were crucified with him, one on either side, with Jesus between them. [19]And Pilate posted a sign over him that read, "Jesus of Nazareth,* the King of the Jews." [20]The place where Jesus was crucified was near the city, and the sign was written in Hebrew, Latin, and Greek, so that many people could read it.

[21]Then the leading priests objected and said to Pilate, "Change it from 'The King of the Jews' to 'He said, I am King of the Jews.'"

[22]Pilate replied, "No, what I have written, I have written."

[23]When the soldiers had crucified Jesus, they divided his clothes among the four of them. They also took his robe, but it was seamless, woven in one piece from top to bottom. [24]So they said, "Rather than tearing it apart, let's throw dice* for it." This fulfilled the Scripture that says, "They divided my garments among themselves and threw dice for my clothing."* So that is what they did.

[25]Standing near the cross were Jesus' mother, and his mother's sister, Mary (the wife of Clopas), and Mary Magdalene. [26]When Jesus saw his mother standing there beside the disciple he loved, he said to her, "Dear woman, here is your son." [27]And he said to this disciple, "Here is your mother." And from then on this disciple took her into his home.

[28]Jesus knew that his mission was now finished, and to fulfill Scripture he said, "I am thirsty."* [29]A jar of sour wine was sitting there, so they soaked a sponge in it, put it on a hyssop branch, and held it up to his lips. [30]When Jesus had tasted it, he said, "It is finished!" Then he bowed his head and released his spirit.

[31]It was the day of preparation, and the Jewish leaders didn't want the bodies hanging there the next day, which was the Sabbath (and a very special Sabbath, because it was the Passover). So they asked Pilate to hasten their deaths by ordering that their legs be broken. Then their bodies could be taken down. [32]So the soldiers came and broke the legs of the two men crucified with Jesus. [33]But when they came to Jesus, they saw that he was already dead, so they didn't break his legs. [34]One of the soldiers, however, pierced his side with a spear, and immediately blood and water flowed out. [35](This report is from an eyewitness giving an accurate account. He speaks the truth so that you also can believe.*) [36]These things happened in fulfillment of the Scriptures that say, "Not one of his bones will be broken,"* [37]and "They will look on the one they pierced."*

19:19 Or *Jesus the Nazarene.* 19:24a Greek *cast lots.* 19:24b Ps 22:18. 19:28 See Pss 22:15; 69:21. 19:35 Some manuscripts read *can continue to believe.* 19:36 Exod 12:46; Num 9:12; Ps 34:20. 19:37 Zech 12:10.

NOTES

19:17 *Carrying the cross by himself.* The church fathers saw a connection between Jesus bearing his own cross and Isaac carrying the wood to his own sacrifice (Gen 22:6).

19:25 *Standing near the cross.* Barrett (1978:551) thinks this story unlikely because the Romans would not have allowed anyone near Jesus due to fear of rebellion. Carson (1991:615-616) points out that the Roman auxiliary would hardly be worried by a few women in deep mourning or by a single disciple without weapons. Also, the sign above the cross was meant to be read, and if people were allowed close enough to read, they would be close enough to converse with Jesus. Another problem is the fact that the women were standing "near the cross," while in the Synoptics they were some distance away (Mark 15:40 and parallels). It is not difficult, however, to imagine them standing at a distance as they saw Jesus suffering and then drawing nearer as the end drew near (so Beasley-Murray, Carson).

19:26 *the disciple he loved.* As already stated (cf. note on 13:23), this was most likely John, who celebrated with a sense of awe the intimate relationship he had with Jesus. The possibility that he was also Jesus' cousin is based on the identification of Salome, the mother of James and John in Matt 27:56, with "his mother's sister" here (cf. Bruce, Morris, Comfort and Hawley, Burge).

19:29 *a hyssop branch.* Since the hyssop stalk was fairly short, some (e.g., Bultmann, Tasker, NEB) have conjectured that the original term was "javelin" (*hussō* [TG5300.1, ZG5726]) rather than "hyssop" (*hussōpō* [TG5301, ZG5727]). This would certainly fit the fact that it was a soldier sharing his wine with Jesus, but there is very little support (two very late cursive mss, 476 and 1242), and there is not much of a possibility that all the earlier mss had the wrong term. Moreover, these were auxiliary troops, and they would not have been issued javelins (so Bruce), leading to the conclusion that this is an interesting but unlikely conjecture. Moreover, the cross was only 7–8 feet tall, and they would not have needed a javelin to reach Jesus' lips.

19:31-37 Many scholars (Westcott, Brown, Bruce, Whitacre) place 19:31-37 with 19:38-42 on the grounds that both passages involve requests and discuss what happened to Jesus' body. John 19:31-37 is more closely related to Jesus' death (19:28-30), however; his body was still on the cross. Here it is the final episode of the Crucifixion narrative. At feast times, measures would have always been taken to ensure that the bodies of the crucified could be removed before sunset (cf. Brown).

19:34 *blood and water flowed out.* Many physicians and others throughout history have speculated on what caused both "blood and water" to flow: (1) The traditional view was that Jesus' heart burst (therefore he died of a broken heart), but that is not likely medically. (2) The lance pierced Jesus' heart, with the blood flowing from the heart and the water from the pericardial sac, along with ascitic fluid from the abdomen accumulated during the process of crucifixion (Edwards et al. 1986:1455-1463). (3) Pleural fluid (that appears like water) would not flow out but rather gather around the lung, so the blood and water had accumulated just inside the rib cage (the effects of the scourging, accumulating while he hung on the cross) between the chest lining and the lung (Sava 1960). Whatever the medical reasons, John was stressing the reality of Jesus' death as well as the horrific nature of it. For water to accumulate in the pericardium, pleural space, or abdomen implies an immense stress on the body far out of the range of any ordinary death (so Dr. John Dunlop, a medical practitioner).

Scholars have long speculated on the symbolic overtones of the blood and water: (1) Historically, it has been common to see a sacramental thrust, with the water symbolizing baptism and the blood the Eucharist (Chrysostom, Augustine, Brown), but this certainly does not fit Johannine themes. (2) In keeping with the use of the symbols in John, the blood could refer to Jesus' sacrificial death as the basis of eternal life, and the water to the cleansing work of the Spirit within (Dodd, Schnackenburg, Morris, Carson, Keener). (3) This is Passover symbolism, in which the legs of the sacrifice are not to be broken (cf. 19:36 below), and the fact that the lamb was a living sacrifice was shown by the flow of blood when the throat was cut (Ford 1969; Grigsby 1982). It is difficult to know if John had intended any special symbolic thrust. If so, either of the last two are good possibilities.

19:35 *He speaks the truth.* There is debate over the referent of the pronoun "he" (*ekeinos* [TG1565, ZG1697], "that one"). The options are as follows: (1) The author referred to himself, the beloved disciple who wrote the fourth Gospel (Westcott, Morris, Carson, Köstenberger). (2) The *ekeinos* refers to Christ, who provides valid testimony to himself (8:14) (Hoskyns). (3) The later church is attesting to the truth of the witness (John) in a manner similar to 21:24 (Michaels, Whitacre). Of these, the first is the most likely. There is nothing in the context to suggest Christ as the witness, and the details of this verse differ enough from 21:24 to make the third option unlikely.

COMMENTARY

John presents a very dramatic, tightly controlled, and unique portrait of Jesus' crucifixion, emphasizing that the central moment in human history had arrived. Its connection with the Synoptic portrait is obvious. John's Gospel parallels them in terms of Jesus bearing his cross, the two criminals crucified with him, the inscription, the dividing of his garments, the women who were witnesses, Jesus' receiving sour wine to drink, and Jesus' death. Yet a great deal is omitted as well—Simon of Cyrene carrying the cross, Jesus refusing the wine at the start, the taunts, the darkness, the cry of dereliction, the earthquake, the tearing of the Temple veil, and the centurion's cry. Moreover, even as John generally followed the synoptic events, he provided new material: the universal witness of the inscription and the consternation it caused, the details in the dividing of the garments, the Scripture-fulfillment quotations, Jesus' giving of his mother to John, the last cry, and the piercing of Jesus' side. John provides his own very stylized portrait, and the theological emphases are central: the sovereign control of Jesus; the Cross as his throne, anointing him as royal Messiah; and the Cross as his exaltation, lifting him up to glory. Culpepper (1997:34-36) believes that the four scenes of the Crucifixion were chosen by John also to illuminate the ecclesiological results: the church originates at the Cross and finds both its meaning and destiny in it.

Jesus Led to the Cross (19:16b-18). Terribly bloodied but unbowed, Jesus began his final walk to the place of execution. He was turned over to the soldiers, who according to the Synoptic accounts, scourged him, mocked him, and then led him away to the place of execution. It was common practice to make the condemned criminal carry the crossbeam to the execution site (so Plutarch *Divine Vengeance* 9— the pole was already standing there), not just out of cruelty but as a message to the condemned that they were as good as dead. It was intended to break their will to live. The Synoptics tell us how Simon of Cyrene was coerced to bear Jesus' cross for him when he collapsed just outside the town due to the scourging, but John omits this, centering instead on Jesus as the one in control of his fate. Mark 15:23 tells us Jesus was offered wine mixed with myrrh (a mild narcotic—this too was normal practice), but Jesus refused it in order to face his destiny in full control of his senses.

The poles for the crucifixions may have stayed upright at the site since it was apparently a regular place for crucifixions. (Some, however argue that it was not the regular site for executions since a Jewish tomb was nearby (19:41) and a tomb would not be placed near an execution site; so Brown). If that was the case, it would have been erected just for this execution. Usually the pole was not more than seven feet high or so—just enough to get the feet off the ground. When they wanted the person to die more quickly (as on this day because the prisoners had to be dead before dusk due to Passover), they would nail the wrists (not the hands) to the crossbeam, hoist it up to the pole, and then nail the feet with one six-inch spike through the ankles to the pole. It is difficult to imagine the pain—Jesus' back was ripped right to the bone by the scourging, and he had nails through his wrists and ankles. The Romans would also place a *sedecula* or seat (a small block of wood placed just above the buttocks) on the cross so the condemned man could rest occasionally and prolong the agony. Death would come by asphyxiation and could take several days if the person was only tied up on the cross. The hands would slowly turn to gangrene since the circulation was cut off, and the agony would be beyond imagination until the victim finally died. Crucifixion is commonly thought to be the worst torture ever devised. Roman citizens could not be crucified except by direct edict of Caesar, and to the Jews it connoted being cut off from the covenant people since it was "hanging from the tree" (Deut 21:23; cf. Gal 3:13).

It is difficult to know why the site was named the "Place of the Skull" (Aramaic, *Golgotha*). It may have had the appearance of a skull, or it could have been named as such because it was a place of execution (though if it was not the regular site [see above], that would not be true). Most agree that the Church of the Holy Sepulchre (inside the walls of the Old City of Jerusalem today) is more likely than Gordon's Calvary (outside the walls of the Old City today) as the locale for it (so Brown, Carson, Blomberg, Keener). The walls of Jerusalem in Jesus' day were in completely different spots than they are today.

Two other criminals were crucified with Jesus, one on each side, fulfilling Isaiah 53:12, "he was counted among the rebels." Mark 15:27 tells us that they, like Barabbas, were insurrectionists or terrorists. John omitted their taunts and the conversion of the one (cf. Luke 23:39-43), again probably in order to center on Jesus.

The Inscription on the Cross: A Universal Witness (19:19–22). It was common to place a *titulus,* or sign, above the cross to explain the crime, and this is how we know Jesus was crucified on a traditional cross-shape rather than a T- or X-shaped cross— this inscription was placed *above* his head. John alone tells us Pilate deliberately had written on the placard, "Jesus of Nazareth, the King of the Jews." He no doubt did this to provoke the Jewish leaders and show his contempt for them, but God had greater plans. He turned this into another unconscious prophecy, a universal proclamation that the cross was Jesus' throne.

It was also common to state the crime in several languages because the Romans wanted to make this a warning to the populace as a deterrent to crime. Hebrew/Aramaic was the language of the populace, Latin the official language of Rome and the military, and Greek the common language of the empire. When the leading priests objected, wanting it to say "He said, I am King of the Jews," Pilate contemptuously dismissed them with "What I have written, I have written" (19:21-22). They wanted to make this no more than Jesus' self-claim, but Pilate wished to humiliate them. In doing so, however, he turned it into a virtually worldwide proclamation of Jesus' kingship. "So here we have another irony: the man who does not have a clue about the truth (18:38) proclaims, unwittingly, the truth about Jesus. And we have the tragedy of the representatives of the one true God, who should have recognized the truth, continuing to reject it" (Whitacre 1999:459).

Dividing Jesus' Clothes (19:23-24). This is briefly mentioned in the Synoptics (Mark 15:24 and parallels) but without this detail. It was common Roman practice for the victim to be crucified nude, but possibly due to Jewish objections regarding nudity, Jesus and the other two were allowed loincloths. Also, the executioners were allowed to keep the personal effects of the condemned. In Jesus' case, that probably would have been his headpiece, belt, sandals, outer robe, and his undergarment or *chitōn* [TG5509, ZG5945]—a seamless tunic "woven in one piece from top to bottom" (not especially expensive or unusual in Palestine). The normal squadron for crucifixion would consist of four soldiers, so they divided up the other four but decided to gamble over the tunic rather than tear it into four pieces. John seems to emphasize the tunic, so commentators have long speculated that the seamless tunic symbolized either the unity of the church (cf. 10:16; 11:52; 17:20-23) or Jesus as the high priest (Josephus [*Antiquities* 3.161] describes the high priest's robe as seamless, cf. Exod 39:27). The unity theme does not fit the context here, however, and the seamless robe was taken away from Jesus rather than given to him. Moreover, the high priest's robe was the outer garment, while this tunic was the undergarment. Neither theme works well here. It is more likely that John emphasized the seamless nature of the tunic to explain why the soldiers gambled for it (they didn't want to rip it into four pieces).

The purpose of the scene is to emphasize how it fulfilled Scripture, specifically Psalm 22:18, "They divide my garments among themselves and throw dice for my clothing" (19:24). This begins a major element of the Crucifixion scene, with four fulfillment passages (19:24, 28, 36, 37). Fulfillment of Scripture is not emphasized in John as much as in Matthew or Luke, so this is unusual. It may be that "in a missionary document addressed to Jews as well as Gentiles a defense of the close of Jesus' life was felt to be necessary. It had to be shown that what happened to Jesus was in accord with a divine plan, as revealed in Holy Writ" (Witherington 1995:308). John, in fact, described the event on the basis of the quote from Psalm 22, with the division of the garments described in 19:23a and the gambling over the tunic described in 19:23b-24a. Moreover, we have here a progressive surrender of Jesus' earthly attachments—first his clothes, then his family (particularly his mother), and finally his life itself (so Michaels).

Giving His Mother to the Beloved Disciple (19:25-27). It is important to remember that Jesus' brothers refused to believe in him (7:5), so Jesus needed to ensure his mother's care when he was gone. (Joseph had probably passed away, as the complete absence of him in the Gospels during Jesus' ministry shows). It was also common to allow the crucified to make a last will and testament with relatives and friends, and even enemies, around them (Stauffer 1960a:111, 179). Since Jesus gave her into the care of his cousin (see note on 19:26) and trusted disciple, John, the scene makes perfect historical sense. Every Gospel has a list of women who functioned as official witnesses of Jesus' death and resurrection. John lists four women, the first pair unnamed (Jesus' mother and her sister) and the second pair named (Mary wife of Clopas and Mary Magdalene). Some have suggested that John lists only three women, with Jesus' mother's sister being the same person as Mary the wife of Clopas, but it is unlikely that the two sisters would have both been named Mary. While the list of names differs somewhat between the Gospels, it is likely there were at least five: (1) Mary the mother of Jesus, (2) Mary the wife of Clopas and mother of James the Younger and Joseph, (3) Salome the sister of Jesus' mother as well as wife of Zebedee and mother of James and John, (4) Mary Magdalene, and (5) Joanna (at the tomb in Luke; cf. Osborne 1984:199).

As Jesus was near death, he looked down and saw his mother standing near the beloved disciple and decided to forge a new family relationship so as to ensure the security of his mother. The language he used ("Dear woman, here is your son . . . Here is your mother") is found in Jewish family law when a person is legally entrusted to another (Stauffer 1960a:113). Needless to say, this is a beautiful scene and demonstrates the incredible love of Jesus for his own, even during the agony of his death. (Family responsibilities in Judaism were taken very seriously.) Mary was being told she had a new son to take care of her. More importantly, they were also related by faith. Roman Catholic exegetes have seen this more as the naming of Mary as the mother of John and therefore of the church (so Brown, Schnackenburg); however, the atmosphere of the passage makes it more likely that Jesus' mother was placed into the care of John, who took her "into his home" rather than vice versa (so Beasley-Murray). With Dodd (1953a:423), it is best to say that all attempts at symbolism (e.g., John and Mary form a new Adam and Eve [Witherington] or portray Jewish and Gentile Christianity [Bultmann]) are "singularly unconvincing." If there is a theological thrust, it is best to say they represent the family relationship that is to typify the new community of the church (so Kysar, Ridderbos, Whitacre).

The Death of Jesus (19:28-30). Jesus "knew that his mission was now finished" (19:28). The "hour" had not just arrived; it had been fulfilled (cf. 7:30; 8:20; 13:1; 17:1). It was time to make his final surrender and give up his life. According to Mark (15:25, 33), Jesus had been on the cross nearly six hours. He was naturally "thirsty," but his declaration here may have been just as much to fulfill Scripture as to assuage his thirst (so Carson, Burge). This statement, "I am thirsty," could allude to Psalm 22:15 ("my tongue sticks to the roof of my mouth"), but a better parallel is Psalm 69:21 ("they offer me sour wine for my thirst"), a psalm already cited in 2:17; 15:25, and alluded to again in 19:29-30 below. The fulfillment of this psalm in 19:29 is nearly exact. The soldiers took a sponge and dipped it in a jar of sour wine to satisfy Jesus' thirst. This was not the myrrhed wine of Mark 15:23, offered as he arrived at the place of execution, but a cheap vinegar wine (*oxos* [TG3690, ZG3954], the same term as in Ps 69:21 [68:22, LXX]) usually drunk by soldiers and the poor.

Only John tells us that the soldiers placed the sponge on a hyssop plant in order to give it to Jesus. Matthew 27:48 and Mark 15:36 say they gave it to Jesus on a "stick" or branch. Probably it was a stalk of hyssop, for a mere sprig of hyssop would not hold the weight of the sponge or allow them to lift it up to Jesus' lips. The stalks did not grow very long, but they would not have to lift it too high since Jesus' feet were only slightly above the ground. A soldier could reach Jesus' mouth easily. Beetham and Beetham (1993:164-167) say the hyssop was placed on a "sprinkle reed," which is linked with purification rites in the Old Testament. Hyssop had important implications at Passover because it was used to put the blood of the lamb on the doorframe and sides of the posts (Exod 12:22). The fact that Jesus died on the first day of Passover is significant, and thus many believe the hyssop symbolized Jesus' death as the paschal sacrifice (so Brown, Grigsby 1982, Bruce, Whitacre, Burge, Köstenberger contra Beasley-Murray, Carson; see also on 1:29).

After he tasted the drink (19:30), Jesus cried out one final time (cf. the "loud cry" in Mark 15:37), "It is finished!" He had completed his mission (finishing the work God gave him; 4:34; 17:4) and fulfilled his destiny. There is both a temporal ("It is ended") and a theological ("It is accomplished") aspect to his words (so Beasley-Murray). If the Passover implications are correct, they emphasize that he had carried out his atoning work on the cross (a major emphasis in John, cf. 1:29; 10:11, 15; 11:50, 52; 18:14). He had become the sacrifice for sin and had procured eternal life for mankind—the age of salvation could begin. Still in sovereign control, even at the last moment, Jesus "bowed his head" and "released his spirit" to the Father (cf. "breathed his last," Mark 15:37 = Luke 23:46). Jesus had earlier said, "No one can take my life from me. I sacrifice it voluntarily" (10:18). That is precisely the case here. Obedient to the Father to the very end, he relinquished his life to him.

Piercing Jesus' Side (19:31-37). If the bodies were still on the crosses after sundown, the Passover celebrations would be seriously compromised, for the Torah demanded that those "hanging from the tree" must not remain overnight (Deut 21:22-23). Moreover, this was the "special Sabbath" during Passover week, so it was even more critical that this injunction be followed. The Jewish authorities did not trust the Romans to observe this and so sent a delegation to Pilate to make certain the victims were dead in time to be removed. Since crucifixion could take several days (in fact, the Romans normally let the bodies rot on the cross as a warning to others), it was necessary to ensure the demise of the three victims. The Jewish leaders asked Pilate "to hasten their deaths by ordering that their legs be broken" (19:31). They would break both legs with a heavy mallet, which sped the victim's death by two means: the physical shock to a system already weakened by scourging and crucifixion; and the inability to push up on the small wooden seat and exhale. Death by asphyxiation would then come quickly. This practice was confirmed by a skeleton discovered in 1968, with one leg fractured and the other totally shattered (Haas 1970). Moreover, the authorities probably reasoned that the mutilation of Jesus' body would emphasize further the fact that he was accursed (so Beasley-Murray).

The soldiers worked from the two sides, breaking the legs of the two criminals first (19:32-33). On the basis of Mark 15:33-34, this was probably shortly after 3 P.M., which would make sense because this would have allowed for the death and removal of the victims before sundown. When they reached Jesus, they undoubtedly said, "He's dead; no need for this here" (so Bruce). Just to make sure, one of the soldiers reached up and thrust his spear into Jesus' side. This was not just a gentle jab but a violent thrust deep within, for "immediately blood and water flowed out" (on the medical and symbolic possibilities, see the note on 19:34). John's primary purpose was certainly to prove the reality of Jesus' death. It is possible that the same docetic heresy confronted in 1 John is answered here. These false teachers denied that the Messiah could be human and asserted that he only appeared to be so (cf. 1 John 2:22-23; 4:2-4; 5:5-6; cf. especially 5:6, "by water and blood"). Such a Messiah could not truly die but only appear to die. John wanted his readers to understand that the royal Messiah had truly died (so Beasley-Murray, Carson, Köstenberger).

John anchors the reality of Jesus' death (and the blood and water flowing out) by telling us that this came from accurate eyewitness testimony (namely his own, 19:35). He wanted his readers to realize the absolute reliability of his account of the Crucifixion. This is important evidence that the early church believed the details to be historically accurate. In John, this is paralleled by 21:24 ("his account of these things is accurate"), which refers more generally to the Gospel as a whole. Other important witnesses are Luke 1:1-4 (where Luke claims to follow eyewitness testimony with historical accuracy) and 2 Peter 1:16 (where Peter says he did not invent "clever stories" when telling the story of Jesus). It is clear that the early church claimed authenticity for the Gospels.

John concluded his Crucifixion narrative with two more fulfillment quotations (19:36-37). The fact that Jesus' legs were not broken fulfills the statement "not one of his bones will be broken" (19:36), which is found in various forms three times in the Old Testament (Exod 12:46 and Num 9:12, both stating that no bone of the Passover lamb is to be broken; Ps 34:20, which states that God protects his righteous people). It is possible that both allusions are intended (so Lindars, Beasley-Murray), but it is difficult to see why the idea of protection would be part of the meaning here, and the first meaning has priority in light of the Passover setting with Jesus as the Paschal lamb (Keener). Second, John notes that the piercing of Jesus' side fulfilled Zechariah 12:10, "They will look on the one they pierced" (19:37). The Zechariah passage talks about Israel looking upon God's representative (the prophet or the Messiah) and mourning for her unbelief. John hoped that Israel would once more repent of her apostasy.

◆   E. The Burial of Jesus (19:38-42)

38Afterward Joseph of Arimathea, who had been a secret disciple of Jesus (because he feared the Jewish leaders), asked Pilate for permission to take down Jesus' body. When Pilate gave permission, Joseph came and took the body away. 39With him came Nicodemus, the man who had come to Jesus at night. He brought seventy-five pounds* of perfumed ointment made from myrrh and aloes. 40Following Jewish burial custom, they wrapped Jesus' body with the spices in long sheets of linen cloth. 41The place of crucifixion was near a garden, where there was a new tomb, never used before. 42And so, because it was the day of preparation for the Jewish Passover* and since the tomb was close at hand, they laid Jesus there.

19:39 Greek 100 litras [32.7 kilograms].   19:42 Greek because of the Jewish day of preparation.

NOTES

19:41 *new tomb.* Burge (2000:536) describes the typical Jewish tomb: (1) A heavy wheel-shaped stone, 4–6 feet in diameter, was rolled into a shallow trough and kept in place by a short wall on both sides of the opening. (2) A burial chamber with a preparation room was encircled with a stone bench on which the body was readied. (3) Burial *niches* (6 feet long and 2 feet high) were cut into the wall either above the bench or in a separate chamber. (4) A decorated limestone "bone box" was placed on the floor to gather the bones after the body had decomposed. The one detail that is problematic here is the burial *niche* cut into the wall. Since two angels would sit at each end of the spot where Jesus' body lay, this makes it difficult to conceive of a *niche* in the wall. More likely it was a *trough-arcosolium*, a sarcophagus placed under a recessed arch (Carson 1991:640). Also, we must note that the actual grave opening would be only about 3 feet high.

COMMENTARY

Since the Cross was the enthronement of the royal Messiah, it was only fitting that Jesus be given a royal burial. Leading the way was Joseph of Arimathea, a wealthy man (Matt 27:57) and member of the Sanhedrin (Mark 15:43 and parallels). He was also a follower of Jesus (Matt 27:57), who anxiously awaited the Kingdom of God and who had opposed the Sanhedrin's decision (Luke 23:51). John added that he "had been a secret disciple of Jesus (because he feared the Jewish leaders)," a recapitulation of 12:42-43, but not as negative here as in chapter 12. In fact, it may well be that John emphasized this in order to draw out (cf. 12:32) other closet Christians who were still in the synagogues and give them the courage to make a public declaration for Jesus (so Brown). Joseph took a step of enormous courage. The Romans usually allowed the crucified to rot, but the Jews had received permission to take them down and place them in a common grave outside the city. Probably so moved by Jesus' solemn death, Joseph traded on his membership in the Sanhedrin and went to Pilate to ask permission "to take down Jesus' body," undoubtedly including permission for burial. It is highly unusual that Pilate acquiesced, but he had been convinced of Jesus' innocence and was disgusted that the Jewish leaders had made him give Jesus up to be crucified. So he gave Joseph permission.

Only John tells us that Nicodemus, "who had come to Jesus at night" (19:39; cf. 3:1ff) and was another secret believer, assisted Joseph (who could hardly have taken the body away himself). It is also possible that they used the service of slaves, since handling the body themselves would have rendered them unclean for seven days, thereby removing them from participation in the Passover (so Brown). Nicodemus brought 100 *litrai* [TG3046, ZG3354] or "seventy-five pounds" (actually 65.45 pounds, so Beasley-Murray) of "perfumed ointment made from myrrh and aloes"—an extraordinary amount. Myrrh was a fragrant resin used by the Egyptians in embalming, and the Jews used it in powder form, mixing it with the aloes, a powder of aromatic sandalwood (Carson). The purpose was to counteract the odor caused by the decaying body, but this amount was very unusual and exceedingly expensive. As such, it parallels the expensive perfume used to anoint Jesus for burial in 12:1-8. There is also a royal motif, for such exorbitant amounts were used to bury kings. For example, there were 500 slaves carrying burial spices at the funeral of Herod the Great (Josephus *Antiquities* 17.199), certainly beyond what even royal burials required. More apropos is the story of Onkelos, who burned 80 *litrai* of spices at the burial of the great rabbi Gamaliel, saying, "Is not Rabbi Gamaliel better than a hundred kings?"

Witherington hypothesizes (1995:312) that "these 'secret disciples' were trying to make up in death for their neglect of Jesus or their lack of courage to support his cause when he was alive." Perhaps this could be called another "unconscious testimony" (as Caiaphas's was in 11:50-52)—this time an unknowing homage to Jesus' genuine royalty by two bashful disciples. The spices were packed in the "long sheets of linen cloth" (*othoniois* [TG3608, ZG3856]) used to wrap Jesus' body (19:40). Some translations (e.g., NIV) have "strips of linen," and at first glance, this seems to contradict the "long sheet of linen cloth" in Mark 15:46, which seems to imply a single sheet. However, it is very possible that this is a generalizing plural for a single sheet (Brown, Keener) or that by "long sheets" or pieces, John includes the face cloth (cf. John 11:44, so Blomberg). Probably they packed the spices in with the cloth and also placed some under and around the body.

The fact that the site of the tomb was "near" the place of execution (19:41-42; most likely both Golgotha and the tomb are covered by the Church of the Holy Sepulchre) was a real boon for Joseph and Nicodemus, since they had only a short time for readying Jesus' body for burial (washing the corpse and wrapping it in the spices and linen) before sunset. Even the description of the site God chose for the tomb would support a royal motif. It was a "new tomb, never used before" (undoubtedly dug into the hillside as was the common Jewish practice), and it was set in a garden, probably some type of olive grove (the same term is used in 18:1 for the grove of Jesus' arrest). Later, Mary Magdalene would wrongly think Jesus was a gardener (20:15). There are Old Testament references to the burial of kings in a garden (2 Kgs 21:18, 26; Neh 3:15-16 of David's tomb), further evidence that the imagery here portrays a royal burial.

◆ VI. The Resurrection of Jesus (20:1–21:25)
   A. Jesus' Appearances in Jerusalem (20:1-31)

Early on Sunday morning,* while it was still dark, Mary Magdalene came to the tomb and found that the stone had been rolled away from the entrance. ²She ran and found Simon Peter and the other disciple, the one whom Jesus loved. She said, "They have taken the Lord's body out of the tomb, and we don't know where they have put him!"

³Peter and the other disciple started out for the tomb. ⁴They were both running, but the other disciple outran Peter and reached the tomb first. ⁵He stooped and looked in and saw the linen wrappings lying there, but he didn't go in. ⁶Then Simon Peter arrived and went inside. He also noticed the linen wrappings lying there, ⁷while the cloth that had covered Jesus' head was folded up and lying apart from the other wrappings. ⁸Then the disciple who had reached the tomb first also went in, and he saw and believed—⁹for

until then they still hadn't understood the Scriptures that said Jesus must rise from the dead. [10]Then they went home.

[11]Mary was standing outside the tomb crying, and as she wept, she stooped and looked in. [12]She saw two white-robed angels, one sitting at the head and the other at the foot of the place where the body of Jesus had been lying. [13]"Dear woman, why are you crying?" the angels asked her.

"Because they have taken away my Lord," she replied, "and I don't know where they have put him."

[14]She turned to leave and saw someone standing there. It was Jesus, but she didn't recognize him. [15]"Dear woman, why are you crying?" Jesus asked her. "Who are you looking for?"

She thought he was the gardener. "Sir," she said, "if you have taken him away, tell me where you have put him, and I will go and get him."

[16]"Mary!" Jesus said.

She turned to him and cried out, "Rabboni!" (which is Hebrew for "Teacher").

[17]"Don't cling to me," Jesus said, "for I haven't yet ascended to the Father. But go find my brothers and tell them 'I am ascending to my Father and your Father, to my God and your God.'"

[18]Mary Magdalene found the disciples and told them, "I have seen the Lord!" Then she gave them his message.

[19]That Sunday evening* the disciples were meeting behind locked doors because they were afraid of the Jewish leaders. Suddenly, Jesus was standing there among them! "Peace be with you," he said. [20]As he spoke, he showed them the wounds in his hands and his side. They were filled with joy when they saw the Lord! [21]Again he said, "Peace be with you. As the Father has sent me, so I am sending you." [22]Then he breathed on them and said, "Receive the Holy Spirit. [23]If you forgive anyone's sins, they are forgiven. If you do not forgive them, they are not forgiven."

[24]One of the twelve disciples, Thomas (nicknamed the Twin),* was not with the others when Jesus came. [25]They told him, "We have seen the Lord!"

But he replied, "I won't believe it unless I see the nail wounds in his hands, put my fingers into them, and place my hand into the wound in his side."

[26]Eight days later the disciples were together again, and this time Thomas was with them. The doors were locked; but suddenly, as before, Jesus was standing among them. "Peace be with you," he said. [27]Then he said to Thomas, "Put your finger here, and look at my hands. Put your hand into the wound in my side. Don't be faithless any longer. Believe!"

[28]"My Lord and my God!" Thomas exclaimed.

[29]Then Jesus told him, "You believe because you have seen me. Blessed are those who believe without seeing me."

[30]The disciples saw Jesus do many other miraculous signs in addition to the ones recorded in this book. [31]But these are written so that you may continue to believe* that Jesus is the Messiah, the Son of God, and that by believing in him you will have life by the power of his name.

20:1 Greek *On the first day of the week.*   20:19 Greek *In the evening of that day, the first day of the week.*
20:24 Greek *Thomas, who was called Didymus.*   20:31 Some manuscripts read *that you may believe.*

NOTES

20:1 *while it was still dark.* As in the Nicodemus episode (3:2), darkness here probably symbolizes their lack of understanding, even spiritual blindness (cf. Brown, Schnackenburg). It may even prepare for "the gradual dawning that is to take place in the following verses, culminating in the self-revelation of Jesus in 20:17" (Mahoney 1974:238).

20:12 *two white-robed angels.* This is not the same scene as the angels appearing to the women in Mark 16:5 and parallels. There the angel gave the women a commission to tell the other disciples, while here the angels have a completely different function. Moreover,

Mary had left the rest of the women and run back. So the first appearance is the one reported in Mark 16, while this is a second appearance to Mary alone. The other women were probably on their way back to the disciples at this time (cf. Westcott, Wenham).

20:17 *Don't cling to me.* This has perplexed commentators for centuries. Brown lists 12 different interpretations. Here are the main ones: (1) Some take this literally; Jesus was asking her not to "touch" him (*mē mou haptou* [TG680, ZG721]) because he had risen from the dead but had not yet ascended (Bultmann), but this is unlikely since he did ask Thomas later to touch him. Others (Brown) believe this means Jesus' ascension occurred between 20:17 and 20:27, so that Thomas might touch him, but there is no hint of that in John or any other Gospel. (2) Mary had perhaps fallen to the ground and was grasping Jesus' feet, so Jesus was telling her to stop clinging or holding on to him—because it was not necessary, for his ascension was in process, and it was a time for joy (Beasley-Murray, Perkins, Carson, Ridderbos, Michaels, Whitacre). (3) Some (Bernard) emend the text to read, "do not fear" (*mē ptoou* [TG3361/4422, ZG3590/4765]), but such a change is speculative and unnecessary. (4) Jesus was saying, "Don't touch me now; instead, take a message to my disciples" (Marxsen), perhaps with an implied, "You will touch me later in eucharistic celebration" (21:11-14, so Hoskyns). This too goes beyond the evidence and ignores the centrality of the Ascension. (5) It means, "Don't cling to me" and indicates Mary was clinging to the old relationships she had with Jesus, her "rabbi" (Dodd, Sanders, Lindars, Barrett, Morris, Forestell, Osborne 1984, Witherington, Burge). The best is probably some combination of 2 and 5. Mary had tried to embrace Jesus in her joy, but Jesus is saying she cannot "cling" to the earthly but must wait for the new age when he will come in the Spirit (Köstenberger). This was the beginning of a new era, and Mary had to be willing to let Jesus go and enter a new relationship.

20:19-26 As some have pointed out (Witherington, Michaels), this scene sums up the promises Jesus made in the farewell discourse: "Jesus was standing there among them" (20:19) fulfills 14:18, 23, 28 ("[I] will come"); "Peace be with you" (20:19, 21, 26) fulfills 14:27; cf. 16:33 ("the peace I give"); "filled with joy" (20:20) fulfills 16:20-22 ("grief [turned] to wonderful joy"); and "receive the Holy Spirit" (20:22) fulfills 14:16-18, cf. 14:26; 15:26; 16:7 ("give you another Advocate").

20:19 *That Sunday evening.* This is undoubtedly the same appearance as recorded in Luke 24:36-49. The time note is interesting. It is possible that "day" (lit., "the first day of the week"; cf. also 20:1, 26) refers to the day of individual decision (Bultmann), a clear theme in this Gospel (1:38; 3:3, 15; 4:24-26; 9:36-38), though it is more likely to connote the offer of Kingdom blessings here (note "peace" and "joy" in vv. 20-21). Less likely is the view of some (Lindars, Brown, Barrett) that there is a liturgical or sacramental motif presupposing the living presence of Jesus in the eucharistic celebration (they see this as the same scene as in Mark 16:14).

20:22 *Receive the Holy Spirit.* The relationship of this giving of the Spirit to the giving of the Spirit at Pentecost in Acts 2 has led to serious debate: (1) Some (Theodore of Mopsuestia, Carson, Witherington, Köstenberger) say there is only one giving of the Spirit (in Acts 2), and so this is a symbol or acted parable pointing forward to that event. Jesus did not give the disciples the Spirit at this time but rather pointed ahead to that future event. This interpretation does not quite fit the text as written, for Jesus said, "Receive the Holy Spirit" rather than "You are going to receive the Spirit." (2) Since there is no article before the word *pneuma* [TG4151, ZG4460] (spirit), some think (Westcott, Johnston) this is a gift of an impersonal power rather than the personal Spirit, but that is to read too much into the absence of the article (in the NT the phrase *pneuma* is found 37 times with the article and 49 times without it; so Comfort). (3) Others simply accept that there are two different early traditions in conflict and that they cannot be reconciled (Bultmann,

Marxsen, Lindars, Brown, Barrett), but that is unnecessary, as the following will show. (4) There were two events of sending the Spirit, with the "Johannine Pentecost" here as a private infilling of the Spirit and Acts 2 as a public empowering by the Spirit (Benoit, Osborne 1984, Morris, Beasley-Murray, Comfort, Burge, Blomberg). This last option makes best sense in light of the reality of the event as portrayed by both John and Luke.

20:23 *If you forgive anyone's sins, they are forgiven.* Roman Catholics have long used this verse, along with Matt 16:19, to support the authority of the priest in the confession booth to forgive sins. Yet the two great Jesuit scholars who have written commentaries on John, Brown (1970:1030-1031) and Schnackenburg (1982:3.326-328) both admit that the meaning here is the proclamation of the Gospel—that is, the church in mission. In addition, J. P. Meier (1996:397-398) thinks it is the mission of the church as a whole that is described here.

20:26 *Eight days later.* This would be the following Sunday (in Jewish reckoning the first and last days are both counted). There may also be a theological motif pointing to "the Lord's Day" (Rev 1:10) as the day of Christian worship (so Plummer, Beasley-Murray, Whitacre).

20:28 *My Lord and my God!* The question of the historical veracity of this statement has divided scholars. It is common to assume that the early church's affirmation of deity came later than this; however, a great deal can be said in favor of the historicity of the scene. Carson (1991:658) notes six things: (1) The view that the Christological titles evolved slowly has long been disproven. (2) The Jews had developed a series of intermediaries between God and men, angels and others, so Thomas had plenty of categories in which to understand this. (3) The use of *kurios* [TG2962, ZG3261] (Lord) for addressing God, as well as a courtesy to others, made this statement possible. (4) *kurios* was an early post-Resurrection title (Rom 10:9; 1 Cor 12:3; Phil 2:9-11) and comes close to ascribing deity. (5) Since *marana* [TG3134, ZG3448] (meaning "our Lord") was used quite early as a reference to Jesus (1 Cor 16:22), there is no reason why "my Lord" should be rejected. (6) The Evangelist was an eyewitness, and there is no reason to reject his witness here.

20:29 *You believe because you have seen me.* Some (NA²⁷, RSV, NRSV) take this as a question, which would highlight Thomas's failure: "Do you believe because you have seen me?" The majority of scholars rightly see this as a direct statement (so NLT). Jesus was simply stating a fact. As Barrett says (1978:573), "In this solemn and impressive pronouncement, Jesus does not ask questions but declares the truth."

20:31 *that you may continue to believe.* There is a text-critical question as to whether the verb is aorist tense (*pisteusēte* [TG4100, ZG4409], "believe"), so ℵ² A C D W 𝔐, or whether it's the present tense of the same word (*pisteuēte*, "continue to believe"), so 𝔓66ᵛⁱᵈ ℵ* B 0250. The stronger mss evidence probably lies with the present tense, but the two have histori- cally become a proving ground for the debate as to whether John was written to evangelize non-believers (aorist tense, "believe") or strengthen believers (present tense, "continue to believe"). In actuality, either tense can connote each of the two meanings. As said in the Introduction, some scholars think John was mainly evangelistic (Carson), others that he mainly addressed believers (Beasley-Murray, Keener). In reality, John probably wrote with both purposes in mind (Köstenberger).

COMMENTARY

Unfortunately, many critical scholars have taken the position that the Resurrection accounts are not historical. Through the centuries, several theories have been devel- oped to explain what "really happened" to Jesus (cf. Osborne 1995:34-38): (1) The conspiracy theory: the Jews spread the rumor that the disciples stole Jesus' body and made up a story of the Resurrection (cf. Matt 28:11-15). Eusebius refuted it, pointing out that the disciples would hardly have been willing to die for a lie. (2) The political theory: H. S. Reimarus in the mid-eighteenth century said the disciples (political opportunists like Jesus was) made up the story in order to gain celebrity and power. Yet again, they would hardly have been willing to die for such a ruse. (3) The swoon theory: The rationalists (e.g., Schleiermacher, Hase) in the nineteenth century (and Muslims too) explained the Resurrection away on the basis of natural causes. Jesus fainted on the cross, recovered in the tomb, and then escaped. For Muslims, he sneaked away to Kashmir, where he preached Islam for 40 years before ascending. This view ignores the fact that Romans were experts at crucifixion; no one survived the experience. (4) The mythical view: D. F. Strauss, in the middle of the nineteenth century (and later Bultmann, Tillich, Crossan), said the Resurrection (like the rest of Jesus' miracles) was a legend fashioned after the manner of Greco-Roman myths—but no "myth" has ever developed so quickly. Five to seven years after Jesus' resurrection, Paul made his first trip to Jerusalem (after his conversion), where he undoubtedly received from the apostles the creed of Christ's death and resurrection (1 Cor 15:3-5). Furthermore, the details of 1 Corinthians 15:3-8 differ strongly from any mythical pattern. (5) The subjective vision theory: Some (Renan, Marxsen, Fuller) believe the disciples had dreams that they interpreted as reality—but Jesus appeared to people who were not believers (James, Paul) and appeared to 500 at once (1 Cor 15:6); such a mass hallucination is highly unlikely. (6) The objective vision theory: Others (Moule, Schweizer, Davies, Schillebeeckx) think the appearances were visions sent from God of Jesus in heaven. It is hard to see why such would be likely; the same God could have Jesus appear on earth, and that is exactly how the Gospel passages portray it. (7) The corporeal resurrection: The best solution by far is that Jesus did indeed rise from the dead and appear to his followers. Nothing else could have propelled those defeated, innocuous disciples to conquer the world with the gospel message.

There have been several successful attempts to harmonize the Resurrection accounts in plausible ways, (cf., in order of length, Wenham 1984; Harris 1990:157-163; Ladd 1975:91-93; Osborne 1995:39-41). For the historicity of the accounts as a whole, see Craig 1989; Keener 2003:1167-1178, 1185-1188. Comfort and Hawley (1994:311-312) list a total of 10 appearances, combining the four Gospels with 1 Corinthians 15:3-8: (1) to Mary Magdalene and the women (20:14ff; Matt 28:9—but these are probably actually separate appearances); (2) to Peter (Luke 24:34; 1 Cor 15:5); (3) to two disciples on the road to Emmaus (Luke 24:13-35); (4) to the disciples in Jerusalem (20:19-23; Luke 24:36-43); (5) to Thomas and the others eight days later (20:26-29); (6) to seven disciples on the Sea of Galilee (21:1-23); (7) to the disciples at the Great Commission appearance on a mountain in Galilee (Matt 28:16-20); (8) to 500 believers (1 Cor 15:6); (9) to James (1 Cor 15:7); (10) to the disciples at the Ascension (Luke 24:44-53; Acts 1:1-12). To some extent, we will place the Johannine story within the larger synoptic framework as we discuss each section.

When we read the resurrection appearances in the four Gospels side-by-side, it is almost as if these are separate stories, for the details are so different. We must understand certain facts, however. First, Jesus appeared to the disciples over a period of 40 days (Acts 1:3), and yet in all four Gospels together, only nine appearances are described. It is doubtful whether Jesus only appeared once every four and a half days during that period. Second, each Gospel writer uses the Resurrection story to sum up the themes of his Gospel. Therefore, they are so different because each writer chose carefully which appearances and details would best summarize and draw to a close his narrative. When we get to heaven, it will be shocking to discover how much was not included in these narratives! John concluded his Gospel with the most detailed narrative of them all. He is the only one to include both Jerusalem appearances (ch 20; parallel accounts in Luke) and Galilee appearances (ch 21; parallel accounts in Matt and Mark).

In keeping with John's style, chapter 20 is a beautifully dramatic portrayal of the problem of faith, this time in believing Jesus' promises about his resurrection from the dead. There are four successive vignettes, and in each of them the problem of faith becomes greater, from the beloved disciple's natural faith to Mary's sorrow, the disciples' fear, and Thomas's doubt. Yet in each case, Jesus meets their need, turns their life around, and guides them into their mission, with the results becoming greater in each scene. Moreover, the chapter also centers upon the Johannine theme of witness, as the empty tomb and then each disciple in turn attest to the reality of the Resurrection as proving the divine nature of Jesus. Köstenberger (2004:558) adds that it centers upon "the commissioning of Jesus' followers, encircled by narratives focusing on Mary Magdalene and Thomas respectively."

The Empty Tomb (20:1-10). In the Synoptics, a group of women started out for the empty tomb just before dawn (John—"while it was still dark"; cf. Osborne 1984:198-199 on the time notes) to anoint the corpse of Jesus, expecting nothing. They saw the stone rolled away and then entered the tomb, at which time they met angels. John centered on one of the women, Mary Magdalene, a formerly demon-possessed woman who became a patron of the apostolic band (Luke 8:1-3) and possibly a leader among the women (her name is always first in the synoptic lists of the witnesses to the death and Resurrection). He was aware of the larger tradition regarding the women (as evidenced in the "we" of 20:2) and chose to center on Mary for dramatic purposes. When Mary saw the tomb empty, she assumed her Lord's body had been stolen, a crime frequent enough to eventually merit the death penalty from the emperor Claudius (so Carson). Leaving the group of women, Mary ran back to the disciples and met Peter and the "other disciple," undoubtedly John, the beloved disciple (cf. 13:23-25; 19:26-27), telling them the body had been taken from the tomb.

The race to the tomb and its aftermath (20:3-9) are found only in John, but two aspects of it are corroborated in Luke: Peter's presence there and his leaving confused (Luke 24:12) and the fact that more than one person had visited the tomb and found it empty (Luke 24:24). Moreover, the vivid, realistic details fit the recollections of the "eyewitness" (19:35, see Ridderbos) and point to historical veracity. The two disciples ran to the tomb, undoubtedly in excitement and anxiety as to what they would find. The fact that the other disciple was faster and arrived first has often been seen as evidence of rivalry between the two, but that is highly unlikely. Both Peter and the beloved disciple are seen as positive figures. John arrived first, but Peter entered the tomb first. The point is their overriding concern for Jesus, in this case for what had happened to his body.

The first thematic emphasis is apologetic (20:5-7). In a series of scenes, the fact that the Lord had risen from the dead is proven. First, John stooped down and saw "the linen wrappings lying there." If grave robbers had stolen the body, they would never have left the expensive linen wrappings. On the basis of 20:8, it seems that this was the time that John began to understand what had actually happened. This is confirmed in the next scene. Peter rushed right into the tomb and saw not only the linen wrappings but also "the cloth that had covered Jesus' head . . . folded up and lying apart from the other wrappings" (20:7). It was not visible until Peter had entered the tomb. This probably means that Jesus' body had been placed on a shelf to the right or left of the tomb entrance with his head toward the entrance wall (so one could not see the cloth from the entrance). Such graphic detail not only points to eyewitness reminiscence on John's part but also has great emphasis in the scene. The whole developing picture suggests that the grave clothes were in the same position on the shelf that they had been in when the corpse of Jesus was lying there, perhaps even retaining some of their shape due to the spices (so Whitacre, cf. Lazarus who came out of the tomb wearing the linens with the cloth still over his face, 11:44). It is almost as if Jesus came to life, perhaps passed through the garments, and then made sure they were laid neatly in the proper place. This means the body could not have been stolen, for grave robbers would never be so neat or leave the wrappings (Keener, Köstenberger). John will later use the characteristic term "signs" of events like this (20:30-31). In fact, Schneiders (1983) thinks the veil constituted a sign for the beloved disciple reminiscent of the "sign-miracles" in chapters 2–12. Moreover, there were now two legal witnesses (Deut 19:15) to the event (possibly, in John's mind, for those unwilling to accept the official witness of the women; so Beasley-Murray).

John then entered the tomb (20:8), and the text says simply that "he saw and believed." It has been debated how much he believed, with some saying he only believed that Mary was correct in saying the tomb was empty (e.g., Augustine). Others say he believed without having knowledge of the Scriptures (Comfort, due to the following 20:9). The conjunction of seeing (see "Salvation" in the Introduction) with believing points to a deep-seated faith and establishes the main theme for the chapter—belief (cf. 20:25, 29, 31). Seeing the empty tomb was enough for John, who believed even though "they still hadn't understood the Scriptures that said Jesus must rise from the dead" (20:9).

Although there is no emphasis on the empty tomb as proof for the Resurrection in the preaching of Acts or in 1 Corinthians 15:3-8, it was certainly important for the early church, and it was enough for John. Still, the main stress is not upon how he believed but the fact that he did so. John's faith was truly a leap of faith since it occurred without knowing the scriptural demand for the Resurrection. Various suggestions have been made regarding Old Testament proof texts referred to by "Scriptures" (20:9)—perhaps Psalm 16:10 (Westcott, Sanders) or Hosea 6:2 (Bruce)—yet the term could also refer to Scripture as a whole, as in Luke 24:7, 25-26, 46 or 1 Corinthians 15:4 (Barrett, Carson). Byrne (1985:91-92) thinks the beloved disciple provides a dramatic portrait of the faith of the Johannine community (based on the connection between his faith and the faith of future believers in 20:29b), and the others (Mary, Thomas, the other disciples,) describe the faith journeys that can culminate in that faith. This makes great sense in light of the theme of belief in this chapter.

Peter apparently returned to Jerusalem, confused and puzzled (Luke 24:12), and one would expect John to walk over and share his newfound faith and understanding with Peter. It would also be natural for John to place his arms around Mary and tell her she need not weep so profusely, but he did neither. The first episode ends in anticlimax, as John simply "went home" with Peter (20:10). In short, he had faith but seemingly did nothing with it. It is common to take this as proof of the inadequacy of John's faith (Schnackenburg, Witherington, Whitacre, Keener), but that is not necessarily the case. There is no real hint that his faith was deficient. John could easily have been so filled with awe that he was dumbstruck. In the narrative, this sets up a contrast with Mary, who did not have this level of faith but who, with the help of Christ, did so much more with it.

Mary Sees the Risen Christ (20:11-18). As the two disciples returned home, Mary remained at the tomb, weeping copiously, still thinking grave robbers had stolen the corpse. Her deep love for Jesus had been turned to sorrow, and as we will see, it virtually rendered her blind. It is likely that she trailed the disciples as they ran, and she arrived only at this point. It is clear she was hoping someone would be able to help her recover the body. In the midst of her tears, she stooped (remember the opening is only three feet high, cf. note on 19:41) and looked into the tomb, unconsciously repeating the actions of Peter. As she looked, however, she was given a supernatural event quite unlike that experienced by Peter and John, for she saw "two white-robed angels, one sitting at the head and the other at the foot of the place where the body of Jesus had been lying." We might conjecture that the burial clothes were lying between them. Whenever angels appear in Scripture, it means heaven itself is deeply involved in the event. It seems evident that God had taken an interest in Mary and sent two messengers to comfort her.

Their question (20:13) was probably an implied rebuke similar to the message to the women in Mark 16:6 ("You are looking for Jesus of Nazareth, who was crucified," meaning, "You are still looking for a corpse?!"). They asked, "Why are you crying?"—implying that there was no longer any need for tears. Mary, however, was so consumed by grief, her eyes so blinded by tears, that she didn't even recognize the heavenly visitors. She repeated much of what she told the two disciples in 20:2:

"They have taken away my Lord, . . . and I don't know where they have put him." The lack of spiritual awareness was complete. Her weeping "is an expression of doubt and spiritual ignorance, especially in contrast to the faith of the 'beloved one'" (Osborne 1984:158).

Then Jesus took over and came to her (20:14). Again her blindness kept her from perceiving the truth. She believed he was the gardener and hoped he might have seen what had happened. It was common for the disciples to fail to recognize Jesus or to doubt when he appeared to them (21:4; Matt 28:17; Luke 24:16ff). This may have been due to the ravages of the crucifixion on his appearance, but it may also have been due to their own lack of expectation and understanding. He repeated the rebuke of the angels ("Why are you crying?") and then asked, "Who are you looking for?" For the third time, Mary repeated her erroneous assumption, this time wondering if perhaps he had something to do with it ("If you have taken him away, tell me where you have put him," 20:15). She may have been hoping that Joseph had his gardener and other servants move the body somewhere, but she was no closer to the truth. Finally, Jesus called out in great compassion, "Mary!" Jesus is the Good Shepherd, who "calls his own sheep by name," so that they "recognize his voice and come to him," 10:3-4.

Mary indeed recognized his voice and cried out "Rabboni"—that is, "My teacher." At this point, she may have reached out to lay hold of his arm or fell down and grasped his feet (as the women do in Matt 28:9), but Jesus wanted to correct her mistaken desire to return to the previous rabbi/disciple relationship (cf. note on 1:38). He said, "Don't cling to me"—that is, to the old relationship (cf. note on 20:17). This was a time for joy and the beginning of an entirely new era. Jesus recognized her love but knew this was the time for moving on rather than going back. The reason for prohibiting her was that he hadn't "yet ascended to the Father." On the surface, there is a contradiction between "I haven't yet ascended" (20:17a) and "I am ascending" (20:17b). The best solution is to take Jesus' ascension in two parts. He ascended to his Father at his resurrection, but the Ascension would not culminate until his physical ascension at the end of his 40 days of appearances. Thus he spoke of being in the process of ascending to his Father (most recent commentators). This was a time of transition, and Mary needed to yield to all the new joyous truths she was about to experience. Köstenberger (2004:569) says that in Mary "the disciples now find themselves in a transition period in which they cannot revert to their familiar pattern of relating to their Master during his earthly ministry; yet at the same time they cannot fully grasp the nature of the new spiritual relationship with their Lord that soon will be mediated to them by the Holy Spirit." When Jesus was raised, he went home to be with the Father, and his appearances were temporary visits from heaven. This was a critical transition time, and the final ascension was to occur 40 days after the Resurrection (Luke 24:51-53; Acts 1:9-11). At that time, the new age would truly begin, for then the Spirit would be given fully (14:16, 26; 16:7).

In the meantime, Mary had the glorious privilege of being the first ambassador of the Resurrection tidings! She was not just ushered into a new age but already was given one of the privileged parts to play. Note that Jesus said, "Go find my *brothers*." In one word, Jesus showed he had already forgiven them and begun the new relationship. In 15:15, Jesus told them, "I no longer call you slaves . . . now you are my friends." Earlier they had been disciples and servants, but they would become "friends." Here Jesus went further: they are not just friends but "brothers"! They are "heirs" with Christ of all the glories that God has awaiting his family (Rom 8:17).

Moreover, Jesus was in the process of ascending to "my Father and your Father, to my God and your God." There is no better way of stating the new relationship of the disciples both to Jesus and to God. The deliberate "my . . . your" language elevates the disciples to a position alongside the Son and further cements this new relationship; at the same time, it also stresses Jesus' unique status as the "Son of God," while the followers are "sons of God" (so Osborne 1984:164). Mahoney (1974:276) thinks the passages in John on Jesus going to the Father (3:13; 6:62; 20:17) build on the son of man imagery in Daniel 7:13, as well as the glorification theme of Psalm 110:1. The Crucifixion as "glory" or being "lifted up" (e.g., 12:23, 32-33; 13:31; 17:24) is intimately connected with Jesus' ascension and "hour" (cf. "time," 7:8; 17:1).

Mary, in obedience to Jesus' command, took the Good News back to the disciples (20:18). This is the astounding reality of the Resurrection event—God chose not the beloved disciple (who "believed" first) but Mary to be the first herald of the Resurrection tidings. John was the first to believe, but Mary was the first to see the risen Lord. Mary told them, "I have seen the Lord!" Note the progression of titles from "Sir" (20:15) to "Rabboni" (20:16) and then "Lord" (20:18). Her faith had come to full maturity as a Resurrection faith.

Jesus Appears to His Disciples (20:19-23). Mary's faith in a sense was clouded by fear, but the ten disciples (Judas was gone and Thomas was absent, cf. 20:24) were in far worse shape spiritually. Two and a half days after the Crucifixion (Sunday evening), they were *still* hiding behind locked doors, filled with fear that they might be arrested. Picture the scene. The doors were locked and the windows possibly shuttered, with the disciples quaking lest they be seen and refusing to believe the women that the Lord had risen (meaning they also failed to remember the numerous times he had prophesied his resurrection). Out of the gloom, "suddenly, Jesus was standing there among them" (20:19). This was another miracle. As Jesus apparently passed through his grave clothes, so he passed through the locked doors! Remember that the others had failed Jesus far more than Peter. He had denied Jesus, but he was the only one with the courage to want to be there for Jesus. We would expect Jesus to rebuke them sharply. Certainly they all deserved to be denounced. Instead he said these wonderful words: "Peace be with you." There is double meaning here. On one level, "peace be with you" was a simple and casual greeting. On a deeper level (and the main one here), Jesus was offering them his messianic peace in keeping with Isaiah 9:6; 52:7 and even more with his own promise of eschatological peace in 14:27 and 16:33.

Mary needed the voice of the Good Shepherd to overcome her sorrow; the disciples in a sense needed more, and Jesus met their need directly, appealing to their sight by showing them "the wounds in his hands and his side" (the actual spot was the wrist, but that can be included in the word "hands," so Carson) so as to prove that he was indeed risen (20:20). At that moment, messianic joy (cf. 16:20-22) was added to their messianic peace. The sacrificial Lamb had become the risen Lord. That is the greatest truth mankind will ever know.

Mary was given a mission (20:17-18), but the disciples were given the very philosophy of mission (20:21-23). This passage culminates John's whole theology of mission and is one of the truly remarkable passages of Scripture. In fact, this is the Gospel of John's Great Commission. Jesus a second time said, "Peace be with you," probably because the disciples were in shock and had not yet experienced that peace. It is the heart filled with God's peace that can engage in his mission. He then passed on his own commission to them, repeating what he had already said in 17:18, "As the Father has sent me, so I am sending you." It has been said over 30 times in this Gospel that Christ was "sent" by God (see e.g., 3:17; 5:23, 30; 8:16, 18), and both the Father and the Son had sent the Spirit as the Paraclete (14:16; 15:26; 16:7). Now the pattern was complete, for the means by which God reveals his Good News passes from Jesus to the Spirit to the disciples (church) to the world. Jesus' ongoing mission is acted out and continued by the Spirit's mission, and the Spirit's mission is acted out and carried on via the church's mission (so Westcott, Carson).

In fact, the mission of each one in this drama is ongoing. The Father authorizes the Son, the Father and Son authorize the Spirit, and the whole Godhead authorizes believers in mission! Köstenberger (1998a:191) sums up the implications: "The disciples are not just to *represent* Jesus (thus the Jewish sending concept is transcended), they are to *re-present* him, i.e., Jesus will be present in and through them in his Spirit as they fulfill their mission in the world" (italics his). Barrett adds (1978:569), "In the apostolic mission of the church . . . the world is veritably confronted not merely by a human institution but by Jesus the Son of God (13:20; 17:18) . . . the church is the apostolic church, commissioned by Christ, only in virtue of the fact that Jesus sanctified it (17:19) and breathed the Spirit into it (20:22) and only so far as it maintains an attitude of perfect obedience to Jesus."

There is no way Jesus' followers in their own strength could fulfill their calling, but Jesus knew that. He gave them the Spirit (the "Johannine Pentecost") when he "breathed on them" and said, "Receive the Holy Spirit." Throughout the farewell discourse, Jesus had promised that he would send the Spirit/Paraclete (14:16-17, 26; 15:26; 16:7), and the Spirit would provide the empowering presence that would enable them to become sent ones. The idea of Jesus breathing on them alludes to God breathing life into Adam at creation (Gen 2:7; cf. Ezek 37:9). Jesus created a new creation by his power to give life (1:3-4; 5:21, 25-26; cf. 1 Cor 15:45, "the last Adam—that is, Christ—is a life-giving Spirit"), and for the disciples that life was manifest not only in eternal life but also in the presence of the Spirit. This is a purification, an empowering, and a prophetic anointing for mission (so Keener), indeed the culmination of John's theology of the Spirit (so Burge). God gave the Spirit to Jesus "without limit" (3:34); Jesus offered the Samaritan woman "living water" (4:10, 14, cf. "water and the Spirit" in 3:5) and then poured out the Spirit from the depths of his being (7:37-39). As Jesus had been empowered by the Spirit in his work on earth, so the disciples must rely on the Spirit's power in their mission.

The authority for the mission is spelled out in 20:23. The reception of the Spirit made the disciples God's agents and bestowed on them the authority to "forgive anyone's sins" or to retain their sins. This is closely connected to Matthew 16:19 and 18:18, where the disciples were given "the keys of the kingdom" and told, "whatever you forbid on earth will be forbidden in heaven." Both in Matthew and here, the actual person doing the forgiving is God (divine passives), and the believers act as his emissaries. While some limit the thrust to forgiveness (and perhaps only within the church community), it is almost certain in this context of sending that it relates to the church's mission to the world (so Carson, Köstenberger). In this respect also, we carry on the work of Jesus: he came to save (3:17), but in encountering every person, he also became the judge (5:22, 30; 9:39) of those who reject him. This continues in the church's mission. We, too, encounter people with the demands of God and force them to decision, and their decision determines whether their sins are "forgiven" or retained.

Jesus Appears to the Disciples with Thomas (20:24-29). In one aspect, Thomas's cynicism was worse than the disciples' fear, for he flatly refused to believe the witness of his fellow disciples. For some unknown reason, he had been absent at the appearance of 20:19-23. When the ten disciples told him, "We have seen the Lord," he was highly skeptical, saying he would not believe unless he could touch "the nail wounds" as well as "the wound in his side." In a sense, Thomas was a philosophy major demanding absolute empirical proof; it was not just *seeing* is believing— Thomas spoke of *touching*. In this way, he was similar to the official at Capernaum to whom Jesus said, "Will you never believe in me unless you see miraculous signs and wonders?" (4:48).

Again, Jesus met his need, but it was eight days later (20:26), and they were still hiding behind closed doors, possibly still afraid (so Carson), though the reason they were in the same place was that they had remained for the weeklong Festival of Unleavened Bread. Mary needed the voice of the Good Shepherd; the Ten needed to see him. Now, Thomas needed to touch him, and as with the others, Jesus accommodated him. Can you imagine the scene? As in 20:19, Jesus miraculously came through the closed door and offered messianic peace. Then he said, "Put your finger here, and look at my hands. Put your hand into the wound in my side" (20:27). This is an extraordinary scene, with Jesus pulling back his robe to show the gaping wounds. There is no record that Thomas actually touched the wounds. It is doubtful he would have needed to at this point. Then Jesus exhorted Thomas, "Don't be faithless any longer. Believe!" Thomas had demonstrated that his faith was the lowest of them all.

Thomas was undoubtedly on his knees, tears coursing down his cheeks, as he uttered one of the great confessions of history, "My Lord and my God!" (20:28).

Some have taken this as an acclamation, part of the developing understanding of the disciples but not a full-fledged statement of deity. Keener (2003:1211) denies this, saying, "The confession of Jesus' deity is unmistakable (Rev 4:11)." While 20:21-23 climaxes the mission theme of John, this scene climaxes his Christology. One could say that the fourth Gospel is framed by statements of Jesus' deity (1:1; 20:28, so Bruce). This affirmation is a high point of the Gospel. It is an astounding utterance; the key is to realize that Thomas was indeed a philosophy major. All the while that he was saying, I won't believe "unless," he was also saying "What if?!" By the time Jesus appeared to him, he had thought through the implications more deeply than the others: if Jesus had risen from the dead, then his teaching was literally true, and he had claimed to be both Lord of all and divine (cf. 10:30, 33). Thomas's statement does not so much reflect the fact that John was written during the reign of Domitian, who encouraged a similar affirmation of himself (*Dominus et deus noster,* "our lord and god"), but instead its origin is almost certainly the Old Testament affirmation, "O Yahweh [Lord] our God" (so Blomberg; cf. e.g., 2 Kgs 19:19; Pss 99:8; 106:47; Isa 26:13; Rev 4:11).

Jesus concluded with a message for future readers (20:29). Thomas did believe but had to "see" in order to believe (Köstenberger [2004:580] calls this a "mild rebuke" of Thomas for needing proof and not believing the other disciples). Jesus drew a comparison with those yet to find faith—namely those who would not have the benefit of seeing the risen Lord—and gave future believers a special blessing from God because they would find faith without the incredible experience of physically seeing the risen Lord. This is the second beatitude in John (cf. 13:17), and interestingly both occur in contexts of admonition. The four episodes leading to belief in chapter 20 have been accompanied by the word "seen" (20:8, 18, 20, 27), but future believers would not have that privilege. Theirs would be a faith engendered by the Good News, and this is perhaps the major theme of the fourth Gospel—the encounter with God in Jesus forces a faith-decision, and that decision brings life. That is the greatest blessing of all. As Peter says so well, "You love him even though you have never seen him. Though you do not see him now, you trust him; and you rejoice with a glorious, inexpressible joy. The reward for trusting him will be the salvation of your souls" (1 Pet 1:8-9).

The Purpose of the Book (20:30-31). John knew of "many other miraculous signs" than just the ones recorded in this book. He wanted the reader to understand that he and the other disciples personally witnessed and were aware of many more miracles than could be recorded (cf. 21:25). John carefully selected those he included in his Gospel. Most likely he would have included in the term "miraculous signs" not just the sign-miracles of chapters 2-12 but also the greatest sign of them all, the death and resurrection of Jesus.

The purpose of all the choices is clear: "that you may continue to believe" (20:31). John's Gospel has always been about faith and the life that results from it. This is the core of Johannine theology, the essence of God's purpose in the world. He "gave his one and only Son" that people might believe and have life (3:16). "No one can come to the Father" any other way (14:6); therefore, those who "listen" and "believe . . . have eternal life" (5:24). John chose the two major titles of Jesus to sum up the focus of faith: "Messiah, the Son of God." The first means to believe Jesus is the Jewish Messiah, probably both the Davidic Messiah and Mosaic Messiah since John contains both emphases (the Davidic or royal Messiah from the Davidic covenant of 2 Sam 7:5-16; the Mosaic from the "prophet like Moses" of Deut 18:15). The second refers not just to the special filial relationship between Jesus and his Father but also to Jesus' complete deity (1:1, 18; 10:30; 20:28) and the fact that he was "sent" by his Father as the divine agent (3:17; 11:42; 16:27; 17:8). The Father-Son relationship in one sense dominates this Gospel. The result of this relationship is that those who believe "will have life by the power of his name." Throughout John, "life" is both an encounter of the unbeliever and a present possession for those who believe because they are under the power of Jesus' name (John's Gospel is intended for both believer and unbeliever).

◆   ## B. Epilogue: Jesus' Appearance in Galilee (21:1-25)

Later, Jesus appeared again to the disciples beside the Sea of Galilee.* This is how it happened. ²Several of the disciples were there—Simon Peter, Thomas (nicknamed the Twin),* Nathanael from Cana in Galilee, the sons of Zebedee, and two other disciples.

³Simon Peter said, "I'm going fishing."

"We'll come, too," they all said. So they went out in the boat, but they caught nothing all night.

⁴At dawn Jesus was standing on the beach, but the disciples couldn't see who he was. ⁵He called out, "Fellows,* have you caught any fish?"

"No," they replied.

⁶Then he said, "Throw out your net on the right-hand side of the boat, and you'll get some!" So they did, and they couldn't haul in the net because there were so many fish in it.

⁷Then the disciple Jesus loved said to Peter, "It's the Lord!" When Simon Peter heard that it was the Lord, he put on his tunic (for he had stripped for work), jumped into the water, and headed to shore. ⁸The others stayed with the boat and pulled the loaded net to the shore, for they were only about a hundred yards* from shore. ⁹When they got there, they found breakfast waiting for them—fish cooking over a charcoal fire, and some bread.

¹⁰"Bring some of the fish you've just caught," Jesus said. ¹¹So Simon Peter went aboard and dragged the net to the shore. There were 153 large fish, and yet the net hadn't torn.

¹²"Now come and have some breakfast!" Jesus said. None of the disciples dared to ask him, "Who are you?" They knew it was the Lord. ¹³Then Jesus served them the bread and the fish. ¹⁴This was the third time Jesus had appeared to his disciples since he had been raised from the dead.

¹⁵After breakfast Jesus asked Simon Peter, "Simon son of John, do you love me more than these?*"

"Yes, Lord," Peter replied, "you know I love you."

"Then feed my lambs," Jesus told him.

¹⁶Jesus repeated the question: "Simon son of John, do you love me?"

"Yes, Lord," Peter said, "you know I love you."

"Then take care of my sheep," Jesus said.

¹⁷A third time he asked him, "Simon son of John, do you love me?"

Peter was hurt that Jesus asked the question a third time. He said, "Lord, you know everything. You know that I love you."

Jesus said, "Then feed my sheep. [18]"I tell you the truth, when you were young, you were able to do as you liked; you dressed yourself and went wherever you wanted to go. But when you are old, you will stretch out your hands, and others* will dress you and take you where you don't want to go." [19]Jesus said this to let him know by what kind of death he would glorify God. Then Jesus told him, "Follow me."

[20]Peter turned around and saw behind them the disciple Jesus loved—the one who had leaned over to Jesus during supper and asked, "Lord, who will betray you?" [21]Peter asked Jesus, "What about him, Lord?"

[22]Jesus replied, "If I want him to remain alive until I return, what is that to you? As for you, follow me." [23]So the rumor spread among the community of believers* that this disciple wouldn't die. But that isn't what Jesus said at all. He only said, "If I want him to remain alive until I return, what is that to you?"

[24]This disciple is the one who testifies to these events and has recorded them here. And we know that his account of these things is accurate.

[25]Jesus also did many other things. If they were all written down, I suppose the whole world could not contain the books that would be written.

21:1 Greek *Sea of Tiberias*, another name for the Sea of Galilee.   21:2 Greek *Thomas, who was called Didymus.* 21:5 Greek *Children.*   21:8 Greek *200 cubits* [90 meters].   21:15 Or *more than these others do?*   21:18 Some manuscripts read *and another one.*   21:23 Greek *the brothers.*

NOTES

21:1-25 There has been a great deal of debate surrounding the origin of this chapter and its place in the fourth Gospel. The majority of scholars conclude that it is non-Johannine and was added at a later date. Many (Brown, Schnackenburg, Kysar) regard it as one of the final additions of the Johannine Circle (cf. "Author" in the Introduction), possibly written after the death of the beloved disciple. Others (Osborne 1984:255-256, Comfort, Witherington) have said that John himself added it as an appendix at a later time. Several points favor the view that John wrote ch 21 as part of his Gospel rather than separately: (1) The language and style are so similar to the rest of John's Gospel that it most likely was written by the same person (cf. Osborne 1981:293-295). (2) While 20:30-31 could be the intended conclusion of the original Gospel, that does not obviate adding further material, and John elsewhere has had purpose statements followed by an epilogue (1 John 5:13; Rev 22:6; so Blomberg). (3) John 21 centers on mission, and thus John ends the same way the Synoptics conclude, with the mission of the church. (4) There is no evidence that the Gospel ever circulated without ch 21. (5) Chapter 21 provides a natural conclusion to the interaction between Peter and the beloved disciple, ending with Jesus prophesying Peter's death. (6) The reinstatement of Peter is a natural denouement to his denials. (7) Chapter 21 makes perfect sense as an epilogue, thus framing the Gospel with the prologue of 1:1-18. Therefore, it is more likely that John wrote ch 21 at the same time as the rest of the book as a conclusion for his Gospel (so Hartman 1984:29, Morris, Carson, Ellis 1992, Ridderbos, Whitacre, Burge, Blomberg, Keener, Köstenberger).

21:1-14 Due to the many similarities with Luke 5 (fishing all night and catching nothing, a command to cast nets, obedience and a miraculous catch, the mission motif) most critical scholars conclude they are one and the same story, and the debate is whether Luke is original (Dodd, Bultmann [1963, *History of the Synoptic Tradition*], Benoit) or John is (Bultmann 1971, Brown, Barrett). Some (e.g., Pesch 1969, Schnackenburg, Beasley-Murray, Perkins) think two separate traditions (a fishing story and a eucharistic meal story) have been combined. However, there are also many differences between Luke and John (different disciples present, the nets almost ripped in Luke, the centrality of the beloved disciple in John, Peter swimming to shore in Luke, the meal fellowship in John), and it is most likely they are separate stories (so Osborne 1984, Morris, Carson, Blomberg, Köstenberger). Keener (2003:1221) says, "If one reads the Gospel as a whole, John 20:30–21:25 can function as a final farewell scene (in which case 20:30-31 and 21:24-25 function as a rather obvious inclusio)."

21:7 *put on his tunic.* There are two possibilities as to what Peter did: he was working naked (perhaps because he was swimming out to secure the nets) and so put on his outer garment to swim or maybe wade to shore; or, he was wearing only a worker's smock and simply tucked it into his belt or wrapped it around himself before swimming in (the same verb is used of Jesus wrapping a towel around him in 13:4). Since the first option involves Peter swimming totally clothed to Jesus (and since 100 yards is a long distance for wading in the Sea of Galilee), the second makes more sense in the situation (cf. Carson, Burge, Keener).

21:11 *153 large fish.* There have been an incredible number of suggestions regarding the meaning of "153" (cf. Brown, McEleney 1977, Beasley-Murray, Burge, Keener): (1) one of the oldest is that proposed by Jerome—that in Jesus' day, they believed there were 153 species of fish and this therefore symbolized the number of nations to be netted; but this has been shown to be untrue. (2) Many have seen *gematria* (the sum of the numerical value of the letters of a word, e.g., 666 in Rev 13:18) in the number, deriving words such as "Jesus Christ, God" (McEleney), "church of love," "children of God," or "Pisgah"—the mountain from which Moses commissioned his followers. (3) Emerton (1958) combines *gematria* and Old Testament background, pointing to Ezek 47:9-10, where a stream flows from Jerusalem to the Dead Sea and is filled with fish from En-Gedi (numerical value of 17) and En-eglaim (= 153). Since 17 is the triangular number of 153 (that is, the sum of the numbers 1–17, a concept well-known to ancients), this has gained some attention. (4) Others have built allegorically on 17 and 153, e.g., Augustine who thought of 153 believers inspired by the seven gifts of the Spirit to obey the Ten Commandments or Origen who thought it signified the Trinity (50 x 3 + 3). (5) Since the options above continue from one imaginative solution to another, it is best to say simply that the number signifies the abundance of the blessings Christ poured out upon the disciples and therefore upon the church in the midst of its mission. This is the view favored by most today.

21:15 *After breakfast.* It is common for critical scholars to assert that this is a separate tradition (perhaps the first appearance mentioned in 1 Cor 15:5) clumsily attached to 21:1-14 by "after breakfast." There is little basis for this other than from critical assumptions that stories like this floated independently in the oral period before the Gospels were written. It was natural, however, for Jesus to reinstate Peter in front of the other disciples since Peter had boasted that he would be true to Jesus before them (13:37-38). John 21:15-17 fits well in the context of the appearance of Jesus on the shore and is not a separate episode (cf. Carson, Köstenberger).

21:15-17 *do you love me? . . . you know I love you.* Many scholars and pastors (e.g., Hunter, McKay 1985) have thought that this episode deals with two levels of love due to the two Greek verbs employed. If this were true, the meaning would be something like this: Jesus asked, "Peter, do you love me with a divine love (*agapaō* [TG25, ZG26])?" and Peter responds, "Lord, I like you a lot (*phileō* [TG5368, ZG5797])." A little discouraged, Jesus tries again, "Peter, do you love me with a divine love (*agapaō*)" and Peter responds, "Lord, I am fond of you (*phileō*)." Jesus gives up, "Peter, do you like me (*phileō*)?" And Peter concludes, "What do you think I've been saying? Of course I like you (*phileō*)."

Of course, this translation is a little free, but it is not far off in showing the inevitable implications of such a reading. Jesus would be surrendering to Peter's lower level of love. That is unlikely. Even more, it does not fit the actual meaning of the passage or the language used. In the fourth Gospel, both words (*agapaō* [TG25, ZG26] and *phileō* [TG5368, ZG5797]) are used for the Father's love for the Son, for the Father's love for the disciples, for Jesus' love for Lazarus and the beloved disciple, and for Christians as "beloved" (Brown 1966:498). The consensus today is that the two terms are synonymous in John (Brown, Carson, Beasley-Murray, Burge, Blomberg, Keener, Köstenberger). Moreover, in these three short verses there are four word pairs—two words for "love," two for "know," two for "tend" (cf. "feed" and "take care of," NLT), and two for "sheep" (cf. "lambs," NLT). By this variety of terms, John was emphasizing the comprehensiveness of the message: deep love for Jesus will produce an intense desire to care for his flock. By restating the point three times, it is given ultimate importance.

21:22 until I return. This is further evidence that John has both a final eschatology centering on Christ's return and the end of the age (cf. 5:25, 28-29; 6:39-40; 14:2-3) and a realized eschatology centering on the present possession of eternal life. There is a greater balance in John's eschatology than many critical scholars are willing to acknowledge.

21:23 this disciple wouldn't die. There are two issues: (1) Some (e.g., Bultmann) believe the beloved disciple was not an actual person at all but a literary construct to typify the ideal disciple (for Bultmann symbolizing the Gentile church). This passage, of course, treats him as an actual historical person, but Bultmann believes this was added by a later redactor (1971:715). This hardly makes sense because at the least it proves the later redactor within a few years considered this disciple to be historical. (2) Others (Beasley-Murray, Carson) assert that this indicates a problem in the church similar to 1 Cor 1-4, in which some were exalting John over Peter or lining up as followers of one or the other (cf. 1 Cor 1:12). This is certainly possible, but there is no hint in this or any other passage in John that the beloved disciple was elevated above Peter; both were on the same level (so Barrett, Blomberg). If that problem did exist, John's testimony here is that both he and Peter were equal before the Lord and the church; each was to find his own destiny within God's will (Ridderbos, Köstenberger).

21:24 the one who . . . has recorded them. The identity of the author noted here as the beloved disciple, John (cf. 19:35), is disputed. Some believe this does refer to the "disciple Jesus loved" as the author of the book (Westcott, Lindars, Morris, Bruce), others that he caused them to be written by someone else (Bernard, Witherington), perhaps as the source of the tradition (Brown, Barrett). In light of the wording of 21:24 and the parallel in 19:35, the first is certainly the meaning here.

we know. Three options exist for the "we" and therefore for the author of these two verses: (1) "we" could be indefinite and equivalent to the expression "as is well-known" (Dodd 1953b:212-213); (2) an editorial "we," like those in 1 John 1:2, 4, 5, 6, 7; 3 John 1:12, referring to John himself (Bernard, Carson, Köstenberger); and (3) the imprimatur of the church, perhaps the elders of Ephesus (Westcott, Hendriksen), to the veracity of this work (Brown, Barrett, Morris, Bruce, Whitacre, Burge, Blomberg, Keener). The first is possible but is an unusual rendering and does not quite fit. The second is more viable but does not quite fit the tone of 21:24, which contains the third person singular as well as first person plural. The most likely is the third option, the witness of the church to the trustworthiness of John's Gospel. This may have been added by the community as an imprimatur similar to 19:35 (see the parallel on the death of Moses in Deut 34—Moses could hardly have chronicled his own death).

COMMENTARY

While chapter 20 centered on the issue of faith, chapter 21 centers on the mission of the church. As we have seen, God's mission to the world is also at the heart of John's

Gospel (cf. "Mission" in the Introduction). Each aspect of these appearance narratives contributes to the mobilization of the church and especially to the task of the leaders as they reach out to God's flock and his world with the Good News. The miraculous catch of fish (21:1-14) reminds us of the similar miracle in Luke 5, with the same message—when God's people surrender to the leading of the Lord, great things will happen for those who are "fishing for people" (Luke 5:10). Then the reinstatement of Peter (21:15-17) also centers on the responsibility of the leaders of the church to "feed" or care for God's flock. Finally, there is the poignant passage (21:18-23) reminding each of us that as we serve the Lord and go through hard times, our response must always be to follow the Lord, no matter what is going on with others. In addition to Jesus, the key characters in this chapter are Peter and the beloved disciple, as all three stories center on them, especially on Peter, who was not just restored but given his commission and told his destiny.

Jesus Appears to His Disciples (21:1-14). John, as elsewhere, was following the historical chronology here. He drew together the Synoptics, with the Jerusalem appearances (Luke = John 20) followed by the Galilee appearances (Mark and Matthew = John 21). The disciples stayed in Jerusalem for about eight days (20:26) until the Passover (and Festival of Unleavened Bread) was finished (Lindars). Then they returned to Galilee as the angels had told them to (Matt 28:7; Mark 16:7). There were seven disciples present (21:2)—the inner circle among the disciples (Peter with James and John, "the sons of Zebedee"), Nathanael (called by Jesus in ch 1), the same Thomas featured in 11:16; 20:24ff, and two unnamed disciples. Now all they could do was wait for Jesus to appear to them, so they decided to go fishing. Some (Hoskyns, Barrett) believe this was an act of disobedience, even apostasy, but that is highly unlikely.

John does not tell us that Peter and Andrew, James and John were fishermen (cf. Mark 1:16-20 and parallels), but that would have been widely known in the early church. It must be remembered that when Jesus called them to "fish for people" (Luke 5:10), that did not mean they were to quit their jobs. Peter and the sons of Zebedee kept their boats and probably fished whenever they were not with Jesus. In fishing, they would use either a hand net (a circular net about 10 or so feet in diameter with weights so that it could be thrown and retrieved by a single person), or a large trawl or seine net with sinkers on the end (as in this scene), which was held between two moving boats (each boat being about 26.5 feet in length and 7.5 feet across—the measurements of one recently discovered in Galilee). The net would trap a large school of fish, and after they were encircled, the fishermen would haul them in with casting nets. In this scene, where the disciples have returned to their "secular work," there is no true atmosphere of aimlessness (Brown), let alone apostasy (Hoskyns). They were simply engaged in their normal activity, while waiting for the Lord to act—and soon he would!

It was normal to fish at night when the fish would come up to the surface to feed (cf. Luke 5:5). When the sun came up, the fish would go deeper, and nets would be useless. As in Luke 5, they fished all night and caught nothing (it is doubtful that "night" here means the time of sin and darkness as in 3:2; 13:30). They again learned the important lesson that apart from Jesus they could do nothing (15:5, so Whitacre). Dawn arrived (21:4), and they were undoubtedly tired and discouraged. Suddenly someone appeared on the shore; it was Jesus. At a hundred yards in the early light (21:8), they could not make out who it was. Disciples being slow to recognize Jesus or initially doubtful about his resurrection is a common feature of the resurrection narratives (e.g., Luke 24:11-16). As in Luke 24:13ff (the Emmaus Road journey), Jesus appeared as a stranger.

Jesus called them *paidia* [TG3813, ZG4086] (21:5), which might be translated colloquially, "lads." It was a term of endearment. When he asked them if they'd caught any "fish" (technically a piece of fish to eat), they had to admit how disappointing the night was. Then the stranger on the shore said an unusual thing, telling them to throw out their casting nets on the right side of the boat, and this without moving the trawl net to gather the fish! It is hard to know why they complied, possibly it was because they thought the stranger had seen something (so Morris). The result was extraordinary. There is little doubt that when we get to heaven, Peter will tell us that the two greatest catches he made in his life were those recorded in Luke 5 and John 21. There were so many large fish (153 in all, 21:11) that they could not even bring the net into the boat. Here and in Luke 5, there is certainly a parabolic or symbolic significance. The message is that when we obey Jesus, even if it doesn't seem logical, wonderful things will happen. The missiological overtones are also obvious.

At this point, the beloved disciple recognized that it was Jesus and said, "It's the Lord!" (21:7). Dodd (1953a:109) called this recognition scene the central element in the pericope. In 21:1 and 14, the story is framed by Jesus revealing himself (cf. "appeared," NLT) to the disciples, and here the beloved disciple responded to that revelation. Impetuous Peter then jumped into the water to swim to Jesus. His eagerness to be with the Lord is evident. He was wearing a worker's smock in the boat and so was naked underneath. He wrapped his smock around himself (possibly tucking it into his belt or putting on a loincloth, so Whitacre) and started swimming (so Brown, Barrett, Burge). The other six disciples rowed the boat to shore with the catch of fish. Interestingly, we are not told what transpired when Peter met Jesus; John wanted to wait until 21:15-17 for that. Also, we are not told what the other disciples did with the huge catch of fish. Presumably, they did what any fisherman then or today does, placing them in some type of bin or tank.

Their focus then shifted to a meal already prepared (21:9). Jesus continued his servant ways: in 13:1-20, he washed their feet; now he prepared them breakfast. The same Lord who ensured their miraculous catch of fish continued to provide for them—another lesson for the reader. Fish cooking in the fire and fresh bread were the basic Galilean meal (the same was provided in the multiplication of the loaves, 6:1-15). Since there were seven disciples, Jesus needed more fish to fix for them, so he asked Peter to fetch some of the fish they had just caught. The disciples shared of their own bounty—the bounty miraculously provided by Christ.

In fact, here we learn that when Peter dragged the net ashore, they discovered two incredible miracles: First, they had caught the astounding number of 153 fish, which certainly sounds like a fisherman's tale! Second, the net had not torn with that incredible weight of fish. Since we have seen symbolism throughout this story, it is no surprise to find more here. Of course, the number is recorded because that indeed was what happened, but as with the 12 baskets of scraps left after the feeding of the 5,000 (6:13, cf. also the seven baskets left after the feeding of the 4,000, Mark 8:8), there is also a symbolic overtone. The number signifies the over-abundant blessing Christ had given to the disciples and therefore to the church in its mission. The unbroken net may signify the unity of the church (so Brown, Kysar, Whitacre) or perhaps that there would be no limit to the number of converts (Bruce; Witherington adds "without losing any").

Then comes the meal scene (21:12-13). Jesus was still in charge; in both their external ministry (the catch of fish) and in their internal needs (the breakfast), it was Jesus alone who could truly provide. The first of the we-petitions in the Lord's Prayer is, "Give us today the food we need" (Matt 6:11), and its meaning is not "gimme, gimme" but rather, "Lord, I rely entirely upon you for my needs." The reaction of the seven disciples is surprising. In spite of the fact that they knew it was the Lord, we are told "none of the disciples dared to ask him, 'Who are you?' They knew it was the Lord" (21:12). Historically, there are several possible explanations as to why the disciples would have asked the Lord who he was. Perhaps they could see Jesus was more than just a man brought back from the dead but had new powers as the Risen One and so were filled with awe; or they still could not come to grips with his death and resurrection; or they were still confused by the reality of the Resurrection (so Carson). Theologically, Albert Schweitzer's classic statement (1968:403) may be the best explanation: "He comes to us as One unknown, without a name, as of old." The emphasis is on Jesus, who now "belonged to another order of existence" (so Bruce; Ridderbos, "wholly-otherness").

The meal itself (21:13) is closely connected to the multiplication of loaves, as in 6:11, "Jesus took the loaves, gave thanks to God, and distributed them to the people. Afterward he did the same with the fish." There is a question as to whether this is a eucharistic celebration (so Brown, Shaw 1974, Pesch, Schnackenburg, Perkins), but that is unlikely because fish did not become a eucharistic symbol until later in the church. In a sense, it is tied to 6:1-15; if that scene is interpreted in a eucharistic direction, this one will be also. But it is doubtful that 6:1-15 is eucharistic (see note on 6:11), so this scene is probably not either. Rather, the emphasis here is on table fellowship—the sharing of a meal as the sharing of life. As Michaels says (1989:356), "The story of the miraculous catch and of the breakfast by the lake is to be understood in connection with the mission and unity of the church . . . and in particular with the expression of this unity in meal fellowship." The mission is conducted by a church that is both dependent on Jesus and in intimate fellowship with him and with one another (cf. 15:4-7; 17:11, 20-23). Hartman (1984:40) connects the meal with the theme of chapter 6: Jesus the Bread of Life who gives eternal life to those who partake of him (and who provides spiritual food for his followers; so Keener).

John then tells us this is "the third time Jesus had appeared to his disciples" (21:14). The appearance to Mary was not "to his disciples," so John was enumerating those appearances found in his Gospel (20:19-23, 24-29). When comparing this to the Synoptics, it would also fit, for Luke 24:36-44 probably describes the same event as 20:19-23 (see commentary on 20:19-23), and Matthew 28:17-20 probably occurred later (cf. Osborne 1995:40-41). Still, there is strong emphasis on the veracity of the appearances: "That there was in the Evangelist's mind some evidential value in this episode as support of Jesus' resurrection is confirmed by this verse, which forms a literary *inclusio* with 21:1" (Carson 1991:674-675). The framing is seen in the term "appeared" (*ephanerōthē* [TG5319, ZG5746]), which means he "was revealed" to them (i.e., he disclosed himself as the risen Lord to them). The emphasis is on the reality and truth behind the Resurrection. The revelation of God in Jesus is another dominant theme of the fourth Gospel.

The Reinstatement and Commissioning of Peter (21:15-17). "After breakfast" was finished, Jesus turned to Peter. We know from Luke 24:34, John 20:19, and 1 Corinthians 15:5 that Jesus had already appeared to Peter, and thus his personal repentance and forgiveness had already taken place by the time of this appearance. This then was a public (six other disciples were present) reinstatement of Peter to ministry (the threefold nature of the encounter offsetting his three denials, so Köstenberger), and even more, it was Peter's marching orders, as he was commissioned to his new ministry. Peter had denied Jesus three times (18:15-18, 25-27), and Jesus here commissioned him three times to "feed" (and "take care of") his flock. The fact that this was indeed a commissioning is reinforced by the opening, "Simon son of John," which repeats the language of Peter's initial call in 1:42. In the first question, "Do you love me more than these?", "more than these" can be understood three ways; (1) "more than you love these other disciples" (Osborne 1981:308; Witherington); (2) "more than you love these other things" (primarily his career in fishing, so Bernard, Keener); or (3) "more than these other disciples love me" (Westcott, Plummer, Carson, Comfort, Blomberg, Köstenerger). It is common to prefer the last on the grounds that Peter had boasted before that he was the most faithful of the group (13:37-38); however, that injects a negative element that I do not find in the context. It is more likely that Jesus was asking if he was first in Peter's life and heart, so it was probably the first or perhaps is a combination of the first two.

When Peter responded positively, "Yes, Lord, . . . you know I love you," then Jesus commissioned him to "feed my lambs." This is the major emphasis of this commissioning service: love for Jesus must result in taking care of his flock. This is stressed by the variation in words for the responsibility of tending Christ's flock: feed/take care of my lambs/sheep. This is stylistic variation for emphasis. Note how Peter "was hurt" (21:17) when Jesus asked the same question three times, replying, "Lord, you know everything. You know that I love you." He did not understand why Jesus kept hammering on the same point. The reason is not just that Peter had failed three times but even more that repetition underscores an important point. The importance of a threefold repetition is best emphasized in the *trisagion*, "Holy, holy, holy" (Isa 6:3; Rev 4:8), rightly labeled by the Greek Orthodox as the heart of the worship of God in Scripture. The threefold repetition emphasizes a superlative truth. So it is here; the heart of ministry is caring for the flock of God, so Jesus drove the point home via his threefold repetition. Köstenberger (2004:597) adds that the threefold repetition reflects "the Near Eastern custom of reiterating a matter three times before witnesses in order to convey a solemn obligation, especially with regard to contracts conferring rights or legal dispositions." So this becomes a virtual covenant obligation for Peter, the disciples, and us.

Maintaining the flock of God is the key to the mission of the church. The lost cannot truly be reached until the saints are deeply fed and mobilized. This was the heart of Paul's message to the Ephesian elders in Acts 20:28 ("Feed and shepherd God's flock") and of Peter's challenge to the leaders in 1 Peter 5:2-4 ("Care for the flock that God has entrusted to you"). One could say that 1 Peter 5:1-4 contains Peter's reflections on the significance of this event (21:15-17) for him. Both passages stress that the flock did not belong to Peter (or to us as leaders in the church) but to God and Christ, who is the "Great Shepherd" (1 Pet 5:4). He gives us a flock as our "assigned" portion (1 Pet 5:3), and it is our privilege to care for that flock as its shepherd. The shepherd image centered, first of all, on God as the Shepherd of Israel (Gen 49:24; Isa 40:11) and on Christ as the Good Shepherd (10:11, 14). The leaders of Israel were also shepherds (2 Sam 5:2; Ezek 34), and through Christ, the leaders of the church are shepherds (Acts 20:28; Eph 4:11). This pastoral care involves every aspect—feeding, protecting, guiding—and it is clear that our reward is not primarily in the here and now (to be had via lording it over the flock; 1 Pet 5:3) but is rather "treasures in heaven" (Matt 6:20; cf. 1 Pet 5:4). We are first of all servant-leaders (see note on 13:1-20), and all authority we have comes from God. Our task is humility and obedience to the will of God (love = obedience, cf. 14:15, 21, 23; 15:10). It is the error of our times to separate evangelism from discipleship and to center on winning the lost rather than building up the church; the best means of reaching the lost is to develop excited Christians who will take the gospel to others.

Prophecy regarding Peter's Death (21:18-23). Jesus apparently took a walk with Peter along the beach (the beloved disciple was following them—see 21:20) to address him privately. In 13:36, Jesus told Peter, "You can't go with me now, but you will follow me later." Peter did not understand and boldly promised that he was "ready to die." Here Jesus spells out his prophecy regarding Peter's death. The double *amēn* [TG281, ZG297] formula (last seen in 16:23) shows the gravity of this proclamation. Peter's call was twofold: to pastor God's flock and to die for the Lord. He would "follow" Jesus not only as shepherd but also in finding glory through dying (a major theme of John's Gospel). Bultmann theorized that this saying was built on a well-known proverb regarding old age (1971:731, cf. also Barrett, Kysar, Burge, Blomberg, contra Carson—but Jesus made the adaptation, not the Evangelist!). If so, Jesus transformed the adage into a prophecy regarding Peter's future.

In Peter's youth (right up to that time), he had been in control and went wherever he wished, but later, like an old man (21:18), he would have no more control over his life. "Stretch out your hands" could mean simply that someone would take Peter where he did not wish to go (so Brown, Blomberg). More likely, it was a metaphor for crucifixion. The verb was used for stretching out the arms on the cross (so Barrett, Carson, Witherington, Keener) and in context prophesies that Peter will be led "where you don't want to go"—namely, to his death, as explained in 21:19. Church tradition says that Peter was crucified upside down during the reign of Nero (*Acts of Peter* 37-39; Eusebius *History* 3.1); while we cannot be sure that he was crucified upside down (the tradition is late), this text would support the likelihood of crucifixion. Note that the emphasis is upon the "kind of death he would [die to] glorify God" (21:19). As Jesus' death was ultimately "lifted up to glory" (cf. 3:14; 8:28; 12:27-28, 32; 13:31-32), Peter's death would share the same "glory." His death would bring glory to God in the way spoken of in Revelation 12:11, "They have defeated him (Satan) . . . by their testimony . . . they were [not] afraid to die." Every martyrdom is a victory over Satan and brings glory to God.

The central theme is expressed twice (21:19, 22): "Follow me." This discipleship command is also used in 1:43 (to Philip) and often connotes discipleship in John (cf. 1:37-38, 40; 8:12; 10:4, 27; 12:26). Peter had to "follow" the Lord in discipleship wherever it led, even to death. As before, Peter always spoke his mind, even when it meant putting his foot in his mouth! He turned around and saw the beloved disciple following, and he blurted out, "What about him, Lord?" He was virtually saying, "Why me and not him?!" This is an important message for all of us. When we face difficult experiences, we so often look at someone for whom everything seems to be going more smoothly and ask a question like Peter's. Jesus' response to Peter is the same message he would give to us: "If I want him to remain alive until I return, what is that to you?" (21:22). Peter's responsibility was to follow Jesus, not to worry about the destiny of his friend. We are not to compare ourselves to others but are simply to seek and accept God's will for us personally. John did in fact live to a very old age (he wrote the book of Revelation in AD 95, close to 30 years after Peter's death), but God was not preferring John to Peter. Rather, he gave each the ministry (and death) that was best. No one would say that John therefore had a greater ministry than Peter's; each fulfilled his call and glorified God accordingly. Whether we are called to a short but intense ministry, dying early like Peter, or to a lengthy life and ministry, like John's, we are also told, "So what? Follow me!" God's commission is not to the life we would like to live but to the life that God in his sovereign wisdom knows is best for us. This is true in many ways—for instance, when a friend is pastor of a big, important church while we have never pastored a church larger than 200. In God's eyes, that does not mean the other pastor is more important to the Kingdom. Small church ministers are just as important to the Lord as are the super pastors! We each must be willing to accept the ministry the Lord has for us.

John also used this to dispel a rumor that had developed, certainly known among his churches (21:23), that he would not die until the Lord returned. This may even have led to a cult following that centered on the Lord's returning soon. Some believe it means the beloved disciple had died, and this had been written later to address the problem his death seemed to cause. However, we have already shown the likelihood that John composed this chapter (see note on 21:1-25), and if he were indeed dead, all the later writer would have to say is that John's grave proves the rumor false (so Carson). Still, fervor (on the basis of this rumor) undoubtedly increased as John's advancing age made it seem likely that Christ's return had to be imminent. John therefore felt it necessary to correct the misunderstanding.

John emphasized the conditional, "*If* I want him to remain alive until I return," saying in effect that this was not Jesus' intention. Jesus' reply may have had a two-fold purpose here: to emphasize the importance of true discipleship and submission to God's will, and to prepare the church of John's day for the time when all the apostolic eyewitnesses would be dead. "Peter and the 'beloved' are symbols of the church as a whole where obedience as well as discipleship remain critical regardless of how long it takes Jesus to return" (Osborne 1984:189; see the excellent chart on the beloved disciple and Peter in relation to Jesus in Köstenberger 2004:599).

Conclusion: The True Witness (21:24-25). The affirmation of the truth or accuracy of the apostolic witness behind John's Gospel is important evidence for the general historical veracity of the Gospels. Along with Luke 1:1-4, John 19:35, and 2 Peter 1:16, this tells us that the evangelists and the early church claimed to be writing factual history. Thus, the burden of proof is upon those who would deny the historical trustworthiness of the Gospels (cf. Blomberg 1987:240-246). This affirmation probably stems from the elders at Ephesus or leaders of the church as a whole (see note on 21:24), to tell the readers that the testimony recorded herein can be trusted. While some believe this refers only to the contents of chapter 21, the whole Gospel is most certainly the intended thrust. As such this concludes the "witness" theme— in chapters 5 and 8, the reader is challenged to accept the testimony of the Baptist, Jesus' works, God, and the Old Testament prophecies, and here the reader is exhorted to accept the eyewitness testimony of John himself. Burge (2000:591) sums it up well: "This Gospel is no fanciful speculation, no whimsical, inspired redrawing of Jesus' portrait. It is an account of what happened, given by a man who had seen it."

Verse 25 changes from the "we" of 21:24 to "I," and some believe it the work of the Evangelist himself (so Carson, Burge). This is quite viable. The point is that no Gospel could even begin to be exhaustive (for parallels in ancient writings see Keener 2003:1241-1242). To record all that Jesus said and did would require so much space that "the whole world could not contain the books that would be written." All John could do was relate a few representative things Jesus said; he did this so that the reader could understand the truth about the God-man, Jesus. John wanted us to understand that no single book could capture the reality and power, the majesty and glory of the Son of God. This is why God inspired four Gospels; each gives us another nuance of Jesus' life and impact.

BIBLIOGRAPHY

Anderson, P. N.
1999 The Having-Sent-Me Father: Agency, Encounter and Irony in the Johannine Father-Son Relationship. *Semeia* 85:33-57.

Appold, M. L.
1976 *The Oneness Motif in the Fourth Gospel.* Tübingen: J. C. B. Mohr.

Bailey, K. E.
1993 The Shepherd Poems of John 10: Their Culture and Style. *Irish Biblical Studies* 15:2-17.

Bammel, E.
1952 Philos tou kaisaros. *Theologische Literaturzeitung* 77:205-220.

Barnhart, B.
1993 *The Good Wine: Reading John from the Center.* New York: Paulist.

Barrett, C. K.
1978 *The Gospel According to St. John: An Introduction with Commentary and Notes on the Greek Text.* 2nd ed. Philadelphia: Westminster.

1982 The Father is greater than I (John 14:28): Subordinationist Christology in the New Testament. Pp. 19-36 in *Essays on John.* London: SPCK.

Bassler, J. M.
1981 The Galileans: A Neglected Factor in Johannine Community Research. *Catholic Biblical Quarterly* 43:243-257.

Bauckham, R.
1993 The Beloved Disciple as Ideal Author. *Journal for the Study of the New Testament* 49:21-44.

1998 John for Readers of Mark. Pp. 147-171 in *The Gospels for All Christians: Rethinking the Gospel Audience.* Editor, R. Bauckham. Grand Rapids: Eerdmans.

Beasley-Murray, G. R.
1987 *John.* Word Biblical Commentary 36. Waco: Word.

Beck, D. R.
1997 *The Discipleship Paradigm: Readers and Anonymous Characters in the Fourth Gospel.* Biblical Interpretation Series 27. Leiden: Brill.

Beetham, F. G. and P. A. Beetham
1993 A Note on John 19:29. *Journal of Theological Studies* 44:163-169.

Belleville, L.
1980 Born of water and spirit, John 3:5. *Trinity Journal* 1:125-141.

Bengel, J. A.
1877 *Gnomon on the New Testament.* Translator, A. R. Fausset. Edinburgh: T & T Clark.

Benoit, P.
1969 *The Passion and Resurrection of Jesus Christ.* Translator, B. Weatherhead. London: Darton, Longman & Todd.

Bernard, J. H.
1928 *The Gospel According to John.* International Critical Commentary. London: T & T Clark.

Beutler, J.
1978 Psalm 42/43 in Johannesevangelium. *New Testament Studies* 25:35-57.

1997 Die Stunde Jesu im Johannesevangelium. *Bibel und Kirche* 52:25-27.

Black, D. A.
1988 On the Style and Significance of John 17. *Criswell Theological Review* 3:141-159.

Blomberg, C. L.
1987 *The Historical Reliability of the Gospels.* Downers Grove: InterVarsity.

2001 *The Historical Reliability of John's Gospel: Issues and Commentary.* Downers Grove: InterVarsity.

Bock, D. L.
2000 *Blasphemy and Exaltation in Judaism: The Charge Against Jesus in Mark 14:53-65.* Grand Rapids: Baker.

Boice, J. M.
1970 *Witness and Revelation in the Gospel of John.* Grand Rapids: Zondervan.

Boismard, M.-E.
1956 *Du baptême à Cana (Jean 1,19-2,11).* Paris: Cerf.

1957 *St. John's Prologue.* Translator, Carisbrooke Dominicans. London: Blackfriars.

Borchert, G. L.
1996 *John,* vol 1. Nashville: Broadman & Holman.

Borgen, P.
1965 *Bread from Heaven: An Exegetical Study of the Concept of Manna in the Gospel of John and the Writings of Philo.* Leiden: Brill.

Brodie, T. L.
1993 *The Quest for the Origin of John's Gospel: A Source-Oriented Approach.* New York: Oxford University Press.

Brown, R. E.
1966, 1970 *The Gospel According to John.* The Anchor Bible 29A-B. Garden City, NY: Doubleday.

1995 *The Death of the Messiah.* 2 vols. Anchor Bible Reference Library. New York: Doubleday.

Bruce, F. F.
1980 The Trial of Jesus in the Fourth Gospel. Pp. 7-20 in *Gospel Perspectives, vol. 1.* Editors, R. T. France and D. Wenham. Sheffield: JSOT Press.

1983 *The Gospel of John: Introduction, Exposition, and Notes.* Grand Rapids: Eerdmans.

Bultmann, Rudolf
1971 *The Gospel of John: A Commentary.* Translator, G. R. Beasley-Murray. Oxford: Blackwell.

Burge, G. M.
1987 *The Anointed Community: The Holy Spirit in the Johannine Tradition.* Grand Rapids: Eerdmans.

1994 Territorial Religion, Johannine Christology, and the Vineyard of John 15. Pp. 384-396 in *Jesus of Nazareth: Lord and Christ: Essays on the Historical Jesus and New Testament Christology.* Editors, J. B. Green and M. Turner. Grand Rapids: Eerdmans.

2000 *John.* The NIV Application Commentary. Grand Rapids: Zondervan.

Byrne, B.
1985 The Faith of the Beloved Disciple and the Community in John 20. *Journal for the Study of the New Testament* 23:83-97.

Cadman, W. H.
1969 *The Open Heaven.* New York: Oxford.

Calvin, J.
1959, 1961 *The Gospel According to Saint John.* 2 vols. Grand Rapids: Eerdmans. (Orig. pub. 1553)

Capper, B. J.
1998 "With the oldest monks . . .": Light from Essenic History on the Career of the Beloved Disciple. *Journal of Theological Studies* 49:1-55.

Carson, D. A.
1979 The Function of the Paraclete in John 16:7-11. *Journal of Biblical Literature* 98:547-566.

1982 Understanding Misunderstandings in the Fourth Gospel. *Tyndale Bulletin* 33:59-89.

1991 *The Gospel According to John.* Grand Rapids: Eerdmans.

2000 *The Difficult Doctrine of the Love of God.* Wheaton: Crossway.

Charlesworth, J. H.
1995 *The Beloved Disciple: Whose Witness Validates the Gospel of John?* Valley Forge: Trinity.

Chilton, B.
1980 John xii 34 and Targum Isaiah lii 13. *Novum Testamentum* 22:176-178.

Coakley, J. F.
1988 The Anointing in Bethany and the Priority of John. *Journal of Biblical Literature* 107:241-256.

Collins, J. J.
1995 *The Scepter and the Star: The Messiah of the Dead Sea Scrolls and Other Ancient Literature.* New York: Doubleday.

Collins, M. S.
1995 The Quest of *Doxa*: A Socioliterary Reading of the Wedding of Cana. *Biblical Theology Bulletin* 25:100-109.

Comfort, P. W.
1994 *I Am the Way: A Spiritual Journey through the Gospel of John.* Grand Rapids: Baker.

2007 *New Testament Text and Translation Commentary.* Carol Stream, IL: Tyndale House.

Comfort, P. W. and D. Barrett
2001 *The Text of the Earliest New Testament Manuscripts.* Wheaton: Tyndale House.

Comfort, P. W. and W. C. Hawley
1994 *Opening the Gospel of John.* Wheaton: Tyndale House.

Conway, C. M.
2002 The Production of the Johannine Community: A New Historicist Perspective. *Journal of Biblical Literature* 121:479-495.

Craig, W. L.
1989 *Assessing the New Testament Evidence for the Historicity of the Resurrection of Jesus.* Lewiston: Mellen.

Cullmann, O.
1976 *The Johannine Circle.* London: SCM.

Culpepper, R. A.
1975 *The Johannine School.* Missoula: Scholars Press.

1983 *The Anatomy of the Fourth Gospel: A Study in Literary Design.* Philadelphia: Fortress.

1997 The Theology of the Johannine Passion Narrative: John 19:16b-30. *Neotestamentica* 31:21-37.

Dahms, J. V.
1981 Isaiah 55:11 and the Gospel of John. *Evangelical Quarterly* 53:78-88.

1983 The Johannine Use of Monogenes Reconsidered. *New Testament Studies* 29:222-232.

Dalman, G.
1935 *Sacred Sites and Ways.* London: SPCK.

Daube, D.
1956 *The New Testament and Rabbinic Judaism.* London: Athlone.

Derrett, J. D. M.
1963 Water into Wine. *Biblische Zeitschrift* 7:80-97.

1993 *Ti ergaze;* (John 6:30), an Unrecognized Allusion to Isaiah 45:9. *Zeitschrift für die neutestamentliche Wissenschaft* 84:142-144.

1999 Advocacy at John 16:8-11. *Expository Times* 110:181-182.

Dodd, C. H.
1953a *The Interpretation of the Fourth Gospel.* Cambridge: Cambridge University Press.

1953b Note on John 21, 24. *Journal of Theological Studies* n.s. 4:212-213.

1963 *The Historical Tradition in the Fourth Gospel.* Cambridge: Cambridge University Press.

Edwards, M. J.
1994 Not Yet 50 Years Old. *New Testament Studies* 40:449-454.

Edwards, R.
1988 *Charin anti charitos* (Jn 1:16): Grace and the Law in the Johannine Prologue. *Journal for the Study of the New Testament* 32:3-15.

1994 The Christological Basis of the Johannine Footwashing. Pp. 367-383 in *Jesus of Nazareth, Lord and Christ: Essays on the Historical Jesus and New Testament Christology.* Editors, J. B. Green and M. Turner. Grand Rapids: Eerdmans.

Edwards, W. D., W. J. Gabel, and F. F. Hosmer.
1986 On the Physical Death of Jesus Christ. *Journal of the American Medical Association* 255:1455-1463.

Ellis, P. F.
1992 The Authenticity of John 21. *St. Vladimir's Theological Quarterly* 36:17-25.

1999 Inclusion, Chiasm, and the Division of John's Gospel. *St. Vladimir's Theological Quarterly* 43:269-338.

Emerton, J. A.
1958 The 153 Fishes in John xxi.11. *Journal of Theological Studies* 9:86-89.

Ensor, P. W.
2000 The Authenticity of John 4:35. *Evangelical Quarterly* 72:13-21.

Evans, C. F.
1990 *St. Luke*. Philadelphia: Trinity.

Fee, G. D.
1978 Once More: John 7:37-39. *Expository Times* 89:116-118.

Feinberg, Paul
1979 The Meaning of Inerrancy. Pp. 267-304 in *Inerrancy*. Editor, N. Geisler. Grand Rapids: Zondervan.

Ford, J. M.
1969 Mingled Blood from the Side of Christ (John XIX. 34). *New Testament Studies* 15:337-338.

Forestell, J.
1974 *The Word of the Cross: Salvation as Revelation in the Fourth Gospel.* Rome: Pontifical.

Giblin, C. H.
1984 Confrontations in John 18:1-27. *Biblica* 65:210-232.

1992 Mary's Anointing for Jesus' Burial-Resurrection (John 12, 1-8). *Biblica* 73:560-564.

Godet, F. L.
1969 *Commentary on the Gospel of John*. Grand Rapids: Zondervan. (Orig. pub. 1893)

Grassi, J. A.
1997 Women's Leadership Roles in John's Gospel. *Bible Today* 35:312-317.

Grigsby, B. H.
1982 The Cross as an Expiatory Sacrifice in the Fourth Gospel. *Journal for the Study of the New Testament* 15:51-80.

Gundry, R. H.
1967 In My Father's House Are Many *Monai* (John 14:2). *Zeitschrift für die neutestamentliche Wissenschaft* 58:68-72.

Gundry, R. H. and R. W. Howell
1999 The Sense and Syntax of John 3:14-17 with Special Reference to the Use of Houtos . . . Hoste in John 3:16. *Novum Testamentum* 41: 24-39.

Haas, N.
1970 Anthropological Observations on the Skeletal Remains from Giv'at ha-Mivtar. *Israel Exploration Journal* 20:38-59.

Haenchen, E.
1984 *A Commentary on the Gospel of John.* 2 vols. Hermeneia. Translator, R. W. Funk. Philadelphia: Fortress.

Harrington, D. J.
1990 *John's Thought and Theology: An Introduction.* Wilmington: Michael Glazier.

Harris, E.
1994 *Prologue and Gospel: The Theology of the Fourth Evangelist.* Sheffield: Sheffield Academic Press.

Harris, M. J.
1990 *From Grave to Glory: Resurrection in the New Testament.* Grand Rapids: Zondervan.

1992 *Jesus as God: The New Testament Use of Theos in Reference to Jesus.* Grand Rapids: Baker.

Hart, H. S. J.
1952 The Crown of Thorns in John 19:2-5. *Journal of Theological Studies* 3:66-75.

Hartin, P. J.
1991 Remain in Me (John 15:5). The foundation of the ethical and its consequences in the farewell discourse. *Neotestamentica* 25:341-356.

Hartman, L.
1984 An Attempt at a Text-Centered Exegesis of John 21. *Studia Theologica* 38:29-45.

Harvey, A. E.
1987 Christ as Agent. Pp. 239-250 in *The Glory of Christ in the New Testament: Studies in Christology in Honour of George Bradford Caird.* Editors, L. D. Hurst and N. T. Wright. Oxford: Clarendon.

Hendriksen, W.
1953 *Exposition of the Gospel According to John.* New Testament Commentary. Grand Rapids: Baker.

Hengel, M.
1989 *The Johannine Question.* Translator, J. Bowden. Philadelphia: Trinity.
2002 Jesus the Messiah of Israel: The Debate about the "Messianic Mission" of Jesus. Pp. 340-351 in *Authenticating the Activities of Jesus.* Editors, B. Chilton and C. A. Evans. Leiden: Brill.

Hofius, O.
1987 Struktur und Gedankengang des Logos-Hymnus in Joh 1:1-18. *Zeitschrift für die neutestamentliche Wissenschaft* 78:1-25.

Hollis, H.
1989 The Root of the Johannine Pun—HYPSOTHENAI. *New Testament Studies* 35:475-478.

Horbury, W.
1982 The Benediction of the *Minim* and Early Jewish-Christian Controversy. *Journal of Theological Studies* n.s. 33:19-61.

Hoskyns, E. C.
1947 *The Fourth Gospel.* 2nd ed. London: Faber & Faber.

Hultgren, A. J.
1982 The Johannine Footwashing (13:1-11) as Symbol of Eschatological Hospitality. *New Testament Studies* 28:539-546.

Hunter, A. M.
1965 *The Gospel According to John.* Cambridge: Cambridge University Press.

Jackson, H. M.
1999 Ancient Self-Referential Conventions and Their Implications for the Authorship and Integrity of the Gospel of John. *Journal of Theological Studies* 50:1-39.

Jaubert, A.
1965 *The Date of the Last Supper.* New York: Alba.

Jeremias, J.
1966 *The Eucharistic Words of Jesus.* London: SCM.

Johns, L. L. and D. B. Miller
1994 The Signs as Witnesses in the Fourth Gospel. *Catholic Biblical Quarterly* 56:519-535.

Johnston, G.
1970 *The Spirit-Paraclete in the Gospel of John.* Cambridge: Cambridge University Press.

Kangas, R.
2000 In My Father's House: The Unleavened Truth of John 14. *Affirmation and Critique* 5:22-36.

Keener, C. S.
1999 Is Subordination within the Trinity Really Heresy? A Study of John 5:18 in Context. *Trinity Journal* 20:39-51.
2003 *The Gospel of John.* 2 vols. Peabody, MA: Hendrickson.

Keller, M. L.
2000 Discipleship in John: An Invitation to See. *Bible Today* 38:87-94.

Kilpatrick, G. D.
1960 The Punctuation of Jn 7:37-38. *Journal of Theological Studies* 11:340-342.

Klauck, H.-J.
1996 Der Weggang Jesu: Neue Arbeiten zu Joh 13-17. *Biblische Zeitschrift* 40:236-250.

Köstenberger, A. J.
1995 The Seventh Johannine Sign: A Study in John's Christology. *Bulletin of Biblical Research* 5:87-103.
1998a *The Missions of Jesus and the Disciples According to the Fourth Gospel.* Grand Rapids: Eerdmans.
1998b Jesus as Rabbi in the Fourth Gospel. *Bulletin for Biblical Research* 8:97-128.
1999 *Encountering John: The Gospel in Historical, Literary, and Theological Perspective.* Grand Rapids: Baker.
2004 *John.* Baker Exegetical Commentary on the New Testament. Grand Rapids: Baker.

Kovacs, J. L.
1995 Now Shall the Ruler of This World Be Driven Out: Jesus' Death as Cosmic Battle in John 12:20-36. *Journal of Biblical Literature* 114:227-247.

Kysar, R.
1975 *The Fourth Evangelist and His Gospel*. Minneapolis: Augsburg.

1986 *John*. Augsburg Commentary on the New Testament. Minneapolis: Augsburg.

2001 As You Sent Me: Identity and Mission in the Fourth Gospel. *Word & World* 21:370-376.

Ladd, G. E.
1975 *I Believe in the Resurrection of Jesus*. Grand Rapids: Eerdmans.

Lagrange, M. J.
1948 *Évangile selon Saint Jean*. 8th ed. Paris: Gabalda.

Lataine, B.
1997 The Son on the Father's Lap. The Meaning of *eis ton kolpon* in John 1:18. *Studien zum Neuen Testament und seiner Umwelt* 22:125-138.

Lenski, R. C. H.
1942 *The Interpretation of St. John's Gospel*. Minneapolis: Augsburg.

Lightfoot, R. H.
1956 *St. John's Gospel: A Commentary*. Oxford: Oxford University Press.

Lindars, B.
1972 *The Gospel of John*. The New Century Bible. Greenwood, SC: Attic.

Loader, W. R. G.
1984 The Central Structure of Johannine Christology. *New Testament Studies* 30:188-216.

Lombard, H. A. and W. H. Oliver
1991 A Working Supper in Jerusalem: John 13:1-38 Introduces Jesus' Farewell Discourse. *Neotestamentica* 25: 357-378.

Maccini, R. G.
1994 A Reassessment of the Woman at the Well in John 4 in Light of Samaritan Context. *Journal for the Study of the New Testament* 53:35-46.

Mahoney, R.
1974 *The Two Disciples at the Tomb. The Background and Message of John 20.1-10*. Frankfurt am Main: Peter Lang.

Marcus, J.
1998 Rivers of Living Water from Jesus' Belly (John 7:38). *Journal of Biblical Literature* 117:328-330.

Marshall, I. H.
1970 *Luke: Historian and Theologian*. Grand Rapids: Zondervan.

Marxsen, W.
1970 *The Resurrection of Jesus of Nazareth*. Translator, M. Kohl. London: SCM.

Matsunaga, K.
1981 Is John's Gospel Anti-Sacramental?—A New Solution in the Light of the Evangelist's Milieu. *New Testament Studies* 27:516-524.

McCane, B. R.
2000 Burial Practices, Jewish. Pp. 173-175 in *Dictionary of New Testament Background*. Editors, C. A. Evans and S. E. Porter. Downers Grove: InterVarsity.

McEleney, N. J.
1977 153 Great Fishes (John 21:11)—Gematriacal Atbash. *Biblica* 58:411-417.

McKay, K. L.
1985 Style and Significance in the Language of John 21:15-17. *Novum Testamentum* 27:319-333.

McKnight, S.
1991 *A Light among the Gentiles: Jewish Missionary Activity in the Second Temple Period*. Minneapolis: Fortress.

Meeks, W. A.
1967 *The Prophet-King*. Leiden: Brill.

Meier, J. P.
1996 John 20:19-23. *Mid-Stream* 35:395-398.

Metzger, B. M.
1994 *A Textual Commentary on the Greek New Testament*. 2nd ed. New York: United Bible Societies.

Metzner, R.
1999 Der Geheilte von Johannes 5—Repräsentant des Unglaubens. *Zeitschrift für die Neutestamentliche Wissenschaft* 90:177-193.

Meyken, M. J. J.
1996 The Origin of the Old Testament Quotation in John 7:38. *Novum Testamentum* 38:160-175.

Michaels, J. R.
1989 *John*. New International Bible Commentary. Peabody, MA: Hendrickson.

Miller, E. L.
1980 The Christology of John 8:25. *Theologische Zeitschrift* 36:257-265.

1999 In the Beginning: A Christological Transparency. *New Testament Studies* 45:587-592.

Moloney, F. J.
1998 *The Gospel of John*. Sacra Pagina 4. Collegeville, MN: Liturgical Press.

2000 The Fourth Gospel and the Jesus of History. *New Testament Studies* 46:42-58.

Morris, L.
1969 *Studies in the Fourth Gospel*. Grand Rapids: Eerdmans.

1995 *The Gospel According to St. John*. New International Commentary on the New Testament. 2nd ed. Grand Rapids: Eerdmans.

1998 The Atonement in John's Gospel. *Criswell Theological Review* 3:49-64.

Motyer, S.
1997 Method in Fourth Gospel Studies: A Way Out of the Impasse. *Journal for the Study of the New Testament* 66:27-44.

Neyrey, J. H.
1996 The Trials (Forensic) and Tribulations (Honor Challenges) of Jesus: John 7 in Social Scientific Perspective. *Biblical Theology Bulletin* 26:107-124.

2001 The Noble Shepherd in John 10: Cultural and Rhetorical Background. *Journal of Biblical Literature* 120:267-291.

Neyrey, J. H. and R. L. Rohrbaugh
2001 He Must Increase, I Must Decrease (John 3:30): A Cultural and Social Interpretation. *Catholic Biblical Quarterly* 63:464-483.

O'Grady, J. F.
1998 The Beloved Disciple, His Community and the Church. *Chicago Studies* 37:16-26.

Oliver, W. H. and A. C. van Aarle
1991 The community of faith as dwelling place of the Father. *Basileia tou theou* as household of God. *Neotestamentica* 25:379-400.

Osborne, G. R.
1981 John 21: Test Case for History and Redaction in the Resurrection Narratives. Pp. 293-328 in *Gospel Perspectives II: Studies of History and Tradition in the Four Gospels*. Editors, R. T. France and D. Wenham. Sheffield: Journal for the Study of the Old Testament Press.

1984 *The Resurrection Narratives: A Redactional Study*. Grand Rapids: Baker.

1991 *The Hermeneutical Spiral: A Comprehensive Introduction to Biblical Interpretation*. Downers Grove: InterVarsity.

1995 *Three Crucial Questions about the Bible*. Grand Rapids: Baker.

2002 *Revelation*. Baker Exegetical Commentary on the New Testament. Grand Rapids: Baker.

2003 *Romans*. InterVarsity New Testament Commentaries. Downers Grove: InterVarsity.

Pamment, M.
1983 John 3:5: Unless one is born of water and the Spirit, he cannot enter the kingdom of God. *Novum Testamentum* 25:189-190.

Pendrick, G.
1995 Monogenes. *New Testament Studies* 41:587-600.

Perkins, P.
1978 *The Gospel According to St. John: A Theological Commentary.* Chicago: Franciscan Herald.

Pesch, R.
1969 *Der Reiche Fischfang.* Düsseldorf: Patmos.

Plummer, A.
1981 *The Gospel According to St. John.* Grand Rapids: Baker. (Orig. Pub. 1882)

Poirier, J. C.
1996 Day and Night and the Punctuation of John 9:3. *New Testament Studies* 42:288-294.

Pope, Marvin H.
1988 Hosanna—What It Really Means. *Biblical Review* 4:16-25.

Porter, C. L.
1962 Papyrus Bodmer XV (𝔓75) and the Text of Codex Vaticanus. *Journal of Biblical Literature* 81:363-376.
1967 John 9:38, 39a: A Liturgical Addition to the Text. *New Testament Studies* 13:387-394.

Pryor, J. W.
1992 *John: Evangelist of the Covenant People: The Narrative and Themes of the Fourth Gospel.* Downers Grove: InterVarsity.

Rahner, J.
2000 Vergegenwärtigende Erinnerung. Die Abschiedsreden der Geist-Paraklet und die Retrospektive des Johannesevangeliums. *Zeitschrift für die Neutestamentliche Wissenschaft* 91:72-90.

Reinhardt, W.
1995 The Population Size of Jerusalem and the Numerical Growth of the Jerusalem Church. Pp. 237-266 in *The Book of Acts in Its Palestinian Setting.* Editor, R. Bauckham. Grand Rapids: Eerdmans.

Ridderbos, H.
1997 *The Gospel of John: A Theological Commentary.* Translator, J. Vriend. Grand Rapids: Eerdmans.

Riesner, R.
1987 Bethany Beyond the Jordan (John 1.28). *Tyndale Bulletin* 38:29-63.

Robinson, J. A. T.
1985 *The Priority of John.* London: SCM.

Rowland, C.
1984 John 1:51, Jewish Apocalyptic and Targumic Tradition. *New Testament Studies* 30:498-507.

Sanders, J. N.
1968 *The Gospel According to St. John.* Black New Testament Commentaries. Edited and Completed by B. A. Mastin. New York: Harper & Row.

Sava, A. F.
1960 The Wound in the Side of Christ. *Catholic Biblical Quarterly* 19:343-346.

Schlatter, A.
1962 *Das Evangelium nach Johannes: Ausgelegt für Bibelleser.* Stuttgart: Calwer.

Schleiermacher, F. E.
1925 *The Life of Jesus.* London: SCM.

Schnackenburg, R.
1968-82 *The Gospel According to St. John.* 3 vols. Translators, K. Smyth, C. Hastings et al. New York: Crossroad.

Schneiders, S. M.
1983 The Face Veil: A Johannine Sign. *Biblical Theology Bulletin* 13:94-97.

Schweitzer, A.
1968 *The Quest of the Historical Jesus.* Translator, W. Montgomery. New York: Macmillan. (Orig. Pub. 1906)

Segovia, F.
1985 The Structure, *Tendenz,* and *Sitz im Leben* of John 13:31-14: 31. *Journal of Biblical Literature* 104:471-493.

Shaw, A.
1974 Breakfast by the Shore and the Mary Magdalene Encounter as Eucharistic Narratives. *Journal of Theological Studies* 25:12-26.

Sherwin-White, A. N.
1965 The Trial of Christ. Pp. 97-116 in *Historicity and Chronology in the New Testament.* Editor, D. E. Nineham. London: SPCK.

Smalley, S. S.
1998 *John: Evangelist and Interpreter.* Downers Grove: InterVarsity.

Smith, D. M.
1992 *John Among the Gospels: The Relationship in Twentieth Century Research.* Minneapolis: Fortress.

Smith, R. A.
1988 Seeking Jesus in the Fourth Gospel. *Currents in Theology and Mission* 15:48-55.

1995 *The Theology of the Gospel of John.* Cambridge: Cambridge University Press.

Staton, J. E.
1997 A Vision of Unity—Christian Unity in the Fourth Gospel. *Evangelical Quarterly* 69:291-305.

Stauffer, E.
1960a *Jesus and His Story.* Translator, D. M. Barton. London: SCM.

1960b Historische Elemente im vierten Evangelium. Pp. 33-51 in *Bekenntnis zur Kirche.* Editor, E.-H. Amberg and U. Kuhn. Berlin: Evangelische.

Stegner, W.
1979 Dikaiosyne in Jo. xvi. 8, 10. *Novum Testamentum* 21:12-19.

Strack, H. L., and P. Billerbeck
1922–61 *Kommentar zum Neuen Testament aus Talmud und Midrasch.* 6 vols. Munich: Beck.

Talbert, C. H.
1992 *Reading John: A Literary and Theological Commentary on the Fourth Gospel and the Johannine Epistles.* New York: Crossroad.

Tasker, R. V. G.
1960 *The Gospel According to John: An Introduction and Commentary.* Tyndale New Testament Commentaries. Grand Rapids: Eerdmans.

Temple, W.
1945 *Readings in St. John's Gospel.* London: Macmillan.

Tenney, M. G.
1960 The Footnotes of John's Gospel. *Bibliotheca Sacra* 117:350-364.

Thomas, J. C.
1991 *Footwashing in John 13 and the Johannine Community.* Sheffield: Journal for the Study of the Old Testament Press.

Thompson, M. M.
1988 *The Humanity of Jesus in the Fourth Gospel.* Philadelphia: Fortress.

1991 Signs and Faith in the Fourth Gospel. *Bulletin for Biblical Research* 1:89-108.

1999 The Living Father. *Semeia* 85:19-31.

2001 *The God of the Gospel of John.* Grand Rapids: Eerdmans.

Tovey, D.
1997 *Narrative Art and Act in the Fourth Gospel.* Journal for the Study of the New Testament Supplement Series 151. Sheffield: Sheffield Academic Press.

Trudinger, L. F.
1982 An Israelite in Whom There Is No Guile: An Interpretative Note on John 1:45-51. *Evangelical Quarterly* 54:117-120.

Trudinger, P.
2001 In My Father's House: Expository Notes on a Johannine Theme. *Expository Times* 112:229-230.

van der Merwe, D. G.
1997 Towards a theological understanding of Johannine discipleship. *Neotestamentica* 31:339-359.

1999 The historical and theological significance of John the Baptist as he is portrayed in John 1. *Neotestamentica* 33:267-292.

Vogler, W.
1999a Johannes als Kritiker der synoptischen Tradition. *Berliner Theologische Zeitschrift* 16:41-58.

1999b The historical and theological significance of John the Baptist as he is portrayed in John 1. *Neotestamentica* 33:293-297.

Walker, W. O. Jr.
1982 The Lord's Prayer in Matthew and in John. *New Testament Studies* 28:237-256.

Wenham, J.
1984 *The Easter Enigma: Are the Resurrection Accounts in Conflict?* Grand Rapids: Zondervan.

Westcott, B. F.
1881 *The Gospel According to St. John.* London: Macmillan.

Whitacre, R. A.
1999 *John.* The IVP New Testament Commentary Series. Downers Grove: InterVarsity.

Wilcox, M.
1977 The Prayer of Jesus in John xi. 41b-42. *New Testament Studies* 24:128-132.

Winter, P.
1974 *On the Trial of Jesus.* Berlin: de Gruyter.

Witherington, B.
1995 *John's Wisdom: A Commentary on the Fourth Gospel.* Louisville: Westminster John Knox.

Zahn, T.
1921 *Das Evangelium des Johannes.* 6th ed. Kommentar zum Neuen Testament 4. Leipzig: Deichert.

Zumstein, J.
1996 Der Prozess der Relecture in der johanneischen Literatur. *New Testament Studies* 42:394-411.

1 John

PHILIP W. COMFORT
AND
WENDELL C. HAWLEY

INTRODUCTION TO
1 John

AFTER READING AND STUDYING John's Gospel, a person might wonder how the great truths presented in it were lived out in the church. Readers might also wonder how they themselves can better understand and experience the truths revealed by Jesus—ideas such as "walking in the light" (John 8:12; 12:35-36), "remaining in Christ" (John 15:4-8), and "loving one another" (John 13:34; 15:12). John's first epistle answers both questions. It tells how Christians in the late first century were practicing (or not practicing) the profound truths proclaimed by Jesus, and it provides key insights into how we today can live in the Spirit of Jesus to experience spiritual transformation and love for the members of Christ's community, the church.

AUTHOR

Since the author does not name himself, the key to determining the authorship of this epistle (as well as that of 2 John and 3 John) is its similarity to the Gospel of John. The similarities between John's Gospel and John's epistles are so remarkable that it would be difficult to argue that these writings were done by two different people. The syntax, vocabulary, and the thematic developments are so strikingly similar that most readers can tell that the epistles were penned by the writer of the Gospel of John. Therefore, the way to establish the authorship of the three epistles is to establish the authorship of the fourth Gospel.

Whoever wrote the Gospel of John was an eyewitness of Jesus and among the very first followers of Jesus. The writer of this Gospel calls himself "the disciple Jesus loved" (John 13:23; 19:26; 20:2; 21:7, 20); he was one of the twelve disciples, and among them he was one of those who was very close to Jesus (e.g., see John 13:23-25 where "the disciple Jesus loved" is said to have been leaning on Jesus' breast during the Last Supper). From the synoptic Gospels we realize that three disciples were very close to Jesus: Peter, James, and John. Peter could not have been the author of this Gospel because the one who called himself "the disciple Jesus loved" communicated with Peter at the Last Supper (John 13:23-25), outran Peter to the empty tomb on the morning of the Resurrection (John 20:2-4), and walked with Jesus and Peter along the shore of Galilee after Jesus' resurrection appearance to them (John 21:20-23). Thus, someone other than Peter authored this Gospel. And that someone could not have been James, for he was martyred many years before this Gospel was written (AD 44; cf. Acts 12:2). This leaves us with John, the son of Zebedee, who, like Peter and James, shared an intimate relationship with Jesus. Most likely, John is also the "other disciple" mentioned in the fourth Gospel (e.g.,

John 18:15). He and Andrew (Peter's brother) were the first to follow Jesus (John 1:35-40), and he was the one who was known to the high priest and therefore gained access for himself and Peter into the courtyard of the place where Jesus was on trial (John 18:15-16). This one, "the disciple Jesus loved," stood by Jesus during his crucifixion (John 19:25-26) and walked with Jesus after his resurrection (John 21:20). And this same disciple wrote the Gospel that today bears his name (John 21:24-25).

The author's claim to have been an eyewitness is just as pronounced in 1 John as it is in the Gospel of John. The author of 1 John claims to be among those who heard, saw, and even touched the eternal Word made flesh (1:1-4). In other words, John lived with Jesus, the God-man. As such, his testimony is firsthand; he was an eyewitness of the greatest person ever to enter human history. As Smith (1979:151) put it: "The author of [1 John] claims to have been an eye-witness of the Word of Life (1:1-3) and speaks throughout in a tone of apostolic authority, and there is abundance of primitive and credible testimony that he was St. John, 'the disciple whom Jesus loved,' and the last survivor of the Apostle-company."

But some scholars have thought that some other John (not the apostle) was the author. They make this judgment on the basis of a quotation from Papias, who was bishop of Hierapolis in the Roman province of Asia Minor (c. AD 100–130). His comment, transmitted through Irenaeus and recorded by Eusebius, is as follows: "If anywhere one came my way who had been a follower of the elders, I would inquire about the words of the elders—what Andrew and Peter had said, or what Thomas or James or John or Matthew or any other of the Lord's disciples say; and I would inquire about the things which Aristion and the elder John, the Lord's disciples, say" (Eusebius *History* 3.39.4-5).

Since two different people named "John" are referred to in this quotation, some scholars have surmised that the first "John" mentioned was John the apostle and the second "John" was an elder but not one of the original twelve disciples. (This was Eusebius's opinion, contra Irenaeus who considered both mentions to refer to the same person, the apostle John—see House 1992:530.) Since the writer of 2 John and 3 John calls himself "the elder," many have thought that the author of the three Johannine epistles was this "John the elder," not John the apostle. Although this could be true, it is not likely. First of all, according to Eusebius's quote, Papias did not say that John the elder was the writer of the three epistles of John. Second, it seems that Papias was speaking of two different categories of sources for his learning. The first was teachings passed down from those who *had been* eyewitnesses of Jesus, his original disciples—namely Andrew, Peter, Thomas, James, John, Matthew, and the other disciples of the Lord. The second source was the ongoing teaching of disciples who were still alive when Papias made this statement—those such as Aristion and John the elder (who was literally much older at this time). Note that Papias spoke of what the first group had "said" (past tense) and what the second group "says" (present tense; cf. Stott 2000:39-40). John the apostle was in both groups. Furthermore, John is lumped together with the other "elders" in the first group (who were also Jesus' apostles), and he is specifically called an elder in the second group.

Later in life, John the apostle called himself an elder. After all, Peter and Paul, both apostles, each called themselves "elder" (1 Pet 5:1; Phlm 1:9, "old man," NLT). The title "elder" probably points to John's position at that time; he was the oldest living apostle and chief leader among the churches in the Roman province of Asia Minor. This is made clear in the First Epistle by the way he addresses the believers as his "dear children" (2:1, 18, 28; 3:7; 5:21).

In any event, whichever John wrote these epistles, he must have been an eyewitness of Jesus. We know, for certain, that John the son of Zebedee was an eyewitness. As for another John, called John the elder—he would have probably been one of Jesus' 72 disciples (Luke 10:1) in order to claim "eyewitness" status. (This would also apply to Aristion.) But then, given the identical style between the epistles and the Gospel, this other "John" would also be the author of the fourth Gospel, and that can't be so, for we know that the disciple who wrote the fourth Gospel was among the inner circle of the Twelve (see the discussion above). Once again, the facts presented in the fourth Gospel and the similarities of the first, second, and third epistles of John to the fourth Gospel press us to conclude that the author of the epistles and the author of the Gospel must be one and the same: John the apostle, the son of Zebedee. The earliest identification of John the apostle as the author of 1 John comes from the late second century, when both Irenaeus (*Heresies* 3.15.5, 8) and the Muratorian Fragment identified 1 John as his work.

Instead of dictating the epistle to an amanuensis, it appears that John himself penned it (2:12-14), as was his habit—as explicitly expressed in 2 John 12 and 3 John 13 and implicitly expressed in the Gospel (John 21:24-25).

DATE AND OCCASION OF WRITING

We really do not know when 1 John was written. For one thing, it could have been written before he wrote the Gospel or after it. In 3 John 9, the apostle says, "I wrote to the church about this." This could refer to 1 John or the Gospel, but the reference (in context) is more likely to 1 John (see note on 3 John 9). Nonetheless, the dating of John's Gospel does bear on the dating of 1 John because the two are written in so similar a style and concern so many of the same issues. Extant manuscript evidence, particularly the papyrus manuscript known as $\mathfrak{P}$52 (P. Rylands 457, dated c. AD 100–120; for details of dating, see Comfort 2005:139-143), shows that the original Gospel had to have been composed before AD 100. The question is, how long before AD 100?

J. A. T. Robinson has placed the composition of the Gospel of John and 1–3 John before AD 70. In fact, Robinson has dated all the New Testament writings to pre-AD 70—primarily on the grounds that not one New Testament writer comments on the destruction of Jerusalem as having already occurred. This significant point, coupled with the fact that John speaks of a certain portico at the sheep gate in Jerusalem that was *still* standing at the time of writing (see John 5:2, where John uses the present tense verb) points to a date of pre-AD 70 for John's Gospel. Based on their relationship to his Gospel, 1–3 John would be dated similarly in Robinson's perspective (see Robinson 1976:277-278).

However, we agree with most other scholars who tend to date the Gospel of John in the 80s, placing it in the following chronology: John and the other apostles were probably forced to leave Jerusalem by AD 70, if not earlier, due to mounting persecution. It is possible that John gathered with some of the Samaritan converts (see John 4:1-45; Acts 8:9-17) and with some of John the Baptist's followers in Palestine, where they continued to preach the word. Sometime thereafter (but probably no earlier than AD 70), they migrated to Asia Minor and began a successful ministry among the Gentiles (see Barker 1981:300-301).

John wrote a Gospel for these Gentiles somewhere around AD 80. Sometime thereafter, some of the members of the community left to form a rival group. John, therefore, wrote 1 John in order to deal with the crisis by encouraging the believers to remain in Christ and in the apostolic fellowship and by denouncing those who had not remained. Thus, the First Epistle was probably written around AD 85–90.

We have early historical records indicating that John wrote his Gospel while living in Ephesus. For example, Irenaeus wrote: "John, the disciple of the Lord, he who had leaned on his breast, also published the Gospel, while living at Ephesus in Asia" (*Heresies* 3.1.2). Irenaeus (who lived AD 130–200) received this information from Polycarp, who in his younger years was personally instructed by John. Thus, it stands to reason that John wrote his three epistles to certain local churches in Asia—especially to those around Ephesus, the church in which John functioned as an elder in his latter days. (The same churches probably include those mentioned in Rev 1:11.)

One of the reasons for this first epistle was that a heretical faction had developed within the church, one that promoted false teachings concerning the person of Christ. Scholars have identified this heresy as Docetism in a general sense and have pointed specifically to Cerinthus as the perpetrator of the specific brand of Docetism that 1 John addresses. Our knowledge of Cerinthus comes from Irenaeus, who cited Polycarp (a disciple of John) as saying that there was an incident once when John discovered that Cerinthus was in the same bath house in Ephesus—John cried out, "Let us save ourselves; the bath house may fall down, for inside is Cerinthus, the enemy of the truth." Irenaeus continued by saying that John proclaimed his Gospel to refute the errors of Cerinthus (*Against Heresies* 3.3.4; 3.11.1; see Brown 1982:766-771 for a full record of the historical evidence concerning Cerinthus). The Docetists denied that Jesus had actually partaken of flesh and blood; they denied that God had come in the flesh (see 4:1-3). They did not deny Jesus Christ's deity; they denied his true humanity (see discussion below under "Major Themes"). John specifically refuted the Cerinthian heresy in 5:5-8. This setting undermines Robinson's dating of John's writings (both Gospel and epistles to pre-AD 70); instead, it points to a date in John's later life, in which he was probably in his 70s or 80s.

AUDIENCE

In recent years various scholars have tried to identify the original Johannine community—the group of believers for whom John wrote his Gospel and the epistles. That there was a Johannine community seems evident from the way John speaks to them and of them in his three epistles. The apostle John and the believers knew each other well, and the believers accepted the teachings of the apostle as "the truth." John encouraged them to stay in fellowship with him (and the other apostles); if they did so, they would enjoy true fellowship with the Father and the Son (1:1-4).

In the Gospel this link between the believers and John and Jesus is also made evident. Throughout the Gospel, John lets his readers know that he had a special relationship with Jesus. As the Son, who was "near to the Father's heart," was the one qualified to explain the Father to mankind because of his special relationship with the Father (John 1:18), so John, who reclined on Jesus' chest, was qualified to explain Jesus and his message to his readers because of his intimate relationship with Jesus. In John's Gospel "the beloved disciple" or "the other disciple" is given a certain kind of preeminence: He is one of the first two followers of Jesus (John 1:35-37); he is the closest to Jesus during the Last Supper (John 13:22-25); he follows Jesus to his trial (John 18:15); and then he alone of the Twelve goes to Jesus' cross and is given a direct command from Jesus to care for Jesus' mother (John 19:26-27). He outruns Peter to the empty tomb and is the first to believe in Jesus' resurrection (John 20:1-8); and he is the first to recognize that it was Jesus appearing to them in the Galilean visitation (John 21:7). Because of his relationship to Jesus, John's testimony to his community could be trusted.

Culpepper (1975:261-290) attempted to reconstruct some of the distinctives of this Johannine community. He conjectured that this community was a kind of school (scholē [TG4981, ZG5391]) that claimed Jesus as its founder and John as its master-teacher. This school studied the Old Testament and was reared on the teachings of John about Jesus, therein absorbing John's esoteric language about mystical experiences with Jesus. This school was also responsible in collaborating with John in producing his written Gospel. As a community, they were detached from Judaism (perhaps several of the members were ex-synagogue members who were expelled for their faith in Jesus), and they struggled with false teachers who denied Jesus as the God-man.

Then Culpepper did another study of John's Gospel based on theories of reader-reception. Adopting Iser's model of the implied reader (see Comfort's evaluation [1997:27-28]), Culpepper was able to sketch the general character of John's intended readers by what information (or lack thereof) the author supplied in the narrative concerning characters, events, language, cultural practices, and so forth. According to Culpepper's study (1983:206-223), John's intended readers were expected to already know most of the characters in the Gospel of John (with the exception of the beloved disciple, Lazarus, Nicodemus, Caiaphas, and Annas). The readers could be expected to know the general regions where the stories take place but would be unfamiliar with the specific locations—for which the author supplies some details. Thus, the readers were not from Palestine. As would be expected, the readers knew Greek but not Hebrew or Aramaic. The author assumed that his readers used a Roman (not a Jewish) system of keeping time and that the readers had little knowledge of Jewish festivals and rituals. However, the readers were expected to know the Old Testament Scriptures and to understand messianic expectations. On the whole, it seems that the readers were not Jewish but Hellenistic Christians who would have been already familiar with many parts of the gospel story.

If the Gospel and epistles were directed to the same audience, then it stands to reason that the readers of John's epistles were primarily Hellenistic Christians. This accords with the tradition that John devoted his last years to ministry in Ephesus, where he was an elder. As such, the recipients of his epistles would have been those in the church in Ephesus and those in the nearby churches. (The same churches probably include those mentioned in Rev 1:11.)

By doing a close study of the epistles, it can be gathered that the readers of John's epistles were close to John—so as to be considered his spiritual family. His readers were believers of all ages (children, young men, and fathers; 2:12-14), who needed to be affirmed as a community in love, life, and truth. They depended on him for his eyewitness account about Jesus and for his insights about his personal relationship with Jesus. They must have been accustomed to his rambling style, and they must have understood certain references that are vague and perplexing to modern readers. For example, we assume that they understood John's words about "he who came by water and blood" (5:6, NLT mg) and about the sin that "leads to death" and the sin that doesn't (5:16-17). We modern readers, however, are forced to conjecture.

It must also be said that the readers of John's first epistle must have known John's Gospel well, especially the upper-room discourse of John 13–17, because there are so many close connections between the two writings (Burge 1996:39; Stott 2000:20-22). John's first epistle is, in effect, a commentary on his Gospel, particularly John 13–17—even more so, an application commentary. John wanted to make sure his readers, whether among the heterodox group or orthodox, were properly understanding Jesus' teachings and applying them in their Christian lives.

CANONICITY AND TEXTUAL HISTORY
Records of the early church indicate that the First Epistle of John was readily received and recognized as John's writing. Polycarp, the disciple of John, quoted 1 John 4:3 (*To the Philippians* 7). Eusebius said of Papias, a disciple of John and a friend of Polycarp: "He used testimonies from the First Epistle of John" (*History* 3.39.17). Irenaeus often quoted this epistle (cf. Eusebius *History* 5.8); in his work *Heresies* (3.15.5, 8), he quoted from John by name (1 John 2:18, etc.), and, in *Heresies* 3.16.7, he quoted 1 John 4:1-3, 5:1, and 2 John 7-8. Clement of Alexandria referred to 1 John 5:16 (*Stromata* 2.66). Tertullian in *Against Marcion* 5.16 refers to 1 John 4:1, and in *Against Praxeas* 15, to 1 John 1:1.

The Muratorian Fragment shows the church's acceptance of two of John's epistles (probably the first and second) by around AD 200. Origen (according to Eusebius *History* 6.25) spoke of the First Epistle as genuine and "probably the second and third, though all [churches] do not recognize the latter two." Eusebius (*History* 3.24) said that John's First Epistle and Gospel were acknowledged without question by those of his day, as well as by the ancients. Jerome said the same thing in his *Catalogue of Scriptures*. The second and third epistles took longer to be accepted into the Canon because they were brief, personal letters. As such, they would not have been in general circulation among the churches. But once they were generally known, they were accepted into the Canon.

The most reliable manuscript for John's epistles is Codex Vaticanus (B), followed by Codex Sinaiticus (ℵ). Other good manuscripts are 𝔓74 and 1739. Codex Alexandrinus (A) tends to be expansive and erratic in John's epistles. Several Western witnesses, especially in the Vulgate manuscripts, have extended interpolations (see notes on 2:17; 4:3; 5:6b, 7b-8a, 9, 10, 20). First John also has one early-third-century witness, 𝔓9, but it is scant, and its textual character is unreliable.

LITERARY STYLE

It is not evident that 1 John is an epistle. It does not contain the name of a sender or addressee in the prescript, and there is no greeting in the conclusion (Schnackenburg 1979:1-3). It is more like a treatise in epistolary format—akin to Romans and Ephesians. However, even those two Pauline epistles have the kind of beginnings and endings (with introductions and greetings, respectively) that are typical of other letters from the time period. First John stands alone among all the New Testament letters (Romans—Jude) in its format. It has a brief poetic prologue and an abrupt ending, lacking any kind of doxology. The whole of the book contains John's full explanation of Christian life and doctrine as a model for all orthodox believers to emulate. The audience is universal in scope—the same audience intended for the fourth Gospel. Thus, when 1 John was published and circulated, it probably went to all the churches in the Roman province of Asia Minor and beyond.

John's first epistle has a very unusual thematic structure. Tenney (1985:377) said, "First John is symphonic rather than logical in plan; it is constructed like a piece of music rather than like a brief for a debate. Instead of proceeding step by step in unfolding a subject, as Paul does in Romans, John selects a theme, maintains it throughout the book, and introduces a series of variations, any one of which may be a theme in itself." Moving in and out of this thematic development is a constant presentation of antithetical proclamations, posed in pairs, such as light versus darkness, love versus hate, truth versus falsehood, righteousness versus sin, Christ versus Antichrist, and so forth. With John, there is no compromise, no blurring of the distinctions; it is all black and white. One who doesn't love, hates, and a hater is a murderer. This kind of extreme posturing is startling and effective in getting the reader's attention. In this regard, John followed his teacher quite well, for Jesus was a master at making bold and startling statements.

MAJOR THEMES

The Believers' Experience of the Triune God. John's epistles are an extension of John's Gospel (especially John 13–17) in that both present details about the relationship between the triune God and the believer. John shows how it was Jesus' primary aim to reveal the Father to those who believe and bring them to truly know the Father and participate in his enjoyment of the Father—as well as enjoy their union with the Son through the Spirit.

God the Father and the Son have always shared the same divine, eternal life and enjoyed each other's love. They created human beings so that they could share this life and love with them. God is glad to give the divine, eternal life to each believer and so beget many lovely and loving children. And God's desire has always been to include these children in the fellowship he has always enjoyed with his one and only Son. Thus, when the Son was sent to earth, he was commissioned by the Father to explain and express him to mankind. His mission was also to bring all the believers into a life-relationship with the Father. But believers could never participate in living fellowship with the Father and the Son without experiencing the Holy Spirit. With the reception of the Spirit comes the reception of life (cf. John 6:63; 7:39) and the ability to experience Jesus in and as the Spirit.

Jesus had told the disciples that he would give them another Comforter (John 14:16-18). Then he told them that they should know who this Comforter was because he was, then and there, abiding with them and would, in the near future, be in them. Who else but Jesus was abiding with them at that time? Then after telling the disciples that the Comforter would come to them, he said, "I will come to you." First he said that the Comforter would come to them and abide in them, and then in the same breath he said that he would come to them and abide in them (see John 14:20). In short, the coming of the Spirit-Comforter to the disciples was one and the same with the coming of Jesus to the disciples.

On the evening of the Resurrection, the Lord Jesus appeared to the disciples and then breathed into them the Holy Spirit (John 20:22). This inbreathing, reminiscent of God's breathing into Adam the breath of life (Gen 2:7), became the fulfillment of all that had been promised and anticipated earlier in John's Gospel. Through this impartation, the disciples became regenerated and indwelt by the Spirit of Jesus Christ. This historical event marked the genesis of the new creation. The believers now possessed Jesus' divine, eternal, risen life. From that time forward, Christ, as spirit, indwelt his believers. Thus, in his first epistle, John could say, "we know he lives in us because the Spirit he gave us lives in us" (3:24), and again, "God has given us his Spirit as proof that we live in him and he in us" (4:13). Christ is in us because his Spirit is in us.

John's emphasis on the Spirit in his Gospel is carried over into his first epistle in the form of practical teaching concerning what is called the discernment of the Spirit. Since all Christians have the Spirit, any Christian could have claimed to be led by the Spirit or receive revelations from the Spirit. In the first century, most Christians did not have a New Testament to affirm or denounce any such leadings or revelations.

Thus, all Christians had to test the spirits of the prophets (i.e., the proclamations of those claiming to be led by the Spirit) as to whether their proclamations were true or false. John said that every Christian has the anointing (the working of the Spirit) and can make such discernments (2:20-21; 3:24–4:6; and see Burge 1996:24-30).

John's epistles are an extension of his Gospel's focus on the triune God but with an added emphasis—the practical, tangible experience of the triune God in the life of the believer as tested by the believer's relationship to the other members of the church community. For example, the Gospel speaks much of the mutual abiding of the triune God and the believers (cf. John 14–17), but there it is spoken of as a nascent revelation. In the epistles, all talk of one's living in God must be tested by how one lives with his or her companions in Christ.

This leads to one of the primary themes in these epistles: Love for God must be exhibited in love for another. If we could ask John what the one message is he wanted us to get from these epistles, he would probably say, "Love one another." This command did not originate from John; it came straight from the lips of Jesus (John 13:34; 15:17). John repeated this command often (2:7; 3:11, 23; 2 John 5-6), reinforcing it with the logic that since "God is love," all who claim to love God must exhibit that nature in their relationship with others.

Christological Orthodoxy versus Heresy. One of the reasons that prompted the writing of John's epistles was that a heretical faction had developed within the church, one that promoted false teachings concerning the person of Christ. Scholars have identified this heresy as Docetism generally and pointed specifically to Cerinthus as the perpetrator of the specific brand of Docetism. The Docetists denied that Jesus had actually partaken of flesh and blood; they denied that God had come in the flesh (cf. 4:1-3). According to Irenaeus, Cerinthus "represented Jesus as having not been born of a virgin, but as being the son of Joseph and Mary according to the ordinary course of human generation, while he nevertheless was more righteous, prudent, and wise than other men. Moreover, after his baptism, Christ descended upon him [*viz.* upon Jesus, the mere human] in the form of a dove from the Supreme Ruler, and that then he proclaimed the unknown Father, and performed miracles. But at last Christ departed from Jesus, and that then Jesus suffered and rose again, while Christ remained impassible, inasmuch as he was a spiritual being" (*Heresies* 3.3.4). John refuted the Cerinthian heresy in 5:5-8 (see comments there).

The heretical faction within the church (or, churches) that John was addressing eventually left the fellowship, and in so doing, they exposed themselves as not genuinely belonging to God's family (2:18-19). But their false teachings still lingered in the minds of the faithful; so John wrote to clear the air of all the falsehoods and bring the believers back to apostolic orthodoxy and to the basics of the Christian life.

Warnings about the Antichrist. According to 1 John, anyone who denies that Jesus is the Christ, that he is the unique Son of God, or that he has come in the flesh, is an antichrist. The biblical term, however, principally refers to a particular person in whom that denial reaches its consummate expression and who will play a key role in the final stage of history.

The word "antichrist" occurs only four times in the New Testament, all in John's epistles (2:18, 22; 4:3; 2 John 7). In 2:18, John refers also to "many such antichrists." John assumed that his Christian readers knew about the Antichrist and had been taught to expect his coming (2:18-27). The presence of many antichrists, in fact, indicated that the end time had arrived. But John warned that a final Antichrist (who, like the others, would deny that Jesus is the Christ) would yet make an appearance.

John further described any person or message that did not confess Jesus as being of the spirit of the antichrist (4:3). In his brief second spistle, John referred to "many deceivers" who would not acknowledge the coming of Jesus Christ in the flesh (2 John 7). Such a person, he wrote, was "a deceiver and an antichrist."

In the book of Revelation, John's symbol for the Antichrist is probably "the beast" (Rev 13:1-18; 17:3, 7-17). The Beast is described not only as one who opposes Christ but more specifically as a satanically inspired Christ-counterfeit. Although the Beast (Antichrist) is clearly distinguishable from the Lamb (Christ), he receives worship from everyone except God's elect. Another probable reference to the Antichrist is "the man of lawlessness" (2 Thess 2:3). The passage is difficult to interpret, but the person described seems to be the same person later designated by John as the Beast. Both the apostle Paul and John saw present events as leading up to the events of the future.

John's thoughts about the Antichrist probably came from the teaching of Jesus in the Gospels. A lengthy passage (Mark 13; paralleled in Matt 24; Luke 21) records the instruction Jesus gave his disciples about the tragic events and persecution to be expected before his return as the glorious Son of Man. His coming would be preceded by the appearance of many "deceivers" and "false messiahs." The term "false messiahs" is used only twice, both times by Jesus (Matt 24:24; Mark 13:22).

THEOLOGICAL CONCERNS

John's theological concerns are very practical in his first epistle. He urges his readers (1) to have fellowship with God in the light (1:7), (2) to confess their sins (1:9), (3) to love God (4:7-10), (4) to love their fellow Christians (4:11-12), (5) to abide in Christ (2:28), (6) to purify themselves from worldly lusts (3:3), (7) to know God personally and experientially (1:3), (8) to appreciate the gift of eternal life (5:11-12), (9) to follow the Spirit of truth (and the anointing) in discerning false teachings (2:2-27), and (10) to esteem Jesus Christ as the true God (5:20). Above all these items, John stressed how necessary it was for the early believers to maintain a proper relationship with those who had been with Jesus. In the prologue to this epistle (1:1-4), he invites all the believers to participate in the one apostolic fellowship. Fellowship is a two-way, simultaneous experience with fellow believers and with God. Fellowship serves to safeguard against pseudospirituality and extreme individualism. Throughout this epistle, it appears that John addressed his comments to those who were claiming to have a relationship with God and yet had left the fellowship of believers and did not love their brothers in Christ. Further, they had rejected the apostolic authority of John.

Throughout this epistle John calls into question all professed spirituality. This element is presented in a series of statements (usually phrased "if we say") that probably mimic what various gnostic believers were claiming about their spiritual experiences (e.g., see 1:6, 8; 2:4, 6, 9). Talk is cheap; reality must be tested by one's relationship with the members of the church community. John urged the believers to know the truth and to live in it.

John's first epistle has much to say to those today who have gnostic tendencies in the sense that they claim to have superior spiritual knowledge (or even experience) beyond that which ordinary Christians have. Indeed, some may even claim to have found the "secrets" to the deeper spiritual life, "secrets" which others can never know unless they become part of their special group. This superior knowledge often leads to an elitist attitude and disdain for other Christians. In short, the superior knowledge leads to rejection (a form of hatred) of other believers. John's epistle exposes this. If one truly knows Christ and lives in him, that person should be loving all fellow Christians. Love, not "superior" knowledge, is the proof that one has a genuine spiritual life.

OUTLINE

This book almost defies being outlined due to its symphonic thematic presentation (cf. "Literary Style," above). Among the many outlines offered by various scholars, some have organized it according to the three tests of life: righteousness, love, and belief. Others have used a simpler outline, generally framing 1 John according to the God proclamations: "God is light" (1:5) and "God is love" (4:8). (For discussions concerning the various outlines, see Brown 1982:764; Burge 1996:42-45). But there is far too much overlapping material to make a clear-cut outline built around this thematic development. We have taken another approach: to organize the epistle around the theme of community fellowship, which is a fellowship that emanates from the triune God and should permeate the members of the believing community.

I. Experiencing Authentic Christian Fellowship (1:1–2:11)
   A. The Prologue (1:1-4)
   B. Living in God's Light with the Community of Believers (1:5-10)
   C. Experiencing the Ministry of Jesus, the Advocate (2:1-2)
   D. Living in the Light Means Loving Fellow Believers (2:3-11)
II. Maintaining the True Fellowship (2:12–3:10)
   A. The Community of Believers Affirmed as a Spiritual Family (2:12-17)
   B. Identifying the False Believers and the True (2:18-27)
   C. Being Prepared for Christ's Return (2:28–3:3)
   D. Recognizing What Kind of Life Prospers the Fellowship and What Contradicts It (3:4-10)

1 John

◆ I. Experiencing Authentic Christian Fellowship (1:1–2:11)
A. The Prologue (1:1-4)

We proclaim to you the one who existed from the beginning,* whom we have heard and seen. We saw him with our own eyes and touched him with our own hands. He is the Word of life. ²This one who is life itself was revealed to us, and we have seen him. And now we testify and proclaim to you that he is the one who is eternal life. He was with the Father, and then he was revealed to us. ³We proclaim to you what we ourselves have actually seen and heard so that you may have fellowship with us. And our fellowship is with the Father and with his Son, Jesus Christ. ⁴We are writing these things so that you may fully share our joy.*

1:1 Greek *What was from the beginning.*   1:4 Or *so that our joy may be complete*; some manuscripts read *your joy.*

NOTES

1:1 who existed from the beginning. Lit., "what was from the beginning" (cf. NLT mg). There are two explanations for John's use of the relative pronoun ("what") instead of the personal pronoun ("who"): (1) John used the relative pronoun because it is more inclusive; it encompasses everything about "the Word of life" that the apostles had come to know and experience (so Westcott 1886:4-7). (2) John used the relative pronoun to point to "the message of life" (so Smalley 1984:5-6) as embodied in Christ, the Word. Since the prologue is a poem, John likely intended both meanings. In any event, this relative pronoun is resumed in the beginning of 1:3, where it is made clear the subject is that which pertains to "the Word of life" (1:1).

we have heard and seen. We saw him with our own eyes and touched him with our own hands. John made a point of saying that they had not only seen and heard the eternal One but had also touched him. In other words, Jesus was truly physical. A certain group of gnostics in John's day (and thereafter), called Docetists (derived from a Gr. word meaning "it seems to be so"—*dokeō* [TG1380, ZG1506]), claimed that the Son of God merely assumed the guise of humanity but was not truly human. Later in this epistle, John says that any person who does not confess that Jesus Christ has come in flesh is a person who does not belong to God (4:2-3).

the Word of life. This title describes the Son of God as the personal expression of the invisible God and the giver of divine, eternal life to the believers. In the prologue to the fourth Gospel, John identified the Son of God as both "the Word" (*logos* [TG3056, ZG3364]) and "life" (*zōē* [TG2222, ZG2437]). The title "the Word of life" is a combination of the two. As "the Word," the Son expresses God; as "life," he imparts God's eternal life to believers.

1:2 was revealed to us. This phrase, which appears twice in this verse, accords with what John said in his prologue to the Gospel of John: "The Word was God . . . and the Word became human . . . and we have seen his glory, the glory of the Father's one and only Son" (John 1:1, 14).

eternal life. The Gr. word translated "life" is *zōē* [TG2222, ZG2437]. In classical Greek, it was used for life in general. There are a few examples of this usage in the NT (Acts 17:25; Jas 4:14; Rev 16:3), but in all other NT instances the word designates the divine, eternal life—the life of God (Eph 4:18). This life resided in Christ, and he made it available to all who believe in him.

with the Father. As in John 1:1, the word "with" (*pros* [TG4314, ZG4639]) suggests that the Word was "face to face with the Father." This connotes intimate fellowship (MM 554). By using this expression, John was implying that the Word (the Son) and God (the Father) enjoyed an intimate, personal relationship from the beginning. In Jesus' intercessory prayer of John 17, he revealed that the Father had loved him before the foundation of the world.

1:3 *We proclaim to you.* The "we" occurring throughout the prologue refers either to John and the apostles (for whom John is the spokesman) or to John and any other believers who saw Jesus Christ in the flesh.

1:4 *that you may fully share our joy.* Lit., "that our joy may be full." This is an attempt to render a variant reading found in ℵ B L 049, but it turns out to be a rendering of a conflated reading because it happens to accommodate another variant reading in other mss (A C P 33 1739), "that your joy may be complete" (as in the TR and KJV). This variant was created by some scribe(s) who thought it strange that John would have penned a letter for his own joy. However, the writer was thinking of their mutual happiness—his and his readers. In other words, he wrote this letter to encourage the readers' participation in the fellowship that he (John) and the other believers were enjoying (cf. 2 John 12). Thus, the NLT rendering gets at the heart of the meaning.

COMMENTARY

The prologue to John's first epistle is poetic, much in the same way the prologue to John's Gospel is poetic. In poetic format, the text of 1:1-3 could be rendered as follows:

> *As to what was from the beginning*
> *as to what we have heard*
> *as to what we have seen with our eyes*
> *and what we have gazed upon*
> *and as to what we have touched—*
> *this is the Word of Life,*
> *for the life was manifested*
> *and we are those who have seen*
> *and give you testimony*
> *as we proclaim to you*
> *the eternal Life that was with the Father*
> *and was manifested to us.*
> *What we have seen and heard*
> *we proclaim to you*
> *so that you may join our fellowship*
> *and have communion with the Father*
> *and with his Son, Jesus Christ.*

As poetry, the prologue presents abstractions that demand the reader's careful interpretation. For example, John did not identify "Jesus" as the subject in the first verse;

rather, he called him "the Word of life." Furthermore, he did not use the personal pronoun, "he who was from the beginning," which would have made the simplest presentation. Rather, he used the relative pronoun, "that which" or "what," so as to be more encompassing—and more compelling. John was speaking of the apostles' total experience of the incarnate God-man, wherein they heard his message, saw his miracles, gazed upon his glory, and even touched him.

John's first epistle opens in the same manner as his Gospel—both begin with a prologue. When John commenced his Gospel, he fondly recollected how he (and the other disciples, for whom he was a spokesman) beheld the Son's glory, the glory of a unique Son from the Father (John 1:14). And then John picturesquely described Jesus as the one who was both God and the Son of God living in the heart of the Father (John 1:18). In both the Gospel and the epistle, John reveals that he (along with the other apostles) has heard, seen, and even handled God in the flesh. In both books, he tells us that the one they experienced is both "the Word" and "eternal life." The apostles had come to the realization that the Word of life, who had been in face-to-face fellowship with the Father for all eternity, had entered into time to be manifest in human flesh to them.

This experience was so life-changing and so memorable that John used the perfect tense verbs ("have seen" and "have heard"—1:1, 3) to convey the idea that the apostles' past experience of the God-man, the incarnate Son of God, was still vivid and present with them. (Such is the force of the perfect tense in Greek.) When the Son entered into time, the eternal fellowship of the Father and Son also entered into time. Thus, to have heard Jesus was to have heard the Father speaking in the Son (John 14:10, 24), to have seen Jesus was to have seen the Father (John 14:8-10), and to have known him was to have known him who was one with the Father (John 10:30, 38). The Son and the Father are so united that they are said to indwell each other (John 14:8-10). Christ perfectly expressed the Father because he lived in perfect union with him. Thus, for the disciples, to know Jesus was to know the Father.

This is why the Son is called "the Word": he is the revealer, the communicator of God to humanity. As the Word, the Son of God fully conveys and communicates God. The Greek term translated "Word" is *logos* [TG3056, ZG3364]; it was primarily used in two ways: "The word might be thought of as remaining within a man, when it denoted his thought or reason. Or it might refer to the word going forth from the man, when it denoted the expression of his thought—i.e., his speech. The Logos, a philosophical term, depended on the former use" (Morris 1971:72-78). As a philosophical term, the *logos* denoted the principle of the universe, even the creative energy that generated the universe. The term *logos* may also have some connection with the Old Testament presentation of "Wisdom" as a personification or attribute of God (Prov 8). In both its Jewish and Greek conceptions, the *logos* was associated with the idea of beginnings—the world began through the origination and instrumentality of the Word (cf. Gen 1:3ff, where the expression "God said" is used repeatedly). John may have had these ideas in mind, but most likely he was originating a new use of this term to identify the Son of God as the divine expression.

Paul had the same idea in mind when he said the Son is "the visible image of the invisible God" (Col 1:15). And the writer of Hebrews was thinking similarly when he said that the Son "expresses the very character of God" (Heb 1:3), which means that the Son is the exact representation (*charaktēr* [TG5481, ZG5917]) of God's nature and being (*hupostasis* [TG5287, ZG5712]). In the Godhead, the Son functions as the revealer of God and the reality of God. He is God made touchable.

During the days of his ministry, Jesus was revealing the Father to the disciples and thereby initiating them into the divine fellowship. Once the disciples were regenerated by the Spirit and received God's eternal life, they actually entered into fellowship with the Father and the Son. Having been brought into this divine participation, the apostles became the new initiators—introducing this fellowship to others and encouraging them to enter into fellowship with them. Whoever would enter into fellowship with the apostles would actually be entering into their fellowship with the Father and the Son.

In summary, the one, unique fellowship between the Father and the Son began in eternity, was manifest in time through the incarnation of the Son, was introduced to the apostles, and then through the apostles was extended to each and every believer. When a person becomes a child of God (through the new life given by the Holy Spirit), he or she enters into this one ageless, universal fellowship—a fellowship springing from the Godhead, coursing through the apostles, and flowing through every genuine believer who has ever been or will ever be.

How much greater is this view of fellowship than is the view commonly held! The true fellowship, having a divine origin, has been extended to people for human participation. How privileged we are to have been included! And we must never forget that this fellowship includes all the believers from the apostles to the present; it is not exclusive. How then can we continue to be so restricted and so sectarian? The Bible does not talk about "this fellowship" and "that fellowship." There is but one fellowship, as there is but one body of Christ. How good it is to come to the Lord's table to enjoy the communion of the believers—communion not just with those present at that particular meeting but communion with all of God's people who lived before us and who live now.

◆   B. Living in God's Light with the Community of Believers (1:5-10)

⁵This is the message we heard from Jesus* and now declare to you: God is light, and there is no darkness in him at all. ⁶So we are lying if we say we have fellowship with God but go on living in spiritual darkness; we are not practicing the truth. ⁷But if we are living in the light, as God is in the light, then we have fellowship with each other, and the blood of Jesus, his Son, cleanses us from all sin.

⁸If we claim we have no sin, we are only fooling ourselves and not living in the truth. ⁹But if we confess our sins to him, he is faithful and just to forgive us our sins and to cleanse us from all wickedness. ¹⁰If we claim we have not sinned, we are calling God a liar and showing that his word has no place in our hearts.

1:5 Greek *from him.*

NOTES

1:5 *the message.* This wording is based on the excellent testimony of ℵ A B. One variant (in C P 33 1739 cop) substitutes "the promise" for "the message." Another variant found in a few mss (ℵ² Ψ) reads "the love of the promise." The idea of "promise" is difficult in this context because the statement that follows can hardly be construed as being a promise: "God is light, and there is no darkness in him at all." Of course, "the promise" could be referring back to 1:3-4, wherein John promised the readers that they would be communing with the Father and the Son if they (the readers) maintained fellowship with the apostles—resulting in full joy for all. Nonetheless, "the message" has better documentary support as the original wording.

God is light. This is a statement of the absolute nature and being of God, as are the statements that he is Spirit (John 4:24) and love (1 John 4:8). To say that "God is light" is to say that God symbolizes truth (compared to darkness that symbolizes error) and righteousness (compared to darkness that symbolizes evil). OT scriptures speak of this: Pss 27:1; 119:130; Isa 5:20; Micah 7:8. In the Gospel of John, Jesus is this light (John 1:4; 8:12; 9:5; 11:9-10; 12:35-36).

there is no darkness in him at all. The Gr. could be translated literally as "darkness is not in him never." God is untainted by any evil or sin (= darkness). John speaks in absolutes, perhaps as no other writer in the NT. So here we have "God is light" and in him is no darkness whatsoever—that is, no change, no sin, no secrecy, no hiding in the shadows.

1:6 *if we say.* This is the first of several instances in which John challenges the claims of the gnostic secessionists (see notes on 1:8; 2:6, 9; see also "Christological Orthodoxy versus Heresy" and "Theological Concerns" in the Introduction). They claimed to be living in God but failed to reflect his moral character. If we have fellowship with God, we should have some of his characteristics—something we share in common. Fellowship is another way of saying "commonality" with God.

1:7 *fellowship with each other.* This is the fellowship among believers that results from each believer having fellowship with the triune God.

the blood of Jesus, his Son. This reading has excellent documentary support: ℵ B C P 1739 syrᵖ copˢᵃ. A variant in the TR (supported by A 33 𝔐. itᵗ·ʷ·ᶻ syrʰ** copᵇᵒ) reads, "the blood of Jesus Christ his Son" (so KJV and NKJV). Since divine names were often expanded by scribes, it is very likely that "Jesus" was expanded to "Jesus Christ" under the influence of John's usual wording (see 1:3; 2:1; 3:23; 4:2; 5:6, 20). The point of using just the human name "Jesus" is that it emphasizes the sacrifice he made in shedding his blood for our sins.

1:8 *If we claim we have no sin.* This is the second false claim of the secessionists (see note on 1:6).

the truth. In order to clarify just what this "truth" is, some scribes expanded this expression to "the truth of God." When John speaks of "the truth" he is speaking of spiritual reality and veracity; it is a spiritual reality in the believer that could be verified by the apostles and other believers as being true (in both life and doctrine) to the teachings of Christ.

1:10 *If we claim we have not sinned, we are calling God a liar.* This verse parallels 1:8, except that here the focus is on the actual acts of sin emanating from the sinful nature. To claim we have no sin goes beyond self-delusion; it is charging that God is a liar! We must acknowledge that God's Word emphasizes the permeating and penetrating nature of sin. So to deny sin is in us indicates God's "word has no place in our hearts" (cf. 2:14; John 8:55; 10:35; 17:6, 14, 17). John is not saying that if we make such a false claim we do not have eternal life. He is saying that a person who makes such a denial of sinful acts does not have the Word of God permeating and changing his or her life.

COMMENTARY

Just as Christ shared the message he heard from the Father, so the apostles, in turn, shared the same message they heard from the Son. John did not use the term usually translated "gospel," but he did use similar words such as "witness" or "testimony," "word," "truth," and "message." The message is God expresses himself as pure light (cf. John 1:4-5, 9; 3:19-21; 8:12; 9:5; 12:35-36, 46). Those who claim to know God must also be living in the light, for darkness and light are incompatible. We cannot live both in the darkness of sin and in the light of fellowship with God in whom is "no darkness at all." First John uses "darkness" seven times to refer to sin (1:5-6; 2:8-9, 11); one cannot live a sinful life and simultaneously claim to be living in the "light."

When Jesus was on earth, his divine life illuminated the inner lives of men. It penetrated people—illumining them to the divine truth and exposing them to their own sin. Everywhere Christ was present, he gave light—light to reveal his identity and light to expose sin (John 3:21; 8:12). No one could come into contact with Christ without being enlightened. His light would either expose or illumine, or both. So it is for the Christian who is indwelt by the Spirit of Christ. In his presence we see our sin and we see his glory. Of course, a person can refuse to receive the light and remain in darkness. But whoever comes to the light will receive Christ's enlightenment.

Since God is pure light, the Son of God lives in pure light and is the light. Those who claim to live in the Son must also live in the light—that is, one must be illumined by the truth of who God is. To live in the light cannot come from imitating God outwardly but from growing more like him in character; it involves transformation. As Paul put it, we are transformed into the image of the one we behold—the Lord, the Spirit (see 2 Cor 3:14-18).

The purpose of "living in the light" (1:7) is not to produce individual mystics but to arouse genuine fellowship among believers. This is important to John's overall argument. True spirituality is manifest in community fellowship. One cannot say he or she communes with God but then refuse to commune with God's people. Such was the case with the gnostics of John's day, and this is the situation with many people in our own times. They claim to get along well with God but can't get along with any of his children. John's point is that the natural result of living in the light (in fellowship with God) is a joyful relationship with other Christians.

Those who live in the light will be enlightened by God's Spirit concerning their sin. Jesus' "blood" (1:7; an expression used throughout the NT to encapsulate Jesus' redemptive death on the cross) cleansed us completely and brought us into fellowship with God; now the same blood of Jesus keeps us clean from every sin that would mar that fellowship. Confession of sin is a sign that truth, which is itself light, has already begun to illuminate our sin-darkened lives. If we refuse to admit that we have sin, we deceive ourselves. We certainly cannot fool God, but by refusing to admit our sin, we can cheat ourselves of fellowship with him.

So confession of sins is necessary for maintaining continual fellowship with God, which, in turn, will enable us to have good fellowship with the members of the church community. The Greek word translated "confess" (*homologeō* [TG3670, ZG3933]) basically means "to say the same thing" or "to acknowledge." Rather than denying our sin nature, we are to confess our sins. God says we are sinners in need of forgiveness. Therefore, to "confess" means to agree with God concerning specific acts of sin we have committed; it is to admit we are sinners. When believers admit their sins, God cleanses them. Forgiveness and cleansing are guaranteed because God is faithful to his promises. God acts on the basis of his justice, not on the basis of how we think he feels about us. Christ has satisfied God's righteous demands on us so that now God is bound to forgive all who believe in his Son. We can depend on this.

Therefore, it is foolish to claim that "we have not sinned" (1:10). However, various Christians throughout the ages have made this claim because they considered Jesus to have abolished their sins once and for all at the moment they believed, or were filled with the Spirit, or were sanctified. But experience teaches against this. Though Jesus condemned sin once and for all, we still sin when we live in the old nature. When we live in the Spirit, we live a sin-defeating life, but no one lives in the Spirit every moment of life. Even Paul struggled with this (see Rom 7).

We may admit to the presence of the sin nature while denying any personal sin and so deny any need for confession. If we do this, we are guilty of calling God a liar. The statement "we have not sinned" (1:10; *ouch hēmartēkamen*, perfect tense) speaks of a denial in the past that continues to the present. Unlike verse 8, which speaks of the guilt of sin or sinful nature, this verse speaks of the denial of particular sins. To make such a claim is to make God a liar because God's Word emphasizes the permeating and penetrating nature of sin. So to deny sin is in us indicates God's "word has no place in our hearts" (1:10). John is not saying that if we make such a false claim, as given in verse 10, that we do not have eternal life. He is saying that a person who makes such a denial of sinful acts does not have the Word of God permeating and changing his or her life.

◆ ## C. Experiencing the Ministry of Jesus, the Advocate (2:1-2)

My dear children, I am writing this to you so that you will not sin. But if anyone does sin, we have an advocate who pleads our case before the Father. He is Jesus Christ, the one who is truly righteous. [2]He himself is the sacrifice that atones for our sins—and not only our sins but the sins of all the world.

NOTES

2:1 *My dear children.* This expresses the tender affection of a father for his own children—the phrase could read, "My own dear children." The expression is patronizing in the best sense of the term.

if anyone does sin. We are all liable to occasional sins. We should not condone these sins, but while condemning them we should not fear to confess them to God.

an advocate who pleads our case. This is an expanded translation of the word *paraklētos* [TG3875, ZG4156] (transliterated in English as "Paraclete"). The word means "one who is called to our side." This could be a comforter, a consoler, or a defense attorney—an advocate. In John 14:26 and 15:26, the Holy Spirit is called our *paraklētos*, our comforter or encourager. Here, "advocate" is the best English equivalent because Jesus is here pictured as the one who represents the believers before the Father.

Jesus Christ, the one who is truly righteous. This is the title "the righteous One," which was used of Jesus Christ from the earliest days of the church (Acts 3:14; 7:52) to describe him as the just and righteous Messiah who was unjustly killed by the Jewish leaders. This righteous One was the perfect man, who fulfilled the law (Rom 10:4) and was the perfect sacrifice for sins. As such, he is the perfect Advocate for sinners.

2:2 the sacrifice that atones. Gr., *hilasmos* [TG2434, ZG2662], the noun form of the verb *hilaskomai* [TG2433, ZG2661]. Though the word meant "to appease" or "to pacify" in classical Greek, it is argued that as used in the NT it means "to atone" or "to expiate" (that is, to make restitution or remove guilt). For example, Westcott (1886:85-87) said, "The scriptural conception of the verb is not that of appeasing one who is angry with a personal feeling against the offender, but of altering the character of that which, from without, occasions a necessary alienation, and interposes an inevitable obstacle to fellowship. Such phrases as 'propitiating God,' [i.e., pacifying him] and 'God being reconciled' [i.e., God being made agreeable] are foreign to the language of the New Testament." However, Stott (2000:87-88) cautions against excluding "appeasement" as being a possible meaning for this in the NT inasmuch as the NT writers did not use it in the sense of appeasing the capricious whims of a god, as was done in pagan societies, but rather of appeasing God's unwavering anger against sin. However the word is to be understood, it should not be lost on us that Jesus himself is the sacrifice for our sins.

and not only our sins but the sins of all the world. John was reminding all believers that Christ's atoning sacrifice is sufficient for the sins of every person in the world. Later in the epistle, John makes the point that Jesus is "the Savior of the world" (4:14).

COMMENTARY

In order to live in the light (1:5, 7), the first step is to confess sin (1:9), and the second is to forsake all sin (2:1). John emphasized our sinfulness in chapter 1 in order to make us despise our sin and try to stay free from it. God's gracious forgiveness is no license to sin. John would say: "Don't sin! Avoid it—flee from it." "It is possible to be either too lenient or too severe towards sin: too lenient encourages us to sin—too severe denies the possibility of sin or the possibility of forgiveness" (Stott 2000:84).

The fact is we sin. And the righteous God has no choice but to hold us accountable for our sins. But Jesus acts as an intermediary between the Father and the confessing sinner to advocate that the sinner be considered righteous—not because the sinner is righteous but because the Advocate, Jesus Christ, is. Because Christ fulfilled the law and paid sin's penalty for us, he can plead for us on the basis of justice as well as mercy. When God raised Christ from the dead, he accepted once for all Christ's plea for our acquittal (cf. Rom 4:23-25).

The whole matter is best viewed in legal terms. That is why Christ is both our Advocate and the propitiatory sacrifice for our sins. First John 4:10 says that God demonstrated his love to us by sending his Son to become the "propitiation" (*hilasmos* [TG2434, ZG2662]) for our sins (cf. 2:2). Propitiation refers to Christ's satisfaction of God's justice, making it "propitious" (or "agreeable") for God to forgive us.

As in the old covenant, wherein God met his people when the blood of the sin offering was sprinkled on the altar, so in the new covenant Christ's sacrificial death has brought us into fellowship with God.

◆ D. Living in the Light Means Loving Fellow Believers (2:3-11)

³And we can be sure that we know him if we obey his commandments. ⁴If someone claims, "I know God," but doesn't obey God's commandments, that person is a liar and is not living in the truth. ⁵But those who obey God's word truly show how completely they love him. That is how we know we are living in him. ⁶Those who say they live in God should live their lives as Jesus did.

⁷Dear friends, I am not writing a new commandment for you; rather it is an old one you have had from the very beginning. This old commandment—to love one another—is the same message you heard before. ⁸Yet it is also new. Jesus lived the truth of this commandment, and you also are living it. For the darkness is disappearing, and the true light is already shining.

⁹If anyone claims, "I am living in the light," but hates a Christian brother or sister,* that person is still living in darkness. ¹⁰Anyone who loves another brother or sister* is living in the light and does not cause others to stumble. ¹¹But anyone who hates another brother or sister is still living and walking in darkness. Such a person does not know the way to go, having been blinded by the darkness.

2:9 Greek *hates his brother;* similarly in 2:11.   2:10 Greek *loves his brother.*

NOTES

2:3 *we can be sure that we know him.* This could also be rendered "By this we come to experientially know that we have experientially known him." The focus is on actual, experiential knowledge of God, contra the theoretical knowledge espoused by various gnostics.

2:4 *If someone claims, "I know God," but doesn't obey God's commandments, that person is a liar and is not living in the truth.* John was likely quoting the claims of the secessionists and/or other spiritual elitists who espoused spiritual knowledge of God (see note on 1:6; cf. notes on 1:8; 2:6, 9). It is possible that they had attained this knowledge from reading John's Gospel. (Knowledge of God through Jesus is a constant theme in John.)
This verse illustrates the principle set out in 2:3. John's answer to those who claim they "know God" but do not obey his commandments is that they are liars. John was very straightforward in his condemnation because he was dealing with gnostics—those who claimed to have special, superior knowledge of God. But if they did not obey the divine command to love others, it is obvious that they do not belong to him.

2:5 *show how completely they love him.* Lit., "the love of God is perfected in these ones." There are three views on the meaning of the phrase "the love of God": (1) it refers to God's love for people (Westcott 1886:49); (2) it is a godly kind of love (Schnackenburg 1979:103); and (3) it is a person's love for God (Marshall 1978:125). All three meanings are acceptable. Behind the NLT's "completely" is *teteleiōtai* [ᵀᴳ5048, ᶻᴳ5457] ("has been perfected," has reached its goal—i.e., has matured). This can mean (1) the believer's love for God is matured in keeping God's Word, or (2) God's love for the believer is matured in the believer who is keeping God's Word. In this context, the point seems to be that as the believer pursues fellowship and obedience, God's love for him or her is more fully appreciated, and, in turn, the believer shows more mature love toward fellow believers. Perfection in the Greek mind did not mean flawlessness, but rather, more fully developed, matured.

Smalley (1984:49) sees the perfect tense here as having the force of the present tense in the sense that the process of fulfillment had already begun and was continuing.

That is how we know we are living in him. By our progress toward this perfect love and obedience we will know that we are living in union with Christ. The idea of living "in him," first mentioned here in 1 John, is a carryover from John's Gospel, where Jesus spoke of the mutual indwelling of God and the believers—he living in them and they in him (cf. John 14:18-23; 15:4-5). John's epistle carries forward the practical implications of his Gospel.

2:6 *Those who say they live in God.* Lit., "the one saying [I] abide in him." John again refers to something that others were claiming (cf. note on 1:6). It is likely that such people were quoting the fourth Gospel (John 15:1-5) and were claiming that they were abiding in Christ.

should live their lives as Jesus did. The word translated "Jesus" is simply *ekeinos* [TG1565, ZG1697] (that one); in 1 John it always refers to Jesus (3:3, 5, 7, 16; 4:17; cf. John 7:11; 9:12, 28; 19:21). Jesus' life on earth, demonstrating his obedience, is held up as the model and example.

2:7 *I am not writing a new commandment for you; rather it is an old one you have had.* This commandment is to love one another (3:11). One of the major themes in 1 John is that of brotherly love (cf. chs 3–4). It is a distinguishing mark of a Christian to serve others rather than one's self.

from the very beginning. For John, the beginning has two meanings: (1) it means from the time the disciples first heard Jesus' command to love one another (John 13:33-34); (2) it also means from the time these same teachings were passed on to the believers, to whom he was writing (see 2:24; 3:11; 2 John 5-6). In other words, the apostles had been faithful to teach others what they had heard from Jesus from the very beginning of his ministry so that their beginning could be as close to the apostles' as possible. Since a lot of new and strange doctrines were circulating in those days, John was encouraging the believers to stay with the primary, fundamental teachings of the apostles.

This old commandment . . . is the same message you heard before. At the end of this clause the majority of late mss repeat the expression "from the beginning," from the first part of the verse (so TR, KJV, and NKJV).

2:8 *Yet it is also new.* The commandment of love is new and different from the old system of the law. The word "new" (*kainēn* [TG2537, ZG2785]) connotes what is new in quality more than what is new in time.

Jesus lived the truth of this commandment, and you also are living it. Vine (1970:27) put it well when he said, "Not only had the commandment been given by him but it had also been exhibited in his example. It is also true in the children of God because it is to be received and fulfilled by them. The new commandment of love finds concrete expression in the daily life of the believer in union with Christ. This love was first shown by Christ in his life on earth, and it is only because he first fulfilled the commandment of love that we can now fulfill it."

the darkness is disappearing, and the true light is already shining. F. F. Bruce's (1970:54) expansion on this is elucidating: "Although 'the true light' is already shining, the darkness has not passed completely away; it is in process of 'passing away.' It is diminishing as the gospel is preached worldwide and the light now shining is from Jesus Christ, the Light of the World. Thanks to the victory of Christ, the outcome of the conflict between light and darkness is a foregone conclusion, but the conflict is still going on. Hence, the tension of the Christian life in the present world is a tension reflected throughout this epistle, not to say throughout the whole New Testament."

2:9 If anyone claims, "I am living in the light." Again, John cites what others were claiming—namely, that they were living in the light (see note on 1:6). It is quite possible that such people were saying that they were experiencing the reality of Jesus' words about him being the light of men, as recorded in John's Gospel (John 8:12; 12:35-36).

but hates a Christian brother or sister, that person is still living in darkness. The hatred mentioned here is probably a form of rejection. For example, when God said, "I loved your ancestor Jacob, but I rejected his brother, Esau" (Mal 1:2-3), he was not speaking of his emotions toward the two but of his election of one and subsequent rejection of the other. In the context of 1 John, "hatred" is tantamount to rejection of other Christians. The secessionists were rejecting John and the community of believers associated with him, while claiming to live an enlightened life—something John makes clear is an impossibility.

2:10 Anyone who loves another brother or sister is living in the light and does not cause others to stumble. Or as it says in the TEV: "There is nothing in him that will cause someone else to sin." Those who hate (i.e., reject) their brothers and sisters are both a stumbling block to themselves and to others. The word John uses here, *skandalon* [TG4625, ZG4998] (stumbling block), indicated the trigger to a trap. Thus, causing one to stumble means to cause them to be ensnared or entrapped.

2:11 anyone who hates another brother or sister is still living and walking in darkness. In the context of this epistle, John was probably referring to those secessionists who had left the fellowship of the church and thereby rejected John and those with him. They claimed to love God, but they hated the other children of God. As such, John perceived that they were living in spiritual darkness.

COMMENTARY

The apostle John's emphasis on the conflict between darkness and light depicts the continuing struggle between the evil one (Satan) and Jesus. The light has come and the darkness has not overcome it (John 1:5). The world is a realm of darkness into which Jesus has brought light (John 3:19; 8:12; 12:46). God himself is light (1:5). True light comes only through Jesus (John 1:9). Anyone, therefore, who does not know God remains in darkness—that is, spiritual ignorance. Jesus had warned the Jewish leaders of his day that the light they thought they had was darkness (Matt 6:23), which meant that their religious truths had blinded them to the spiritual illumination they could have received from Christ. In like manner, certain gnostics thought they were enlightened, but they were actually darkened by their so-called illuminations. They made wonderful claims—such as "I know God," "I abide in him," and "I am in the light"—probably all drawn from John's Gospel (see notes on 2:4, 6, 9), but their rejection of John and the other believers showed that they were lying. Ironically, their claims show that they knew Jesus' teachings as communicated by John and had even appropriated some of the most central ideas—knowing God, abiding in God, and living in the light.

However, all such claims are tested by adherence to one commandment, also put forth by Jesus and recorded by John in his Gospel: "I am giving you a new commandment: Love each other. Just as I have loved you, you should love each other" (John 13:34-35). But where is the newness of this command, since a command to love one another had already been mandated in the Old Testament (Lev 19:18, 33-34)? The newness of Jesus' command rests upon the reality that, because our hearts have been changed by experiencing the love of Jesus, we reach out in reciprocal fashion to all those touched by that same love. It may not be easy to do, but grace helps us. Jesus commanded the disciples to love one another "as I have loved you." This love would be the mark of distinction: "Your love for one another will prove to the world that you are my disciples" (John 13:35). Tertullian said that the Gentiles saw this love and commented, "How they love one another!" (*Apology* 39.3.46).

The Christian rule of love is new because our love for others is motivated by our love for Christ, who first loved us. He demonstrated what true love is by coming into our world and giving his life for all of us. Christians should, then, follow this supreme example by showing their love for fellow believers. Those who reject other Christians reject Christ's exemplary model. This rejection is the kind of hatred John was talking about. If we hate any of these brothers or sisters, then we are not in the light.

Those who left the community of fellowship did so out of spiritual pride. They disdained those "common" believers who had only "common" knowledge of God. Many people with this sort of gnostic bent had infiltrated the churches and, in some form or another, disrupted the fellowship by their claims of having spiritual knowledge that was superior to that taught by the apostles. John pointed out that these people were deceived—living in the darkness, not in the light. In our own times, many leave the Christian community for some cult and think that, spiritually speaking, they are way ahead of those they left. But all the while they are in darkness. So darkened are their minds that they don't know where they are going. John's irony shows itself again—those who espouse superior knowledge are those who don't know! Such people are in darkness, not light, in sin and not in fellowship with God. They live there and do not know where they are going because they have lost their spiritual perspective and sense of direction (cf. 2 Pet 1:9).

◆ II. Maintaining the True Fellowship (2:12–3:10)
    A. The Community of Believers Affirmed as a Spiritual Family
        (2:12–17)

¹²I am writing to you who are God's children
    because your sins have been forgiven through Jesus.*
¹³I am writing to you who are mature in the faith*
    because you know Christ, who existed from the beginning.
I am writing to you who are young in the faith
    because you have won your battle with the evil one.

¹⁴I have written to you who are God's children
    because you know the Father.
I have written to you who are mature in the faith
    because you know Christ, who existed from the beginning.
I have written to you who are young in the faith
    because you are strong.
God's word lives in your hearts,
    and you have won your battle with the evil one.

¹⁵Do not love this world nor the things it offers you, for when you love the world, you do not have the love of the Father in you. ¹⁶For the world offers only a craving for physical pleasure, a craving for everything we see, and pride in our achievements and possessions. These are not from the Father, but are from this world. ¹⁷And this world is fading away, along with everything that people crave. But anyone who does what pleases God will live forever.

2:12 Greek *through his name.* 2:13 Or *to you fathers;* also in 2:14.

NOTES

2:12 *I am writing to you who are God's children.* The term "children" has no reference to age here; rather, it is a term of endearment. Jesus used the same phrase when speaking to his disciples (cf. John 13:33).

2:13 *you who are mature.* Lit., "fathers." The various interpretations of this term are described in the commentary section below.

Christ, who existed from the beginning. Lit., "the one from [the] beginning." The NLT correctly identifies this one as Christ, the eternal Word of life (1:1-2), but notice that John now speaks of "the one who is from the beginning," and not "that which was from the beginning" (as in 1:1). This signifies an emphasis on Jesus' person here.

you who are young. The various interpretations of this phrase are described in the following commentary section.

2:14 *I have written.* This reading is strongly supported by 𝔓74ᵛⁱᵈ ℵ A B C L P 33. The Majority text reads, "I write"—the result of harmonization to 2:12 and 2:13. John's shift to the aorist tense is stylistic. It is called the epistolary aorist; it represents the idea that by the time the readers read what is written in the epistle, the writing will be a past event.

Christ, who existed from the beginning. Lit., "the one from [the] beginning." This is the reading in several mss (𝔓74 ℵ A C). A few other mss, including B, read "that which was from the beginning," as in 1:1 (see comments there).

2:15 *Do not love this world.* In this verse, the "world" (*kosmos* [TG2889, ZG3180]) is the morally evil system that is opposed to all that God is. In this sense, the world is the satanic system opposing Christ's Kingdom on this earth. It is the dominating order of things—a system and a people. It is activity apart from and against God. It is anything that arouses "the lust of the flesh, the lust of the eyes, and the pride of life" (2:16 lit. translation; 3:1; 4:4; 5:19; cf. John 12:31; 15:18; Eph 6:11-12; Jas 4:4).

nor the things it offers you. This statement would convict those who deny that they love the world but care keenly about some particular thing the world offers, such as wealth, honor, or pleasure.

for when you love the world, you do not have the love of the Father in you. God and the sinful world are such opposites that it is impossible to love both at once.

2:16 *craving for physical pleasure.* This refers to any kind of fleshly desire but especially "the craze for sex" (TLB) to which young people are particularly liable. We dare not excuse ourselves of lustful thoughts because they are not from God.

craving for everything we see. Satan tempted Christ this way by showing him all the kingdoms of the world (Matt 4:8-9).

and pride in our achievements and possessions. Many commentators have noted that the three evils mentioned here were the elements in Satan's temptation of Eve (Gen 3:6) and of Jesus (Luke 4:1-12). Others see them as simply three categories of sin or three examples of sins characteristic of the world.

2:17 *anyone who does what pleases God will live forever.* In contrast to the three evil desires of the world, which are already "fading away," the one who does God's will remains forever united to God.

COMMENTARY

These verses contain a pair of triplets that describe John's readers as "children," "fathers," and "young men." (Accordingly most translations, including the NLT, set 2:12-14 as poetry.) These three classifications are not physical age groups (John calls all his readers "dear children"—see 2:1) and their order is not chronological. Therefore, it seems that each group is a reference to all John's readers. For example, viewed as little children, they know their sins are forgiven. Viewed as fathers, they not only have a relationship with God, they have knowledge of God that came from obedience to his commandments. Viewed as young men, they are strong. At the same time, John was being purposely ambiguous, as is inherent in poetry. Another understanding (which is secondary) is that these represent stages of spiritual maturity—for it is the children (the youngest believers) who would be most conscious of having their sins forgiven and of coming to know the Father; and it is the young, strong believers who would be engaged in spiritual warfare by means of God's Word; and it is the fathers who would have experientially known Christ, the one from the beginning (as this suggests antiquity). It is possible that the "fathers" were the ones who saw and heard Jesus while he was on earth.

The main thrust of the section is to encourage the believers in their pursuit of knowing God experientially. The young children are seen in relation to God as their Father, whom they could know only through the Son (cf. Matt 11:27). The fathers and the young men are said to have known God; this is experiential knowledge. No one can know God the Father apart from the Son. This knowledge, as well as knowledge of the Scriptures, gives them the strength to overcome the evil one (2:14). This strength is not the natural physical vigor of young men but the power of God's Word in them through the Holy Spirit (Isa 40:30-31). They can enjoy this power and this victory over Satan, John goes on to affirm, only by freeing themselves from the grasp of the evil things of the world.

John makes an unmistakable contrast: Those who love this world do so by pursuing the lust of their flesh, the lust of their eyes, and the pride of possessions (see notes on 2:15-16). They love a world that is passing away; whereas those who love the Father and obey him are those who live forever. Since Satan is in control of the world (5:19), believers must constantly guard against his assaults by becoming saturated with God's Word (cf. John 17:15-17). We are strong only because the Word of God abides in us.

◆ ## B. Identifying the False Believers and the True (2:18-27)

¹⁸Dear children, the last hour is here. You have heard that the Antichrist is coming, and already many such antichrists have appeared. From this we know that the last hour has come. ¹⁹These people left our churches, but they never really belonged

with us; otherwise they would have stayed with us. When they left, it proved that they did not belong with us.

²⁰But you are not like that, for the Holy One has given you his Spirit,* and all of you know the truth. ²¹So I am writing to you not because you don't know the truth but because you know the difference between truth and lies. ²²And who is a liar? Anyone who says that Jesus is not the Christ.* Anyone who denies the Father and the Son is an antichrist.* ²³Anyone who denies the Son doesn't have the Father, either. But anyone who acknowledges the Son has the Father also.

²⁴So you must remain faithful to what you have been taught from the beginning. If you do, you will remain in fellowship with the Son and with the Father. ²⁵And in this fellowship we enjoy the eternal life he promised us.

²⁶I am writing these things to warn you about those who want to lead you astray. ²⁷But you have received the Holy Spirit,* and he lives within you, so you don't need anyone to teach you what is true. For the Spirit* teaches you everything you need to know, and what he teaches is true—it is not a lie. So just as he has taught you, remain in fellowship with Christ.

2:20 Greek *But you have an anointing from the Holy One.*   2:22a Or *not the Messiah.*   2:22b Or *the antichrist.*   2:27a Greek *the anointing from him.*   2:27b Greek *the anointing.*

NOTES

2:18 *the last hour.* John and other NT writers called the period that began with Christ's first coming "the last days" (cf. Acts 2:17; Heb 1:2; 1 Pet 1:20). They understood this to be the final era in world history because neither the former prophecy of the OT nor any new revelation predicted the coming of another era before Christ's second coming.

You have heard. They had heard from the apostles (e.g., see 2 Thess 2:3-10).

the Antichrist. This is the reading in some mss (א² A 33 𝔐); others do not include the definite article (א* B C 1739), which could be rendered in English, "an antichrist." The absence of the article points to character—"one who is antichrist"; the inclusion of the article points to identity—the specific Antichrist. Either way, an Antichrist is one who is "instead of Christ"; he claims for himself what belongs to Christ and poses as a substitute for Christ. The person called "Antichrist" is probably the same as "the man of lawlessness" in 2 Thess 2:3 and "the beast" in Rev 13:1-10.

already many such antichrists have appeared. As precursors to the one Antichrist, these many antichrists are the false teachers who deny (1) that Jesus is the Christ (2:22); (2) that Jesus is God's Son (2:23); and (3) that Jesus was God manifest in the flesh (4:2; 2 John 7). They are deceivers and liars.

2:19 *These people left our churches.* Lit., "they departed from us." This describes the secessionists. See discussion in the following commentary section.

2:20 *the Holy One has given you his Spirit.* Lit., "you have an anointing (*chrisma* [TG5545, ZG5984]) from the Holy One" (cf. NLT mg). As "Christ" means "the anointed one," the one on whom the Spirit was poured out (cf. Luke 4:18), so Christians are anointed ones in that they partake of the Spirit of Christ (2 Cor 1:21-22).

all of you know. This is the reading according to some ancient Gr. mss (א B). Other mss read "you know everything" (A C 33 1739 𝔐 it syr cop^bo). According to the first reading, John was affirming that all the members of the church community know who is a genuine believer and who isn't (see 2:19). The emphasis of the second reading is on the anointing and how it enables believers to know everything.

2:22 *And who is a liar? Anyone who says that Jesus is not the Christ.* The great central truth of all Christian truth is that Jesus is the Christ. To deny this is blatant heresy. The heretic Cerinthus taught that "Jesus" and "the Christ" were two separate beings who were united only from the time of Jesus' baptism until the time he was crucified—at which point, Cerinthus taught, "the Christ" left Jesus.

Anyone who denies the Father and the Son is an antichrist. The wordplay is interesting here: Anyone denying that Jesus is the "Christ" (2:22a) is "an antichrist" (2:22b). Those who reject the Son cannot know the Father, since the Father is known only through the Son (John 14:6-9). The Son is the expression of the Father—God made visible, God made known. To see the Son is to see the Father (John 14:8-10). He is the image of the invisible God (Col 1:15), the express image of God's substance and radiance of his glory (Heb 1:2-3). Thus, the claim of any religious person to worship God the Father while denying that Jesus is his Son is simply a false claim.

2:23 Anyone who denies the Son doesn't have the Father, either. But anyone who acknowledges the Son has the Father also. In both this epistle and his Gospel, John makes it very clear that the Father can be known only through the Son (cf. John 14:6-10).

2:24 So you must remain faithful to what you have been taught from the beginning. If John's readers would let the truth that they had learned from their initiation into the Christian faith and the truth that was proclaimed by John *remain* in them, then they would *remain* in the Son and in the Father. The message is that Jesus is the Christ (2:22), the Son of God (2:22) come in the flesh (1:1-4). If the believers resisted the lies of the antichrists and remained in the truth they had begun in, they would also "remain in fellowship with the Son and with the Father." By clinging to the truth about God the Father and Christ his Son, we can be sure we will never be separated from fellowship with God.

2:25 And in this fellowship we enjoy the eternal life he promised us. See John 3:15, 36; 6:40, 47, 57; 17:2, 3 for examples of promises related to eternal life. The expression "eternal life" is both quantitative (illimitable time) and qualitative (eternal in nature—as in the nature of God).

2:26 I am writing these things to warn you about those who want to lead you astray. As in 2:12-14 and 21, John took pains to make it clear that his purpose in writing was to combat the seduction of the believers by false teachers and to affirm the practical import of his teachings.

2:27 But you have received the Holy Spirit. Lit., "you have received the anointing" (*chrisma* [TG5545, ZG5984]); see note on 2:20. One ancient ms (B) reads, "you have received the *charisma* [TG5486, ZG5922] (spiritual gift)." This was probably a transcriptional mistake (with a one-letter difference in the two words) because the scribe did not make the same change in the next occurrence of the same word later in the verse.

the Spirit teaches you. Lit., "the anointing teaches you." One ancient ms (ℵ*) reads, "his Spirit teaches you."

COMMENTARY

This section gives us the reason behind John's appeal in the opening verses of the epistle (1:1-4). John had invited all the believers to remain in fellowship with him and his fellow eyewitnesses as the means of guaranteeing their genuine fellowship with God the Father and his Son. For people to purposely cut themselves off from having fellowship with the apostles was tantamount to cutting themselves off from God. Since the apostles *were* in fellowship with God, one could not leave their fellowship and still claim to be in fellowship with God. Thus, their departure was a sign that they never really knew God in the first place.

According to John's statement in 2:19, some had, in fact, already left the fellowship of the apostles and the churches established by them. These were the secessionists. At one point, they had been part of the church community, in fellowship with

John and the other eyewitnesses. Then they left that fellowship and evidently became promoters of false teachings about Jesus (cf. 4:1; 2 John 7). But just who were these people that left the fellowship? In 2:19, John speaks of "us" and "they" (lit., "they departed from us"). The plural pronoun "us" refers either to the apostolic circle or to both John and his readers. In other places in the epistle, the "us" is the apostolic community, with John's readers being the "you" of the epistle (see especially 1:1-4). If this is so here, John may be saying that the false teachers were among those individuals still alive late in the first century who had been eyewitnesses of Jesus. Yet at some point they broke away from John and his coworkers. If the "us" refers to the entire church community (i.e., John and his readers), then the false teachers would not have necessarily been part of the apostles' early contemporaries. Either way, these people had once been part of the church community and then left. Their departure was a clear indication that they never really belonged.

But those who departed weren't just secessionists; they were antichrists (2:18, 22). This means that they were deceptive teachers and false prophets (cf. 4:1; Mark 13:22—Jesus predicted such false Christs and false prophets). These antichrists must have tried to seduce various church members to believe their heretical teachings about Jesus. In John's day, one such antichrist was Cerinthus, who was an avowed enemy of John the apostle. Polycarp, a disciple of John, said that John once left a bath house when he heard that the heretic Cerinthus was inside, for fear that the house would fall in ruins since "the enemy of truth" was there. (This story comes from Irenaeus's *Against Heresies* 3.3.4). Cerinthus denied that Jesus was the Christ. He spoke of "Jesus" and "the Christ" as two separate beings who were united only from the time of Jesus' baptism to the time he was crucified—at which point, Cerinthus taught that "the Christ" left Jesus (see comments on 5:6-12 and "Christological Orthodoxy versus Heresy" in the Introduction). According to John's epistles, any denial that Jesus is the Christ includes a denial that he had come in the flesh (1:1-3; 4:3; 2 John 7). Cerinthus had clearly departed from the apostolic truths and fellowship, and there were others who had also done likewise.

It is a relief to the church when members who have already left the truth and cut themselves off from spiritual fellowship finally leave publicly. But not until the resurrection will the church be completely free of such people. One should not get upset over false believers within the church. They will always be present, but God knows those who are truly his (cf. Matt 13:24-30, 36-43). In the meanwhile, we should not quickly judge everyone who leaves the church. There are those who love Jesus and are truly saved but leave the church because they have been hurt or "burned out," but they still belong to God's family. Then there are those who leave the church and deny its teachings about Christ. Furthermore, they parade their contempt for the people of God. They remain agnostic or perhaps join some cult. These are the kind of people John wrote about. They should be refuted and opposed, while the discouraged ones should be encouraged and restored.

The anointing that each and every one of the believers has received helps them to discern the false from the true. Thus, the emphasis is on shared, communal knowledge. There is nothing "secret" that is kept from most Christians and revealed to only a select few. The false believers claimed to have special knowledge and probably a special anointing from God. But all the true Christians share the same anointing (see note on 2:20). As Christians, now indwelt by the Holy Spirit, we are joined to Christ, "the Anointed One," and share in his anointing (2 Cor 1:21-22). This anointing from the Holy Spirit enables believers to know everything that pertains to false and true teaching. Furthermore, it enables us to discern who the antichrists might be. Jesus promised that he would send the believers his Spirit, who would teach them of the truth (John 16:12-15).

The second part of the antichrist heresy that John was dealing with was the false teaching that denied the Father and the Son (2:22-23). To do so meant that one would claim to know God the Father apart from the Son and thereby reject the Son as the Father's revelation to mankind. Many of the Jewish religious leaders of Jesus' day rejected him as the Father's "Word," the Father's revealer to mankind (see John, chs 5, 8). Most Jews have persisted in this disbelief. Denying any notion of the Trinity, especially the Father–Son relationship, they claim that only Yahweh is true God. In other words, they believe that only the Father is deity.

Other notable antichrists throughout history espousing this same heresy are Muslims and Jehovah's Witnesses. Muhammad explicitly denied that Jesus was the divine Son of God, stripping him of his deity and labeling him with the title "prophet"— albeit a prophetic forerunner to Muhammad himself, the culmination of all prophets. The Qur'an espouses the one true God as Allah and denounces the Trinity. As such, he denied God's revelation to humanity in the incarnation of the Son of God, Jesus. While the Qur'an does speak of Jesus as Messiah (Suras 3:45-47; 5:72), the denial of his divinity is patent heresy—John would have labeled Muhammad an antichrist.

Jehovah's Witnesses posit a similar heresy. They believe that only Yahweh (Jehovah) is true God, not Jesus, the Son of God. They deny Jesus' deity. Church historians point to Arius (died AD 336) as the earliest example of this heresy (consequently known as the Arian heresy). Arius taught the following: "The Father existed before the Son. There was a time when the Son did not exist. Therefore, the Son was created by the Father. Therefore, although the Son was the highest of all creatures, he is not the essence of God" (Douglas, Comfort, and Mitchell 1992:35-36).

The Nicene Creed (AD 325) rejected Arius's heresy and upheld the apostolic teaching that the Father and Son are coeternal and share the same essence (*homoousios*). Both the Father and Son are eternal God. All who deviate from this teaching—especially in the direction of diminishing the Son's deity—would be considered by John to be antichrists promoting heresy.

By the power of the anointing, Christians can discern lying antichrists. We do not need another teacher because the Holy Spirit, the Spirit of truth, is our teacher; so we will remain in Christ and in what he has taught us (cf. Jer 31:34; John 6:45; 16:13). This does not mean that a Christian has no use for teachings from others; it means that a believer is able to discern and reject what is false (2:21). The better we know the truth, the more easily will we be able to identify a lie.

◆ **C. Being Prepared for Christ's Return (2:28–3:3)**

28And now, dear children, remain in fellowship with Christ so that when he returns, you will be full of courage and not shrink back from him in shame.

29Since we know that Christ is righteous, we also know that all who do what is right are God's children.

CHAPTER 3

See how very much our Father loves us, for he calls us his children, and that is what we are! But the people who belong to this world don't recognize that we are God's children because they don't know him. 2Dear friends, we are already God's children, but he has not yet shown us what we will be like when Christ appears. But we do know that we will be like him, for we will see him as he really is. 3And all who have this eager expectation will keep themselves pure, just as he is pure.

NOTES

2:28 *dear children, remain in fellowship with Christ.* John repeated this command (cf. 2:27); the term of endearment ("dear children") reveals how deep his loving concern was for these Christians. He was so anxious for their spiritual lives that he said over and over, "Remain in him; don't let anyone lead you away from him."

2:29 *Since we know that Christ is righteous, we also know that all who do what is right are God's children.* John's reasoning is that God alone is truly righteous, and therefore he is the source of righteousness. If a person's actions demonstrate righteousness, we know he or she acquired this righteousness from God by being given a new nature.

3:1 *See how very much our Father loves us.* The word behind the English expression "how very much" is *potapēn* [TG4217, ZG4534], a term that speaks of something that has come from another country. In other words, it is "exotic, extraordinary." The translation could read, "Behold, what extraordinary love the Father has poured on us."

his children. The Gr. word translated "children" (*tekna* [TG5043, ZG5451]) emphasizes birth rather than infancy. John is here calling attention to the wonderful fact, carried over from the last verse (2:29), that God has spiritually begotten us as his children.

and that is what we are! God gives us both the title and the reality. This clause was dropped in several late mss (K L 049 69 𝔐), probably because it was perceived as being redundant with the next clause, which says, "we already are." But the clause is present in 𝔓74vid ℵ A B C 33 1739, an excellent array of witnesses.

COMMENTARY

Although we already have fellowship with Christ through his indwelling Spirit, a time is coming when we will see him face to face, in all his glory (3:2). Just as he could be seen, heard, and touched in his first manifestation, so it will be true at his second appearing. John's statement implies that Christ may come at any time, so we must always be ready. Though guaranteed eternal life (5:11-12), true believers will nonetheless give account to God (Heb 13:17) and be judged by their works (Matt 16:27; 2 Cor 5:10).

At this time in our lives, the world may not fully recognize us as the children of God, but it will when we are fully glorified with Christ. Nonetheless, our lives should display the fact that we are God's children now. Contrary to the belief of the Pelagians, we do not become children of God by doing right. Rather, doing right is a sign that we have already become God's children—because we cannot do right on our own.

In this section, John declares that something inconceivably wonderful is waiting for us—even more glorious than what we now have as God's children. And of this prospect we can be sure: In eternity we will be with Christ and be like Christ. We already have a hint of what this future glory will be like, though the world is completely ignorant of it. Christ will be revealed to us and in us, in all his glory (2 Cor 4:4). In the same way, believers will be revealed to the world as God's children, sharing in Christ's glory and honor. This is the hope of every believer, even of all creation itself. As the apostle Paul said, the whole creation is waiting for the day when the children of God will be revealed in all their glory, reflecting the image of Christ (cf. Rom 8:18-30).

But seeing Christ is something that begins in the earthly life of the believer. The idea is not that we see him physically but that by constantly gazing at Christ, we will become like him and reflect his glory (2 Cor 3:17-18). As John said it, "we will see him as he really is" (3:2). This means more than a merely physiological occurrence; it means "perceiving," "recognizing," even "appreciating." In order to know someone—to see them as they really are—you have to pass through similar experiences. Therefore, in order to see Jesus as he really is, we must experience the power of his resurrection and the fellowship of his sufferings. This was Paul's aspiration, and it should be ours (Phil 3:7-14). Of course, this was also John's aspiration, as expressed in the following verse: "All who have this eager expectation will keep themselves pure, just as he is pure" (3:3). Everyone who has the hope of seeing Christ and being like him realizes that Christ is morally pure and therefore pursues purity now. We can do this only through Christ's Spirit in us—as Jesus said, "Apart from me you can do nothing" (John 15:5). This is an ongoing purification process, which begins at rebirth and continues until the day we see Jesus. The more pure we become, the clearer our view will be of Jesus, who is pure through and through.

◆ **D. Recognizing What Kind of Life Prospers the Fellowship and What Contradicts It (3:4-10)**

⁴Everyone who sins is breaking God's law, for all sin is contrary to the law of God. ⁵And you know that Jesus came to take away our sins, and there is no sin in him. ⁶Anyone who continues to live in him will not sin. But anyone who keeps on sinning does not know him or understand who he is.

⁷Dear children, don't let anyone deceive you about this: When people do what is right, it shows that they are righteous, even as Christ is righteous. ⁸But when people keep on sinning, it shows that they belong to the devil, who has been sinning since the beginning. But the Son of God came to destroy the works of the devil. ⁹Those who have been born into God's family do not make a practice of sinning, because God's life* is in them. So they can't keep on sinning, because they are children of God. ¹⁰So now we can tell who are children of God and who are children of the devil. Anyone who does not live righteously and does not love other believers* does not belong to God.

3:9 Greek *because his seed.*   3:10 Greek *does not love his brother.*

NOTES

3:4 *Everyone who sins is breaking God's law.* This statement is probably aimed at the gnostic secessionists who considered themselves to be free from sin (see 1:8, 10, and notes).

for all sin is contrary to the law of God. Lit., "sin is lawlessness"; grammatically, this could also be inverted to read "lawlessness is sin." Here is a basic definition of sin and lawlessness. The word *hamartia* [TG266, ZG281] (sin) was used by Homer and other ancient Greek writers of "missing the mark" (BDAG 49). One picture of sin, then, is that God's law is this mark or standard that we aim at and miss. The term *anomos* [TG459, ZG491] (lawlessness) in this context signifies reckless disregard of God's principles for righteousness.

3:5 *you know that Jesus came to take away our sins.* The term translated "came" (*ephanerōthē* [TG5319, ZG5746]) more precisely means "was manifested." The coming of the Son of God was his manifestation in human form among humans. He became flesh so as to express God to humanity (1:1-4; John 1:1, 4, 18; 14:9). He also became flesh in order to take away the sins of the world (John 1:29, 36). As such, he fulfilled the OT picture of both the sacrificial lamb and the scapegoat by taking away our sins once for all.

3:6 *Anyone who continues to live in him will not sin.* John's argument here is that those who are joined to Christ should live as Christ lived—pure, without sin. The word rendered as "continues to live" (*menōn* [TG3306, ZG3531]) indicates "abiding" and "remaining." This is the same verb John used in his Gospel when Jesus illustrated the believers' dependence on him by speaking about branches remaining in the Vine. As a branch lives in the Vine, it draws its life from the Vine.

anyone who keeps on sinning does not know him or understand who he is. John is again presenting the ideal. In this verse, John purposely used the present tense verb to denote the sin he speaks of as an ongoing, repeated action. He was not saying that a person who sins even once has never known God, but he insists that, as far as we continue in sin—to that degree—we do not know God.

3:7 *don't let anyone deceive you about this.* Many scholars think this is a concluding statement for vv. 4-6, with the rest of v. 7 being a summary statement. Apparently, the false teachers who were denying the doctrine of Christ (2:22) were also claiming that they knew God, yet they were living unrighteous lives (cf. 1:6). The believers should not be deceived by such people.

When people do what is right, it shows that they are righteous, even as Christ is righteous. It is not doing righteousness that makes us righteous, but rather our righteousness given to us by Christ that naturally leads to doing righteous acts. This principle can function as a tool for discernment: a tree that bears good fruit is a good tree; it is not that the fruit makes the tree good, but it shows that the tree is good (cf. Matt 7:15-20).

3:8 *But when people keep on sinning, it shows that they belong to the devil.* "The Devil is the source of sin, and therefore the one who leads a sinful life is spiritually connected with him" (Vine 1970:56). It is in this sense that the person who continually sins belongs to the devil. The devil cannot create or produce children, but people become children of the devil by imitating him. This was Jesus' argument against the Jewish religious leaders who wanted to kill him; these evil intentions showed that they were children of the devil, a murderer (cf. John 8:39-44).

who has been sinning since the beginning. Since the beginning of creation—and probably before—the devil has lived a life in opposition to God.

But the Son of God came to destroy the works of the devil. As in 3:5, the word translated "came" is *ephanerōthē* [TG5319, ZG5746] (was manifested). The repetition of the verb here suggests that the Son of God's appearance on earth was to die for sins and, in so doing, to overthrow the power of the devil. The word behind "destroy" (*lusē* [TG3089, ZG3395]) does not mean to annihilate; rather, it means "to break down" (cf. Eph 2:14), "to undo," "to render ineffective." In other words, the works of the devil have been deprived of force, rendered inoperative, conquered, and overthrown (Stott 2000:129).

3:9 *Those who have been born into God's family do not make a practice of sinning, because God's life is in them. So they can't keep on sinning, because they are children of God.* At first glance, this appears to completely contradict what John said earlier: "If we claim we have no sin, we are only fooling ourselves" (1:8). Here he is saying that "we do not sin." Do we sin or don't we? Experience tells us that we do, but our spirits tell us that we aspire not to sin. This aspiration comes from "God's life" within each believer. The Gr. phrase here is *sperma autou* [TG4690, ZG5065] (his seed); it signifies God's life and God's nature. Since we have God's nature in us, we can become partakers of the divine nature and thereby live a sin-free life (see 2 Pet 1:3-4). This is also called *regeneration* (Titus 3:4-5, NLT mg).

3:10 *Anyone who does not live righteously.* Living righteously means living in a right relationship with God. This does not mean that we live perfect lives but that we keep ourselves in a good relationship with God. When we sin, we confess our sins. Then we continue to live in fellowship with God.

COMMENTARY

Early in his first epistle, John not only exposes the false teaching of the gnostics but offers corrective instruction to true believers regarding the nature of sin. His main point in 3:4-10 is that a life of sin is incompatible with the new life in Christ.

Sin is rebellion against God; it is the recurring, irrational impulse to do anything rather than obey God. This aspect of sin is incompatible with being born of God. Sin is the Christian's enemy. It removes the believer from the light. It must be resisted; it cannot be tolerated. Where failure occurs, sin must be confessed to the Lord and then abandoned. The purpose and intent of the believer always remains the same—to commit no sin. But if any believer should fail and commit sin, they should neither deceive themselves about it, nor lie about their actions, nor give up walking in the light. The response to a lapse into sin is not to deny it but to seek the forgiveness of God, made available through Jesus Christ.

No one born of God can continue in sin or practice a life of sin. In fact, a life of sin (that is, active rebellion against God's known will) is evidence that one is not really God's child. The continual practice of sin is incompatible with the new nature derived from the new birth. Those who continue in sin are lawbreakers; they live unrighteous lives because they live in sin. Living in sin and living in God are mutually exclusive, like darkness and light. The way to be free from sin is to live in Christ. When believers commit sins (1:8-10; 2:1-2), these sins do not come from, or belong to, their life in Christ because they cannot sin as long as they are living in Christ. Complete union with Christ bringing complete separation from sin is the ideal for each and every Christian. This ideal, while never perfectly attained in this life, differs from that claimed by the gnostics who professed sinlessness by denying sin's existence. According to John's perspective, the degree to which one sins is the degree to which one is still in darkness and therefore still exhibits the characteristics of evil. John believed in transformation—from darkness to light, from sin to sinlessness, from hate to love.

The devil sinned even before the creation of the world; and ever since, as the prince of this world, he has been both sinning and causing people to sin. John's words here are very similar to what Jesus told the Jewish leaders who refused to accept his message. In John 8:44, Jesus told them, "You are the children of your father the devil, and you love to do the evil things he does." This statement, which is developed in 3:7-15, indicates that a person's actions are a manifestation of his true source of being. The intent to murder comes from the father of murder, the devil. The devil was the instigator of Jesus' murder and the perpetrator of the lies the Jews believed about Jesus. The devil, Jesus said, "was a murderer from the beginning. He has always hated the truth, because there is no truth in him. When he lies, it is consistent with his character, for he is a liar and the father of lies." The devil, through his lies to Eve (Gen 3:4-5), paved the way for death to enter into the world, causing Adam and Eve and all their posterity to be alienated from God. In this sense, the devil was a murderer and a sinner from the beginning.

Though we might have hoped that Christ would have obliterated Satan, he didn't; rather, Christ came to undo Satan's work and thereby free people from sin and all its awful consequences. John is therefore arguing that Christians cannot be involved in what Christ came to destroy—that is, lies and unrighteousness.

When we were "born again," a new life was born within us. The new life, or nature, which is "born of God" does not habitually practice sin and is entirely incompatible with sin. It gives us a hatred for sin, and though at times we may give in to sin, we are continually fighting against it. Sin is still active, but it no longer has complete control over us. The normal direction of a Christian's life is against sin and toward God. The Holy Spirit works, through the Word of God, to sanctify us or to make us holy and pure, as Christ is (3:3; cf. 5:18.)

Some teachers have wrongly affirmed that 3:9 teaches that the Christian does not sin in the new nature, although the physical body may sin. This is gnostic dualism: a division of the physical from the spiritual. The text does not say that the new nature does not sin but that the person himself does not sin. Other teachers—especially in the holiness movement—have used this verse to say that a person, once regenerated, can never sin. If he or she does, they have lost their salvation and must get saved and be regenerated all over again. To avoid this dilemma, many in this movement will never confess to having sinned; instead, they will call their sins "errors" or "mistakes." Both of these views misunderstand this passage. Each person lives only one life, and it is ultimately characterized by either abiding in Christ or practicing sin. One must look at the habitual, volitional characteristics of those who profess the new birth; if they can be characterized as rebellious, then they are not born of God.

In the end, we all must admit that one of the greatest tensions in the Christian's life is the presence of sin. Various theological answers have been purported—all the way from total eradication, on one hand, to acquiescent cohabitation on the other. Both are extreme positions, unsatisfactory to the sincere believer. Though believers are absolutely and totally forgiven for sin, the marks of sin are still on them. Christ died to deliver the redeemed from sin's guilt, and he now lives to save the believers from sin's power. Regenerated people are new creations in Christ and, as such, a new principle of life has been implanted in them. They have an awareness of God, a desire for God, and responsiveness to God. At the same time, the Holy Spirit is constantly at work in the believers' lives, purifying and cleansing their nature from the pollution and uncleanness of sin, renewing in them the image of God. This is a life-long renovation of our natures by the Holy Spirit, as we yield to God. Such a cooperative effort between the believer and the Holy Spirit is called "sanctification" and is defined in the Westminster Shorter Catechism (Question 35) as "the work of God's free grace, whereby we are renewed in the whole man after the image of God, and are enabled more and more to die unto sin, and live unto righteousness."

John was well aware of the difficulties involved in living the purified life and of the power of opposition from the evil one. Nevertheless, the evil one need not prevail. One must negate the innate, carnal self-will and the rebellious, egocentric behavior patterns that develop from birth. We need to keep the Word of God, value it, obey it, and live by it. As we do so, Christ promises to keep us (Rev 3:10) and preserve us (Ps 25:21). It is not the quality of strength in the life of the believer that gives one hope of prevailing against sin but the mighty presence and power of God.

◆ III. Loving One Another in the Community of Believers (3:11-4:21)
A. Loving the Members of the Community: A Sign of Divine Life (3:11-18)

¹¹This is the message you have heard from the beginning: We should love one another. ¹²We must not be like Cain, who belonged to the evil one and killed his brother. And why did he kill him? Because Cain had been doing what was evil, and his brother had been doing what was righteous. ¹³So don't be surprised, dear brothers and sisters,* if the world hates you.

¹⁴If we love our Christian brothers and sisters,* it proves that we have passed from death to life. But a person who has no love is still dead. ¹⁵Anyone who hates another brother or sister* is really a murderer at heart. And you know that murderers don't have eternal life within them.

¹⁶We know what real love is because Jesus gave up his life for us. So we also ought to give up our lives for our brothers and sisters. ¹⁷If someone has enough money to live well and sees a brother or sister* in need but shows no compassion—how can God's love be in that person?

¹⁸Dear children, let's not merely say that we love each other; let us show the truth by our actions.

3:13 Greek *brothers.* 3:14 Greek *the brothers;* similarly in 3:16. 3:15 Greek *hates his brother.* 3:17 Greek *sees his brother.*

NOTES

3:11 *This is the message.* This is the reading according to A B 049 33 𝔐. Several other mss (ℵ C P 1739 cop) read, "This is the promise." The same textual variant in nearly the same mss occurs in 1:5.

you have heard from the beginning. This "beginning" does not refer to the time Jesus first told his disciples to love one another (see John 13:34-35; 15:17); it refers to the time when John's audience first became believers and heard the message of the gospel (see note on 2:7).

We should love one another. This is the central theme of this section.

3:12 We must not be like Cain, who belonged to the evil one and killed his brother.
John returns to the thought of 3:8, and he gives an example of the works of the
devil—the actions of Cain.

And why did he kill him? Because Cain had been doing what was evil. "Cain, who
murdered his brother (Gen 4:8), showed by that act that he hated him, and his hatred
indicated quite clearly to which spiritual family he belonged" (Bruce 1970:94).

and his brother had been doing what was righteous. Abel made sacrifices to God that
God approved because Abel acted in faith (Heb 11:4).

3:13 So don't be surprised, dear brothers and sisters, if the world hates you. Jesus told his
disciples the same thing—and in the same context (John 15:18; 17:14). Hatred from the
outside world should serve to increase the believers' love for one another.

**3:14 If we love our Christian brothers and sisters, it proves that we have passed from
death to life.** John now reduces the world to two spheres, that of death and that of life.
Love for fellow believers is experiential evidence that one has passed from the realm of
death to the sphere of life. "Passed" is a perfect tense verb indicating that something experienced in the past has continuing and abiding results in the present. Christians experience a
permanent passage from death to life at the time of regeneration.

But a person who has no love is still dead. This translation has the excellent ms backing
of ℵ A B 33 1739 it cop. Other mss supply "the brother," (C 044 𝔐) or "his brother"
(P syr) so as to qualify the idea: ". . . has no love for [his] brother." To have no love speaks
of the spiritual condition of the unregenerate—that is, such people are spiritually dead.
If a person does not have any love for other Christians, it shows that the person does not
share the same life as the others—it reveals that the person has not migrated from death
to life.

3:15 Anyone who hates another brother or sister is really a murderer at heart. The dark
image of Cain still lingers. To not love (3:14) is to hate—there is no middle ground (cf.
Matt 5:21-22).

3:16 We know what real love is because Jesus gave up his life for us. Christ's example
shows us that real love involves self-sacrifice, which, as 3:17-19 points out, must result in
self-sacrificial actions. Reduced to the absolute minimum, love gives and hate takes.

So we also ought to give up our lives for our brothers and sisters. We do this by becoming
truly concerned about the needs of our Christian brothers, and by unselfishly giving time,
effort, prayer, and possessions to supply those needs. Such an attitude would result in actually dying for a brother or sister if this were ever necessary. Our lives should not be more
precious to us than God's own Son was to him.

**3:17 If someone has enough money to live well and sees a brother or sister in need but
shows no compassion—how can God's love be in that person?** If we are to give our very
lives for our brothers and sisters, we certainly should not hold back money or anything we
own from Christians who are in need.

COMMENTARY

This section thematically follows the previous one in its message that the presence or
absence of brotherly love is a sure way to tell a true child of God from a pretender.
Our nature has consequences; eventually we act the way we really are. To love the
brothers and sisters in the believing community demonstrates that we belong to God;
to reject the brothers and sisters demonstrates that we don't really belong to God.

   Our love for one another is a constant manifestation that we are living in Christ.

John never tired of telling the brothers and sisters to love one another. In his *Commentary on Galatians* (6.10), Jerome said that even when the apostle John was very old and had to be carried to the church meetings, he continued to remind the believers of Christ's command: "My little children, love one another." The brothers and sisters may have grown tired of always hearing the same instruction, but John insisted that this was the command of the Lord Jesus (see John 13:34) and that, if we could attain just this one thing, it would be enough.

Hatred toward other Christians is a clear indication of a person's alignment (perhaps unwitting) with the devil. Those who hate (that is, reject) other Christians belong to their father, the devil (3:10, 12, 15). This statement accords with Jesus' indictment made against the Jewish leaders who wanted to kill him. Jesus told them that they were children of the devil for wanting to murder him because the devil was a murderer from the beginning (John 8:43-44). John used "Cain" as an exemplary brother-hater and murderer. Cain, Abel's brother, was jealous of Abel receiving approval from God. This jealousy led to murder (Gen 4:8). If we hate someone, we wish he or she were dead, and the Lord sees the inner desire as equal to the outward act that would result from it (cf. Matt 5:21-22). Therefore, those who hate are murderers. Perhaps the foothold the devil used in Cain's case was Cain's intense desire to outdo Abel, to show himself better than Abel. The devil always uses some foothold to get us to sin. It is possible that the secessionists from the Johannine community left because they were jealous of John. After departing, their goal was to poison others against John and those with him. Diotrephes was likely such a poisoner (see comments on 3 John 9).

It is notable that Jesus had reminded his disciples that the world would hate them after telling them to love one another (John 15:17-18). The world hates us because it can see the difference between our godly lives and its own evil. The world would prefer that we were like them; since we are not, they hate us (see 1 Pet 4:3-4). Any professing Christian who is warmly embraced by the world at large should reexamine the reality of his claim to discipleship (2:15-17; 3:1; 4:5-6; 2 Tim 3:10-12; Jas 4:4). The world's hatred for the believers should increase believers' love for one another. This love does not cause us to have eternal life, but it is evidence that we already have it. We must each ask ourselves if we have this love. If we do, then we can be sure that we have eternal life and that this will be publicly revealed when Christ comes. Those who do not love do not abide in light but in darkness (2:11); they are not abiding in life but in death (3:14). Their source is not God but the devil (3:8). Thus, the eternal life inside them is not living because it is not the controlling factor in their lives.

To summarize: Hatred characterizes the world, whose prototype is Cain. Hatred originates in the devil, issues in murder, and is evidence of spiritual death. Love characterizes the church, whose prototype is Christ. It originates in God, issues in self-sacrifice, and is evidence of eternal life (Stott 2000:146-147). Interestingly and significantly, John uses three different Greek words meaning "life" in 3:15-17. The three words are *zōē, psuchē, bios*. The word *zōē* [TG2222, ZG2437] is used in the New Testament to designate divine, eternal life—the life of God. This life resided in Christ, and he made it available to all who believe in him (cf. 3:15). In 3:16, *psuchē* [TG5590, ZG6034] (soul, personality, life) designates the natural life that all human beings are born with; as a human, Jesus had a *psuchē* or "soul." He gave up his soul (*psuchē*) in death so that we might have the *zōē*, the eternal life of God. In 3:16-17, John states that believers should likewise sacrifice their *psuchē* (life, soul) by giving their *bios* [TG979, ZG1050] (life, livelihood) to those in need. The word *bios* refers to one's "livelihood" or "that which is necessary to sustain physical life" (cf. NLT, "enough money to live well"; 3:17). John shows these three aspects of life to be inextricably intertwined: believers demonstrate that they have eternal life (*zōē*) by imitating Christ in surrendering their earthly life (*psuchē*), specifically in giving of their livelihood (*bios*) to sustain the lives (*psuchē*) of other believers. This is the truest and best manifestation of love. Our actions of taking care of others in need are true demonstrations of our love.

◆ ## B. Maintaining a Relationship with God by Being Faithful to Him and Living in Christ (3:19-24)

¹⁹Our actions will show that we belong to the truth, so we will be confident when we stand before God. ²⁰Even if we feel guilty, God is greater than our feelings, and he knows everything.

²¹Dear friends, if we don't feel guilty, we can come to God with bold confidence. ²²And we will receive from him whatever we ask because we obey him and do the things that please him.

²³And this is his commandment: We must believe in the name of his Son, Jesus Christ, and love one another, just as he commanded us. ²⁴Those who obey God's commandments remain in fellowship with him, and he with them. And we know he lives in us because the Spirit he gave us lives in us.

NOTES

3:19 *Our actions will show that we belong to the truth.* Lit., "By this we will know that we are of the truth." The best mss (א A B C 33 1739) support the verb tense as being future. In inferior mss (K L 049 𝔐—so TR), the tense is present, "we know"; this displays assimilation to the present tense verb, "we know," used predominantly in this epistle (see 2:3, 5, 18; 3:24; 4:6, 13; 5:2). John deviated from the present tense in this instance because he wanted to include a notion of future accountability as well as ongoing accountability.

3:20 *Even if we feel guilty, God is greater than our feelings, and he knows everything.* As is discussed in the commentary section below, this statement has two possible interpretations—one positive and one negative, each depending on how the expression "God is greater than our feelings [lit., hearts]" is understood. The positive interpretation is that the believer can take consolation in God's beneficent greatness (cf. Brooke 1912:100; Stott 2000:150-152). The negative interpretation is that the believer should recognize that God, who is greater than us, would echo any condemnation and do so in greater fashion (cf. Alford 1976:4.479-481). The context would seem to support the positive interpretation inasmuch as John was trying to encourage the believers, not discourage them. Certain scholars would repunctuate 3:19-20 to make it even clearer that John intended a positive interpretation. Burge (1996:164), following Marshall (1978:198), suggests this format:

19a: "In this [the love and obedience we exhibit, vv. 11-18] we will know that we are of the truth."

19b-20: "We will reassure our hearts in his presence whenever our hearts condemn us, because (1) God is greater than our hearts, and (2) God knows all things."

3:22 *And we will receive from him whatever we ask because we obey him and do the things that please him.* This statement follows what Jesus uttered in his final discourse to his disciples, as recorded in John 15:7—"If you abide in me and my words abide in you, ask for whatever you wish, and it will be done for you" (NRSV).

3:23 *We must believe.* This reading is based on the aorist verb, *pisteusōmen*, [TG4100, ZG4409] found in B 𝔐. The more likely reading is a present subjunctive, *pisteuōmen* (we should continue to believe), found in ℵ A C 044 0245 33 1739. The variant reading has better support and suits the context. John was not asking his readers to begin to believe (which is the force of the aorist); he was asking them to continue in their faith.

3:24 *remain in fellowship with him, and he with them.* Lit., "abides in him [Christ] and he [Christ] in him [the believer]." This is the first time in this epistle that John mentions the mutual indwelling of Christ and the believer. This was a major theme in Jesus' last discourse, as recorded by John in his Gospel (John 14:20; 15:5; 17:21-26).

And we know he lives in us because the Spirit he gave us lives in us. The way in which Christ lives in the believer is by his indwelling Spirit. In Jesus' last discourse, he told the disciples that he would give them the Spirit of truth to live in them. In the same breath, he told them that he would come to them (John 14:16-20). The coming of the Spirit to indwell the believers is none other than the coming of Christ in his invisible, spiritual presence to live in the believers. John's mention of the Spirit in this verse prepares the way for 4:1-3, which deals with the Spirit of truth versus the spirit of error.

COMMENTARY

In this section, John continues to affirm that life must match doctrine. One can claim to be in the truth, but one's deeds prove or disclaim that profession. We can be assured that we are practicing what we preach if we have active love toward other Christians. The person who loves in truth (3:18) knows that his behavior has its source in truth and has confidence before God (3:21). If we are demonstrating love by our actions, we will not constantly wonder whether God condemns us or condones us. John could speak this way because he was not speaking to people whose consciences were dead by continual, deliberate sin (1 Tim 4:2); he was speaking to Christians who knew Christ's commands and were testing themselves by them.

God's knowledge of our thoughts and motives should relieve us, not terrify us (see note on 3:20). This is the interpretation favored by the NLT rendering. As written, this passage functions to console the believer whose heart (or, conscience) accuses him or her of sin because God, in his greatness, assures the believer of his love. But it is also possible to read this passage in another way: "And by this we know that we are of the truth, and shall assure our hearts before him. For if our heart condemns us, God is greater than our heart, and knows all things" (NKJV). In this rendering, the phrase "God is greater than our heart" intensifies John's warning. The condemning voice of our conscience merely echoes the judgment of God, who knows our lives better than we do. Thus, we cannot gloss over or excuse our sin as insignificant. No matter which interpretation we are convinced of, we can come confidently to God when we recognize that his grace and mercy are greater than our guilt.

Furthermore, when believers live (abide) in Christ, their prayers will be answered. This does not mean that all requests are granted; the context of a parallel passage, John 15, suggests that the prayers should pertain to fruit-bearing and glorifying the Father. The same holds true for John's statement: "We will receive from him whatever we ask." Our requests will be honored by God when they are focused on accomplishing God's will. This accords with how Jesus taught his disciples to pray: "May your will be done on earth, as it is in heaven" (Matt 6:10).

Continual abiding engenders continual faith (see note on 3:23 above). Our faith in Christ must be ongoing. To believe in the name of Jesus Christ is to believe in his person—who he is and what he represents. We must believe in Jesus as the Son of God; we must be careful not to believe in him according to our own conceptions but according to the biblical presentation of his person. The result of believing in Jesus is that we love all others who also believe. This comes not only from Jesus' command (John 13:34; 15:17) but from Jesus' new life imparted to us by the Spirit.

John concludes this section of his epistle with an affirmation of what theologians call "mutual indwelling." Mutual indwelling means that God and the believers live in one another. This is made possible by the presence of the Spirit in the believer's life. The Christian lives in the Spirit, and the Spirit lives in the Christian (3:24). An appropriate—albeit limited—analogy is a human being's relationship to air: We must live in the air so that the air can come into us and live in us.

The indwelling Spirit provides us with the presence of the indwelling Christ. For the Spirit to live in us is to have Christ live in us (see Rom 8:9-11). When Christ gave us his Spirit to live in us, he gave us himself to live in us (cf. John 14:16-20; 1 Cor 15:45; 2 Cor 3:17-18). The Holy Spirit manifests himself in our lives and conduct. It is he who inspires us to confess Jesus as the Christ. It is he who empowers us to obey God's commandment, which is to love our brothers and sisters.

In summary, this section is John's reiteration and application of Jesus' upper room discourse, wherein Jesus first gave the disciples the commandment to love one another (John 13), then revealed to them that he would indwell them by his Spirit (John 14), and finally encouraged the disciples to practice abiding (living) in him so that he could live in them and their prayers could be answered (John 15–16).

◆   ## C. Community Fellowship Protected by Watchfulness for Deceivers (4:1-6)

Dear friends, do not believe everyone who claims to speak by the Spirit. You must test them to see if the spirit they have comes from God. For there are many false prophets in the world. ²This is how we know if they have the Spirit of God: If a person claiming to be a prophet* acknowledges that Jesus Christ came in a real body, that person has the Spirit of God. ³But if someone claims to be a prophet and does not acknowledge the truth about Jesus, that person is not from God. Such a person has the spirit of the Antichrist, which you heard is coming into the world and indeed is already here.

⁴But you belong to God, my dear children. You have already won a victory over those people, because the Spirit who lives

in you is greater than the spirit who lives in the world. ⁵Those people belong to this world, so they speak from the world's viewpoint, and the world listens to them. ⁶But we belong to God, and those who know God listen to us. If they do not belong to God, they do not listen to us. That is how we know if someone has the Spirit of truth or the spirit of deception.

4:2 Greek *If a spirit;* similarly in 4:3.

NOTES

4:1 *do not believe everyone who claims to speak by the Spirit.* The literal expression here is "do not believe every spirit" (used also in 4:2 and 4:3); "every spirit" is a metonymy for "every prophet" in the sense that the prophet is an instrument for the spirit's utterance (cf. Acts 4:25). First Timothy 4:1 has a parallel expression inasmuch as the words "the Holy Spirit tells us clearly" is tantamount to saying "prophecy indicates." Paul conveys nearly the same idea in 1 Cor 14:29-32 (NASB), where he conjoins "the prophet" exercising his or her gift with "the spirit."

You must test them. Lit., "test the spirits." The plural "spirits" does "not refer to a multiplicity of divine spirits or even of evil spirits but to a multiplicity of human beings who may be inspired in their spirits by the Spirit of God or the spirit of falsehood" (Marshall 1978:2004). The test question is made explicit in 4:2-3.

many false prophets. This is probably another name for the many antichrists (see comments on 2:18-19).

4:2 *If a person claiming to be a prophet.* Lit., "Every spirit that" (cf. also NLT mg). The NLT understands this correctly; the reference is to the spirit of the speaker, the spirit of the prophet.

acknowledges that Jesus Christ came in a real body. There are three parts to this confession: (1) Christ had an existence prior to becoming flesh; (2) Jesus is the Christ; and (3) he became a man. In other words, Jesus was the Christ come in the flesh (Stott 2000:154-156). The verb "came" (a perfect active participle in Greek: *elēluthota* [TG2064A, ZG2262]) implies the coming of Jesus Christ from God, as well as the preexistence of Christ before the Incarnation (Marshall 1978:205).

4:3 *if someone claims to be a prophet.* Lit., "every spirit that." The reference is to the spirit of the prophet.

does not acknowledge . . . Jesus. In this context, refusing to "acknowledge Jesus" or "confess Jesus" means denial of Jesus' true person as both God and man. This is the true reading according to the best ms support (ℵ A B C 33 1739* 𝔐). A few other witnesses, however, read, "annuls Jesus" (1739ᵐᵍ Vulgate [which reads *solvit* = "severs"] Irenaeus, Clement, Origen [per 1739ᵐᵍ], Augustineᵐˢˢ [per Socrates]). This variant, which is noted in NRSVmg and NJBᵐᵍ, is an anti-gnostic statement. Those "annulling Jesus" or "severing Jesus" destroy the orthodox teaching about Jesus' incarnation. Some church fathers thought the severing would be to divide "Jesus" from "the Christ," as was done by Cerinthus and later by Nestorius (cf. discussion in Smalley 1984:214-215).

Such a person has the spirit of the Antichrist. In the Gr., there is no word for "spirit" here; rather, just the neuter article *to* [TG3588, ZG3836] (the), which is used substantively to refer back to *pneuma* [TG4151, ZG4460] (spirit) in the first part of the verse. The spirit operating in the false prophets is the spirit of the antichrist (2:18), the spirit of error (4:6).

which . . . is already here. The relative pronoun "which" is neuter in the Gr., again referring to *pneuma* [TG4151, ZG4460] (spirit). John says "it [the spirit] is already here" because the spirit of the antichrist is already present, while the appearing of the Antichrist himself is yet impending.

4:4 *you belong to God.* This is said in emphatic contrast to the false teachers who were enemies of Christ.

You have already won a victory over those people. Christians don't have to overpower false prophets to conquer them; rather, they can overcome them and their teachings by recognizing them and then refusing to follow them. The believers in the churches John was writing to had already done this; they had not succumbed to the false prophets.

the Spirit who lives in you is greater than the spirit who lives in the world. The NLT specifically identifies what the Greek text leaves unclear: "The one who is in you is greater than the one in the world." This one could be God the Father, Jesus, or the Spirit—or all three, the triune God (Smalley 1984:227).

4:5 *Those people belong to this world.* In John's Gospel and epistles, the term *kosmos* [TG2889, ZG3180] (world) describes the world system in which every human being lives, and it refers to this system as it stands in opposition to God and the people in the system. This system is opposed to God's realm because Satan exerts his influence over it.

4:6 *we belong to God.* John was primarily speaking of himself and those with him, who were the true teachers of Christ, but his statement also includes all those who speak from God and therefore speak the truth.

those who know God listen to us. John was following Jesus in this proclamation, for Jesus declared, "Anyone who belongs to God listens gladly to the words of God" (John 8:47).

they do not belong to God. "They" refers to the false prophets (4:5); since they do not know God, they cannot speak for him.

the Spirit of truth. According to the Gospel of John (John 14:17, 26; 15:26; 16:13-15), the "Spirit of truth" is the Holy Spirit, who proceeds from God and teaches the truth about Christ (cf. 1 John 2:20, 27).

the spirit of deception. This expression is unique in the NT; the closest parallel is found in 1 Tim 4:1 (deceptive spirits). The spirit of deception is the spirit of the antichrist present in the false prophets; it is the spirit that leads people away from the truth about Christ.

COMMENTARY

The statement "And we know he lives in us because the Spirit he gave us lives in us" (3:24) serves as a transition to chapter 4. Those who are indwelt by the Spirit have the ability to discern the Spirit of truth from the spirit of error because the anointing of the Spirit teaches them about these things (see comments on 2:20, 27). In John's day, the secessionists may have claimed to speak Spirit-inspired messages. Those messages had to be tested. The same holds true throughout all church history.

Those who have the Spirit of God confess that Jesus is God's Son come in the flesh. In other words, they acknowledge the full reality of the Incarnation. This is John's "litmus test" for distinguishing heresy from orthodoxy. This doctrinal test of orthodoxy is spelled out clearly: A person must confess that "Jesus Christ has come in the flesh." This means that a person must acknowledge Jesus' divinity and preexistence as the Son of God (that he "has come"; cf. 4:15), as well as Jesus' incarnation and true humanity (that he has come "in the flesh"). This truth is made explicit in John 1:1 and 1:14—"the Word was God . . . the Word became human." It is also affirmed in John's prologue to this epistle (1:1-4).

Jesus did not merely appear to be a man; he actually became a man, with a human body. John's "statement is directed against the gnostic error promulgated by Cerinthus, that 'the Christ' descended into an already existing man" (Vine 1970:75). John was also speaking against this heresy in his Gospel when he said, "the Word *became* human" (John 1:14). "The verb is in the perfect tense in the Greek ('has come'); it represents an abiding effect. From his incarnation onward, Christ was, and ever is, possessed of true Manhood" (Vine 1970:76). God the Son is forever fully God and fully man, though in immortal, incorruptible flesh. A denial of Jesus' full and true humanity proves that a prophet is not "of God." The church has fought the battle for this truth concerning Christ's person ever since John's day—the late first century. Indeed, the earliest extant quote of 1 John comes from Polycarp (*To the Philippians* 7.1), who quotes 4:2-3: "Everyone who does not confess that Jesus Christ has come in the flesh is antichrist."

The responsibility for testing the spirits does not rest solely on scholars or church leaders but on every Christian. Whenever we hear someone teaching about Jesus, our spiritual "antennae" ought to be operating so that we can sense whether truth or falsehood is being spoken. The church does not now have any of the apostles present to correct error, but we do have the Holy Spirit and Scriptures written by the apostles. All those who are indwelt by the Spirit of truth and anointed by the Spirit can know the truth; it is not reserved for a special few. The greater the number of believers who know the truth and can discern error, the stronger the church will be against deception. Those who have the Spirit should be able to discern true prophets from the false. Whereas a true prophet is one who receives direct revelation from God (cf. Deut 13, 18), a false prophet is one who claims to have received direct revelation from God but actually has not.

False teachers and false prophets, being a part of the world system, will be accepted by the world. This is why so many cults are readily accepted in the world; they offer something new and distinctive to a world that is looking for novelty and speciality. The presence, even in our own times, of false prophets, false teachers, and even antichrists should not surprise us. Jesus warned his disciples of their coming (Matt 24:15, 24-26), and the apostles, in turn, warned the believers (cf. 2 Thess 2:3-12; 2 Pet 3:3ff). They will enter our churches, speak on our radios, and appear on our televisions. We can discern them and reject them if we know the truth and pay attention to the inward teaching of the Spirit. If something they say doesn't "sit right" with our spirit, we should compare their teachings against the apostolic truths as presented in Scripture. We should be especially sensitive to remarks made about the person and work of Jesus Christ. In John's day, many rejected Jesus' humanity; in our day, many reject Jesus' deity.

◆   ## D. God's Love Expressed in Community Love (4:7-21)

[7]Dear friends, let us continue to love one another, for love comes from God. Anyone who loves is a child of God and knows God. [8]But anyone who does not love does not know God, for God is love.

[9]God showed how much he loved us by

sending his one and only Son into the world so that we might have eternal life through him. ¹⁰This is real love—not that we loved God, but that he loved us and sent his Son as a sacrifice to take away our sins. ¹¹Dear friends, since God loved us that much, we surely ought to love each other. ¹²No one has ever seen God. But if we love each other, God lives in us, and his love is brought to full expression in us.

¹³And God has given us his Spirit as proof that we live in him and he in us. ¹⁴Furthermore, we have seen with our own eyes and now testify that the Father sent his Son to be the Savior of the world. ¹⁵All who confess that Jesus is the Son of God have God living in them, and they live in God. ¹⁶We know how much God loves us, and we have put our trust in his love.

God is love, and all who live in love live in God, and God lives in them. ¹⁷And as we live in God, our love grows more perfect. So we will not be afraid on the day of judgment, but we can face him with confidence because we live like Jesus here in this world.

¹⁸Such love has no fear, because perfect love expels all fear. If we are afraid, it is for fear of punishment, and this shows that we have not fully experienced his perfect love. ¹⁹We love each other* because he loved us first.

²⁰If someone says, "I love God," but hates a Christian brother or sister,* that person is a liar; for if we don't love people we can see, how can we love God, whom we cannot see? ²¹And he has given us this command: Those who love God must also love their Christian brothers and sisters.*

4:19 Greek *We love.* Other manuscripts read *We love God;* still others read *We love him.*   4:20 Greek *hates his brother.*   4:21 Greek *The one who loves God must also love his brother.*

NOTES

4:7 *for love comes from God.* God is love (4:8) and the source of all love.

Anyone who loves is a child of God. In Greek, the present tense verb here indicates ongoing action: "Everyone loving has been born of God." This verse is not saying that every person who experiences any kind of love has, therefore, been regenerated by God. Even the worst people can have loving moments. What this is saying is that like begets like. Those born of God, who is love, will also love and be characterized by love.

and knows God. The verb indicates an ongoing knowledge, as in "getting to know God" (*ginōskei* [TG1097, ZG1182] *ton theon*). This is a continual, growing, spiritual knowledge based on actual experience of God in our lives.

4:8 *anyone who does not love does not know God.* A person who does not love Christians has never known the God whom Christians love. The verb translated "know" in this verse is in the aorist tense, thereby indicating that such a person not only doesn't know God now but has never known him.

God is love. We cannot turn this around to say, "Love is God," or weaken it by saying, "God is loving," as if this were just one of God's attributes. Rather, God is love in his very essence. Those who do not love other children of God do not know God. "God is love" is the second description of God's absolute nature in 1 John; the first is "God is light" (1:5).

4:9 This verse nearly replicates the well-known statement in John 3:16, thereby showing that John wrote both the fourth Gospel and this epistle. The main thrust of this verse, as well as of John 3:16, is that God was motivated by love for humanity when he sent his only Son to give eternal life to all who will believe.

his one and only Son. The Greek is *ton huion* [TG5207, ZG5626] *autou ton monogenē* [TG3439, ZG3666]. The term *monogenē* is a title for Christ found only in John's writings (John 1:14, 18; 3:16, 18; cf. 5:18 and note); this title expresses the Son's unique position as the

Father's beloved Son (cf. Smalley 1984:241-242). The NLT translation rightly avoids the old KJV rendering, "only begotten Son," because the term *monogenē* does not emphasize "birth" (begotten) as such but speciality (the one and only). Jesus Christ is God's uniquely favored Son.

4:10 *This is real love.* In the ancient Greek language there were four words for love that generally focused on four different aspects of love: (1) *eraō* for fervent longings, esp. sexual passion; (2) *phileō* [TG5368, ZG5797] for friendship; (3) *stergō* for benevolent devotion, esp. among family members; and (4) *agapaō* [TG25, ZG26] for loving kindness. The fourth word is the term used by John to characterize God's love.

not that we loved God, but that he loved us. Initiating love is greater than responding love (cf. Rom 5:10).

and sent his Son as a sacrifice to take away our sins. The supreme manifestation of God's love was demonstrated in sending his Son to die for us to take away our sins. By removing our sins, God removed the barrier between him and us (Rom 5:1-2; Eph 2:18) so that he could live within us and we could live within him. The word *hilasmos* [TG2434, ZG2662] (sacrifice) is the noun form of the verb *hilaskomai* [TG2433, ZG2661], which in classical Greek meant "to appease" but in the NT means "to atone" or "to expiate" (see note on 2:2).

4:12 *No one has ever seen God.* This statement reiterates what John said in the prologue to his Gospel (John 1:18), which recalls what God said to Moses in Exod 33:20. Moses wanted to see God's glory, but he was not allowed to gaze directly upon God's glory; God told him that no man could see God's face and live. In John 6:46, Jesus said that no one has seen the Father except he who is of God—this one has seen the Father. This means that only the Son, who is himself God, has seen God and can communicate his glory to people.

his love is brought to full expression in us. This means that the believers' love for each other, finding its source in God's love, has ripened and matured so as to find expression in self-sacrifice.

4:13 *God has given us his Spirit as proof that we live in him and he in us.* Lit., "He has given us . . ." The subject of this sentence could also be "Jesus" because the mutual abiding is often spoken of as a spiritual reality between Jesus Christ and the believers. If so, it could be rendered "Jesus gave us of his own Spirit." This means that the Spirit is not some anonymous source of inspiration but the representative of Christ himself. After Jesus' resurrection, his Spirit could live in the believers and the believers could live in his Spirit. According to John 14:16-20, the disciples would begin to experience what it meant to live in God and have God live in them once they had received the Paraclete, the Spirit of truth. Thereafter, they would know that the Son is in the Father, and they are in the Son, and the Son is in them (John 14:20). See comments on 3:24.

4:14 *we have seen with our own eyes and now testify that the Father sent his Son.* The "we" refers to the apostles and other eyewitnesses of Christ's life on earth (see comments on 1:1-4). They were appointed by Christ to testify to others about their firsthand, eyewitness experiences (1:3). Therefore, Christians have two proofs of God's love for us: (1) the indwelling presence of God's Spirit and (2) the testimony of the apostles and other eyewitnesses of Jesus.

to be the Savior of the world. The expression "Savior of the world" occurs only one other time in the NT—in John's Gospel in the passage where the Samaritans recognize that Jesus is the Messiah (4:42). John made it clear that Jesus was not just the Jews' Messiah but the world's Savior, the Deliverer of all those who put their trust in him.

4:15 *All who confess that Jesus is the Son of God.* The verb translated "confess" is an aorist subjunctive (*homologēsē* [TG3670, ZG3933]). This *could* imply that this confession is done once for all; however, the aorist does not always signal once-for-all action. When a person confesses that Jesus is the Son of God, he or she is declaring that they believe that Jesus is God's unique Son.

have God living in them, and they live in God. The person who believes in Christ is indwelt by God and simultaneously dwells in God. This mutual indwelling, experienced by the Father and Son (John 10:38; 14:10; 17:21), is a special privilege for the believers (cf. John 14:20; 15:5; 17:21-24).

4:16 We. This pronoun refers to John and his readers, rather than just the apostles and/or John's coworkers.

know how much God loves us. John is not so much speaking of the degree ("how much") of love but of the specific quality of love God has for us.

God is love. Only three times in the NT is such a short definition of God given, all in the writings of John. According to John, "God is Spirit" (John 4:24), "God is light" (1 John 1:5), and "God is love" (1 John 4:8, 16).

4:17 as we live in God, our love grows more perfect. The word "perfect" here does not mean "that which is flawless" but that which is "mature and complete." This perfection develops our relationship with God, who is love.

So we will not be afraid on the day of judgment, but we can face him with confidence. Confidence is the opposite of "fear" (4:18). The result of living with Christ and growing more perfect in love is confidence in the day of judgment, which is terrifying to other people (Acts 24:25; Rom 2:16).

because we live like Jesus here in this world. Lit., "because as that One [Jesus] is, so are we in this world." This causal explanation is astounding because it says that Christians are like Jesus in the sense that they bear his likeness in this world. This, of course, is the ideal of Christlikeness, which exists to one degree or another in various believers. But John did not qualify his statement, so it could be read to mean that all Christians—regardless of maturation—are now even as Christ is, when experience tells us that this is not so. Noting this difficulty, several scribes tried to fix it in various ways. One eleventh-century ms (2138) exhibits, in one way or another, all the changes found in several other mss (including ℵ). Ms 2138 reads, "We may have confidence in the day of judgment, because just as that One was blameless and pure in the world, so we, who [also] have human nature, will be in this world" (cf. Comfort 2007:[1 John 4:17]). This fix allows for the believers to be like Christ with respect to his humanity and also allows for a maturation process (note the future tense: "will be").

4:19 We love each other. Cf. NLT mg: "Greek We love. Other mss read We love God; still others read We love him." These three variant readings are supported by different mss: (1) "We love" (A B 1739); (2) "We love God" (ℵ 048 33); and (3) "We love him" (Ψ 𝔐—so TR). Textual criticism favors the simple expression, "We love." Ancient scribes felt compelled to provide a direct object and chose "God" or "him." The NLT translators supplied "each other" because the context of 1 John 4 speaks about community love. However, it is best to omit any direct object—John was emphasizing that we are now able to truly *love* because God demonstrated what love is when he sent his Son to die for our sins (cf. Comfort 2007:[1 John 4:19]).

because he loved us first. God is always the initiator (see comments on 4:9-10).

4:20 If someone says, "I love God." This is a very rare statement, found only here in the NT. John, again, was probably quoting those spiritual elitists who made boasts about their relationship with God. This boast—"I love God"—can be tested by one's love for the community of God. If such a person rejects other believers or refuses to fellowship with them, his or her love for God should be questioned. Such was the case with Diotrephes, who refused to have fellowship with John and his coworkers (cf. 3 John 9-10).

4:21 *he has given us this command: Those who love God must also love their Christian brothers and sisters.* This is a powerful summary statement. Not only is it natural to love God's children if we love God (4:20); it is also God's command.

COMMENTARY

From 3:11 through 3:23 John's major theme is love. At 3:23 he mentions the Spirit and went into a brief excursus in 4:1-6 concerning the discernment of false spirits. At 4:7 John resumes and elaborates on a major theme in this epistle: Love among Christians demonstrates love for God and love from God, for God is love. And that love was demonstrated unmistakably in Jesus in order to solve the problem of sin.

Our recognition of Jesus as the Son of God and the Savior of the world leads believers to know the love of God. This love flows through us to others and is evidence of our relationship to God. This love also gives us the assurance of being accepted by God, to the extent that even our fears of the final judgment are overcome.

"God is love" (4:8) is one of the three great Johannine expressions of the nature of God. The other two are "God is light" (1:5) and "God is Spirit" (John 4:24). The statement "God is love" is certainly one of the most profound divine revelations. Our inability to fully grasp its import lies in our defective use and understanding of the term "love." We tend to think of love as an emotion, a feeling, or maybe a fluctuating attribute. However, "God is love" is properly interpreted as meaning that God, self-conscious and moral, creates, sustains, and orders all things in love. Love is the very essence of God. Of no other person could it possibly be said that "he is love" or "she is love." Only God is completely loving because love is his very entity, nature, and character. When John writes "God is love," he is giving the reader the clearest, briefest, most comprehensive expression possible of the nature of God.

Nothing in God is in the slightest way incompatible with love; in him there is no malice, no malignity, no coldness, no indifference, no malevolence, no spite, no rancor. Rather, his nature demonstrates consistency in fidelity, tenderness, compassion, active favor, loyalty, covenant-keeping, longsuffering, and gracious giving. God's love is ever abounding, ever present, and ever beneficial; his love can never be diminished in the slightest way. God's love is so boundless that it is impossible either by experience or by definition to scale its heights or fathom its depths (cf. Eph. 3:17-19).

"God is love" manifested itself singularly in his gracious act of sending his only Son, Jesus Christ, into the world to take upon himself the consequences of peoples' sins, thereby to absolve them of their guilt and to free them to live eternally in his love. In other words, God loved in a way that resulted in a gift. The Word made flesh is Love Incarnate. Love moved to action so efficaciously that it has reached the darkest, most dismal, most unheavenly people. "God is love" is basic to the gospel message. God loves and thus gives—his Son, forgiveness, salvation, fellowship, eternal life. It is in the crucifixion and resurrection of Jesus Christ that we see most clearly the love of God. Love is written all over the Cross. It is the gospel. There would be no gospel—no Good News—without love.

True fellowship with God is based on love (4:11). The Son showed love for the Father by obeying his commands. The believer shows love for the Son by obeying his command to love one another. Love is a divine reality coming to believers from the Father, through the Son, returning from them through Christ to the Father, marking them as true believers and proving the authenticity of Christ's mission.

In all of this it must be remembered that John's exposé on love (*agapē* [TG26, ZG27]) is not primarily to encourage individuals to love God privately but to motivate the brothers and sisters in God's community to love one another. This love proves the reality of one's personal love for God. Those who have received God's gift of life are endowed with the nature of God and thereby become partakers of the divine love. Our love for fellow Christians provides proof of our spiritual birth and relationship with God (4:20). Anyone in whom God lives will naturally reflect his character. To claim to know God while failing to love is a false claim. It is just as false as claiming to know God, who is light, while still living in darkness (1:5-6).

God's supreme love for us is the motive of our love to one another (4:11). Remember, God's great initiating love is an expression of true and real love, and in our appreciation and gratitude of such love, we should be the initiators of loving fellow believers. It is in loving one another that we really demonstrate our love for God.

The apostles had the privilege of seeing God manifest in the flesh (1:1-3; 4:14; John 1:14), a privilege that later believers do not have in this life. Nonetheless, having never seen Jesus, we still love him, even as Peter said (1 Pet 1:8). But we cannot claim to love someone we have never seen and at the same time despise those who belong to him. Evidently, John made this point to expose the secessionists to the Johannine community (see "Date and Occasion of Writing" in the Introduction; and comments on 2:19). They must have talked about their great "love for God." So John said to them: "How do you measure your love for God?" The evidence of one's love for God is one's love for fellow believers. That is measurable, evidential, and observable. If we do not love our Christian brothers and sisters, who are God's visible representatives, how can we love the invisible God?

All believers need to reach maturity in love for God and love for each other. As we mature in love, we will be motivated by love to please God. Until we mature, we will be motivated by fear—fear of God's punishment. But John affirms that it is love, not fear, that should motivate us (4:17-18). We are in a new era—of the new covenant—where God is the initiator and supplier. As he supplies the love, we receive, and in that receiving, fear is cast out. Eventually, we will have "perfect" love—that is, our love will have reached maturity. We must not think of "perfect" as meaning flawless. A fully developed apple is mature, "perfect," even if it has bumps, scabs, and bruises. None of us will be flawless and faultless in this lifetime, but we can become mature in our love for God and his people.

John's words are challenging, especially those in 4:17-18, because he himself could not have said these things if they were not real to him. Thus, we gather that he probably considered himself to have matured to the extent that (1) he was a living representative of Jesus Christ on earth, and (2) he was motivated by pure love, not fear, to please the Lord. Because he knew that he was motivated by love, he did not fear the day of judgment. The extent to which we fear the day of judgment is a converse measure of how truly we are living in God's love. Let us take John as our example to live in God, who is love, and thereby love one another. May this love be perfected in us.

◆ IV. Overcoming Hindrances to Community Fellowship (5:1-21)
A. Overcoming the World (5:1-5)

Everyone who believes that Jesus is the Christ* has become a child of God. And everyone who loves the Father loves his children, too. ²We know we love God's children if we love God and obey his commandments. ³Loving God means keeping his commandments, and his command-ments are not burdensome. ⁴For every child of God defeats this evil world, and we achieve this victory through our faith. ⁵And who can win this battle against the world? Only those who believe that Jesus is the Son of God.

5:1 Or *the Messiah.*

NOTES

5:1 *Everyone who believes that Jesus is the Christ.* Here, as in the Gospel of John, people are called upon to believe first that Jesus is the Christ, God's Anointed One, and then also to believe that he is the Son of God (cf. 5:5; John 20:31). It is possible that John was addressing the proto-gnostics who denied the Incarnation (see note on 5:6).

And everyone who loves the Father loves his children, too. Lit., "Everyone loving the One who gives birth loves also the one born of him." This is the reading supported by A P 1739 𝔐 syr. Other mss (B 044 048^vid 33 cop) read, "Everyone loving the One who gives birth loves also the one born." Two mss (א 69) read, "Everyone loving the One who gives birth loves also that which is born." This last reading means that everyone who loves the Father (the One who has begotten) loves the collective community of believers (see note on 5:4 for a similar collective construction; cf. Comfort 2007:[1 John 5:1]). All other mss have the masculine singular rather than this neuter construction.

5:2 *We know we love God's children if we love God and obey his commandments.* "Obey" is a synonym for "keep" (*tērōmen* [TG5083, ZG5498]), a reading found in א P (048) 𝔐. A reading found in other mss (B 044 81 1739) is "do" (*poiōmen* [TG4160, ZG4472]). The first reading ("we keep") is probably the result of scribal assimilation to 5:3 (as well as to 2:3-5; 3:22, 24). The meaning of the verse, however, is not affected greatly.

Just as our love for our brothers and sisters is the sign and test of our love for God, so our love for God, tested by obedience, is the only basis of our love for our brothers and sisters. John was not contradicting what he said in 4:20-21; rather, he was insisting that love for God and love for our brothers and sisters cannot be separated.

5:3 *Loving God means keeping his commandments, and his commandments are not burdensome.* This is an extension of what Jesus said to his disciples, as recorded in the Gospel of John. He really only had one preeminent commandment for them: Love one another (John 13:34; 15:17).

5:4 *For every child of God defeats this evil world.* This is one way to interpret the text, but it misses a significant point. The Greek literally reads, "Whatever is born of God conquers the world" (as in NRSV). The Greek term for "whatever" is *pan to* [TG3956/3588, ZG4246/3836]. John used this collective neuter construction to designate the collective unit of believers, not just a single believer. In other words, it refers to the whole body of those begotten by God (cf. Manson 1947:27). In the next verse he speaks of the individual. This same pattern—of first speaking of the collective body of believers and then of each individual believer—is found in John 6:37, 39; 17:2, 24 (cf. Comfort 1994:191).

COMMENTARY

In this section, John encourages faith in Jesus as the Christ and as the Son of God. John concluded his Gospel (at the end of ch 20, before adding a prologue) in the same way. In the Gospel he said, "These are written so that you may continue to believe that Jesus is the Messiah, the Son of God, and that by believing in him you will have life by the power of his name" (John 20:31). When John speaks of believing in Jesus as the Christ, he means that people must believe that Jesus of Nazareth was God's one and only Anointed One. He was anointed by God's Spirit to preach the gospel, heal the sick, raise the dead, die on the cross for our sins, and rise from the dead to become our life. When John speaks of believing in Jesus as the Son of God, he means that people must believe that Jesus of Nazareth was God become human, God come from heaven to earth in human flesh. They must believe that he has always been the Son of God, coeternal with the Father, sharing the Father's glory from everlasting. And they must believe that he and he alone is the unique Son of God. No one else can legitimately make that claim because no one else has proven to be deity by rising from the dead (cf. Rom 1:3-4).

The belief John speaks of is not a one-time event. According to him, both in his Gospel and this epistle, faith in Christ must be ongoing and perpetual. This is indicated by his habitual use of the present tense for "believe" (the present participle *pisteuōn* [TG4100, ZG4409] is used both in 5:1 and 5:5). Though Christians can point to a day when they first began to believe, they must continue to be believers every day.

We must always remember that all who believe that Jesus is the Christ, the Son of God, are our brothers and sisters—no matter what they think about other biblical matters, such as the Rapture, the millennial kingdom, speaking in tongues, baptism, eternal punishment, and so on. We should love all those who share the same faith we have in Jesus as the Christ, the Son of God, because we all have the same Father and the same divine life.

As was noted above (see notes on 5:1 and 5:4), John calls upon the believers to love the collective community of believers. This love proves each believer's love for God. And, furthermore, it is in this community that we have the power to overcome the evil forces of the world because the community of faith keeps encouraging each of us to stay believers, to remain faithful to Christ. It is by this kind of believing that we gain victory over the world system, which is permeated with false, anti-Christian teachings. By holding fast to our faith in Jesus as God's Son, we will not be steered away to false teachings. It is belief, not activity, that overcomes the world, and absolutely no one overcomes the world apart from believing that Jesus is the Son of God. And no one can do this alone. The collective body of regenerated believers—the community as a unit—has the power to conquer.

◆   B. Discerning Truth from Falsehood and Keeping Eternal Life (5:6-12)

⁶And Jesus Christ was revealed as God's Son by his baptism in water and by shedding his blood on the cross*—not by water only, but by water and blood. And the Spirit, who is truth, confirms it with his testimony. ⁷So we have these three witnesses*—⁸the Spirit, the water, and the blood—and all three agree. ⁹Since we believe human testimony, surely we can believe the greater testimony that comes from God. And God has testified about his Son. ¹⁰All who believe in the Son of God know in their hearts that this testimony is true. Those who don't believe this are actually calling God a liar because they don't believe what God has testified about his Son.

¹¹And this is what God has testified: He has given us eternal life, and this life is in his Son. ¹²Whoever has the Son has life; whoever does not have God's Son does not have life.

5:6 Greek *This is he who came by water and blood.*   **5:7** A few very late manuscripts add *in heaven—the Father, the Word, and the Holy Spirit, and these three are one. And we have three witnesses on earth.*

NOTES

5:6 *Jesus Christ was revealed as God's Son by his baptism in water and by shedding his blood on the cross.* Lit., "This is the one coming by water and blood" (cf. NLT mg). As in 4:2 (see note), this points to Christ's incarnation, as well as to his entire life in the flesh. "John is not, of course, thinking narrowly of the mere moment when the Incarnation became a reality at the birth of Jesus; he is thinking of the total act of his coming into the world" (Marshall 1978:231).

The phrase "water and blood" can mean one of two things in this context: (1) The phrase may refer to Christ's death on the cross, at which time he was pierced and blood and water flowed out (John 19:34-35). John witnessed this, and asserted the importance of this occurrence. (2) The phrase "water and blood" could refer to Christ's baptism (water) and crucifixion (blood). This is more likely the correct interpretation (see commentary below for discussion.)

And the Spirit, who is truth, confirms it with his testimony. The Spirit bears witness to the truth of Christ's life and work (cf. John 15:26; 16:13-15). This is why he is called "the Spirit of truth." The Spirit's primary role is to reveal Christ to the believers and to affirm Christ's message. This statement also affirms that the truth proclaimed by John is the truth proclaimed by the Spirit. Others could claim to have the Spirit and thereby speak certain truths, but all so-claimed "speaking from the Spirit" must accord with the apostolic truths (cf. 2:20, 27).

5:7-8 As is noted in the NLT mg, there is a substantially longer version of this passage, which appears in the KJV and NKJV as follows (the italic type shows the extra words):

> For there are three that bear witness *in heaven: the Father, the Word, and the Holy Spirit; and these three are one. And there are three that bear witness on earth:* the Spirit, the water; and the blood, and the three agree as one.

This famous passage, called "the heavenly witness," has been the object of much discussion. The textual evidence against its inclusion is substantial: ℵ A B (044) 𝔐 syr cop arm eth. As such, it does not appear in any of the earliest Greek mss nor in the majority of Greek mss; furthermore, it does not appear in any of the translations, except some of the Latin versions. The first time this passage appears in the longer form (with the heavenly witness) is in the treatise entitled *Liber Apologeticus* (ch 4), attributed to the Spanish heretic Priscillian (died c. 385) or his follower, Bishop Instantius. Metzger said, "Apparently the gloss arose when the original passage was understood to symbolize the Trinity (through the mention of the three witnesses; the Spirit, the water, and the blood), an interpretation which may have been written first as a marginal note that afterwards found its way into the text" (1994:648). The gloss showed up in the writings of Latin Fathers in North Africa and Italy (as part of the text of the epistle) from the fifth century onward, and it found its way into more and more copies of the Latin Vulgate. But "the heavenly witnesses" cannot be found in any Greek ms prior to the eleventh century, and it was never cited by any Greek Father.

Erasmus did not include "the heavenly witnesses" in the first two editions of his Greek NT. He was criticized for this by defenders of the Latin Vulgate. Erasmus, in reply, said that he would include it if he could see it in any one Greek ms. In turn, a ms (most likely the Monfort Ms, 61) was especially produced to contain the passage. Erasmus kept his promise; he included it in the third edition of his Greek NT. From there it became incorporated into the TR and hence was translated in the KJV (as well as in the NKJV).

5:9 *Since we believe human testimony.* The law required two or three witnesses as adequate testimony to decide what was true.

God has testified about his Son. This is fully developed in John 5:31-47, where Jesus affirms his Father's witness.

5:10 *All who believe in the Son of God know in their hearts that this testimony is true.* Lit., "Those who believe in the Son of God have the testimony in themselves." When a person becomes a child of God (by believing that Jesus is the Son of God), he or she knows it without any doubt because the Spirit who regenerated them gives them an inner witness to that reality (cf. Rom 8:16; Gal 4:6).

Those who don't believe this. Lit., "those who do not believe God"; this is supported by ℵ B P 044 1739mg. Other witnesses (A 1739* Vulgate), showing assimilation to the first clause, read, "those who do not believe the Son of God."

5:11 *And this is what God has testified: He has given us eternal life, and this life is in his Son.* The divine, eternal life (Eph 4:18) resides in Christ, who makes it available to all who believe in him. Jesus Christ is life (John 1:4; 14:6)—life is available in him (2 Tim 1:10) and in no other (see note on 5:12). Those who do not have him remain in death.

5:12 *Whoever has the Son has life; whoever does not have God's Son does not have life.* Human beings do not have life in themselves; they receive their life from God's Son. The Son of God does not receive his life from any exterior source; he has life in himself and is life; he is the source of his very own life, a uniquely divine characteristic, unshared by any created being. Those who have the Son of God living in them have eternal life now—not life someday, not life later on, not conditional life, but life, eternal life, now.

COMMENTARY

In our day, we hear people left and right denying that Jesus is God. In the days of the early church, there were just as many denying that Jesus was a true human being. They did this because they could not conceive of God, being a pure spirit, taking on actual human flesh, for that would mean that God had tarnished himself with sin. Therefore, they believed that Jesus had only the appearance of humanity—that is, he *seemed* to be human but wasn't really. (Hence, the name "Docetists," from the Greek word *dokeō* [TG1380, ZG1506], "appear, seem").

In John's day the Docetists (and specifically a man named Cerinthus, who was a Docetist) denied Christ's true and lasting humanity, saying that Christ could not have had real flesh and real blood. Refuting this heresy, John affirmed that he saw Jesus in the flesh (see 1:1-4 and comments), and he saw Jesus shed his blood and die (see comments on 4:2).

In order to accommodate his teachings, Cerinthus developed the heresy (later known as the adoptionist heresy) that Jesus of Nazareth became "the Christ" at his baptism and ceased being "the Christ" prior to his death. In other words, he taught that "the Christ" descended into the man Jesus after his baptism and then left him prior to his crucifixion. Cerinthus's heresy comes to us through the writings of Irenaeus:

> [Cerinthus] represented Jesus as having not been born of a virgin, but as being the son of Joseph and Mary according to the ordinary course of human generation, while he nevertheless was more righteous, prudent, and wise than other men. Moreover, after his baptism, Christ descended upon him in the form of a dove from the Supreme Ruler, and that then he proclaimed the unknown Father, and performed miracles. But at last Christ departed from Jesus, and that then Jesus suffered and rose again, while Christ remained impassible, inasmuch as he was a spiritual being." (*Heresies* 3.3.4)

In countering this heresy, John argued that Jesus was the Christ, the Son of God "through water" (= prior to, during, and after his baptism), as well as "through blood" (= prior to, during, and after his death on the cross). F. F. Bruce (1970:118-119) elaborates:

> The sequence "water and blood" is not accidental, but corresponds to the historical sequence of our Lord's baptism and passion. Cerinthus, we recall, taught that "the Christ" (a spiritual being) came down on the man Jesus when He was baptized but left Him before He died. The Christ, that is to say, came through water (baptism) but not through blood (death). To this misrepresentation of the truth John replies that the One whom believers acknowledge to be the Son of God (verse 5) came "not with the water only but with the water and with the blood."

The One who died on the cross was as truly the Christ, the Son of God, as the One who was baptized in the Jordan. In words that must have been clear to his original readers, John said, "And Jesus Christ was revealed as God's Son by his baptism in water and by shedding his blood on the cross—not by water only, but by water and blood. And the Spirit, who is truth, confirms it with his testimony" (5:6). What we can gather from this statement is that John was speaking of three critical phases in Jesus' life where he was manifested as God Incarnate, the Son of God in human form. This was made evident at his baptism (= the water), his death (= the blood), and his resurrection (= the Spirit). At his baptism, the man Jesus was declared God's beloved Son (cf. Matt 3:16-17). At his crucifixion, a man shedding blood was recognized by others as "God's Son" (cf. Mark 15:39). In resurrection, he was designated by the Spirit as the Son of God in power (Rom 1:3-4). This tri-fold testimony is unified in one aspect: Each event demonstrated that the man Jesus was the divine Son of God.

These divinely given witnesses should convince us that Jesus is the Son of God. According to Jewish law, the testimony of one man was not a valid witness. Truth or validity has to be established by two or three witnesses (Deut 17:7; 19:15). Therefore, Jesus' self-witness would not validate his claims; he needed the witness of another. That other witness was his Father. Of course, he had more witnesses than just one. In the Gospel of John, Jesus defended his deity with a five-fold witness. In response to the Jewish leaders who had questioned his authority and assaulted his identity, Jesus indicated that he had five very reliable witnesses: (1) the Father himself (John 5:31-32, 37), (2) John the Baptist (John 5:33-35), (3) his own works (John 5:36), (4) the Scriptures (John 5:39-40), and (5) Moses (John 5:45-47). But of all these witnesses the greatest one comes from the Father. And his witness is transferred to us when we receive the Spirit. God's Spirit, alive in our spirits, gives witness to the fact that everything Jesus said and did is true. In fact, that is the primary function of the Spirit—to testify and reveal Jesus to each and every believer (cf. John 14:26; 15:26; 16:7-13).

Those who do not believe that Jesus is the Son of God should realize that by rejecting what God has so plainly told us, they are calling God a liar (5:10). This has two aspects: refusing to believe what God has said about his Son, and in consequence, refusing to believe in Christ who, because he is God's Son, is the only one who can save people. What better reason can we have for believing something than that God says it is true?

Those who believe receive the greatest gift from God: eternal life. This is not something we have to wait to get. We have eternal life now; we possess a new nature and enjoy fellowship with God. Therefore, a believer need not be uncertain about whether he or she has eternal life. Those who have eternal life now (as a present reality and experience) are assured of everlasting life in the future.

◆   ## C. Conclusion: Helping the Wayward Return to the Fellowship (5:13-21)

13I have written this to you who believe in the name of the Son of God, so that you may know you have eternal life. 14And we are confident that he hears us whenever we ask for anything that pleases him. 15And since we know he hears us when we make our requests, we also know that he will give us what we ask for.

16If you see a Christian brother or sister* sinning in a way that does not lead to death, you should pray, and God will give that person life. But there is a sin that leads to death, and I am not saying you should pray for those who commit it. 17All wicked actions are sin, but not every sin leads to death.

18We know that God's children do not make a practice of sinning, for God's Son

holds them securely, and the evil one cannot touch them. [19]We know that we are
children of God and that the world around
us is under the control of the evil one.

[20]And we know that the Son of God has
come, and he has given us understanding
so that we can know the true God.* And

now we live in fellowship with the true
God because we live in fellowship with his
Son, Jesus Christ. He is the only true God,
and he is eternal life.

[21]Dear children, keep away from anything that might take God's place in your
hearts.*

5:16 Greek *a brother.*   5:20 Greek *the one who is true.*   5:21 Greek *keep yourselves from idols.*

NOTES

5:13 *I have written this to you who believe in the name of the Son of God, so that you may know you have eternal life.* This has excellent documentary support: ℵ* (A) B 0296. This is expanded in the TR (following P 𝔐) as follows: "and that you may continue to believe in the name of the Son of God" (NKJV; see also KJV). The expansion was intended to make this verse more closely follow John 20:31 (see commentary below). In its shorter form, this verse sufficiently concludes the previous section on eternal life and introduces the conclusion, which also pertains to eternal life (5:16, 20).

5:15 *And since we know he hears us when we make our requests, we also know that he will give us what we ask for.* We should not think that these requests are for our personal benefit. Prayer in line with God's will is prayer for the benefit of God's Kingdom, as the next verses (5:16-17) illustrate.

5:16 *sinning in a way that does not lead to death . . . a sin that leads to death.* What is the difference between the "sin that leads to death" and "the sin that does not lead to death"? Some commentators (Marshall 1978:274; Burge 1996:216) point out that these two kinds of sin are spoken of in the OT: (1) unconscious or accidental sins (Lev 4:2, 13, 22, 27; 5:15-18; Num 15:27-31); and (2) intentional sins, which could be punished by exile (Num 15:30-31) or death (Deut 17:12). But how this applies to Christians is not totally clear. (See commentary for further discussion.)

5:18 This verse appears in two ways in various translations because of a textual variant in the Greek mss: (1) Most modern versions (RSV, NRSV, NASB, NIV, NEB, NJB) read, "We know that any one born of God does not sin, but He who was born of God keeps *him,* and the evil one does not touch him." (This follows A* B it.) (2) The KJV and NKJV read, "We know that whoever is born of God does not sin; but he who has been born of God keeps *himself,* and the wicked one does not touch him." (This follows ℵ A^c P 044 33 1739.) The difference between the two readings revolves around the pronouns "him" (*auton* [TG846, ZG899]) and "himself" (*heauton* [TG1438, ZG1571]). The difference in meanings also stems from the interpretation of the phrase "the one born of God" (*ho gennētheis* [TG1080, ZG1164]), which could be a reference to Christ or to the Christian. The first reading affirms the inter-pretation that it is Christ; the second reading supports the interpretation that it is a Chris-tian. The first reading indicates that the Son of God keeps the believer from sin. The second reading indicates that the believer, as a son of God, keeps himself from sin.

Many commentators (see Marshall 1978:252; Smalley 1984:293; Schnackenburg 1979:280; Metzger 1994:650) favor the first reading because (1) the first clause of this verse already mentions the believer who is born of God, (2) John consistently used the perfect tense to describe the believer who has become a son of God (2:29; 3:9; 4:7; 5:1, 4, 18a) whereas here the aorist is used (*ho gennētheis*), and (3) there is little or no security in the fact that the believer must keep himself. Rather, it is the One begotten of God, the Son of God, who keeps each believer from the evil one. This interpretation is made explicit in the NLT.

5:20 *we can know the true God.* This is based on the textual variant found in A Ψ 33 1739. The more likely reading, as found in ℵc B 81 syrᵖ copᵇᵒ, is simply, "We can know the true one."

we live in fellowship with the true God because we live in fellowship with his Son, Jesus Christ. To be in God is to be in God's Son; for when we are united to the Son, we are also united to the Father (cf. John 17:21-24).

Jesus Christ. He is the only true God. The word behind "he" is *houtos* [TG3778, ZG4047], meaning "this one" (the nearest one just mentioned); thus, it refers to the person just named, "Jesus Christ." A large number of scholars are convinced that *houtos* refers to Jesus Christ and therefore think that John was unequivocally asserting that Jesus Christ is "the true God" (*ho alēthinos theos* [TG228/2316, ZG240/2536]). A full list with bibliography is supplied by Harris (1992:249). I also hold that John was saying that Jesus Christ is the true God. Jesus' deity is elsewhere affirmed in John's writings (John 1:1, 18; 8:58; 10:30; 20:28) as well as in other NT passages, such as Rom 9:5; Titus 2:13; 2 Pet 1:1. Harris (1992:250-252), however, thinks the wording here is saying that "God" (5:19) is the "true God" noted in 5:20. But what is the point of saying this? Of course, God is the true God. John would not have needed to say this. Rather, he was affirming Jesus' deity, as he had earlier affirmed Jesus' humanity (4:1-6). This is the more natural reading of the Greek.

and he is eternal life. While the Father is the source of eternal life, Jesus Christ reveals that life and through his death makes that life available to the believers. He himself is the "eternal life" (John 14:6; cf. John 1:4).

5:21 *keep away from anything that might take God's place in your hearts.* Lit., "keep yourselves from idols" (cf. NLT mg). The thrust of the functionally equivalent translation is to help the modern reader understand that John was probably not talking about actual idols but about those things that rob Jesus of the worship due him as true God (5:20). It should also be noted that this ending is unlike all the other endings to NT epistles, which conclude either with a doxology or personal greeting or both. The abruptness of the ending affirms the idea that 1 John was not ever written as a letter; rather, it was a kind of treatise or manifesto, like a pamphlet.

COMMENTARY

The final nine verses of John's epistle comprise the epilogue. This particular epilogue has two functions: to summarize the main body of the writing and to prompt the believers to apply what they have heard.

First John 5:13 provides John's reason for writing the epistle. Remarkably, the wording is nearly identical to that found in John 20:31, John's purpose in writing his Gospel. But there is a difference. Whereas the Gospel encourages the continuance of faith in the Son of God as the means to enjoying the divine life, the verse in the epistle affirms the possession of divine life for all who believe in the Son of God. In both cases, John wanted his readers to be sure that they had eternal life. And this security is the basis for the other aim of John's letter: that they would be full of joy (1:4).

Because Christians possess and enjoy the life of God, we have the confidence that we are his children, which gives us confidence and boldness when we make our requests to God. When we choose to place our wills in line with God's will, the Holy Spirit in us will teach us to understand God's will more completely, and he will enable us to pray in line with God's will. This is the key to getting our prayers answered. Jesus himself was a model of this: He taught us to pray for God's will to be accomplished on earth (Matt 6:10). And he chose God's will over his own in accepting the bitter cup—death on the cross (Matt 26:39-42).

This much, as modern readers, we can understand quite clearly. But what John asked his readers to specifically pray for is somewhat beyond our ability to grasp because we are not told what the sin that "leads to death" is (5:17). Evidently, his readers knew what he was saying, but we don't exactly know. F. F. Bruce said, "The distinction is one which John's readers were expected to recognize. But it is difficult to see how they could recognize the distinction except by the result. Elsewhere in the NT instances occur of sins which caused the death of the persons committing them, when these persons were church members" (1970:124). But the context of 1 John leads us to believe that John was not talking about physical death but spiritual death. The sin that led to this kind of death was the sin of leaving the apostolic truths concerning Jesus and pursuing Docetic gnosticism. A brother in Christ could be deceived to follow this errant way, as indeed many early Christians did. Such brothers and sisters could see the errors of this way and return to the truth. Thus, John encouraged the believers to pray for such people before these straying believers went all the way down the road that leads to death. Of course, some people had already gone that way. These were those who had left the community of true believers, thereby exposing the fact that they never really belonged among God's people (see 2:19 and comments). There was no point in praying for them because they had denied that Jesus is the Christ, the Son of God, thereby leaving themselves in a condition of spiritual death.

Only those who have faith in Jesus Christ as God's Son have eternal life. This life empowers all the children of God to overcome the evil in the world around us. This life also gives us a true understanding of God and his Son, Jesus Christ. There are two kinds of knowledge mentioned by John in 5:20, one that is absolute and the other that is ongoing. Using the Greek word *oidamen* [TG1492, ZG3857], John said that we absolutely know that the Son of God has come in the flesh. The purpose of his coming to earth was to reveal God the Father and to enable the believers to know him experientially (cf. John 17:3). Then, John uses the Greek word *ginōskōmen* [TG1097, ZG1182]—that "we may get to know" the true one (i.e., God the Father). And how is it that we can know God? It is because we live in him by virtue of living in his Son (5:20b). This is one of the primary themes of John's Gospel and first epistle. The Son came to earth to bring the believers into God the Father by way of coming to live in him. The Son declared that he was the visible expression of the Father and the way for the believers to live in the Father (cf. John 14:1-18). To be in Jesus Christ is to be in God because Jesus Christ is "the true God" and he is "eternal life." Life is not a commodity. Life is a person—as Jesus said, "I am the way, the truth, and the life" (John 14:6). All three of these elements come together here at the end of John's epistle. Jesus is the way to the Father because he is the truth—the true One, the true God; and he gives eternal life to all who take this way!

Only God's life can truly be called "life" because all else that is called life eventually dies. God's life is eternal. The Greek New Testament has a special word for this eternal life; it is called *zōē* [TG2222, ZG2437]. The word *zōē* in classical Greek was used for life in general. There are a few examples of this meaning in the New Testament (Acts 17:25; Jas 4:14; Rev 16:3), but in all other instances in the New Testament the word was used to designate the divine, eternal life—the life of God (Eph 4:18). The word *zōē* is used to describe the eternal life, the divine life—present in Jesus and available as a gift to all who believe in Jesus as the Son of God. To receive *zōē* is to have God's life now and to be guaranteed eternal life in the future. All those who have received this life are true members of God's family.

To close, John tells his readers to keep themselves from idols. Though this ending is abrupt and lacks the kind of doxologies or conclusions found in other New Testament letters (see note on 5:21 and "Literary Style" in the Introduction), it is a fitting conclusion. Given the context of this epistle, "idols" is probably a general reference to false teachings that present false images of Jesus Christ, who is "the only true God, and he is eternal life" (5:20). To replace Jesus with heresy is idolatry. Even today readers must take heed that they let nothing turn their faith from the Jesus of the apostles—the divine Messiah, both God and man.

BIBLIOGRAPHY

See page 401, the bibliography for the Johannine epistles.

2 & 3 John

PHILIP W. COMFORT
AND
WENDELL C. HAWLEY

INTRODUCTION TO
2 & 3 John

THE TWO SHORTEST EPISTLES in the New Testament, 2 and 3 John, are gems in their own right. Second John, a miniature version of 1 John, extols those who live in the truth and live in love and warns against those who do not teach the apostolic truths about Jesus Christ—who, in some fashion or another, deny that he is the unique Son of the Father, the Son of God come in the flesh. Third John, giving us a window into the early church, presents us with two kinds of leaders: one that serves the Lord and others by living in the truth and practicing love, and another that refuses apostolic authority and loves himself more than the church.

AUTHOR

These two epistles were written by the same author, as is evident from their similarity of tone, style, and thematic development—all of which are also extremely similar to 1 John, which is undeniably similar to the fourth Gospel. The grammar, style, and vocabulary of 2 John compare very closely to 1 John. Five of the 13 verses of the second letter are almost identical with verses in 1 John (cf. 2 John 1 with 1 John 3:13; 2 John 2 with 1 John 2:4; 2 John 5 with 1 John 2:7 and 5:3; 2 John 7 with 1 John 2:18 and 4:2; 2 John 9 with 1 John 2:23-24). Third John has vocabulary and expressions that are distinctly similar, if not identical, to 2 John (cf. 3 John 4 with 2 John 4; 3 John 13-14 with 2 John 12), as well as to 1 John (cf. 3 John 11 with 1 John 3:6, 10). The style and voice are also markedly similar. Thus, we must conclude that the same writer who composed 2 John and 3 John also composed 1 John, the author of which was most likely John the apostle, the son of Zebedee (see "Author" in the Introduction to 1 John). In fact, it must be said that these two short letters would hardly have been included in the New Testament canon if their author was not the apostle John. Their authorship—by the beloved disciple—is what warranted their inclusion in the New Testament canon.

In both 2 John and 3 John, the writer calls himself an "elder" (2 John 1; 3 John 1). Quite literally, John was an old man at this point in his life. If he were 10 years (or so) younger than Jesus (who was born between 6 and 4 BC), then John would have been in his 80s (or thereabouts) when he wrote these two epistles (see below on date of writing).

DATE AND OCCASION OF WRITING

There is very little in the letters of 2 John or 3 John to point us to a date of writing. The similarities to 1 John strongly suggest a similar time period, around the late 80s or early 90s. The Second Epistle must have been written in the same time period as 1 John because it deals with the same issue—heresy regarding the human nature of Jesus Christ (2 John 7). It is a special warning for believers to not receive the traveling teachers who would be spreading the false teachings of the secessionists addressed in 1 John. The Third Epistle addresses related concerns: John cautioned Gaius about Diotrephes, who had evidently been affected by the secessionists to have a negative attitude about John and his coworkers.

The purpose of 2 John is manifold. In the first place, the recipient is urged to live in the truth and to continue practicing Christian love. The second and more compelling reason for the epistle is its warning against the deceivers who refused to acknowledge Jesus as the Christ and were actively recruiting others to join them. This same concern to prevent and correct false teaching prompted Paul to write Galatians (Gal 1:6), Colossians (Col 2:16-23), 2 Thessalonians (2 Thess 2:1-3), and 1 Timothy (1 Tim 4:1; 6:20-21). Other epistles were also written to deal with false teachers and their doctrines (cf. 2 Pet 2:1ff; Jude 3-4). John's first two epistles were written specifically as antidotes to the poisonous effects of Docetic gnosticism, which was infecting many of the early churches. Third, the epistle was written to exhort the Christians to close their home meetings to false teachers (2 John 9-10).

Third, John was written by John to commend Gaius and the other Christians in the same local church for living in the truth. He also commended Gaius for the hospitality he had given to those who were traveling "for the sake of the Name" (3 John 7, NIV). These traveling teachers had spoken well of Gaius's love for the church. In contrast to Gaius stood Diotrephes, whose love of power and authority motivated him not only to defy the authority of the elder John, but also to convince others to follow his defiance. He had refused to receive the coworkers sent by John. (Interestingly, Diotrophes was doing to John's emissaries the very thing John had told his churches to do to the false teachers in 2 John. He was treating John and his coworkers as false teachers.) Thus, John indicated in this letter that he would come to the church and set things in order.

AUDIENCE

Second and Third John have been placed among the General Epistles (also known as the Catholic Epistles) by virtue of their association with 1 John. But they are not, by content, General Epistles. Second John was addressed to an individual or a specific local church, and 3 John was addressed to a specific individual, Gaius.

Second John was written to a "chosen lady and to her children" (2 John 1). Some commentators think this refers to a specific woman and her actual, physical children (Smith 1979:162; Morris 1970:1271). Accordingly, some think that the Greek word for "lady" (*kuria* [TG2959, ZG3257]) is a proper name, "Cyria"; this view was held by Athanasius (see note on 2 John 1). Clement of Alexandria in *Adumbrations* (see *Fragments of Clement of Alexandria* 1.4) said, "John's Second Epistle was written to a certain Babylonian lady named Electa," thus taking the word for "chosen" or "elect" as a proper name.

Most modern commentators think John was using this address as a surrogate for a particular local church, as perhaps Peter also did in 1 Peter 5:13 (cf. Smalley 1984:318; Marshall 1978:10; Burge 1996:232). They argue that the nature of the epistle points to a corporate personality, the local church (see comments on 2 John 5, 6, 8, 10, 12). As such, 2 John was probably sent to one of the churches in the Johannine community of churches, which was a cluster of churches in Asia Minor that were the recipients of John's apostolic ministry.

Another approach to identifying the addressee is to view this letter as being addressed to a specific woman *and* a local church that met in that woman's house. The New Testament gives us a picture of the early church wherein believers met in houses. This is the case in the book of Acts (cf. 2:46; 5:42; 8:3; 12:5, 12), and it can be gathered from reading the New Testament epistles that there were similar situations elsewhere (cf. Rom 16:3-5, 14-15; 1 Cor 16:19-20; Col 4:15-16; Phlm 1-2). We know that some of these homes, where the church gathered, belonged to women—or, at least were known by the name of the lady of the house. The church in Jerusalem gathered in the house of Mary (the mother of John Mark) to pray for Peter (Acts 12:5-12), and the natural conclusion is that the church habitually gathered there. The church in Corinth at one time assembled in the home of Priscilla and Aquila (Rom 16:3-5), and when Priscilla and Aquila lived in Ephesus, an assembly gathered in their home there (1 Cor 16:19-20). According to Colossians 4:15, the church in Laodicea assembled in the home of Nymphas—indeed, Paul specifically calls it "the church in her house." (For more discussion on "house churches" in the NT, see Comfort 1993:153-158.) In light of this, the addressee in 2 John could very likely be a woman who housed an assembly of believers, who then are metaphorically and affectionately called "her children." This position is further reinforced by 2 John 10, where John makes a specific point of telling the woman and her children not to receive false teachers "into the house" (*eis oikian* [TG1519/3614, ZG1650/3864]). In historical context, this would refer to the house wherein the believers assembled.

Third John was written to Gaius. Although the New Testament mentions several men with the name Gaius (Acts 19:29; 20:4ff; Rom 16:23; 1 Cor 1:14), it would be difficult to say that any one of these was the same as the Gaius in 3 John, especially since Gaius was a popular name in the first century. At any rate, Gaius was commended for his Christian life and hospitality and so was Demetrius (3 John 12), both of whom stand in sharp contrast to Diotrephes, who is literally called "the one loving to be first" (3 John 9).

Even though 2 John and 3 John were addressed to particular individuals or churches, John had his entire community of churches in mind. These churches had been infected by the false teachings of the gnostics, particularly those who were propagating a heretical view about the nature of Jesus Christ such as Cerinthus (see "Date and Occasion of Writing" and "Major Themes" in the Introduction to 1 John). John sent out various coworkers to promote the apostolic truths and to reunite the community in Christian love. Diotrephes rejected these coworkers and was even cutting off those in his church who were receiving them. Though it is not stated explicitly, one can surmise that he was sympathetic to the secessionists and thereby was causing divisions among the Johannine community. Third John was written to announce John's intentions to go directly to that church and deal with this situation head on.

John's statement in 3 John 9, "I wrote to the church about this," indicates that 3 John builds upon a previous correspondence (likely 1 John). As such, both 1 John and 3 John were written to deal with the issue of teachers and leaders who opposed John and the apostolic teaching; Diotrephes was one of those leaders.

CANONICITY AND TEXTUAL HISTORY

In the early centuries of the church, 2 John and 3 John were not as well known as 1 John. Each epistle, written on only one sheet of papyrus, was a personal letter. As such, these writings would not have been circulated in the churches like 1 John was. Nonetheless, 2 and 3 John were recognized as John's epistles as early as the second century. Irenaeus quoted 2 John 7 and 10 and 11 in his works (*Heresies* 1.16.3; 3.16.8), and Dionysius of Alexandria observed that John never named himself in his epistles, "not even in the second and third epistles, although they are short epistles, but simply calls himself the presbyter" (Eusebius *History* 7.25.11). Although their brevity and the personal nature of their contents caused 2 and 3 John to be less widely read and less likely to be quoted by the early church fathers, their personal nature also makes them less likely to be spurious, for they would serve no purpose as forgeries.

Eusebius (*History* 3.24.17) reckoned both epistles among the *Antilegomena* or controverted Scriptures, as distinguished from the *Homologoumena* or universally acknowledged Scriptures. Eusebius's personal opinion, however, was that the two short epistles were genuine. In *Demonstration of the Gospel* 3.5, Eusebius said that in John's "epistles" he does not mention his own name, nor call himself an apostle or evangelist but an "elder" (2 John 1; 3 John 1). Origen (according to Eusebius's *History* 6.25.10) mentioned the second and third epistles but added, "not all admit their genuineness"—implying that most authorities did take them as genuine. These two epistles were eventually recognized as canonical, soon after the Council of Nicea (AD 325). Thus, Cyril of Jerusalem (AD 349) enumerated fourteen epistles of Paul, and seven Catholic (or, General) Epistles, including 2 and 3 John. So did Gregory of Nazianzus in AD 389, the Council of Hippo (AD 393), and the Council of Carthage (AD 394).

The most reliable and earliest manuscript for 2 John and 3 John is Codex Vaticanus (B), followed by Codex Sinaiticus (א), 𝔓74, and 1739. Codex Alexandrinus (A) tends to be expansive and erratic in these epistles. The earliest extant copy of 2 John is the uncial manuscript 0232, a miniature codex dated to the early fourth century. Its testimony is also reliable.

LITERARY STYLE

Of all the New Testament writings, these are the two shortest letters. We know that the author himself wrote these letters with "pen and ink" on papyrus (cf. 3 John 13; cf. 2 John 12), as opposed to dictating the letters to an amanuensis. Both of these letters would have taken no more than one sheet of papyrus (averaging about 6" x 8"), written on both sides. Furthermore, these two letters have a format that is typical of letters written during the Hellenistic period. This is especially true of 3 John. It begins with an identification of the writer (the elder), then of the recipient (Gaius), followed by a statement of well-wishing: "I hope all is well with you and that you are as healthy in body as you are strong in spirit" (3 John 2). Examples of this abound in the extant papyri. For example, one second-century papyrus reads as follows:

> *Antonius Maximus to Sabina his sister, many greetings. Before all things I pray that you are in health, for I myself also am in health . . . When I knew that you fared well, I rejoiced greatly. And I at every occasion delay not to write to you concerning the health of me and mine. Salute Maximus much, and Copres my lord. There salute my life's partner, Aufidia, and Maximus my son.* (Deissmann 1978:184)

Other examples of ancient letters are provided in the commentary on 3 John 1-2.

In both 2 John and 3 John, John got to his point quickly and then concluded that he would rather communicate face to face than by letter, so he cut his writing short. Their vocabulary, syntax, and style completely accord with that found in 1 John.

MAJOR THEMES

John's second epistle can be described as a miniature version of 1 John. The same major themes that one finds in 1 John appear in 2 John. In both epistles John wants his readers to (1) live in the truth, (2) love one another, (3) be on guard against false teachers, and (4) adhere to the apostolic teachings—especially about Jesus, God's Son come in the flesh—in the face of gnostic infiltration into the church. Marshall (1978:3) tells us that 2 John "presents us with a cameo of John's chief concerns; on one hand, the importance of adherence to the truth, especially believing the truth about Jesus as the Son of God, and of living in Christian love, and, on the other hand, the dangerous threat posed by heresy. Truth and love constitute the two main positive features of John's Christianity."

Third John focuses on a problem addressed in 1 John—namely, spiritual elitism bucking against apostolic authority. A certain man named Diotrephes (who probably sympathized with the false teachers who had left the church) was undermining the authority of the apostle John and was trying to frustrate his leadership by ousting all who were sent to the church by John and by excommunicating those in the church who did receive John's emissaries. So John wrote this letter to Gaius, who was still loyal to John, to encourage him to receive the teachers and workers sent by John, for they were, in fact, messengers of Christ.

THEOLOGICAL CONCERNS

The same theological motifs appear in 2 John that are in 1 John. In both epistles, heresies are denounced, and the church is warned not to support the messengers of the heresy. Third John provides a window into first-century church leadership problems. The concerns it addresses have more to do with the practical administration of the church than with theological doctrines, but it nonetheless affirms the theology of 1 and 2 John—namely, that one cannot claim to know God and yet reject the people of God.

John's letters "contain theological, ethical, and practical truths which are fundamental to the Christian position in every age: that Jesus is one with God as well as one with us; that love and righteousness are indispensable to the believer who seeks as a child of God to walk in the light; and that unity, however flexible, is a demand laid upon the whole Church at all times" (Smalley 1984:xxxiv).

OUTLINE OF 2 JOHN
  I. Greetings (vv. 1-3)
 II. Live in the Truth (vv. 4-11)
III. John's Final Words (vv. 12-13)

OUTLINE OF 3 JOHN *(Commentary begins on p. 393)*
  I. Greetings (vv. 1-2)
 II. Caring for the Lord's Workers (vv. 3-12)
III. John's Final Words (vv. 13-15)

2 John

◆ **I. Greetings (vv. 1-3)**

This letter is from John, the elder.*

I am writing to the chosen lady and to her children,* whom I love in the truth—as does everyone else who knows the truth—²because the truth lives in us and will be with us forever.

³Grace, mercy, and peace, which come from God the Father and from Jesus Christ—the Son of the Father—will continue to be with us who live in truth and love.

1a Greek *From the elder.*   1b Or *the church God has chosen and its members.*

NOTES

1 John, the elder. The Greek text does not include the word "John" (cf. NLT mg); it was added for clarification. In *Demonstration of the Gospel* 3.5, Eusebius said that in John's "epistles," John did not mention his own name, nor call himself an apostle or evangelist, but an "elder" (2 John 1; 3 John 1). The title "elder" probably points to John's position at that time; he was the oldest living apostle and chief leader among the churches in the Roman province of Asia Minor. For further discussion concerning the title "elder," see "Author" in the Introduction to 1 John and in the Introduction to 2 & 3 John.

chosen lady. In ancient Greek, all words were written entirely in capital letters; thus, one cannot tell from the ancient page whether the phrase *eklectē kuria* ("chosen lady") referred to a specific woman—either "Eclecta, a woman" or "elect Kyria"—or whether it denotes simply "an elect lady" or "chosen lady." Clement of Alexandria thought her name was "Electa" (*Adumbrations* 4 [i.e., *Fragments* 1.4]). Athanasius thought her name was the elect "Kyria." One modern English version (TLB) follows this, naming her "Cyria." It is likely that *kuria* [TG2959, ZG3257] should be understood as "lady" inasmuch as this was a common term used in the papyri of that time period when a writer was addressing a woman (cf. examples in Hunt and Edgar 1959:302-303).

Most commentators do not identify the recipient of the letter as an individual because the epistle does not speak of the woman with any particular details (in contrast to 3 John, which speaks specifically of Gaius, Diotrephes, and Demetrius). Rather, they see this as being a symbolic way of speaking about a local church (cf. Marshall 1978:60; Schnackenburg 1979:306-307). This interpretation is reinforced by John concluding the letter with the salutation, "Greetings from the children of your sister, chosen by God" (v. 13). However, it is possible that the "elect lady" receiving the letter could be a reference to a particular woman in whose home a local church met, and the elect sister sending greetings also to a particular woman in whose home a local church met (see "Audience" in the Introduction).

her children. If the recipient was a woman, these would have been her actual children; if the recipient was a local church, these would have been the members of the church. This understanding is reflected in the NLT mg: "Or *the church God has chosen and its members.*"

But it seems more plausible to consider that this "lady" was an actual woman and that her "children" were those who met in her home.

2 *the truth lives in us.* This language personifies "truth." Since Jesus Christ is the full expression and embodiment of truth (John 14:6; Eph 4:21), truth dwells in us because Christ dwells in us as the Spirit of truth (John 16:13). The word translated "lives" is *menousan* [TG3306, ZG3531], which can also be translated "abiding" or "remaining"—a primary emphasis in this epistle is that believers remain in the truth and not stray from it.

3 *Grace, mercy, and peace.* This is a unique constellation of blessings, found only here in the NT. The only other time John mentions "grace" is in John 1:16-17, which says that "grace . . . came through Jesus Christ," so that "from his fullness we have all received grace upon grace" (NRSV). John nowhere else mentions "mercy." "Peace" is found a few times in John's Gospel; each time Jesus appeared to the disciples after his resurrection, he blessed them with "peace" (John 20:19, 26).

Jesus Christ. Divine titles in the text of the NT were often subjected to scribal expansion. In this case, "Jesus Christ" (found in A B 048 0232 81 1739) was expanded to "Lord Jesus Christ" in Codex Sinaiticus (ℵ) and the majority of late mss. Then it was popularized by its inclusion in the TR and KJV.

the Son of the Father. This reading is based on the strong textual support of ℵ A B 048 0232 81 1739. The uniqueness of this expression (it occurs only here in the NT), prompted scribes to shorten it to "the Son" (found in a few late minuscules) or change it to "the Son of God" (1881 and some Vulgate mss). But the title "the Son of the Father" functions to show the unique relationship between the Son and the Father.

in truth and love. John speaks more directly about truth in v. 4 and about love in v. 5.

COMMENTARY

The opening verses display the typical format used for letters in the Hellenistic period: identification of the writer, identification of the recipients, and a greeting and blessing (the commentary on 3 John 1-2 gives two other examples of letters from the Hellenistic period).

In this informal letter, John did not stand on his authority as an apostle but instead identified himself as "the elder," one who watched over the believers with loving concern for their spiritual well-being. The word "elder" (*presbuteros* [TG4245A, ZG4565]) was also a reference to John's age; he must have been an old man at the time he wrote this epistle (perhaps in his 80s). As discussed in the notes, the identification of the recipients as "the chosen lady and her children" probably refers to a specific Christian woman in whose home a church assembled. The other two options are (1) a specific woman and her actual children, or (2) a local church (see comments on vv. 6, 12, and 13). This elect lady and her children were loved by all the believers who had come to know the truth. The "truth" John speaks of is the sum total of orthodox teachings concerning Jesus Christ, the Son of God, as defined by the apostles. All who have embraced the truth concerning Jesus' true deity and humanity are true members of the household of God.

Secular writers of the time often greeted their recipients with words of blessing such as these: "may good things be yours from the gods"; "may you have absence of conflict and good health." Contrast that with the richness of this greeting and blessing: "May you have grace, mercy, and peace from God the Father and from Jesus

Christ, the Son of the Father." The apostle Paul often used "grace" and "peace" in his opening greetings; John also adds "mercy" here.

Though John does not speak of grace and peace as frequently as Paul does, he does mention them in his Gospel. The Greek text of John 1:16 indicates that grace is given to the believer as a continual supply—just when one measure of grace is used up, another replaces it. This grace keeps on giving, like a spring-fed well that never runs dry. Christ's dispensation of grace to every believer can never be exhausted because he is full of grace, which means he is full of God's kindness extended to us. God's mercy is seen in forgiving us and freeing us from sin, and peace is the result, providing cessation of turmoil and anxiety. These are gifts from God the Father and from the Father's Son, Jesus Christ. These blessings are transmitted to us from the Father through the Son. Some may claim to receive peace directly from God, apart from Jesus Christ, but no one can experience the Father apart from the Son. This is a consistent theme in John's Gospel (John 8:18; 14:6-10; 17:3) and John's epistles (see commentary on vv. 7-9).

"Truth" and "love" are appended to this blessing, as if they were afterthoughts, but this is not really the case because these words actually serve to introduce the next verses, where John emphasizes that it is necessary for all God's children to know the truth and live it out in their lives by practicing brotherly love.

◆ II. Live in the Truth (vv. 4-11)

⁴How happy I was to meet some of your children and find them living according to the truth, just as the Father commanded.

⁵I am writing to remind you, dear friends,* that we should love one another. This is not a new commandment, but one we have had from the beginning. ⁶Love means doing what God has commanded us, and he has commanded us to love one another, just as you heard from the beginning.

⁷I say this because many deceivers have gone out into the world. They deny that Jesus Christ came* in a real body. Such a person is a deceiver and an antichrist.

⁸Watch out that you do not lose what we* have worked so hard to achieve. Be diligent so that you receive your full reward. ⁹Anyone who wanders away from this teaching has no relationship with God. But anyone who remains in the teaching of Christ has a relationship with both the Father and the Son.

¹⁰If anyone comes to your meeting and does not teach the truth about Christ, don't invite that person into your home or give any kind of encouragement. ¹¹Anyone who encourages such people becomes a partner in their evil work.

5 Greek *I urge you, lady.*   7 Or *will come.*   8 Some manuscripts read *you.*

NOTES

4 *How happy I was to meet some of your children and find them living according to the truth.* Though we do not know the individuals John was referring to, he was probably speaking of believers he met at some place other than the local church itself—or other than the home of the elect lady. His joy at meeting them and then discovering that they were living in the truth prompted him to write this epistle. In identifying only "some" of the children, he was not necessarily saying that others were not living in the truth. Rather, he was probably speaking only of those he met.

just as the Father commanded. The commandment to live in the truth came from the Father through the Son to the disciples (cf. John 15:15), who passed it on to the believers (cf. 1 John 3:23).

5 *I am writing to remind you.* This expression implies some degree of authority and shows John's deep concern. The pronoun "you" is singular here, which could designate a particular woman or refer to an individual church as a whole (see note on v. 1).

that we should love one another. This was Jesus' command to the apostles (John 13:35; 15:12), which John passed on to the believers (cf. 1 John 3:11-18). For the secessionists to reject the apostolic truths was tantamount to hating those who accepted these truths. By contrast, loving one another is a sign of accepting the truth and living by it.

This is not a new commandment, but one we have had from the beginning. In light of what John says in the next verse, the expression "we have had from the beginning" primarily refers to the time the apostles first heard Jesus give them this commandment of love (see John 13:35; 1 John 2:7).

6 *Love means doing what God has commanded us, and he has commanded us to love one another.* This virtually repeats what Jesus told his disciples (John 15:9). Those who really love God do what he says, and his command is that we love one another.

just as you heard. The Gr. expression translated "you heard" is grammatically plural (*ēkousate* [TG191, ZG201]), indicating that John was speaking to several individuals. It should also be noted that the writer places himself among those who first proclaimed the gospel. Second-generation Christians (i.e., those not among Jesus' eyewitnesses), such as Luke and the writer of Hebrews, spoke of themselves as having heard the gospel from those who had heard and seen Jesus directly (cf. Luke 1:1-4; Heb 2:3).

from the beginning. Christians had been taught this commandment of love from the time they first heard the gospel preached by the apostles (cf. 1 John 2:7; 3:11 and notes).

7 *many deceivers have gone out into the world.* Jesus predicted that many false Christs would come (Matt 24:5). Some historically known deceivers were Theudas (Acts 5:36), Judas the Galilean (Acts 5:37), and one called "the Egyptian" (Acts 21:38). Another well-known Jewish messianic pretender was Bar Kochba, who led a second Jewish revolt against Rome, which ended in AD 135 with the banishing of all Jews from Jerusalem (Josephus *Antiquities* 20.97-99, 160-172, 188). Other unnamed false teachers are alluded to in 1 Tim 4:1; 2 Tim 4:3; 2 Peter 2:1; Jude 3-4. We do not know if these men were propagating teachings that denied Jesus Christ's true humanity. One man who did this was Cerinthus (see commentary below).

They deny that Jesus Christ came in a real body. John spoke of the same heresy in his first epistle (see comments on 1 John 4:2-3).

Such a person is a deceiver and an antichrist. These false teachers foreshadow the final personal Antichrist, who will embody all the evil of earlier anti-Christian systems and teachers (see comments on 1 John 2:18ff; 4:3).

8 There are three textual variants on this verse: (1) "Watch out that you do not lose the prize that we [the apostles] worked for but that you receive a full reward" (B syrʰᵐᵍ); (2) "Watch out that you do not lose the prize that you worked for but that you receive a full reward" (א A 044 0232 33 1739 it syr); (3) "Watch out that we do not lose the prize that we worked for but that we receive a full prize" (𝔐; so also TR).

The shift from "you" (in the first clause) to "we" (in the next clause) is more likely due to the author than to copyists because scribes would have wanted to simplify matters, not complicate them. Thus, the first reading is most likely original. As such, John was speaking of the labor that he, the apostles, and any other coworkers had done for the benefit of the believers. Since the apostles' work was to raise up churches, the loss of a church to heresy was a loss of the apostles' work. These laborers (the "we") proclaimed the truth, defined the truth, and defended the truth against heresy—all so that the church could get off to a good start and be built up. The believers, in turn, were admonished to exercise care in protecting that work from the destructive teachings of deceivers (v. 7). John feared that the apostatized deceivers would disrupt the community of faithful believers.

Several modern versions have adopted the second reading (or, at least, noted it—so NLT mg). The point of this reading is that it admonishes the believers to hold fast to the truths they know to be real and effective in their spiritual lives and not to give in to any kind of deception that would rob them of their reward. The third reading, found in the TR, is the result of a scribal adjustment.

9 *Anyone who wanders away from this teaching.* Lit., "everyone going beyond and not remaining in the teaching of Christ." This is the reading in the four earliest mss of 2 John (א A B 0232). Later mss replace the participle *proagōn* [TG4254, ZG4575] ("going before" or "going beyond") with *parabainōn* [TG3845, ZG4124] ("trespassing" or "transgressing"). This reading was adopted by the TR and so the KJV and NKJV. The word *proagōn* (NLT, "wanders away") literally means "leading forward"—hence, "to go before" or "to run ahead." This may be a sarcastic remark about the way in which the false teachers proudly claimed to be offering advanced teaching—so advanced that they went beyond the boundaries of true Christian belief.

10 *don't invite that person into your home.* This is very likely a reference to a house meeting of the church. Several such home meetings are mentioned in the NT. The church in Jerusalem must have had several groups at separate home meetings (cf. Acts 2:46; 5:42; 8:3; 12:5, 12), as did the church in Rome (cf. Rom 16:3-5, 14-15). A small local church may have had only one home gathering—as was probably the case with the church at Colossae (cf. Phlm 2). As mentioned in the Introduction, the house church to which John was writing this epistle could have been one and the same as the one in Laodicea. (For a fuller discussion on house churches, see "Audience" in the Introduction; Comfort 1993:153-158).

COMMENTARY

By the time we have read the first four verses of this epistle, we should have noticed that the word "truth" is used five times: "whom I love in the truth," "everyone else who knows the truth" (v. 1), "because the truth lives in us" (v. 2), "in truth and love" (v. 3), and "living according to the truth" (v. 4). The threat of gnosticism infiltrating the church prompted John to counter their falsehoods with strong admonitions to the believers about knowing the truth concerning Jesus Christ and living in it.

Since there were many false teachings about Jesus Christ in the days of the early church, the apostles had to describe what teachings about Jesus were true and what teachings were false. The true teachings could be labeled as orthodox and apostolic; the false teachings were heretical. Those believers who adhered to the apostolic teachings—both in doctrine and in practice—were those who were living in the truth.

One of the prominent signs of living in the truth is that a believer loves the other members of God's family. The one command "to love one another" sums up all of God's commands. John repeatedly made the same proclamation in his first epistle (see comments on 1 John 3:11, 16-19). Since love is volitional, we can be *commanded* to love fellow believers. We don't have to *feel* like we love others; we need to *decide* to love others. This choice strengthens the unity of the church.

The believers needed to be encouraged to live in the truth because many false teachings were infiltrating the church. In John's day, the worst infection was coming from a specific group of gnostics known as Docetists. These people denied Jesus Christ's real humanity; they promoted the falsehood that Christ only *seemed* to have a human body (see "Christological Orthodoxy versus Heresy" in the Introduction to 1 John). To deny Jesus' true humanity is to eradicate the fact that he actually shed real blood on the cross for the sins of the world. Thus, denial of Jesus Christ's humanity is denial of his redemption.

One such false teacher in John's day was Cerinthus (who died c. 100). Probably born in Egypt and reared as a Jew, Cerinthus was leader of a group of Christians that had gnostic tendencies. He taught that Jesus was an ordinary man upon whom "the Christ" descended at his baptism. This divine power revealed the transcendent and unknown God. This "Christ" then abandoned Jesus before his crucifixion (cf. Hicks and Winter 1992:148).

False teachers such as Cerinthus proudly claimed to be offering "advanced" teaching—teaching that went beyond what Jesus and the apostles had taught. John drew a line in the sand, so to speak: Those who go beyond the apostolic teachings concerning Christ are deceivers and antichrists; those who stay with the apostles remain in the truth. This is why John could say, "Anyone who remains in the teaching of Christ has a relationship with both the Father and the Son" (v. 9). The "teaching of Christ" is the true apostolic teaching concerning Christ, which was based on the teachings the apostles received from Christ. To remain in this teaching is to remain in the Son and the Father (see comments on 1 John 2:22-23). To depart from this teaching is a sign of apostasy, but it is more subtle than apostasy because these people claim to see more than what has been revealed in the New Testament. They claim to have special knowledge about spiritual things. The apostolic teachings concerning the person of Jesus Christ, however, are clear and simple: Jesus is God come in the flesh; he is God Incarnate, the God-man. A denial of either his full humanity or his full divinity is heresy.

John told his readers to be on guard against the deceivers. This was nothing new. Christ had previously warned his disciples, "Don't let anyone fool you. For many will come claiming to be the Messiah, and will lead many astray . . . so that if it were possible, even God's chosen ones would be deceived" (Matt. 24:4-5, 24, TLB). Paul had also previously warned the believers at Colossae (a church in the region where John ministered in his later days) about gnostic heresies:

> Don't let anyone capture you with empty philosophies and high-sounding nonsense that come from human thinking and from the spiritual powers of this world, rather than from Christ. For in Christ lives all the fullness of God in a human body. So you also are complete through your union with Christ, who is the head over every ruler and authority. (Col 2:8-10)

Paul was giving the same warnings that John later gave: Beware of anyone who denies the full deity or full humanity of Christ. We are complete in Christ Jesus; we need nothing beyond him. To be taken from Christ is to be robbed of our reward. It also robs the apostles of their reward (v. 8), for they were the ones who brought the precious truths concerning Christ to the believers in the first place.

In John's day, the false teachers would infiltrate the church by entering into home meetings and spreading their deceptive teachings. In the early days of the church, the believers met in homes (cf. Rom 16:5; Col 4:15). These meetings could be corrupted and become spiritually detrimental due to the presence of false teachers and false prophets (cf. 2 Pet 2:1, 13; Jude 12). The only way to deal with such people was to not accept them into the fellowship (v. 10). By helping them in any kind of way (such as providing housing or even a meal), the early Christians would have been promoting their cause. But John said it was worse than that—they would have actually been partners with them in their evil deeds (v. 11). John practiced what he preached: Polycarp, a disciple of John, said that John once left a bath house when he heard that the heretic Cerinthus was inside, for fear the house would fall in ruins since "the enemy of truth" was there (Irenaeus *Heresies* 3.3.4).

In our own day, there are many aberrant and heretical groups that have deviated from basic Christianity. Most of these, in some fashion or another, have heretical and/or extremely unorthodox views about the person of Jesus Christ. Of course, these views will often be presented as "new light" or "special revelation." And those who hold these views will look down on other Christians because they are not as "enlightened" as they are. We must not be deceived by such special "light" or special insights; rather, we must check to see if everything they say about Jesus Christ accords with Scripture. If it goes beyond what the apostles wrote, then we must judge it to be heretical. Our course of action is to refuse to participate in their movement so as not to promote error and falsehood.

◆ III. John's Final Words (vv. 12-13)

¹²I have much more to say to you, but I don't want to do it with paper and ink. For I hope to visit you soon and talk with you face to face. Then our joy will be complete. ¹³Greetings from the children of your sister,* chosen by God.

13 Or *from the members of your sister church.*

NOTES

12 *I have much more to say to you.* The word for "you" is plural in Greek, indicating a plural recipient—either a family of believers or the members of a particular local church.

but I don't want to do it with paper and ink. Lit., "not with a sheet of papyrus and ink." The modern idiom would be "sheet of paper" (BDAG 1081). This sheet (*chartēs* [TG5489, ZG5925]) would not have been "paper" but a sheet of papyrus, onto which this entire short epistle could have been written (front and back). The term was frequently used in Hellenistic times (cf. MM 685). For a similar expression, see 3 John 13.

talk with you face to face. Our English idiom "to speak face to face" parallels the Greek idiom here: "to speak mouth to mouth."

Then our joy will be complete. John made a similar statement in his first epistle (1 John 1:4). John's joy was fulfilled by the fellowship he had with other believers.

13 *Greetings from the children of your sister, chosen by God.* Since the sister was not named, John was probably referring to the sister church where he was staying. This is why the NLT mg reads, "Or *from the members of your sister church.*" This sort of reading also shows up in some mss of the Vulgate and in codex 307. A parallel greeting is found at the end of 1 Peter, where the apostle says, "she who is in Babylon, chosen together with you, sends you her greetings" (1 Pet 5:13, NIV). Convinced that this was speaking of a sister church, the translators of the TEV translated the clause, "Your sister church in Babylon, also chosen by God, sends you greetings."

The TR (followed by the KJV and NKJV) appends an "amen" to the end of the epistle, but this is completely out of character for this kind of personal letter.

COMMENTARY

This letter closes almost as quickly as it began. John's desire to speak with the believers—rather than write more—accounts for the brevity of the entire letter. He concluded the letter with a promise of further communication in person; thus, he and his recipients would complete each other's joy. John's love for the believers was not satisfied merely by writing a letter; he still longed (even in his advanced age) to visit them personally and discuss the truths of the gospel more fully.

As we all know, it is much better to be together in person with those we love than to only correspond by mail. Unfortunately for us, we don't get to read in this epistle as much as we might like, but there is enough here to give us a window into some important matters in the early church. By reading this short letter, we realize that the apostles were fighting for the basic truths concerning the person of Jesus Christ and that they were doing this on a house-by-house basis. Heretics and false teachers were prevalent and infectious. The only antidote was the apostle's living word. In our times, the antidote is the written word of the apostles. We should be thankful that we have their writings, even this one, though it is so short. From a theological perspective, Second John is a condensed version of 1 John. To repeat what was said in the introduction, 2 John is 1 John in a nutshell. In both epistles John calls his readers to (1) live in the truth, (2) love one another, (3) be on guard against false teachers, and (4) adhere to the apostolic teachings—especially about Jesus, God's Son come in the flesh—in the face of gnostic infiltration into the church.

3 John

◆ **I. Greetings (vv. 1-2)**

This letter is from John, the elder.*
    I am writing to Gaius, my dear friend, whom I love in the truth.

²Dear friend, I hope all is well with you and that you are as healthy in body as you are strong in spirit.

1 Greek *From the elder.*

NOTES

1 John, the elder. The Greek text does not include the word "John" (see NLT mg). It was added for clarification. In *Demonstration of the Gospel* 3.5, Eusebius writes that John, in his epistles, does not mention his own name, nor call himself an apostle or evangelist but an "elder" (2 John 1; 3 John 1). The title "elder" probably points to John's position at that time; he was the oldest living apostle and chief leader among the churches in the Roman province of Asia Minor. For further discussion concerning the title "elder," see "Author" in the Introduction to 1 John and in the Introduction to 2 & 3 John.

Gaius. Several people with the name Gaius are mentioned in the NT: (1) a Macedonian traveling companion of Paul (Acts 19:29); (2) a native of Derbe in Lycaonia, who traveled with Paul from Ephesus to Macedonia (Acts 20:4); (3) a prominent believer who hosted Paul and the whole church in Corinth (Rom 16:23; 1 Cor 1:14). The Gaius in 3 John was probably a different person than these three inasmuch as "Gaius" was a common name in those days.

2 Dear friend, I hope all is well with you and that you are as healthy in body as you are strong in spirit. The first part of this statement is a typical "well-wishing" found at the beginning of many letters written in the Hellenistic era. The second part, which literally reads, "as it is with your soul," is also found in many Hellenistic letters. The NLT rendering is a "Christianization" of it.

COMMENTARY

Of all the New Testament letters, this one has a format that is most typical of letters written during the Hellenistic age (325 BC–AD 325). The format for personal letters remained fairly constant for hundreds of years. Here is a letter dated 258/257 BC which came from a mummy's cartonnage (the plastered layers of linen or papyrus covering the body):

> Philotas to Epistratos, greeting. You do well if you are in health; we also are in health; Pleistarchos also is well and was gladly received by the king. You would please us if you take care of your health. Also remember us, just as we also remember you always. This will please us greatly. (Papyrus BGU XIV 2417)

Another papyrus manuscript (from the second century AD) demonstrates the continuation of the same style:

> Apollinarius to Taesis, his mother and lady, many greetings. Before all I pray for your health. I myself am well and make supplication for you before the gods of this place. (Hunt and Edgar 1959:302-303)

The opening of John's letter hardly differs from these in form. The writer is first identified; then the recipient. What usually follows is a "well-wishing" concerning one's health, which is usually followed by the writer asking the recipient to increase their mutual joy or pleasure in some way or another.

The writer of 3 John did not name himself; he simply identified himself as "the elder," just as he did in 2 John. The term "elder" (*presbuteros* [TG4245A, ZG4565]) connotes that the writer was one who watched over the spiritual well-being of the believers. The word "elder" is also a reference to John's age; he must have been an old man at the time he wrote this letter (see "Author" in the Introduction). The recipient of the letter, Gaius, was probably an elder in a local church because he was in the position of receiving the traveling teachers or coworkers (see v. 5 and comments). Three times in the first two verses John speaks of Gaius in very loving terms. He was loved by the congregation, loved by other believers, and loved by John.

John's personal greeting to Gaius indicates that they must have had a close relationship. John cared about Gaius's physical health and total well-being (v. 2) and wished him well in regard to both. This is a good way for Christians to express their concern for each other. We should not care just for each other's souls but for each other's bodies as well. This is linked with the principle of incarnation—God taking on a human body—which is a major theme in all of John's epistles. Our attitudes toward the physical must reflect our relationship to the spiritual (1 John 3:14-18). We should not neglect the body under the pretense that we care only for that which is immaterial.

◆ II. Caring for the Lord's Workers (vv. 3-12)

3Some of the traveling teachers* recently returned and made me very happy by telling me about your faithfulness and that you are living according to the truth. 4I could have no greater joy than to hear that my children are following the truth.

5Dear friend, you are being faithful to God when you care for the traveling teachers who pass through, even though they are strangers to you. 6They have told the church here of your loving friendship. Please continue providing for such teachers in a manner that pleases God. 7For they are traveling for the Lord,* and they accept nothing from people who are not believers.* 8So we ourselves should support them so that we can be their partners as they teach the truth.

9I wrote to the church about this, but Diotrephes, who loves to be the leader, refuses to have anything to do with us. 10When I come, I will report some of the things he is doing and the evil accusations he is making against us. Not only does he refuse to welcome the traveling teachers, he also tells others not to help them. And when they do help, he puts them out of the church.

¹¹Dear friend, don't let this bad example influence you. Follow only what is good. Remember that those who do good prove that they are God's children, and those who do evil prove that they do not know God.*

¹²Everyone speaks highly of Demetrius, as does the truth itself. We ourselves can say the same for him, and you know we speak the truth.

3 Greek *the brothers;* also in verses 5 and 10.   **7a** Greek *They went out on behalf of the Name.*   **7b** Greek *from Gentiles.*   **11** Greek *they have not seen God.*

NOTES
3 traveling teachers. Lit., "the brothers" (cf. NLT mg), but the context implies that these must have been the same ones who traveled from church to church, teaching the apostolic truths (see notes on v. 5 and v. 10).

your faithfulness. Lit., "the truth in you." This truth was his "loyalty to Christ and the gospel by which his life was marked" (Bruce 1970:148). The NRSV reads "your faithfulness to the truth."

you are living according to the truth. Gaius conducted his life in the truth—he lived it, or as we might say today, "He was really into it." This is in clear contrast to Diotrephes, whose conduct was contrary to the truth.

4 I could have no greater joy. This reading has excellent textual support: A © L P (1739) syr cops. Another reading, "I could have no greater thanks," is supported by B (1243 2298) it copᵇᵒ. Westcott and Hort, showing their preference for Codex Vaticanus (B), selected this reading for their text (see WH), but the textual evidence speaks against it.

my children. John was fond of calling the believers under his care "my children" (cf. 1 John 2:12-14). This use of the phrase supports the view that in 2 John the dear woman and her children, and the sister and her children, also refer to local churches.

5 traveling teachers who pass through, even though they are strangers to you. This is a justified interpretive translation of what is more literally "the brothers, especially [when] strangers." The context indicates that Gaius was caring for Christian workers, previously unknown to him, as they traveled from local church to local church.

6 the church. This is the first occurrence of the word "church" in all of John's writings (see also vv. 9-10). This was most likely John's home church, perhaps the church in Ephesus. The context and wording point to a particular assembly of this local church (note the anarthrous expression, *ekklēsias* [ᵀᴳ1577, ᶻᴳ1711]), during which some brothers told the believers about Gaius's kindness, which was then held up as an example for others.

Please continue providing for such teachers. Lit., "to send them on their way." This is an idiom for providing needed supplies for a journey. Since the traveling teachers were servants of the Lord Jesus, they were worthy of support.

7 the Lord Lit., "the Name" (see NLT mg). The writer did not need to identify whose name he meant; every believer knew that "the Name" denoted "Jesus Christ." Other NT writers did the same; they simply said "the Name" and expected their readers to know whose name they meant—the name of Jesus Christ (cf. Heb 1:4; 6:10; 13:15; Jas 2:7; 1 John 2:12).

accept nothing from people who are not believers. Lit., ". . . from the Gentiles" (*ethnikos* [ᵀᴳ1482, ᶻᴳ1618]). At this time in church history (AD 80 at the earliest), non-Christians may very well have been considered to be "Gentiles"—just as previously all non-Jews were categorized as "Gentiles." Apparently these traveling missionaries had a self-imposed restriction to not take anything offered from unbelievers.

8 we ourselves should support them. This is the reading in ℵ A B C* 33 1739. A variant reading is "We ought to receive such men," found in C² P 𝔐. (so TR and KJV, NKJV). A mere one-letter difference (upsilon/alpha) separates the two readings: (*[h]upolambanein* [ᵀᴳ5274, ᶻᴳ5696] versus *apolambanein* [ᵀᴳ618, ᶻᴳ655]). But there is a significant difference in meaning. The text, which has superior attestation, provides an encouragement for the believers to support traveling teachers by giving them hospitality (cf. BAGD 845) and an opportunity for ministry. The variant, which has inferior, late attestation, provides encouragement for the believers to welcome (cf. BAGD 94) the traveling teachers. The former speaks of a greater commitment on the part of the believers.

we can be their partners as they teach the truth. This reading is attested by only a few late mss (614 1505); it makes the people the coworkers with one another, not with the truth. Better textual attestation (ℵᶜ B C) supports the reading, "that we may become partners with the truth." Two mss (ℵ* A) read "that we may become partners with the church." This last variant obfuscates the personification of the truth by substituting "the church" for "the truth" (The same change occurred in v. 12—see note). The idea of the text is that the believers can promote and partner with the truth by supporting the traveling teachers who affirm the apostolic truths.

9 I wrote to the church about this. Lit., "I wrote something to the church." This reading has the support of ℵ* A B 048ᵛⁱᵈ 1739. Other mss read, "I wrote to the church" (C P Ψ 𝔐 [so TR]), and still others read, "I would have written to the church" (ℵ² 33 81 323 614 630 945 Vulgate syr). The first variant omits "something," probably so that readers won't think to trivialize any writings of the apostles. The second variant is probably an attempt to circumvent any queries about why John's previous letter to the church is not extant. Of course, if 1 John or 2 John were that letter, then there would be no perceived problem. But it is a matter of conjecture whether or not this correspondence "to the church" (the second use of *ekklēsia* [ᵀᴳ1577, ᶻᴳ1711] in all of John's writings; cf. v. 6) refers to one of John's previous epistles or to some lost epistle. Most scholars (e.g., Stott 2000:228-229; Marshall 1978:88) reject 1 John as an option because, though it is a letter to the church or churches in the Johannine community, it says nothing about the reception or rejection of traveling teachers (the subject at hand in 3 John). And though 2 John is probably a letter to a specific church, most scholars also reject it as an option because it, too, says nothing about traveling teachers (e.g., Smalley 1984:353-354). Most scholars, therefore, conclude that the letter John previously wrote got lost or was destroyed by Diotrephes.

However, John does not explicitly say that his previous letter dealt with the issue of receiving the traveling teachers. The text does not say, "I have written something to the church *about this.*" Rather, it simply indicates that John wrote something to the church and that his letter to the church was not received by Diotrephes because he did not receive John and his coworkers. This situation coincides with a major theme in 1 John—namely, John's insistence that those who claim to have enlightened fellowship with God while disdaining fellowship with the children of God are liars. Such was Diotrephes. So, 1 John could very well be the previous correspondence that John was referring to. With this as a possibility, the variant "I would have written to the church" could mean that John wrote to Gaius instead of to the church because he knew that Diotrephes would have interfered with his message to the church.

Diotrephes, who loves to be the leader. Lit., "Diotrephes loving to be first among them." Diotrephes apparently had an important position in the church. Maybe he was an elder or wanted to be; either way, he was blinded with pride and self-importance (cf. 1 Tim 3:6) and was acting against the apostle's teaching.

refuses to have anything to do with us. Given the context, this is a correct interpretation of "does not receive us."

10 *when I come, I will report some of the things he is doing.* John was prepared to publicly denounce Diotrephes before the whole church. (See v. 14 for John's anticipation of soon visiting the church Gaius belonged to.)

evil accusations he is making against us. The verb *phluareō* [ᵀᴳ5396, ᶻᴳ5826], used only here in the NT, "has the meaning of making false accusations in a garrulous way" (Vine 1970:126).

11 *those who do evil prove that they do not know God.* As John made known in his first epistle (1 John 2:29), the works of evil done by men such as Diotrephes prove that they do not really know God.

12 *Everyone speaks highly of Demetrius.* The placement of Demetrius's name at the end of the letter suggests that he was the one who carried John's letter to Gaius. The fact that John commends Demetrius to Gaius seems to imply that he was better known to John than he was to Gaius. He may, in fact, have been one of the "traveling teachers" John had sent earlier.

as does the truth itself. This reading has excellent support (𝔓74ᶜ ℵ Aᶜ B P 044 049 33 1739). The truth is depicted as a witness of the good works of Demetrius, for Demetrius had advanced the cause of truth. The scribes of two mss (𝔓74 A) changed "the truth" to "the church"; later, these mss were corrected to read "the truth."

you know we speak the truth. It was typical for John to use the plural "we" when affirming the veracity of his testimony (cf. John 19:35; 21:24; 1 John 1:4-5).

C O M M E N T A R Y

The main body of the letter has three purposes: (1) The first paragraph (vv. 3-4) commends Gaius and the other Christians meeting with him for living in the truth. (2) The second paragraph (vv. 5-8) commends Gaius for his hospitality given to those who were traveling "for the sake of the Name." These traveling teachers had spoken well of Gaius's love for the church. (3) The third paragraph (vv. 9-12) condemns the deeds of Diotrephes. His love of power and authority led him to defy the authority of John, the elder, and he had even refused to receive the coworkers sent by John. It is quite likely that Demetrius was one of the coworkers sent by John because John commends him to Gaius. (He also may have been the carrier of this letter, 3 John.) After Gaius received him and gave him hospitality, Demetrius (as representing John) could make a significant impact on the church by bringing apostolic truth to the members.

This short letter gives us a window into some interesting and significant features of the early church. What we can gather is that there were several traveling Christian workers going from church to church, teaching the apostolic truths of the gospel. Since these workers would not accept any support from the Gentiles (i.e., non-Christians), they needed to be helped financially by the churches. The coworkers' attitude about not receiving monetary help from unbelievers could have been motivated by Jesus' statement to his disciples: "Freely you have received, freely give" (Matt 10:8, NIV). The same principle is stated in *Didache* 11 which instructs traveling preachers not to take anything but food from their hosts. If they asked for money they were considered to be false prophets. By way of example, Paul did not want to take money from those to whom he preached the gospel (1 Cor 9:11ff;

1 Thess 2:9). Because the pure and true Christian workers did not get money from unbelievers, John was calling upon the believers to care for them financially.

In this epistle, specifically, it seems that the coworkers were part of John's community and therefore had been sent out by John. Their task was to carry his message to the churches in the Roman province of Asia. To receive them would be to complete the link between John and the churches, and thereby all would become colaborers in advancing the cause of truth (and halting the spread of heresy). To reject these traveling teachers would be to reject John and the truth. Thus, Diotrephes was not merely guilty of refusing to give hospitality to traveling teachers; he was guilty of separating himself (and members of his local church) from the apostle John.

It is quite possible that John had Diotrephes in mind when he was writing 1 John. Immediately after John said, "I wrote to the church about this" (v. 9; a possible reference to 1 John), he added, "but Diotrephes, who loves to be the leader, refuses to have anything to do with us" (3 John 9). In 1 John, the apostle urged the believers to continue in their fellowship with the apostles as a means to having true fellowship with God. These urgings may have been prompted by Diotrephes's attempts to keep the members of his church away from John and his coworkers. In 1 John, the apostle also condemned those who claimed to have fellowship with God while rejecting full fellowship with all the members of God's family. Diotrephes was thereby exposed. One cannot claim to love God while rejecting (the true meaning behind "hating") other members of God's family.

In one particular local church, Gaius had promoted church unity and solidarity with the apostle John by receiving the coworkers he sent. By contrast, Diotrephes was destroying the unity by rejecting those sent by John. As such, Diotrephes is a clear example of one who may have claimed to be spiritual but really was not because he did not love the brothers and because he rejected those who truly knew Jesus Christ. The lesson for us is that we cannot claim to love God if we don't love the church of God, the members of the Father's family.

Gaius stood in stark contrast to Diotrephes. He welcomed the brothers sent by John, and thereby promoted the cause of Christ and the propagation of the truth. Demetrius, one of John's coworkers and probably the carrier of the Third Epistle, also stood in contrast to Diotrephes because Demetrius had a good reputation among all the believers.

The situation described in 3 John has much to teach us about church leadership. It helps us to distinguish authoritarian leadership from the kind of leadership that arises from a spirit of servanthood. From the time of the apostles, the Christian church has always been served by leaders, however varied in status, title, or function. At the very onset of Christian gatherings, the believing community of the first century acknowledged some individuals as leaders. Sometimes these leaders emerged on the basis of their charisma; sometimes they were appointed by the apostles; and in some cases, they were elected by the church community. They certainly were not "clergy" in the modern sense. They were not rulers "over" the church, nor in charge of the church. Most often, they were gifted by the Holy Spirit to teach and edify the believers.

In 3 John we have a powerful example that juxtaposes two styles of church leadership: authoritarian self-promotion (Diotrephes) versus servanthood (Gaius). The first runs absolutely counter to the teaching of Christ and the apostles, while the second sets a pattern for all to emulate. An authoritarian leader exercises an undue influence on the decisions and lifestyles of other believers. This leads to manipulation and the dictating of a behavioral pattern that usurps the authority of the head of the church, Jesus Christ. A natural by-product of such dominance is that the word of the leader becomes more important than the Word of God. Often, the ambitious leader degenerates into a petty tyrant. To guard against this, each local assembly must seek its direction and authority from the New Testament Scriptures, and their historical interpretation by the collective body of Christ.

It seems to be an American obsession for church members to admire a strong and powerful church leader. His word is law. He acts swiftly and persuasively. He gets things done. Committees are for those minor details that do not concern him. He sets the program, and the program operates around him. Many are quite willing to meekly follow, giving modified support to this ecclesiastical superstar. One-man ministries abound for several reasons: tradition, lazy parishioners, and the attitude that "the pastor's paid to do it." Almost by default, some pastors become builders and defenders of their own little kingdoms.

Diotrephes knew nothing of the New Testament pattern of shared ministry. He loved to be first, to have the preeminence. He actively engaged in a gossip campaign against the apostle John. In his arrogance he expelled some believers from the local congregation and was inhospitable to the visiting teachers. Diotrephes leads the way for those domineering, authoritarian leaders who blatantly violate the scriptural admonishment to servanthood.

Gaius, on the other hand, embodies the New Testament standard of servant leadership. He lived the truth, gave hospitality to the Lord's servants, and was known for his loving deeds. With a heart truly devoted to God, Gaius demonstrated that spiritual leadership is concerned more with the service one renders to God and fellow believers than with the benefits one can gain from a leadership role.

Those who lead would do well to bear in mind our Lord's words, "Whoever wants to be a leader among you must be your servant, and whoever wants to be first among you must be the slave of everyone else" (Mark 10:43-44), or as Luke records Jesus' words, "the leader should be like a servant" (Luke 22:26). Jesus provided his disciples an example of servanthood when he washed their feet (John 13:3-5); he was visibly demonstrating the spirit of servanthood. Such a model made an impact on Simon Peter, who, years later, would write in his epistle to the churches: "Care for the flock that God has entrusted to you. Watch over it willingly, not grudgingly—not for what you will get out of it, but because you are eager to serve God. Don't lord it over the people assigned to your care, but lead them by your own good example" (1 Pet 5:2-3).

◆ III. John's Final Words (vv. 13-15)

¹³I have much more to say to you, but I don't want to write it with pen and ink. ¹⁴For I hope to see you soon, and then we will talk face to face.

¹⁵*Peace be with you.

Your friends here send you their greetings. Please give my personal greetings to each of our friends there.

15 Some English translations combine verses 14 and 15 into verse 14.

NOTES

13 *I don't want to write it with pen and ink.* The pen would have been a stylus, shaped from a "reed" (*kalamos* [^{TG}2563, ^{ZG}2812]). The "ink" (*melanos* [^{TG}3188, ^{ZG}3506]) would have probably been a black or dark carbon-based ink. At the conclusion of 2 John, the writer also said he wanted to communicate further, but not with "paper and ink" (see note on 2 John 12).

14 *face to face.* The English idiom "face to face" parallels the Greek idiom here, which is lit., "mouth to mouth."

15 *friends.* Gr., *philoi* [^{TG}5384, ^{ZG}5813]. The term "brothers" is usually used in the greetings found in NT epistles, but "friends" is appropriate in this friendly letter to Gaius.

COMMENTARY

This letter closes in a manner quite similar to what has been found in any number of letters from Hellenistic times. It was a letter from one friend to another. This shows that John and Gaius had a close relationship. John did not use his apostleship to command Gaius to do anything. Rather, he spoke to him as a friend. The same kind of spirit is exhibited in Paul's letter to Philemon.

Many Christians will testify of the same reality: their closest friends are their brothers and sisters in Christ—even closer (in some ways) than their blood brothers and sisters. Jesus set the example. He called his disciples "friends." And because they were his friends, he expected that they would do whatever he commanded them (John 15:14-15). So it is true among Christian friends: We hear each other's requests and we respond, because we are friends.

BIBLIOGRAPHY

Alford, Henry
1976 *The Greek Testament.* Grand Rapids: Guardian. (Orig. Pub. 1852.)

Aune, David
1987 *The New Testament in Its Literary Environment.* Philadelphia: Westminster.

Barker, G. W.
1981 1 John, 2 John, 3 John. Pp. 293–377 in *The Expositor's Bible Commentary,* vol. 12. Grand Rapids: Zondervan.

Barrett, C. K.
1978 *The Gospel according to St. John.* 2nd ed. Philadelphia: Westminster.

Beasley–Murray, George R.
1987 *John.* Word Biblical Commentary. Waco: Word.

Brooke, A. E.
1912 *A Critical and Exegetical Commentary on the Johannine Epistles.* Edinburgh: T & T Clark.

Brown, Raymond E.
1966 *The Gospel According to John,* vol. 1, chs. 1–12. Anchor Bible. New York: Doubleday.

1970 *The Gospel According to John,* vol. 2, chs. 13–21. Anchor Bible. New York: Doubleday.

1979 *The Community of the Beloved Disciple.* Toronto: Paulist.

1982 *The Epistles of John.* New York: Doubleday.

Brown, Raymond E., Joseph Fitzmyer, and Roland Murphy
1990 *The New Jerome Biblical Commentary.* Upper Saddle River, NJ: Prentice Hall.

Bruce, F. F.
1970 *The Epistles of John.* Old Tappan, NJ: Revell.

1983 *The Gospel of John.* Grand Rapids: Eerdmans.

Bultmann, Rudolf
1971 *The Gospel of John: A Commentary.* Translator, G. R. Beasley-Murray. Oxford: Blackwell.

Burge, Gary M.
1987 *The Anointed Community.* Grand Rapids: Eerdmans.

1996 *Letters of John.* NIV Application Commentary. Grand Rapids: Zondervan.

Carson, D. A.
1989 *The Gospel According to John.* Grand Rapids: Eerdmans.

Comfort, Philip
1993 The New Testament Ecclesia: The House Church and the Local Church. Pp. 153-158 in *The Topical Encyclopedia of Christian Worship,* vol. 1. Editor, Robert Webber. Nashville: Abbott Martyn.

1994 *I Am the Way: A Spiritual Journey through the Gospel of John.* Grand Rapids: Baker Book House. (Reprinted by Wipf and Stock, 2001.)

1997 "The Scribe As Reader: A New Look at New Testament Textual Criticism according to Reader Reception Theory." D. Litt. Dissertation, University of South Africa.

2005 *Encountering the Manuscripts: An Introduction to New Testament Paleography and Textual Criticism.* Nashville: Broadman & Holman.

2007 *New Testament Text and Translation Commentary.* Carol Stream, IL: Tyndale House.

Comfort, Philip and Wendell Hawley
1992 *Opening the Gospel of John.* Wheaton: Tyndale House. (Reprinted by First Books, 2001.)

Conway, C. M.
2002 The Production of the Johannine Community: A New Historicist Perspective. *Journal of Biblical Literature* 121:479-495.

Cullman, Oscar
1975 *The Johannine Circle.* Translator, John Bowden. Philadelphia: Westminster.

Culpepper, R. Allen
1975 *The Johannine School.* Missoula, MT: Scholars Press.

1983 *Anatomy of the Fourth Gospel: A Study in Literary Design.* Philadelphia: Fortress.

Deissmann, Adolf
1978 *Light from the Ancient East: The New Testament Illustrated by Recently Discovered Texts of the Graeco-Roman World.* Translator, Lionel R. M. Strachan. Grand Rapids: Baker. (Orig. Pub. 1922.)

DeYoung, James B.
1989 1–3 John. Pp. 997-1079 in *Evangelical Commentary on the Bible.* Editor, Walter Elwell. Grand Rapids: Baker.

Dodd, C. H.
1946 *The Johannine Epistles.* London: Hodder & Stoughton.

1953 *The Interpretation of the Fourth Gospel.* Cambridge: Cambridge University Press.

Douglas, J. D., Philip Comfort, and Donald Mitchell
1992 *Who's Who in Christian History.* Wheaton: Tyndale House.

Dunn, J. D. G.
1975 *Jesus and the Spirit.* Philadelphia: Westminster.

Elwell, Walter and Philip Comfort
2001 *Tyndale Bible Dictionary.* Wheaton: Tyndale House.

Giles, Kevin
1997 Prophecy, Prophets, False Prophets. Pp. 970-977 in *Dictionary of the Later New Testament and Its Developments.* Editors, Ralph P. Martin and Peter H. Davids. Downers Grove: InterVarsity.

Gundry, R. H.
1967 In My Father's House Are Many *Monai* (John 14:2). *Zeitschrift für die Neutestamentliche Wissenschaft* 58:68-72.

1994 *A Survey of the New Testament* (3rd ed.). Grand Rapids: Zondervan.

Harris, M. J.
1992 *Jesus As God: The New Testament Use of Theos in Reference to Jesus.* Grand Rapids: Baker.

Hicks, C. and M. Winter
1992 Cerinthus. P. 148 in *Who's Who in Christian History.* Editors, J. D. Douglas, P. W. Comfort, D. Mitchell. Wheaton: Tyndale House.

House, W. H.
1992 Papias. P. 530 in *Who's Who in Christian History.* Editors, J. D. Douglas, P. W. Comfort, D. Mitchell. Wheaton: Tyndale House.

Howard, W. F.
1947 The Common Authorship of the Johannine Gospel and Epistles. *Journal of Theological Studies* 48:12-25.

Hunt, A. S. and C. C. Edgar
1959 *Select Papyri.* Cambridge: Harvard University Press.

Johnston, G.
1970 *The Spirit-Paraclete in the Gospel of John.* Cambridge: Cambridge University Press.

Law, R.
1914 *The Tests of Life: A Study of the First Epistle of John.* Edinburgh: T & T Clark.

Manson, T. W.
1947 Entry into Membership in the Early Church. *Journal of Theological Studies* 48:25-33.

Marshall, I. H.
1978 *The Epistles of John.* New International Commentary on the New Testament. Grand Rapids: Eerdmans.

Metzger, Bruce
1994 *A Textual Commentary on the Greek New Testament* (2nd ed.). Stuttgart: German Bible Society.

Morris, Leon
1970 1 John, 2 John, 3 John Pp. 1259-1273 in *The New Bible Commentary.* (Rev. ed.) Grand Rapids: Eerdmans.

1971 *The Gospel According to John.* Grand Rapids: Eerdmans.

Oliver, W. H. and A. C. van Aarle
1991 The Community of Faith As Dwelling Place of the Father: *Basileia tou theou* as Household of God. *Neotestimentica* 25:379-400.

Painter, J.
1993 *The Quest for the Messiah: The History, Literature and Theology of the Johannine Community.* Edinburgh: T & T Clark.

Richards, W. L.
1971 *The Classification of the Greek Manuscripts of the Johannine Epistles.* Society of Biblical Literature Dissertation Series. Missoula, MT: Scholars Press.

Roberts, C. H.
1935 An Unpublished Fragment of the Fourth Gospel in the John Rylands Library. Manchester.

Robinson, J. A. T.
1976 *Redating the New Testament.* London: SCM. (Reprinted by Wipf and Stock, 2000.)
1985 *The Priority of John.* London: SCM.

Schnackenburg, Rudolph
1979 *Die Johannesbriefe.* Freiburg: Herder.
1980, 1982 *The Gospel According to St. John.* 3 vols. Translator, Kevin Smyth. New York: Crossroad.

Smalley, Stephen S.
1984 *1, 2, 3 John.* Word Biblical Commentary. Waco: Word.

Smith, David
1979 *The Epistles of John. The Expositor's Greek Testament,* vol. 5. Editor, W. R. Nicoll. Grand Rapids: Eerdmans. (Orig. pub. 1910.)

Stott, John R. W.
2000 *The Letters of John.* Tyndale New Testament Commentaries (rev. ed.). Leicester: Inter-Varsity.

Stowers, Stanley K.
1986 *Letter Writing in Greco-Roman Antiquity.* Philadelphia: Westminster.

Strecker, Georg
1995 *The Johannine Letters.* Hermenia. Philadelphia: Fortress.

Talbert, C. H.
1992 *Reading John: A Literary and Theological Commentary on the Fourth Gospel and the Johannine Epistles.* New York: Crossroad.

Tenney, Merrill
1985 *New Testament Survey.* Rev. ed. Grand Rapids: Zondervan.

Thompson, M. M.
1992 *1–3 John.* IVP New Testament Commentary. Downers Grove: InterVarsity.
2001 *The God of the Gospel of John.* Grand Rapids: Eerdmans.

Vine, W. E.
1970 *The Epistles of John.* Grand Rapids: Zondervan.

Westcott, B. F.
1881 *Gospel According to St. John.* London: Macmillan.
1886 *The Epistles of St. John.* London: Macmillan.